Physical and Virtual Learning Spaces in Higher Education:

Concepts for the Modern Learning Environment

Mike Keppell
Charles Sturt University, Australia

Kay Souter
La Trobe University, Australia

Matthew Riddle
La Trobe University, Australia

Senior Editorial Director:	Kristin Klinger
Director of Book Publications:	Julia Mosemann
Editorial Director:	Lindsay Johnston
Acquisitions Editor:	Erika Carter
Development Editor:	Michael Killian
Production Editor:	Sean Woznicki
Typesetters:	Keith Glazewski, Natalie Pronio, Milan Vracarich, Jr.
Print Coordinator:	Jamie Snavely
Cover Design:	Nick Newcomer

Published in the United States of America by
Information Science Reference (an imprint of IGI Global)
701 E. Chocolate Avenue
Hershey PA 17033
Tel: 717-533-8845
Fax: 717-533-8661
E-mail: cust@igi-global.com
Web site: http://www.igi-global.com

Library of Congress Cataloging-in-Publication Data

Physical and virtual learning spaces in higher education: concepts for the modern learning environment / Mike Keppell, Kay Souter, and Matthew Riddle, editors.
    p. cm.
  Includes bibliographical references and index.
  Summary: "This book documents real-world experiences of innovators in higher education who have redesigned spaces for learning and teaching, including physical, virtual, formal, informal, blended, flexible, and time sensitive factors"--Provided by publisher.
  ISBN 978-1-60960-114-0 (hardcover) -- ISBN 978-1-60960-116-4 (ebook) 1. College environment. 2. Classroom environment. 3. Virtual reality in higher education. 4. Blended learning. I. Keppell, Mike, 1961- II. Souter, Kay, 1952- III. Riddle, Matthew, 1969-
  LB2324.P47 2012
  378.1'01--dc22
                                        2011014040

British Cataloguing in Publication Data
A Cataloguing in Publication record for this book is available from the British Library.

All work contributed to this book is new, previously-unpublished material. The views expressed in this book are those of the authors, but not necessarily of the publisher.

Table of Contents

Section 1
Space Perspectives

Chapter 1
Mike Keppell, Charles Sturt University, Australia
Matthew Riddle, La Trobe University, Australia

Chapter 2
Warren Sellers, La Trobe University, Australia
Kay Souter, La Trobe University, Australia

Chapter 3
Merilyn Childs, Charles Sturt University, Australia
Regine Wagner, RMIT University, Australia

Chapter 4
John M. Rafferty, Charles Sturt University, Australia

Section 2
Physical and Virtual Learning Spaces

Section 3
Blended Learning Spaces

Detailed Table of Contents

Section 1
Space Perspectives

Chapter 1

Mike Keppell, Charles Sturt University, Australia
Matthew Riddle, La Trobe University, Australia

This chapter examines distributed and personal learning spaces across the spectrum of physical, blended and virtual learning spaces in the higher education context. We suggest that higher education is no longer defined by tangible boundaries of a 'physical campus' but by the entire student experience, whether that involves negotiating the physical corridors of the campus, attending face-to-face classes, participating in fully online courses or a blend of both face-to-face and online courses. In addition the student experience may also involve connecting to virtual environments from home, a local cafe, on the train or participating in professional practice hundreds of kilometers from the physical campus. This chapter attempts to account for the diverse range of spaces that are enriching the learning and teaching experience for both academics and students and suggests the need to recognise the changing nature of learning spaces in higher education.

Chapter 2

Warren Sellers, La Trobe University, Australia
Kay Souter, La Trobe University, Australia

Many discussions about teaching and learning spaces research concern what happens at an educational place. This chapter looks less at the physical place and more into potential spaces – the notional margins, interstices, and liminalities that are outside, between, and on the fringes of defined places. It advocates looking at spaces to bring new and different understandings, like "smooth and striated" (Deleuze & Guattari, 1987) to what learning and teaching spaces might mean for dramatically changing global educational environments and practices. Rather than seeing a student's classroom, workroom, lecture hall, and lab as a singular person's situation or place, the authors of this chapter propose seeing and thinking conceptually about spatial-dimensional multiplicities for identities. That is seeing various coextensive situations and sites both out and indoors (where 'doors' may also be 'walls') as activities and areas not pre-bounded or specified for particular individual purposes, and thinking about these by bringing different mind-views to conceptualising collaborative activities in spaces as complex knowledge generating affects.

Chapter 3

Merilyn Childs, Charles Sturt University, Australia
Regine Wagner, RMIT University, Australia

In this chapter, the authors argue that a disjuncture has emerged between the look of learning spaces within learning spaces discourse, definitions of learning spaces, and the aspirations of learning spaces as a design concept that transforms higher education. Using Visual Studies methodology and photographs, the chapter contrasts the hegemonic look of learning spaces with a viral learning space – learning that is not designed or controlled by the institution. The authors argue that the Learning Spaces agenda will fail to transform higher education in the twenty first century if its proponents do not adequately conceptualize lifelong and lifewide learning achieved by learners outside the institution.

Chapter 4

John M. Rafferty, Charles Sturt University, Australia

This chapter explores the environmentally sensitive design characteristics of Charles Sturt University's Albury Wodonga campus and the outdoor learning spaces it provides. Attention will be given to exploring how the holistic and integrated nature of the campus and the environmental functionality of the site provide unique opportunities for learning within learning spaces. Examples are provided of how the natural and built environments of the campus are used as learning spaces to promote social interactions, conversations, and experiences that enhance student learning. The chapter highlights the value of outdoor environments as legitimate and critical spaces for learning within higher education. The chapter explores the benefits of designing teaching space based on strategies that are defined by personal pedagogic repertoires and practical wisdom. By enacting such strategies, it is argued that universities can develop diverse, locally appropriate, and inclusive pedagogies.

Section 2
Physical and Virtual Learning Spaces

Chapter 5

Robert Fox, The University of Hong Kong, Hong Kong
Paul Lam, The Chinese University of Hong Kong, Hong Kong

This chapter explores the changing needs for university learning spaces and the resultant designs to maximize opportunities for student learning, taking into account the special needs and learning culture of the local context and the changing curriculum needs of all higher education institutions in Hong Kong. The chapter outlines a study of these needs and an institution's plans to better use space to support both flexible and interactive learning environments to enhance active student learning.

Chapter 6

This chapter discusses the purposes, design and implementation of a physical experimental learning and teaching space which forms part of the University of Southern Queensland's Australian Digital Futures Institute (ADFI). It identifies challenges associated with the initial design and offers some recommendations for addressing these challenges. The concept and principles of the PaSsPorT design model which has been developed to guide the redesign of the space are introduced, and a brief description of another ADFI space, the software research and development laboratory follows. This chapter also introduces a process for evaluating the design and implementation of learning, teaching, and research spaces using design-based research to frame the model.

This chapter introduces the idea of networked learning environments and argues that these environments provide the totality of surrounding conditions for learning in digital networks. It provides illustrative vignettes of the ways that students appropriate networked environments for learning. The chapter then examines the notion of networked learning environments in relation to the idea of infrastructure and infrastructures for learning and sets out some issues arising from this perspective. The chapter suggests that students and teachers selectively constitute their own contexts and that design can only have an indirect effect on learning. The chapter goes on to argue that design needs to be located at the meso level of the institution and that a solution to the problem of indirect design lies in refocusing design at the meso level and on the design of infrastructures for learning.

Chapter 8

In this chapter, the currently dominant virtual learning spaces employed in institutions of higher education are explored and contrasted with the virtual social spaces provided by Web 2.0 tools. Guided by the increasing focus on lifelong learning skills in the world of work and in higher education, the gap that exists between institutional and social virtual spaces is identified. It is then argued for filling this gap by providing access to institutional e-Portfolio systems to students in higher education, giving students an institutionally supported student-focused virtual learning space. By examining the perspectives of stakeholders involved in higher education, the challenges inherent in the adoption of institutional e-Portfolio systems are identified and recommendations for overcoming these based on practical experience and research findings are made.

Chapter 9

Nathan Wise, University of New England, Australia
Belinda Tynan, University of New England, Australia

Our concept of 'virtual learning spaces' is changing, as are the practices that are adopted within these spaces. To understand these changes, this chapter will provide an exploration of the conceptualisation and creation of an interactive, online, social network community of practice. The case that will be used is based around the Distance Education Hub (DEHub) which is both virtual and physical. DEHub is in the simultaneous process of constructing and facilitating a virtual space to support and encourage both knowledge dissemination and knowledge creation. The DEHub space focuses on learning as a cooperative, constructive, and dynamic process involving engaged communities of scholars, learners and practitioners. It will tackle the question of why this virtual learning space is defined as a niche social network and how this impacts on the conceptualisation and consequent development of virtual spaces — in this instance, co-development by the community. Finally, it will demonstrate through this analysis how changing concepts of 'virtual learning spaces' are put into practice through 'virtual space' design and development for creating and supporting niche social networks.

Section 3
Blended Learning Spaces

Chapter 10

Kerryn Newbegin, Monash University, Australia
Leonard Webster, Monash University, Australia

The development of physical and virtual learning spaces is prominent in the current higher education context, however a preoccupation with the design of these environments must not be at the cost of the learner. This chapter proposes that new ways of thinking need to be adopted and new strategies for collaborating need to be developed to enable students and teachers to traverse the physical and virtual environments. In traversing these spaces, learners must use them to best advantage, both within the higher education context, and then later in the professional arena in which they will be operating. Specifically this chapter will examine the use of one collaboration tool—blogs— to bridge the gap between the physical and the virtual, the formal and the informal learning spaces. Strategies for using blogs will be presented as a tool for students and educators to enable and promote knowledge creation, and to develop a habit of reflective practice both during and after formal study.

Chapter 11

Steve Dillon, Queensland University of Technology, Australia
Deidre Seeto, University of Queensland, Australia
Anne Berry, Queensland University of Technology, Australia

eZine and iRadio represent knowledge creation metaphors for scaffolding learning in a blended learning environment. Through independent and collaborative work online participating students experience a simulated virtual publishing space in their classrooms. This chapter is presented as an auto-ethnographic account highlighting the voices of the learning designer and the teacher. Using an iterative research design, evidence is provided for three iterations of each course. A collaborative approach to the development, planning, implementation, and evaluation of two tertiary music elective courses between lecturers, tutors, learning and technological designers is narrated. The student voice is embedded in the methodology, which involved an innovative approach that blends software development and pedagogy in iterations of software and experience design. The chapter describes how the teachers and learning designers translate these data into action and design. A blended learning space was incorporated within each of these elective music courses and the movement between these learning spaces is described and problematized. The research suggests that learning design, which provides real world examples and resources integrating authentic task design, can provide meaningful and engaging experiences for students. The dialogue between learning designers and teachers and iterative review of the learning process and student outcomes has engaged students meaningfully to achieve transferable learning outcomes.

Chapter 12

Lynne Hunt, University of Southern Queensland, Australia
Henk Huijser, University of Southern Queensland, Australia
Michael Sankey, University of Southern Queensland, Australia

This chapter shows how virtual and physical learning spaces are shaped by pedagogy. It explores the shift in pedagogy from an orientation to teaching to an emphasis on student learning. In so doing, it touches on Net Generation literature indicating that this concept has a poor fit with the diverse nature of student populations engaged in lifelong learning. The argument is that the skill set required for lifelong learning is not age related. At the core of the chapter is a case study of the University of Southern Queensland (USQ) which describes a history of learning environments that have been variously shaped by pedagogy and the limits of technology. It refers to the concept of the 'edgeless university', which acknowledges that learning is no longer cloistered within campus walls, and it describes how USQ is engaging with this concept through the development of open source learning materials. An important point in the chapter is that the deliberate design of quality learning spaces requires whole-of-institution planning, including academic development for university teaching staff, themselves often ill-equipped to take advantage of the potential of new learning environments. The import of the discussion is that higher education learning spaces are shaped by deliberate design, and that student learning is optimised when that design is pedagogically informed and properly managed.

Section 4
Authentic Learning Spaces

This chapter examines how assessment spaces must change in response to the rapid development and uptake of new virtual learning spaces. Students are engaging in collaborative, cooperative learning activities in a spatially distributed environment, yet their assessment tasks are often delivered in traditional assessment spaces that bear little resemblance to their learning spaces. The assessment of students in virtual worlds, virtual laboratories, role-plays and serious games is examined and the case is presented for the wider use of evidence-centered assessment designs and stealth assessment techniques.

This chapter presents an overview of an innovative teaching approach in an undergraduate nursing degree at Charles Darwin University (CDU). The authors describe the development and initial integration into the first year clinical nursing subject of a virtual learning space using a case-based approach to address some of the issues associated with an externalised Bachelor of Nursing program. In addition, the use of the CDU vHospital® in supporting early role socialisation into nursing and professional identity of first year nursing students will be explored. The findings and outcomes of formal and informal evaluations of the resource are also presented. Lastly, the authors identify recommendations for future development and areas for potential future research.

New technology-enriched learning spaces are a focus of institutional investment to address the identified shortcomings of traditional teaching and learning environments. Academic development, an area that has received little attention in this context, can be designed to provide strong opportunities for university teachers to re-imagine their teaching for these new spaces while also building their leadership capacity. This chapter discusses challenges that teachers face in transforming their teaching practices and proposes a model for academic development to support this. Two case studies demonstrate the flexibility and efficacy of the model and provide pointers for further adoption in the higher education context

The description of learning environments as physical or virtual spaces focuses on the tools and infrastructure that support learning as opposed to the learning interactions. The authors of this chapter advocate the view that to maximise the potential of any learning environment, educators need to understand how students learn in the first instance and then design the learning environment based on these insights. Throughout this chapter, formal learning is conceived as an individualised experience within an organised learning community, and as such, it is suggested that this learning environment is described as an experiential space. Within this chapter, an approach to designing an experiential space that uses problem based learning to engage students and facilitate their active construction of knowledge is described. The Holmesglen built environment degree program is used as a case study to illustrate a particular solution to designing an experiential learning space.

This chapter explores the human element in the learning space through the notion that once a learning space is inhabited, it becomes a learning place of agency, purpose and community involving both staff and students. The School of Languages and Learning at Victoria University in Melbourne has initiated a multifaceted peer learning support strategy, 'Students Supporting Student Learning' (SSSL), involving the deployment of student peer mentors into various physical and virtual learning spaces. The chapter discusses the dynamics of peer learning across these learning space settings and the challenges involved in instituting the shift from teacher- to learning-centred pedagogies within such spaces. Both physical and virtual dimensions are considered, with the SNAPVU Platform introduced as a strategy for facilitating virtual learning communities of practice in which staff, mentors, and students will be able to engage in mutual learning support. The chapter concludes with calls for the explicit inclusion of peer learning in the operational design of learning spaces.

Foreword

Howard Rheingold was asked to comment on a number of questions in relation to learning spaces. His insightful reflections serve as the foreword to the book and a recognition of the importance of spaces for learning and teaching in higher education.

What are some important features of learning spaces? Traditional learning spaces perpetuate the power hierarchy and the innate assumptions of pedagogy which are built into the architecture of the lecture hall. You have the authority standing at the front and everybody is focused toward them and if the student wants to hide out, you hide out in the back row. To me the most important part of the classroom is that you can fold up the tables and the chairs and move them out of the way... No matter what other fancy technology you've got in the classroom, if the chairs and tables are bolted down, you're in trouble. In other words, I like re-configurability, whether you're talking about the physical equipment or the online aspects of learning and teaching. For me, moving the students' chairs in a circle has an explosive effect as there is no back row and you are all seeing each other. It is important to move away from the movie theatre effect, where all of the screens are in the front and everyone has to face the same direction...

How have learning spaces changed? The change that overshadows all other changes is the availability of broadband wireless internet access. In addition, the increased diversity and range of devices allows student and teacher access, which was unanticipated. This ubiquity of wireless access and the range of devices create both a challenge and an opportunity because it wasn't planned from a pedagogical perspective. However, we can capitalize on this opportunity as the technology affords a much richer opportunity for peer-to-peer interaction, collaboration, and of course a connection with the world of other people and information that is available across the globe.

Do you think universities understand collective intelligence? Collective intelligence suggests that everybody finds a piece of the puzzle, and collaboratively, everyone pieces together the puzzle utilizing the contributions of the many. Collaborative inquiry is particularly called for in the 21st century as it optimizes collective intelligence to solve problems. However, because anyone can publish to the Web, the degree of authority, credibility, and accuracy that you can assign to a text needs to be determined individually as well as collaboratively and socially. Science, scholarship, business, and education are increasingly dependent on more collaborative work and less individually authored work. This is a trend that is a traumatic change for students who are used to being the sole author of a work and who perceive their role as performing for the instructor. For example, a Wiki collaboration is radically new in that you don't have an author so much as you have a revision history, and I use it in my own teaching as a collective action problem. I've got a different team every week who co-teach with me and who stimulate active discussion. In terms of education, there are tools yet to be invented that will make more visible how these collaborations happen and make it visible for the students so that they can see collaboration in action.

How do you think university learning environments might change in the future? I don't see learning institutions having an in-built incentive for changing anywhere near the pace at which technology is changing. When I first started teaching at Stanford I was surprised at how many students really didn't know how to blog or use a Wiki. I assumed that they were all like my daughter and her friends, that is, digital natives. However, as I found, you can't assume they know how to use a blog or wiki. From the teachers' perspective there is no incentive for innovating in pedagogy, and this is a major issue.

Do you have a metaphor to describe learning spaces in higher education? What comes to mind immediately is the learning community, which of course can be virtual and/or physical. The agora is the gathering place, a marketplace of ideas and a place of exchange. The agora is not the auditorium with the podium. It's not the passive audience and the active "sage on the stage." The locus of authority and the lines of communication in the agora are very different from the auditorium.

Howard Rheingold

Howard Rheingold *is a critic, writer, and teacher; who specialises in the cultural, social and political implications of modern communication media such as the Internet, mobile telephony and virtual communities (a term he is credited with inventing). Howard worked on and wrote about the earliest personal computers. In 1985 he published Tools for Thought and The Virtual Community and he co-authored Out of the Inner Circle: A Hacker's Guide to Computer Security. In 1991, he published Virtual Reality: Exploring the Brave New Technologies of Artificial Experience and Interactive Worlds from Cyberspace to Teledildonics. He was the editor of The Whole Earth Review; Editor in Chief of The Millennium Whole Earth Catalog; and founding Executive Editor of HotWired. In 1996 he founded Electric Minds which was named one of the ten best web sites of 1996 by Time magazine. In 1998, he created Brainstorms, a private successful webconferencing community. He published Smart Mobs in 2002, and in 2008, he became the first research fellow at the Institute for the Future. He is a visiting lecturer at Stanford University and a lecturer at U.C. Berkeley.*

Preface

INTRODUCTION

Higher education is facing a renaissance in terms of its approaches to teaching and learning and the use of physical and virtual spaces. This book will address the question of how higher education institutions and administrators need to re-conceptualize, re-design, and rethink the use of space for students entering university in the 21st Century. Higher education institutions are no longer defined by the physical boundaries of their traditional campus but the entire student experience, whether that be negotiating the physical corridors of the campus or connecting to virtual environments. The design of spaces to support the generation of knowledge by students themselves is an important and neglected field. With lectures and tutorials still predominant in higher education, the organization of space and time configures students as receivers of knowledge until the point of graduation, at which time they are expected to produce knowledge of their own. Rather than lecture halls with rowed seats being the predominant physical learning space for learning and teaching in higher education, learning spaces need to include: physical/virtual, formal/informal, blended, mobile, personal, and professional learning spaces that need to consider flexibility, adaptability, and time. They need to mirror contemporary learning and teaching strategies that emphasize independent and peer-based learning in both physical and virtual learning spaces, and need to account for how students perceive and utilize space in higher education settings. In meeting these priorities, it is essential for universities to support synchronous and asynchronous, multi-disciplinary, multi-campus, and inter-institutional collaboration amongst students, between students and teaching staff, and amongst teaching staff.

THE TARGET AUDIENCE

The target audience of this book will be composed of professionals and researchers working in the field of physical and virtual learning spaces in higher education (e.g. university academics teaching in higher education, librarians, educational designers, academic developers, learning and teaching centre staff, online professionals focused on the design and development of educational technology projects, architects who design buildings and spaces in university environments, and IT administrators). Moreover, the book will provide insights and support university senior management who make decisions about learning space and building projects, heads of departments, faculty deans, and facility managers at universities concerned with the management and design of physical and virtual learning spaces in higher education.

HOW THIS BOOK IS ORGANISED

This book is divided into four sections: Section I. Space Perspectives; Section II. Physical and Virtual Learning Spaces; Section III. Blended Learning Spaces; and Section IV. Authentic Learning Spaces.

Section 1: Space Perspectives

Section 1 examines theoretical and practical perspectives in relation to learning spaces. The first four chapters examine distributed learning spaces, the continual emphasis of 'place' in learning spaces, viral learning spaces, and outdoor learning spaces. The chapters attempt to push the boundaries of what we mean by learning spaces from both a theoretical and practical perspective.

In Chapter 1, Mike Keppell and Matthew Riddle examine distributed and personal learning spaces across the spectrum of physical, blended, and virtual learning spaces in the higher education context. They suggest that higher education is no longer defined by the physical boundaries of a 'physical campus,' but the entire student experience, whether that involves negotiating the physical corridors of the campus, attending face-to-face classes, participating in fully online courses, or a blend of both face-to-face and online courses. In addition the student experience may also involve connecting to virtual environments from home, a local café, on the train, or participating in professional practice hundreds of kilometers from the physical campus. This chapter attempts to account for the diverse range of spaces that are enriching the learning and teaching experience for both academics and students and suggests that we need to recognize the changing nature of learning space and broaden our mental models of learning spaces in higher education. In Chapter 2, Warren Sellers and Kay Souter focus on differences between educational places for learning and spaces for learning. They suggest that discussions about teaching and learning spaces continue to concern themselves with what happens at an educational "place." This chapter looks less at the physical place and more into potential spaces – the notional margins, interstices, and liminalities that are outside, between, and on the fringes of defined places. Rather than seeing a student's classroom, workroom, lecture hall, and lab as a singular person's situation or place, they propose seeing and thinking conceptually about spatial-dimensional multiplicities for identities. In Chapter 3, Merilyn Childs and Regine Wagner examine viral learning spaces which are spaces neither designed nor controlled by the institution. They suggest that a disjuncture has emerged between the look of learning spaces within learning spaces discourse, definitions of learning spaces, and the aspirations of 'learning spaces' as a design concept that transforms higher education. They argue that a current emphasis on designing learning spaces will fail to transform higher education in the twenty first century if its proponents do not adequately conceptualize the end of the institution and the rise of viral learning spaces. In Chapter 4, John Rafferty examines the design of outdoor and environmentally integrated learning spaces. He emphasizes the need to explore how the holistic and integrated nature of the campus and the environmental functionality of the site provide unique opportunities for learning within learning spaces. The chapter highlights the value of outdoor environments as legitimate and critical spaces for learning within higher education. Examples are provided of how the natural and built environments of the campus are used as learning spaces to promote social interactions, conversations, and experiences that enhance student learning.

Section 2: Physical and Virtual Learning Spaces

Section 2 examines the diversity of physical and virtual learning spaces. The five chapters examine institutional spaces for learning, using design-based research to evaluate spaces, networked learning environments, lifelong learning through e-portfolios, and learning community spaces.

In Chapter 5, Robert Fox and Paul Lam explore the changing needs for university learning spaces and the resultant designs to maximize opportunities for student learning, taking into account the special needs and learning culture of the local context and the changing curriculum needs of all higher education institutions in Hong Kong. The chapter outlines a study of these needs and an institution's plans to better use space to support both flexible and interactive learning environments to enhance active student learning. In Chapter 6, Shirley Reushle discusses the purposes, design, and implementation of a physical experimental learning and teaching space which forms part of the University of Southern Queensland's Australian Digital Futures Institute (ADFI). It identifies challenges associated with the initial design and offers some recommendations for addressing these challenges. The chapter examines the principles of the PaSsPorT design model which has been developed to guide the redesign of space. The chapter also introduces a process for evaluating the design and implementation of learning, teaching, and research spaces using design-based research to frame the model. In Chapter 7, Chris Jones introduces the idea of networked learning environments and argues that these environments provide the totality of surrounding conditions for learning in digital networks. He provides illustrative vignettes of the ways that students appropriate networked environments for learning. The chapter then examines the notion of networked learning environments in relation to the idea of infrastructure and infrastructures for learning and sets out some issues arising from this perspective. The chapter suggests that students and teachers selectively constitute their own contexts and that design can only have an indirect effect on learning. In Chapter 8, Eva Heinrich and Yuliya Bozhko explore the dominant virtual learning spaces employed in institutions of higher education and contrast them with the virtual social spaces provided by Web 2.0 tools. Guided by the increasing focus on lifelong learning skills in the world of work and in higher education, the authors identify the gap that exists between institutional and social virtual spaces. Heinrich and Bozhko argue for filling this gap by providing access to institutional e-Portfolio systems to students in higher education, and giving students an institutionally supported, student-focused virtual learning space. In Chapter 9, Nathan Wise and Belinda Tynan explore the conceptualisation and creation of an interactive, online, social network community of practice. The Distance Education Hub (DEHub) is both a virtual and physical community space. DEHub is in the simultaneous process of constructing and facilitating a virtual space to support and encourage both knowledge dissemination and knowledge creation. The DEHub space focuses on learning as a cooperative, constructive, and dynamic process involving engaged communities of scholars, learners, and practitioners.

Section 3: Blended Learning Spaces

Section 3 examines the concept of bridging the gap between physical and virtual learning spaces and the movement of the learner between the spaces. The three chapters examine blogs for traversing physical and virtual spaces, a simulated virtual publishing space and blending space with pedagogy.

In Chapter 10, Kerryn Newbegin and Leonard Webster use blogs to traverse physical and virtual spaces. The chapter proposes that new ways of thinking need to be adopted, and new strategies for collaborating need to be developed to enable students and teachers to traverse physical and virtual environments. In traversing these spaces, learners must use them to best advantage, both within the higher education context, and then later in the professional arena in which they will be operating. Specifically, this chapter will examine the use of one collaboration tool—blogs—to bridge the gap between the physical and the virtual, the formal and the informal learning spaces. Strategies for using blogs will be presented as a tool for students and educators to enable and promote knowledge creation, and to develop a habit of reflective practice both during and after formal study. In Chapter 11, Steve Dillon, Deidre Seeto and Anne Berry describe knowledge creation metaphors for scaffolding learning in a blended learning environment. Through independent and collaborative work, online participating students experience a simulated virtual publishing space in their classrooms. This chapter is presented as an auto-ethnographic account highlighting the voices of the learning designer and the teacher. Using an iterative research design, evidence is provided for three iterations of each course. A collaborative approach to the development, planning, implementation, and evaluation of two tertiary music elective courses between lecturers, tutors, learning, and technological designers is narrated. A blended learning space was incorporated within each of these elective music courses, and the movement between these learning spaces is described and problematized. The research suggests that learning design, which provides real world examples and resources integrating authentic task design, can provide meaningful and engaging experiences for students. In Chapter 12, Lynne Hunt, Henk Huijser, and Michael Sankey examine blending space with pedagogy. This chapter shows how virtual and physical learning spaces are shaped by pedagogy. It explores the shift in pedagogy from an orientation to teaching to an emphasis on student learning. In so doing, it touches on Net Generation literature indicating that this concept has a poor fit with the diverse nature of student populations engaged in lifelong learning. The argument is that the skill set required for lifelong learning is not age related. The chapter refers to the concept of the "edgeless university," which acknowledges that learning is no longer cloistered within campus walls. An important point in the chapter is that the deliberate design of quality learning spaces requires whole-of-institution planning, including academic development for university teaching staff, themselves often ill-equipped to take advantage of the potential of new learning environments.

Section 4: Authentic Learning Spaces

Section 4 examines the concept of authentic learning spaces. The five chapters examine assessment in virtual learning spaces, creating an authentic learning environment for nurses, academic development for learning spaces, designing experiential learning spaces, and utilizing student mentors in learning spaces.

In Chapter 13, Geoffrey Crisp examines assessment in virtual learning spaces. The chapter examines how assessment spaces must change in response to the rapid development and uptake of new virtual learning spaces. Students are engaging in collaborative, cooperative learning activities in a spatially distributed environment, yet their assessment tasks are often delivered in traditional assessment spaces that bear little resemblance to their learning spaces. The assessment of students in virtual worlds, virtual laboratories, role-plays, and serious games is examined, and the case is presented for the wider use of evidence-centered assessment designs and stealth assessment techniques. In Chapter 14, Gylo (Julie) Hercelinskyj and Beryl McEwan present an overview of an innovative teaching approach in an under-graduate nursing degree at Charles Darwin University (CDU). The authors describe the development and initial integration of a virtual learning space into the first year clinical nursing subject using a case-based approach in order to address some of the issues associated with an externalised Bachelor of Nursing program. In addition, the use of the CDU vHospital® in supporting early role socialisation into nursing and professional identity of first year nursing students will be explored. In Chapter 15, Caroline Steel and Trish Andrews suggest that academic development can be designed to provide strong opportunities for university teachers to re-imagine their teaching for these new spaces while also building their leadership capacity. This chapter discusses challenges that teachers face in transforming their teaching practices and proposes a model for academic development. Two case studies demonstrate the flexibility and efficacy of the model and provide pointers for further adoption in the higher education context. In Chapter 16, Chris Cheers, Chen Swee Eng, and Glen Postle advocate that to maximise the potential of any learning environment, educators need to understand how students learn in the first instance and then design the learning environment based on these insights. Formal learning is conceived as an individualised experience within an organised learning community, and it is suggested that this learning environment is described as an experiential space. Within this chapter, the authors describe an approach to designing experiential space that uses problem based learning to engage students and facilitate their active construction of knowledge. In Chapter 17, Keith Kirkwood, Gill Best, Robin McCormack, and Dan Tout explore the human element in the learning space through the notion that once a learning space is colonised, it becomes a learning place of agency, purpose, and community involving both staff and students. The chapter discusses the dynamics of peer learning across learning space settings and the challenges involved in instituting the shift from teacher- to learning-centred pedagogies within spaces. Both physical and virtual dimensions are considered, with the SNAP-VU Platform introduced as a strategy for facilitating virtual learning communities of practice in which staff, mentors, and students will be able to engage in mutual learning support. The chapter concludes with calls for the explicit inclusion of peer learning in the operational design of learning spaces.

Mike Keppell
Charles Sturt University, Australia

Kay Souter
La Trobe University, Australia

Matthew Riddle
La Trobe University, Australia

Acknowledgment

We would like to thank our colleagues who contributed the diverse range of chapters to the book. The response to the call for chapters was overwhelming and we were pleasantly surprised that other colleagues shared our interest, passion, and enthusiasm for learning spaces. These contributions demonstrate the importance of community and the quality of work that is being undertaken across a broad spectrum of roles and professions. We would also like to thank the authors for willingly reviewing chapters and providing extensive feedback to improve the quality of each chapter. Within the academic community this is a priceless contribution.

We wish to thank Professor Jan Herrington and Professor Ron Oliver for assisting with the review of chapters.

In particular we wish to thank Dr. Dominique Parrish for her significant contribution to the book in terms of project management, administration, and communication with authors and IGI.

We would also like to thank the staff at IGI Global for their patience and guidance in the process of editing this book.

We would also like to thank the many people we have worked with on the *Spaces for Knowledge Generation Project* http://www.skgproject.com which was the inspiration for the development of the book.

Mike Keppell
Charles Sturt University, Australia

Kay Souter
La Trobe University, Australia

Matthew Riddle
La Trobe University, Australia

Section 1
Space Perspectives

Chapter 1
Distributed Learning Spaces:
Physical, Blended and Virtual Learning Spaces in Higher Education

Mike Keppell
Charles Sturt University, Australia

Matthew Riddle
La Trobe University, Australia

ABSTRACT

This chapter examines distributed and personal learning spaces across the spectrum of physical, blended and virtual learning spaces in the higher education context. We suggest that higher education is no longer defined by tangible boundaries of a 'physical campus' but by the entire student experience, whether that involves negotiating the physical corridors of the campus, attending face-to-face classes, participating in fully online courses or a blend of both face-to-face and online courses. In addition the student experience may also involve connecting to virtual environments from home, a local cafe, on the train or participating in professional practice hundreds of kilometers from the physical campus. This chapter attempts to account for the diverse range of spaces that are enriching the learning and teaching experience for both academics and students and suggests the need to recognise the changing nature of learning spaces in higher education.

INTRODUCTION

Higher education institutions are no longer defined by the physical boundaries of their campus but by the entire student experience, whether that involves negotiating the physical corridors of the campus, attending face-to-face classes, participating in fully online courses or a blend of both face-to-face and online courses. In addition to the formal institutional physical and virtual spaces utilised by staff and students, the informal physical and virtual spaces may now encompass a wider range of distributed learning spaces. These distributed

DOI: 10.4018/978-1-60960-114-0.ch001

learning spaces could involve a complex web of on-campus experiences, connecting to virtual environments from a variety of locations such as home, a local cafe, on the train or participating in professional practice hundreds of kilometers from the physical campus. Distributed learning spaces recognise that we are seeing a disintegration of the distinction between face-to-face learning and teaching and distance education. There is increased recognition that learning does not just occur in the formal university setting but increasingly at work, home and within the community and that the principles of lifelong learning are being embraced by society. There is also a proliferation of approaches emerging including 'flexible', 'open', 'distance' and 'off-campus' that assist the ubiquity of learning in a wide range of contexts (Lea & Nicholl, 2002).

The blurring of face-to-face learning and teaching and online learning is a significant shift for both students and staff of universities. This disintegration of the distinction and the growing acceptance that learning occurs in different 'places' presents both exciting and challenging opportunities for higher education. The recognition of blended and flexible learning is significant for traditional face-to-face institutions as well as distance education universities. For the purposes of this chapter the premise that flexible learning provides *opportunities* to improve the student learning experience through flexibility in time, pace, place (physical, virtual, on-campus, off-campus), mode of study (print-based, face-to-face, blended, online), teaching approach (collaborative, independent), forms of assessment and staffing is accepted. It may utilise a wide range of media, environments, learning spaces and technologies for learning and teaching. "Blended and flexible learning" is a design approach that examines the relationships between flexible learning *opportunities*, in order to optimise student engagement and equivalence in learning outcomes regardless of mode of study (Keppell, 2010).

The growing acceptance of life-long and life-wide learning also have a major influence on distributed learning spaces. Lifelong learning encompasses both formal and informal learning, self-motivated learning, self-funded learning and universal participation (Watson, 2003). There is growing acceptance and recognition of life-wide learning in informal settings. "The idea of life-wide learning is proposed to highlight the fact that at any point in time, for example while a learner is engaged in Higher Education, an individual's life contains many parallel and interconnected journeys and experiences and that these individually and collectively contribute to the ongoing personal and potentially professional development of the person" (Jackson, 2010, p. 492). We can no longer assume that school leavers are the major demographic group that universities need to cater for as mature age students are increasingly represented in higher education settings. We can also not assume that all students will desire the campus experience for their learning and that many students may choose flexible learning opportunities to suit their life circumstances which may mean that they do not physically visit the university campus.

This chapter recognises the ubiquity of spaces that are enriching the learning and teaching experience for both academics and students and suggests that we need to begin by exploring the pedagogical interactions and considerations that are possible in distributed learning spaces. This chapter will begin with an examination of the role of the university, the utopian university in relation to learning and teaching, and the ecological university (Barnett, 2011). Secondly we will examine the assumptions and principles underlying higher education. These assumptions and underlying principles form the default basis for making decisions about learning and teaching in the higher education environment. Thirdly, pedagogy needs to be examined to understand the nature of distributed learning spaces. Fourthly, rather than lecture halls with rowed seats being the predominant physical space for learning and teaching in higher education, this chapter explores a diverse range of alternate learning spaces including: physical/virtual, formal/informal, blended, mobile, outdoor, academic, personal and practice-based spaces and considers the importance of flexibility, adaptability and time in these settings. The chapter traverses physical, blended and virtual spaces and examines the perceived and actual affordances of these learning spaces. Fifthly, a case study is presented outlining a range of spaces utilised by students. It examines the use of spaces from the student experience as opposed to the technology or physical space perspective. Gaining a clear understanding of where, how, and why students use these technologies is more elusive and how students use space in their everyday lives provides a fascinating insight into the use of space by students (Riddle & Howell, 2008). Finally, the chapter will examine implications for the use of distributed learning spaces in higher education.

ROLE OF UNIVERSITIES IN RELATION TO DISTRIBUTED LEARNING SPACES

The role of universities has been traditionally focused on research, teaching and service to the community. At the core of their values is that the needs of society are central to their activities. A core value of universities is that they focus on enhancing society and influencing students to become fully functioning members of their professional community. There would be little disagreement with the notion that universities should contribute to the well-being of society and strive to develop students who are both confident and forward-looking in their aptitude to continue to learn once working in their chosen profession. The major distinctive feature of a professional is their ability to reflect on a daily basis on their work and then action forward-looking thinking for the benefit of their own professional practice. In

other words universities seek to develop graduates who will continue to develop intellectually, professionally and socially beyond the bounds of formal education. To achieve this goal we need to explicitly teach university students skills in life-long learning and life-wide learning in order for them to continue to learn once outside the bounds of the physical or virtual boundaries of the institution. In addition, university curriculum, learning and teaching services need to be responsive to the diverse cultural, social and academic needs of students in order to enable them to adapt to the demands of university education and to provide them with cultural capital for life success. In essence we seek sustainability or as Barnett (2011) suggests, we seek the utopia of the ecological university.

Barnett (2011) suggests that the ecological university represents an orientation to sustainability, interconnectedness, wellbeing and care for the university environment that encompasses all aspects of its functioning including the environment, social relations and knowledge. It is a networked university that values and fosters its networks and their interconnectedness and feels a responsibility to the wellbeing of these networks. "Through its interest in promoting understanding through learning and inquiry, it seeks to contribute what it can so as to advance the wellbeing of each aspect of the world upon which it might have an effect" (Barnett, 2011, p. 142). Instead of 'having an impact' on the world, ecological universities seek sustainability and more importantly self-sustainability in multiple levels of interactions. It adopts a 'care for the world' as opposed to an 'impact on the world' approach (Barnett, 2011).

The underlying principles for achieving the goal of the ecological university include at least five aspects: access and equity; equivalence of learning outcomes; student learning experience; constructive alignment and discipline pedagogies. Universities have ethical obligations to cater for students of all ages, geographical location and technological access. Distance education universities usually cater for all students by providing options for face-to-face students, students in blended learning environments (combination of face-to-face and online interactions), online environments and also students who require print-based resources due to their lack of internet access or technological proficiency. In other words universities have an ethical obligation in relation to 'access and equity' in the provision of courses (degrees) and subjects for all students.

In addition to access and equity, university education has an ethical obligation to have 'equivalence of learning outcomes' across the range of options mentioned previously. Universities are now seeing a higher percentage of part-time students juggling family, work and studies as well students who may study by distance education using online technologies and who may seldom visit the physical campus. This means that no two students may have exactly the same educational experience, yet it is expected that students will graduate with comparable knowledge, skills, competence and attitudes in their chosen area. Instead of examining sameness of the educational experience (whatever that means) we need to focus on 'equivalence of learning outcomes'. Learning and teaching in all these spaces (face-to-face, blended, online, resource-based) needs to be underpinned by optimal design practices to ensure equivalent learning outcomes for all students.

Another key principle that naturally flows from the previous principle is that the 'contemporary student experience traverses physical, blended and virtual learning spaces'. This includes students studying at traditional face-to-face universities as well as distance education universities that should be naturally embracing distributed learning spaces. 'Place' is becoming less important in the student experience and it may be that academics will need to embrace this multiplicity of spaces for learning and teaching. The recognition of distributed learning spaces in higher education will have enormous implications for all universities and particularly those universities that believe

face-to-face learning and teaching in physical buildings is superior to other forms of learning and teaching.

The concept of 'constructive alignment' (Biggs & Tang, 2007) is another principle that underpins learning and teaching in the ecological university. It suggests that students construct meaning through their interactions in learning and teaching and that all aspects of the learning context should be aligned to achieving the desired learning outcomes. For this reason the learning environment, curriculum, degree, learning and teaching activities, assessment and learning outcomes should be designed in conjunction with each other to guarantee the richness of the student experience.

Another principle that will influence the use of spaces in higher education is the discipline pedagogy unique to the specific profession. Shulman (2005) refers to these unique approaches as the 'signature pedagogies' of the professions. "A 'signature pedagogy' is a mode of teaching that has become inextricably identified with preparing people for a particular profession" (Shulman, 2005, p. 5). A 'signature pedagogy' has a number of unique characteristics. Firstly, it is an approach distinctive to the profession (e.g. clinical rounds in medicine). Secondly, the approach is pervasive in the curriculum and thirdly, the approach is pervasive across institutions and therefore essential in the education of the profession.

In addition to the principles above, contemporary learning and teaching needs to account for the type of interactions that are occurring or could occur in subjects and degree programs. Information access (course and subject expectations) conveys/delivers information to the individual learner through the learning management system. This may include course design information as well as the subject related requirements in relation to subject information, learning outcomes, assessment and a rationale for the use of online tools. Information access allows easy access by learners to information or resources and the ability to review the content at anytime through the learning management system. Interactive learning (learner-to-content interactions) determines the blends that are appropriate at subject level, taking into account factors such as the learning space (on-campus, at a distance, workplace learning, the level of learner engagement with the resources within the learning management system environment, and other connected environments such as eportfolio, Web 2.0 tools, online meeting spaces and so on). It involves an individual interaction with the resources. These resources would be embedded within the online environment or may involve standalone CD-ROMs, DVDs which are delivered to distance education learners or utilised by learners in face-to-face classes. Networked learning (learner-to-learner, learner-to-teacher interactions) enhance communication between learners; and between learners and teachers within the learning management system, and other connected environments such as eportfolio, Web 2.0 tools, online meeting spaces and so on. Peer learning is central to this approach where it is expected that there would be two-way dialogue/feedback between learners and/or two-way dialogue/feedback between learners and the teacher. Within the learning management system this may include: forums, chat, group tasks, reflective journals, blogs, online debates, online presentations, virtual tutorials, wikis. Student-generated content (learners-as-designers, assessment-as-learning) emphasises the design, development and presentation of products and artefacts which may also be associated with the formal assessment of the subject. These artefacts may include student-generated: reports, concept maps, reflective journals, digital stories, presentations, e-portfolios, group projects as well as photographs, video and audio artefacts and web 2.0 technologies. Individual, partner and group developments may be utilised in this approach (Keppell, 2010).

DISTRIBUTED LEARNING SPACES

Learning and teaching in higher education should occur in a range of learning spaces rather than the predominant physical learning space being the lecture halls with rowed seats. These learning spaces should include: physical/virtual, formal/informal, blended, mobile, outdoor, academic, personal and practice-based spaces and should consider flexibility, adaptability and time. This section traverses physical, blended and virtual spaces and examines the perceived and actual affordances of these learning spaces.

Throughout this chapter four key aspects will define our definition of learning spaces. Learning spaces are:

- physical, blended or virtual learning environments that enhance as opposed to constrain learning;
- physical, blended or virtual 'areas' that motivate a user to participate for learning benefits;
- spaces where both teachers and students optimize the perceived and actual affordances of the space; and
- spaces that promote authentic learning interactions.

Physical Learning Spaces

These spaces often have a preconceived function that is determined before they are designed for learning and teaching. They are often determined by traditional conceptions of teaching and learning that place a premium on the teacher as authority and disseminator of knowledge and the student as passive recipient of knowledge. Typical of these approaches are the use of lectures and tutorials where students listen and write notes. Although there is a place for lecturing in any learning and teaching strategy and within any institution, the focus tends to be on content as opposed to student engagement and learning. A high proportion of

Figure 1. Distributed learning spaces that students and academics are increasingly traversing in higher education

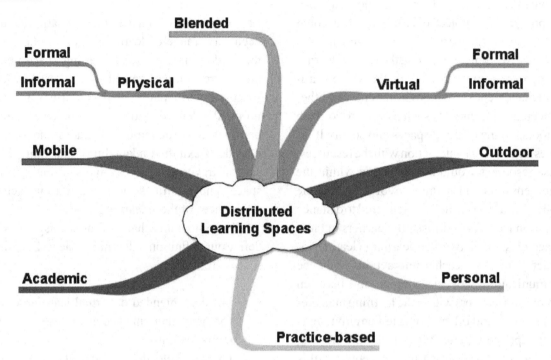

lecture halls within universities reinforce this traditional approach to disseminating content which is in opposition to the interactive formal learning spaces that encourage knowledge generation by students. Innovative formal learning spaces that explicitly encourage peer-learning may adopt problem-based learning or project-based learning approaches.

To enhance learning, universities have traditionally used physical learning spaces (lecture theatres, labs, tutorial rooms) to prepare students for their future careers and professions. To motivate learners and provide diverse teaching approaches, formal physical learning spaces need to be adaptable and flexible for learning and teaching as opposed to being designed for one purpose. This allows both learners and teachers to use the space to suit the learning activities as opposed to constraining the learning and teaching opportunities in the subject or course. Ideally, learning activities should focus on authentic learning interactions

which are directly relevant for the future career of the student. Informal physical learning spaces include libraries and learning commons (see Figure 2) that have been explicitly designed to encourage students to engage in both independent and peer-learning. Ideal informal spaces provide sufficient flexibility so that students can design the informal space to suit their own learning needs. Chairs, tables, access to wi-fi and power points need to be considered to allow this adaptability. In addition, different weeks of the semester may require totally different spaces as students progress through stages of their learning. One learning space may need to promote quiet, independent, self-reflective study for the individual student while the same space on another day may need to allow group-based and peer learning. This is ideal when spaces enhance, motivate and promote authentic learning interactions. These aspects are important for existing spaces as well as spaces that are being designed or repurposed.

Souter, Riddle, Keppell, Sellers (2010) suggest seven principles of learning space design which support a constructivist approach to learning: and support a learning environment that is student-centred, collaborative, and experiential. These include:

- *Comfort*: a space which creates a physical and mental sense of ease and well-being.
- *Aesthetics*: pleasure which includes the recognition of symmetry, harmony, simplicity and fitness for purpose.
- *Flow*: the state of mind felt by the learner when totally involved in the learning experience.
- *Equity*: consideration of the needs of cultural and physical differences.
- *Blending*: a mixture of technological and face-to-face pedagogical resources.
- *Affordances*: the "action possibilities" the learning environment provides the users, including such things as kitchens, natural light, wifi, private spaces, writing surfaces, sofas, and so on.
- *Repurposing*: the potential for multiple usage of a space.

Virtual Learning Spaces

Many higher education universities use institutional virtual learning environments (e.g. Sakai, Blackboard, Moodle) to complement the face-to-face learning and teaching experience via blended learning or to provide distance education using blended or totally online subjects and courses (degree programs). Coates, James and Baldwin (2005) suggest a number of factors that have been drivers behind the adoption of learning management systems (LMS) within higher education settings. These include:

- LMS suggest a means of increasing the efficiency of teaching

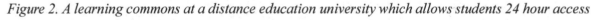

Figure 2. A learning commons at a distance education university which allows students 24 hour access

- The attractiveness of LMS is associated with the promise of enriched student learning
- Universities are driven by new student expectations
- Competitive pressure between institutions has been a driver behind the adoption of LMS
- LMS are sometimes proposed as a key means of responding to massive and increasing demands for greater access to higher education
- LMS are part of an important culture shift taking place in teaching and learning in higher education (p. 24-25).

Associated with this culture shift in teaching and learning has been the important decisions that need to be made by institutions in choosing a LMS that best matches their 'specific context'. This is not a simple decision, as evidenced by the calibre of personnel who need to be involved in the decision making process. "In incorporating online learning systems into university teaching programmes, it is important to consider whether commercially available systems are adaptable to the needs of diverse academic cultures and communities" (Coates, James & Baldwin, 2005, p. 31). Debate still occurs as to whether an institution should adopt a proprietary LMS (with so-called constraints) or an open source LMS (which may provide too much freedom).

Virtual learning spaces provide unique opportunities that are unavailable in physical learning spaces and can enrich the student experience. These affordances or 'action possibilities' allow a richer range of learning interactions and may include online discussion forums, blogs, wikis, podcasts and diverse media-rich environments. The notion of space in this context is not bounded by physical walls but by virtual spaces that have different affordances. An affordance is a design aspect of an object which suggests how an object should be used (Norman, 1988). An affordance is often influenced by context, culture, instinct and mental models. When designers make use of affordances the user knows what to do just by looking. The concept of affordance has been widely discussed in relation to ICT (Boyle & Cook, 2004; Conole & Dyke, 2004a, 2004b; Hill, 2006; John & Sutherland, 2005; Oliver, 2005). A crucial aspect of the concept is that both the teacher and learner must understand how a space can be utilised which means that it is necessary to understand both the perceived and actual affordance of a space. For example, a student needs to recognise and understand the perceived affordance of a wiki (i.e. collaboration) and be able to use this affordance in the actual development of a project that involves three students dispersed across different states and time zones of Australia.

Informal virtual learning spaces are becoming increasingly utilised in higher education. Facebook, Flickr, YouTube and Twitter allow users to personalise and customize their own virtual spaces and network and socialise with others. Madge, Meek, Wellens and Hooley (2010) suggest that "Web 2.0 applications are increasingly embedded in the daily routines of everyday life, particularly for young people in many places and a variety of different social settings" (p. 142). Universities are recognising the value of web 2.0 tools to enhance the formal virtual learning environment and many are utlising both vendor supplied and community-driven tools. Madge, Meek, Wellens and Hooley (2010) research on the use of Facebook for streamlining the transition of new students into university also found that "online and offline worlds are clearly coexisting, but used in different ways for developing and sustaining different types of relationships. For example, face-to-face friendships from home have been developed and sustained through continued online interactions, whilst newer online relationships have flourished at university and developed into face-to-face in-depth relationships" (p. 145).

Blended Learning Spaces

Blended learning involves the integration of both on-campus face-to-face learning and teaching and on or off-campus virtual learning environments utilising the affordances of each environment to enhance the student experience. A combination of physical/virtual, formal/informal would be considered in these spaces to optimise the student experience. "Blended and flexible learning" is a design approach that examines the relationships between flexible learning opportunities, in order to optimise student engagement and equivalence in learning outcomes regardless of mode of study (Keppell, 2010). Gerbic and Stacey (2009) suggest that the introduction of blended learning is challenging as "the face-to-face setting is foundational in all contexts, and has a historical and experiential legitimacy" (p. 302). They also suggest that "it is far more difficult to create or develop the same kind of fidelity, comfort or social presence in online spaces" (p. 302).

Other perspectives suggest that blended learning is "a design approach whereby both face-to-face and online learning are made better by the presence of each other" (Garrison & Vaughan, 2008, p. 52). Blended learning and teaching can occur at four levels of granularity. These include: activity-level blending, subject-level blending, course-level blending and institutional-level blending (Graham, 2006). A blended learning design may also be enabling, enhancing or transformative. Enabling blends would address issues of access and equity to provide equitable opportunities in face-to-face, print-based, blended and fully online learning environments. Enhancing blends focus on incremental changes to the existing teaching and learning environment. Transformative blends focus on a major redesign of the teaching and learning environment (e.g. online, problem based learning). Littlejohn and Pegler (2007) suggest that "blended e-learning offers the possibility of changing our attitudes … as to *where* and *when* learning takes place" (p. 2).

In addition it offers an "integration of *spaces*" (p. 2) and allows flexibility in the time when learners are involved in subjects or courses.

Mobile Learning Spaces

The use of mobile technology such as Smartphones and iPods represents a promising area in which to explore the concept of space. Mobile technologies will provide further flexibility to the student experience in higher education and they will become increasingly important as students and academics traverse physical, blended and virtual learning environments. "With its strong emphasis on learning rather than teaching, mobile learning challenges educators to try to understand learners' needs, circumstances and abilities even better than before. This extends to understanding how learning takes place beyond the classroom, in the course of daily routines, commuting and travel, and in the intersection of education, life, work and leisure" (Kukulska-Hulme, 2010, p.181).

The Horizon Report (2011) suggests that there is a shift in the means that users are connecting to the internet due to: "the growing number of internet-capable mobile devices, increasingly flexible web content, and continued development of the networks that support connectivity." It is also suggested that 100% of university students utilise mobile phones and their portability and ubiquity are powerful tools for learning and teaching. Their ability to be used as electronic book readers, annotation tools, creation, composition, social networking, image, video and audio capture tools is becoming increasingly sophisticated (Horizon Report, 2011). In addition "learning when mobile means that context becomes all-important, since even a simple change of location is an invitation to revisit learning, in both a literal sense (to apply it, reflect on it, reinforce it, share it) and metaphorical, to reconsider what constitutes learning or what makes it effective in a given situation" (Kukulska-Hulme, 2009, p. 159). Conversely, it is possible to argue that the context becomes immaterial when mobile technologies make any place a learning space.

Outdoor Learning Spaces

The need to think 'outside the box' as to what constitutes a learning and teaching space will become increasingly important particularly as mobile learning will continue to grow in usage. Outdoor spaces represent one of the unexpected 'places' where rich learning may occur. Most university campuses focus time and energy on the formal learning spaces of the buildings for learning and teaching with both students and staff often gazing across manicured gardens and fields surrounding the buildings. It is somewhat ironic that few academics and students may consider and utilise these open spaces as formal/informal learning spaces that provide unique opportunities for learning in all disciplines.

Rafferty (2011) eloquently suggests that "these pathways, thoroughfares and occasional rest areas are generally given a functional value in traffic management and are more often than not developed as an after thought in campus design. As such the thoroughfares and rest areas are under valued (or not recognised) as important spaces for learning and teaching." Importantly, with the pervasiveness of wifi and mobile devices, outdoor learning spaces can create a blended learning experience that models distributed learning and provides learning opportunities which may not be possible within the boundaries of physical classrooms.

Academic Spaces

Barnett (2011) suggests that "today's university lives amid multiple time-spans, and time-speeds" (p. 74). He suggests that the arrival of constant email would be considered one of these multiple time-spans, and other time spans might include historians who focus on the past and researchers who may focus on the future of their research. Academic developers may focus on 12 months of workshops and seminars and distance education

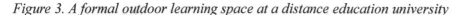

Figure 3. A formal outdoor learning space at a distance education university

universities may need to be conscious of the 24/7 existence of their students across the globe, each in their own unique time-span. In other words there are a 'plurality of durations' and 'time-spans' for individual academics who often work evenings and weekends. Increasingly, academics need to focus on activities that do 'double-time', in order to manage multiple time-spans. These activities fulfill more than one function, such as researching one's own teaching. Academics may also use their 'multiple time-spans' to 'open spaces' through collaborations across the country and globe with academics within other universities.

Barnett (2011) suggests that academics may be active in university spaces that may include:

- *Intellectual and discursive space* which focus on the contribution to the wider public sphere.
- *Epistemological space* which focuses on the "space available for academics to pursue their own research interests" (p. 76).
- *Pedagogical and curricular space* focuses on the spaces available to trial new pedagogical approaches and new curricular initiatives.
- *Ontological space* which focuses on 'academic being' which is becoming increasingly multi-faceted beyond the research, teaching and community commitments. Terms such as manager, mentor, facilitator and curriculum designer suggest boundaries which are changing. In fact "the widening of universities' ontological spaces may bring both peril and liberation" (p. 77).

Increasingly due to the dispersed student population spread across the globe, timezones, physical and virtual learning spaces, universities may be seen as "intersecting time zones and space zones" (Barnett, 2011, p. 78). Barnett (2011) combines time and space to create three formations. These include:

- *Practical time/practical space* is the work diary time that is scheduled for individual academics and the university calendar. It is the predominant "visible felt time and visible space" (p. 78) in universities.
- *Virtual time/virtual space* is the 'hidden time' and space that includes the papers and books written at home, reading undertaken on the train to work or plane commuting to other campuses, communication via Skype and other such activities that go unseen. This 'hidden time' may impinge on the life/work balance of the academic if it is not managed by the individual academic.
- *Imagined time/imagined space* is the time spent thinking of possibilities which are 'new spaces and timeframes' (Barnett, 2011).

The academic who imagines possibilities, lives with uncertainty when they travel (physically or virtually) as they are putting themselves forward into new spaces. International conference presentations, working in different cultural contexts all represent new spaces and a stretching of thoughts and perspectives. Universities need to encourage this entry into new spaces, new thoughts and new possibilities in order to continue thinking about what will work toward the goal of the ecological university.

Personal Learning Spaces

Personal learning environments (PLE) integrate formal and informal learning spaces but more importantly they are customised by the individual to suit their needs and allow them to create their own identities. They comprise all the tools we use in our daily lives. Figure 4 is an attempt to map the tools that are used for learning in the role of a university academic. A PLE recognises ongoing learning and the need for tools to support life-long and life-wide learning. "PLE are based on the idea that learning will take place in different contexts and situations and will not be provided by a single learning provider" (Attwell, 2007, p. 1). PLE are individually-constructed and customised and they stand in stark contrast to learning management systems which both enhance and constrain learning due to their inherent structure, configuration and imposed organisation. PLE may also foster self-regulated learning "which refers to the ability of the learner to prepare for his/her own learning, take the necessary steps to learn, manage/evaluate his/her learning and provide self-feedback and judgement, all while maintaining a high level of motivation (McLoughlin & Lee, 2009, p. 639).

PLE may also require new ways of learning as knowledge has changed to networks and ecologies (Siemens, 2006). The implications of this change is that improved lines of communication need to occur. "Connectivism is the assertion that learning is primarily a network-forming process" (p. 15). It is a theory of learning in the digital age that attempts to filter and offload

knowledge to trusted members of a personal network. Some of the principles of connectivism include:

- Learning requires a diversity of opinions;
- Learning is a network formation;
- Knowledge rests in networks;
- The capacity to know more is essential; and
- The capacity to remain current is valued.

Practice-Based Spaces

Universities are increasingly educating learners to participate in professional practice before entering the workforce. Learners are immersed in practicums or work-integrated learning activities in schools, hospitals, practice environments etc. These work-integrated activities are undertaken in spaces often at a distance from the university campus, sometimes without direct supervision.

Figure 4. Personal learning spaces that may regularly be traversed

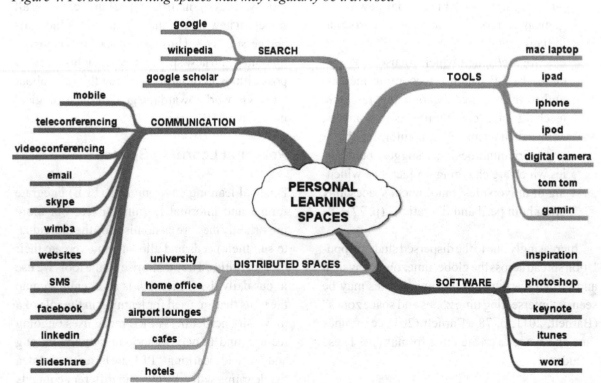

The student within the practicum learns the culture of the profession through this immersion and often interacts at a distance from university academics. The use of mobile devices and personal learning environments has enormous potential for connecting the student during their practicum. The use of eportfolios also provides a mechanism for the student to provide reflections, complete formal assessments and use multiple forms of media to document, reflect and share their ongoing learning within the practice-based space with other students and academic staff.

CASE STUDY: STUDENT EXPERIENCE

A Day In the Life of a Student

In September and October 2008, 19 students from La Trobe University in Melbourne became co-researchers in an experiment about the use of technologies in their daily lives. After a short briefing, they carried a kit designed to assist them to record one twenty-four hour period of their student experience. The kit included, a short list of instructions, a paper diary, and a digital camera with voice recording capability. Each student also carried a mobile phone.

This project used the 'day experience method' (Riddle & Arnold, 2007) and is based on a combination of the 'experience sampling method' (Hektner, Schmidt & Csikszentmihalyi, 2006), 'cultural probes' (Gaver, Dunne, & Pacenti, 1999) and the 'day reconstruction method' (Kahneman, Krueger, Schkade, Schwarz, & Stone, 2004). The method was developed to examine student perspectives of technologies in their daily lives, as part of the Learning Landscape Project (2008) at the University of Cambridge.

Four different groups of students participated over the university week. Each student was sent a text message between eight and ten times at irregular intervals over a twenty-four hour period,

excluding the hours between 10pm and 8am, prompting them with the following questions.

1. What time is it?
2. Where are you?
3. Who are you with? (friends, colleagues, family etc.)
4. What are you doing?
5. What technologies or techniques are you using? (including pen & paper or face-to-face communication)
6. How do you feel about it?
   - Use the camera!
   - Use the voice recorder if you like!
   - Use the diary!

These instructions encouraged the participants to provide as rich and detailed an account as possible of their experience. At the end of the twenty-four hour period, the students were invited to present their photos and discuss their 'day' with each of the other students in the cohort. In groups of five or six, they sat around a table and a facilitator invited them to show the group their photographs using a computer and projector. As each slide appeared, the student who had taken the photograph talked about where they were at the time and what they were doing, as well as any technologies they happened to be using at the time. The slides showed lecture halls, tutorial rooms, and library carrels, but most of them showed informal 'places' off campus including pizza shops, trams, swimming pools and cars, with many photos taken indoors at home.

Fitting Everything Into the Day

Freda is a 20-year old full time student who is studying tourism management. During the focus group, Freda presented her photos which included a photo featuring her iPod while she was at the gym. The conversation turned to the topic of using music players while doing other things, and to the general topic of doing many things concurrently, often involving technologies. When asked, Freda explained that it was quite normal for her to have an iPod, an iPhone, a met ticket, and shopping bags under her arms while she was trying to catch a bus, and even when using her computer she often used an iPod while chatting to friends on Facebook. The other students agreed that this was normal practice. Eddie suggested that listening to music on his laptop headphones assisted him to concentrate, but Chanelle complained that listening to music while doing other things could also be a distraction.

Freda showed another slide with some books, and explained that she was studying at work while "it's pretty quiet and the bosses aren't around". A discussion with the group about time management followed and Freda pointed to a small red leather bound book on top of the pile. "That's my organiser, the red thing's my organiser which I write in all the time to juggle commitments…". None of the other students had an organiser to manage hourly appointments, but some of the other students commented that they write down tasks or add reminders to their phones for important appointments.

Bernice, a 21-year old law and management graduate diploma student, described being alone at home on her computer writing an essay while at the same time messaging a friend and organising a limousine for her sister's wedding.

During the focus group discussion almost all of the group identified themselves as multi-taskers, with only one student, Harvey, seeing himself as more focused. A little later in the discussion, he explained why.

Harvey: I run a pet wholesaling business, so I'm … on-call for 60 hours from Thursday morning to Sunday night, so it's just go, go, go!

Facilitator: How much of that [time] will you be … unable to study?

Harvey: …probably 80% of the time.

Harvey: It's just, I'm on call literally, I'll have orders that I have to fill and be all over Melbourne doing deliveries… It's pretty full on.

Facilitator: Are you studying full time?

Harvey: Yes. From Monday to Wednesday I'm here, and Thursday to Sunday I work … a 60 hour week, so it's pretty full on!

Laptops and Wifi

Eddie is 27, and is a full time business information management systems student at La Trobe in his second year of a masters degree. He lives nearby the university, only four stops away on the tram. Like all his friends, Eddie carries a mobile phone with him at all times. Eddie's diary shows that in the early afternoon he walked to the library to do research for his assignments. At the time of the first text prompt, Eddie was waiting outside the library and regretted his decision to leave his laptop at home because the queues were so long to get onto a library workstation. He sat outside the library and was embarrassed to ask a friend to borrow his laptop to check his email.

During the focus group discussion, Eddie explained that he had trouble accessing wifi on campus during the semester. Alexandra, a 22-year old international student suggested that the staff have told her that undergraduates cannot access the internet from outside the library, whilst postgraduates could do so. Eddie confirmed that he could use the internet sitting outside the library, but Alexandra complained that she could not access wifi even from inside the classrooms.

Studying in Comfort

Chanelle complained that when students do take laptops outside, they can't use them for very long because the battery dies. She also mentioned that there are no power points available on the campus to accommodate students outside of the library. While examining a photo of a study area outside the library, Eddie suggested that 'when the library closes, many students move outside to finish off their work, but because of the lack of power they can only study for a short while'. The students also discussed how well the university meets their needs in terms of private study. The students expressed frustration about finding a comfortable place to study on the campus.

Chanelle: There's just no ... place for large numbers [of students] to sit. The university is not providing for the number of people that actually attend [the campus]. Because it is so far 'out' I guess it benefits people who live ... locally ... but people that have ... to travel ... far ... they're going to spend the whole day here. If they leave the library they lose their spot in the library and there's nowhere else to go.

Where are You?

The 'day experience method' is useful for a consideration of the theme of space, as it provides a snapshot of where students are spending their time during a typical day (Howell, 2008; Riddle & Howell, 2008). Table 1 illustrates the number of times students mentioned their location in diaries or voice recordings. The most prominent location for studying was home (66). The second most prominent location was the library (25), followed by the car (13) tutorial (12) and lecture (11). One other notable aspect of this data is that the students in this study spent a significant amount of time in places outside home, work or their university,

such as the car, on the tram, at a friend's place, or pursuing a hobby.

Adapting Learning Space Designs

A number of challenges arise from the data collected in this study. In particular, student expectations of their study environment may be 'out of step' with university provision, and students are dissatisfied with some particular aspects of private study spaces. They often lack suitable places to work on their assignments, which demand independent, focused research as well as collaborative study. Because students are dividing their time between work, study, home and social commitments, they often find it difficult to juggle these commitments.

A subsequent project has now been initiated at La Trobe University under the banner of Faculty Based Learning Commons, which is addressing some of these student concerns. The project involves the development of several 'eddie spaces'

Table 1. Frequencies of the responses to the question "Where are you?"

Location	Responses
Bank	1
Cafe	6
Car	13
Car park	1
Computer lab	2
Friend's residence	8
Home	66
Lecture	11
Library	25
Public transport	6
Recreation venue	8
Shopping	4
Tutorial	12
University	5
Walking	2
Workplace	10

around the Melbourne campus, and includes provision of group and individual study spaces in corridors and building overpasses. A centerpiece of this development is the design of a new student hub (Figure 5). This hub includes an indoor space with a combination of fixed banquette seating to form café style booths with power hubs, alongside flip top tables and lightweight durable seating that can be easily reconfigured for group or private study. The space will include a kitchen area for tea and coffee, powered lockers, and card entry for extended hours thereby enabling students to use the space in comfort over the course of an entire day. The design calls for wifi zones to extend to an outdoor seating area which will also include comfortable powered work areas. In this way the 'day in the life of a student study' has influenced the design of distributed spaces across the campus.

IMPLICATIONS

There are a number of implications that should be considered in relation to distributed learning spaces.

Adaptability of Learning Spaces

Flexible learning and teaching spaces should allow adaptability over time for different uses. For example distance education universities may require spaces to be used for students who are both physically present and students who never visit the campus but participate via videoconferencing in group learning activities. Balancing the experience of students who traverse face-to-face, blended and virtual learning spaces will be increasingly important in the future.

Figure 5. Concept drawing for a faculty based learning commons including indoor and outdoor spaces with wifi zones, powered booths, and flexible furniture. Image authored by Baldasso Cortese Architects.

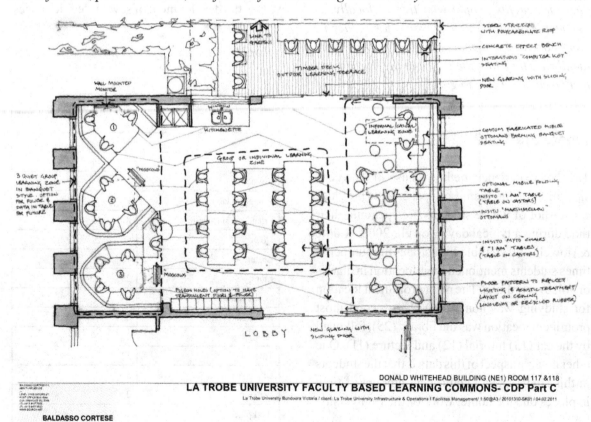

Ubiquity of Spaces

It is essential that we recognise the diversified nature of learning and teaching spaces. Homes, cars, buses, hotels, cafes become mobile spaces where the student may undertake learning. Studying while travelling to work via train or bus may represent the learning space for some students. The need for careful thought about how students will interact with universities will need to be considered in the future.

Study Time and Space

In addition to the notion of physical/virtual and formal/informal, the concept of time also needs to be considered. Students' use of space during a semester will be influenced by time of day, day of week and week of semester. Students may utilise space dependent on their other constraints of work and family and timing of classes and travel. Distance education students may budget only certain days to study on-campus or virtually. For example, the early stages of a subject may encourage students to discuss content with other peers, while group assessment tasks will also require students to work in teams and use space for discussion and negotiation. When exams are nearing, students may revert to quiet individual spaces for self-study as opposed to peer learning.

Decision-Making

Decision makers who determine physical and virtual infrastructure for higher education institutions need to be cognizant of the emergence of distrib-

Figure 6. Multi-dimensional and integrated nature of distributed learning spaces

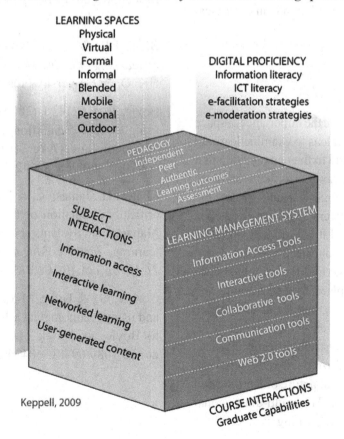

uted learning spaces in order to plan and cater for future students. Adaptability of spaces will be the key aspect required of both physical and virtual spaces. The acceptance of blending face-to-face and virtual learning environments across degree programs will also be an essential component of the learning landscape. In addition, the need to provide students with a wider range of options to suit their idiosyncratic circumstances will also be a necessity. Senior managers in higher education will need to recognise space from the student and academic perspectives when decisions are made about space in higher education institutions. These decisions will require careful evaluation of major trends occurring in the learning and teaching environment in order to design spaces that are useful, beneficial and sustainable. To assist this process the underlying principles of higher education need to always underpin decision-making in relation to choosing, designing and constructing the types of spaces that universities utilise for educational interactions in order to evolve into an ecological university.

CONCLUSION

This chapter has discussed the importance of space in higher education as a lens to examine learning and teaching, and to add to the conversation that we need to rethink the campus as the 'workplace of learning'. The personal learning spaces that learners occupy are diverse and unprecedented in higher education and it is time that we begin changing our thinking about the 'place' of learning. We need to let go of the tradition of universities as being a 'singular place' where learning and teaching occur. It is also time for us to embrace distributed learning spaces.

In order to embrace distributed learning spaces more fully we also need to recognise the complexity and multi-dimensional nature of learning and teaching (see Figure 6). The multi-dimensional nature of learning and teaching is a complex interrelationship of course/degree strategy and planning. It also includes the interrelationship of subject interactions with learning spaces, pedagogy, digital proficiency and the affordances of the learning management system. Academics need to consider the interrelationship of all these dimensions when conceptualising their teaching as all of these factors will influence the learning and teaching nexus. Learning spaces are an essential aspect of the learning and teaching landscape and their design will become increasingly important as learners choose to learn in 'places' that best suit their needs and lifestyle.

REFERENCES

Attwell, G. (2007). The personal learning environment: The future of elearning? *Elearning papers, 2*(1), 1-7.

Barnett, R. (2011). *Being a university*. New York, NY: Routledge.

Biggs, J. B., & Tang, C. (2007). *Teaching for quality learning at University* (3rd ed.). Maidenhead, UK: Open University Press/McGraw Hill.

Boyle, T., & Cook, J. (2004). Understanding and using technological affordances: A commentary on Conole and Dyke. *ALT-J, 12*(3), 295–299. doi:10.1080/0968776042000259591

Coates, H., James, R., & Baldwin, G. (2005). A critical examination of the effects of Learning Management Systems on university teaching and learning. *Tertiary Education and Management, 11*, 19–36. doi:10.1080/13583883.2005.9967137

Conole, G., & Dyke, M. (2004). Understanding and using technological affordances: A response to Boyle and Cook. *ALT-J, 12*(3), 301–308. doi:10.1080/0968776042000259609

Conole, G., & Dyke, M. (2004). What are the affordances of information and communication technologies? *ALT-J, 12*(2), 113–124. doi:10.1080/0968776042000216183

Garrison, R., & Vaughan, H. (2008). *Blended learning in higher education: Framework, principles and guidelines*. San Francisco, CA: Jossey-Bass.

Gaver, W., Dunne, T., & Pacenti, E. (1999). Design: Cultural probes. *Interaction, 6*(1), 21–29. doi:10.1145/291224.291235

Gerbic, P., & Stacey, E. (2009). Conclusion. In Stacey, E., & Gerbic, P. (Eds.), *Effective blended learning practices: Evidence-based perspectives in ICT-facilitated education* (pp. 298–311). Hershey, PA/New York, NY: Information Science Reference. doi:10.4018/978-1-60566-296-1.ch016

Graham, C. (2006). Blended learning systems. Definitions, current trends and future directions. In Bonk, C., & Graham, C. (Eds.), *The handbook of blended learning: Global perspectives, local designs*. San Francisco, CA: John Wiley and Sons.

Hektner, J. M., Schmidt, J. A., & Csikszentmihalyi, M. (2006). *Experience sampling method: Measuring the quality of everyday life*. London, UK: Sage.

Hill, J. (2006). Flexible learning environments: Leveraging the affordances of flexible delivery and flexible learning. *Innovative Higher Education, 31*, 187–197. doi:10.1007/s10755-006-9016-6

Howell, C. (2008). *Space*. Project Report. Learning Landscape Project, University of Cambridge. Retrieved March 15, 2011, from http://www.caret.cam.ac.uk/blogs/llp/wp-content/uploads/llp_public_t1report_l3_space_final_v06.pdf

Jackson, N. J. (2010). From a curriculum that integrates work to a curriculum that integrates life: Changing a university's conceptions of curriculum. *Higher Education Research & Development, 29*(5), 491–505. doi:10.1080/07294360.2010.502218

John, P., & Sutherland, R. (2005). Affordance, opportunity and the pedagogical implications of ICT. *Educational Review, 57*(4), 405–413. doi:10.1080/00131910500278256

Johnson, L., Smith, R., Levine, A., & Haywood, K. (2010). *The 2010 horizon report: Australia–New Zealand edition*. Austin, TX: The New Media Consortium.

Johnson, L., Smith, R., Willis, H., Levine, A., & Haywood, K. (2011). *The 2011 horizon report*. Austin, TX: The New Media Consortium.

Kahneman, D., Krueger, A. B., Schkade, D. A., Schwarz, N., & Stone, A. A. (2004). A survey method for characterizing daily life experience: The day reconstruction method. *Science, 306*(5702), 1776–1780. doi:10.1126/science.1103572

Keppell, M. J. (2010). *Blended and flexible learning standards*. Charles Sturt University.

Kukulska-Hulme, A. (2010). Mobile learning as a catalyst for change. *Open Learning: The Journal of Open and Distance Learning, 25*(3), 181–185. doi:10.1080/02680513.2010.511945

Lea, M. R., & Nicoll, K. (2002). *Distributed learning: Social and cultural approaches to practice*. New York, NY: RoutledgeFalmer.

Learning Landscape Project Team. (2008). *The Cambridge pathfinder journey: The experience of the learning landscape project*. Retrieved March 15, 2011, from http://www.caret.cam.ac.uk/blogs/llp/wp-content/uploads/llp_pathfinder_journey_v03.pdf

Littlejohn, A., & Pegler, C. (2007). *Preparing for blended e-learning*. London, UK: Routledge.

Madge, C., Meek, J., Wellens, J., & Hooley, T. (2009). Facebook, social integration and informal learning at university: It is more for socialising and talking to friends about work than for actually doing work. *Learning, Media and Technology, 34*(2), 141–155. doi:10.1080/17439880902923606

McLoughlin, C., & Lee, M. J. W. (2009). Personalised learning spaces and self-regulated learning: Global examples of effective pedagogy. In R. Atkinson & C. McBeath, *Same places, different space. Proceedings ascilite Auckland 2009* (pp. 639-645). Retrieved March 29, 2011, from http://www.ascilite.org.au/conferences/auckland09/procs/mcloughlin.pdf

Norman, D. (1988). *The psychology of everyday things*. New York, NY: Basic Books.

Oliver, M. (2005). The problem with affordance. *E-learning, 2*(4), 402–413. doi:10.2304/elea.2005.2.4.402

Rafferty, J. (2011). Design of outdoor and environmentally integrated learning spaces. In Keppell, M. J., Riddle, M., & Souter, K. (Eds.), *Physical and virtual learning spaces in higher education. Concepts for the modern learning environment*. Hershey, PA: IGI Global.

Riddle, M., & Arnold, M. (2007). *The day experience method: A resource kit*. Retrieved July 29, 2008, from http://www.matthewriddle.com/papers/Day_Experience_Resource_Kit.pdf

Riddle, M., & Howell, C. (2008). You are here: Students map their own ICT landscapes. In R. Atkinson & C. McBeath (Eds.), *Hello! Where are you in the landscape of educational technology? Proceedings ascilite Melbourne 2008* (pp. 802-808). Retrieved March 29, 2011, from http://www.ascilite.org.au/conferences/melbourne08/procs/riddle.pdf.

Shulman, L. S. (2005). Signature pedagogies in the professions. *Daedalus*, (June): 52–59. doi:10.1162/0011526054622015

Siemens, G. (2006). *Knowing knowledge*. Lulu.com.

Souter, K. Riddle, M., Keppell, M. J., & Sellers, W. (2010). *Spaces for knowledge generation*. Retrieved March 29, 2011, from http://www.skgproject.com/

Watson, L. (2003). *Lifelong learning in Australia (3/13)*. Canberra, Australia: Commonwealth of Australia.

Chapter 2
Changing Approaches to Educational Environments:
Valuing the Margins, Interstices and Liminalities of Learning Spaces

Warren Sellers
La Trobe University, Australia

Kay Souter
La Trobe University, Australia

ABSTRACT

Many discussions about teaching and learning spaces research concern what happens at an educational place. This chapter looks less at the physical place and more into potential spaces – the notional margins, interstices, and liminalities that are outside, between, and on the fringes of defined places. It advocates looking at spaces to bring new and different understandings, like "smooth and striated" (Deleuze & Guattari, 1987) to what learning and teaching spaces might mean for dramatically changing global educational environments and practices.

Rather than seeing a student's classroom, workroom, lecture hall, and lab as a singular person's situation or place, the authors of this chapter propose seeing and thinking conceptually about spatial-dimensional multiplicities for identities. That is seeing various coextensive situations and sites both out and indoors (where 'doors' may also be 'walls') as activities and areas not pre-bounded or specified for particular individual purposes, and thinking about these by bringing different mind-views to conceptualising collaborative activities in spaces as complex knowledge generating affects.

INTRODUCTION

For they inquire of the parts... but they inquire not of the secrecies of the passages. (Francis Bacon, The advancement of learning, 1605)

DOI: 10.4018/978-1-60960-114-0.ch002

The concept of learning spaces expresses the idea that there are diverse forms of spaces within the life and life world of the academic where opportunities to reflect and analyse their own learning position occur... [s]uch learning spaces are places of engagement where often disconnected thoughts and ideas, that have been inchoate, begin to cohere as a result of some kind of suspension from daily life (Savin-Baden, 2008, p. 7).

[In anatomy], potential space ... is commonly used to describe a space which is not evident until it is created by distension or blunt dissection. ... it could be argued ... that potential space is both an abstract concept and an oxymoron (Farinon, 2005).

The place where cultural experience is located is in the potential space between the individual and the environment. ... The same can be said of playing. Cultural experience begins with creative living first manifested as play (Winnicott, 1971, p. 100).

Learning for earning has for too long been a predominant educational premise. As David Perkins (2008) poignantly remarks "...the world would be a better place if more people energetically integrated merely competent knowledge [rather than excellent possessive knowledge] from diverse sources on such fronts as political, economic and ecological responsibility" (p. 16). In this chapter we contend that the growing concern about problematics of living in the contemporary world presages a tectonic shift in educational approach, a move "beyond understanding" (p. 3) to insight and adaptation of our learning tools. In expectation of such a shift, there is a need to review and reconceptualise how education works for teaching and learning, especially with regard to the complex interactions between people and environments.

Here, drawing on a variety of recent theoretical work, we briefly explore and discuss new and different ways of thinking about identities, activities, spaces and organisation that affect teaching and learning (Bauman, 2000; Castells, 1996, 1997, 1998; Castells, et al., 1999; De Landa, 2002; Deleuze, 1993; Deleuze & Guattari, 1987; Land, Meyer, & Smith, 2008; Lefebvre, 1991; Lefebvre

& Goonewardena, 2008; Meyer & Land, 2006). We also touch on impacts of complex pedagogical and technological change in higher education and explain implications of this for educational environments, practices and policies (Barnett, 2000, 2005; Laurillard, 2002; Prosser & Trigwell, 1999; Temple, 2008).

Educational structures have, in principle, remained much the same for centuries (Figure 1). However, although the two structures in this illustration are familiar there is considerable difference in what is happening in each realm: one displays constructed ordered space, the other imaginative chaotic space. Our chapter tries to imagine the relationship between the two. We introduce concepts about spaces that are becoming imagined rather than undergoing construction, and the creative tension that can exist when designers address the tensions and interplay between imagination, space and construction. The importance of such concepts are their helpful commensurability with emerging theories and practices involving issues and matters of dynamic systems, chaos and complexity that are increasingly perturbing society at large – extreme volatility in global economics and climate conditions, for example.

To be specific, the main issue is that ever-increasing anachronisms, redundancies and tensions now extend beyond education into current and future understandings of 'place', 'playing' and 'working'. Traditional concepts such as lectures, seminars, transmission, conduit, receivers, schedules, experiments, readings, essays and examinations can become problematic, impoverished, or obstacles to learning. More often now, challenging teaching situations (large mixed-age/culture/ language cohorts, for example) call for practice inquiries using different conceptions of thinking and working as ways for generatively affecting new technologies and practices such as Peer2peer, wiki and work-learning. This invites collaborative thought-work for generating practice, space production and software rather than vice-versa.

When this happens, we see practice inquiries becoming synthesised as affective moments in

Figure 1. Academic construction and educative chaos (Illustrative montage by Warren Sellers)

temporal and spatial sites. That is, the feelings surrounding practice become more obvious. This is particularly so when and where changing emerges as enabling enactive and performative differences. Rather than privileging the logical, the rational, or cause-effect problem analysis of known variables, approaches which value the unstable, the irrational and/or the interpersonal can introduce methodologies and discourses which are able to account for highly variable ways of knowing in dynamic, complex and self-organising systems. That is, when thinking and feeling are foregrounded in the design of learning spaces it becomes possible to understand more about classroom and learning experiences. Although contested, such approaches demonstrate recognisable and helpful commensurabilities with emerging scholarly research.

These ways of thinking and working anticipate a changed approach to the idea of what can constitute a learning space. *Change* characterises the twenty-first century and the generations growing within it. While humans historically resist change until acute awareness of different conditions forces thinking differently about action, new conditions of global communication and connectivity have

brought about unprecedented scales of acuteness and awareness about change which require exceptional approaches to understanding difference through thinking differently. The reconceptualizing of learning spaces as paradoxical–simultaneously internal and external, interpersonal and architectural, stable and transformative–provides one such approach.

BACKGROUND

Learning spaces are characteristically represented as three-dimensional architectural-technological constructs or, alternatively, as virtual environments that provide a learning experience analogous to that of the classroom and transcend some of the interpersonal limitations of time and space. A careful consideration of the nature of physical and virtual learning spaces conceived of in this way obliges us to expand the usual range of offerings and to look at "the role of spaces such as faculty offices, hallways, plazas, courtyards, dormitories, and food service areas... [and] the instructional implications of these spaces" (Johnson & Lomas, 2005) not to mention the airport lounges, public transport, bedrooms, kitchen tables and so on that supplement the on-campus environment.

Whatever the physical and virtual landscape, however, the primary learning space is mental, both intra-psychic and interpersonal. D.W. Winnicott (1953) describes the concept of potential or transitional space as the transformation of a brute material world into one where objects or spaces may become highly charged emotionally and in which psychologically meaningful things happen. Any space can become meaningful to people, as is shown by the customs of erecting shrines at the sites of fatal car crashes or of making pilgrimages to farmlands which were once battlegrounds. Unless learning spaces take on at least some of the emotional aspects of potential space, it is hard to imagine that anyone could or would want to learn. For many individuals, classrooms, libraries, sheets of blank paper, computer screens, can all readily provide potential space. A major issue in thinking about learning spaces is therefore to maximize the ease with which spaces can be reconfigured so as to become psychologically available for large numbers of different people: to take on, in short, what we will call spatial-dimensional multiplicities for identities.

This complexity of various notions of space is our focus. We are interested in the intersection of these spaces: the mental, interpersonal, virtual and physical. How do they interact? How do qualities of mental space vary within various different types of physical and virtual space? In place of the more traditional what and why questions we prefer to ask: how does this space work and how do we work with it? (Deleuze & Guattari, 1983, p. 109).

THINKING(...)SPACES

Mental space is a notion that owes much to Henri Lefebvre's (1991) insight of space as including complex socially produced phenomena affecting practices and perceptions: "Not so many years ago, the word 'space' had a strictly geometric meaning...it evoked...an empty area...[t]o speak of 'social space', therefore, would have sounded strange" (p.1).

No limits at all have been set on the generalization of the concept of mental space: no clear account of it is ever given and, depending on the author one happens to be reading, it may connote logical coherence, practical consistency, self-regulation and the relations of the parts to the whole, the engendering of like by like in a set of places, the logic of container versus contents, and so on (p. 3).

Lefebvre was concerned to reveal the complexity of space; as a power effect (hegemony) and for liberating affect (discourse). Although highly critical of what he called 'epistemo-philosophical' thinking, which he associated with Husserl, Foucault, Derrida, Barthes, Chomsky and Kristeva and regarded as a sort of ascientific absolutism occupying mental space, Lefebvre worked to understand a 'science of space' incorporating political (social), ideological (mental) and technological (physical) attributes towards a "unitary theory" or rather a theory of interrelated "fields" (p. 11). Other works by philosophers such as Deleuze and Guattari (1987) complement Lefebvre's ideas by introducing various figurations of space such as folds, rhizomes, striations and smoothness that bring meaning to intermediating concepts such as liminality, marginality and interstitiality. Notions and concepts such as these open understandings about interactions in physical and virtual properties and generate some sense of unusual qualities.

The physicality of potential space, for example, is apparent in a balloon. When 'flat' the balloon has very little space, but with inflation it expands into its potential space, which varies according to the flexibility of the balloon. Furthermore, as balloon artists demonstrate, the entire space can also be manipulated in ways that give varying form to sub-spaces. That is, the artist can envision how twisting and knotting one simple volume can reconfigure it into a more complex series of volumes.

MULTISTABILITY

Reconfigurability calls attention to a *multistable* quality, which is an inhering aspect of the experience of space. The space which can protect its inhabitants can provide a good fit, or a bad one: can crush, asphyxiate, endanger; contents can rupture the container, be so small as to be inappropriate or abandon it altogether, leaving it functionless. The dynamic interaction of container and contained enables creative mental life (Bion, 1984). The fundamental process concerns the cross-checking: is the container protective/inspiring/enabling at this point? Are the contents filling/satisfying/enhancing the container at this moment? If not, can mutual adjustments be made? From this point of view, the comfortableness of learning spaces actually depends on the ability to keep the interactive ambiguity constantly in mind, or to continually check-adjust the fit. When this is the case, interactive and multistable learning space design can actually free up mental space

for learning, as environment and mind mutually shape, rather than impinge upon, each other.

Space can be a transitional, allusive/elusive notion that is difficult to apprehend, as Figure 2 suggests. Perceptions and interpretations of space often depend on what is being attended to, or where attention is directed, thereby obscuring inherent complexities that can afford deeper and richer understandings.

Lefebvre's explorations of space help to understand why and how space affects and is affected by and effects humans, society and life in the interplay of physical, virtual and potential (transitional) spaces. An indication of the complexity of these interplays is shown in Figure 3. Here we see expanding coincidences of spatial relations that show a triadic tendency following Lefebvre's proposal of three relations: *Spatial practice, representations of space* and *representational spaces*.

Spatial practice characterizes what happens where, for example travel via airports and shop-

Figure 2. Illustrating potential space

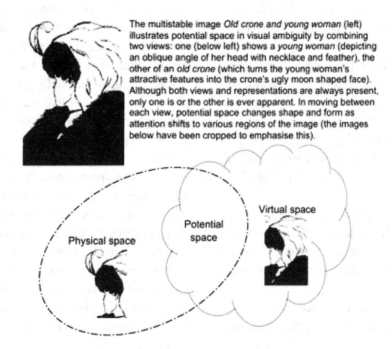

The multistable image *Old crone and young woman* (left) illustrates potential space in visual ambiguity by combining two views: one (below left) shows a *young woman* (depicting an oblique angle of her head with necklace and feather), the other of an *old crone* (which turns the young woman's attractive features into the crone's ugly moon shaped face). Although both views and representations are always present, only one is or the other is ever apparent. In moving between each view, potential space changes shape and form as attention shifts to various regions of the image (the images below have been cropped to emphasise this).

Physical space

Potential space

Virtual space

Figure 3. Spatial complexity

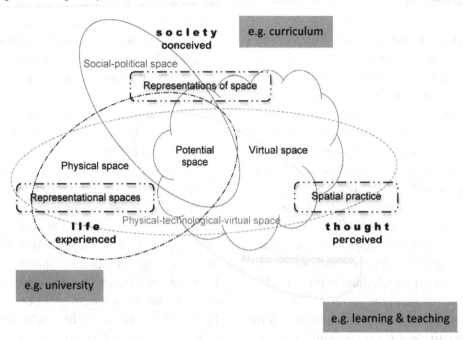

ping in malls. It also examines where it is perceived, for example, air traffic control around airports, production assembly lines in factories, computer aided design for mall shop layout. *Representational spaces* characterize manifestations of habitation and its lived uses, for example: farm house, Catholic church and a university campus.

Notice that although these characterizations are discrete they also intersect and overlap, so, for example, as well as a university campus being a representational space and a physical space, learning and teaching is a spatial as well as an interpersonal practice and curriculum is a representation of space as well as a pedagogical document.

This brings into focus the complex interrelationships involving these spaces and how to see this through the locus of potential space, which penetrates and coheres into assemblages of multiplicity.

In order to create potential space – affectively[1] the intersection/cession of these practices and representations – as many of these modalities as possible need to be brought into play. Another way of putting this is to note that the 'physical-technical-virtual' needs to be overlaid and interpenetrated by the ideological and emotional, that the concrete needs the psychological element to be included. Further, the various emphases in planning learning spaces will always need to be reconfigured at any given time. As in anatomy, potential spaces need to be opened up from their passive 'non-space'- like status as necessary to come into being. While this may sound unnecessarily complicated, we are attempting to explain complex occurrences involving dynamic changes in timing-and-spacing, a notion which is conceptually at odds with linear and hierarchical constructions of time and space as discrete and singular.

In practical teaching and learning terms, this means that single purpose 'classrooms' or 'lecture theatres' need to be rethought. The conventional use of non-didactic spaces as passages or thoroughfares explicitly militates against a multistable configuration of space. For the University campus, and at the simplest level, it is important that all spaces can link up as reconfigurable learning spaces. To affect teaching and learning, this means that spaces must contain the potential and possibility of becoming their opposites, so that public spaces can be reconfigured to become private and active spaces can become didactic.

SMOOTH AND STRIATED

Deleuze and Guattari discuss the concept of smooth and striated space (1987) which is useful in influencing our thinking about this issue. This concept doesn't indicate an oppositional binary where one state is completely unlike the other. Rather, it emphasizes a complex interrelationship between differences; "not that of a quantifiable scientific determination but of a condition that is coextensive to science and that regulates both the separation and the mixing of the two models" (p. 371). Striated spaces are highly regulated and externally organised; smooth spaces are available for free personalised configuration.

As Figure 4 shows, both fluids and solids can demonstrate smooth space within striated space, and vice versa. Transferred to teaching and learning the concept affirms that active learning can be coextensive with the didactic paradigm, as can private spaces within the classroom. For this to be recognized calls for a different and more inclusive approach in which diverse ways of thinking accept that the didactic acknowledges question/conversation/discussion and the classroom includes cafe/cushions and booths.

In this space, the eddy space becomes a profound potential space. In streams, eddies are areas where a current moves against the direction of the main current, in a circular motion, forming relatively quiet circling pools out of the main flow. They are said to form downstream of an obstruction. In educational buildings, these can become the spaces where smokers congregate, where broken equipment is left to pile up, where rubbish gets blown into piles. In essence the eddy space provides small areas of informal, reformable spaces in which to recoup before venturing out into the stream. If provided with some basic necessaries of potential space (power, Wi-Fi, a chair,

Figure 4. Fluid (left) and solid (right) eddy space as smooth space within striations (Warren Sellers, photo left; Natasha Wheatfield, photo right: used with permission)

Fluid

Solid

a table, shelter), they can provide a series of links to allow thoughtful process down the thoroughfare, or affective moments within a formal trajectory. They can link the extra-institutional with the didactic space.

Deleuze and Guattari (1987) argue "nothing is ever done with: smooth space allows itself to be striated and striated space reimparts a smooth space…but all becoming occurs in smooth space" (p. 486). This implies that within its striations educational institutions must provide for these pockets of smoothness. The striations of highly regulated lecture theatres can be simply reconfigured by allowing chairs to move; halls can have sliding doors (as is the case at the Stata centre, MIT); walls can be writable, panels can be everywhere, outdoor spaces can have shelter and power, libraries can have cafes and sleeping spaces.

This is to argue that the University campus needs to be seen not as a series of formal time-tableable spaces linked by corridors, like a freight train or a string of beads, but as an infinite collection of repurposeable space. Spaces designed for a single purpose are the enemy of active learning, in that such design militates against easy psychological use: the user must make the space 'smooth' each time it is used, a tiring and often challenging business.

As Figure 5 shows, young people are highly adept at 'smoothing' striated spaces and turning them to their own purposes, making the unfriendly spaces their own learning space. They perch on window sills, seek out quiet spaces in the corners of corridors unplug equipment to use laptops, colonize understair spaces and so on. These young women were eager to be photographed when it was explained to them that the photographer (KS) was interested in seeing how students repurposed blank, unlikely or even forbidding institutional spaces. It would ease and enrich their experience, however, if the institution could signal its enthusiasm for their repurposing, making it clear that all campus spaces are learning spaces and providing hints and resources: writing surfaces, perches, demarcations of various sorts.

TOWARDS A SEA-CHANGE IN UNDERSTANDINGS OF TEACHING AND LEARNING

Recent inquiries of international academic and technology professionals involved with design and operations of new higher education learning spaces (as for example in this volume) consistently report concerns for generating ways to engage both teachers and learners in facilitating a sea-change in their understanding of how teaching and learning works and how to work with such changed understandings. Educational technologists remark that there is no single techno-pedagogical solution as hardware and software and pedagogical practices are always changing. Instead, their interest is in facilitating understandings of how to better affect teachers and learners work with technology, environments and each other. Similarly, higher education academics comment that the concept of a single generalizable teaching method, style or approach is an anachronism. Teachers unfamiliar with the diverse complexities of learning and teaching scholarship may struggle to enjoy the new cooperative, collaborative realms of practice.

All of this highlights not so much a 'paradigm shift' where scientific knowledge is transformed, as a 'sea-change' where comprehension modulates and enlarges[2], and the subtle and significant, complex and simple difference in understandings between the views these two expressions characterize are crucial to what follows.

THRESHOLD CONCEPTS AND TROUBLESOME KNOWLEDGE

Thomas Kuhn's (1957, 1962) revolutionary thinking about scientific knowledge introduced major changes in what is often called technological know-how. Although he too used multistable images[3] to demonstrate variation in view points, his focus was on anomaly and confrontation that shifted acceptance from one position to another, superior one. This determinist view is not one

Figure 5. Students (Kay Souter, photos)

we share. Rather, our view recognizes diversity and difference as co-implicated and cooperating, always already emerging and dispersing. Such a position is often negated as relativist, and from a paradigmatic position this indeed appears to be the case. This present explication offers another view.

Rather than regarding changing viewpoints as revolutionary, which suggests an over turning of specific positions, we prefer to see changing as momentous, that is more about continuing physical/ temporal turning towards other paths. Such a view could be seen as indecisive, but we see it as an exemplar of "troublesome knowledge" involving "threshold concepts" (Land, et al., 2008; Meyer & Land, 2003; Perkins, 1999). David Perkins (1999) explains different kinds of "troublesome knowledge" involving "pragmatic constructivism" "as a toolbox for problems of learning...invit[ing] constructivist responses to fit the difficulties–not one standard constructivist fix" (p. 11), which Jan Meyer and Ray Land elaborate on to propose interdisciplinary linkages to different ways of thinking and practicing. A threshold concept is characterized as a 'portal' or way through to new thinking, without which further knowing remains closed and hidden.

SOLUTIONS AND RECOMMENDATIONS

The setting up of the physical and virtual spaces to create and energize this multi-stable dynamic, where potential spaces can be opened and closed as needed, has occupied a great deal of institutional attention of recent decades. Celebrated exemplar sites, such as Stanford University's Wallenberg Hall or MIT's Stata Centre use lightweight furniture that is readily moved and folds flat which saves time in designing learning interactions. Harvard provides for the chalk-to-plasma interface in their eponymous heritage lecture theatres. University libraries incorporate sleeping, chill-out and café facilities; refurbishment of 'lost' or cellar-like spaces provide cosy student retreats. All these have in common multiple opportunities for rethinking the uses of spaces. Nevertheless, the spaces in question have formal, designated learning spaces but we are also interested in how can we energize whole campuses.

We imagine 'Guides to Using your Campus': handouts, posters, signboards giving suggestions. In the physical world, campuses should provide cues, such as

- deckchairs, cushions, folding low tables, sun-shades for loan in various areas;
- landscaping designating potential spaces (mounds, logs, outdoor furniture);
- perching sites: single or double hard surfaces at seat height projecting from walls, with small table-like surfaces, power and perhaps a writable board beside them;
- multiple small focuses for gatherings: sculptures, water-features, coffee carts.

Virtual learning spaces should include
- campus buses with Wi-Fi
- institutional SMS features
- blogs, wikis for various student cohorts
- 'ask us' online sites

Campuses should embrace opportunities for 'anytime, anyplace' learning, making it clear that the campus environment is designed to invite students to continually consider and remake their learning needs. This will be economically and efficiently completed by highlighting eddy spaces.

CONCLUSION

In this chapter we have proposed that learning spaces invite and challenge their occupants to see the world differently. Emerging theories, practices and tools for learning and teaching are not singular components to be added to existing overfilled resources. Instead they must be recognized as multiplicities of performance modelling. Technology is not some 'machine that goes ping', as Monty Python has it, a fetishized box with wires and buttons to be used for a specific task; rather, it provides a way of helping to explain an idea. A classroom is not a room with tables and chairs for teachers to assemble students, it offers a space for teachers and students to engage in learning. However, adopting new ways of seeing the world differently is challenging in a way we have referred to as a sea-change. This sea-change calls for very

different understandings of tactics and tools that have been commonplace for many years.

Although this may seem difficult and even perhaps daunting at first, encouragement can be found in substantive research that is producing helpful advice and good practice modelling. Knowledge generation is much more than a fancy term for teaching and learning, it signals a new becoming that reconceptualises spaces for how and where learning meets teaching.

REFERENCES

Barnett, R. (2000). *Realizing the university in an age of supercomplexity*. Buckingham, UK & Philadelphia, PA: Society for Research into Higher Education & Open University Press.

Barnett, R. (2005). *Reshaping the university: New relationships between research, scholarship and teaching*. Maidenhead, UK & New York, NY: Society for Research into Higher Education & Open University Press.

Bauman, Z. (2000). *Liquid modernity*. Cambridge, UK: Polity Press.

Bion, W. R. (1984). *Elements of psycho-analysis*. London, UK: Karnac.

Castells, M. (1996). *The rise of the network society* (*Vol. 1*). Oxford, UK: Blackwell.

Castells, M. (1997). *The power of identity* (*Vol. 2*). Oxford, UK: Blackwell.

Castells, M. (1998). *End of millennium* (*Vol. 3*). Oxford, UK: Blackwell.

Castells, M., Flecha, R., Freire, P., Giroux, H. A., Macedo, D., & Willis, P. (1999). *Critical education in the new information age*. Lanham, MD: Rowan & Littlefield.

Colman, F. (2005). Affect . In Parr, A. (Ed.), *The Deleuze dictionary* (pp. 11–13). Edinburgh, UK: Edinburgh University Press.

De Landa, M. (2002). *Intensive science and virtual philosophy*. New York, NY: Continuum International Publishing Group.

Deleuze, G. (1993). *The fold: Leibniz and the baroque*. Minneapolis, MN: University of Minnesota Press.

Deleuze, G., & Guattari, F. (1983). *Anti-Oedipus: Capitalism and schizophrenia* (Hurley, R., Seem, M., & Lane, H. R., Trans.). Minneapolis, MN: University of Minnesota Press.

Deleuze, G., & Guattari, F. (1987). *A thousand plateaus: Capitalism and schizophrenia* (Massumi, B., Trans.). Minneapolis, MN: University of Minnesota Press.

Farinon, A. M. (2005). *Endoscopic surgery of the potential anatomical spaces*. Dordrecht, The Netherlands & London, UK: Springer. doi:10.1007/1-4020-2846-6

Johnson, C., & Lomas, C. (2005). Design of the learning space: Learning and design principles. *EDUCAUSE Review, 40*(4), 16–28.

Kuhn, T. S. (1957). *The Copernican revolution: Planetary astronomy in the development of Western thought*. Cambridge, MA: Harvard University Press.

Kuhn, T. S. (1962). *The structure of scientific revolutions* (1st ed.). Chicago, IL: University of Chicago Press.

Land, R., Meyer, J., & Smith, J. (2008). *Threshold concepts within the disciplines*. Rotterdam, The Netherlands: Sense Publishers.

Laurillard, D. (2002). *Rethinking university teaching: A conversational framework for the effective use of learning technologies* (2nd ed.). London, UK & New York, NY: Routledge Falmer. doi:10.4324/9780203304846

Lefebvre, H. (1991). *The production of space*. Oxford, UK: Blackwell.

Lefebvre, H., & Goonewardena, K. (2008). *Space, difference, everyday life: Reading Henri Lefebvre*. New York, NY: Routledge.

Meyer, J., & Land, R. (2003). Threshold concepts and troublesome knowledge: Linkages to ways of thinking and practicing within the disciplines. In C. Rust (Ed.), *Improving student learning theory and practice - 10 years on* (pp. 412-424). Oxford, UK: Oxford centre for Staff & Learning Development Oxford Brookes University.

Meyer, J., & Land, R. (2006). *Overcoming barriers to student understanding: Threshold concepts and troublesome knowledge*. London, UK & New York, NY: Routledge.

Perkins, D. (1999). The many faces of constructivism. *Educational Leadership, 57*(3), 6–11.

Perkins, D. (2008). Beyond understanding . In Land, R., Meyer, J., & Smith, J. (Eds.), *Threshold concepts within the disciplines* (pp. 3–19). Rotterdam, The Netherlands: Sense Publishers.

Prosser, M., & Trigwell, K. (1999). *Understanding learning and teaching: The experience in higher education*. Buckingham, UK & Philadelphia, PA: Society for Research into Higher Education & Open University Press.

Savin-Baden, M. (2008). *Learning spaces: Creating opportunities for knowledge creation in academic life*. Maidenhead, UK: Open University Press.

Temple, P. (2008). Learning spaces in higher education: An under-researched topic. *London Review of Education, 6*(3), 229–241. doi:10.1080/14748460802489363

Winnicott, D. W. (1953). Transitional objects and transitional phenomena. *The International Journal of Psycho-Analysis, 34*, 89–97.

Winnicott, D. W. (1971). *Playing and reality*. London, UK: Tavistock.

KEY TERMS AND DEFINITIONS

Interstices: Small interceding spaces between adjacent states or objects that distinguish them from each other. Cords in a rope, for example.

Liminalities: Thresholds of transition between differing objects, conditions and states. A doorway is a threshold. As a conceptual term, it characterizes a de-emphasizing of typical differences to allow for alternative and changing views to emerge.

Mental Space: A move to understand conceptual space as a complex of interrelated fields comprising *Spatial practice, representations of space* and *representational spaces* (see below).

Multiplicities: Philosophical concept that distinguishes multiplicity as a complex comprising continuous and discrete aspects. Continuous multiplicities are qualitative, virtual, subjective, fused; discrete multiplicities are quantitative, actual, subjective, juxtaposed.

Potential Space: In anatomy: space that is not evident until an intervention takes place that brings it about; can be regarded as both an abstract concept and an oxymoron. In psychology: space that is infused with potential, where something meaningful can be expected to take place; an intermediate space between reality and fantasy which is the location of culture and cultural life.

Representations of Space: Characterizes how spatial practice is perceived. University course curriculum, for example.

Representational Spaces: Physical manifestations of habitation and lived uses. House for dwelling, University campus for study, for example.

Sea-Change: A gradual and/or dramatic change of state or condition involving a substance or understanding that maintains its overall existence, from calm seas to tempest, for example. Used here to emphasize an analogous change of state in conceptualising educational teaching and learning.

Smooth and Striated: Expression that characterizes complex interrelationships between differing but coextensive objects, conditions and states. Clouds, for example, can appear striated but are also smooth volumes of water droplets.

Spatial Practice: Describes what happens where. Teaching and learning in school, for example.

Threshold Concept: Involves a perception, experience, apprehension, understanding, without which further related knowing remains elusive.

Troublesome Knowledge: Counterintuitive, paradoxical, interpretations that are often symptomatic of engaging with a threshold concept.

ENDNOTES

[1] In the Deleuzian sense of 'additive processes' (Colman, 2005, p. 11), where multiplicities generate assemblages of becoming events.

[2] Kuhn's (1962) paradigm shift concerned a structural revolution in hard science terms, which is at odds with a more poststructuralist move towards a humanities notion suggested by 'Nothing of him that doth fade But doth suffer a sea-change Into something rich and strange. (Shakespeare, 1610)

[3] He used the duck/rabbit image.

Chapter 3
Beyond the Look:
Viral Learning Spaces as Contemporary Learning Environments

Merilyn Childs
Charles Sturt University, Australia

Regine Wagner
Charles Sturt University, Australia

ABSTRACT

In this chapter, the authors argue that a disjuncture has emerged between the look of learning spaces within learning spaces discourse, definitions of learning spaces, and the aspirations of learning spaces as a design concept that transforms higher education. Using Visual Studies methodology and photographs, the chapter contrasts the hegemonic look of learning spaces with a viral learning space – learning that is not designed or controlled by the institution. The authors argue that the Learning Spaces agenda will fail to transform higher education in the twenty first century if its proponents do not adequately conceptualize lifelong and lifewide learning achieved by learners outside the institution.

THE LOOK OF LEARNING SPACES

In her chapter *Learning How to See*, Obliger (1996, italics added) gives thanks to the Dean of the College of Design at North Carolina State University for helping her to understand that "design is a *way of seeing* things". Grummon (2009) for example, asked his readers to "look around your campus", and

....you'll rapidly discover that students are studying and learning in many places. Visit the library,

a coffee shop, a residence hall lounge, a dining room, and the quad. You'll discover students with books open, laptops humming, and text messages flying — while intensely discussing their views on social issues. The characteristics of these informal learning spaces are ones that need to be translated into classrooms, labs, and other built environments. [1]

Seeing may be physical – the tour of the built environment – but it is often representational using still photographs, floor plans and mud maps. Photographs are used to give 'visual voice' and an "aesthetic lens" (Warren, 2002, p. 224) to learn-

DOI: 10.4018/978-1-60960-114-0.ch003

ing spaces within the institution so that others, particularly those sharing ideas on the web, can see (Figure 1). This chapter listens to this visual voice and argues that, even with the exception of images of cafes and students sitting under trees; formal, institutionalized education dominates how photographs see and construct learning spaces. This dominance constructs an aesthetic lens that is blind to learning spaces outside the institution. This is an important blindness, as there appears to be strong agreement that the way in which learning spaces are designed reflects the way in which institutions understand, and respond to, how students learn.

In order to explore this disjuncture visually, we need to explore the way in which people talk about 'learning spaces'. As long ago as 1994, Hunkins wrote of his vision of learning spaces;

I see misty outlines of spaces that suggest unity, integration of knowledge realms, not discontinuity, the atomization of information. I see spaces that suggest prolonged inquiry under the control of students, with teachers as consultants, coaches, guides. I see spaces that allow for emergence and chaos, that give students time and space for developing patterns of meaning, projects.

In it, learning is "under the control" of students, and there is space "for emergence and chaos" (Hunkins, 1994). In their vision for 2020, Miller, Shapiro and Hilding-Hamann (2008) argued "Learning spaces are the new school" and that "in 2020, Learning Spaces will enable people to construct their identities as inter-dependent and inter-connected social beings and on this basis to produce the wealth and community that sustain their well-being". Such an approach will be achieved in two key ways – "(a) the abandonment of the technocratic, hierarchical and exclusive approach to education and skill achievement, and (b) the marginalization of institutionalized learning". In this vision, Learning Spaces are characterized by "permeable, connected, and modular spaces

that enable a wide range of learning, including synchronous and asynchronous, face-to-face and virtual, subjective and inter-subjective" (Miller et al., 2008, p. viii-ix).

According to Siemens (2008, p.1, italics added) learning spaces provide "space for learning that extends *beyond the classroom*". In this space, teaching moves away from hierarchy and class-rooms, a pedagogy of participation is achieved, and emphasis is placed increasingly on accreditation rather than content (Siemens, 2008). Brown and Long (2006, p 9.1, italics added) argue that "learning spaces are not mere containers for a few, approved activities; instead, they provide environments for people" and that "learning spaces encompass the *full range of places* in which learning occurs, from real to virtual, from classroom to chat room." Learning spaces include but are not limited to classrooms. For example, Hammons (2008) argued that "learning now takes place wherever the learner is inspired" and that "learning occurs in classrooms (formal learning); other times it results from serendipitous interactions among individuals (informal learning). Space - whether physical or virtual - can have an impact on learning." Recently the University of Brighton proposed that learning spaces involve "the social and spatial practices of post-compulsory teaching and learning within and beyond the built environment" (University of Brighton online, 2010).

Strong general agreement exists that learning spaces are physical and virtual; exist within and outside the institution; engage pedagogy that supports self-direction; engage learners in participatory, collaborative learning processes; are permeable; involve synchronous and asynchronous learning; may be digital; and are designed (by educators as well as learners). They provide a challenge to didactic and mono-directional approaches to education (teacher to learner) in response to "knowledge fluidity" (Siemens 2008, p. 3, ellipses added) where "the world of expert, clearly-defined, and well-organized knowledge formed by ancient philosophers and deciphered by subsequent thinkers [and transmitted to learners], has today given way to continual flux" and knowledge produced through multiple places/voices. Learning spaces engenders *a vision* of learning that is derived in complex ways through learning-by-doing, experimentation, collective intelligence, reflection, complexity, personal learning – not through a reliance on formal, hierarchical Higher Education. This is a vision we hold in our mind's eyes. But as the narrative unfolds, we wonder if the images used to illustrate Learning Spaces through photography reflect this vision?

METHODOLOGY: VISUAL STUDIES

Introduction

Visual images *do something* (Rose, 2001, p. 10). They invite the viewers into a text by offering something to look at that goes beyond and beneath words into a deeper understanding of how things *look*. They invite a "kind of seeing" (Berger, 1972, p. 9) and through this seeing they construct meaning. The purpose an author or designer gives to the placement of an image within a text varies enormously, as the image itself becomes an extension of the author's argument or story, whether the author is the photographer or not. The choice of image, as much as the taking of it, constructs meaning, and invites meaning construction by the viewers. As such photographs may be used to teach the viewers "a new visual code" because "photographs alter and enlarge our notion of what is worth looking at and what we have the right to observe" (Rose, 2001, p. 3). During the past decade, digital photography has rapidly transformed the ethic of seeing world events, as "photo-essays make us feel as if we can see what really happened" (Childs, 2006). Ordinary people now create traces of reality through mobile phone cameras, digital SLRs, and easy to carry digital video cameras – reports from the catastrophic aftermath of the earthquake in Haiti (14th January

2010) for example, were derived almost universally from personal mobile devices. These traces become codified further when uploaded onto social media sites, inserted within site pages, or uploaded into image sites such as *Flickr*. Photographs give to online text a sense of realness – the viewers can see 'evidence' of what is really going on, what was really done, how things really work, what things people really did – the camera, in this view, appears to "simply duplicate what the eye can see" (Childs, 2006, p. 206). The act of constructing, and of viewing photographic images can be understood as "a patterned social activity" (Schwartz, 1989, p. 119) that is inter-subjective in that it is shaped by subject, photographer, editor, author, group norms, viewers.

Prosser (1998) argued that "[t]aken cumulatively, images are signifiers of a culture; taken individually they are artifacts that provide us with very particular information about our existence" (p. 2). Images, such as those produced by still photography, can be used as a methodological tool (Prosser, 1998; Pink, 2001; Rose, 2001) that provides an opportunity to explore a wide range of compositional attributes, such as the content of the image, the relationships portrayed within the image, and the way in which series of images construct social relations and cultural meanings and take on the feeling of "evidence" within texts that possess "universal relevance" (Rose, 2001, p 9). In the case of educational images, that relevance may establish pedagogy. Photographs can imply a "set of principles of right conduct". Giroux (2004) for example, argued that a politics of public pedagogy were embedded within the infamous images of Abu Ghraib, and that these representations needed to be made visible.

Photographs demand more than a response to the specificity of an image; they also raise fundamental questions about the sites of pedagogy and technologies that produce, distribute and frame these images in particular ways, and what the operations mean in terms of how they reso-

nate with established relations of power and the identities and modes of agency that enable such relations to be reproduced rather than resisted and challenged (p. 9).

Photographs provide an important means by which relations of power and identity might be understood, through analysis.

Approach

Our aim was to use still photographs in two ways (Schwartz, 1989, p. 119). Firstly, as a method-ological tool to better understand *the look* of still photography in virtual learning spaces narratives; and secondly, as a means whereby this look might be questioned. In the former, we adopted a sampling approach whereby numbers of pho-tographs were analyzed and counted based on visual information about locale. In the latter, we provide a set of photographs of a Learning Space designed virally and collaboratively by thousands of people involved in the Copenhagen climate change rallies, at which 968 protesters were de-tained in mid December 2009. We acknowledge the limitations of our sampling method of viral learning spaces. We chose and sought permission to use one series of photographs of a particular event, rather than exploring viral learning spaces through single photographs of various unrelated events. We wanted to give aesthetic and compo-sitional depth to our argument – space constraints means that this choice has limited the breadth of our argument.

Figure 1, shown at the start of this chapter, provides an example of a normative still photo-graph representing a learning space. Firstly, the look implies *locale*. The learning space is within a building, in this case a Learning Common, and it is fair to speculate that it is an institutional building, possibly in a University Library. It is therefore inside a building, and the building is an institution. The viewer sees a cluster of three stools, sug-gesting recent human use, near a moveable table

Figure 1.

with wheels, and wireless laptop computers. The stools and table are shown within the context of an open space possibly called a learning commons or a library. Furniture is moveable; arrangements are flexible, and includes computers, learning is self-directed; people learn alone, from each other, through hypertext, and so on. Seen in this way, *the look* suggests open, egalitarian social relations, learners are self-directed, engaged, involved and in control. This second look reflects the *compositionality* (Rose, 2001, p. 19, *italics in original*) of learning spaces photographs. We use both these approaches to understand photographs in this chapter.

Sampling Method

How can we ascertain *the look* of learning spaces? We faced a methodological challenge – which still photographs should we choose? We made the decision to adopt a purposive sampling approach (Merriam, 1998, p. 61) on the basis that criterion based selection of information was appropriate to the visual study of learning spaces. We chose one purposive, and three randomly selected sources of publications online. These are shown in Table 1.

Table 1. Sampling methods

Method	Source
Purposive Sample Method	Oblinger S [Ed.] (2006) book, *Learning Spaces*, Chapters 1-13.
Random Sample method	The first ten images produced as a result of the key words "learning spaces" in Google Images
	An analysis of the images used in the first 5 Australian University websites retrieved as a result of the keyword terms "learning spaces" AND .edu.au

Content Analysis

For the purposes of this paper, we adopted the question "what is the 'look' of the image, including the background setting and its artifacts?" drawing on Childs' study of disaster photography following the Boxing Day Tsunami (2006, p. 206). Our aim was understand the cumulative nature of the photographs using "a simple head count" (Childs, 2006, p. 207) as this constructed a sense of what the photographer and the user of the photograph saw as important. Given that Learning Spaces narrative argues that spaces and places for learning exist in multiple locations, we wanted to find out if these were portrayed through photograph.

Therefore, we analyzed the photographs using a simple tally of *locale* using the following categories:

1. Inside the institution, within a building
2. Inside the Institution, within a classroom
3. Outside the Institution
4. Virtual Space

Our analysis focused on the relationship between the learning space and the institution rather than on describing what was taking place within each photograph (for example, human activity). It was therefore not relevant to our analysis to examine the compositionality of the photographs.

SEEING LEARNING SPACES

Purposive Sampling: Oblinger's (2006) Learning Spaces

We counted the still photographs used within the first thirteen chapters of Oblinger's book. In total, 42 images were shown (see Table 2), as well we conducted an analysis based on the four categories previously described.

Of the 42 photographs used within the chapters, 36 were of learning spaces within the institution, 21 within open spaces; and 15 within classrooms, or rooms. Although we did not do a content analysis, it is the case that many photographs included a screen, laptops or computers, and therefore compositionally, these may be used to imply 'outside the institution' in the virtual sense (sitting at a computer, within a lab, and accessing the internet). 4 photographs showed learners working in environments that might be outside the institution (sitting on grass, learning in context), but we suspect these are photos of students learning informally on campus.

The First Ten Images in Google Images Using "Learning Spaces" as the Search Term

The key word search within Google Images resulted in 10 photographs (Table 3), 8 of which were of the built environment, with the look of an institution with contemporary architectural aesthetics (lights, furniture, glass and pine melamine as well as the presence of screens and technology and moveable furniture).

Table 2. Categories used to analyse locale

Chapter	Inside the Institution, within a building	Inside the Institution, within a classroom	Outside the Institution	Virtual space
1	0	0	0	0
2	0	3	4	0
3	3	3	0	0
4	3	0	0	0
5	0	0	0	0
6	0	0	0	2
7	4	3	0	0
8	4	1	0	0
9	0	0	0	0
10	6	4	0	0
11	1	0	0	0
12	0	0	0	0
13	0	0	0	0
TOTAL	**21**	**15**	**4**	**2**

Table 3. An analysis of Google images as a result of a key word search "learning spaces"

Google Images	Description	Source	Inside the Institution	Outside the Institution
1	Inside the institution, showing a variety of arrangements of tables and people in a large space	uq.edu.au	1	
2	Cover of Oblinger's Learning Spaces book.	scup.org	0	
3	Curved tables in a digitized classroom	uq.edu.au	1	
4	4 photographs showing young adults walking, sitting, talking in a variety of contemporary aesthetic spaces	designshare.com	unknown	unknown
5	Young adults sitting in a high-tech, contemporary internal space	heyjude.wordpress.com	1	
6	Mudmap of institutional learning spaces	educause.edu	1	
7	Compilation of images showing floor plans, layouts and young adults in institutional settings in a variety of social arrangements	*designshare.com*	1	
8	Young people in a classroom with flexibly arrangement furniture	cilass.group.shef.ac.uk	1	
9	A library of learning commons with large white seating spaces and other arrangements	spokenword.ac.uk	1	
10	A learning studio, with a variety of arrangements of furniture.	emc.maricopa.edu	1	
TOTAL			**8**	**0**

Table 4. Five Australian University websites retrieved as a result of the keyword terms "learning spaces" and .edu.au that also contain images of learning spaces

University	Description	Inside the Institution	Outside the Institution	Source
University of Queensland	6 site pages were visited, as well as subpages from virtual proceedings of a 2008 Conference (1-4). Photos showed moveable furniture, screens and computers, learning commons, and digitized lecture theatres.	23	0	http://www.uq.edu.au/next-generationlearningspace/ http://www.uq.edu.au/nextgenera-tionlearningspace/proceedings
University of Wollongong	1 site page, 3 images showing students in a tutorial, a computer lab (circular) and a large study area (computers and furniture)	3	0	http://www.uow.edu.au/student/el-earning/learningspaces/index.html
University of Melbourne	3 pages visited, each shows a teaching space (room).	3	0	http://trs.unimelb.edu.au/room/
Monash University	1 site page visited, image of students in a digitized lecture theatre	1	0	http://www.its.monash.edu.au/staff/teachingspace/
Bond University	1 site page visited, image of green modular furniture arranged in café style for student collaboration,	1	0	http://www.bond.edu.au/about-bond/teaching-and-learning/con-text/learning-spaces/index.htm
TOTAL		31	0	

The First Five Australian University Websites Retrieved as a Result of the Keyword Terms "Learning Spaces" and .edu.au That Also Contain Images of Learning Spaces

The key word search lead to numerous results from one domain name with numerous child pages (University of Queensland) so we made the decision to visit this site once via http://www.uq.edu.au/nextgenerationlearningspace/ and to skip other University of Southern Queensland or University of Queensland (UQ) sites in search of a further 9 sites. The UQ site included a comprehensive publication of Learning Spaces, so we included four chapters from this publication in our analysis. We visited 12 URLs, plus child pages associated with the UQ publication. 31 photographs were used of Learning Spaces, all of which were within buildings, within institutions (Table 4).

CUMULATIVE INSIGHTS

The 3 data sets chosen as a basis for this chapter included 59 images of which 55 were of Learning Spaces shown within institutional locales (Table 5). These locales were of open spaces (such as learning commons and open flow through spaces) as well as rooms (computer labs, tutorial rooms, lecture theatres). Screens, laptops and computers were common. Some photos showed human occupation, others were of tables, chairs, arrangements of furniture. Only 4 of the 59 images showed people in outside settings such as on a park bench. Only 1 photo showed people doing what might have been a 'real world' activity (possibly working in a laboratory).

The purposive sampling method used to develop this data was undoubtedly limited. It is possible that another method, using a different key word search, may have lead to alternative images. At the time of writing, Google Images alone indicated that there exist 8,710,000 images of 'learning spaces' within schools, technical

Table 5. Cumulative insights about the look of the locales of learning spaces photographs

Sample	Images of Inside the Institution	Images of Outside the Institution
Oblinger's Chapters 1-13.	36	4
The First Ten Images in Google Images Using "Learning Spaces" as the search term	8	0
The first 5 Australian University websites retrieved as a result of the keyword terms "learning spaces" AND .edu.au that also contain images of learning spaces	31	0
TOTAL	**55**	**4**

colleges and universities; and represented as photographs, drawings, mud maps, and floor plans. We only accessed 55! Some, like the image at http://elearning.osu.edu/mobilelearning/images/oval_girl_bike_final_cut.jpg [retrieved 12 January, 2010], of a girl riding a bike through landscape, with three laptops flying in the air behind her, clearly show an alternative view of learning spaces. But such images are rare. As a common sense 'test' of the approach we took – we ask the reader to use the key words "learning space" or "learning spaces" using *Google Images*, to quickly test our findings. We remain comfortable asserting that over 90% of the images found will construct a view of learning spaces as occurring within educational institutions within the built environment, augmented with screens, laptops and computers. Google functions on the basis of keywords; and the *Google Adwords* analysis of the number of searches using the term "learning spaces" is predicted as 3,600 per month, (at 13th January 2010). The responses we achieved to this search term would be those achieved by 3,600 other users per month searching for the same materials.

Learning spaces rhetoric defines physical and virtual spaces as affording learning within and *beyond* the built and virtual environments. Learning spaces, according to the rhetoric, occur where students learn – not simply within designed space, or as formal learning, but in spaces designed by learners within other social contexts. Photographs of learning spaces construct a vision of formal education within educational institutions. They do not construct a vision of learning beyond the institution. They maintain institutional blindness to learning outside the built environment, outside formal education, and outside the boundaries and control of institutions. Undoubtedly the built environment is aesthetically enhanced with light, mobility, flexibility, clean lines and order; and learning is enhanced with socially engaging and egalitarian settings that afford collaboration, interaction, self-direction, presence and withdrawal as well as access to digital resources. Photographs of computers no doubt are used to convey virtual spaces beyond the built environment; but in truth this is the *only* approach to showing learning outside the institution in all but a few of the images we interpreted.

SEEING LEARNING SPACES BEYOND THE INSTITUTION

Obligner (2006) asked her readers to *see* learning spaces in their mind's eye:

When thinking about colleges and universities, what do you see? [....] when asked to describe a learning space, we often revert to a mental image of the classroom—technology enhanced, perhaps—with all seats facing the lectern. If we are committed to transforming learning, perhaps we should practice Da Vinci's saper vedere—knowing how to see. What should we see?

Figure 2.

Figure 3.

In asking her readers "what should we see?" Oblinger acknowledged the power of the mental image in the process of transforming learning for students. She wanted her readers to see a "mental image" that does not have "all seats facing the lectern". We want to radicalize what we see further so that we can see a vision of Higher Education *outside* the institution (and by outside, we are not simply talking about accessing the outside through *html*). We borrow Oblinger's question, and ask again what should we see? We would also add; how can photographs be used to construct this view? We propose the partial "abandonment of the

Figure 4.

institution" (Miller, Shapiro & Hilding-Hamann, 2008) as the lens through which we gaze.

The following set of photographs (Figures 2, 3 and 4) shows a Learning Space that was designed virally and collaboratively by thousands of people who travelled physically or virtually to Copenhagen to demand action on climate change at the United Nations Climate Change Conference. Millions participated in the space virtually via networking sites (see http://www.avaaz.org/en/ or http://tcktcktck.org/about), and photographs of the space were shared virally through social media sites, as well as *Flikr*.

In Figure 2, hundreds of mostly young, white people are lined up in close body contact, sitting on the road, their hands are cuffed on their backs. The rows are gender segregated. They are surrounded by a large number of police. It appears to be blocked off by vehicles and a police cordon. The scene is brightly lit. The scene has been designed by the state, and by protesters, captured by a photographer. What we cannot see but can imagine is the temperature, the sounds, the history and progression of the story. It is December,

it would have been very cold, there would have been shouts, yelling, swearing and some people would have cried, police dogs would have barked, sirens may have gone off. There may have been some chanting or singing in an attempt to keep the spirit up[2].

Figure 3 is of a young woman, made up and dressed as a clown – she stands behind a police van. Her posture signals 'stop', her expressions are serious. Other activists, dressed in colorful clothes are visible in the background. The van appears to be stopped on a main road. In contrast to image 6, the activists appear to be in control of the moment. We do not know if the clowns are engaged in coordinated and planned or spontaneous action, but we can assume a relationship between the clowns. We can imagine strategic discussions about the clown outfits, the implied and communicated meanings. We can imagine the fun in putting together make-up and outfits and the associated visceral experiences. These are 'designer' clothes and 'designed' learning spaces with an action outcome.

Figure 4 shows a group of demonstrators marching along carrying placards. One placard, in German, reads: it is time for climate justice. In the centre of the image walks a smiling older male. Many in the group are smiling. Some walkers wear rain ponchos of the same color, possibly identifying some group membership. The mood appears optimistic. We do not know where these demonstrators come from and how they got to Copenhagen but we can imagine the organizational, logistic, material effort involved in getting the group to coalesce. In situ, the group's viral learning space is joined by thousands of others, leading to new network formations. These, in turn, provide new opportunities for action. In this physical and connected place and space, perhaps we are invited to see, and construct, through the gaze of the photograph, a "fleeting utopia" of struggle;

[....] people have experienced a brief sense of solidarity, of living one's full potential, of being oneself but fully integrated into a collectivity. These solidarities, inevitably beget a sense of disillusion because life is not like that; daily life resumes and reality sets in. But for a moment we have experienced something well beyond it; living a sense of justice, becoming fully moral and fully who we want to become (Aronson, 1999, pp. 492-493).

VIRAL LEARNING SPACES AND STUDENT-CENTRED LEARNING

The Copenhagen photographs challenge us to *see* Learning Spaces with a new gaze. They represent what we think are usefully termed *Viral Learning Spaces* – those designed outside the institution, by people who probably do not call themselves 'students' or 'learners' at the time of the activity, engaged in learning in and through the world (Figure 5). In *Viral Learning Spaces*, learning is contagious rather than contained; spreadable and self-directed; networked and uncontrollable (in a

Figure 5.

similar view to viral marketing). It involves the construction of knowledge "associated with our acting and existing in a biologically and phenomenological constructed world" (Davis & Sumara, 1997, p. 109) and learning that embodies *enactivist cognition* represented by conversations that unfold "within the reciprocal, codetermined actions of the persons involved" (Davis & Sumara, p. 110). These conversations

...might be thought of as a process of 'opening' ourselves to others, at the same time opening the possibility of affecting our understandings of the world – and hence our senses of our identities that are cast against the background of this world (p. 110).

Figure 6.

Viral Learning Spaces like the Copenhagen Space, where people engage in participatory citizenship, can be seen in our mind's eye *everywhere*. They involve complexity, everyday passion, physicality, cognitive engagement and " […] the capacity to undergo spontaneous self-organization, in the process somehow managing to transcend themselves. Collective properties such as thought and purpose emerge, and these sorts of properties might never have been manifested by any of the subsystems" (Davis & Sumara, p. 118). In recognizing the complex nature of *Viral Learning Spaces* as represented by the selected images, it seems possible to think again about the place of student-designed learning, connected, digitized and collaborative, within Learning Spaces design.

The absence of *Viral Learning Spaces* within Learning Spaces photographs suggests that Learning Spaces are seen through institutional eyes. This profoundly limits the transformative possibilities of Learning Spaces within Higher Education. For example, Figure 6 shows a Learning Space from 1981, not markedly different to the normative photos of Learning Spaces today. Students sit in a relaxed informal space doing self-directed study in a Library (now often called a Learning Commons). They are accessing the technologically available materials of the day – books. The furniture is made of wood, and is not modular or colorful. The photograph has been digitally altered, so that snap shots of computers have been added to the picture. Is this all that has changed between 1981 and 2010?

Photographs of Learning Spaces appear to be located within the institution, yet student-centred learning exists in a state of acute flux along a continuum inside as well as outside formal education; and connected to other spaces and places through hypertext. Learning Spaces can be designed by the institution (through subjects, learning outcomes, qualifications, assessments and so on) and by the learner (through social contexts, work-based learning, professional practice, democratic participation, and so on). We found that student-designed, and socially-designed spaces were not portrayed.

Student-centred learning challenges the institution to enact permeability and flexibility not only through formally designed and controlled physical and virtual space, but through the process of valuing and validating viral learning gained elsewhere, beyond and outside the control of Higher Education. High quality, deeply informed content as well as reflected action are *everywhere*. Disciplinary expertise and quality public commentary is no longer the sole province of the University. It is not enough to create high quality learning environments inside the university that reach out through virtual worlds and field placements to external spaces. External spaces must be able to reach into Higher Education. The logical extension of Learning Spaces discourse is the development of quality design principles that enable learning to be valued and validated, regardless of who owned or controlled the original design. It should be possible, for example, for a learner to demonstrate they have achieved a three year undergraduate degree through self-designed learning in their own time; rather than as an outcome of a lock-step, three-year, 24- subject degree, offered across levels 1-3 – even if studied while sitting on comfortable beanbags or in Learning Commons! In other words, we have to get better at integrated assessment, dealing with evidence, and appreciating application-derived disciplinary knowledge.

How might this be achieved? 'Learning spaces' discourse opens up the possibility of genuine institutional reform – but only if designers are able to see differently. 'Seeing differently' includes seeing viral learning spaces as legitimate sites of learning and developing course design principles, courses and subjects, and assessment practices that engage with viral learning in meaningful ways. The single series of virtual learning spaces we have presented here provide indicators of qualitative aspects of viral learning. First and foremost, they let us *see* learning spaces as action/interaction by people involved in shared projects with complex outcomes. Designing learning spaces with these qualitative indicators in mind aims to transform our lens and focus and move us metaphorically from 'still life' representations of learning within institutions to 'action shots'. We propose the following set of principles to enable the inclusion

of viral learning spaces and viral learning within Higher Education course design.

- Value viral learning and viral learning spaces (value student-designed learning; or context-lead learning).
- Develop assessment strategies that enable learners to achieve graduate attributes and learning outcomes through evidence.
- Develop benchmarks that provide tertiary teachers with ways of valuing viral learning. These benchmarks for recognition of viral learning might include evidence that indicates:
  - Learning was constructed through shared meaning within communities or networks. That is, it was situated and connected.
  - Learning was developed through real life problems/activities/concerns. That is, it was solution-focused and aimed to transform practice.
  - Situated learning included multiple domains of human activity (cognitive, emotional, sensual, and physical).
  - Learning was developed across a spectrum of learner identities. That is learners moved in and out of various roles as students, educators, professionals, researchers, institutional actors, political actors, consumers, performers.
  - Learning was diachronic. That is, it can be shown to have developed and changed over time.
  - Learning was hypertextual and intertextual.
  - Actions were conducted as a consequence of a reasoned rationale.
  - Multiliteracies were evoked and demonstrated.

Imagination plays a part. For example, imagine designing a Viral Learning Spaces strategy based on The Day Experience Method (Riddle & Arnold, 2007). Imagine designing an ePortfolio strategy that purposefully encourages learners to provide evidence of learning outcomes achieved in viral learning spaces, as well as institutional learning spaces.

CONCLUSION

In this chapter we used still photography in two ways. We used photography to ascertain 'the look' of Learning Spaces as represented online within Learning Spaces narratives using a simple tally. We also used photographs of the Copenhagen Climate Change Rallies that occurred in 2009 to provide an example of a *Viral Learning Space* as a conceit that allowed us to question the narrowness of the look of Learning Spaces photographs. Our aim was to challenge the look of Learning Spaces photography. The photographs we considered for this chapter constructed an aesthetic lens that appeared blind to learning spaces outside the institution. This blindness falls short of the promise offered by Learning Spaces to transform Higher Education in the twenty-first century.

The choice to use the Copenhagen Protest photographs was shaped by our own political leanings and our shared background as researchers and advocates of the Recognition of Prior Learning in Higher Education in Australia (Childs, Ingham & Wagner, 2002). We understand that our lens provided only one of many ways of seeing *the look* of Viral Learning Spaces – but our aim was to open up dialogue, rather than conclude it. Valuing learning achieved outside the institution through lifelong and lifewide learning remains a challenge; but one that remains central to the future of Higher Education. We also appreciate the limitations of our argument - we have not taken to these photographs an evidentiary lens in order to ask how might what was learnt at Copenhagen be used as evidence within a formal course of study? This question falls outside the parameters of our chapter, but it is nevertheless an essential corollary to our argument and one we leave with the reader and with recommended readings.

The construction of the Learning Spaces narrative needs to care about the ethics of seeing Learning Spaces, and we need to 'see' learning in new ways, through a different lens. Such seeing is not simply about the built environment – it is about how and what we see as legitimate sites of learning. We offer this final thought, and in doing so, we revisit Oblinger's (2006) speculative question "[w]hat if you 'saw' something different?" when looking at learning spaces? What if students were given cameras and asked to capture the Learning Spaces within which they felt most engaged, challenged and inspired, and they were instructed to go outside the institution for such a set of photographs – *what would we see*? Perhaps we would be challenged to see Learning Spaces in ways that would allow our blindness to knowledge produced through environments within which people learn outside the institution to be resolved. Perhaps finally, we could come to understand the importance of places and spaces *outside* the institution, in the design of Higher Education, and develop our capacities to understand lifelong and lifewide learning and reflected actions that were not manufactured inside our designed environments.

REFERENCES

Aronson, R. (1999). Hope after hope? *Social Research, 66*(2), 471–494.

Berger, J. (1972). *Ways of seeing*. London, UK: Penguin Books.

Brown, M., & Long, P. (2006). Trends in learning space design. In D. Oblinger (Ed). *Learning spaces*. Retrieved October 25, 2009, from http://www.educause.edu/ learningspacesch9

Childs, M. (2006). Not through women's eyes: Photo-essays and the construction of a gendered tsunami disaster. *International Journal of Disaster Prevention and Management, Special Tsunami Edition, 15*(1), 202–212.

Childs, M., Ingham, V., & Wagner, R. (2002). Recognition of prior learning on the Web - a case of Australian universities. *Journal of Adult Learning, 42*(1), 39–56.

Davis, B., & Sumara, D. J. (1997). Cognition, complexity, and teacher education. *Harvard Educational Review, 67*(1), 105–125.

Freire, P. (1970). *Pedagogy of the oppressed.* New York, NY: Continuum.

Giroux, H. (2004). What might education mean after Abu Ghraib: Revisiting Adorno's politics of education. *Comparative Studies of South Asia, Africa and the Middle East, 24*(1), 3–22. doi:10.1215/1089201X-24-1-5

Grummon, P. T. H. (2009). Best practices in learning space design: Engaging users. Retrieved April 24, 2010, from http://www.educause.edu/ EDUCAUSE+Quarterly/ EDUCAUSEQuarterlyMagazineVolum/ BestPracticesinLearningSpaceDe/ 163860

Hammons, A. (2008). *Transforming informal learning spaces – blog entry.* Retrieved January 10, 2010, from http://edtechconnect.mst.edu/ learning_spaces/

Hunkins, F. (1994). Reinventing learning spaces. *New Horizons for Learning.* Retrieved May 4, 2010, from http://www.newhorizons.org/ strategies/ learning_environments /hunkins. html#author

Lorenz, W. (1994). *Social in work a changing Europe.* London, UK: Routledge.

Merriam, S. B. (1998). *Qualitative research and case studies applications in education.* San Francisco, CA: Jossey-Bass Publications.

Miller, R., Shapiro, H., & Hilding-Hamann, K. E. (2008). School's over: Learning spaces in Europe in 2020: An imagining exercise on the future of learning. In Y. Punie, K. Ala-Mutka, & C. Redecker (Eds.), *JCR scientific and technical reports* (pp. 1-80). Luxembourg: Office for Official Publications of the European Communities. Retrieved December 10, 2009, from ftp://ftp.jrc. es/ pub/ EURdoc/ JRC47412.pdf

Oblinger, D. (Ed.). (2006). *Learning spaces.* Retrieved May 4, 2010, from http://www.educause. edu/ LearningSpaces.

Oblinger, D. (2006). Learning how to see. In D. Oblinger (Ed.). *Learning spaces.* Retrieved May 4, 2010, from http://www.educause.edu/ learningspacesch14

Pink, S. (2001). *Doing visual ethnography: Images, media and representation in research.* London, UK: Sage Publications.

Prosser, J. (Ed.). (1998). *Image-based research: A sourcebook for qualitative researchers.* Philadelphia, PA: Taylor and Francis.

Riddle, M., & Arnold, M. (2007). *The day experience method: A resource kit.* Retrieved February 15, 2010, from http://www.matthewriddle.com/ papers/ Day_Experience _Resource_Kit.pdf

Rose, G. (2001). *Visual methodologies: An introduction to the interpretation of visual materials.* London, UK: Sage.

Schwartz, D. (1989). Visual ethnography: Using photography in qualitative research. *Qualitative Sociology, 12*(2), 119–154. doi:10.1007/ BF00988995

Siemens, G. (2008). *New structures and spaces of learning: The systematic impact of connective knowledge, connectivism, and networked learning.* Retrieved May 4, 2010, from http://elearnspace. org/ Articles/ systemic_impact.htm

Thornborrow, J., & Coates, J. (2005). *The socio-linguistics of narrative.* Amsterdam, The Netherlands: John Benjamin Publishing Company.

University of Brighton. (2010). *Reshaping Learning Conference.* Retrieved May 4, 2010, from http://arts.brighton.ac.uk/ whats-on/ news/ reshaping-learning-the-future -of-learning-spaces -in-post-compulsory -education-conference-21 -23-july-2010

Warren, S. (2002). Show me how it feels to work here: Using photography to research organizational aesthetics. *Ephemera: Critical Dialogues on Organization, 2*(3), 224–245.

ADDITIONAL READING

Adorno, T. W., & Horkheimer, M. (1969). *Dialektik der Aufklärung. Philosophische Fragmente. [Dialectic of Enlightenment].* Frankfurt/Main, Fischer: Neuauflage.

Cameron, R., & Miller, P. (2004, October 29). *RPL: Why has it failed to act as a mechanism for social change?* Paper presented to the Social Change in the 21st Century Conference, Centre for Social Change Research, Queensland University of Technology, Australia, Retrieved, January 15, 2010, from http://www.humanities.qut.edu.au/ research/ socialchange/ docs/ conf_papers2004/ cameron_ros.pdf

Dewey, J. (1916). *Democracy and education. An introduction to the philosophy of education* (1966 ed.). New York: Free Press.

Dewey, J. (1933). *How we think. A restatement of the relation of reflective thinking to the educative process* (Revised ed.). Boston, DC: Heath.

Illich, I. (1970). *DeSchooling society.* New York: Harper & Row. Retrieved October 10, 2010, http:// www.preservenet.com/ theory/ Illich/ Deschooling/ intro.html

Illich, I., & Verne, E. (1976). *Imprisoned in the global classroom,* London: Writers and Readers Publishing Co-operative.

Michelson, E., & Mandel, A. (2004). *Portfolio development and the assessment of prior learning: Perspectives, models and practices.* Sterling, VA: Stylus Publishing.

Otero, M. S., McCoshan, A., & Junge, K. (Eds.). (2005). *European Inventory on Validation of non-formal and informal learning A Final Report to DG Education & Culture of the European Commission,* Birmingham, United Kingdom: ECOTEC, Research & Consulting Limited http:// www.educacion.es/ educa/ incual/ pdf/ 3/ european_inventory_2005_ECOTEC.pdf

Wenger, E. (1998). Communities of practice. Learning as a social system, systems thinker, Retrieved December 5, 2009, http://www.co-i-l. com/ coil/ knowledge-garden/ cop/ lss.shtml.

White, M. (1999). *A philosopher's story.* Philadelphia: Pennsylvania University Press.

KEY TERMS AND DEFINITIONS

Enactivist Cognition: Enactivist Cognition is a term developed by Davis and Sumara, (1997, p.109) to describe the construction of knowledge "associated with our acting and existing in a biologically and phenomenological constructed world" and learning that embodies *enactivist cognition* represented by conversations that unfold "within the reciprocal, codetermined actions of the persons involved". These conversations…"might be thought of as a process of 'opening' ourselves to others, at the same time opening the possibility of affecting our understandings of the world – and hence our senses of our identities that are cast against the background of this world" (Davis & Sumara, p.110).

Formal Education: We use the term Formal Education to refer to education that is conducted within the Institution's codes, rules, monetary systems and accreditation processes. Formal education assumes that *learning* "has a beginning and an end; that it is best separated from the rest of our activities; and that it is the result of teaching" (Wenger 1998, p.3).

Higher Education: We use the term Higher Education to refer to Universities. We acknowledge that Vocational Education forms an important part of Higher Education, but our visual study was limited to Universities.

Informal and Experiential Learning: We have purposefully avoided using these terms in this chapter, despite our prior research using these terms (Childs, Ingham & Wagner 2004). Higher Education in Australia continues to struggle to value and validate learning gained outside the institution. For this reason, we have worked to reposition these forms of learning within the *Viral Learning Spaces* rubric to form part of the Learning Spaces narrative.

Institution: We use the term Institution in this chapter to refer to the systems, processes and practices that shape the identity, activities, codes and narratives of actors and actions within Higher Education, specifically Universities that construct the student experience of formal education; as per Street (2001, p.63, cited in http://www.infed.org/biblio/b-socped.htm1991, p.163): *When we participate in the language of an institution, whether as speakers, listeners, writers, or readers, we become positioned by that language; in that moment of assent, myriad relationships of power, authority, status are implied and reaffirmed. At the heart of this language in contemporary society, there is a relentless commitment to instruction. Our language use as workers, and the way in which we define space can act to constrain exploration and to subordinate people.*

Learning Spaces: Learning spaces encompass the full range of places and spaces in which learning occurs, both inside and external to the institution, designed by educators and by people who may at some time be students, and including digitized learning.

Narrative: In this chapter we use narrative in a socio-linguistic sense, in that proponents of Learning Spaces construct a community of interest, often informally through the WWW, using stories and case studies of Learning Spaces; thereby constructing definitions, stories and artifacts that provide a basis whereby the culture of Learning Spaces, and people's places within it, are constructed (Thornborrow & Coates, 2005, p.7).

Student-Centred Learning: Student-Centred Learning places the focus of design on the individual and socially-mediated and socially-constructed needs and 'enactivist cognition' of student. Student-Centred Learning exists in a state of acute flux along a continuum inside as well as outside formal education; and connected to other spaces and places through hypertext. Our thinking reflects the philosophies and practices associated with sozial pädagogik; usefully defined by Lorenz (1994) who uses the term "social pedagogy" as an attempt to compute the more critically aligned term sozial pädagogik: *Social pedagogy defines the task and the process of all 'social activity' from theoretical positions beyond any distinct institutional setting and instrumental interest, and thereby safeguards the autonomy of the profession and appeals to the reflective and communicative abilities of the worker [and people within society] as the key to competence (p. 97, ellipses added).* In this way of thinking, student-centred learning is not simply a matter of enhancing participation of 'the student' within the institution. Rather it extends to include Illich's notion of *de-schooling* (learning outside and without the institution); Freire's (1970) concepts of *dialogue, praxis* and *conscientization* (learning through the word and the word; to build a socially just society); and Dewey's (1916, 1933) ideas associated with learning that emerges from thinking, experience and interaction, as well as democratic participation (1933).

Viral Learning Spaces: Those designed outside the institution, by people who probably do not call themselves 'students' or 'learners' at the time of the activity, engaged in learning in and through the world. In Viral Learning Spaces, learning is contagious rather than contained; spreadable and self-directed; networked and uncontrollable (in similar view to viral marketing). Viral Learning Spaces afford informal and experiential learning.

ENDNOTES

[1] Note however, that Grummon makes no mention of accrediting the learning that may have been achieved in experiential learning environments.

[2] Prior to the climate summit the Danish policy force was granted the right to preemptive arrest; they could arrest people without a crime having been committed. Special cages for the demonstrators had been built and set up at a Copenhagen prison in anticipation of large numbers of arrestees. In planning its street actions, the Danish Police would have taken global media attention into account; the lesson was designed to be a global one.

ATTRIBUTIONS

Image 1: <div xmlns:cc="http://creativecommons.org/ns#" about=" http://www.flickr.com/photos/cyprien/43544086/in/photostream/ "><a rel="cc:attribution URL"href=" http://www.flickr.com/photos/cyprien/"> http://www.flickr.com/photos/cyprien/</a>/ <a rel="license" href="http://creativecommons.org/licenses/by-sa/2.0/">CC BY-SA 2.0</ a></div>

Image 2-5: We gratefully acknowledge the Photographer, *kk* for giving us Copyright Permission. For a full exposition of kk's photographic work, see http://www.flickr.com/photos/kk/

Image 6: No known copyright issues, http://www.flickr.com/photos/lselibrary/3989341477/

Chapter 4
Design of Outdoor and Environmentally Integrated Learning Spaces

John M. Rafferty
Charles Sturt University, Australia

ABSTRACT

This chapter explores the environmentally sensitive design characteristics of Charles Sturt University's Albury Wodonga campus and the outdoor learning spaces it provides. Attention will be given to exploring how the holistic and integrated nature of the campus and the environmental functionality of the site provide unique opportunities for learning within learning spaces. Examples are provided of how the natural and built environments of the campus are used as learning spaces to promote social interactions, conversations, and experiences that enhance student learning. The chapter highlights the value of outdoor environments as legitimate and critical spaces for learning within higher education. The chapter explores the benefits of designing teaching space based on strategies that are defined by personal pedagogic repertoires and practical wisdom. By enacting such strategies, it is argued that universities can develop diverse, locally appropriate, and inclusive pedagogies.

INTRODUCTION

The purpose of this chapter is to extend discussion about learning space design, particularly in relation to spaces without walls and ceilings. In particular the chapter demonstrates and promotes the validity of outdoor and environmentally integrated environments as learning space. This chapter is structured into several sections. The first section provides the background to the chapter by highlighting the tensions that exist between the managerial and ecological discourses that com-

DOI: 10.4018/978-1-60960-114-0.ch004

pete within the university campus environment. The second section presents the main focus of the chapter and begins by explaining the environmentally sensitive characteristics of Charles Sturt University's Albury Wodonga campus. The section then examines the development of existing learning space design guidelines from an ecological discourse perspective. The chapter then reports on the engagement of learningscapes and hears from students who participated in outdoor multi-sensory mobile learning experiences. The final section considers how learning space design benefits from engaging with the tensions encountered particularly when competing discourses are engaged. The conclusions are a practical reflection on the role of the competing discourses in learning space design and the role of the University as a space for higher education. The need to counter the assumptions shaped by managerial discourses within learning space design concludes the chapter.

BACKGROUND

Ball (1994) argues that 'discourses are about what can be said and thought, but also about who can speak, when, where and with what authority' (p. 21). The Albury Wodonga campus of Charles Sturt University (CSU) is a deliberate attempt to construct critical educational and social responses to ecological issues. At the time of planning the campus ecological discourse had great currency within University management at CSU. Ecological discourse, according to Jørgensen and Philips (2002) is a discourse that stresses the importance of protecting the environment on the basis of a holistic understanding of the world. The discourse ascribes individuals and organisations with a 'green identity' whereby they should be actively engaged in environmental problems and recognize their role as an integrated part of nature. According to this discourse engagement, protecting the environment is a moral necessity and lack of engagement is illegitimate (p. 166). The Albury

Wodonga campus has developed a 'green' identity within higher education in Australia. However, the capacity of the ecological discourse to influence University management has diminished as managerial discourse increasingly sets the agenda of higher education.

University management has long been dominated by the business-like accountability discourses (Etzkowitz, 2004; Clark, 2004; Rosenzweig, 2001; Soley, 1995; Steck, 2003). These business-like discourses are referred to as the discourse of accountability or managerial discourse. It is argued that managerial discourse reflects the neoliberal ideology that dominates government policy and the educational landscape of countries with advanced economies (Marginson, 1997). Managerial discourse holds firmly to the notion that the practices of private enterprise can be applied to the public sector, especially education. Universities are, as Clegg, Hudson and Steel (2003) contend, "exhorted to open up for business in order to play their role in the knowledge economy" (p. 41). The managerial discourse ascribes individuals and organisations an entrepreneurial identity (Sachs, 2001). According to Ball (1995), from a policy perspective, the

...entrepreneur is committed to the application of certain technical solutions [to] organizations and contexts which are taken a priori to be in need of structural and/or cultural change (p. 265).

Managerial discourse points to the efficient, responsible and accountable management practices (Gay, Salaman, & Rees, 1996). Reducing education issues and dilemmas into their simplest definition and engineering precise solutions based on models of efficiency and accountability are intrinsic characteristics of managerial discourse (Rafferty, 2007). In many ways, University education is now understood and known in terms consistent with the language of the market and business and can be regarded as a commodity (Allen, 1998). Within this commodification of

University education, risk minimization, maximization of outputs, accountability and efficiency become the key drivers. This means that certainty, evidence and replication are the strategies that are expressed through managerial discourse and dominate University management. From the perspective of managerial discourse the characteristics of ecological discourses are problematic because they come with a degree of uncertainty and offer unacceptable levels of risk. To minimize the threat posed by alternative discourses, like ecological discourses, managerial discourse redefines their characteristics and invests them with new meaning.

The Albury Wodonga campus was designed to function autonomously, drawing minimally on external services, using material resources sparingly and generating significantly less waste. The comprehensive, environmentally sensitive design process that encompassed all stages from site planning to the selection of materials, succeeded in creating a campus based on far more rigorous principles of sustainability than any project of comparable size in Australia. The campus comprises academic buildings, teaching rooms, and student accommodation, all of which are designed so that the 'green agenda' is symbolically declared in the built forms. The wetlands, drains, swales and reed beds that comprise the water management systems provide habitat for a wide variety of native flora and fauna. Constant restoration of native vegetation to indigenous levels is critical in ensuring the ecological integrity of the environment required for the water management system.

The campus facilities and the environment needed to enable the campus to develop and maintain such an environmentally sensitive and sustainable approach to higher education is significant in two ways. Firstly, the unique design of the campus extends the traditional role of universities through the engagement of management strategies that relied upon an innovative commitment to environmental sustainability. Secondly, the outside environment simultaneously provides stimulating and effective learning space(s) and extends contemporary discussions concerning learning space design. The capacity of the campus to extend the role of the University as well as discussions on learning space will be examined directly.

THE CAMPUS IN FOCUS

The Albury Wodonga campus of CSU is located in southern NSW near the Murray River. The land for the campus was dedicated as the site of the campus in the early 1980s. The site comprises 87 hectares of north facing, sloping land. The aspect and topography are considered to be ideal for sustainable development (Mitchell, Croft, Harrison, & Webster-Mannison, 2001). Indeed, passive design techniques associated with low energy technologies, minimizing the consumption of scarce resources in the choices of materials and having regard to the social and environmental costs and benefits were considered routine rather than exceptional factors in the construction of the Albury Wodonga campus (CSU Annual Report, 2003). Construction programs on the site up to 2007 saw the construction of buildings that reflect passive energy usage principles and are made from rammed earth. Buildings constructed since 2007 share in design principles of the earlier buildings but employ recently developed technologies. As a result, the latest buildings are very different in form and materials from the earlier constructions. The facilities of the campus allow the university to fulfill its traditional role by a providing physical setting that fosters academic research and opportunities for students to attain a high level of education (Allan, Kent & Klomp, 2004). However, as well as providing a physical setting for the University to fulfill its traditional role, the buildings also provide a dynamic model for sustainable living and unique opportunities for community and student engagement. The buildings on the campus have won several awards including the 2001 Environment and Architecture

Figure 1. The Albury Wodonga campus

Awards from institutions that include the NSW Chapter of Royal Australian Institute of Architects and the national Master Builders Association. One of the most recently constructed buildings, the Academic Accommodation Stage 3 (AA3) was awarded a 6 star Green Star - Office Design rating from the Green Building Council of Australia. This award represents "World Leadership" in environmental sustainability. The AA3 building engages the same thermal mass principles as the rammed earth buildings. However, instead of rammed earth, AA3 uses lightweight gypsum plasterboard that is permeated with phase change microcapsule (PCM). Also, the newly constructed Learning Commons and Teaching and Learning hub are made from conventional building materials and operate conventional heating and cooling systems, albeit in innovative ways. The end result is a campus with a very visible commitment to sustainability. While the buildings take on different physical forms and use different technologies, they are designed to demonstrate and promote pro environmental behaviour through the responsible management of resources. As well as awards for its buildings the campus has also won the NSW

government Award for Excellence for the water management systems that define and dominate the campus. The campus buildings and the environment built to support it are a local response to global issues.

Water management is a critical component of the campus's environmentally sensitive design. In fact, the campus is physically shaped to accommodate the water management practices of the campus due to its unique gentle slopes which assures optimal collection of water. The principles of water management on the campus are twofold; minimize waste and pollution and maximize the holistic aspects of onsite water treatment retention. Water entering the campus as rainfall (run-off) is either harvested from buildings and stored in water tanks or channelled through a system of connected open drains, swales and contoured banks to wetlands and deposited into three reservoirs that were built along natural drainage lines. The management of run-off significantly reduces issues concerning erosion across the campus site and provides water for irrigation. Wind and solar energy technologies are mobilized to pump the water to a reservoir constructed at the highest point of the campus for storage and distribution through irrigation. Much of the grey water produced on the campus is collected from the wash-basins, showers, baths, kitchen sinks and laundries throughout the campus and plumbed into an artificial wetland drainage system, consisting of reed beds, before joining the runoff water system. Perhaps the most innovative characteristic of the rammed earth buildings in regard to water management is the use of composting toilets. Conventional toilet systems contaminate high quality drinking water and were considered to be too resource intensive and environmentally unsound. The design, construction and operation of the composting toilets ensure waterless and odorless toilets. The compost produced in the toilet system is shallow buried, mixed with other organic matter and over time develops into a mulch used as a soil conditioner. The cisterns of most of the conventional toilets on the campus use harvested water, further reducing the usage of valuable potable water. The onsite management of black water (sewage) dramatically minimizes water usage, waste and pollution from the campus. It also exemplifies the pro-environment actions and behaviours that are required by communities dealing with diminishing water supplies. Considering the campus is located within a regional community experiencing unprecedented water shortages the water management practices provide a model of sustainability that is very relevant to the community.

The Rationality of Learning Space Design

The development of the campus as a self-contained system and the responsible management of resources is an expression of ecological discourse. The campus provides opportunities for staff, students and the wider community to adopt pro-environmental behaviour. As Allan et al (2004) contend the campus invites staff and students to experience sustainable living and incorporate

this experience into their own lives. This invitation extends the role of the university beyond a traditional role as a place of research and higher learning. With the Albury Wodonga campus and its commitment to tread lightly on the earth, CSU provides a reference point for researchers, students, business, governments and the wider community in developing capacity to manage the effects of climate change (Allan et al, 2004). In effect, through the Albury Wodonga campus CSU is satisfying the expectation of a 21st century University as described by Levin (2008) in leading community responses to environmental issues. However, despite the magnitude of the looming global environment crisis, the influence of ecological discourse in shaping the development of a university campus is not the norm.

In determining what constitutes a suitable learning environment the emergence of guidelines for developing learning space can be regarded as a sensible practice, ensuring resources are maximized and learning is optimized. In this sense they can be regarded as an entrepreneurial response. Jamieson, Fisher, Gilding, Taylor and Trevit (2000) offer a set of guiding principles for the development of on-campus teaching and learning facilities.

1. Design space for multiple uses concurrently and consecutively
2. Design to maximize the inherent flexibility within each space
3. Design to make use of the vertical dimension in facilities
4. Design to integrate previously discrete campus function
5. Design features and functions to maximize teacher and student control
6. Design to maximize alignment of different curricula activities
7. Design to maximize student access to, and use and ownership of the learning.

The Designing Spaces for Effective Learning report (JISC, 2006) argues that "a learning space should be able to motivate learners and promote learning as an activity, support collaborative as well as formal practice, provide a personalized and inclusive environment, and be flexible in the face of changing needs." It states that the design of individual spaces within an educational building needs to be:

- **Flexible:** to accommodate current and evolving pedagogies;
- **Future proofed:** to enable space to be re-allocated and reconfigured;
- **Bold:** to look beyond tried and tested technologies and pedagogies;
- **Creative:** to energize and inspire learners and tutors;
- **Supportive:** to develop the potential of all learners; and
- **Enterprising:** to make each space capable of supporting different purposes.

Oblinger (2005) takes a more focused and learner centered approach to the design of facilities:

- Design learning spaces around people;
- Support multiple types of learning activities;
- Enable connections, inside and outside;
- Accommodate information technology;
- Design for comfort, safety and functionality; and
- Reflect institutional values

The development of such guidelines can be regarded as rational expressions of managerial discourse. It is argued that such guidelines have potency because they fit comfortably with the business like accountability schemes that dominate university management. The very nature of the dominant managerial discourses makes them highly impervious to critiques, given that they ap-

pear to be so inevitable, normal and natural, they are difficult to oppose (Larsen, 2010). As Kress (1989 as cited in Larsen, 2010) writes:

If the domination of a particular area by a discourse is successful it provides an integrated and plausible account of that area, which allows no room for thought; the social will have been turned into the natural. At that stage it is impossible to conceive of alternative modes of thought.

In other words, managerial discourses sanction particular systems of rationality. In regard to pedagogy and learning space design managerial discourses define what is rational and sensible. It is difficult to argue against or question practices and procedures that are considered to be 'commonsensical'. Universities and those who manage and inhabit them have little option but to embrace the prescribed rationality.

The pace of change and acceptance of technology in higher education has been rapid with limited empirical research and theoretical explanation supporting the changes (Pratt, 2003). It is argued that the rationality sponsored by managerial discourses is comprised of a series of myths or assumptions about learning and the most suitable environment and physical resources required to facilitate it. Managerial discourse, assumes learning occurs inside buildings, involves technology and rely on an individualistic "sight based" pedagogy. These assumptions have tremendous potency because the managerial discourses that sponsor them are an expression of the neoliberal ideologies of the systems that govern Universities. In essence managerial discourse reduces learning space design to its simplest definition and attempts to engineer learning space based on models of efficiency and accountability.

Further, it is argued that some principles of learning space design are often aspirational while others imply they are based on experience and that there is little objective data based or analysis that can be used to test these principles (Radcliffe,

Wilson, Powell & Tibbetts, 2008). Learning space design principles are drawn from a set of accepted assumptions about teaching and learning. For example, the provision of a variety of platforms to engage with a wide range of technologies is a clear priority for Universities (Alexander, 1999; Daniel, 1996; McCann, Christmass, Nicholson & Stuparich, 1998). It seems that engaging emerging technologies provide a critical element of 'convenience' and 'access' in the educative process at a University. However, through further analysis it becomes evident that with such guidelines the understanding of 'convenience' is skewed towards the convenience of the teacher, rather than the convenience of the learner. Further there is considerable complexity involved in determining what exactly technology gives "access" to (McWilliam, 1998). Moreover, the guidelines like those offered by Jamieson et al (2000), Oblinger (2005) and JISC (2006) are structured around an exclusive focus on "sight based" approaches to pedagogy. Learning space design principles make little affordance to multi-sensory pedagogical practices. In fact the focus on 'sight based' approaches to pedagogy have become the 'normal' unquestioned given of learning space design. Ultimately, it is argued, guidelines on learning space facilitate approaches to learning that are decontextualised and excessively individualistic to such a degree that little attention has actually been paid to student learning (Phillips, 1998).

The argument is that learning space design in tertiary education is dominated by managerial discourse and that assumptions concerning teaching and learning that underpin managerial discourse are generally accepted as commonsensical approaches to tertiary education, despite the lack of supporting data. In regard to developing learning spaces, efficiency and effectiveness are the key concepts that shape design. Assumptions about learning that do not align with managerial discourse have little potency because the managerial discourse defines what is accepted and what is not. The personal pedagogical repertoires of

the educators who use the 'learning spaces' are limited by the parameters of the guidelines. For example, using outside space as learning spaces and engaging students' corporeal experience into a pedagogical framework are not even part of the discussions concerning the design of learning space.

The domination of managerial discourse in the design of learning spaces is not necessarily a negative aspect of university management. Universities operate within a political and social environment that places particular demands on Universities. With the neoliberal inspired quasi market environments Universities are forced to compete against each other for students and funding. Managerial discourses provide a way of thinking and acting that allow universities to satisfy the demands that the neoliberal ideologies require of them. As a result of this dominance the learning spaces in universities have a particular universality or "sameness" in internal form and function. For example, despite the environmental sensitivity of the Albury Wodonga campus the actual learning spaces it provides are more or less indistinguishable from the learning spaces offered on other CSU campuses or indeed the learning spaces offered on any other Australian university campus. This "sameness" is not necessarily a negative characteristic, nor is it the intention of this chapter to argue that it is. However, this "sameness" indicates the surrounding environments of a campus are excluded from discussions concerning learning space design. In the case of the Albury Wodonga campus the exclusion of outdoor environments as 'learning space' inhibits the ability of Universities to provide locally appropriate and inclusive pedagogies. As McWilliam (2005) contends the re-enacting of pedagogical habits promotes a culture of teaching and learning that is predictable and regular. The Albury Wodonga campus was designed from an ecological discourse; making it a unique campus reflective of and responsive to the local environment. The use of outdoor spaces on the Albury Wodonga campus as a learning space(s) or learningscapes will be the focus of the next section of this chapter. It will be argued that the sensuality and desensitizing qualities of various outdoor spaces should be included within guidelines concerning the development of learning space.

Models for Learning Space

Existing guidelines concerning learning space encompass a broad range of physical environments (James, 2008). Discussions around learning space are often binary with "formal spaces" and "informal spaces" used to loosely group types of space. James (2008) defines formal spaces, or 'teaching-spaces', as typically including tutorial rooms, lecture theatres and laboratories, and used for 'in-class' teaching and learning. Informal spaces can include just about everything else. The informal spaces currently receiving design attention range from libraries and learning commons, to corridors and outdoor spaces (James, 2008). The Albury Wodonga campus's recently constructed informal learning spaces include the Teaching and Learning Hub and the Learning Commons which reflect the principles offered by Jamieson et al (2000), Oblinger (2005) and JISC (2006). They also demonstrate environmentally sensitive design innovations. The use of natural light, passive heating and cooling, thermally re-active walls, recycled water and solar power are features of CSU's informal spaces (Klomp, 2008). In a sense such efforts to engage all things natural are an attempt to make the 'inside' as much like the 'outside' as possible. However, within learning space design guidelines outdoor space seems only to extend to passive recreation areas. It is argued that outdoor spaces should be given greater consideration in learning space design. Further, it will be will argued that the principles that guide the design of learning space should be extended to include the corporeal experiences of students.

Defining Space and Multi Sensory Outdoor Experiences

Space, according to Le Grew (2008), is an abstract notion and only becomes a place when it is injected with identity and meaning. Learning spaces are places of learning because they are given that identity. Within Universities, learning spaces are usually found in heavily concentrated areas and actually occupy a small portion of a campus. For example, less than 10% of the total area of the Albury Wodonga campus's 87 hectares has actually been developed for use. The combined area of the buildings, car parks, roads and pathways that comprise the 'university' occupy no more than 4 hectares. Within this development only a minute area of the total land available is referred to as a "learning space" – all of which is within buildings. While not all of the remaining space is accessible (wetlands, etc) there remains a substantial area of land that could potentially be understood as learning space. It is noted that not all Universities have the extensive acreage of the Albury Wodonga campus however, all University campuses do have surrounding or local environments. Some of these local environments may consist of well-maintained traditional lawns, gardens and fields, while others may be dense urban environments. What follows provides an example of how a local environment can be identified as a space that becomes a 'learning space'.

The principles that shape the Albury Wodonga campus situate students within an integrated and unique environment that provides opportunities for students to learn from multi-sensory outdoor experiences. As explained earlier a key component in planning the ecologically sensitive nature of the campus was the establishment and preservation of wetlands, native grasslands and remnant woodlands. Criss-crossing the campus is a network of pathways that link buildings and lead to sites that have a specific environmental functionality. Some of these sites are located near the buildings while others are located within the natural environment.

Figure 2. Aerial image of the Albury Wodonga campus. The circle indicates the area used as the learningscape.

All of these sites have an aesthetic quality and a unique defining characteristic and functionality. These places do not have any of the features usually expected in a "learning space" as defined by guidelines examined earlier but they are indeed places where learning occurs.

This outdoor environment is used as the designated "learning space" for at least one University subject on the Albury Wodonga campus.

CSU Bachelor of Education students on the Albury Wodonga campus participate in a subject (EMS301) that is designed to prepare them to teach science and technology in primary schools. As with most primary curriculum subjects in teacher education programs, the content of EMS301 is regulated by the New South Wales Institute of Teachers (NSWIT). As a result, students in EMS301 must be able to demonstrate competency in content knowledge and teaching skills. The development of these skills is a mandatory component of teacher registration. They include science concepts and specific pedagogical practices, areas where students are expected to attain and demonstrate competency.

Peripatetic Expeditions

Conventional notions of a lecture followed by supporting tutorials have been abandoned in the delivery of EMS301 in favour of a peripatetic approach. Aristotle provides the earliest example of peripatetic pedagogy where he would walk around the Lyceum teaching as his students followed. In a similar way staff and students involved in EMS301 walk, talk and learn in and around the outdoor spaces of the Albury Wodonga campus. These walks, or expeditions, provide opportunities for the students to explore the campus from a sensual perspective and be immersed the environment. The tradition of physical boundaries and territo-

Figure 3. Outdoor learning space

Figure 4. Outdoor learning space

riality associated with 'in-door' learning spaces are challenged by this pedagogical approach. In metaphorical and physical ways the students enter a new world for learning. The everyday lived experiences of the students become the focus of all activities. Students are encouraged, through discussion, to draw on the many situational encounters they experience on these peripatetic expeditions.

In situating EMS301 within the learningscapes of the campus, diverse, locally appropriate and inclusive pedagogies can be developed and engaged. Many of the EMS301 students are from inland Australia and have witnessed and experienced the effects of climate change and global warming on their environment and communities. Their experience with climate change and the environmentally sensitive and passive design of the campus provides a critical backdrop for this subject. In order to develop and maintain enthusiasm for science and science education as much of the course work as possible is based on interactions with the built and natural environments that comprise the campus. The pedagogical approach is locally appropriate as it relies upon making explicit the links between science concepts and the student's daily experiences. The students have opportunities to think and talk with the educational leader and peers and are afforded time to listen, talk and think within the environment. As Russell and Hodson (2002, p. 489) claim, 'it is not enough for students to be armchair critics; they need to get their hands dirty and learn how to take action. This action-orientation extends the campus's capacity to provide 'education for the environment'. Such an approach draws on the educational leader's teaching experience, knowledge of the campus environment and a passion for ecology and sustainability. The educational leader has a fundamental belief that knowledge is socially constructed and adopts a 'constructivist' mindset toward learning.

EMS301 is allocated 1 three-hour session per week. At the start of the three-hour session the students and staff meet in a conventional learning space. This room serves as an administrative meeting place. At the start of the three-hour block the students negotiate the schedule for the session. As the subject prepares the students to be science and technology educators the features and systems of the campus provide a rich platform to bring science and technology into focus. Negotiations consider a number of meteorological variables. Firstly the outside temperature and prevailing conditions plays an important role in determining what part of the campus the class use. The students must dress appropriately for the conditions so student thermal comfort is the students' responsibility. There are no air conditioners, heaters or ergonomic considerations within the learningscapes. Obviously when extreme weather conditions are encountered students' movement around the campus is restricted.

Understanding scientific concepts is a core outcome for the subject and attaining the learning objectives of the subject is paramount. However, the commitment to educational attainment does not exclude notions of enjoyment and fun from the process. Warm spring days provide opportunities to monitor and investigate native flora and fauna populations in pleasant and relaxed conditions. Connections are made between science phenomena and the student's daily interactions with campus. On different days and at different times, certain areas of the campus are more pleasant and interesting for seasonal or ecological reasons than other areas of the campus. The class identifies and spends time in whatever part of the campus is determined to be the most suitable at that time. On cool spring days the earthen roof of the main lecture theatre is a comfortable place to be as it is warmed by the sun, while in summer, the area nearer the largest trees close to the wetlands is cooled by shade and soft breezes; providing welcome relief from the heat. On occasion students will meet with the lecturer on campus very late at night or early in the morning, depending on the activity. For example, sampling the population levels of small marsupials is often more success-ful after dark and ornithological surveys are most successful when they start at dawn. Whether the students are on campus early in the morning or late night or within regular hours students are en-couraged to read and be prepared for the learning spaces they will utilise.

The weather is also an important consideration in determining the structure as well as the content of the expedition. For example, rainy days provide opportunities to investigate water management techniques around the campus. The drains and swales catch and direct all surface water to the wetlands. These investigations open opportunities for the students to talk about and share knowledge concerning the water cycle, the properties and characteristics of water, water ecology, etc. In practical terms a rainy day expedition starts at the highest point of the campus and literally follows the water down hill. In turn such adventures may lead into discussions concerning erosion, which in turn lead into discussions of the physical and chemical changes that water initiates.

In preparation for expeditions students are expected to participate in at least 6 hours of pri-vate study time outside the three-hour block for EMS301. During private study time students are encouraged to work in whatever space or time that best suits their requirements either on campus or off campus. If the students wish to talk with the subject convener during private study time (in groups or individually) they usually find them-selves walking around the campus in his company. The subject is supported by an electronic forum within the university learning management sys-tem. Students are encouraged to post questions, insights, concerns and understandings concerning expeditions. The Internet offers the opportunity for students to be part of a 'virtual community' of learners (Dillenbourg, 1999). The use of the Internet in this subject is a secondary support for the students.

Student Experiences

The students respond positively to the mobile learning expeditions and the opportunity to share their learning spaces. Interspersed with the text below are quotes from students who have partici-pated in EMS301. The comments were offered as part of the CSU subject evaluation procedures. Student evaluations generally rate the subject highly and student comments below provide some insight into the value of the EMS301 experience. (All comments below are from EMS301 students).

During expeditions incidental interactions with native flora and fauna create excitement and curiosity among the students. From casual encounters with large lizards to observing the behaviour of native bees, connections to ac-cepted scientific thinking are constantly being made during the journeys around the campus. It is interesting to note that there is no need to create a realistic simulation through technology. Encounters are explored from an inquiry-based approach and students are encouraged to engage with their senses. That is, the lecturer initiates discussions with and among the students about what has been observed and why the phenomena occurred. Students are encouraged to reflect on their level of awareness and learning.

The practical side was amazing. I loved discover-ing new science concepts on our walks. Looking at animal scats, finding spider webs –it all makes sense when you see it in real life.

You get really attentive when something exciting is happening in front of you or you see something exciting in what you thought was an ordinary event.

The student's knowledge of the local environ-ment is often drawn upon to enrich discussions and students can validate understandings with accepted scientific perspectives. The value of the discussions as a tool for learning is discussed at the start of the semester. The discussions are a collaborative process with students expected to initiate discussions and make scholarly contributions.

The discussions and conversations were really useful and helped to make sense of some 'big' ideas and complicated concepts. I learnt a lot from my friends and myself.

These formal and informal conversations can also highlight alternative conceptions that the students may hold in regard to particular scientific phenomena. Determining and understanding the nature of any alternative conceptions that learners may hold is critical to further learning in science (Skamp, 2008). When the expeditions and associated discussion do draw attention to an alternative understanding of a particular ecological phenomenon the students are guided through investigations and discussion, to reach evidence based conclusions.

The theoretical side of science was a little overwhelming but the discussions helped me to understand more. Like, I always knew the water cycle BUT I never really 'understood' it fully until I saw how we manage water.

Improving scientific understanding and appreciating the importance of science education practices is an important component of the expeditions.

I came away from this subject with more than just knowledge about science, but an understanding of the value of science.

The peripatetic approach builds on Social Constructivist learning theory (Vygotsky & Cole, 1978) which argues that learning is more than the accumulation of facts. Instead it involves a process of enculturation through social discourse and situated cognition (Brown, Collins, & Duguid, 1989).

The discussions on justifying science education and designing a philosophy for science education made me think about the science content but also the methodology behind teaching it. My thinking changed a lot.

Social Constructivist learning theory requires trust-based relationships to develop. The expeditions provided opportunities for all involved to develop a relationship that promoted engagement and discussion at meaningful levels.

Well done on student - teacher relationships, your professionalism is one to be very proud of, and I thoroughly enjoyed your class and joking around with you.

During the expeditions the students are required to be physically active. The actual journey to the identified areas is an important component of the session and many opportunities to explore scientific concepts present themselves as the students move through the environment. However, while seemingly haphazard the expeditions require the leader to be prepared to facilitate discussions across a broad spectrum.

The walks showed me that science is really everywhere. I understand that now better than I did before. Just walking around buildings is like being in a giant lab and I was really switched on.

The value of exercise in the educational enterprise is well documented (Radloff, 1998) and the expeditions around campus are designed to be pleasant and afford opportunities for relaxation as well as learning.

Loved attending this class due to the relaxed, easy nature teaching style. The design of the subject makes the class always enjoyable and fun. There was never a rush to 'do' something. It was great being out and about.

The pathways, thoroughfares and occasional rest areas that exist throughout the campus are generally given a functional value in traffic management and passive recreation. More often than not, these have been developed as an afterthought in campus design. As such the thoroughfares and rest areas are under valued (or not recognized) as important spaces for teaching and learning. Moving around the campus afforded opportunities for discussions that promoted the development of relationships. The relationships allow trust to develop and discussions to be robust.

The aesthetic quality of the natural environment is accompanied by the sound of native birds, the scent of native flora, interactions with native fauna. Sensory stimulation by the atmospheric conditions and the energy spent walking causes the release of endorphins, which heightens awareness.

This was a fantastic subject – EMS301. I think that the subject design creates the perfect, comfortable learning and teaching environment. Apart from bringing science alive being outside relaxes and stimulates you.

An important component of EMS301 involves local primary school students coming to the learningscape to be guided by EMS301 students. EMS301 students take the primary students on their own peripatetic expeditions. These tours often involve hands-on activities and provide the EMS301 students with opportunities to demonstrate the necessary skills and competencies in teaching science and technology to primary students.

Thanks for creating an awesome learning experience that was not only practical and useful but also fun. I see things differently now. I know I can teach science well and I know how to teach it.

The spaces that serve an environmental function become key sites for learning in EMS301. Discussion and contemplation are promoted as a critical component of learning. Discussions vary from practical classroom issues and basic science concepts to issues about the very nature of science and its value to society.

The lecturer's passion for the subject shone through our discussions, and enabled me to develop a deeper understanding of why science and technology is so important.

The process of scholarship is central to the expeditions. The quality of the discussion is an important consideration in this pedagogical approach. The students are afforded time to think, contemplate, reflect on and discuss key components of the subject.

The lecturer had obvious passion about the subject, which made the discussions and walks really positive experiences. I learned lots while walking, talking and thinking.

Critical reflection is an important component of the educative processes and the way that expeditions take the students to physical and metaphorical places that increase one's capacity for reflection.

I found all components assisted my learning, particularly the time to think and be in nice places.

The stimulation provided by the learningscape is critical in ensuring the students are motivated and engaged.

The subject reminded me that learning can (and needs to be) fun. There is more to learning than just reading and listening. I was motivated to learn. There is something about being outside that makes you feel good.

The Albury Wodonga campus affords opportunities to develop outdoor learning spaces that engage students sensually, offer eclectic experiences, and promote 'face to face' discussions.

Students report that the time and space to think and contemplate is beneficial to their learning. The EMS301 students get experience and exposure to a different approach to learning and how to inject identity into space to make a place for learning. The peripatetic expeditions provide a valuable learning experience for the students. The nature of the subject, the pedagogical repertoire of the educational leader, and the environment of the campus combine to create an alternative education experience. Such experiences have value and broaden discussions concerning learning space design. It is important to note that the educational leader's role in the learning process is important but not central to the enterprise. Electronic technologies have a small contributing role within this approach. The students are cognitively and physically active during the process. The students are engaged with all their senses, not just the sense of sight. The students' value the 'face to face' discussions and the time they are afforded to think.

Solutions and Recommendations

This chapter argues the need for Universities to redefine their situations when contemplating the design of learning spaces. The challenge for Universities is to develop ways of anticipating and analyzing the risks that attend all systems of rationality. The discourse that underpins learning space design principles must be identified. Such risk analysis involves the critical investigation of the social and political context of learning space design guidelines, the research paradigms that support them, and the external authorities that fund them in order to assess the possible impact they will have on the University beyond providing learning spaces. This needs to be recognized as part of the core business of Universities. The question for Universities considering designing learning space is not about choosing guidelines; it is about choosing systems of rationality, choosing beliefs and understandings that define and pre-

scribe a role for Universities. The intention of this chapter is not to discredit existing learning space design guidelines. This analysis of the guidelines is an example of managerial discourse and how it demonstrates how the values of efficiency, standardization and accountability endorsed by a market economy sponsor assumptions about learning and learning space. If Universities are to provide leadership to communities, they need to identify and interrogate the discourses that dominate them. Unless they can do this, Universities may inadvertently imprison themselves within a rationality upon which they may not have necessarily reflected on to a sufficient degree.

FUTURE RESEARCH DIRECTIONS

While the Albury Wodonga campus can be regarded as a bold departure from conventional approaches to campus design and celebrated as a reference point for other institutions and the wider community as a model of the 21st century University, it must be able to validate itself. The effectiveness of the campus on student learning requires greater empirical research and theoretical explanation. Ecological discourses sponsor a particular rationality and set of assumptions and therefore require as much interrogation as managerial discourses. Future research should be directed towards investigating the value of 'alternative' discourses in enhancing university management practices, learning space design, student outcomes and teaching and learning strategies. Considering the dominance of managerial discourse and its capacity to marginalize and discredit competing discourses, it would be useful to investigate strategies needed to nurture and promote alternative discourses.

FUTURE AND EMERGING TRENDS

It is reasonable to expect that neo-liberal inspired educational policies will place increasing demands on Universities to provide evidence of improvement in student outcomes and to behave in business like ways. The expectation for Universities and to respond to educational issues through neo-liberal notions of measurement, accountability is likely to continue. As Universities search for a response to these ideological pressure guidelines offering 'rational' solutions will become increasingly attractive. However, as this chapter argues, within the neo-liberal dominated landscape particular pedagogies and practices are valued and sanctioned. Practices and pedagogies that are outside the rationality managerial discourse are regarded as an intolerable and unproductive extravagance that higher education can no longer afford. In order to avoid narrow approaches to education and the design of learning space it is essential that Universities retain an awareness of all outcomes associated with engaging particular rationalities.

CONCLUSION

The intention of this chapter is to demonstrate that challenging the parameters of what constitutes learning space within a university context provides positive outcomes for students. Ecological discourse advances the concept of learningscapes to encompass the multiple dimensions of a student's on–campus existence which is an important consideration when designing learning space. As a result of its environmentally sensitive design the Albury Wodonga campus is fortunate to be surrounded by a unique environment that provides opportunities to define and engage 'space' in innovative ways.

The expeditions are essentially a pluralistic approach to learning that relies on ecological discourses to empower personal pedagogies and practical wisdom. This pedagogy approach facili-

tates learning through stimulating the senses and being in the natural environment. The learning experiences are negotiated and choreographed to accommodate a number of variables. As result the process is organic and unpredictable. Contingencies must constantly be enacted. Indeed for leaders and students the expeditions require an open mind. It would be unreasonable to expect these peripatetic expeditions to be replicated either on the Albury Wodonga campus or any other University campus. However, it is reasonable to expect that all Universities have the capacity to reflect upon and challenge the underlying ideology of the dominant discourses.

The capacity of managerial discourse to intentionally and non-intentionally dominate the thinking and action is particularly relevant to this chapter. The development of the Albury Wodonga campus highlights the struggle between managerial discourse and ecological discourses. The development of the Albury Wodonga campus was shaped by ecological discourses. The passive form of buildings and rigorous implementation of principles of sustainability represent tangible expressions of a genuine vision concerning the role of Universities in leading communities through times of extreme change related to global warming. The visionary practice involved with building such a campus requires a preparedness to embrace change and challenge (Klomp, 2008). Embracing change requires a critical stance to be taken toward the discourse that dominates management practices. Alternative discourses play an important role in providing the discursive spaces required to challenge the assumptions sponsored by dominant discourses. In this case, the design of learning space benefits from the insights generated by ecological discourse. Alternative discourses and the tensions they create by challenging the prevailing rationality should be nurtured and celebrated.

REFERENCES

Alexander, S. (1999). An evaluation of innovative projects involving communication and information technology in higher education. *Higher Education Research & Development, 18*(2), 173. doi:10.1080/0729436990180202

Allan, C., Kent, K., & Klomp, N. (2004). Walking the talk in environmental management. In *University Regional and Rural Engagement. Conference Proceedings 2004.* Sydney, Australia: Australian Universities Community Engagement Alliance.

Allen, M. (1998). Has the discourse of teaching/ learning killed the radical and the spontaneous in university education? In B. Black, & N. Stanley, (Eds.), *Teaching and learning in changing times. Proceedings of the 7th Annual Teaching Learning Forum* (pp. 12-16). Perth, Australia: The University of Western Australia.

Ball, S. J. (1994). *Education reform: A critical and post-structural approach.* Buckingham, UK: Open University Press.

Ball, S. J. (1995). Intellectuals or technicians? The urgent role of theory in education studies. *British Journal of Education, 43*(3), 255–271.

Brown, J. S., Collins, A., & Duguid, P. (1989). Situated cognition and the culture of learning. *Educational Researcher, 18*(1), 32–42.

Clark, B. R. (2004). Delineating the character of the entrepreneurial university. *Higher Education Policy, 17*(4), 355–370. doi:10.1057/palgrave. hep.8300062

Clegg, S., Hudson, A., & Steel, J. (2003). The emperor's new clothes: Globalisation and e-learning in higher education. *British Journal of Sociology of Education, 24*(1), 39–53. doi:10.1080/01425690301914

CSU. (2003). *Charles Sturt University annual report. For the public good.* Retrieved April 8, 2010, from http://www.csu.edu.au/ division/ marketing/ annualreports/ ar03/ index.html

Daniel, J. S. (1996). *Mega-universities and knowledge media: Technology strategies for higher education.* London, UK: Kogan Page.

Dillenbourg, P. (1999). What do you mean by collaborative learning? In Dillenbourg, P. (Ed.), *Collaborative-learning: Cognitive and computational approaches* (pp. 1–19). Oxford, UK: Elsevier.

Etzkowitz, H. (2004). The evolution of the entrepreneurial university. *International Journal of Technology and Globalisation, 1*(1), 64–77.

Gay, P., Salaman, G., & Rees, B. (1996). The conduct of management and the management of conduct: Contemporary managerial discourse and the constitution of the competent manager. *Journal of Management Studies, 33*(3), 263–282. doi:10.1111/j.1467-6486.1996.tb00802.x

James, R. (2008). The theories of teaching and learning underpinning space and design decisions. In Huijser, H., Elson-Green, J., Reid, I., Walta, C., Challis, D., & Harris, K.-L. (Eds.), *Places and spaces for learning seminars (draft report).* Sydney, Australia: Carrick Institute for Learning and Teaching in Higher Education.

Jamieson, P., Fisher, K., Gilding, T., Taylor, P. G., & Trevitt, A. C. F. (2000). Place and space in the design of new learning environments. *Higher Education Research & Development, 19*(2), 221–237. doi:10.1080/072943600445664

JISC. (2006). *Designing spaces for effective learning: A guide to 21st century learning space design.* Retrieved April 8, 2010, from http:// www.jisc.ac.uk/ media/ documents/ publications/ learningspaces.pdf

Jørgensen, M., & Phillips, L. (2002). *Discourse analysis as theory and method.* London, UK: Sage.

Klomp, N. (2008). Learning places and head spaces – are we leading by example? In Huijser, H., Elson-Green, J., Reid, I., Walta, C., Challis, D., & Harris, K.-L. (Eds.), *Places and spaces for learning seminars (draft report).* Sydney, Australia: Carrick Institute for Learning and Teaching in Higher Education.

Larsen, M. (2010). Troubling the discourse of teacher centrality: A comparative perspective. *Journal of Education Policy, 25*(2), 207–231. doi:10.1080/02680930903428622

Le Grew, D. (2008). The place of learning. In Huijser, H., Elson-Green, J., Reid, I., Walta, C., Challis, D., & Harris, K.-L. (Eds.), *Places and spaces for learning seminars (draft report).* Sydney, Australia: Carrick Institute for Learning and Teaching in Higher Education.

Levin, C. (2008). *Leading by example: From sustainable campuses to a sustainable world.* Climate Lecture Series, University of Copenhagen. Retrieved April 8, 2010, from http://opa.yale.edu/president/ message.aspx? id=1

Marginson, S. (1997). *Markets in education.* Melbourne, Australia: Allen & Unwin.

McCann, D., Christmass, J., Nicholson, P., & Stuparich, J. (1998). *Educational technology in higher education.* Canberra, Australia: Department of Employment, Education, Training and Youth Affairs.

McWilliam, E. L. (1998). Teacher IM/material: Challenging the new pedagogies of instructional design. *Educational Researcher, 27*(8), 29–35.

McWilliam, E. L. (2005). Unlearning pedagogy. *Journal of Learning Design, 1*(1), 1–11.

Mitchell, D. S., Croft, I., Harrison, T., & Webster-Mannison, M. (2001). *Water management on the Thurgoona campus of Charles Sturt University.* Paper presented at the Advancing On-site Wastewater Systems, University of New England, Armidale.

Oblinger, D. (2005). Leading transition from classrooms to learning spaces. *Educause 28*(1). Retrieved April 8, 2010, from http://www.educause.edu/EDUCAUSE+Quarterly/EDUCAUSEQuarterlyMagazineVolum/LeadingtheTransitionfromClassr/157328

Phillips, R. (1998). What research says about learning on the Internet. In McBeath, C., & Atkinson, R. (Eds.), *Planning for Progress, Partnership and Profit. Australian Society for Educational Technology. EduTech 98* (pp. 203–207). Perth, Australia: Australian Society for Educational Technology.

Pratt, J. G. (2003). Decision making, rationality, and the adoption of online learning technologies in Australian higher education. In *Conference Proceedings - Surfing the Waves: Management Challenges, Management Solutions, 17th Annual Conference of the Australian and New Zealand Academy of Management (ANZAM)* (pp. 1-11). Fremantle, Australia. ANZAM.

Radcliffe, D., Wilson, H., Powell, D., & Tibbetts, B. (2008). *Designing next generation places of learning: Collaboration at the pedagogy-space-technology nexus.* Retrieved March 6, 2010, from http://www.uq.edu.au/ nextgenerationlearning-spaces

Radloff, P. (1998). Proceedings of the 7th Annual Teaching Learning Forum. In B. Black & N. Stanley (Eds.), *Teaching and learning in changing times.* Perth, Australia: The University of Western Australia. Retrieved April 30, 2010, from http://lsn.curtin.edu.au/ tlf/ tlf1998/ radloff-p.html

Rafferty, J. M. (2007). *The continuing myth of school reform*. Paper presented at the Australian Association for Research in Education International Education Research Conference, Fremantle, Western Australia.

Rosenzweig, R. M. (2001). *The political university: Policy, politics, and presidential leadership in the American research university*. Baltimore, MD: Johns Hopkins University Press.

Russell, C., & Hodson, D. (2002). Whalewatching as critical science education? *Canadian Journal of Science, Mathematics and Technology Education, 2*(4), 485–504. doi:10.1080/14926150209556537

Sachs, J. (2001). Teacher professional identity: Competing discourses, competing outcomes. *Journal of Education Policy, 16*(2), 149–161. doi:10.1080/02680930116819

Skamp, K. (2008). *Teaching primary science constructively* (3rd ed.). South Melbourne, Victoria, Australia: Cengage Learning.

Soley, L. (1995). *Leasing the ivory tower: The corporate takeover of academia*. Boston, MA: South End Press.

Steck, H. (2003). Corporatization of the university: Seeking conceptual clarity. *The Annals of the American Academy of Political and Social Science, 585*(1), 66–83. doi:10.1177/0002716202238567

Vygotsky, L. S., & Cole, M. (1978). *Mind in society: The development of higher psychological processes*. Cambridge, UK: Harvard University Press.

ADDITIONAL READING

Agarwala, S. P. (2006). *Environmental studies*. Oxford, England: Alpha Science International.

Azeiteiro, U. (2008). *Science and environmental education: Towards the integration of science education, experimental science activities and environmental education*. Oxford, England: Peter Lang.

Ben-Peretz, M. (2009). *Policy-making in education: A holistic approach in response to global changes*. Lanham: Rowman & Littlefield Education.

Blewitt, J. (2006). *The ecology of learning: Sustainability, lifelong learning and everyday life*. London, England: Earthscan.

Cressey, P., & Docherty, P. (2006). *Productive reflection at work: Learning for changing organizations*. New York, NY: Routledge.

Curtis, D., & Carter, M. (2003). *Designs for living and learning: Transforming early childhood environments*. St. Paul, Minn: Redleaf Press.

Eriksson, I. V. (2008). *Science education in the 21st Century*. New York: Nova Science Publishers.

Freeman, G. T., & Council on Library and Information Resources. (2005). *Library as place: Rethinking roles, rethinking space*. Washington, DC: Council on Library and Information Resources.

Ganderton, P. S., & Coker, P. (2005). *Environmental biogeography*. Sydney: Pearson Education.

Gough, S., & Scott, W. (2007). *Higher education and sustainable development: Paradox and possibility*. London: Routledge.

Gray-Donald, J., & Selby, D. (2008). *Green frontiers: Environmental educators dancing away from mechanism*. Rotterdam, Netherlands: Sense Publishers.

Harper, S. R., & Quaye, S. J. (2009). *Student engagement in higher education: Theoretical perspectives and practical approaches for diverse populations*. New York: Routledge.

Kagawa, F., & Selby, D. (2009). *Education and climate change: Living and learning in interesting times*. New York: Routledge.

Lang, J. R., & Curriculum Corporation (Australia) (2007). *How to succeed with education for sustainability*. Carlton South, Vic: Curriculum Corporation.

Littledyke, M., Taylor, N., & Eames, C. (2009). *Education for sustainability in the primary curriculum: A guide for teachers*. South Yarra, Vic: Palgrave Macmillan.

Lyth, A., Nichols, S., & Tilbury, D. Australian Research Institute in Education for Sustainability, & Australia. Dept. of the Environment and Water Resources. (2007). *Shifting towards sustainability: Education for climate change adaption in the built environment sector*. North Ryde, NSW: Australian Research Institute in Education for Sustainability (ARIES).

Reid, A., & Scott, W. (2008). *Researching education and the environment: Retrospect and prospect*. Oxford, UK: Routledge.

Sernau, S. (2008). *Contemporary readings in globalization*. Thousand Oaks: Pine Forge Press.

Steiner, F. R. (2008). *The living landscape: An ecological approach to landscape planning* (2nd ed.). Washington, DC: Island Press.

Stone, M. K., & Barlow, Z. (2005). *Ecological literacy: Educating our children for a sustainable world*. San Francisco: University of California Press.

Tilbury, D., Crawley, C., & Berry, F. Australia. Dept. of the Environment and Heritage, & Australian Research Institute in Education for Sustainability. (2005). *Education about and for sustainability in Australian business schools*. Canberra: Dept. of the Environment and Heritage.

Wheatley, N., & Searle, K. (2007). *Going bush*. Crows Nest, NSW: Allen & Unwin.

KEY TERMS AND DEFINITIONS

Discourse: The language, knowledge and practices used in and around institutions constitute various discourses. Discourses constitute a particular patchwork of thoughts, words and actions and interactions that give them a unique entity and promote specific identities.

Ecological Discourse: A discourse that stresses the importance of protecting the environment on the basis of a holsitic understanding of the world.

Entrepreneurial: Showing committment to the application of certain technical solutions [to] organizations and contexts which are taken to be in need of structural and/or cultural change.

Learningscapes: Outdoor and natural spaces used as learning sites.

Managerial Discourse: A discourse that reflects the neoliberal ideology that dominates government policy and the educational landscape of countries with advanced economies.

Neoliberal Ideology: An ideology that promotes market logic and business like strategies to all levels of governance.

Peripatetic Expeditions: Pedagogical strategies that facilitate learning opportunities that involve physical activity, multi-sensory stimulation and discussion to generate knowledge.

Section 2
Physical and Virtual Learning Spaces

Chapter 5

Balancing Context, Pedagogy and Technology on Learning Space Designs:
Opportunities Amidst Infrastructural Developments in Hong Kong

Robert Fox
The University of Hong Kong, Hong Kong

Paul Lam
The Chinese University of Hong Kong, Hong Kong

ABSTRACT

This chapter explores the changing needs for university learning spaces and the resultant designs to maximize opportunities for student learning, taking into account the special needs and learning culture of the local context and the changing curriculum needs of all higher education institutions in Hong Kong. The chapter outlines a study of these needs and an institution's plans to better use space to support both flexible and interactive learning environments to enhance active student learning.

INTRODUCTION

The concept of learning spaces in the higher education context has attracted much attention and discussion in recent years as a range of physical environments has been identified as affording different student opportunities to learn (e.g. Bransford, Brown, & Cocking, 2000; Brown, 2005). As Brown and Lippincott (2003) note, understanding where teaching and learning takes place is both "expanding and evolving" (p. 14). The concept is expanding because learning spaces are no longer restricted to predominantly traditional teaching venues (e.g. classrooms)

DOI: 10.4018/978-1-60960-114-0.ch005

and formal self-study places (e.g. the library). At the same time, what constitutes good designs of learning spaces is changing, in part influenced by technology developments as well as research into student learning and changing space requirements for both teaching and learning.

LEARNING ACTIVITIES AND STUDENT PROFILES

The learner-centred paradigm of teaching and learning (e.g. Laurillard, 2002; Biggs, 2003) highlights the importance of students actively engaging in the manipulation and construction of knowledge. This view de-emphasizes the role of teacher-led activities and increases the importance of providing opportunities for students to work with each other. This learner-centred paradigm identifies learning as a social constructivist process (Vygotsky, 1978; Collins, Brown & Newman, 1989) as students co-construct knowledge through communicating their own interpretations of concepts and ideas. In planning a major expansion of teaching and learning facilities, different types of learning spaces were investigated that would best afford this more active and interactive learning process (Brawn, 2006). Van Note Chism (2006) questioned typical assumptions of traditional education, including:

- Learning only happens in classrooms
- Learning only happens at fixed times
- Learning is an individual activity
- What happens in classrooms is pretty much the same from class-to-class and day-to-day
- A classroom always has a front
- Learning demands privacy and the removal of distractions

Higher education students are juvenile: they destroy or steal expensive furnishings; they need to be confined to tablet arm chairs to feel like students; and they are all small, young, nimble, and without disabilities (p. 2.3).

However, increasing numbers of studies argue that higher education practices are far removed from the above stereotype understandings. For example, Bransford, Brown and Cocking (2000)'s extensive collated study of educational research states that students greatly benefit from physical environments that encourage group interaction. Goldschmid and Goldschmid (1976) emphasize the benefits accrued when students spend increased time with their peers and work collaboratively. Simsek and Hooper (1992) state that students are able to develop more complex examples and explanations related to set contexts when they work with their peers. In addition Poole (2008) argues that much of this deep collaborative learning takes place outside formal learning venues and spaces should be created on campus to facilitate this learning.

Students need places where they can work collaboratively, on their own, in quiet and noisy areas and in multiple settings. These learning spaces can be broadly categorized as formal and informal learning spaces. Formal learning spaces are normally managed and staffed by service units in a university. The 'learning commons' housed in or associated with the library and the 'living-learning spaces' that facilitate learning in student halls of residences as described by Van Note Chism (2006) are good examples of these formal learning spaces. But there is also a growing need for more 'informal' and 'seriously cool' places (Dittoe, 2006) such as suitably furnished discussion areas that can be the open spaces outside classrooms, or comfortable gathering places with sofas and with the provision of food and drink facilities or increased seating in Starbucks-style café settings, to encourage lengthened group discussions.

Learning spaces can also be virtual as well as physical. According to Oblinger (2006), the need to consider virtual learning spaces is the result of changes in student habits and study practices and the advances and ubiquity of technologies, supported by cross campus internet connectivity. Most students own their own computers and almost all have their own mobile and increasingly smart phones with good internet connections in many countries. "Browsing, downloading, and messaging happen anywhere and anytime" (Oblinger, 2006, p. 1.2). University students today are sometimes labeled "the net generation" (Tapscott, 1998) or "digital natives" (Prensky, 2001). However, not all digital natives are fully 'techno-savvy' nor have they all acquired the multi-literacy skills needed to make the most of technology affordances to support their learning (Kennedy et al., 2008). However, Oblinger (2006) argues that a growing student population in universities today consists of mature students and many study part-time. These students predominantly live off campus and not in halls of residence. The virtual learning environment is important to them as it increases flexibility in when and where they learn.

The emphasis of this chapter is on physical learning spaces. However, virtual and physical learning spaces are not two separate entities but influence the designs of each other. For example, physical space needs for learners are influenced by the increased use of virtual learning environments and subsequent blended learning opportunities (Osguthorpe & Graham, 2003) that supplement and take the place of face-to-face teaching and learning, whether students live on- or off-campus. Dillenbourg, Schneider and Synteta (2002) argue that the virtual learning environment is a very real space for student learning, and it influences the kinds of physical places students need for their studies. For example, the ease of use of technology and access to the internet is a prime consideration in many physical learning space designs.

DESIGNING NEW SPACES FOR LEARNING

A number of excellent research and development studies on what constitutes good designs in today's learning spaces have been published (e.g. JISC, 2006; Eberhard & Patoine, 2004; AMA, 2006). These publications draw attention to changing teaching and learning needs and outline broad considerations necessary in new designs. Van Note Chism (2006), for example, suggested the following as important guiding principles in modern learning space designs:

- Flexibility: learning activities can be diverse and the flow from one activity to another can be immediate. It is thus important to construct spaces that are capable of quick reconfigurations.
- Comfort: comfortable chairs and tables with ample working surfaces facilitate group study and individual learning.
- Sensory stimulation: natural lighting, colours and pleasant designs make spaces interesting and stimulating, encouraging students to stay longer.
- Technology support: increasingly students bring their own mobile digital devices to university and need basic technical support.
- Electricity supply: students need convenient places to plug-in and re-charge their devices.
- Wireless connectivity: increasingly this is required across campus and especially in formal and informal learning spaces.
- Interest groups: in designing new learning spaces all stakeholders (managers, architects and especially teachers and students should be involved).

Bickford and Wright (2006) investigated learning space designs that can facilitate interactions in the form of learning communities. They define these learning communities as "a group of people with a common purpose, shared values and agreement on goals…[and that] a community has the power to motivate its members to exceptional performance" (p. 4.3). They argue that learning communities benefit from access to rich physical environments that encourage groups to gather. Learning spaces in universities should therefore be designed to foster such community gatherings. Learning spaces at universities, they state, should also be inviting and roomy and should encourage cross-disciplinary contacts by providing spaces in interdisciplinary buildings.

At the same time, teachers need be encouraged to make use of these new learning spaces to support student work and encourage learning activities. A growing number of universities have established rich learning environments to facilitate both students and teachers to study and interact outside the classroom in well provisioned and comfortable surroundings (e.g. Poole, 2008; Fox & Stuart, 2009). One challenge universities face is in helping teachers become aware of the potential and make full use of these new learning spaces to support their own teaching as well

as their students' learning. McNaught and Lam (2009) note some factors that may hinder the use of such innovations include the commitment to a university research life and teacher peer groups in departments not favouring any change. Figure 1 illustrates a model used in the exploration of learning spaces.

The dotted oval, 'A' in Figure 1 illustrates the traditional view of learning spaces. This view does not support the more innovative and interactive types of teaching and learning. For example, immovable or hard to move chairs and tables in a classroom simply discourage group work in class. The dotted lines around 'B' in Figure 1 includes the new designs for learning spaces that facilitate more styles and activities. Based on the orientations provided, the investigations into new learning space needs within a single university in Hong Kong was carried out, where the majority of the teaching approaches is considered traditional and didactic. Our learning space designs however do not only support the existing dominant teaching and learning approaches, but the expected changes and transformations of the teach-

Figure 1. Compatibility of the new learning spaces

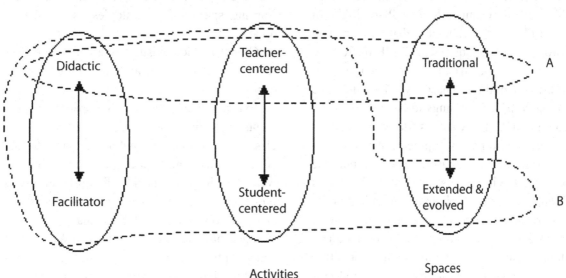

ing and learning culture at universities in future years.

CONTEXTUAL CHALLENGES IN A HONG KONG HIGHER EDUCATION INSTITUTION

Education in Hong Kong is often seen as adopting a rather traditional teacher-centred approach. However, Hong Kong is undergoing major curriculum change in secondary and post-secondary education. The new curriculum dictates that secondary schooling will be shortened from seven to six years and undergraduate programmes be lengthened from three to four years starting in 2012. Preparations are underway in every aspect by universities in order to accommodate a larger student population and to accommodate them for the extra year. The main universities are planning for major building expansion and this has focused attention on rethinking what new spaces are needed to support the new curriculum. At CUHK, the University has developed an overall Campus Master Plan (2009) for phased building developments up to and including 2021.

Planning for new teaching and learning therefore needs to take into account the phases outlined in the Campus Master Plan (ibid). In the first phase, it is estimated that an extra 100 classrooms will be required at CUHK by 2012 to cater for the estimated extra 3000 students (AMI, 2008). Later building phases will include more teaching complex buildings to be completed by 2015 and 2021. The Campus Master Plan (ibid) and phased building developments offer the University a unique opportunity to rethink the purpose of teaching environments and to align the design with approaches to teaching and learning which are more appropriate for the new curriculum. University campuses worldwide and the majority of their teaching environments built before 2000 were designed to enable and privilege a predominantly teacher-centred pedagogy which resulted

in a more passive approach to learning (Edwards, 2000; AMA, 2006). However, teaching environments built in the last eight years have included more student-centred designs, taking into account more constructivist approaches to learning and the introduction of ubiquitous mobile technologies and the internet and their subsequent impact on student learning practices (JISC, 2006; Temple & Barnett, 2007).

There is now a recognized need at CUHK to create a new generation of teaching and learning environments, to meet the changing imperatives of a university education in knowledge-based economies (Fox, 2005 & 2007; Lawson, 2001). CUHK and the new outcomes-based curriculum expect students to graduate with additional attributes including: critical and creative thinking, problem solving, self-managed learning, adaptability and collaborative and communication skills. These abilities require a rethink in the design of teaching places that encourage more student-centred interactive learning opportunities.

The University's teaching and learning and educational research unit, the Centre for Learning Enhancement And Research (CLEAR) identified the need to make evidence-based recommendations to the University that guide and coordinate the developments of the various initiatives about learning spaces. The strategies used included reviews of:

Global practices: visits to international centres, review of the literature and consulting overseas experts.

Existing teaching and learning spaces: arrangements of relatively new (less than ten years-old) classrooms on campus, and a number of formal and informal learning spaces across the university were investigated. A checklist for observation was prepared beforehand. Investigators recorded and analysed topics such as tables, chairs, shelving, storage, computer setup, internet and WiFi access and quality, electrical outlets, lighting, access to natural light, projection and screen facilities, flooring, window fixtures, and air-conditioning.

Common learning activities: the nature and amount of individual and group work as well as computer facilities and their usage in shared learning spaces (Lee, Lam, Lee, Ho & Fox, 2009).

The needs of various stakeholders: Flutter (2006) emphasized the importance of including student voices and Callahan (2004) noted that "teachers and students are the people who spend the most amount of time in these learning environments, not the architects, designers, and facility planners. Therefore, the needs of the users must be taken into consideration in the programming and pre-design phases" (p. 70). The investigation team therefore held meetings over a ten-month period with teachers and teacher groups, students, fresh graduates and a student leader group. In addition, meetings and workshops were held with the University senior and middle managers, Library staff, commissioned architects, and administrative groups such as the campus development and estates office staff. In each of the meetings, the investigators started by introducing concepts and plans, preliminary findings and suggestions for new learning spaces. The informants' comments were then solicited. Multi-stakeholder meetings will continue to be held at different stages of the learning spaces development and until the initial buildings, rooms and spaces have been completed, used and evaluated by all concerned.

PRELIMINARY RESULTS

Existing Arrangements of Teaching and Learning Spaces

In 2009, the investigation team reviewed existing classrooms, learning space provision in the main library, and six existing or potential informal learning spaces across the campus. The investigators found the majority of existing classrooms lacked any real flexibility in the seating arrangements. Tables and chairs were generally heavy and difficult (and noisy) to move. A standard teacher-centred seating arrangement predominated in classrooms. On occasions, when the rooms had been re-organised to afford student-centred activities (desks arranged in groups), the following day, the room cleaners had re-arranged the furniture in line with the traditional teacher-centred layout. Notices in all classrooms inform teachers to reset all tables and chairs to the default teacher-centred arrangement every time they finish a lesson. However, several special classroom layouts that favoured class interaction and group work were also identified. Students using these rooms were asked their opinions on how well these alternative arrangements worked for their classes. Their comments were mixed. Some liked the layout, which encouraged teachers to get students to interact with each other. However, students also noted that most of their teachers still taught in a traditional teacher-dominant way and the student grouped tables had meant that some students had to either sit with their back to the teacher or had to sit awkwardly to face the teacher. So despite the more interactive design, the difficulty in easily moving the desks and chairs to suit different phases of the class resulted in desks and chairs remaining in the way they were originally placed in the room.

Outside classroom investigations of existing informal learning spaces where furniture had been placed, led us to identify many low or no cost improvements in order to create more useful learning spaces. For example, sofas that were heavy and were placed too far apart (Figure 2) to encourage discussion between students sitting at the sofas.

Other spaces were identified as being crowded with tables and chairs (Figure 3). Students commented that they used the space for individual work only. If the place was used for group discussions, noise in groups interfered with other group discussions. By sharing these small but significant points with administrators and cleaners, simple changes can be easily made to make the space more useful. It was also a little surprising that students themselves had not moved the

Figure 2. Space with heavy sofas set too far apart

furniture to suit their immediate needs. When asked, one student commented that he felt had no right to make any changes to the way the furniture was laid out. There is clearly a need to create places across campus where students feel free to move and re-position the furniture to suit different needs.

The University has many different spaces in the open air, in between buildings that have the potential to be used to support student study. Outside areas that have comfortable seating, shading from the sun, open to through breezes and close to food and drink facilities were favoured by students. At the same time, students pointed out that some cafes across campus actively dis-

Figure 3. Space cramped with tables and chairs

courage students from using tables and chairs for group work near the facilities as they take up seats of potential paying customers.

Other spaces were identified that could be effectively used as informal learning spaces across campus. Figure 4 shows vast empty air-conditioned spaces with excellent WiFi in front of classrooms in a recently built teaching complex.

Learning Space Developments and Discussions

The data from various investigations above have helped inform us of learning space needs across the University. Together with data collected from across the world, from visits to other universities, from bringing in outside consultants and from research into new learning spaces, the University is continually adjusting its designs for new buildings and new spaces to support student learning. In 2010, the University proposed to build four new Learning Commons, strategically positioned across campus to provide students with flexible, well equipped facilities and services, staffed 24/7. A discussion document on the requirements of the first new 100 classrooms to be built over the next two years at the University has been circulated and discussed (Fox, 2009). No decisions have yet been made, but through dialogue across the University, requirements for the new classrooms is becoming clearer. One key outcome to-date is that most stakeholders at all levels want the new classrooms to be different from the existing classrooms.

Key points from this discussion document (Fox, ibid) on requirements for the new classrooms is outlined below. In making these suggestions, reference has been made to take into consideration classroom layout designs and settings in the literature (e.g. Prosser & Jamieson, 2008; Callahan, 2004; McCroskey & McVetta, 1978). Important physical elements such as windows, lighting, facilitator's desk, display, surface and students seating identified by Allen et al., (1996) and others were also identified and included in the designs.

Prosser and Jamieson (2008) identified four main types of spatial settings for teaching rooms at universities, outlined in Table 1. Type 1 is the traditional theatre arrangement that enables large

Figure 4. Empty space identified as potential learning spaces

scale lecture delivery. Type 2 is a modified theatre, affording some interaction between students and groups. This design is often favoured in casebook style presentations. Type 3 provides a modified theatre arrangement, facilitating greater flexibility for students to turn round and talk to individuals and form multiple groups for discussion. Type 4 offers a seminar classroom-style arrangement, suited for presentation as well as small group work. Prosser and Jamieson (ibid) identified this spatial setting being most suited to rooms with a capacity of up to 70 seats. The design of grouped tables affords small group interaction and the ability to easily change seating arrangements. Analysis of institutional needs identified the smaller rooms most suitable (AMI, 2008) and therefore Type 4 is recommended as the basic setting for all the 100 new classrooms at CUHK.

Classrooms, generally, need to cater for different teaching and learning practices that support both instructivist and constructivist approaches to teaching (McNaught, 2005). In order to cater for multiple practices and to maximize flexibility (Gale, 2006), classrooms need to be designed to enable quick re-configuration from one activity to another *during* individual classes (Van Note Chism, 2006). Furniture in all classrooms should facilitate mobility as well as flexibility (Haw-

Table 1. Spatial-pedagogy matrix for different types of classroom settings

Spatial Types	Primary Use Mode & Indicative Capacity	Key Educational Interactions								
		Teacher – Student			Student - Student			Student - Environment		Student - Learning Content
		With individual student	With small groups	With class	With individual student	Within small group	Between small groups	Physical setting	Facilities in setting	
Type 1 Traditional theatre arrangement for presentation mode. Large capacity possible. Room arrangement fixed.				👍	?					
Type 2 Modified theatre / casebook arrangements for presentation mode enabling limited interaction. Ideal for medium to smaller groups. Room arrangement fixed.				👍	👍					
Type 3 Modified theatre arrangements (double-row per terrace) for presentation mode enabling good interaction. Large capacity possible. Room arrangement fixed / furniture mobile?			👍	👍	👍	👍		?		👍
Type 4 Seminar mode with capacity for presentation & small-group work. Suggested capacity 70 max. Room arrangement adaptable.		👍	👍	👍	👍	👍		👍		👍

(adapted from Prosser & Jamieson, 2008)

thorne, 2002). To support group interaction as well as increase mobility, two-seater trapezoid or rectangular desks *designed for adults* with lockable wheels and stackable chairs are recommended for most classrooms, though some variation in classroom furniture is also recommended. Some classrooms would benefit from hinged desktops that can be stacked together or used as mini-walls between study groups in the room.

The location of where the new classes will be built was also explored. Generally, a balance between locating classrooms in multi-faculty teaching buildings and single faculty buildings was discussed and a key consideration explored was maximising efficient use of energy and resources, for example, whether the building or part of the building can easily be sealed off and closed during vacations and university close down. If too many classrooms are located in centrally scheduled teaching blocks, the buildings may be underused during non-teaching times. On the other hand, multi-faculty classroom block buildings may facilitate faster changeover for students between classes.

General purpose classrooms differ in size, shape and orientation. In general, the proposed 40-seater classrooms are rectangular and can be oriented

in two main ways as in Figures 5 and 6. Some teachers in the study stated they favoured square-shaped classrooms as this shape was perceived and allowing teachers increased ease of access to interact with individual students and groups across the classroom. Larger or smaller classrooms will need different designs. For example, classes smaller than 30-seats may not require two access doors while 60-seat classrooms may need more than two entrances/exits. One key area discussed was the need for doors to be placed to facilitate entrance and exit of the room, while a class is in progress without disrupting the rest of the class.

All classrooms will use two walls for whiteboards or equivalent, to increase flexibility in room orientation while projection screen size recommended is no less than one fifth of the length of the classroom. Some classrooms will need two screens and two projectors as in Figure 6. The two projectors need to allow for more than one source with at least one projector plug-in facility for laptops and other connections digital connections.

All classrooms will have WiFi connectivity but also need plenty of double power plugs distributed around the room to enable students to plug in personal digital devices. As one teacher commented, "you can never have too many plugs

Figure 5. Standard classroom design (long)

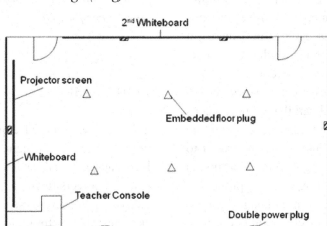

Figure 6. Standard classroom design (wide)

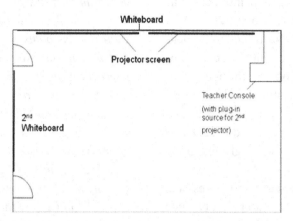

....the more increases flexibility and safety, reducing chances of students tripping over each other's power leads." It is preferable for some power plugs to be embedded in the floor in strategic places to enable students, grouped around tables, easy access to power (see Figure 5).

To encourage a more student-centred environment, the teacher desk or console should be no higher than the student tables (approx 74 cm high). The console should be located horizontal alongside rather than perpendicular to the wall to reduce unnecessary physical barriers between teachers and students.

The type of flooring was also discussed at length. Thick linoleum flooring will reduce noise of moving furniture, while at the same time be long lasting and easy to maintain and keep clean, especially in Hong Kong where the humidity reaches 95% in the summer. Wall-to-wall carpets, unless in the form of replaceable carpet squares, in classrooms are not recommended due to hygiene, maintenance and longevity matters.

Natural light sources are necessary for all classrooms and standard parallel lighting is considered adequate, though all require additional control over lighting zones across the room to increase flexibility in changing room focal points as well as avoiding lighting with the projection screens. This is particularly important in the more technology-rich interactive classrooms described below. These classrooms will need additional spot lighting installed.

The institution is considering establishing several 'technology-rich' classrooms for teachers and students to experiment with new ways of teaching and learning. Figure 7 offers a sample layout. To increase flexibility and control in these classrooms, the teacher console could include a portable remote control panel for different projection and other facilities including the lighting control. Facilities will include LCDs, interactive and standard whiteboards on wheels as well as technology such as Clickers and ECHO360 as required. To support teacher professional development and innovation, it has been proposed that the professional development centre will be given priority booking of one of these technology-rich classrooms for their workshops and activities.

CONCLUSION

This chapter outlined expanding and evolving opportunities to influence the design of new learning spaces, taking into account the changing needs of universities and those that use university campuses. We saw ourselves in a unique position as educators, to stimulate debate across campus

Figure 7. Sample hi-technology interactive classroom of the future

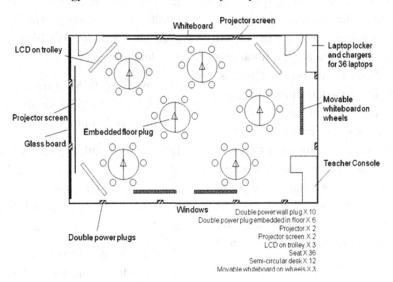

about what new learning spaces we need to create in order to provide the best environment for learning for today and for the future. We also saw ourselves in a unique position to influence the designs of new university buildings, rooms and spaces where students study. We noted that technology advancements and recent research into student learning has thrown open new possibilities and new imperatives in thinking about physical learning environments. What was once taught solely through face-to-face, in lecture theatres or read in books in libraries and halls of residence, can increasingly be found online, as video presentations in YouTube, as PowerPoint presentations in Slideshare, Google Docs, or read in online journals, debated in electronic forums, through social networking and referenced in collective shared online bookmarking.

The ubiquity of technology and in Hong Kong's case, the near 100 per cent student ownership of laptops, cell phones and other digital devices, have all impacted on the way we work, on the way that we teach, on the way that we learn and interact, and on the physical learning environments we need. We still, of course, need physical spaces at universities, but we no longer need to make these

spaces look like the Victorian, industrial age rooms of yesterday, as Corcoran (1993) points out:

The traditional classroom ...... is singularly ill suited to producing lifelong learners: "Right now, you've got 30 little workers who come into a room, sit in rows, follow instructions from a boss, and can't talk to one another. ... [This is] the last time they'll ever see that model" (para. 1)[1]

In exploring new space needs, we identified the need for flexibility and mobility, providing ease of opportunity to change furniture settings, re-orient and re-focus rooms to meet instant needs. We need full connectivity to the internet, for all at all times, through WiFi, we need convenient sources to plug-in digital devices to re-charge batteries. Physical environment affords different educational approaches and while many of our teachers may still want to predominantly teach in traditional teacher-centred ways, we want to provide them with new spaces, new opportunities to interact with students, new opportunities to enable their students to move around spaces to increase opportunities for active group work. We recognize the importance of involving multi-stakeholders in the debate about what new learning spaces we really need. We held public and private meetings with different interest groups across campus, from students and student leaders, teachers, librarians and managers, architects and estate planners, maintenance staff to classroom administration staff. And through interaction, in teasing out ideas and proposing new ones, we have been able to gain acceptance that new learning spaces need to be different from old ones. Providing new learning spaces is just the first step and the ongoing challenge is to work with teachers and students in finding new ways of using these new learning spaces that best affords learning. However, we feel we have successfully made the first step.

REFERENCES

Allen, R., Bowen, J. T., Clabough, S., DeWitt, B., Francis, J., Kerstetter, J., & Rieck, D. (1996). *Classroom design manual* (3rd ed.). College Park, MD: Academic Information Technology Services, The University of Maryland.

AMA (Alexi Marmot Associates). (2006). *Spaces for learning. A review of learning spaces in further and higher education*. Edinburgh, UK: Scottish Funding Council.

AMI. (Academic Management Information Section, Office of Registry Services). (2008). *A projection of the number of classrooms required for the 334 curriculum*. Hong Kong: The Chinese University of Hong Kong.

Bickford, D. J., & Wright, D. J. (2006). Community: The hidden context for learning. In D. G. Oblinger (Ed.), *Learning spaces*, (pp. 4.1 – 4.22). Retrieved September 9, 2009, from http://www.educause.edu/learningspaces

Biggs, J. (2003). *Teaching for quality learning at university* (2nd ed.). Buckingham, UK: SRHE and Open University Press.

Bransford, J., Brown, A., & Cocking, R. (Eds.). (2000). *How people learn: Brain, mind, experience and school*. Washington, DC: National Academy Press.

Brawn, R. (2006). From teaching spaces to learning spaces. [University of Bristol Learning Technology Support Service]. *Interact, 32*, 3–4.

Brown, M. (2005). Learning spaces. In D. G. Oblinger & J. L. Oblinger (Eds.). *Educating the Net generation*. Boulder, CO: EDUCAUSE. Retrieved April 25, 2010, from http://www.educause.edu/LearningSpaces/6072

Brown, M., & Lippincott, J. (2003). Learning spaces: More than meets the eye. *EDUCAUSE Quarterly, 26*(1), 14–16.

Callahan, J. (2004). *Effects of different seating arrangements in higher education computer lab classrooms on student learning, teaching style, and classroom appraisal*. Unpublished Master's thesis, University of Florida, Gainesville, FL.

Collins, A., Brown, J. S., & Newman, S. E. (1989). Cognitive apprenticeship: Teaching the crafts of reading, writing and mathematics. In Resnick, L. B. (Ed.), *Knowing, learning and instruction: Essays in honor of Robert Glaser* (pp. 453–494). Hillsdale, NJ: Lawrence Erlbaum Associates.

Corcoran, E. (1993). Why kids love computer nets. *Fortune*. Retrieved March 18, 2010, from http://money.cnn.com/magazines/fortune/fortune_archive/1993/09/20/78335/index.htm

Dillenbourg, P., Schneider, D., & Synteta, P. (2002). Virtual learning environments. In A. Dimitracopoulou (Ed.). *Proceedings of the 3rd Hellenic Conference: Information & Communication Technologies in Education* (pp. 3–18). Greece: Kastaniotis Editions.

Dittoe, W. (2006). Seriously cool places: The future of learning-centered built environments. In Oblinger, D. (Ed.), *Learning spaces*. Washington, DC: Educause.

Eberhard, J. P., & Patoine, B. (2004). Architecture with the brain in mind. *Cerebrum*, 6(Spring), 71–84.

Edwards, B. (2000). *University architecture*. London, UK: Spon Press.

Flutter, J. (2006). This place could help you learn: Student participation in creating better school environments. *Educational Review*, 58(1), 183–193. doi:10.1080/00131910600584116

Fox, R. (2005, June). *Universities in knowledge-based economies: The challenge for change*. Invited keynote speech at the International Conference on Capacity Building for Information Technology Integration in Teaching and Learning, Hong Kong Baptist University, Hong Kong.

Fox, R. (2007). Teaching through technology: Changing practices in two universities. *International Journal on E-Learning*, 6(2), 187–203.

Fox, R. (2009). *CUHK future classrooms*. Shatin, Hong Kong: The Chinese University of Hong Kong, Centre for Learning Enhancement And Research.

Fox, R., & Stuart, C. (2009). Creating learning spaces through collaboration: How one library refined its approach. *Educause Quarterly*, 32(1). Retrieved April 27, 2010, from http://www.educause.edu/EDUCAUSE+Quarterly/EDUCAUSEQuarterlyMagazineVolum/CreatingLearningSpacesThroughC/163850

Gale, H. (2006). Flexible learning needs flexible spaces. [University of Bristol Learning Technology Support Service]. *Interact*, 32, 14–15.

Goldschmid, B., & Goldschmid, M. L. (1976). Peer teaching in higher education: A review. *Higher Education*, 5(1), 9–33.

Hawthorne, J. (2002). What about the tables and chairs? [Oxford Brookes University]. *Teaching Forum*, 50, 46–47.

JISC. (2006). *Designing spaces for effective learning: A guide to 21st century learning space design*. Bristol, UK: JISC Development Group. Retrieved February 27, 2010, from http://www.jisc.ac.uk/eli_learningspaces.html

Kennedy, G. E., Judd, T. S., Churchward, A., Gray, K., & Krause, K. L. (2008). First year students' experiences with technology: Are they really digital natives? *Australasian Journal of Educational Technology*, 24(1), 108–122.

Laurillard, D. (2002). *Rethinking university teaching: A framework for the effective use of educational technology* (2nd ed.). London, UK: Routledge Falmer. doi:10.4324/9780203304846

Lawson, B. (2001). *The language of space*. Oxford, UK: Architectural Press.

Lee, C. H., Lam, P., Lee, W. K., Ho, A., & Fox, R. M. (2009). Role of computers in student learning. In W. Kwan, R. Fox, A. Chan, et al. (Eds.). *ICT2009*, (p. 12). Hong Kong, Hong Kong SAR: Open University of Hong Kong.

McCroskey, J. C., & McVetta, R. W. (1978, April 25–29). *Classroom seating arrangements: Instructional communication theory versus student preferences*. Paper presented at the annual meeting of the International Communication Association, Chicago, IL.

McNaught, C. (2005). *Criteria for the design of a classroom for active and interactive teaching and learning*. Unpublished paper, CLEAR, The Chinese University of Hong Kong.

McNaught, C., & Lam, P. (2009). Institutional strategies for embedding blended learning in a research-intensive university. *Proceedings of the elearn2009 Conference, Bridging the development gap through innovative eLearning environments.* St Augustine, Trinidad and Tobago: The University of the West Indies. Retrieved April 27, 2010, from http://elearn2009.com/public/downloads/papers/MCNAUGHT_Carmel.pdf

Oblinger, D. G. (2006). Space as a change agent. In D. G. Oblinger (Ed.), *Learning spaces*, (pp. 1.1 – 1.4). Educause. Retrieved September 9, 2009 from http://www.educause.edu/learningspaces

Osguthorpe, R. T., & Graham, C. R. (2003). Blended learning environments definitions and directions. *The Quarterly Review of Distance Education, 4*(3), 227–233.

Poole, G. (2008). *A place to call a learning home.* Key address at ASCILITE 2008, Hello! Where are you in the landscape of educational technology, Melbourne, Australia. Retrieved February 27, 2010, from http://www.ascilite.org.au/conferences/melbourne08/keynotegary.htm

Prensky, M. (2001). Digital natives, digital immigrants. *Horizon, 9*(5), 1–6. doi:10.1108/10748120110424816

Prosser, M., & Jamieson, P. (2008). *Spatial-pedagogy matrix for different types of classroom settings.* Unpublished manuscript, The University of Hong Kong.

Simsek, A., & Hooper, S. (1992). The effects of cooperative versus individual videodisc learning on student performance and attitudes. *International Journal of Instructional Media, 19*(3), 209–218.

Tapscott, D. (1998). *Growing up digital: The rise of the net generation.* New York, NY: McGraw-Hill.

Temple, P., & Barnett, R. (2007). Higher education space: Future directions. *Planning for Higher Education, 36*(1), 5–15.

The Chinese University of Hong Kong. (2009). *Campus master plan.* Retrieved March 10, 2010 from http://www.cuhk.edu.hk/cmp/en/

Van Note Chism, N. (2006). Challenging traditional assumptions and rethinking learning spaces. In D. G. Oblinger (Ed.), *Learning spaces*, (pp. 2.1 – 2.12). Educause. Retrieved February 27, 2010, from http://www.educause.edu/learningspaces

Vygotsky, L. (1978). *Mind in society: The development of higher psychological processes.* Cambridge, MA: Harvard University Press.

ADDITIONAL READING

McNaught, C., Storey, C., & Leung, S. (2004). Embedding information literacy into the curriculum: A case study of existing practice and future possibilities at a Hong Kong university. *Journal of Library and Information Science, 30*(1), 5–13.

KEY TERMS AND DEFINITIONS

Learner-Centred Paradigm: Student focused approaches to teaching and learning.

Learning Spaces: Spaces where students go to study. These can be physical or virtual.

Physical Spaces: Spaces on-campus students can actually go.

Virtual Spaces: Spaces online, mostly via the internet.

ENDNOTE

[1]   This article is only available online and does not have a page no. Reference: http://money.cnn.com/magazines/fortune/fortune_archive/1993/09/20/78335/index.htm

Chapter 6
Designing and Evaluating Learning Spaces:
PaSsPorT and Design–Based Research

Shirley Reushle
University of Southern Queensland, Australia

ABSTRACT

This chapter discusses the purposes, design and implementation of a physical experimental learning and teaching space which forms part of the University of Southern Queensland's Australian Digital Futures Institute (ADFI). It identifies challenges associated with the initial design and offers some recommendations for addressing these challenges. The concept and principles of the PaSsPorT design model which has been developed to guide the redesign of the space are introduced, and a brief description of another ADFI space, the software research and development laboratory follows. The paper also introduces a process for evaluating the design and implementation of learning, teaching, and research spaces using design-based research to frame the model.

INTRODUCTION

The University of Southern Queensland (USQ) is a regional, multi-campus institution with more than seventy-five percent of its twenty-six thousand students studying at a distance in local, national and international locations. Given the geographical

DOI: 10.4018/978-1-60960-114-0.ch006

spread of the students, the focus on an equitable student learning experience has always been a priority. Evidence indicates that USQ's students tend to be connected, active, resourceful learners familiar with interacting in a complex world of multi-tasked, community-focused activity. As USQ is not constrained by 'place', the need to further explore hybrid (physical and virtual) learning spaces is obvious. Grummon (2009, as cited in Bradwell, 2009, p. 63) makes the point that the world is in a "neutral zone" which she views as a time of "maximum uncertainty and time for creative possibility between the ending of the way things have been and the beginning of the way they will be" supporting the idea that infrastructure should not be built only around the needs of institutions as they exist already.

Developing effective spaces for 21st century learning is a key challenge across the world. Programs in Australia such as the Digital Education Revolution (DEEWR, 2009) and the Building the Education Revolution (DEEWR, 2009a) have been seen as opportunities to consider what effective 21st century learning spaces can look like and to implement strategies for achieving this vision. This is particularly the case for those working with learning technologies who have yet to see significant transformational change in education despite seeing profound change in society, the workplace and how learners live and work. In today's interconnected, technology-supported and driven world, learning typically takes place in physical, virtual and remote places. It is often an integrated, highly technical environment in which learners learn. There is a need for a broad spectrum of opportunities for learners and teachers to interact and collaborate – through virtual and physical spaces using multiple communication streams and the ability for spaces to be accessed and used to cater for the continuum of difference in terms of learners, teachers and discipline areas.

This chapter does not examine all of the learning spaces at USQ but focuses primarily on one space which is part of USQ's Australian Digital Futures Institute (ADFI) - a physical, technology-rich learning and teaching space - the Technology-Enhanced Learning Laboratory or TELL. It also briefly explores how the findings reported in this chapter can be used to evaluate another ADFI space, the software research and development laboratory (SRDL) where both physical and virtual activities occur. The purposes, design and implementation of the TELL are dis-

cussed and issues associated with the initial design are identified. The concept and principles of the PaSsPorT (Pedagogy-Space-People-Technology) design model (Reushle, 2009), an adaptation of Radcliffe's (2009) Pedagogy-Space-Technology (PST) framework are then applied to the review and redesign of this space. A model for evaluating the design and implementation of USQ learning spaces using design-based research is also introduced (Reushle, 2009a).

BACKGROUND

ADFI is a research and innovation Institute established in 2008. The scope, focus and strategic intent of the Institute align with the University's 2020 vision to be recognised as a world leader in open and flexible higher education. ADFI contributes to both the eLearning and the eResearch agendas and aims to form strong links and networks locally, nationally and internationally with like-minded individuals and groups. It has two physical environments: the Technology Enhanced Learning Laboratory (TELL), which provides a facility for staff and students to investigate technology-enhanced learning innovations and the Software Research and Development Laboratory (SRDL) which accommodates the software development team and provides some access to software and hardware for trial purposes. ADFI's goals are underpinned by research with the relationship between learning and innovation at the heart of its overall agenda.

Technology Enhanced Learning Laboratory (TELL)

The increasing access to a variety of technologies and the need to investigate innovative approaches to learning and teaching led to the conception of the TELL. An initial proposal for a technology enhanced 'sandpit', submitted by two academics from the Faculty of Education to the Information

Technology division marked the beginning of planning for the TELL. Soon after, a small reference group participated in several brainstorming sessions to determine the purpose, design principles and functionality of the space. However, due to limited funds, the project stalled and when plans were later drawn up, hardware and software configurations designed and equipment acquired, there was little input from those who might use the space – the teachers and the students. As Radcliffe, Wilson, Powell and Tibbetts (2008, p. 3) note, "While many new facilities start out with sound pedagogical intent, the actual spaces often reflect the imperatives of technology, or architecture, or operational considerations". This observation is also reflected in comments by MacPhee (2009, p. 2) who notes that, in many designs, people "make mistakes or compromises because of budget and time constraints, space limitations [and] failure to anticipate the way the facility will be used". This was the unfortunate sequence of events for the TELL but this did provide valuable lessons when it came to evaluating the process and the impact of the facility on the USQ academic community.

In the last few years, a number of design principles for creating learning spaces has been generated (Oblinger, 2005; Jamieson, 2005). However, as identified by Radcliffe (2009), there is no generally agreed approach with some of the proposed principles being aspirational while others imply they are based on experience. The design principles which guided the initial development of the TELL learning space were both aspirational and based on experience. They recommended that the space must:

1. be flexible to accommodate differences in discipline, learning and teaching requirements and activities.
2. have intuitive, user-friendly interfaces.
3. provide social spaces for collaboration and other interactive activities.
4. address creature comforts and ambience. According to Jamieson (2008), people create identity through their association with space and it is important to keep some space empty to accommodate 'possibilities'.
5. ensure that equipment, facilities and furniture is accessible to both teachers and learners and inclusive of diverse needs.
6. support and enable the exploration of new and emerging technologies not yet present in learning, teaching and research environments.

The purpose of the TELL was to provide a safe, experimental, ICT-enabled environment where teachers could explore the pedagogical applications of technologies and be challenged to rethink the possibilities of using spaces and technologies for learning and teaching. The term 'learning laboratory' was chosen because it conveys a sense of innovation, exploration, experimentation and prototyping to maximise student learning. Those responsible for the initial conceptualisation of this space believed that bringing learning and teaching exploration into the 'open' could lead to the deprivatisation of the teaching experience and provide serendipitous opportunities for people to learn from each other through demonstration, discussion and the sharing of expertise. The intention was not for the TELL to be regarded as a modern teaching facility with set furnishings and a variety of technologies, risking the perpetuation of the traditional classroom model, but rather as an enabler of change, a place to explore the appropriate use of new and emerging technologies to support contemporary pedagogical practices (see Figure 1).

An assumption was made that teachers, learners and researchers would 'drive' the space in terms of how and why it was used. Some preliminary evaluative questions were formulated by one of the academics who proposed the concept of the TELL to help guide how the space might be used and for what purposes. These were:

Figure 1. TELL in use for group brainstorming sessions

- What pedagogies might be supported by certain space-technology elements?
- What space-technology elements might enhance student engagement?
- How might space-technology configurations support interactive and collaborative activity?
- How might physical and virtual spaces and technologies be brought together to enhance learning and teaching?
- How might flexible learning space-technology configurations enhance student motivation and satisfaction?
- What space-technology configurations might support ease of use and encourage participation and exploration by teachers?
- Would access to a flexible space with new and emerging technologies promote and encourage teachers to engage in reflective activity on their pedagogical practice?

- How might the ability to observe others' practice (e.g., through the physical observation deck in the TELL or via video link) support and encourage teachers' inspiration and enthusiasm for exploring new ways of 'doing' and thinking about their own practice?
- What might be achieved with flexible space-technologies that cannot be achieved in existing institutional spaces?

An important objective in the conceptualisation of the TELL was for continuous and vigorous usage by teachers, students, collaborators, researchers and presenters. This, however, has not occurred.

Interim Evaluation Findings: Challenges

A review of the TELL was conducted in early 2009. It was examined using the six design principles outlined in the previous section. Findings are reported in Table 1.

The analysis of the planning documentation revealed that the first iteration of this space was created on a 'lightweight' budget relying predominantly on the updating or relocating of existing infrastructure, hardware and software. Although the human element (that is, the users of the space) should have been of primary consideration in the design of the TELL space, it was evident that this was not the case with the creation of the space receiving little input from students, teachers, or researchers after initial consultations had been conducted.

Solutions and Recommendations

The motivation to use and continue to re-use a learning space is essential to ensure its sustainability (users need to see a reason for its 'being'). Planning for and using the space should not be an onerous task with innovative pedagogy and research activity supported by technology and administrative structures, not hindered by them. According to the MCEETYA Learning Spaces Framework (2008, p. 2), "Spaces shape and change practice. Engaging, adaptable spaces energise students, teachers and the community. Well-designed learning spaces inspire creative, productive and efficient learning". However, as the experience of USQ's development of the TELL has shown, without the added element of the 'people' dimension to the pedagogy-space-technology consideration, the design can be right off the mark.

Table 1. Interim evaluative findings of TELL

Design principles	Findings from interim evaluation
Be flexible, user friendly and intuitive	Much of the infrastructure and technologies were not as appropriate or effective as they could be and usage by practitioners was low. Feedback from users referred to the 'intimidating' appearance of the TELL and a feeling of unease in terms of identifying what they would like to do and how they would like to do it.
Spaces suitable for collaboration and interaction	There appeared to be the idea that collaboration and interaction equated to flexible furnishings. Opportunities to explore contemporary pedagogies and innovative learning and teaching strategies that promoted new ways of communicating, interacting and collaborating had not occurred. Even access to wireless technologies was limited by the existing technological infrastructure.
Empty spaces provided for 'possibilities'	This was evident in the design but the size of the space limited the provision of 'empty' spaces.
Accessible equipment and facilities	As is sometimes the case when learning and teaching spaces are developed by technicians, the interface between user and technology did not account for those with limited technological knowledge and skills. The interface between hardware, software and user was not seamless and use of the technologies required a level of technical knowledge and support that was not readily accessible or sustainable.
Support exploration of new and emerging technologies	Little of this had occurred due to the inflexibility of the space, lack of ongoing funds, issues with technology infrastructure and an absence of an official facility 'owner' or 'driver'. As mentioned previously, an assumption had been made that teachers, learners and researchers would drive the space but because they had little involvement in the design and had no access to long-term funding, there has been reluctance by those groups to assume any ownership or responsibility for the space.

PaSsPorT for Design

Radcliffe's (2009) PST (Pedagogy-Space-Technology) framework (Figure 2) provides a simple and flexible instrument that can be used by a wide variety of stakeholders to reflect on ideas and outcomes at every stage in the life-cycle of a learning space. This framework recognises "the nexus between pedagogy, technology and the design of the learning space" (p. 11) and explores the relationship between the types of activity stakeholders are seeking to encourage, the physical design of the learning space and the role of technology in supporting learning, teaching and research. The PST Framework takes account of the three factors of pedagogy, space and technology in informing the conceptual design and post-occupancy evaluation of either discrete learning environments (e.g. individual rooms) or networks of places. Oblinger (2005, p. 14) has also recognised that "the convergence of technology, pedagogy and space can lead to exciting models of campus interactions."

The concept of the PaSsPort (Pedagogy-Space-People-Technology) for designing learning spaces (Reushle, 2009) is an extension of Radcliffe's PST framework with 'People' having been added to the mix (Figure 3). This is not to suggest that the human element in not evident in the PST framework as it is indeed implied and Radcliffe et al. (2008, p. 13) make the point that "many groups have a stake in the success of ... learning spaces including students, staff, senior administrators, technology managers, architects, builders, facilities and security manager, and time-tablers". The addition of the extra 'P' in the PaSsPort model is not a revelation as Long and Ehrmann (2005, as cited in Radcliffe, 2009, p. 14) emphasised how important a space should be "designed for people, not for ephemeral technologies". The PaSsPorT model merely makes the implied explicit.

Figure 2. Radcliffe's PST framework (Radcliffe, 2009)

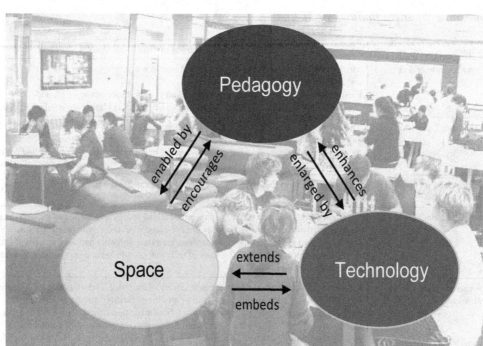

Radcliffe (2009) reports that there is a tendency for many learning space initiatives to be technology-driven rather than pedagogy-driven. Although the human ('people') element should be a given in learning space design, the USQ experience with the TELL suggests otherwise. As noted earlier, the final design decisions were not made in consultation with a broad sector of the university community and there was little evidence of consultation with the student body.

Where contemporary pedagogies are the focus, learning space initiatives typically adopt some explicit form of learner-centred or constructivist pedagogy paradigm. With PaSsPorT as a model for redesign, USQ will extend and enhance the functionality and capabilities of the TELL space using a collaborative design team of students, teachers, other researchers and technicians (that is, 'people') to guide the revised specifications for the TELL and people (a broad spectrum of stakeholders) will continue to be intimately associated with the TELL's ongoing maturity.

How might this be conducted to ensure a far-reaching but inclusive consultative process? As noted by MacPhee (2009), planning ahead and involving all stakeholders from the beginning can avoid all manner of problems. It is critical that those who design and build learning spaces really listen to those who will support, teach and learn in them and recognise that the university of today and tomorrow should not be the place it was 20 (or even five) years ago.

As part of the interim evaluation of the TELL, discussions were held with several stakeholder groups through informal focus groups (USQ teachers, ICT support personnel and managers). They indicated that the acceptance and successful uptake of the facility would be influenced by:

- institutional buy-in;
- ease of use;
- sustainable support structures; and
- evidence of pedagogical enhancement.

The main purpose of conducting these informal focus groups was to offer an open forum to draw upon participants' attitudes, feelings, beliefs, experiences, and reactions to the TELL concept and space design. From an analysis of these findings and a scan of more recent literature, the author has been able to draw together some guidelines for ensuring the next stage of development reflects an inclusive consultative process.

An important principle in devising inclusive and engaging planning strategies is the recognition that the stakeholder groups are diverse in terms of background and expertise, assumptions, expectations/interests, requirements, understandings and

Figure 3. PaSsPorT learning space design model (Reushle, 2009)

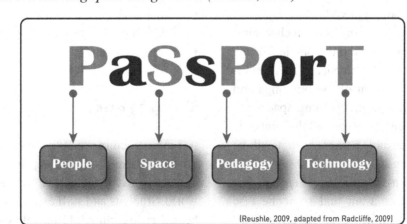

(Reushle, 2009, adapted from Radcliffe, 2009)

practices. This means that a variety of approaches must be in place to ensure broad representation from these groups. Guidelines for engaging all interested parties in the design and development process include:

- Form a cross-institutional, representative group as early as possible to contribute to the planning, design and development process. Adopt a 'work-in-progress' approach.
- Do not under-estimate the significance of the student voice.
- Work towards a shared vision.
- Build an 'awareness campaign' to ensure open, effective communication and to promote institutional interest and buy-in. Establish a flexible communication mechanism to promote ongoing contribution and maintain shared understanding of the project progress. This might be done through face-to-face meetings, informal gatherings, focus groups, email, online discussion groups, Web 2.0 technologies such as blogs and wikis, diagrammatic illustrations, public presentations, and so on.
- Take advantage of what an institution already has in terms of infrastructure, human capital, achievements – but do not dwell on historical events.
- Review other learning space concepts and models and establish contacts and networks with others working and researching in the area – be receptive to advice.
- Avoid the assumption that a technology-rich environment is the domain of the technologists and a physical, 'built' environment the domain of the buildings and facilities department. Learning spaces are for learners and teachers and their input is critical to the whole process as they will be the ones using it.
- We all dream of projects where we describe what we want and someone else makes it happen. However, effective learning space design and development takes a lot of people, a lot of talent, a lot of time and resourcing (Weaver, 2009), a lot of tolerance, goodwill and some compromise.
- Ensure credit is given where credit is due – everyone enjoys sharing ideas, learning from others, and sharing credit for a good idea or a job well done.
- Encourage teachers to bring their students to the space and test out strategies in an authentic environment.
- Conduct ongoing evaluation of usage and gather user feedback to enable constant, incremental improvement.

Radcliffe et al. (2008) PST framework is a question-driven inquiry process which follows each stage of the life cycle of a learning space, from conception through stages of design, construction, operation and review. Table 2 illustrates how the questions associated with the PST framework outlined in the Australian Learning and Teaching Council (ALTC) project report have been extended to make explicit the 'People' element of the PaSsPorT model.

Some useful guiding principles for space design put forward in the MCEETYA (2008) Learning Spaces Framework provide further guidance. Put simply, these high-level guidelines refer to the following for effective space design:

- flexibility;
- inclusivity,
- collaboration;
- creativity; and
- efficiency.

Managing Risk

ICT infrastructure in a 21st century learning institution is a strategic asset. ICT capabilities are integral to success in a connected, fast-moving, demanding world. Students and staff expect environments to be ICT-rich, compatible and interconnected, user

Table 2. Questions associated with the PaSsPorT for designing learning spaces

	Focus	Conception and design	Implementation and operation
	Overall	What is the motivation for the initiative? What and who initiated the idea? Who has to be persuaded?	Is the facility a success? What is the evidence? What lessons have been learned?
P a	**Pedagogy**	Why type(s) of learning and teaching are we trying to foster? Why? What impact will this have overall on learning/teaching/research? What education and training is required?	What type(s) of learning and teaching are observed taking place? What is the evidence? What evaluation methods are used to gauge worth and guide future decision making?
S s	**Space**	What aspects of the design of the space will foster these types of learning and teaching? How?	Which aspects of the space design and equipment worked and which did not? Why? What were the unintended and unexpected uses of the space that emerged?
P o r	**PEOPLE**	Who are the stakeholders in this space? (Students? Teachers? Other scholars? Technicians? Visiting professionals?) What are their characteristics? What do they need? What are their skills – pedagogical; technical?	Who is using the space and for what purposes? Why are they using/not using the space? What changes are required to support the use of the space – what are the people asking for? How are suggestions by stakeholders for future use of the space/s being captured – and enacted?
T	**Technology**	What technologies have been/will be deployed and why? How is technology deployed to complement the space design in fostering the learning and teaching outcomes?	What technologies were most effective in enhancing learning, teaching and research? Why? How will decisions be made on what technologies to adopt, and what technologies to reject? What other technologies will be explored?

*(Adapted from:*Radcliffe et al., 2008, p. 3)

friendly and reliable. However, Mitchell, Winslett and Howell (2009) report that there should be a healthy tension between safety in IT (security, etc.) and risk experimentation when providing and supporting technologies associated with innovation in learning, teaching and research (Figure 4). Mitchell et al. (2009) encourage IT managers to challenge the security/risk issues rather than allow them to stifle innovation. Their belief in the focus on encouraging technological innovation rather than 'managing risk' reflects a growing trend in higher education. Mitchell et al. (2009, p. 92) make the point that "risk management and

innovation are not necessarily good companions" and that to fully explore experimental learning and teaching spaces, new policy may be required to enable the exploration of innovative ideas that are not necessarily consistent with previous practice. Using digital technologies blurs boundaries between learning and teaching, learners and teachers, formality and informality (MCEETYA, 2008).

This acceptance and adoption of a more flexible approach to risk is also an imperative for academic and administrative fundamentals of an educational institution and reflect Bradwell's (2009, p. 58) view that "being able to develop

Figure 4. Managing risk

new ways of teaching depends on the capacity to experiment". This requires a planned strategy for the institutional asset of technology – a strategic plan for ICT usage and development which involves all stakeholder groups and accommodates best practice, standards, opportunities, encourages innovation and is able to adapt to pedagogical and technological possibilities, changing demographics and educational advances beyond today's horizon.

An important objective at USQ is to increase the usage of the TELL by teachers, students, researchers, collaborators, and presenters, and to promote the TELL across the University as a dynamic, usable space for exploration and experimentation. The facility is not limited to those technologies and other resources associated with a physical learning space. This broader focus encompasses the exploration of virtual world technologies, the ever-increasing numbers of mobile devices, the proliferation of web applications and the growing focus on personal learning environments requiring a flexible ICT infrastructure that can accommodate and support these explorations.

Evaluation of Space Design to Nurture and Progress Innovation

Many 'flexible' classroom designs are now in operation around the globe but often assertions of effectiveness are not accompanied by objective data or empirical evidence. As identified by Lee, Dixon and Andrews (2008), evaluations of learning spaces have tended to focus on individual indicators, such as student satisfaction, frequency of use or successful technological integration. While these indicators are useful in the evaluation of particular aspects of learning spaces from the perspectives of specific stakeholders, they do not provide a substantial, systematic or rigorous model for evaluation of the impact across a range of criteria related to design intent, practical implementation or staff and student learning. Without such a model, the development of coherent and

credible theory and transfer of knowledge to drive future development is problematic. As various researchers (MacPhee, 2009; Radcliffe et al., 2008) in the learning space arena have noted, one of the primary goals of the design and redesign of learning spaces is to improve student learning outcomes. This can be achieved by designing spaces (virtual as well as physical) that foster certain models of learning and teaching. An effective evaluation will determine whether changes in practice are observed and which aspects of the space (configurations, technologies) enable, encourage and empower these models of learning and teaching.

In recent years, educators have been attempting to narrow the chasm between research and practice because traditional research paradigms tend not to meet the real needs of practicing educators. Part of the challenge is that research that is detached from practice "may not account for the influence of contexts, the emergent and complex nature of outcomes, and the incompleteness of knowledge about which factors are relevant for prediction" (DBRC, 2003, p. 5). It is the role of educators "to predict and evaluate the learning impact of current and emerging technologies to determine the best use of ICT in their context" (MCEETYA, 2008, p. 11).

The pragmatic, yet rigorous method of Design-Based Research (DBR) provides an appropriate framework for conducting evaluation of learning spaces as it focuses on the design, construction, implementation and adoption of an initiative and its effects in multiple contexts. DBR is an important methodology for understanding how, when, and why educational innovations work in practice; DBR methods aim to bridge the gaps between educational research theory, designed artifact, and practice, thus addressing the relationships between teaching and learning. The method bears a strong resemblance to action research but is considered by its proponents to be more aligned to research in educational contexts that focuses on the design, construction, implementation, and adoption of a teaching/learning intervention. According to Anderson (2005, p. 1), design-based research is "an effective educational research tool with … potential to aid in the development, and assessment of innovations in education".

A contextually appropriate model (see Figure 5) to evaluate USQ projects such as the TELL has been developed by the author based on Bannan-Ritland's (2003) interpretation of design-based research. This model (eValuation model) is being used to step the evaluation of the TELL through the stages of informed exploration, enactment, local impact evaluation and broader impact evaluation and the process is illustrated in brief in Table 3 in terms of questions asked and sources of data to be collected. The redesign and development of the TELL is currently at Stage 1, Informed Exploration and some work has been done on the Enactment

stage. Outcomes of this evaluation design will be reported upon in future work.

Software Research and Development Laboratory

The Software Research and Development Laboratory (SRDL) houses the Australian Digital Futures Institute software development team whose skills range from technical writing, computer programming in most modern languages through to project management and advising clients on technological requirements. This space has initially served little more than as a technology-enabled location where the programming team has been able to go about their daily work including software development, interacting with each other and clients. However, as the findings of this work have emerged, it is

Figure 5. eValuation model using Design-Based Research

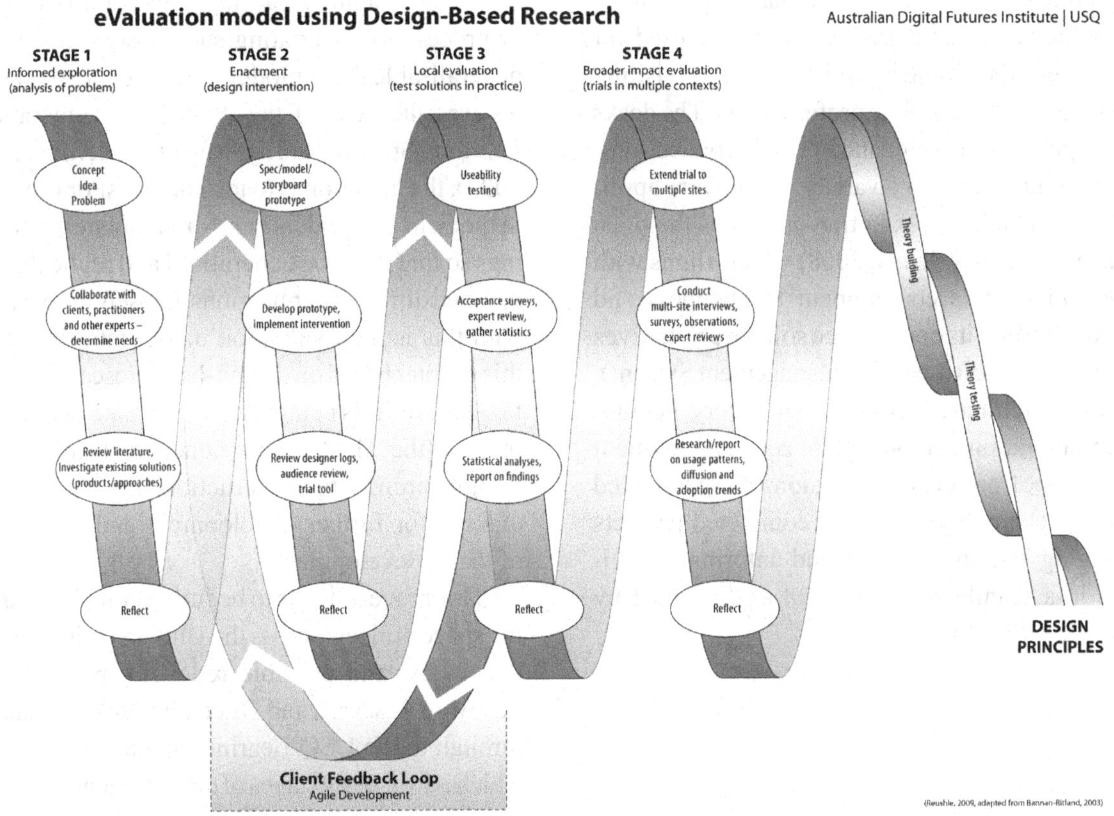

Table 3. Application of eValuation model

Stages	Examples of Process	Data Sources
1 Informed exploration (concept/idea &/or problem identification)	Collaborate with practitioners and other experts to determine needs. Review the literature; investigate and benchmark existing solutions. Review budget considerations/availability. Conduct reflection on findings to guide each stage of the process.	Qualitative - interviews, focus groups. Quantitative - survey of experts. Literature, e.g., existing cases.
2 Enactment	Design space using diagrams, flowcharts, design specifications, costings, etc.	Design documentation
3 Evaluation – local impact	Survey questions to determine usefulness of space; usability of space and technologies; purposes – planned, emerging. Statistics on questions submitted by students; on student access to tool; on key words used.	Qualitative – usability testing; acceptance survey; expert review. Quantitative – statistical analyses of support required, usage of space. Reports
4 Evaluation - broader impact	Usage pattern reports; diffusion and adoption trends to guide review and future directions	Qualitative - surveys, observations; expert panel review. Research reports

evident that this space can and will play a vital role in the development of innovative learning, teaching and research endeavours in ADFI. For example, the physical space that is the SRDL now includes 'hot desks' which can be used for short periods of time by University staff, visiting scholars or other mobile professionals. The desks have phone, computer and network connections, along with access to a variety of software applications. The hot desk notion embraces the open place concept (Velocity, 2008) which aligns with the University's commitment to openness and flexibility and its open source software initiatives (e.g., the Moodle Learning Management System). The research and development laboratory includes a collaboration/demonstration zone and frequent displays of projects. Discussions are conducted around planned, current and completed projects bringing together formal and informal activities in a seamless environment as described by Oblinger (2006).

RESEARCH DIRECTIONS

Although this chapter aims to articulate a generic model for designing learning spaces and a strategy or process for evaluating such spaces, just how generalisable these models are is not yet evident. As was the goal of the 2006 Next Generation Learning Spaces Priority Project (Radcliffe et al., 2008), the intention is to test the PaSsPorT model in the field and evaluate and disseminate the findings so that it can be generalised and replicated in new and different applications. Closely associated with this is the eValuation model introduced in this chapter based on design-based research. Thus far, this model is being used to evaluate one ADFI project (the TELL) from conceptualisation and design through to construction, trial, decision-making for further development and outcomes of that redevelopment.

This process needs to be fully applied to learning space projects across the University including the review and possible redevelopment of the Software Research and Development Laboratory through to the USQ Learning Commons project which is in its early stages of development. Already it is evident that some of the lessons learnt from the TELL experience could assist those contributing to the Learning Commons project and this should be addressed with some urgency. Further research could focus on how these models can be successfully applied to other institutional projects and across into other educational contexts.

CONCLUSION

Space design needs to facilitate changing demands and building single-purpose spaces has proven not to be an effective use of resources. Student learning preferences are hard to predict but spaces designed around flexible fittings and technologies allow students and teachers to design and redesign spaces to suit their specific and changing needs. As noted in the JISC (2006, p. 30) report, "Spaces are themselves agents for change. Changed spaces will change practices". Mobility of resources increases utilisation. Stringent risk management and innovation are not necessarily good companions and changing needs which may not necessarily be consistent with previous practice should lead to the development of new policies and procedures. Enlisting the support of users as co-design partners is both feasible and provides for highly interesting and useful outcomes recognising that space design is a process, not a product and must involve all interested parties (Oblinger, 2006). Ongoing evaluation of these spaces ensures that resources are responsive and adaptable to the changing needs of all stakeholders.

REFERENCES

Anderson, T. (2005). Design-based research and its application to a call center innovation in distance education. *Canadian Journal of Learning and Technology, 31*(2). Retrieved March 6, 2010, from http://www.cjlt.ca/index.php/cjlt/article/view/143/136

Bannan-Ritland, B. (2003). The role of design in research: The integrative learning design framework. *Educational Researcher, 32*(1), 21–24. doi:10.3102/0013189X032001021

Bradwell, P. (2009). *The edgeless university: Why higher education must embrace technology*. Retrieved March 6, 2010, from http://www.demos.co.uk/publications/the-edgeless-university

Department of Education. Employment and Workplace Relations (DEEWR). (2009). *Experience the digital education revolution*. Retrieved March 6, 2010, from http://www.digitaleducationrevolution.gov.au

Department of Education. Employment and Workplace Relations (DEEWR). (2009a). *Building the education revolution*. Retrieved March 6, 2010, from http://www.deewr.gov.au/Schooling/BuildingTheEducationRevolution

Design-Based Research Collective. (2003). Design-based research: An emerging paradigm for educational inquiry. *Educational Researcher, 32*(1), 5–8. doi:10.3102/0013189X032001005

Jamieson, P. (2005). *Understanding a happy accident: Learning to build new learning environments. Report of ECE Research Project on Learning Communities*. Brisbane, Australia: TEDI, The University of Queensland.

Joint Information Systems Committee (JISC). (2006). *Designing spaces for effective learning: A guide to 21ˢᵗ century learning space design.* Retrieved March 6, 2010, from http://www.jisc.ac.uk/media/documents/publications/learning-spaces.pdf

Lee, N., Dixon, J., & Andrews, T. (2008). *A comprehensive learning space evaluation model: ALTC project proposal.* Retrieved March 6, 2010, from http://www.altc.edu.au/project-comprehensive-learning-space-swinburne-2008

MacPhee, L. (2009). Learning spaces: A tutorial. *Educause Quarterly, 32*(1). Retrieved February 2, 2010, from http://www.educause.edu/EDUCAUSE+Quarterly/EDUCAUSEQuarterlyMagazineVolum/LearningSpacesATutorial/163854

MCEETYA. (2008). *Learning in an online world: Learning spaces framework.* Retrieved March 2, 2010, from http://www.mceecdya.edu.au/verve/_resources/ICT_LearningOnlineWorld-LearningSpacesFWork.pdf

Mitchell, G., Winslett, G., & Howell, G. (2009). Lab 2.0. In D. Radcliffe, H. Wilson, D. Powell, & B. Tibbetts (Eds.), *Learning spaces in higher education – positive outcomes by design. Proceedings of the Next Generation Learning Spaces 2008 Colloquium* (Ch. 5.9). Brisbane, Australia: University of Queensland.

Oblinger, D. (Ed.). (2006). *Learning spaces.* EDUCAUSE. Retrieved March 6, 2010, from www.educause.edu/learningspaces

Oblinger, D. G. (2005). Leading the transition from classrooms to learning spaces. *EDUCAUSE Quarterly, 28*(1), 14–18.

Radcliffe, D. (2009). A pedagogy-space-technology (PST) framework for designing and evaluating learning spaces. In D. Radcliffe, H. Wilson, D. Powell, & B. Tibbetts (Eds.), *Learning spaces in higher education – positive outcomes by design. Proceedings of the Next Generation Learning Spaces 2008 Colloquium* (Chapter 1.0). Brisbane, Australia: University of Queensland.

Radcliffe, D., Wilson, H., Powell, D., & Tibbetts, B. (2008). *Designing next generation places of learning: Collaboration at the pedagogy-space-technology nexus.* ALTC Priority Project #627. The University of Queensland. Retrieved March 6, 2010, from http://www.uq.edu.au/nextgenerationlearningspace/

Reushle, S. (2009). *PaSsPorT for designing learning spaces.* Unpublished USQ discussion paper.

Reushle, S. (2009a). *eValuation model using design-based research.* Unpublished USQ discussion paper, University of Southern Queensland, Queensland.

Velocity Magazine. (2008). *Hot desking.* Retrieved March 6, 2010, from http://vlmmagazine.com/2008/11/01/hot-desking/

Weaver, B. (2009). Collaboration with users to design learning spaces: Playing nicely in the sandbox. *Educause Quarterly, 32*(1). Retrieved February 2, 2010, from http://www.educause.edu/EDUCAUSE+Quarterly/EDUCAUSEQuarterlyMagazineVolum/CollaboratingwithUserstoDesign/163855

ADDITIONAL READING

AMA Alexi Marmot Associates. (2006). *Spaces for learning: A review of learning spaces in further and higher education.* Scottish Funding Council. Retrieved March 6, 2010, from http://www.jiscinfonet.ac.uk/Resources/external-resources/sfc-spaces-for-learning

Anderson, T. (2005). Design-based research and its application to a call center innovation in distance education. *Canadian Journal of Learning and Technology, 31*(2). Retrieved March 6, 2010, from http://www.cjlt.ca/index.php/cjlt/article/view/143/136

Brown, M. (2005). Learning spaces. In D. G. Oblinger & J. L. Oblinger (Eds.), *Educating the Net Gen.* Boulder, Colo: EDUCAUSE. Retrieved March 6, 2010, from http://www.educause.edu/LearningSpaces/6072

Huijser, H., Elson-Green, J., Reid, I., Walta, C., Challis, D., Harris, K.-L., & McCafferty, M. (2008). *Places and spaces for learning seminars (Draft report).* Sydney, Australia: Carrick Institute for Learning and Teaching in Higher Education. Retrieved March 6, 2010, from http://www.altc.edu.au/resources-places-and-spaces-for-learning-seminars-altc-2008

Radcliffe, D., Wilson, H., Powell, D., & Tibbetts, B. (Eds.). (2009). Learning spaces in higher education – Positive outcomes by design. *Proceedings of the Next Generation Learning Spaces 2008 Colloquium.* Brisbane: University of Queensland. Retrieved March 6, 2010, from http://www.uq.edu.au/nextgenerationlearningspace/proceedings

Reushle, S., Kissell, B., Fryer, M., & King, D. (2009). TELL us all about it: Establishment of a technology enhanced learning laboratory. In D. Radcliffe, H. Wilson, D. Powell, & B. Tibbetts (Eds.), *Learning spaces in higher education – Positive outcomes by design. Proceedings of the Next Generation Learning Spaces 2008 Colloquium* (Ch. 5.13). Brisbane: University of Queensland.

KEY TERMS AND DEFINITIONS

ADFI: Australian Digital Futures Institute, a research and innovation institute at the University of Southern Queensland.

Design-Based Research (DBR): Research methodology for understanding how, when, and why educational innovations work in practice.

Evaluation: The systematic examination of the worth, relevance, effectiveness, impact and sustainability of a program, policy, initiative, or service in order to support decision-making about its future.

Learning Spaces: Learning spaces encompass the full range of places in which learning occurs, from real to virtual, from classroom to chat room.

PaSsPorT: Pedagogy-Space-People-Technology learning space design model.

SRDL: Software Research and Development Laboratory.

TELL: Technology Enhanced Learning Laboratory.

Chapter 7
Networked Learning Environments

Chris Jones
The Open University, UK

ABSTRACT

This chapter introduces the idea of networked learning environments and argues that these environments provide the totality of surrounding conditions for learning in digital networks. It provides illustrative vignettes of the ways that students appropriate networked environments for learning. The chapter then examines the notion of networked learning environments in relation to the idea of infrastructure and infrastructures for learning and sets out some issues arising from this perspective. The chapter suggests that students and teachers selectively constitute their own contexts and that design can only have an indirect effect on learning. The chapter goes on to argue that design needs to be located at the meso level of the institution and that a solution to the problem of indirect design lies in refocusing design at the meso level and on the design of infrastructures for learning.

INTRODUCTION

This chapter focuses on the idea of a learning environment from the perspective of networked learning. The term has been developed and defined in a number of publications and a series of international conferences and the definition of networked learning arising out of this tradition is that networked learning is:

learning in which information and communication technology ... is used to promote connections: between one learner and other learners, between learners and tutors; between a learning community and its learning resources (Goodyear, Banks, Hodgson & McConnell, 2004, p. 1).

The central terms in this definition are *connections* and *information and communication technologies* because the interactions the defini-

DOI: 10.4018/978-1-60960-114-0.ch007

tion points towards are human interactions but they include human interactions with materials and resources and interactions that are mediated through digital networks. In this definition interactions with materials and resources alone are insufficient and networked learning requires aspects of human-human interaction even when they are mediated through digital technologies. This definition of networked learning takes a relational stance in which learning takes place in relation to others and in relation to artifacts in the form of both communications media and learning resources.

The chapter argues that networked learning *environments* are critical for networked learning but that the environment is always selectively appropriated by students and tutors participating in it to make their own learning contexts. Environments are understood from this perspective in a straightforward way as the totality of surrounding conditions. The term learning environment points to the human, social, physical and virtual aspects of a setting, and the characteristics or arrangements of those elements of that setting, within which learning can take place. This definition is not restricted to the social environment and includes technological artifacts and the physical arrangements of things. Of course learning can take place anywhere and at any time and the idea of a learning environment implies that such settings are intentionally designed and arranged to allow learning to take place. Recently the debate about design has focused on the term Learning Design (Koper & Tattersall, 2005) which has at least two distinct meanings. The first more technical approach is often distinguished by the use of capital letters, Learning Design (LD), and the second usage in lower case refers to learning design in a more general sense. In this chapter I argue for the use of the idea of indirect design for learning and by implication I dismiss the idea that learning design in either sense is an appropriate approach. Learning Design in the stronger sense of Learning Design (LD) arose out of the experi-

ence of the Open University in the Netherlands and its desire to reduce institutional complexity by developing a "pedagogical meta-language" (Koper & Tattersall, 2005, p. vii). Other approaches compete with Learning Design for attention as researchers search for ways to abstract general design principles, such as pedagogical design patterns (McAndrew, Goodyear & Dalziel, 2006) and scripts (Tchounikine, 2008). Beyond design the term learning environment is explored further in relation to recent usages within educational research literature. For example one use of the term learning environment would include the totality of resources on which the learner can draw. This view is found widely in educational literature and is particularly strongly associated with the relational or phenomenographic approach to learning (see for example Laurillard, 2002). Laurillard comments that:

The epistemological position ... requires a relational view of knowledge and of learning, and emphasizes the situated character of all learning. (Laurillard, 2002, p. 62)

To a large extent this is the position taken in this chapter with a small variation which is that I would separate the environment, the totality of surrounding conditions, from the context which I understand as being constituted in an active process by participants in the environment. For example, two students in an identical learning environment may make quite different contexts from the same set of resources according to their orientation and intentional engagement with the learning environment and consequently we regularly find students studying the same course interpreting, even well designed, assessment criteria in divergent ways (see for example Jones & Asensio, 2001).

NETWORKED LEARNING ENVIRONMENTS

Networked learning environments are the totality of surrounding conditions, *mediated by digital networks*, within which education or learning can take place. They may be composed of intentionally organized elements and in some cases elements that are specifically designed for learning but a networked learning environment can be composed of contingently arranged components that are drawn on for educational and learning purposes without themselves being the outcome of a design process. For the purposes of this chapter all networked learning environments include networked and digital technologies. A networked learning environment would include a school classroom incorporating computers and network connections, but it would also include an Internet café, a study bedroom and many largely informal settings. Within a university students move between a variety of environments and as networks extend to include mobile technologies many, if not all, of these environments become networked learning environments which allow access to a range of study materials, resources and organizational aids. In some ways as mobile communications develop it becomes increasingly difficult to leave a networked learning environment in network societies (Castells, 2000; Castells, Fernández-Ardèvol, Qiu, & Sey, 2007).

The assumption of network connectivity is no longer unusual but equally it is not yet universal and care needs to be taken to ensure some equality of access. It is becoming commonplace for surveys of students at university in the US, Australia and the UK to show high levels of ownership of networked devices including laptop computers and sophisticated mobile (cell) phones (Salaway, Caruso & Nelson, 2008, Kennedy, Judd, Churchward, Gray & Krause, 2008, Jones, Ramanau, Cross & Healing, 2010). Even in these countries ownership and access to networked computing is not universal and in developing countries the evidence is that network access is still restricted, even though students are prepared to make exceptional efforts to obtain access (Czerniewicz, Williams & Brown, 2009). A central question for the design of learning spaces in Higher Education is how these learning environments, infused with networked and digital technologies are being inhabited by students. The next section examines one popularized approach to the relationship between young students and technology, the Net Generation and Digital Natives debate.

Technological Impacts and Student Agency

The following section examines a widely referenced set of ideas using the terms Net Generation and Digital Natives (see for example Tapscott 1998 & 2009; Palfrey & Gasser, 2008, Oblinger & Oblinger, 2005). The idea of a Net Generation and Digital Natives suggest that because young people have grown up in a world infused with networked and digital technologies there has been a clear impact, in terms of attitudes and orientation to learning, on an entire generation of young people, many of whom are now students at university. This set of ideas has a strongly determinist essence in which young people's ideas and attitudes are affected as a whole by the introduction of new technologies. This view of the new generation of students has been qualified by recent empirical research and by theoretical work questioning the terms in which the Net Generation and Digital Natives debate has taken place (see for example Kennedy et al., 2008; Bennett, Maton & Kervin, 2008; Jones et al., 2010). The recent empirical work points to two key features of new students entering university. Firstly there are age related differences amongst students, even within the Net Generation age group. Secondly that these differences cannot be smoothed into a single generational shift and they remain complex and related to specific contextual factors including student choice, gender, institutional mode (distance or place-based) and design. The newer critical work on the Net Generation and Digital Natives suggests we should be cautious about generalizing to an entire generation of students and points to the existence of variations within Net Generation age students and to the agency of students in negotiating their engagement with new technologies (Jones et al., 2010, Czerniewicz, 2009).

In the spring of 2009, as part of a research project investigating first year students, 18 students at four English Universities were asked to respond to text messages over a 24 hour period. This intervention was based on the Day Experience Method (Riddle & Arnold, 2007). The project team also interviewed 58 students in the winter of 2008 and spring of 2009. Drawing from the interviews, and from the students own reports from the Day Experience intervention, a picture emerged of the kinds of contexts that students constituted in the learning environments supplied by universities. Such a picture contrasts with and complements the literature that has grown up describing Net Generation or Digital Native students. We have drawn two illustrative vignettes from our research and whilst not fully representative, they are included to illustrate the potential variety of students' engagements with current technologies. They provide accounts of how students actively make use of the environments, both the physical spaces and the networked ones, to constitute their own contexts.

A Young 'Net Generation' Place-Based Student

Beth is a young student studying a science based course. Like many students she balances a busy social life that includes sport and a range of leisure activities with academic work. Her study room is a comfortable space with a range of technologies at hand including a laptop computer and a mobile phone. The day moves between different spaces but often within the confines of this room.

Arrangements are made on Facebook for sports activities and email is checked for both study and social purposes. The Virtual Learning Environment (VLE) is accessed at the end of a sequence of activities that, despite being a first year student, is already described as a habit that moves from social activities in towards her work.

Right, I've just flicked on to the internet and I'm just checking my Tiscali e-mails which is the first thing I usually do and see whether anybody interesting has bothered to contact me. Usually there are only Facebook notifications - looks as though there is one from my football team which means I probably will actually go on to Facebook which is never a good idea to see what all that's about. I usually follow the same thing each day, I log on to my Tiscali e-mail see whether anything interesting is on there, usually there isn't. Then I go on to BBC sport because I'm a bit of a sport addict and see what's happening there. Then I check my [University] student e-mails because there's usually a lot more going on there. That could be if there is any lecture changes or exam results out that I need to be aware off. Then I log into [local VLE] and the lecture writing up begins.

This is the portal home page, got all sorts of stuff on that, my e-mail, [local VLE] my life saver, random announcements that may be of interest to us, not really. Here's [local VLE], if it wasn't for this it would be so difficult because I'd be scrambling down notes in my lectures and I really wouldn't be paying much attention. So thanks for this, it's an absolute life saver.

I think I've missed the last couple of texts, I've been far too busy playing football need a good respite from all of this hard work. I think I left to go to football at about quarter to seven and I've just got back at quarter past nine, so back to the hard work, I've got to continue with the lecture I was doing earlier. If there is anything.. I need back up I need to actually look that up on the Internet, I just need to look up a few definitions...

A Mature Student Place-Based Student

Helen is a busy Mum. She moves from university to home and then picks up the children. Her early evening is full of domestic work and engagement with her children while they use their own technologies, mainly games. Later in the evening when the children have gone to bed she begins to work in a corner of a domestic room that is equipped with a laptop computer and a desk. Work goes on for a couple of hours before bed and includes working online as well as reading for the next day's classes. In the morning Helen goes to the lecture theatre early after dropping the children off and works on her laptop online until the lecture theatre fills up for the first class.

It's just gone seven o'clock and I've just turned on the laptop ready to start some work. The children are busy on Nintendo DS's. Ok we'll talk again later...

Hi the time now is 20.16 and I've just started work on my CV. The children have now gone to bed so there should be peace and quiet.

Hi its me, I'm still working on my CV the time now is nine o'clock and now I'm getting tired. [Camera moves around the room showing books on a shelf to the left and the laptop in front. As the camera pans right the scene moves from a work station to a living room in dim light with a TV turned on to the rear of the workstation without sound]

Not much has changed from before, still working.

As you can see the fish are going to sleep, it's very quiet. I don't think you can see the dragon who's fast asleep. The television is off, the Wii is off, and I'm still in my corner on the computer. Just put

all the washing to dry, made a cup of coffee, and going to start my next lot of work. Everybody else has left me, so I'm very tired now, bye.

The time is now 23.15 ...as you can see [laptop screen showing graphs and data] I'm working on cinema attendances and I'm very, very tired now and I'm going to bed in a moment.

These two vignettes point towards the way students actively engage with technologies, in relation to their learning, within the overall pattern of their lives. There is no sense that the technology imposes itself on the user or that the technology can be considered alone. The student is faced with a learning 'landscape', that consists of organizational and institutional requirements, academic interests, social and leisure activities, etc within which the technological tools and services sit. The technologies form just one part of this landscape in which students selectively appropriate different elements they consider appropriate for their learning. When the students use their laptop it is as a multi-functional device that facilitates a variety of activities and social engagements from which the students choose to constitute their own personal repertoire of activity.

Students from the same course and university manage their environments in notably different ways. For example consider these two computing students studying at the same university:

B: I prefer to work in the lab because the software is there and everything's working. So it's easier for me that way.

Interviewer: And your choice was?

C: I kind of prefer to do it in my room because in the labs there's certain things you can't do and on your own computer you can.

Both students were studying the same computing course and confirmed that they had different working practices based on considerations of reliability and a lack of distraction in the first case (B) and greater control over what can be done in the second (C). Later in the same interview the same two students contrasted their use of cut and paste for programming:

C: ... I use quite a lot of online books because if I do code ... if you have a book on paper you have to copy the code in, type it in yourself.

Interviewer: You have to retype it, yeah?

C: But then if you make like one mistake, if you like miss out a dot or something, it messes up and you can't understand why. But if they provide you with an example on the Internet and you copy and paste and then you know it works because it's exactly what they give you, if you know what I mean.

B: I prefer to do both. I like the books because it's something you can read. When I type it and if I get it wrong after a couple of attempts I'll just go to the website and copy the exact same code but I prefer to type it because it's like a learning process isn't it.

Clearly these students even when studying under the same conditions general conditions still engaged in significantly different practices which accorded with a largely personal selection from the learning environment.

A commonly made comment from the students during de-briefing following the Day Experience intervention was how it had drawn attention to technologies that they used but usually didn't consider. For example:

I found it quite interesting like getting the text and then having to record what I'm doing and trying to identify what technology I'm actually using... and in parts I thought 'what technology am I actually using?', it turned out I was using more than I thought and how much it's incorporated into my everyday life without me even realising it ... it was quite surprising. (Accounting student Day Experience De-briefing group interview)

This was most remarked on in relation to the mobile (cell) phone but it applied to other technologies too. It suggests that technology is becoming naturalized such that students are less aware of the technologies themselves and have to be prompted to notice them (JISC, 2007).

Networked Learning Environments and Infrastructure

The way that the technology fades into the background suggests that many of the elements that compose a networked learning environment fit the traditional conception of an infrastructure as something that is already in place, ready-to-use, completely transparent and not requiring consideration. Infrastructure though often out of sight comes into sharp focus when it fails. Infrastructure can be thought of simply as an object, something that is built and maintained and then sinks into the background becoming almost invisible. Edwards (2003) describes infrastructures as socio-technical systems, which are reliant on complex organizational practices for maintenance and for making the infrastructure meaningful in practice. In networked learning digital technologies are integrated into social structures and practices and these structures and practices are rapidly becoming naturalized for both teaching staff and students. Technological infrastructures in tertiary education now reach well beyond particular tasks and processes and there are development programs aimed at both staff and students intended to make the networked learning infrastructure an integral part of university practices. The installed base of networked technologies in universities has now been in place for many years and it is part of a process of continuous renewal. For many staff and students it is the experience of a sudden or unexpected breakdown of the standard technologies that makes it clear just how much networked and digital technologies now form part of a widespread infrastructure in university education.

The general conception of an infrastructure has been developed with a specific focus on learning (Guribye 2005; Guribye & Lindström, 2009).

An infrastructure for learning is a set of resources and arrangements – social, institutional, technical – that are designed to and / or assigned to support a learning practice. (Guribye & Lindström, 2009)

Elsewhere Guribye points out that infrastructures for learning do not have to be designed by the users for specific tasks and might commonly be designed by a variety of actors (Guribye, 2005, pp. 63 & 64). Guribye's approach is a useful way to examine those internal infrastructures that form part of the learning environment as it is experienced by students. It is also useful for considering the way infrastructures influence the teaching environment experienced by academic staff. However caution needs to be exercised because this approach explicitly excludes those areas that are neither designed for nor specifically assigned to support learning but which are arguably of central importance in networked learning environments (Jones, 2009). Examples of this are the routine use of Google as the search engine of choice by both students and academics and the use of Wikipedia for quick answers, even when this is officially frowned upon within the university. Currently services such as Facebook, You Tube and iTunes are being integrated into educational institutions, and student learning practices, but they are still largely outside institutional control. Universal services such as You Tube and iTunes now have institutional aspects and the Open University (UK) has, for example, launched an iTunes U service in June 2008 (http://www.open.ac.uk/itunes/) and materials are also available via a YouTube channel (http://uk.youtube.com/theopenuniversity).

Universities will have to make choices about the relationship they have to universal services. They may find that they cannot easily rely on external systems and services because they depend on decisions taken elsewhere and because these systems and services can be unilaterally withdrawn or altered by their suppliers. Externally supplied systems and services may not comply with university regulations, such as those in relation to access for students and staff with disabilities. The need for an institutional 'backbone' is related to one of the core functions of a university which is to provide credentials and to stand behind those credentials by having warranted procedures (Brown & Duguid, 2000). In this context decisions about the boundaries of institutional provision have to be made by universities between two forces that are in tension. Firstly there is a need for infrastructures for learning and the provision of 'quality assured' safe areas in which media and technologies are under institutional control. Secondly there is a need to incorporate and manage the universal service infrastructures, such as Google, Wikipedia and social networking sites, which routinely breach institutional boundaries.

Networked Learning and Virtual Learning Environments

The area of institutionally bounded infrastructures for learning, and the provision of quality assured areas, concerns the provision of technologies such as virtual or managed learning environments (VLE), which are strongly identified with commercial products and open source software (often known outside the UK as Learning or Course Management Systems e.g. Blackboard, Moodle etc).

Virtual learning environments (VLEs) are learning management software systems that synthesise the functionality of computer-mediated communication software and on-line methods of delivering course materials (Britain & Liber, 1999, p. 3).

The use of VLEs in UK universities has developed in the last ten years in ways that have emphasized the management aspects of online learning environments with the integration of a variety of administrative and organizational features. Weller places the VLE at the heart of a complex process of change that has surrounded the term e-learning:

...underlying all of these activities is the environment in which e-learning takes place, the VLE or LMS... The pedagogical, political, technical and economic arguments that pervade e-learning are reflected in the choice, deployment and development of a VLE in an organization. (Weller, 2007, p. 1)

Weller defines a VLE, like Britain and Liber as a software system that combines a number of different tools that are used systematically to deliver content online but he adds that a VLE also facilitates the learning experience around that content (Weller, 2007, p. 5). The VLE in both definitions includes aspects of delivery and of communication with the latter being clearly identified by Weller as enabling facilitation of learning around content.

The development and deployment of VLEs in place-based universities has shifted debate away from the 'virtual' university to the ways in which networked and digital technologies interpenetrate physical learning spaces.

The enhancement of face-to-face teaching with the use of CITs (sic) [Communication and Information Technologies] represents a shift from campus-bound activities, enabling increased flexibility over when, where, what, how and with whom students learn... In this context, what types of built environments are universities offering students? (Jamieson, Taylor, Fisher, Trevitt & Gilding, 2000, p. 221)

Crook used the term learning 'nests' to describe the student study bedroom equipped with networked computers (Crook, 2002). He noted how the term learning nests caught on, perhaps because it implied a cosy, personalized space that was still connected to a larger world. Crook also commented that the feature that distinguishes networked learning from "mere 'electronic learning' is the promise of interpersonal communication" (Crook, 2002, p. 296). Other authors have also noted that we should expect students to customize designed learning spaces and make their own "local habitations" (Nardi & O'Day, 1999). The tension built into Virtual Learning Environments and the emergent study bedroom setting is one between networks as sources of delivery and networks as conduits for communication. Weller dubs these two views the broadcast and discussion viewpoints (Weller, 2007, p. 6) and it clearly relates to the much broader and philosophically inspired debate between transmission models of learning and participative models. Sfard, 1998 for example has discussed these issues in terms of two metaphors for learning and argued that there is a danger in just choosing one. The contrast Sfard makes is between what she calls an 'acquisition' metaphor and a 'participation' metaphor but like Weller she argues that the metaphors are not mutually exclusive and that strength lies in combining the two perspectives rather than relying on one.

The institutional location of VLEs suggest that they need to be understood as being at intermediate levels of scale, somewhere between macro and micro levels of the environment, i.e. at the meso level (see Mouzelis 1995; Sibeon, 2004; Jones, Dirckinck-Holmfeld & Lindström, 2006). Embedded at an institutional level a VLE is neither a small-scale self-contained learning environment, nor does it encompass a totality of resources, sitting as it does within a broader learning environment that would include a range of externally designed and supplied elements, for example iTunesU and YouTube. The nature of the VLE also suggests that it needs to be understood as an infrastructure rather than as a technology or tool. Infrastructure, as noted above, suggesting something that is already in place and immediately available for use, readily understood and requiring little thought. In other contexts infrastructure would apply to the water system, the electricity supply, the railway, the mail services and more recently the Internet.

Issues Arising from Networked Learning Environments

The concept of a networked learning environment suggests that the technological and physical environment is best understood as intertwining and constantly interacting with the social organization of the setting. It also points towards the socially and physically networked nature of learning environments that are distributed over both space and time. The introduction of digital and networked technologies has generated a number of issues concerning their impact on learning environments which include:

- Time shifts: Computer networks used in education affect the usual time patterns of education. Many courses delivered across networks are asynchronous.
- Place: The introduction of mobile and ubiquitous computing devices have begun to make the idea of education occurring at anytime, anyplace, and anywhere seem more feasible.
- Digital preservation: The outputs of synchronous and asynchronous activity are easily preserved in transcripts, logs and a variety of other forms including the archiving of web casts and audio interviews/podcasts.
- Public/Private boundaries: The preservation of what would otherwise be ephemeral materials alters the boundaries between what is public and what is private. Tutors

can now view and preserve the details of student's interactions during group activities, making these available as tools for assessment.
- Forms of literacy: The still largely text based world of networked learning has generated new forms of writing that are neither simple text replications of informal conversation nor are they formal written texts. The integration of images and audio into digital environments has suggested new forms of multimedia literacy.
- Content: The boundary between content and process is shifting. Blogs and wikis can provide elements of content and cut and paste re-use is common practice. The idea that there is a clear distinction between activity/process and artefact/content is becoming strained. (Jones & Dirckinck-Holmfeld, 2009, p. 13)

Participants in a computer network whilst they are simultaneously situated at a real point in time and space are also displaced from that physical point in a virtual space configured through the network. In contrast Hine (2000) points out that despite the generic nature of Internet spaces the local is very much embedded in particular uses of the Internet, e.g., homepages or social networking site profiles such as those on Bebo, Facebook and MySpace. People using network spaces are never completely disembedded or separated from their off-line activities and spatial locations. Rather offline spaces interpenetrate online netscapes and together they configure new hybrid forms. Moreover the properties of space as experienced offline are used to inform the design of online environments. Overall the standpoint taken in this chapter is that computer networks disrupt and disturb traditional boundaries in education. If this is so then it is important to consider how this might affect the parameters of design.

Solutions and Recommendations: Contexts for Learning and Indirect Design

Networked learning environments disrupt traditional boundaries and place the emphasis for designers in different parts of the environment. A networked learning environment rekindles disputes between individual and social perspectives on learning with advocates of the VLE pitching themselves against advocates of personal learning environments (Weller, 2007; Sclater & Weller, 2009). Networked learning environments also disrupt institutional boundaries with advocates of Web 2.0 technologies suggesting that VLEs perpetuate a 'walled garden' of provision when the new technologies that are becoming available allow for a wider variety of provision and for services to be sourced from outside the academy (Jones, 2008). This kind of thinking is only enhanced by the current shift in emphasis towards cloud computing and a number of universities in the UK, including the Open University, are currently shifting some of their institutional provision of services to Google apps and placing them, at least partially, outside the institution.

I have argued that networked learning environments are composed of the totality of resources and that contexts for learning are constituted from this totality selectively by students and teachers acting in ways that are informed by their own histories, purposes and intentions. In relation to design I argue that as a consequence of this selective appropriation of the learning environment learning itself can never be directly designed, only designed *for* (i.e. planned in advance) (see Beetham & Sharpe, 2007). Learning itself is only indirectly related to our activities, communities and places and these in turn are indirectly related to those aspects that can be designed and planned. The tasks, spaces and organizations that we design rely on being inhabited by the teachers and learners who will 'enact' our designs. Goodyear has summarized these distinctions as an indirect approach to learning and their relationships are shown in Figure 1.

In a networked learning environment place and space become highly contingent factors as I have illustrated in relation to students learning nests and the vignettes derived from our research. As a consequence place and space require detailed attention in terms of the design of all types of learning environments that are affected by digital networks, whether learners are co-located, distant or in a combination of the two (see, for example, Goodyear et al., 2001).

The first suggestion for design is to focus further away from the learning in networked learning

Figure 1. Indirect approach to learning (Goodyear, Jones, Asensio, Hodgson & Steeples, 2001)

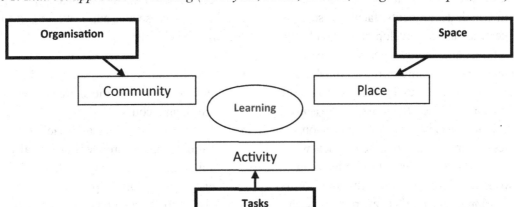

environments and to concentrate on designing those aspects of the learning environment that are clearly under the designers control such as organization, space and task. Given what I have also argued about the way new technologies form a netscape, that is a composite of various technologies aggregated in services and accessed through particular devices, it also suggests that a focus for design should be on meso level features such as infrastructures and infrastructures for learning rather than on the particular practices, tools and services situated at a micro level of activity.

FUTURE RESEARCH DIRECTIONS

Networked learning environments are becoming the basis of much university education in the advanced industrial countries and even more broadly as networked technologies inform and infuse many aspects of the world. I would argue that to understand the changes in learning environments that are continuing to disrupt traditional patterns of learning we need to understand learning infrastructures rather better. Educational research has a tendency to focus on either micro level activity by teachers and learners or on broad social and policy issues that occur at the macro levels of national or regional political policy and broad, even global social and technological changes. The arguments presented here suggest that the focus should be at the meso level of institutional and collective agency in which departments, faculties, schools and universities act to develop and provide the infrastructures and environments for learning that students and academic staff then inhabit and enliven with their activities. Furthermore the shift from place-based forms of organization to a more networked form based more closely on person-to-person ties requires the development of new ways of thinking about the organization of learning.

Networked and complex internetworked forms of organization signal a shift away from space and locality to more networked forms. Part of this shift

is towards networked individualism, the move from place-to-place to person-to-person forms of organization (Castells, 2000). However caution needs to be exercised in interpreting the idea of the person not to slide into a form of methodological reduction and the diminution of social forms into aggregates of individuals. For example research should explore whether designers respond to networked individualism by the development of Personal Learning Environments (PLE). Weller has noted that personalisation can be interpreted as either the personalisation of information or the personalisation of tools and services (Weller, 2007, p. 111). It is the second view that links to the suggestion that design needs to consider the institutional and infrastructural level.

The idea behind a PLE is that users amass or create a collection of tools for themselves, which constitute their own learning environment... The PLE provides a way of linking these together for the user and then integrating them with institutional systems (Weller, 2007, p. 114).

Research will need to examine the ways in which new network forms relate to institutional boundaries and whether greater personalisation will lead to the disaggregation of university functions or to a new integration with networked technologies finding a place within institutional forms whilst allowing for greater personalisation.

Weller notes four downsides to the concept of a PLE and these also suggest topics for future research in this area:

- Commonality of experience. PLEs may threaten or loosen the shared experience of studying a course.
- Exposure to different approaches. The educational gain of broadening a local and personal experience may be lost. PLEs may encourage a narrow private view that is resistant to change and encourage a 'customer' focus that relies on consumer choice of

'educational goods' that are often not appreciated until after the educational experience has taken place.

- Privacy. Personalisation requires the collection of user data and raises serious concerns in terms of privacy and surveillance. It may also have unintended consequences as once it is known that a system is monitored, user behaviour will adapt to the perceived requirements of the monitoring.
- Content focus. The drive behind PLEs is one that emphasises delivery of personalised content at the expense of communication with others

The PLE is one current design area that is closely related to the idea of networked individualism. However networked learning may offer an alternative vision to personalization, a vision of the social potential of learning environments infused with digital and networked technologies. The same technological forms that afford an enhanced personalization also emphasize connectivity and suggest new networked social forms that contrast with notions of community (Wittel, 2001). Network forms of organization can enable both the strong ties that are found in collaboration and community and the weak links found in looser more networked forms of organization.

CONCLUSION

This chapter has touched on a current debate in education about what might be called the limits of design. This chapter should be read in this context as an acceptance that design is an appropriate activity in networked learning, even if I have argued against the approaches that come under the banner of learning design in both its forms. All of the mentioned approaches to design illustrate the challenges that are arising in higher education with the disruption caused by the introduction of networked and digital technologies on a broad

scale. One of the most pressing problems that remains is to work out how a systematic design approach can be applied to the highly idiosyncratic and personalised practices of learning in higher education.

The chapter has also argued that design should shift focus towards institutional and infrastructural aspects of the networked learning environment. This implies that both research and design need to change focus to a different level of granularity, away from the detailed practices that occur at micro level of classroom interaction and equally away from the macro level technology and policy issues that provide the framework within which networked learning environments are developed. The appeal is for a focus on the meso level of learning characterised as residing at an institutional level of scale and open to design interventions at a collective rather than an individual level. The suggestion is that infrastructure for learning at a whole institution level should be one focus of attention, in the form of the design of VLEs and PLEs and that smaller units such as Departments, Faculties and Schools should provide another level of focus in the development of procedures and patterns of local practices.

Students already inhabit networked learning environments when they arrive at university. They bring with them habits of social engagement that are already mediated by digital networks. At university students engage with the institutional infrastructure for learning and within that designed elements of networked and e-learning. As mobile technologies become increasingly available students will construct their learning environment away from the buildings and settings that have been purposely designed for learning. The lecture theatre, seminar room and library will remain in use but they will be inhabited in different ways by students who can interact during face-to-face classes using networked devices. The library which can now be accessed from anywhere using the network will become less place-based and more of a network service available at all times from anywhere with network access. While these technological shifts are possible they are not inevitable and students cannot be simply described as a new Net Generation of Digital Natives. The task remains to find suitable ways to introduce design features into networked learning environments without prescribing the kinds of detailed interactions that teachers and learners undertake in these settings.

REFERENCES

Beetham, H., & Sharpe, R. (Eds.). (2007). *Rethinking pedagogy for a digital age: Designing and delivering e-learning*. London, UK: Routledge Falmer.

Bennett, S., Maton, K., & Kervin, L. (2008). The 'digital natives' debate: A critical review of the evidence. *British Journal of Educational Technology, 39*(5), 775–786. doi:10.1111/j.1467-8535.2007.00793.x

Britain, S., & Liber, O. (1999). *A framework for pedagogical evaluation of virtual learning environments*. Retrieved March 30, 2010, from http://www.jisc.ac.uk/publications/reports/1999/pedagogicalvlefinal.aspx

Brown, J. S., & Duguid, P. (2000). *The social life of information*. Boston, MA: Harvard Business School.

Castells, M. (2000). *The rise of the network society* (2nd ed.). Oxford, UK: Blackwell.

Castells, M., Fernández-Ardèvol, M., Qiu, J. L., & Sey, A. (2007). *Mobile communication and society: A global perspective*. Cambridge, MA: MIT Press.

Crook, C. (2002). The campus experience of networked learning. In Steeples, C., & Jones, C. (Eds.), *Networked learning: Perspectives and issues* (pp. 293–308). London, UK: Springer.

Czerniewicz, L., Williams, K., & Brown, C. (2009). Students make a plan: Understanding student agency in constraining conditions. *ALT-J, 17*(2), 75–88. doi:10.1080/09687760903033058

Dirckinck-Holmfeld, L., Jones, C., & Lindström, B. (2009). *Analysing networked learning practices in higher education and continuing professional development*. Rotterdam, The Netherlands: Sense Publishers B.V.

Edwards, P. N. (2003). Infrastructure and modernity: Force, time, and social organization in the history of sociotechnical systems. In Misa, T. J., Brey, P., & Feenberg, A. (Eds.), *Modernity and technology* (pp. 185–225). Cambridge, MA: MIT Press.

Goodyear, P., Banks, S., Hodgson, V., & McConnell, D. (2004). *Advances in research on networked learning*. Dordrecht, The Netherlands: Kluwer.

Goodyear, P., Jones, C., Asensio, M., Hodgson, V., & Steeples, C. (2001). *Effective networked learning in higher education: Notes and guidelines*. Lancaster, UK: CSALT, Lancaster University. Retrieved April 10, 2011, from http://csalt.lancs.ac.uk/jisc/

Gurlbye, F. (2005). *Infrastructures for learning - ethnographic inquiries into the social and technical conditions of education and training*. Doctoral Thesis, University of Bergen, Norway. Retrieved April 10, 2011, from http://hdl.handle.net/1956/859

Guribye, F., & Lindström, B. (2009). Infrastructures for learning and networked tools - The introduction of a new tool in an inter-organisational network. In Dirckinck-Holmfeld, L., Jones, C., & Lindström, B. (Eds.), *Analysing networked learning practices in higher education and continuing professional development* (pp. 103–116). Rotterdam, The Netherlands: Sense Publishers.

Hine, C. (2000). *Virtual ethnography*. London, UK: SAGE Publications Ltd.

Jamieson, P., Taylor, P., Fisher, K., Trevitt, A. C. F., & Gilding, T. (2000). Place and space in the design of new learning environments. *Higher Education Research & Development, 19*(2), 221–236. doi:10.1080/072943600445664

JISC. (2007). *Student expectations study: Key findings from online research.* Discussion evenings held in June 2007 for the Joint Information Systems Committee. London, UK: JISC. Retrieved April 10, 2011, from http://www.jisc.ac.uk/publications/publications/studentexpectations

Jones, C. (2008). Infrastructures, institutions and networked learning. In V. Hodgson, C. Jones, T. Kargidis, D. McConnell, S. Retalis, D. Stamatis, & M. Zenios (Eds.), *Proceedings of the Sixth International Conference on Networked Learning 2008*. Lancaster, UK: Lancaster University.

Jones, C. (2009). A context for collaboration: The institutional selection of an infrastructure for learning. In C. O'Malley, D. Suthers, P. Reimann, & A. Dimitracopoulou (Eds.), *Proceedings of the 8th International Conference on Computer Supported Collaborative Learning Practices (CSCL2009)*. Rhodes, Greece: Lulu.com.

Jones, C., & Asensio, M. (2001). Experiences of assessment: using phenomenography for evaluation. *Journal of Computer Assisted Learning, 17*(3), 314–321. doi:10.1046/j.0266-4909.2001.00186.x

Jones, C., & Dirckinck-Holmfeld, L. (2009). Analysing networked learning practices: An introduction. In Dirckinck-Holmfeld, L., Jones, C., & Lindström, B. (Eds.), *Analysing networked learning practices in higher education and continuing professional development* (pp. 1–28). Rotterdam, The Netherlands: Sense Publishers B.V.

Jones, C., Dirckinck-Holmfeld, L., & Lindström, B. (2006). A relational, indirect, meso-level approach to cscl design in the next decade. *International Journal of Computer-Supported Collaborative Learning, 1*(1), 35–56. doi:10.1007/s11412-006-6841-7

Jones, C., Ramanau, R., Cross, S. J., & Healing, G. (2010). Net generation or digital natives: Is there a distinct new generation entering university? *Computers & Education, 54*(3), 722–732. doi:10.1016/j.compedu.2009.09.022

Kennedy, G., Judd, T. S., Churchward, A., Gray, K., & Krause, K. (2008). First year students' experiences with technology: Are they really digital natives? Questioning the net generation: A collaborative project in Australian higher education. *Australasian Journal of Educational Technology, 24*(1), 108-122. Retrieved April 20, 2009, from http://www.ascilite.org.au/ajet/ajet24/kennedy.html

Koper, R., & Tattersall, C. (Eds.). (2005). *Learning design: A handbook on modeling and delivering networked education and training*. Berlin, Germany: Springer.

Laurillard, D. (2002). *Rethinking university teaching: A conversational framework for the effective use of learning technologies* (2nd ed.). London, UK: Routledge Falmer. doi:10.4324/9780203304846

McAndrew, P., Goodyear, P., & Dalziel, J. (2006). Patterns, designs and activities: Unifying descriptions of learning structures. *International Journal of Learning Technology, 2*(2–3), 216–242. doi:10.1504/IJLT.2006.010632

Mouzelis, N. (1995). *Sociological theory: What went wrong?* New York, NY: Routledge.

Nardi, B., & O'Day, V. (1999). *Information ecologies: Using technology with heart*. Cambridge, MA: MIT Press.

Oblinger, D. G., & Oblinger, J. L. (2005). *Educating the Net generation, an Educause e-book*. Retrieved April 10, 2011, from http://www.educause.edu/ir/library/pdf/pub7101.pdf

Palfrey, J., & Gasser, U. (2008). *Born digital: Understanding the first generation of digital natives*. New York, NY: Basic Books.

Riddle, M., & Arnold, M. (2007). *The day experience method: A resource kit.* Retrieved April 10, 2011, from http://www.matthewriddle.com/papers/Day_Experience_Resource_Kit.pdf

Salaway, G., Caruso, J. B., & Nelson, M. R. (2008). *The ECAR study of undergraduate students and Information Technology, 2008. Research study* (vol. 8). Boulder, CO: EDUCAUSE. Retrieved April 10, 2011, from http://www.educause.edu/ecar

Sclater, N., & Weller, M. (2009). *Podcast for H800 Technology-enhanced learning: Practices and debates.* Retrieved April 11, 2011 from http://nogoodreason.typepad.co.uk/no_good_reason/2009/04/vle-vs-ple-fight-club.html

Sfard, A. (1998). On two metaphors for learning and the dangers of choosing just one. *Educational Researcher, 27*(2), 4–13.

Sibeon, R. (2004). *Rethinking social theory.* London, UK: Sage publications.

Tapscott, D. (1998). *Growing up digital: The rise of the Net generation.* New York, NY: McGraw-Hill.

Tapscott, D. (2009). *Grown up digital: How the Net generation is changing your world.* New York, NY: McGraw-Hill.

Tchounikine, P. (2008). Operationalising macro-scripts in CSCL technological settings. *International Journal of Computer-Supported Collaborative Learning, 3*(2), 193–233. doi:10.1007/s11412-008-9039-3

Weller, M. (2007). *Virtual learning environments: Using, choosing and developing your VLE.* London, UK: Routledge.

Wittel, A. (2001). Towards a network sociality. *Theory, Culture & Society, 18*(6), 51–76.

ADDITIONAL READING

Bielaczyc, K. (2001). Designing social infrastructure: The challenge of building computer-supported learning communities. In P. Dillenbourg, A. Eurelings & K. Hakkarainen (Eds.), *European perspectives on computer-supported collaborative learning. The proceedings of the First European Conference on Computer-Supported Collaborative Learning* (pp. 106-114). University of Maastricht.

Bielaczyc, K. (2006). Designing social infrastructure: Critical issues in creating learning environments with technology. *Journal of the Learning Sciences, 15*(3), 301–329. doi:10.1207/s15327809jls1503_1

Britain, S. (2004). *A review of learning design: Concept, specifications and tools.* A report for the JISC E-learning Pedagogy Programme. Retrieved April 11, 2011, from http://www.jisc.ac.uk/uploaded_documents/ACF83C.doc

Brown, C., & Czerniewicz, L. (2008, September). *Trends in student use of ICTs in higher education in South Africa.* Paper presented at the 10th Annual Conference of WWW Applications, Cape Town, SA. Retrieved April 11, 2011, from http://www.cet.uct.ac.za/files/file/ResearchOutput/2008_wwwApps_UseTrends.pdf

Brown, J. S. (2006). New learning environments for the 21st century: Exploring the edge. *Change, 38*(5), 18–24. doi:10.3200/CHNG.38.5.18-24

Brown, J. S., & Duguid, P. (2001). Knowledge and organization: A social-practice perspective. *Organization Science, 12*(2), 198–213. doi:10.1287/orsc.12.2.198.10116

Cornford, J. (2000). The Virtual University is … the University made Concrete? *Information Communication and Society, 3*(4), 508–525. doi:10.1080/13691180010002314

Edwards, P. N., Jackson, S. J., Bowker, G. C., & Knobel, C. P. (2007, January). *Understanding infrastructure: Dynamics, tensions and design.* Report of a workshop on History & theory of Infrastructure: Lessons for New Scientific Cyber-infrastructures. NSF and University of Michigan. Retrieved April 11, 2011, from http://pne.people.si.umich.edu/PDF/ui.pdf

Hanseth, O., & Lundberg, N. (2001). Designing work oriented infrastructures. *Computer Supported Cooperative Work, 10,* 347–372. doi:10.1023/A:1012727708439

Harrison, S., & Dourish, P. (1996). Re-place-ing space: The roles of space and place in collaborative systems. In [New York, NY: ACM.]. *Proceedings of CSCW, 96,* 67–76.

Hemmi, A., Bayne, S., & Land, R. (2009). The appropriation and repurposing of social technologies in higher education. *Journal of Computer Assisted Learning, 25,* 19–30. doi:10.1111/j.1365-2729.2008.00306.x

Jones, C. (2004). Networks and learning: communities, practices and the metaphor of networks. *ALT-J Association for Learning Technology Journal, 12*(1), 82–93. doi:10.1080/0968776042000211548

Jones, C., Ferreday, D., & Hodgson, V. (2008). Networked learning a relational approach – weak and strong ties. *Journal of Computer Assisted Learning special section, 24*(2), 90–102.

Kapur, M., Hung, D., Jacobson, M., Voiklis, J., Kinzer, C., & Chen, D.-T. (V). (2007). Emergence of learning in computer-supported, large-scale collective dynamics: A research agenda. In C. A. Clark, G. Erkens & S. Puntambekar (Eds.), *Proceedings of the International Conference of Computer-Supported Collaborative Learning* (pp. 323-332). Mahwah, NJ:Erlbaum.

Lakkala, M., Paavola, S., & Hakkarainen, K. (2008). Designing pedagogical infrastructures in university courses for technology-enhanced collaborative inquiry. *Research and Practice in Technology Enhanced Learning., 3*(1), 33–64. doi:10.1142/S1793206808000446

Lash, S. (2001). Technological forms of life. *Theory, Culture & Society, 18*(1), 105–120. doi:10.1177/02632760122051661

Liljenström, H., & Svedin, U. (Eds.). (2005). *Micro, meso, macro: Addressing complex systems.* London: World Scientific Publishers. doi:10.1142/9789812701404

Ryberg, T., & Larsen, M. C. (2008). Networked identities: Understanding relationships between weak and strong ties in networked environments. *Journal of Computer Assisted Learning* special section, *24*(2), 103–115.

Schatzki, T. R., Knorr Cetina, K., & Von Savigny, E. (Eds.). (2001). *The practice turn in contemporary theory.* London: Routledge.

Sclater, N. (2008). Large-Scale Open Source E-Learning Systems at the Open University UK. *Educause Centre for Applied Research Research Bulletin* Issue 12. Boulder, CO: Centre for Applied Research. Retrieved April 10, 2011, from: http://www.educause.edu/ecar

Sclater, N. (2008a). Web 2.0, Personal Learning Environments and the Future of Learning Management Systems. *Educause Centre for Applied Research Research Bulletin* Issue 13. Boulder, CO: Centre for Applied Research. Retrieved April 10, 2011, from: http://www.educause.edu/ecar

Star, S. L., & Ruhleder, K. (1996). Steps toward an ecology of infrastructure: Design and access for large information spaces. *Information Systems Research, 7*(1), 111–134. doi:10.1287/isre.7.1.111

Steeples, C., & Jones, C. (Eds.). (2002). *Networked learning; perspectives and issues.* London: Springer Verlag.

Weller, M., & Daziel, J. (2007). Bridging the gap between web 2.0 and higher education. *Proceedings of the 2nd International LAMS conference, Sydney*. Retrieved April 10, 2011, from http://lams-2007sydney.lamsfoundation.org/pdfs/04g.pdf

Wellman, B., Quan-Haase, A., Boase, J., Chen, W., Hampton, K., Isla de Diaz, I., et al. (2003). The social affordances of the internet for networked individualism. *JCMC, 8*(3). Retrieved April 10, 2011, from http://jcmc.indiana.edu/issues.html

KEY TERMS AND DEFINITIONS

Context: The active constitution of an understanding of the available elements in an environment by an agent acting for a purpose.

Design for Learning: The process by which those interested in the support of learning, plan, structure or design environments to enable or allow for learning.

Indirect Design: The process of designing those aspects of a learning environment open to design (organization, space and tasks) and expecting these features to be enacted by learners and teachers (in communities, places and activities) and understanding that these enacted contexts are themselves only loosely related to learning.

Infrastructure: A mature socio-technical system that has become naturalized in the background. These socio-technical systems have become infrastructures in relation to organized practices.

Infrastructure for Learning: An infrastructure for learning is a set of resources and arrangements – social, institutional, technical – that are designed to and / or assigned to support a learning practice.

Learning Context: The constituted understanding by an agent of an environment for the purpose of learning

Learning Environment: The human, social, physical and virtual aspects of a setting, and the characteristics and arrangements of those elements, within which learning can take place.

Networked Learning: Learning in which information and communication technology is used to promote connections: between one learner and other learners, between learners and tutors; between a learning community and its learning resources.

Networked Learning Environment: The totality of surrounding conditions, mediated by digital networks, within which education or learning can take place.

Chapter 8
The Role of Institutions in Creating Student–Focused Virtual Learning Spaces with ePortfolio Systems

Eva Heinrich
Massey University, New Zealand

Yuliya Bozhko
Massey University, New Zealand

ABSTRACT

In this chapter, we explore the currently dominant virtual learning spaces employed in institutions of higher education and contrast them with the virtual social spaces provided by Web 2.0 tools. Guided by the increasing focus on lifelong learning skills in the world of work and in higher education, we identify the gap that exists between institutional and social virtual spaces. We argue for filling this gap by providing access to institutional e-Portfolio systems to students in higher education, giving students an institutionally supported student-focused virtual learning space. By examining the perspectives of stakeholders involved in higher education, we identify challenges inherent in the adoption of institutional e-Portfolio systems and make recommendations for overcoming these based on practical experience and research findings.

INTRODUCTION

To develop our arguments we need to explore a number of core areas and their relationship with each other. Figure 1 displays these core areas and provides key questions that are indicative of the issues we examine in the chapter in relation to creating student-focused virtual learning spaces with ePortfolio systems.

DOI: 10.4018/978-1-60960-114-0.ch008

THE DIFFERENT WORLDS OF INSTITUTIONAL AND OPEN LEARNING SPACES

The virtual learning spaces of institutions are dominated by Learning Management Systems (LMS) which support course related work. In addition students also have access to library systems and learning support. LMS are often closed systems that require user accounts and permissions to access the learning space. These closed systems contrast to open learning spaces provided by Web 2.0 and in particular its social networking tools which are characterised by open access allowing an individual to participate under their own direction in contributing information. Social networking includes sharing, exchanging and re-

flecting which provides benefits for learning. In the following sections we examine characteristics of these learning spaces and describe the barriers in utilising closed and open access environments within the higher education environment.

LEARNING MANAGEMENT SYSTEMS IN HIGHER EDUCATION

Higher education institutions have embraced computer systems to support teaching and learning as indicated by an OECD survey in which 89% of responding institutions (across 13 countries) used university-wide LMS (OECD Centre for Educational Research and Innovation). Further indications of uptake can be seen when visiting

Figure 1. Core areas and key questions for deliberation in this chapter

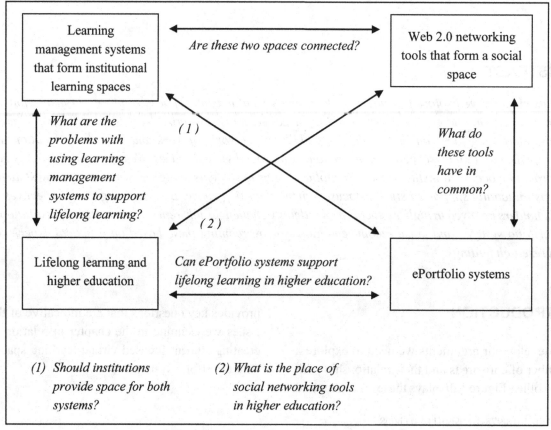

institutional websites, examining user statistics provided by system suppliers (for example, http://moodle.org/sites/ or http://sakaiproject.org/community-overview) or by following discussions in the academic literature (Browne, Jenkins & Walker, 2006; Collis & De Boer, 2004).

The systems are referred to as Virtual Learning Environments, Course Management Systems or Learning Management Systems (LMS), the term we use throughout the rest of this paper. LMS create a virtual space that is shared by staff and students of a particular course (discrete unit of study such as a subject) and are used for providing access to teaching and learning materials such as lecture slides. They form a platform for course discussions and facilitate assessment, both via online testing and for submission and return of assignments.

The use of LMS in higher education is characterised by a strong institutional focus. Access to the LMS is dependent on current enrolment with the institution and is organised around course structures. This means students have access to only the courses they are enrolled in and only for the duration of these courses because LMS are based on a hierarchy of user access rights. For example, the lecturer determines the 'toolset' for their course and sets the parameters that define the involvement of the students. In addition the lecturer has access to all course information while the student space is prescribed.

WEB 2.0 SOCIAL NETWORKING TOOLS

Outside the higher education sector, in the open Internet domain, Web 2.0 social networking tools have been firmly established and tools are available for the sharing of images, photos and video clips. Individuals can communicate with others in synchronous and asynchronous forms, and in access-protected as well as open formats. Individuals can consume and contribute information on a wide range of topics. Web 2.0 is characterised by open access availability to anyone who has an Internet connection and the level of participation is determined by the individual. This freedom also means that the individual should act in responsible ways in the Web 2.0 space.

Web 2.0 plays an important role in today's society and is used for social and commercial purposes. Examples from a variety of areas show the popularity and impact of Web 2.0: Virtual sports leagues attract millions of participants (Holahan, 2006); politicians use blogs and podcasts in fighting for voters (Capell, 2006); communication with customers is used to increase revenue (Havenstein, 2007); communication pathways in research communities are changing (Ashling, 2007); video-blogging facilitates new ways of sharing Social video: Videoblogging & YouTube, 2007); the music industry is being transformed (Holahan, 2007); genealogy research has become accessible to the public (MacMillan, 2007).

Web 2.0 spaces are conducive for learning in the higher education context particularly in relation to lifelong learning skills expected from today's higher education graduates. This potential is confirmed by: Churchill (2009) who examines the use of blogs in support of learning; Wheeler, Yeomans and Wheeler (2008) who examine student-generated content using wikis. In addition, Boulos and Wheeler (2007) investigate Web 2.0 tools for social communication in a learning context. It is essential that the skill levels of students are considered when designing education that integrates Web 2.0 technologies. While it is widely assumed that today's student generation is Internet savvy, it has to be acknowledged that quite a number of students have limited Web 2.0 skills. They are either not familiar with the technologies, or have only basic level skills (Kennedy et al., 2008).

THE SEPARATION OF THE ENVIRONMENTS

Students in higher education have access to both closed and open access environments, the institutionally focused LMS and the individually focused Web 2.0. However, these two virtual worlds often remain separate, both in the students' and the institutions' minds, with a distinction being made between 'serious learning' and 'play'. In addition, students may not be able to transfer their technology skills utilised in a social Web 2.0 context into academic learning, which is both a motivational and a skill transfer issue (Katz, 2005). The information technology sections of institutions often draw a clear line between institutionally provided, controlled and supported LMS services and the 'wild west' of the Web. While they cannot effectively restrict access to Web 2.0 tools they can deny institutional support and responsibility for quality of service. Educational researchers and individual academics have identified the potential of social networking tools for teaching and learning yet institutions are often unsure how to use these tools in the formal education setting.

In response to the popularity of Web 2.0 tools and their potential for learning, LMS system providers have started to integrate social networking functionality into their systems. Discussion forums, blogs and wikis have been added to the toolsets of LMS. Yet, the important Web 2.0 characteristic of open access has been removed as these tools have been bound into the institutional LMS framework. Access is linked to course enrolment and under institutional control. Student generated content is accessible to the lecturers in charge and tool use is directed by relevance to the respective course. This allows the teaching and learning interactions but still confines learning to the boundaries of course content and purpose.

Overall, we argue that there is a clear separation between the virtual spaces of institutional learning and social networking (see Figure 2).

LIFELONG LEARNING AND HIGHER EDUCATION

Before continuing the discussion on virtual learning spaces we need to consider the importance of lifelong learning. The notion of lifelong learning consists of a variety of meanings, models and ideas (Jarvis, 2004). The concept of lifelong learning is based on the principle of the self-motivated pursuit of knowledge or skills that occurs throughout one's life (European Commission, 2000; Knapper & Cropley, 2000; Longworth, 2003). It encompasses the elements of self-direction and life-wide learning, recognizing the fact that learning also takes place outside the formal education system and

Figure 2. Barrier between institutional learning and social networking

Institutional focus LMS		Individual focus Web 2.0

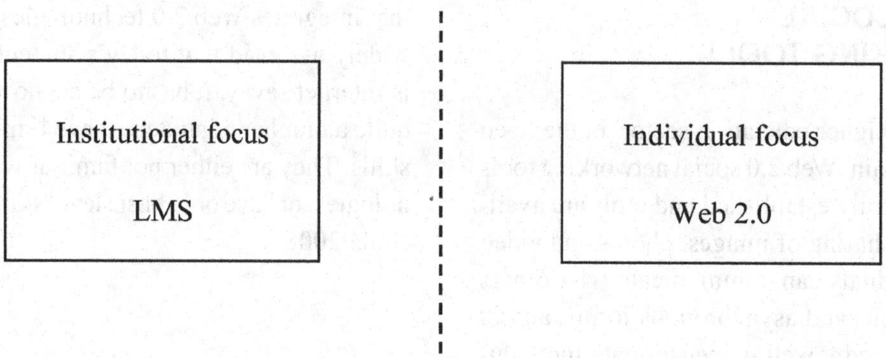

is focused on and guided by learners themselves (Schuetze & Casey, 2006). Over recent years the skills that provide lifelong learning ability have been identified. They include problem solving, critical thinking, utilizing technology, and information literacy; working with others in teams, communication skills, leadership and social interaction skills; self-management; collecting, analyzing and organizing information; planning and organizing activities; cultural awareness and understanding (Brooks & Everett, 2008; Heinrich, Bhattacharya & Rayudu, 2007; Otala, 1997; Pitman & Broomhall, 2009).

The concepts of 'lifelong', 'life-wide' and 'self-directed' learning carry significant implications. In the widest sense 'lifelong' implies the full life span of an individual. The higher education institutions should provide lifelong learning support covering the formal years of study, without withdrawing access during non-semester or interruption-of-study times if we are serious about life-long learning. Life-wide learning implies that learning is not restricted to formal university study. Personal and professional development occurs in many contexts. A lifelong learning environment needs to acknowledge this and allow learners to record and reflect on experiences from all these contexts. For the higher education institution this may mean re-evaluating access and the scope of the virtual learning environment provided. The need for learning does not stop with degree completion. Graduates have to be equipped with the skills for ongoing personal and professional development, which requires the ability to learn self-directed. While higher education institutions should provide assistance and guidance for learning, there is the need to nurture independence and self-sufficiency.

The importance of these lifelong learning skills in addition to academic and subject knowledge has found increasing emphasis in the workplace and public policy over the last decade (Morgan-Klein & Osborne, 2007; Sutherland & Crowther, 2006). Individuals today need to continue to update and upgrade their skills and knowledge, even after

completing formal education, in order keep pace with an ever changing world. Otala states that the flexibility and adaptability required to adjust to these rapid changes are gained through "better developed learning skills and the right attitudes that help individuals quickly and easily learn new things" (1997, p. 456). Current students need to "possess something more than skills which grow obsolete as technology advances" (Field & Leicester, 2003, p. 195).

Higher education institutions have responded to the need for lifelong learning skills by defining their own strategies to promote lifelong learning. Many institutions in Europe, the United States, Australia and New Zealand now explicitly express the lifelong learning characteristics they strive for in their graduates (Scanlon, 2006). Australian universities, such as Curtin University, have made policy declarations committing to graduate attributes across their programmes (Curtin University, 2006). The College of Sciences of Massey University has formulated a draft lifelong learning policy (Massey University, 2008) that expresses values, support and expectations in regards to lifelong learning. Graduate profiles, naming lifelong learning skills such as critical thinking, effective communication, teamwork and leadership have been established for many degree programmes (Davies & LeMahieu, 2003; McAlister & Alexander, 2003). The accreditation criteria for engineering degrees now refer to and demand soft skills (Aller et al., 2005; Muffo, 2001). The need for a holistic education and the development of students beyond technical competency is requested (Brakke & Brown, 2002; Davies & LeMahieu, 2003; Dowling, 2006; Fallows, 2003; Grabowski, 2004; Hernon, 2006).

In order to enact policy academics need to incorporate development opportunities for these skills into their teaching and learning designs. While individual academics succeed in doing so by using techniques such as group work, reflective journals and authentic assessment (Clarke, 2003; Lombardi, 2008), the sector is far from achieving the required levels of lifelong learning skills in its graduates. We see the following reasons for this.

While graduate profiles express graduate attributes and lifelong learning skills, the individual courses making up the degrees have not been adjusted accordingly. One consequence of this is that students are not presented with a coherent picture across their courses and that it is too easy to disregard the messages given in single courses. In our observations, some academics may lack awareness, skills and support to fully incorporate the development of lifelong learning skills into their teaching. Academics who do not consciously practice their own lifelong learning skills development will find it difficult to lead and to inspire their students. Yet, students need guidance in developing lifelong learning skills, both to recognise their importance and to acquire the knowledge 'how to' study. The currently dominant academic systems are in conflict with the characteristics of lifelong learning skills. The academic system is assessment-driven and focuses on course content and duration. On the contrary, lifelong learning needs to be self-directed, life-wide and lifelong.

Following from these discussions on lifelong learning and higher education we want to emphasise three key points: the importance of lifelong learning skills is more and more recognised; higher education institutions are attempting to promote and support lifelong learning; at this stage, lifelong learning support provided in higher education is not sufficient.

In the next section we intend to explore the connections between social virtual spaces and learning in higher education.

SOCIAL VIRTUAL LEARNING SPACES IN HIGHER EDUCATION

Previously we have suggested that social learning spaces and Web 2.0 virtual environments offer promise for lifelong learning. They provide learners with opportunities of collecting and organizing various pieces of their work, showcasing and sharing it with others, reflecting and getting feedback (Barrett, 2009).

Yet, from our deliberations on the relationship of higher education to Web 2.0 we can also see that the gap between these two environments is wide and not easily bridged. To give an example: an integrated application using the Facebook social networking platform was included into the Blackboard Learn software. Blackboard Inc. believed that such an approach would enable students to stay connected, not only inside their classroom, but also outside (Blackboard Inc., 2009). However, reviewing users' feedback on the Web (as can be found by searching for the keywords 'Blackboard', 'Facebook' and 'integration') shows that this integration approach was not accepted by the learner community. Users were concerned about application security and the privacy of information stored in this social networking environment. A number of students hesitated conducting their social communication in such close proximity to their classroom work.

Based on the considerations we have outlined we see the need for a virtual space that meets several requirements to facilitate the development of lifelong learning skills. It has to be integrated within higher education institutions and accepted by student learners. The space has to bridge institutional and personal learning.

The virtual space has to be safe, secure and have long-term accessibility to the students. It should also facilitate both formal and informal learning and allow for social networking and for collaboration. Such space needs to put students in charge of their learning and offer them privacy for exploration. It should allow students to continue learning informally even when they complete their formal courses (and lose access to the LMS artefacts). This space has to provide a long-term accessible, safe repository for storing artefacts demonstrating achievements. It needs to be a 'professional' space that remains uncluttered from purely social communication. Taking into account all the requirements mentioned above, we suggest drawing on 'institutional' ePortfolio systems for providing such a virtual space. To justify this suggestion we use the next sections of this chapter to introduce portfolios and ePortfolio systems in general before focusing on the characteristics of institutional ePortfolio systems.

ePORTFOLIOS AS STUDENT-FOCUSED VIRTUAL LEARNING SPACES

To develop our arguments for using ePortfolios as student-focused virtual learning spaces we introduce the key ideas behind 'portfolios' and outline the common features of ePortfolio systems. We then describe characteristics of 'institutional' ePortfolio systems and give examples of how ePortfolios are currently being used in further and higher education and for personal development in learning contexts. We then examine how ePortfolios should be introduced into a higher education context.

Portfolios and ePortfolio systems have a strong history in the arts and in professional areas such as nursing, engineering and teaching, where they play an important role in professional registration. We acknowledge the importance of portfolio use in these areas, but focus our deliberations on the higher education sector and the support of students.

CHARACTERISTICS OF PORTFOLIOS AND ePORTFOLIO SYSTEMS

The term portfolio is used in many different ways. One important distinction can be made along the lines of purpose of a portfolio, namely for development, showcase, assessment or competences. Development portfolios or repositories support the learning and development of a learner and contain material and artefacts related to learning, reflections and feedback. It is important that the material stored in these repositories is private to the learner. It is up to the learner to decide when and what to share with whom. The learner needs to reflect on the material collected and on his/her development in relationship to criteria or skills. The giving and receiving of feedback are important aspects of the learning processes around development portfolios. Showcase or presentation portfolios allow the learner to present their work and development to others. These presentations contain reflection and supporting evidence. They are composed for a specific purpose and audience, e.g. an assessment committee or a potential employer.

Portfolios are often linked to assessment including subject specific work, reflections, lifelong learning skills, or presentations. The type of portfolio and type of assessment have to be carefully adjusted to each other. Development portfolios are suited to a formative assessment approach where the learner documents work on a task and reflections and the assessor provides feedback that assists the learner in future development. Showcase portfolios can be linked to summative assessment where the work of the learner is assessed according to predefined criteria.

Portfolios for competences combine elements of both development and showcase portfolios and are, to a certain degree, linked to assessment. In professional areas, like health services, teacher education or engineering, the accreditation of graduates and the continuing accreditation of professionals are often linked to the demonstration of competencies. Portfolios have proven to be excellent tools for this process. The candidate collects evidence, reflects on their practice and might invite feedback, all processes covered by portfolio approaches. The accreditation occurs based on the information provided in the portfolio.

Despite these variations there are several key processes included in most if not all portfolio work, as is displayed in Figure 3.

While portfolio work can be conducted without the help of electronic systems, such systems assist with many tasks around document collection, recording of information, sorting through data and communicating with others. Many systems, from general Web tools to specialised applications, can be used to support portfolio work. A comprehensive overview can be found at Helen Barrett's ePortfolio site (Barrett, 2008). In our chapter we concentrate on systems specialised for portfolio work.

ePortfolio systems focus on the individual as they provide the individual with a space for storing documents of any electronic format. In this space the user creates a repository of artefacts related to all aspects of their learning and professional development. There are tools for reflection, commonly in the form of blogs. In contrast to open Web 2.0 systems, access to both files and reflections is by default set to the individual. There is no hierarchy between users in which one higher-level user could see the work of a lower-level user. The individual can select to share their work with others and has full control over sharing and the period of time it is accessible by others. ePortfolio systems also provide tools for constructing presentations that combine artefacts and reflections and that can be shared with others. The systems allow each individual to form groups and identify partners

for exchange. To a varying degree the ePortfolio systems incorporate guidance towards reflection and self-directed learning. ePortfolio systems provide a set of features that in combination are well suited to support lifelong learning. Each of the individual features can be found in other computer systems or Web 2.0, but their combination within one system makes ePortfolios systems extremely valuable.

CHARACTERISTICS OF INSTITUTIONAL ePORTFOLIO SYSTEMS

The types of tasks that need to be supported in portfolio work and the long-term nature of engagement lead us to four parameters for discussing ePortfolio systems. The first parameter involves web-based versus stand-alone applications. The vast majority of ePortfolio systems are web-based which facilitates access to documents independent of physical storage location and opens up possibilities for communication with others. The opportunities are not existent with stand-alone applications.

Our second parameter looks at the composition of ePortfolio community. A key feature of portfolio work is the interchange with others.

Figure 3. Key processes in portfolio work

Collection	Collect artefacts related to one's learning
Selection	Select material that best displays certain characteristics
Reflection	Reflect on learning in the context of learning goals and link reflections to selected artefacts
Planning	Plan new learning steps in response to reflections
Feedback	Invite others to give feedback on any of the previous steps and take this feedback into consideration

The technical setup of an ePortfolio system and the policies around its use determine the potential community for interchange. This can mean completely open access or access restricted to certain groups of users.

The need for provision of system services provides the third parameter. The long-term value of any computer system is closely linked to the maintenance and support of the system. Tasks included are system upgrades, monitoring of security, conducting backups, performing technical maintenance and giving technical support.

Our fourth parameter examines system ownership. The owner of a system decides on the nature of access to the system, including who can participate, the duration of this participation and who carries the costs of participation. It is the role of the owner to provide the system services. The conduct of the system owner is critical for system acceptance.

Based on these parameters we can characterise institutional ePortfolio systems. Such systems are web-based. They are owned by an institution, in our context an educational institution which provides the system services. The ePortfolio community is formed by members that are students and staff of the institution. Well-known examples of such institutional ePortfolio systems are Mahara (http://mahara.org/) and Pebblepad (http://www.pebblepad.co.uk/). The work undertaken at the Queensland University of Technology in Australia provides an excellent example of employing an institutional ePortfolio system for institution-wide support of lifelong learning (http://www.studenteportfolio.qut.edu.au/).

In the context of system ownership we want to briefly mention an alternate approach that is being followed in New Zealand, with the establishment of the MyPortfolio service (http://myportfolio.ac.nz/). Here, the Mahara ePortfolio system is maintained by a commercial company that provides an ePortfolio service to the whole tertiary sector of New Zealand. There are a number of potential advantages to this approach

as the community of learners is not restricted to one institution as learners can continue to use the same learning environment when moving between institutions. The learner can feel more comfortable in their life-wide- learning as the learning environment is not being controlled by one institution (Heinrich, 2008). This alternate ownership approach could be promising for the provision of student-focused virtual learning spaces and will require more comprehensive discussion and the establishment of appropriate policy frameworks on a national level.

EXAMPLES OF ePORTFOLIO USE IN FURTHER AND HIGHER EDUCATION

To illustrate the application of ePortfolios we proceed with introducing examples of ePortfolio use in further and higher education from the UK context. The UK has a strong tradition in personal development planning, progress files and competence development. Since the 1990s projects have been undertaken to investigate the use of information and communication technologies to support these traditions. This has led to projects at all levels of the education system, in transition from secondary to further and tertiary education, in competence development, especially in the health and medical areas and in teacher development.

PERSONAL DEVELOPMENT PLANNING (PDP) AND PROGRESS FILES

The University of Newcastle has been a centre of activity in the areas of PDP and progress files since the 1990s. In the first EPICS project (Newcastle University, 2007) several universities, further education colleges and regional authorities combined to investigate the implementation of a region-wide infrastructure for the transfer of progress files, ePortfolios and PDP information among stakeholders. Information available from the EPICS project and related websites (University of Leeds, 2008b) indicate that there is an active community in the UK who are using ePortfolio and related electronic systems for supporting progress files and PDP. The PADSHE project (University of Nottingham, 2005) describe a range of activities conducted at the University of Nottingham in the areas of progress files and the use of web technologies for electronic Personal and Academic Records (ePARs). In the ISLE project (ISLE, 2005) ten universities and colleges worked together towards an ePortfolio supported approach to PDP. ePortfolios are employed to provide structure and support to the individual.

PERSONALISED LEARNING

The EPICS-2 project (Newcastle University, 2009) is investigating the use of ePortfolio systems and Web2.0 technologies for supporting personalised learning pathways in under- and postgraduate education. In the MOSEP project (MOSEP, 2006) a European grouping of tertiary institutions with UK participation is working on the use of ePortfolios to support adolescent learners and their advisors in the transition phase into upper secondary education or vocational training. With the help of ePortfolios the learning is personalised which should lead to greater motivation and empowerment.

ADMISSION PROCESSES, TRANSITION, CROSS-INSTITUTIONAL LEARNING

The DELIA project (Centre for International ePortfolio Development, 2007) is investigating the use of ePortfolios for presenting admission information and therefore allowing consideration of much richer applicant data. The Enhancing

Learner Progression Project, eLP, at the School of Medicine at the University of Leeds (2008a) uses ePortfolios at key stages in student transmission. Students, who are competing for entry into the medical programmes, are provided with career information, advice and guidance to assist with the admission process. The students complete exercises and are provided with feedback from medical staff and career advisors. In the JOSEPH (Centre for International ePortfolio Development, 2006) project several colleges work together on exploring the use of ePortfolio approaches for facilitating the transition from vocational to higher education in context of the 14-19 diploma in engineering. This project includes the use of ePortfolios as one platform for recording learning that takes place at multiple institutions or workplaces.

EMPLOYABILITY, SELF-DIRECTED LEARNING

The context for the eReturn project (JISC, 2009) is the return into the workforce after a career break. It investigated how ePortfolios can assist the sharing of information on personal and professional development planning between job seekers, educators, advisors and employers. Projects like the ones by the City of Nottingham (Passportfolio, 2008) or by Careers Wales (Careers Wales Association, 2006) provide citizens with an electronic environment to reflect on their skills and to record information online. Guidance on career options and learning choices and assistance in preparing for job applications is provided. Access to such systems for all citizens, regardless of employment and education status, facilitates social inclusion.

LIFELONG AND LIFE-WIDE LEARNING

The RIPPLL project (JISC, 2006) has investigated support for lifelong learning by investigating the transfer of progress files and personal development planning data from further to higher education and between study and employment. In various regions of the UK Lifelong Learning Networks have been established (see Higher Education Funding Council for England, 2009) for an overview and University of Leicester (2007) for an example of a regional network). These networks target areas of regional need. They assist individuals in making the transition from further education, vocational courses or work into higher education by helping them to recognise and present their skills and mapping out a learning pathway. The EAQUALS-ALTE Portfolio Project on European language portfolios (Association of Language Testers in Europe, 2005) provides an example of UK involvement on a European level. The advantages of electronic versions instead of paper portfolios provide access to a full range of character sets, privacy protection and histories of learning. One aspect of the European language portfolio is the deliberate inclusion of language and cultural proficiencies that have been developed outside formal learning situations.

INTRODUCING PORTFOLIOS AND ePORTFOLIO SYSTEMS INTO A HIGHER EDUCATION CONTEXT

The introduction of any e-learning environment requires careful planning and institutional support (Kenny, 2002). The same is true for the introduction of portfolio or ePortfolio programmes. Issues such as faculty buy-in, policy development, resourcing, software selection and intellectual property ownership need to be resolved for successful programmes (Schwartz, 2006). Of particular importance are the challenges faculty are facing with implementation. One danger related to the introduction of new programmes or teaching methods is that discussions are often confined to working parties and advisory groups while individual academics are tasked with the implementation. These academics are often concerned about the impact on curriculum content and their own ability to facilitate learning via the new methods (Fallows, 2003).

The motivation for the introduction of portfolios stems from the new emphasis on lifelong learning skills and the suitability of portfolios in nurturing these skills. Academics must find ways to effectively integrate the new learning outcomes into courses. They must shift their focus from providing input via lecturing to giving feedback to facilitate learning (Bouslama et al., 2003). Part of the new role of academics is to coach students towards reflection. Students are initially not aware of the valuable learning processes that are occurring. They need to be prompted to reflect and need to be taught to recognize and value not just formal but informal learning as well (Guest, 2006). Students must be made aware of the opportunities that lie in the development of personal and transferable skills, as they otherwise do not appreciate the importance of these skills (Overton, 2003).

USING INSTITUTIONAL ePORTFOLIO SYSTEMS TO PROVIDE STUDENT-FOCUSED VIRTUAL LEARNING SPACES

Lifelong learning skills are of critical importance for today's graduates and higher education institutions have recognised the need to facilitate such skill development. Portfolio thinking and ePortfolio systems are well suited to the development of lifelong learning skills. Learning management systems (LMS), as the dominant e-learning tools in higher education institutions, do not provide the best context for lifelong learning. Web 2.0 tools provide elements of what is needed to support lifelong learning but are dominated by social use.

Based on these arguments we propose the use of institutional ePortfolio systems for supporting lifelong learning skills development in a higher education context. Such systems can fill the gap between the institutional focus of an LMS and the social networking world of Web 2.0 (see Figure 4). In combination, the three approaches will lead us towards Personal Learning Environments.

Referring back to our system parameters, the following aspects are important. The student must have long-term access to the ePortfolio system. While this access is likely to be linked to enrolment at the institution it should be independent of enrolment in individual courses. Access has to be continuous, covering breaks between study years. The student should be seen as member of the institution's community. At the end of the association with the institution the student must be allowed to retain access to their ePortfolio data, either within the same ePortfolio system as a member of the alumni of the institution, or by exporting their data to a comparable system of their choice. Throughout their association with the ePortfolio system the student must have ownership of their data stored in the system. The privacy of all data stored in the ePortfolio system must be guaranteed. In particular, no-one in charge of courses or teaching should have access to any of the material in the ePortfolio system unless explicitly authorised by the student. Besides these system parameters many other factors need to be

considered for a successful adoption of institutional ePortfolio systems as student-focused virtual learning systems which we will examine in the next section.

SUCCESS FACTORS FOR STUDENT-FOCUSED VIRTUAL LEARNING SPACES

In the previous sections of this chapter we have created an argument for using ePortfolio systems in an institutional context to support the lifelong learning of students. The introduction of student-focused virtual learning spaces into higher education will require a major culture shift in higher education institutions. To succeed all stakeholders involved will have to overcome challenges:

- Policy makers: The responsibility of academics in terms of facilitating the development of lifelong learning skills has to be clearly defined and related workload issues have to be addressed.
- Programme committees: Programme committees have to recognise the nature of lifelong learning skills which stretch course and even degree boundaries. Development opportunities for these skills have to be planned on programme level and the extent and nature of assessment has to be decided on.

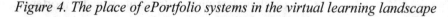

Figure 4. The place of ePortfolio systems in the virtual learning landscape

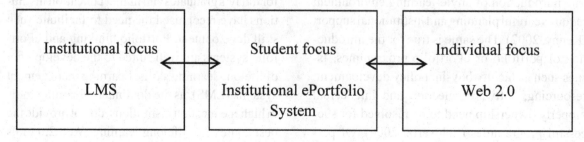

Institutional focus	Student focus	Individual focus
LMS	Institutional ePortfolio System	Web 2.0

- Academics: Academics have to take on board the directives of their programme committees and have to integrate development opportunities into their teaching. Further, academics should model lifelong learning in their own practice, for example, by maintaining teaching portfolios and by communicating their own teaching reflections to students and colleagues.

- Learning support: Learning support sections have to support lecturers in the pedagogy of ePortfolio work and have to guide students in the use of the system.

- Institutional IT sections: The provision of ePortfolio access can mean less control over access and content as compared to the currently used LMS. The duration of access can stretch beyond the immediate student enrolment. To use the full potential in sharing and feedback 'outsiders', such as industry advisors, have to be given system access. The appropriate level of technical support has to be provided, both to students and staff.

- Students: Students need to take charge of their own learning and development. They need to move away from being pushed along by assessment. They need to widen their horizons from a short-term assessment view towards a longer-term development view.

- Employers and professional groupings: These groups are required on two fronts. First, they need to make it clear what skills they require from future employees to provide students with guidance for their learning. Second, they need to be prepared to accompany students during their time at higher education institutions by providing ongoing feedback.

CONCLUSION

In this chapter we have explored and contrasted various virtual spaces. We have examined institutional learning spaces such as learning management systems that dominate e-learning in higher education. We have also explored the virtual social networking spaces provided by Web 2.0 tools. Finally, we have examined ePortfolio systems and have defined the characteristics of institutional ePortfolio systems. Guided by the explorations of these virtual spaces and systems, we have suggested making institutional ePortfolio systems an integral part of the systems provided by higher education institutions, providing student-focused virtual learning spaces. To motivate our arguments we have examined the characteristics of lifelong learning and have made the link to ePortfolios, showing how these can facilitate the development of lifelong learning skills. We have looked at examples from the education sector to demonstrate what efforts are already undertaken in regards to lifelong learning and ePortfolio approaches.

We acknowledge that the provision of student-focused virtual learning spaces with ePortfolio systems in higher education institutions will only be a first step. The successful adoption of these spaces for lifelong, life-wide and self-directed learning will require changes across institutional structures and stakeholders. Our current degree and assessment structures are in many ways counterproductive to lifelong learning efforts. Academics need to learn how to guide students in different ways and would best lead by example, practicing and showcasing their own lifelong learning efforts. Maybe most importantly, we need to inspire students to see the value of investing their energy into the development of their lifelong learning skills.

REFERENCES

Aller, B. M., Kline, A. A., Tsang, E., Aravamuthan, R., Rasmusson, A. C., & Phillips, C. (2005). WeBAL: A Web-based assessment library to enhance teaching and learning in engineering. *IEEE Transactions on Education, 48*(4), 764–771. doi:10.1109/TE.2005.858390

Ashling, J. (2007). Transforming research communication. *Information Today, 24*(5), 29–30.

Association of Language Testers in Europe. (2005). *EAQUALS-ALTE Portfolio Project*. Retrieved Novemver 13, 2009, from http://www.eelp.org/eportfolio/index.html

Barret, H. (2008). *Categories of ePortfolio tools*. Retrieved November 13, 2009, from http://electronicportfolios.com/categories.html

Barrett, H. (2009). *Researching lifelong ePortfolios and Web 2.0*. Retrieved April 26, 2010 from http://electronicportfolios.org.

Blackboard Inc. (2009). *Blackboard release 9*. Retrieved September 6, 2009, from http://www.blackboard.com/Release9/Release-9/What-is-New-in-9/Facebook.aspx

Boulos, M. N. K., & Wheeler, S. (2007). The emerging Web 2.0 social software: An enabling suite of sociable technologies in health and health care education. *Health Information and Libraries Journal, 24*(1), 2–23. doi:10.1111/j.1471-1842.2007.00701.x

Bouslama, F., Lansari, A., Al-Rawi, A., & Abonamah, A. A. (2003). A novel outcome-based educational model and its effect on student learning, curriculum development, and assessment. *Journal of Information Technology Education, 2*, 203–214.

Brakke, D. F., & Brown, D. T. (2002). Assessment to improve student learning. In Narum, J. L., & Conover, K. (Eds.), *Building robust learning environments in undergraduate science, technology, engineering, and mathematics: New directions for higher education* (pp. 119–122). San Francisco, CA: Jossey-Bass.

Brooks, R., & Everett, G. (2008). The impact of higher education on lifelong learning. *International Journal of Lifelong Education, 27*(3), 239–254. doi:10.1080/02601370802047759

Browne, T., Jenkins, M., & Walker, R. (2006). A longitudinal perspective regarding the use of VLEs by higher education institutions in the United Kingdom. *Interactive Learning Environments, 14*(2), 177–192. doi:10.1080/10494820600852795

Capell, K. (2006). Europe's politicians embrace Web 2.0. *BusinessWeek Online*. Retrieved 24 October, 2006, from http://www.businessweek.com/bwdaily/dnflash/content/oct2006/db20061024_653130.htm

Careers Wales Association. (2006). *E-progress file project*. Retrieved November 13, 2009, from http://www2.careerswales.com/progressfile/

Centre for International ePortfolio Development. (2006). *Joining up organisations supporting engineering pathways into higher education*. Retrieved November 13, 2009, from http://www.nottingham.ac.uk/eportfolio/JOSEPH/

Centre for International ePortfolio Development. (2007). *DELIA*. Retrieved November 13, 2009, from http://www.nottingham.ac.uk/eportfolio/delia/

Churchill, D. (2009). Educational applications of Web 2.0: Using blogs to support teaching and learning. *British Journal of Educational Technology, 40*(1), 179–183. doi:10.1111/j.1467-8535.2008.00865.x

Clarke, M. (2003). *The reflective journal: Implications for professional learning*. Paper presented at the NZARE/AARE Conference, Auckland, New Zealand.

Collis, B., & De Boer, W. (2004). E-learning by design. *Teachers as learners: Embedded tools for implementing a CMS, 48*(6), 7-12.

Curtin University. (2006). *Graduate attributes policy* Retrieved September 7, 2009, from http://policies.curtin.edu.au/policies/teachingandlearning.cfm

Davies, A., & LeMahieu, P. (2003). Reconsidering portfolios and research evidence. In Segers, M., Dochy, F., & Cascallar, E. (Eds.), *Optimising new modes of assessment: In search of qualities and standards* (pp. 141–170). Dordrecht, The Netherlands/ Boston, MA/ London, UK: Kluwer Academic Publishers. doi:10.1007/0-306-48125-1_7

Dowling, D. (2006). Designing a competency based program to facilitate the progression of experienced engineering technologists to professional engineer status. *European Journal of Engineering Education, 31*(1), 95–107. doi:10.1080/03043790500429542

European Commission. (2000). *A memorandum on lifelong learning*. Retrieved April 20, 2009, from http://www.bologna-berlin2003.de/pdf/MemorandumEng.pdf

Fallows, S. (2003). Teaching and learning for student skill development. In H. Fry, S. Ketteridge, & S. Marshall (Eds.). *A handbook for teaching and learning in higher education: Enhancing academic practice* (2nd ed.) (pp. 121-133). London, UK & Sterling, VA: Kogan Page.

Field, J., & Leicester, M. (2003). *Lifelong learning: Education across the lifespan*. London: UK RoutledgeFalmer.

Grabowski, U. (2004). Erfolgsfaktor persönlichkeit: Anforderungen an eine ganzheitliche ingenieurausbildung. *Global Journal of Engineering Education, 8*(3), 269–274.

Guest, G. (2006). Lifelong learning for engineers: A global perspective. *European Journal of Engineering Education, 31*(3), 273–281. doi:10.1080/03043790600644396

Havenstein, H. (2007). Customers courted with Web 2.0. *Computerworld, 41*(8), 1–36.

Heinrich, E. (2008, July 1-4). *Supporting continuous improvement in teaching development through electronic teaching portfolios*. Paper presented at the 31st HERDSA Annual Conference, Rotorua, New Zealand.

Heinrich, E., Bhattacharya, M., & Rayudu, R. (2007). Preparation for lifelong learning using ePortfolios. *European Journal of Engineering Education, 32*(6), 653–663. doi:10.1080/03043790701520602

Hernon, P. (2006). Methods of data collection. In Hernon, P., Dugan, R. E., & Schwartz, C. (Eds.), *Revisiting outcomes assessment in higher education* (pp. 135–150). Westport, CT & London, UK: Libraries Unlimited.

Higher Education Funding Council for England. (2009). *Lifelong learning networks*. Retrieved November 13, 2009, from http://www.hefce.ac.uk/widen/lln/

Holahan, C. (2006). Fantasy football 2.0. *BusinessWeek Online*, p. 6. Retrieved November 11, 2009, from http://www.businessweek.com/technology/content/sep2006/tc20060901_880554.htm

Holahan, C. (2007). Close harmony: Bands and Web 2.0. *BusinessWeek Online*, p. 10 Retrieved November 11, 2009, from http://www.businessweek.com/technology/content/mar2007/tc20070326_958216.htm

ISLE. (2005). *Individualised support for learning through e-Portfolios*. Retrieved November 13, 2009, from http://isle.paisley.ac.uk/default.aspx

Jarvis, P. (2004). From adult education to lifelong learning: A conceptual framework. In Jarvis, P. (Ed.), *Adult education and lifelong learning: Theory and practice* (pp. 39–65). London, UK & New York, NY: Routledge Falmer.

JISC. (2006). *Regional interoperability project on progression for lifelong learning*. Retrieved November 13, 2009, from http://www.nottingham.ac.uk/rippll/

JISC. (2009). *E-return*. Retrieved November 13, 2009, from http://www.jisc.ac.uk/whatwedo/programmes/elearningcapital/xinstit2/ereturn

Katz, R. (2005). Foreword: Growing up digital. In J. B. Caruso & R. Kvavik (Eds.), *ECAR study of students and information technology, 2005: Convenience, connection, control, and learning* (pp 5-8). EDUCAusE. Retrieved November 11, 2009, from http://net.educause.edu/ir/library/pdf/ers0506/rs/ERS0506w.pdf

Kennedy, G. E., Judd, T. S., Churchward, A., Gray, K., & Krause, K.-L. (2008). First year students' experiences with technology: Are they really digital natives? *Australian Journal of Educational Technology, 24*(1), 108–122.

Kenny, J. (2002). Managing innovation in educational institutions. *Australian Journal of Educational Technology, 18*(3), 359–376.

Knapper, C. K., & Cropley, A. J. (2000). *Lifelong learning in higher education* (3rd ed.). London, UK: Kogan Page.

Lombardi, M. M. (2008). *Making the grade: The role of assessment in authentic learning*. Retrieved April 26, 2010, from http://net.educause.edu/ir/library/pdf/ELI3019.pdf

Longworth, N. (2003). *Lifelong learning in action: Transforming education in the 21st century. London, UK & Sterling*. VA: Kogan Page.

MacMillan, D. (2007). Family trees 2.0. *Business-Week Online*, p. 23 Retrieved November 11, 2009, from http://www.businessweek.com/technology/content/jun2007/tc20070617_133514.htm

Massey University. (2008). *Lifelong learning policy*. Retrieved November 13, 2009, from http://science.massey.ac.nz/eportfolios/lllPolicy.asp

McAlister, G., & Alexander, S. (2003). Key aspects of teaching and learning in information and computer sciences. In H. Fry, S. Ketteridge, & S. Marshall (Eds.), *A handbook for teaching and learning in higher education: Enhancing academic practice* (2nd ed.) (pp. 278-300). London, UK & Sterling, VA: Kogan Page.

Morgan-Klein, B., & Osborne, M. (2007). *The concepts and practices of lifelong learning*. London, UK & New York, NY: Routledge.

MOSEP. (2006). *More self esteem with my e-Portfolio*. Retrieved November 13, 2009, from http://www.mosep.org

Muffo, J. A. (2001). Assessing student competence in engineering. In Palomba, C. A., & Banta, T. W. (Eds.), *Assessing student competence in accredited disciplines* (pp. 159–175). Sterling, VA: Stylus.

Newcastle University. (2007). *The first EPICS project*. Retrieved November 13, 2009, from http://www.eportfolios.ac.uk/EPICS/?pid=173

Newcastle University. (2009). *EPICS-2: North East regional collaboration for personalised, work-based, and life-long learning*. Retrieved November 13, 2009, from http://www.eportfolios.ac.uk/EPICS

OECD. (2005). E-learning in tertiary education: Where do we stand? In OECD (Ed.), *IT infrastructure: Use of learing management system (LMS) and other applications* (pp. 138-178). Paris, France: OECD Publishing.

Otala, L. (1997). Implementing lifelong learning in partnership with the educational sector and the work place. *The International Information & Library Review, 29*(3-4), 455–460. doi:10.1006/iilr.1997.0063

Overton, T. (2003). Key aspects of teaching and learning in experimental sciences and engineering. In H. Fry, S. Ketteridge, & S. Marshall (Eds.), *A handbook for teaching and learning in higher education: Enhancing academic practice* (2nd ed.) (pp. 255-277). London, UK & Sterling, VA: Kogan Page.

Passportfolio. (2008). *Passportfolio project.* Retrieved November 13, 2009, from https://www.passportfolio.com

Pitman, T., & Broomhall, S. (2009). Australian universities, generic skills and lifelong learning. *International Journal of Lifelong Education, 28*(4), 439–458. doi:10.1080/02601370903031280

Scanlon, L. (2006). Graduate attributes and the transition to higher education. In Hager, P. J., & Holland, S. (Eds.), *Graduate attributes, learning and employability* (*Vol. 6*, pp. 125–148). Netherlands: Springer. doi:10.1007/1-4020-5342-8_7

Schuetze, H. G., & Casey, C. (2006). Models and meanings of lifelong learning: Progress and barriers on the road to a learning society. *Compare: A Journal of Comparative and International Education, 36*(3), 279-287.

Schwartz, C. (2006). Managing electronic portfolios. In Hernon, P., Dugan, R. E., & Schwartz, C. (Eds.), *Revisiting outcomes assessment in higher education* (pp. 151–164). Westport, CT & London, UK: Libraries Unlimited.

Stevens, M. (2007). Social video: Videoblogging & YouTube. *Library Technology Reports, 43*(5), 52–57.

Sutherland, P., & Crowther, J. (2006). *Lifelong learning: Concepts and contexts.* London, UK & New York, NY: Routledge.

University of Leeds. (2008a). *The enhancing learner progression project.* Retrieved November 13, 2009, from http://www.leeds.ac.uk/medicine/meu/elp/index.html

University of Leeds. (2008b). *Leeds practice.* Retrieved November 13, 2009, from http://www.leeds.ac.uk/PDP/leedspractice.htm

University of Leicester. (2007). *Skills for sustainable communities lifelong learning network.* Retrieved November 13, 2009, from http://www.le.ac.uk/ssclln/

University of Nottingham. (2005). *PADSHE project.* Retrieved November 13, 2009, from http://www.nottingham.ac.uk/padshe/

Wheeler, S., Yeomans, P., & Wheeler, D. (2008). The good, the bad and the wiki: Evaluating student-generated content for collaborative learning. *British Journal of Educational Technology, 39*(6), 987–995. doi:10.1111/j.1467-8535.2007.00799.x

Chapter 9

The DEHub Virtual Learning Space:
A Niche Social Network Community of Practice

Nathan Wise
University of New England, Australia

Belinda Tynan
University of New England, Australia

ABSTRACT

Our concept of 'virtual learning spaces' is changing, as are the practices that are adopted within these spaces. To understand these changes, this chapter will provide an exploration of the conceptualisation and creation of an interactive, online, social network community of practice. The case that will be used is based around the Distance Education Hub (DEHub) which is both virtual and physical. DEHub is in the simultaneous process of constructing and facilitating a virtual space to support and encourage both knowledge dissemination and knowledge creation. The DEHub space focuses on learning as a co-operative, constructive, and dynamic process involving engaged communities of scholars, learners and practitioners. It will tackle the question of why this virtual learning space is defined as a niche social network and how this impacts on the conceptualisation and consequent development of virtual spaces — in this instance, co-development by the community. Finally, it will demonstrate through this analysis how changing concepts of 'virtual learning spaces' are put into practice through 'virtual space' design and development for creating and supporting niche social networks.

INTRODUCTION

Annette Lorensten (in Bernath et al., 2009) briefly noted, "the two most promising new learning contexts to replace the traditional classroom setting seem to be virtual learning spaces and situated learning in learning communities where learning and work are combined and intertwined" (p.60). This chapter focuses specifically upon our understanding of 'virtual learning spaces' and the practices adopted within these spaces through an exploration of the conceptualisation and creation

DOI: 10.4018/978-1-60960-114-0.ch009

of an interactive, social network, research community of practice. The case that will be used is based around the Distance Education Hub (DEHub) which is both virtual and physical. Through an exploration of the structure and purpose of the DEHub space (DEHub, 2010), this chapter will uncover issues surrounding 'engagement' and the 'relevance' of virtual spaces situated against the theoretical knowledge base around communities of practice and the co-generation of knowledge. Through an analysis of the DEHub space this chapter will uncover contemporary practices surrounding the design and development of online spaces. It will reveal considerations that take place in facilitating the creation and ongoing support of a sense of 'value' amongst participating community members and provide insight into the decisions that are made to ensure practical application of such spaces. The work presented here does not aim, nor is there space, to address in detail criticisms of virtual spaces in the contexts of the use of personal learning tools such as blogs, wikis or repositories and no doubt others in this book have done so. Nor is a full exploration of the substantive literature around repositories presented. Rather the case presented here uses that work as the starting point and attempts to locate the development of the DEHub 'virtual' social niche network from the view of relevance and purpose.

Background

One of DEHub's primary starting goals was to establish a central agency for the provision of best practices in distance education for the Australian higher education sector. There was a need to bring practitioners together to reduce overlap and duplication, identify common goals/objectives, work together cooperatively and collaboratively to aggregate research and address these issues, and then disseminate their findings to a national and international audience who may be able to draw lessons and implement practical changes relevant to their environment. The delivery of

these findings, originally conceived along the lines of a 'clearinghouse' model, was later developed to a vision whereby visitors would personally contribute their experiences, theories, and arguments and thus contribute to the development of knowledge through a virtual community. The term 'virtual learning space' is hereafter used to distinguish the broad, multi-faceted design of the DEHub space apart from 'virtual learning environments', or VLEs. VLEs are often fixed systems with finite boundaries and structures, whereas the DEHub space incorporates a range of different environments within a borderless, highly dynamic and undefined 'space', as explained in more detail further below.

The innovative design of the DEHub space sought to address some of the primary concerns surrounding pedagogical practice in distance education environments, in particular, skill development surrounding technological innovation, workloads in e-learning spaces, and the construction of online communities ('of practice' and 'of learning'). Today's rapidly changing educational environments, and the knowledge and skills needed to maintain these environments, have been well documented by the pedagogical literature. Teghe and Knight (2004, p. 152) argued that institutions must remain up to date with technological advances if they are to remain competitive. In addition, there is also pressure to provide students, whatever their course of study, with the additional skills needed for employment (Leitch, 2006, pp. 3-4). More recently Tynan, Lee and Barnes (2008) suggested that, on an individual level, instructors must maintain an advanced level of knowledge and be "on the new wave" if they are to meet the new challenges (p. 3560). There are ample examples in the literature which describe professional development approaches but as Collom, Dallas, Jong and Obexer (2002) observed in their analysis of existing practice, most development was reactive, non-flexible, piecemeal and poorly targeted academic development programmes which were constrained by the client base with competing interests in the delivery of flexible learning. As the virtual space we have chosen is 'open' it is an aim to target the specific interest of a community and at the same time in their participation, they engage in the use of technologies that may be relevant to their teaching as well as their research. It is hoped that through participation individuals will also be learners.

DEHub commenced activities in February 2009 as a research consortium between the University of New England (UNE), Charles Sturt University (CSU), Central Queensland University (CQUniversity), and the University of Southern Queensland (USQ); Massey University (based in New Zealand) later joined as a fifth partner. DEHub's physical presence stretches across the consortia. Central offices, hosting about a dozen academic and general staff on a mixed full-time, part-time and casual basis, are based at the University of New England, but the research network consists of representatives and academics from all five partners. In terms of a virtual presence, from the outset DEHub sought to provide a space that would promote and facilitate what Lombardo (2007) described as 'the desire for *adventure and change*' amongst practitioners engaged in distance education. Thus, a key priority in this design was the need for a community-driven space where review, feedback and support were ongoing processes. Conceptualisation of this space gave recognition to the epistemological debates surrounding the changing form of pedagogical knowledge and included consideration of the range of educational needs both in the Australian tertiary sector and indeed worldwide (Brownlee & Berthelsen, 2008; Schwarz, Meyer & Sharma, 2007). In 2001 a meeting of 23 international experts, organised by UNESCO and LEARNTEC, made the following recommendation on The State of Distance Education in the World:

The past need for distance education to achieve parity of esteem with the traditional schooling systems has often led to the adoption of distance education practices that are based on the same outdated assumptions that underlie those schooling systems. Now that distance education has reached its desired level of recognition and esteem vis-á-vis traditional educational alternatives, time has come for it to take a critical look at itself, asking questions about how existing experience fits in with the requirements of and opportunities inherent in present day society and how it reflects the current state of knowledge about how people learn. It is recommended that such a critical attitude drive any future development in the field of distance education in UNESCO and its Member States (UNESCO, 2001, p. 4).

Whilst it has been a number of years since this recommendation was made, there will always be a need for practitioners to ask questions of themselves, critically review their activities, and look across the broader environment to improve their understanding of how people learn (Tynan & Lee, 2009). Thus, in the early stages of the DEHub project it was decided that one of the most practical ways to assist in this 'critical review' and improve distance education practices was through the development of a virtual learning space to facilitate a dynamic, online environment that would support a combined *community of practice* and *community of learning*, both of which will be explored in more detail below.

In tune with this practical approach, the site was also designed along the DEHub project's operational priorities (*ease-of-access, ease-of-understanding,* and *ease-of-implementation*) to present a clear and fresh portal to best aid the different learning styles and research priorities of visitors within the one environment. The design of the space (see Figure 1) sought to simultaneously meet the need for a range of educational support systems and pedagogical approaches and the requirement for visitors to be able to quickly access, engage and interact in these new environments without difficulty.

The design of the DEHub virtual learning space also took into consideration the ongoing debate surrounding e-teaching workloads. Tynan *et al.* (2008) recently argued that without careful planning the changes that new technologies bring can place increased pressures on tertiary educators and, far from reducing academic workloads, can actually create further complexities as educators wrestle with new and constantly changing systems and protocols. It was with this argument in mind that the above mentioned DEHub operational priorities came about and these have since in part driven the design of the DEHub space. The design of the space envisioned an environment where interested parties could quickly and easily access relevant information, readily digest the most appropriate information relevant to their field of study, and implement any newfound knowledge into their existing work patterns and culture with minimal time-investment or disturbance. At the same time, the space was designed to support a community for those interested in investing more time. Visitors can become members of the space and thus contribute to the ever expanding body of information, as explained in more detail below.

Virtual Learning Space: A Social Network Community

Technological developments have had a profound impact on the modes of delivery of educational material. In particular, the proliferation of internet access and the integration of the internet into software developments have created a new range of 'virtual learning spaces' and a new, tech-savvy society to tap into. However, the transition to these new environments has not been smooth. Technologies are advancing at a rate faster than

Figure 1. The main DEHub website: www.dehub.edu.au

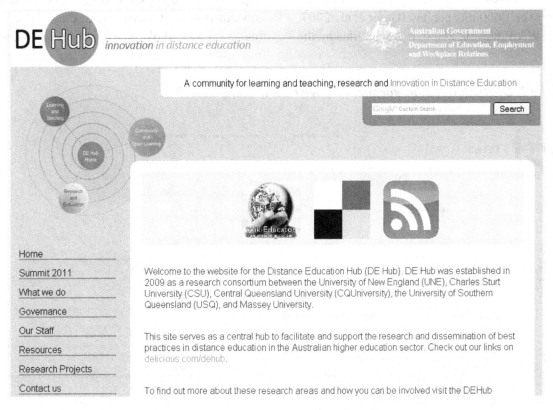

the average academic can keep up with, meaning that few are up to date with the 'latest and greatest' teaching practices associated with these technologies (Hanna 2007 in Moore, p. 503). Furthermore, as Hanna (2007, p. 503) argues, the restructuring of staff and resources around these changes adds to the complexity. As technologies change, so too do the pedagogical theories surrounding their use. Practitioners are expected to not only 'know the technology', but also know how to use the technology most effectively in their teaching. The DEHub virtual learning space presents a dynamic environment where practitioners can use technologies and engage with an online community, network with potential research partners, contribute personal experiences with teaching, and learn from the comments and experiences of others.

A core feature of the DEHub virtual learning space is the use of the WikiEducator project. The WikiEducator (WikiEducator, 2009) was established in 2006 and by September 2008 had grown to over 5,000 worldwide users, over 11,000 articles, and reportedly had an average of well over 1,000 hits per day (Geser et al., 2007, p. 4; WikiEducator, 2009). It is supported by the

Commonwealth of Learning (COL) and has a global network of active and supportive partners. The DEHub page was developed by DEHub staff and a range of practitioners across the consortia. The establishment of this node was an important step towards developing an online Australian community within WikiEducator (See Figure 2).

In seeking to address the learning needs, styles and research opportunities of anticipated participants, an early consideration in the development of the site was the need to reconsider the nature of the spaces within which the development of this community and the desired information bases could take place. This demonstration through utilisation approach enables visitors to engage in dynamic online communities and to practice with such tools as they learn about them. For example, an online visitor clicks through to the DEHub WikiEducator site from the DEHub website, reviews the information on the use of Wikis in teaching and learning, and in providing comments on the Wiki page actively practices such tools, expands the body of knowledge, and contributes towards the broader dynamic of the DEHub virtual space as a whole. The result envisioned was

Figure 2. DEHub's WikiEducator site: www.wikieducator.org/DEHub

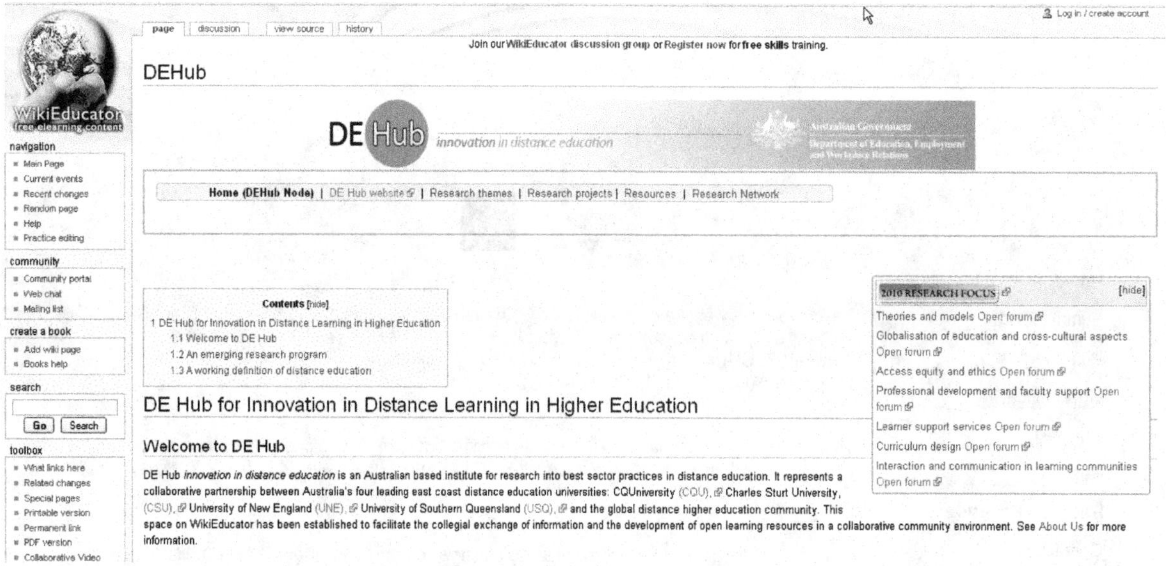

that the community of visitors/participants would develop their knowledge of best practices through direct personal practice — that is, learning by being actively involved.

In presenting information *about* technologies, *through* technologies the DEHub virtual learning space addresses several critical areas: it implements the 'best practices' in learning that it promotes (thus 'practicing what it preaches'); it provides specific practical examples of technological use within an educational environment; it presents examples of the integration of different technologies together; and it uses Web 2.0 technologies as a resource for the clear (and dual) purposes of learning and teaching and not for the purposes of using technology for technologies' sake. Perraton and Moses argued that in determining what technologies are appropriate one needs to start with the curriculum (Perraton & Moses, 2004, p. 144). In this instance DEHub is supporting the social group or those we feel will want to participate by situating the research of and about the use of technologies through the use of technology which is similar to Schwarz *et al.* (2007) who argued that the incorporation of technology using research-based pedagogies will encourage new teachers, albeit in the school sector in this example to consider their future integration into their classroom practice.

A similar theory was behind the design of the DEHub space. Through the integration of technological resources and pedagogical approaches in the DEHub virtual learning space we hope that visitors/participants will quickly gain an understanding of *what* such resources and approaches look like and *how* they can implement similar structures within their personal educational environment.

Wenger, McDermott and Synder (2007) argued that it is not enough simply to create an online environment and expect a community to develop. Within the DEHub environment it was anticipated that visitors and participants would each share the roles of 'contributor', 'learner' and 'practitioner'

— *contributing* to the debate on pedagogical approaches, *learning* from the comments and experiences of others, and *practicing* the knowledge gained from this community within a real world environment. To facilitate this, DEHub sought to introduce practitioners to WikiEducator through 'open forums'. These allow new users of Wikis to begin editing online and contributing to discussion without having to commit long periods of time.

In April 2009 DEHub began the process of constructing and facilitating a virtual space to support and encourage both knowledge *creation* and knowledge *dissemination*. Throughout conceptualisation and development the focus of the DEHub space was on learning as a cooperative, constructive and dynamic process involving engaged communities of scholars, learners and practitioners. The vision of the end design was of a space connecting individuals around the world to a central, communal hub within which ideas, theories and practices can be exchanged, reviewed and developed.

A Niche Social Network

The DEHub space seeks to bring together a broad range of diverse and differing real world experiences, both positive and negative, in the development of an online *community of practice*. As Wenger (2003) argued, "Participating in these 'communities of practice' is essential to our learning. It is at the very core of what makes us human beings capable of meaningful knowledge" (p. 80). Furthermore, Wenger adds, "By participating in these communities, we define with each other what constitutes competence in a given context" (p. 80). DEHub sought to combine the three elements that Wenger identified as working together best in this process: the creation of a 'collective' of members holding each other accountable in a '*joint enterprise*'; building the community, networks, and relationships of '*mutuality*'; and producing a '*shared repertoire* of communal resources' that is accessible and functional (p. 80). DEHub sought to support Wenger's three elements by bringing them together and ensuring integration. Through the development of a community of practice, DEHub aimed to facilitate a powerful, practical, and enjoyable learning environment that would benefit distance education practices in the higher education sector.

In many ways this community of practice will serve as a practical real world experience for educators. The behaviours they exhibit and encounter through the DEHub virtual learning space will provide experiences that can be translated to other educational environments. By applying Chickering's (2008) conceptual argument to pedagogical practices in higher education settings, concrete experiences and reflection on the use of the niche social network is a critical component of the virtual learning space *for* academics, these educators can apply and test 'concepts, principals and theories' that can be related back to units and courses they operate or indeed inform research.

Campbell's (2008) case study of a community of practice for individuals in Charles Sturt University's School of Policing Studies provides some valuable lessons for the development of similar practical communities. As a positive, Campbell argues that "Communities of practice provide a framework for the socialisation of knowledge sharing and therefore improved organisational outcomes" and "The creation of a safe space for unhindered discussion and the devolution of leadership were imperative to the evolution of the community and the building of networks". However, he also warns that there is a wide range of areas where such communities can be tested and risk falling down if they cannot meet the needs of users. Campbell (2008, p. 71), citing the argument of Wenger, McDermott and Snyder, noted that "a community is driven by the value members get from it, so people need to see how their passion will translate into something useful". Furthermore, Campbell argues that communities need to have a core group of motivated and interested people and can become divided if they fail to understand

each others' "backgrounds, concerns, strengths and limitations".

With Campbell's arguments in mind, DEHub sought to design a space that members would value and feel valued within, and feel comfortable contributing to and learning from. The DEHub environment places great emphasis on the multiple roles of community members. As noted briefly earlier, visitors and participants serve as contributors, learners and practitioners. This shared role is at the core of the view of learning as a social process; as Brockbank and McGill (2007, p. 4) argue, "Learning is a social process which will influence the degree of 'agency' experienced by the learner". DEHub seeks to facilitate this process and thus support the agency of visitors within their own educational environment. It seeks to empower professionals to engage with the world's best pedagogical practices and make positive changes to their personal pedagogical approaches.

There are numerous examples of excellent websites that allow potential users to engage productively in the social process of co-construction of meaning. Increasingly websites have social networking tools attached to them. It was an aim of the DEHub website to ensure that a community could develop and for this purpose a range of tools has been attached to the site as enablers for this process. Social networking is a key aspect of the creation of the site. Careful consideration of how individuals engage with social networking tools was necessary in order to understand the possible full range of possible engagement and assist us in our selection of tools. Social networkers differ in their attitudes to social networking sites and in their behaviour while using them. Ofcom's qualitative research indicates that site users tend to fall into five distinct groups based on their behaviours and attitudes. These are as follows:

- Alpha Socialisers: (a minority) people who used sites in intense short bursts to flirt, meet new people, and be entertained.

- Attention Seekers: (some) people who craved attention and comments from others, often by posting photos and customising their profiles.
- Followers: (many) people who joined sites to keep up with what their peers were doing.
- Faithfuls: (many) people who typically used social networking sites to rekindle old friendships, often from school or university.
- Functionals: (a minority) people who tended to be single-minded in using sites for a particular purpose (Ofcom, 2008, p. 6).

The importance of giving members 'value' within their communities is a critical issue that DEHub sought to address. As noted, learning is a form of social participation and in an online environment facilitators must ensure that they provide a space where healthy levels of 'social participation' can be encouraged and maintained (Woudstra & Adria, 2008, p. 573). A core factor in social participation is the degree to which an individual feels valued by the community they are contributing to. Within the DEHub virtual learning space, visitors and participants may set up a member profile, including a member page, allowing them to provide details on their personal approach to teaching and research, the theories they incorporate, and the tools and resources they commonly utilise. In this respect, DEHub is consistent with the format of most social networking sites. Our decision to use WikiEducator means that individuals are not limited to one tool but rather can connect outwards to other social networking tools that they may already have relationships with so as to reduce duplication of their profiles. This is a voluntary option, allowing users to engage with the space on a wide range of levels. Visitors can 'drop in' to the site for a quick visit, find the specific information they need on a certain issue, and then 'drop out'. Alternatively, they may find on visiting information on a certain issue that

they would like to contribute to the discussion, or add details on their personal positive or negative experiences. After further exploration of the site, they may decide to set up a member profile to link them in with a range of other online resources accessible from the DEHub space.

Ofcom (2008) also found that effective social networking requires users to create well-developed profiles as the basis of their online presence. Ofcom (2008, p. 7) states that "users derive significant enjoyment from the process of building a social network, collecting a list of their friends and using this list of friends to browse others' profiles". However, this Ofcom report also noted that, whilst people most commonly communicate with those they already know, "17% of adults used their profile to communicate with people they do not know" (p. 7). DEHub's challenge will be to see whether the social networking of researchers and practitioners can build on those who may know each other and further extend its value to those who may like to become a member of this community.

The DEHub space also distinguishes itself from being a *purely* 'social networking' site; a point that Boyd and Ellison (2007) neatly define:

We define social network sites as web-based services that allow individuals to (1) construct a public or semi-public profile within a bounded system, (2) articulate a list of other users with whom they share a connection, and (3) view and traverse their list of connections and those made by others within the system. The nature and nomenclature of these connections may vary from site to site (Boyd & Ellison, 2007, p. 1).

Rather, DEHub identifies a broader agenda in the design and development of their online space that incorporates the above distinction as only part of their activities. The *purpose*, whilst partly to facilitate social networking, is largely upon helping to facilitate a collaborative learning space and dissemination point. The creation of a niche social network helps to facilitate these activities but it is not necessarily the primarily *raison d'être*. The DEHub space seeks to bring people together to create a unique research and practitioner group with a focus on distance learning. An important aspect of the space is to enable ownership by the contributors. For example, contributors can explore tacit knowledge through the blog and contribute to the wiki and receive feedback on how their work is being received. This enables individuals and groups to adjust and perhaps challenge their thinking in almost the same real time. It is both disruptive and pre-emptive. The cycle of continually learning and adapting could be more akin to 'just-in-time'. It also allows groups to develop their own identity. One example of this can be found in the Virtual Worlds Working Group, which is a small group of individuals who work together on mutual concerns and who developed their own wiki which branches off wikieducator. A new layer of autonomy and collaboration is forged.

CONCLUSION

This chapter has focused specifically upon our understanding of 'virtual learning spaces' and the practices adopted within these spaces through an exploration of one project's conceptualisation and creation of an interactive, social network research community of practice. The case used is based around the development of a niche social network community for the Distance Education Hub (DEHub) which, while both virtual and physical, intends to develop primarily through user interaction based around key themes of mutual interest. The decision to draw upon and aggregate other social network tools and Web 2.0 technologies creates an innovative way in which researchers and practitioners can co-construct knowledge around distance education together. By drawing upon theoretical knowledge of communities of practice and social networking a clear

case is made for how niche interest groups can be created based on demand, interest and mutual knowledge dissemination and development. It remains to be seen whether this approach will realise the expectations and evaluation of the progress of the virtual space will be ongoing. There is enormous opportunity to research the development and evaluation of social network sites that have niche markets. In particular their sustainability as virtual sites that create community where knowledge is democratised. While the focus in this book is multifarious there can be no doubt that the web is a modern learning environment and as such demands attention in the way it might support learning and research.

The key tools used within the DEHub virtual space are expanding as the community itself develops confidence. It is intended that a group of people will no doubt create their own culture and way of working. In the first instance the following tools are being used. The DEHub virtual site will evolve from the main website. Wenger (2003) argues that "Communities of practice deepen their mutual commitment when they take responsibility for a learning agenda, which pushes their practice further" (p.83). Primarily the website includes basic project information and the intent is to add to the site via WikiEducator by ensuring information is accessible, with a practical focus — end-user, implementation orientated. The site has a simple architecture as follows and is constantly evolving based on the community needs.

REFERENCES

Bernath, U., Szücs, A., Tait, A., & Vidal, M. (2009). *Distance and e-learning in transition*. London, UK: ISTE.

Boyd, D. M., & Ellison, N. B. (2007). Social network sites: Definition, history, and scholarship. *Journal of Computer-Mediated Communication, 13*(1). Retrieved April 28, 2010, from http://jcmc.indiana.edu/vol13/issue1/boyd.ellison.html

Brockbank, A., & McGill, I. (2007). *Facilitating reflective learning in higher education*. Maidenhead, UK: Open University Press.

Brownlee, J., & Berthelsen, D. (2008). Developing relational epistemology through relational pedagogy: New ways of thinking about personal epistemology in teacher education. In Khine, M. S. (Ed.), *Knowing, knowledge and beliefs: Epistemological studies across diverse cultures* (pp. 404–421). Perth, Western Australia: Springer Science and Business Media.

Campbell, M. (2008). Teaching, communities of practice and the police. In Barrow, M., & Sutherland, K. (Eds.), *HERDSA 2008: Engaging Communities* (pp. 106–116). Milperra, NSW: HERDSA.

Chickering, A. W. (2008). Strengthening democracy and personal development through community engagement. *New Directions for Adult and Continuing Education, 118*, 87–95. doi:10.1002/ace.298

Collom, G., Dallas, A., Jong, R., & Obexer, R. (2002, December). *Six months in a leaky boat: Framing the knowledge and skills needed to teach well online*. Paper presented at the ASCILITE 2002 - Winds of Change in the Sea of Learning: Charting the Course of Digital Education, Auckland, NZ. Retrieved March 3, 2010, from http://www.ascilite.org.au/conferences/auckland02/proceedings/papers/181.pdf

DEHub (2010). *About*. Retrieved February 17, 2010, from http://dehub.edu.au

Geser, G., Hornung-Prähauser, V., & Schaffert, S. (2007). Observing open e-learning content: A roadmap for educational policy and institutions and hands-on tips for practitioners. In *Proceedings of the Interactive Computer Aided Learning Conference (ICL)*. Villach, Austria.

Hanna, D. E. (2008). Organizational change in higher distance education. In M. G. Moore (Ed.), *Handbook of distance education* (pp. 501-514). Mahway, NJ & London, UK: Lawrence Erlbaum Associates.

Leitch, S. (2006). *Leitch review of skills: Prosperity for all in the global economy - world class skills*. London, UK: HM Treasury. Retrieved August 25, 2009, from http://www.hm-treasur,/.gov.uk/media/6/4/leitch finalreport051206.pdf

Lombardo, T. (2007), *Understanding and teaching future consciousness*. Retrieved August 25, 2009, from http://oth-newlearning.wikispaces.com/Understanding+and+Teaching+Future+Consciousness

Ofcom. (2008). *Social networking: A quantitative and qualitative research report into attitudes, behaviours and use*. Retrieved September 29, 2009, from http://www.ofcom.org.uk/advice/media_literacy/medlitpub/medlitpubrss/social-networking/report.pdf

Perraton, H., & Moses, K. (2004). Technology. In Perraton, H. D., & Lentell, H. (Eds.), *Policy for open and distance learning* (pp. 141–157). London, UK: RoutledgeFarmer. doi:10.4324/9780203464403_chapter_8

Schwarz, C. V., Meyer, J., & Sharma, A. (2007). Technology, pedagogy, and epistemology: Opportunities and challenges of using computer modeling and simulation tools in elementary science methods. *Journal of Science Teacher Education, 18*(2), 243–269. doi:10.1007/s10972-007-9039-6

Teghe, D., & Knight, B. A. (2004). Neo-liberal higher education policy and its effects on the development of online courses. *Campus-Wide Information Systems*, *21*(4), 151–156. doi:10.1108/10650740410555025

Tynan, B., & Lee, M. J. W. (2009). Tales of adventure and change: Academic staff members' future visions of higher education and their professional development needs. *Horizon*, *17*(2), 98–108. doi:10.1108/10748120910965485

Tynan, B., Lee, M. J. W., & Barnes, C. (2008). Polar bears, black gold and light bulbs: Creating stable futures for tertiary education through instructor training and support in the use of ICTs. In *Proceedings of World Conference on Educational Multimedia, Hypermedia and Telecommunications*, (pp. 3557-64). Chesapeake, VA: AACE.

UNESCO. (2001). *Report on the UNESCO Programme — LEARNTEC 2001*. Retrieved August 23, 2009, from http://webworld.unesco.org/e_learning/new/report.shtml

Wenger, E. (2003). Communities of practice and social learning systems. In D. Nicolini, S.Gherardi, & D. Yanow (Eds.), *Knowing in organizations: A practice-based approach* (pp. 76-99). New York, NY: Armonk.

Wenger, E., McDermott, R. A., & Snyder, W. (2002). *Cultivating communities of practice: A guide to managing knowledge*. Boston, MA: Harvard Business School Press.

WikiEducator. (2009). *About*. Retrieved February 17, 2010, from http://wikieducator.org/WikiEducator:About

Woudstra, A., & Adria, M. (2008). Network and virtual forms of distance education. In M. G. Moore (Ed.), *Handbook of distance education* (pp. 501-514). Mahway, NJ & London, UK: Lawrence Erlbaum Associates.

ADDITIONAL READING

West, J. A., & West, M. L. (2008). *Using wikis for online collaboration: The power of the read-write web*. San Francisco, CA: John Wiley and Sons.

Section 3
Blended Learning Spaces

Chapter 10
Using Blogs to Traverse Physical and Virtual Spaces

Kerryn Newbegin
Monash University, Australia

Leonard Webster
Monash University, Australia

ABSTRACT

The development of physical and virtual learning spaces is prominent in the current higher education context, however a preoccupation with the design of these environments must not be at the cost of the learner. This chapter proposes that new ways of thinking need to be adopted and new strategies for collaborating need to be developed to enable students and teachers to traverse the physical and virtual environments. In traversing these spaces, learners must use them to best advantage, both within the higher education context, and then later in the professional arena in which they will be operating. Specifically this chapter will examine the use of one collaboration tool—blogs— to bridge the gap between the physical and the virtual, the formal and the informal learning spaces. Strategies for using blogs will be presented as a tool for students and educators to enable and promote knowledge creation, and to develop a habit of reflective practice both during and after formal study.

INTRODUCTION

A recent trend in Australian higher education has been the creation of physical learning spaces that are claimed to be flexible, engaging and efficient, and which will attract students and teachers to them. Concurrently personal and social technologies are prominent within society and it is inevitable that these physical spaces will incorporate these social collaboration technologies based on assumptions of improving the learning experience for students.

It can be argued that these environments are not being designed with the view of supporting students in the variety of learning environments in which they find themselves from day to day (Wilson et al, 2007; Attwell, 2007; Mazzoni & Gafurri, 2009). For some students, the learning

DOI: 10.4018/978-1-60960-114-0.ch010

space will be these physical spaces provided by, and at, the University campus. For others, the physical spaces will be of their own choosing—the lounge room, the train, the tea-room, the café, the office or the playground. For many it will be a combination of spaces and learning strategies, and the supportive technologies provided will need to traverse these spaces.

The consistent element in the traversing of spaces is the student. In order to negotiate the challenges inherent in this variety of learning spaces, both the educator and the student will benefit from a shared space which transverses the physical and virtual and is arguably most easily facilitated in the virtual space.

The virtual learning space is today commonly conceptualised by reference to Web 2.0, so named as it is said to represent the second generation of web software. Web 2.0 refers to social software such as blogs, wikis, podcasts, Real Simple Syndication (RSS), social bookmarking (e.g. Delicious. com), and media sharing software (e.g. Flickr). In the educational context McLoughlin and Lee (2007) suggest that the essence of Web 2.0 is "about linking minds, communities and ideas, while promoting personalisation, collaboration and creativity leading to joint knowledge creation" (p. 668). Mazzoni and Gafurri (2009) suggest that Web 2.0 technologies are less restricted by and to formal learning than were the Web 1.0 technologies. It is generally accepted that Web 2.0 technologies provide enhanced opportunities for online collaboration, peer assessment, individual and group reflection, and development of e-portfolios (for examples see Table 1).

This chapter examines the ways in which blogs have been conceptualised and strategies to enable blogs to place the student in the role of 'knowledge prosumer' (Farmer, Yue & Brooks 2008; Klamma et al, 2007; McLoughlin & Lee, 2007; Wilson et al, 2007). This is discussed in the context of an Australian university with a number of national and international campuses that have embarked on a number of physical learning space redesign

projects. In particular, this chapter will discuss the use of blogs as a key tool in enabling the learner to effectively integrate the physical, virtual, informal and formal learning spaces to take advantage of the significant investments and interest in both these areas.

BACKGROUND

Traversing the Physical and Virtual: One Case Study of a Large Global University

Monash University provides one case study where the traversing of the physical and virtual space is presenting challenges to conceptualising the next development of its virtual environments. Monash is an international institution with eight campuses across three culturally diverse countries, with research and teaching centres across the world. Monash is focused on providing a dynamic environment that allows students and educators to engage with their peers, their community and their learning, a focus encapsulated in the Monash Passport. The Monash Passport is "a master-key for experiences in plural campuses, countries and disciplines … a passport to employment; to engagement; to course and unit flexibility" (Shoemaker, 2008). Fundamental to the Monash Passport model is "the marshalling of technology by pedagogy: learning to impart knowledge in vastly different ways; visualising futures through E-Research and E-Learning" (Shoemaker, 2008).

To 'marshal technology by pedagogy' Monash has established a Learning Spaces Taskforce which is charged with developing "a strategy for future learning space design, upgrades and refurbishment" (Monash University, 2009). Within the scope of their stated strategy, the Taskforce has been involved in redeveloping existing teaching spaces to facilitate the student-centred approach. The Earth Sciences Teaching Laboratory enables learning across four domains (fieldwork, wet

Table 1. Selection of research concerning blog use in education

Study	Field of practice	Ownership	Reported Blog Usage
Hernández-Ramos, 2004	Pre-service teacher training	Individual student blog	Reflective tasks
Williams & Jacobs, 2004	MBA	Group student blog	Reflective tasks; peer interaction
Chong & Soo, 2005a (as cited in Chong, 2008)	Music education	Individual student blog	Individual research reports; peer review and interaction; reflective tasks
Chong & Soo, 2005b (as cited in Chong, 2008)	Music education	Group student blog	Collaborative research; peer interaction
Chong, 2008	Music education	Individual student blog	Analytical discussion; peer review and interaction; reflective tasks
Farmer et al, 2008	Cultural studies	Individual student blog; Teacher blog	Reflective tasks; peer review and interaction
Ladyshewsky & Gardner, 2008	Physiotherapy	Group student blogs with teacher moderation	Reflective journal
Tekinarslan, 2008	Computing	Individual student blogs; Teacher blog	Online research reports
Sun, 2009	English language education	Group student blog	Voice posts; Voice based peer comments
Richardson, 2009	Journalism	Individual student blog	Reflective journal; assessment submission; peer and expert review and interaction
Richardson, 2009	American Literature	Group student blog	Analytical discussion; peer and expert interaction; online community
Dickey, 2004	Pre-service teacher training	Group student blog	Peer interaction; online community
Young & Delves, 2009	Social work	Group student blogs	Online community

laboratory, the classroom and the mobile environment), providing a highly interactive classroom experience that can be digitally captured and replayed for improved learning. In other areas, a lecture theatre has been retasked as a large, flexible, unscheduled space for staff to explore the features of new spaces and associated technologies, and a suite of tutorial rooms have been redesigned to bring together staff and first-year students with a view to increasing interaction and communal spirit.

The Taskforce's strategic focus may suggest that Monash's key concern is the physical space however, the Taskforce are also engaged in a number of projects within the virtual space. It is recognised that the investment in the virtual learning space at Monash University is essential and that the virtual learning space should be considered as important to the student experience as the physical spaces. Monash's virtual learning landscape includes learning management systems, such as Moodle and Blackboard, in-house developed learning environments, such as InterLearn and Pharmacopia, and an assortment of individual tools such as online lecture recordings, unit websites, wikis, discussion forums, online quizzes, digital library resources and blogs. All these tools are provided to students and teachers to enable the goals of the Monash Passport to be realised. However, this has also revealed a lack of research and frameworks of practice as to how collaboration tools such as blogs can be used to support the traversing of learning spaces. Further, it can be argued that higher education is at the 'cusp' of a new era in virtual environments. Monash University is currently reviewing its traditional approach to Learning Management Systems (LMS) and how it might move to more Personalised Learning Environments (Webster, Fraser & Smith, 2009) including an amalgamation of publicly available tools such as Google Wave into an alternative, powerful and efficient solution to future learning needs. Future online environments even in the 'hard to predict' scenarios are likely to incorporate blogs. An understanding of blogs and their learning features is one critical step to inform the next stage of developing virtual environments in the higher education context.

BLOGS

Features of Blogs

Blogs, or "web logs", are often defined as online diaries or journals, however their application has become more varied in recent years. Essentially a blog is a self-published website, where content is provided by one or more authors. Blog content can include text, hyperlinks, RSS feeds, images, and videos provided in the format of 'posts', which are dynamic webpages within the blog site, or of pages, which are static within the blog site. Readers of the blog can provide comment or opinion on the posts, thereby enabling conversation to occur within the blog. The static pages do not enable commentary and therefore can be used by the blog owner to ensure an important level of personal control over specified content (Ferdig & Trammell, 2004; McLoughlin & Lee, 2007).

To facilitate ease of navigation and following of updates, blog posts are ordinarily presented in reverse chronological order. The sidebar is an important area of the blog, in which the blog owner can determine customisations to their blog's functionality. The sidebar may include a listing of the most recent posts, the static content pages, and the blogroll. The blogroll is a list of links to important, useful or otherwise relevant websites or blogs as determined by the blog owner. Further customisation and personalisation of the blog, both in appearance and functionality, can be achieved through the use of widgets, also referred to as gadgets or plugins. Some examples of widgets

include search, an RSS feed, and categorisation of posts. This customisation provides the student further control over the learning space.

Distinguishing Blogs, Wikis and Discussion Forums

Blogs are often confused with wikis. A wiki is a website that can be authored and edited by numerous people, without specific web authoring software. In essence it is a collaboration tool that enables quick and relatively unstructured web editing. It is similar to a blog in the sense that it enables self-publishing, and for numerous participants to engage in the content creation. The ability for anyone, with the appropriate permissions, to edit any content on a wiki is a key feature which sets it apart from a blog. Within the context of a blog, multiple authors are enabled and they may comment upon the entry of other authors, but they cannot simply change the original entry.

A wiki enables groups of learners to co-create and reach a shared understanding. The blog enables each individual learner to express their own learning development and maintain control over their personal learning space, while contextualising their learning through links to other resources, such as a shared wiki. McLoughlin and Lee (2007) and Ferdig and Tramell (2004) stress the importance of this individual, personal control.

Blogs have also been likened to discussion forums in their ability to provide the online conversation and exchange of ideas. Essentially, a discussion forum is a highly structured, asynchronous communication tool which allows authors to post a message and comment upon other messages. Discussion forums, considered to be a tool of the Web 1.0 era (McLoughlin & Lee, 2007), have been widely used in higher education for many years. Discussion forums have been found to generate conversation and engage students in higher order learning (e.g. Hernández-Ramos, 2004; Ma, 2009); assist in collaborative thinking (Nicholson & Bond, 2003); and create a social space in which students feel supported (Greyling, Kara, Makka & van Niekerk, 2008).

It can be seen that discussion forums and blogs enable similar tasks to be undertaken, however Ferdig and Trammell (2004) suggest that the blog is superior to the discussion forum as the blogger has ultimate control over the blog and its content. Mazzoni and Gafurri (2009) propose that the blog allows the learner to "determine(s) and (delimit) … multiple levels of engagement in collective activities, and multiple spaces for sharing and exchanging knowledge" in a more powerful way than Web 1.0 tools. Further, Farmer and Bartlett-Bragg (2005) suggest that when used in conjunction with RSS, blogs are preferred as collaborative tools over discussion forums.

Blogs and the Learning Environment

The blog fulfills the definitions presented by Piccoli, Ahmas and Ives (2001) and Burbules (2006) and also allows for the specific features that Dillenbourg, Schneider and Synteta (2002) argue must be present in a Virtual Learning Environment (VLE). Specifically a blog:

- is a designed information space;
- is a social space;
- is explicitly represented, with relationships between elements being overt and obvious;
- includes navigation supports for users, such as the recent post listings, blogrolls, and the ability to add permanent links to particular postings or pages, known as "permalinks";
- is a place in which learners are prosumers, or consumers who are actively involved in the creation, as well as the consumption of knowledge;
- can be equally useful in face-to-face and distance teaching;
- can integrate multiple and differing technologies and pedagogical approaches; and

- enables users to utilise and incorporate physical resources and activities within the virtual environment, thus overlapping the physical space.

Wilson et al (2007) contrast a VLE, which they believe to be driven by the learning institution in design, context, information management and accessibility, with a Personalised Learning Environment (PLE). They present the PLE as a learning space in which the primary focus is on "the practices of users in learning with diverse technologies" (p. 31), within multiple contexts and across their lifetime.

Attwell (2007) sees the driver of the PLE as the need to facilitate learning across multiple situations and contexts, and to recognise the increase in informal learning. As has been previously discussed, blogs enable users to incorporate learning artefacts from numerous diverse contexts, including their formal study materials, practice examples, and workplace experiences. The inherent sharing and communication within the blog provides ample opportunities for informal, unguided learning to occur.

Wild, Mödritscher and Sigurdarson (2008) suggest that the key to a successful learning environment is the ability for the user to adapt the environment to their needs, that is that the user is in control of the learning environment. Ferdig and Trammell (2004) propose this as a key strength of the blog. Wilson et al (2007) suggest that a PLE must encourage users to make "'playlists' of resources and to share them with others for collaborative knowledge construction" (p. 33), thereby becoming knowledge prosumers. This notion of knowledge prosumers also fits within the framework presented by Vygotsky (1978) in which the expert and the student are required to work together to reach a shared meaning.

Blogs have been described as the vehicle by which learners can become prosumers of knowledge (Farmer et al, 2008; Klamma et al, 2007; McLoughlin & Lee, 2007) rather than simply consumers. The ability to selectively incorporate all manner of resources within the blog environment empowers learners to traverse their physical, virtual, formal and informal learning spaces in the process of knowledge construction. It is the blog which provides an overlap or bridge between the varied external learning spaces that the student must negotiate. The learner, in using the blog, brings together their chosen resources, enabling them to be the prosumers of knowledge. As Farmer and Bartlett-Bragg (2005) suggest "education may not be a location anymore — it will be an activity — discretely embedded in the lifestyles of our learners" (p. 202).

USE OF BLOGS IN HIGHER EDUCATION

Academic research into the use of blogs in the education sector has been rapidly increasing over recent years, with proponents advocating for the widespread introduction of blogs as key tools in educational design (Boulus, Maramba & Wheeler, 2006; Duffy & Bruns, 2006; Farmer & Bartlett-Bragg, 2005; Ferdig & Trammell, 2004; Godwin-Jones, 2003; McLoughlin & Lee, 2007; Richardson, 2009). Fields of practice in which blogs have been utilised include music education (Chong, 2008), pre-service teacher training (e.g. Hernández-Ramos, 2004), cultural studies (Farmer et al, 2008), physiotherapy (Ladyshewsky & Gardner, 2008), business (Williams & Jacobs, 2004), social work (Young & Delves, 2009), English language learning (Sun, 2009), journalism (Richardson, 2009), and literature (Richardson, 2009) to name a few.

Chong (2008) in discussing the work of Hewitt and Scardamalia (1998) argues that blogs can provide "access to distributed expertise" (p. 186), and that blog posts are effective participant artefacts that can be used by the whole community to build knowledge, and foster feedback, by way of blog comments. The persistent nature of blog pages, posts and comments, by way of permalinks, mean that these artefacts are available for the community as a whole to reflect upon and interpret and are an example of externalised knowledge (Chong, 2008).

The studies that have investigated aspects of blogs such as the purposes and uses of blogs, and the positive outcomes experienced in using blogs are varied. Some of the foci for investigation include: personal reflection; an exchange of cultural understandings; sharing experiences and expertise; developing students' ability to conduct online research; developing students' writing skills; providing and seeking support in practice; as an e-portfolio; to facilitate knowledge creation by students; to gain access to external experts; as a classroom portal; and to create a community of practice amongst students. Some studies that describe these uses are listed in Table 1.

Guidelines for Using Blogs in Higher Education

Richardson (2009) makes a clear distinction between what he terms "journaling" via social software such as MySpace or Facebook, and blogging. In an education context, he presents blogging as engaging learners in "a process of thinking in words" (p. 20). Farmer et al (2008) provide guidelines for the application of blogging technology within the higher education context that will provide authentic student-centred learning activities rather than "the simple phatic discourse of online sociability and the prosaic 'daily diary' experience" (p. 134) enabling learners to become prosumers of knowledge.

Guidelines for the successful application of blogs are:

- Teachers should first use blogs themselves (Richardson, 2009; Young & Delves, 2009)
- Assessment requirements must be clear (Farmer et al, 2008; Hernández-Ramos, 2004)
- Students should be encouraged to set blogging goals that go "above and beyond a quantity measure" (Farmer et al, 2008, p134)
- Adequate technical support must be provided (Farmer et al, 2008)
- Facilitators must ensure that adequate feedback, as to purpose and progress, is provided early on (Chong, 2008; Farmer et al, 2008; Ladyshewsky & Gardner, 2008; Song & Chan, 2008)
- Adequate training, guidelines and scaffolding must be provided (Chong, 2008; Farmer et al, 2008; Hernández-Ramos, 2004; Ladyshewsky & Gardner, 2008), particularly where there may be students from a non-native English speaking background (Song & Chan, 2008)
- Blog environments must be monitored to ensure that a safe and supportive environment is being created, where risks are encouraged and mistakes accepted (Song & Chan, 2008)
- Implementation of the blog aspect of a class must be fundamental to the learning experience, rather than just an "add-on" (Chong, 2008; Ladyshewsky & Gardner, 2008)
- Aggregation or RSS should be incorporated into the blogging experience (Farmer & Bartlett-Bragg, 2005)
- Where the full advantage of learner customisation of blogs is encouraged, the nature of the blogging task should have an individual focus, rather than a group based focus (Farmer & Bartlett-Bragg, 2005).

A Framework for the Use of Blogs in Traversing Physical and Virtual Spaces: Spaces of Influence

Green (2005) further developed Vygotsky's work to suggest that where the expert, or teacher, is moving within an area where they too are the learner there needs to be an environment in which the construction of knowledge is facilitated thus enabling learners to be knowledge prosumers. Green (2005) calls these environments spaces of influence. Spaces of influence are dynamic places where shared understandings are negotiated between participants, and in which participants share and swap within the roles of 'teacher' and 'student' as required. Green (2005) building on the scaffolding work of Wood, Bruner and Ross (1976) presents five spaces of influence, as seen in Table 2, this framework provides an excellent model for examining the usefulness of blogs within the learning context.

A *space of action* is categorised by the learner's ability to be in control of their learning and to determine the way in which they interact with an activity. Learners sharing such a space of action will be motivated toward a similar goal, thus forming a "community of actively engaged learners" (Green, 2005, p. 301). McLoughlin and Lee (2007) argue that in order for students to truly have the control over their own learning environment, they need to have control over the tools that they use to learn and the ways in which they apply them. Blogs allow for personalisation of not only the content but also of the appearance and functionality of the space by customised inclusion of widgets. The inherent flexibility of the structure and appearance of a blog and the tools added to it, as well as the ability of the blogger to publish their own learning artefacts, such as text, images, videos, and audio, and add hyperlinks to external content, give the student control of their own learning environment (Ferdig & Trammell, 2004). Students in Alm's (2009) study reportedly took great pride in the creation of their blog and con-

Table 2. Green's (2005) five spaces of influence

Spaces of Influence	Key elements in supported Learning	Application to Blogs
Spaces of action	Engaging learners Motivating others Balance between autonomy and dependence	Creation of personal learning artefacts Personalisation of content, appearance and functionality
Spaces of explicit discourse	Engaging in explicit discourse practices	Creation, viewing and changing content Anchored, contextualised discussion Richly embed content within commentary, and vice versa RSS feeds for immediacy Draft/edit/publish cycle
Spaces of learning	Providing examples (content based) Understanding and working from people's capabilities Providing a forum for critical feedback	Direction, through hyperlinks, to resources or practice examples Embed practice examples Elicit student feedback/discussion on content sticking points Continuous, contextualised feedback and commentary
Spaces of practice development	Providing examples (practice based) Understanding and working from people's capabilities	Post examples of practice development Report and reflect on practice experiences
Spaces of trust	Reflexivity Empathy	Provision of support and empathy to peers via posts and commentary

sidered it their personal space over which they maintained control.

Spaces of explicit discourse are those in which the learning context is made explicit through reading, writing and conversation (Green, 2005). A blog clearly provides an entry into a space of explicit discourse through the ability to read and write textual posts and hyperlinks, listen to and/or watch, as well as create, image, audio and video artefacts. A blog, unlike a standard discussion forum (Brush, Bargeron, Grudin, Borning & Gupta, 2002), enables anchored discussions, where the content and the conversation are contextualised jointly (Guzdial & Turns, 2000). This contextualisation is achieved by allowing the blogger, whether expert or learner, to provide a rich post or commentary of interest to readers by directly embedding hyperlinks, images, video and/or audio to their comments within the post. This explicit discourse can be further supported within the blog via RSS feeds to allow readers and bloggers to "keep up with the discussion", and to draft and edit posts, the lack of which are shortcomings of many discussion forums (Guzdial & Turns, 2000).

Within a *space of learning*, learners are engaged with the content knowledge required to reach the learning objectives (Green, 2005). In the context of a blog, the expert can direct learners to relevant content resources or provide practice examples. Blogs could also be used to elicit from students and then expand upon and encourage discussion of the areas of course content that students are having most trouble with, as was the case in Greyling et al's (2008) "muddiest point" surveys. Further content can also be provided through the blogroll. The community may engage in the space of learning by providing one another with feedback and additional content, by way of comments or new posts, thus engaging in the "cycle of growth" (Green, 2005, p. 302). Tekinarslan's (2008) students were required to perform literature searches in order to develop content for their blogs, thus compelling them to engage directly with content knowledge.

A *space of practice development* is, as may be expected, where the learner practices the processes of their given field. The space must allow for variation in methodology or application of the process used, and for feedback to guide the development of the practice (Green, 2005). A blog provides ample opportunity for learners to demonstrate development of practice. Tekinarslan (2008) found that his students were able "to practise and advance their skills in writing" (p. 410) within their individual blogs, as well as practicing their literature search skills in preparing their blog content. In the case of pre-service teachers, use of a blog during the course of their study, as described by Hernández-Ramos (2004), illustrates to future teachers how they can utilise blogs in their own teaching, and allows them to practice potential uses. Further, a blog will allow a learner to report and reflect on practice experiences, as may be seen in studies of pre-service teachers (Hernández-Ramos, 2004) and physiotherapy students (Ladyshewsky & Gardner, 2008).

As the name suggests, *spaces of trust* are those in which learners are comfortable to take risks, with expectation of support and without fear of criticism (Green, 2005). Both the expert and the learner's peers are able to provide support and empathy for risks taken with the blog environment. Care needs to be taken to develop and protect trust formed within the blog. Where this space of influence is a dominate need, thought should be given to the way in which the blog is set up and presented to learners (Chong, 2008) including allowing or disallowing bloggers to be anonymous, restrictions that may need to be applied and the degree of moderation the expert engages in. These issues will be key considerations, particularly early on, to encourage the new-comer or even the "lurker", or passive participant, to move into the space of trust. Studies have shown that feelings of trust and confidence can take time to build within blogs (Ladyshewsky & Gardner, 2008). Alm (2009) reported that the participants in her German language course felt safe to express themselves within the blog environment, and students in Dickey's (2004) study reported feeling part of a supportive community.

Employing Blogs to Ease the Pressures on Universities and Students

There is a gap between the study practices of today's students and those traditionally seen in Australian universities, with reduced attendance a common complaint of teachers (for example, Rogers, 2001; Pearce, 2004). In part this may be attributed to increased pressures imposed on students to work and study simultaneously (Barrett, Rainer & Marczyk, 2007; Wyn, Cuervo, Smith, Beadle & Woodman, 2008) and the inherent difficulty that presents for timetabling. It has been acknowledged that distance education learners can experience varying levels of isolation and distress (Dickey, 2004) and it is not inconceivable that time pressured students choosing non attendance will experience similar feelings. Dickey (2004) shows that blogs can assist in reducing negative experiences providing the learner with a feeling of community and support.

Universities Australia (2005) data shows that the majority of students entering university are within the age range commonly referred to as Generation Y, and that they are also the largest single cohort of enrolled students. While it would be simplistic to assume members of Generation Y are all the same, Wyn et al (2008) argue that "it is important to know the distinctive impact of their social context on their lives and it is implied that this experience will continue to shape their lives well into the future" (p. 496).

Members of Generation Y (Gen Y) have been characterised as "techno-savvy, connected...24/7, self-confident, optimistic, hopeful, independent, comfortably self-reliant, determined, goal oriented, success-driven, lifestyle-centred, diverse, inclusive, service-oriented, entrepreneurial, and global-, civic- and community minded" (Deloitte Development 2006, as cited in Alloway & Dalley-Trim, 2009, p. 51). Saulwick and Muller (2006) suggests that the typical Generation Y student looks on education, including higher education, as a means to an end, rather than being driven by the gaining of knowledge.

There is a need to attract students and to provide them with the engaging learning experiences to ensure that they are active participants in their learning as, for Gen Y students at least, the learning is not their chief concern. Barrett et al (2007) showed that provision of online learning resources did not affect student attendance on campus, however time pressured students did appreciate the availability of the resources.

Universities are also trying to forge long term relationships with students, to encourage them to further study or research, to entice them back from within their professions to undertake professional development, or to teach. Blogs, as spaces of professional development and of learning can be employed to foster and manage many types of relationships between teachers, students and alumni. For example, later year students may play a supportive role to early year students via a university or discipline wide blog. In addition, more experienced students or alumni may mentor early and middle year students via a blog. Students at any level may post samples of their work or commentary on their work experience and seek support or critique from teachers, alumni and other students. Such relationships between students, teachers, alumni and the university can be formed and maintained for extended periods, regardless of physical constraints, by way of the blog.

These pressures have seen a move toward more flexible physical spaces which can be used to service multiple needs with minimal changes. The investment in virtual spaces is seen as beneficial because it can reduce the burden on the physical spaces, and enable students to reach a wider potential student body outside of their physical geographic region.

Blogs can provide the means by which universities can reach a wider student body, as well as foster communities made up of current and past students, teachers and researchers. Blogs also enable universities to foster knowledge creation, lifelong learning, and a sense of continued belonging for alumni, which is a key goal of many universities today.

FUTURE RESEARCH

Higher education, and education at all levels is challenged in this dawn of a new era containing increased social networking tools. Challenges facing students, teachers and institutions alike include the internationalised and global higher education context, mobility of students, lifestyle expectations, changes in technologies such as tablet computers, and new developments such as the Apple iPad. Although there are a number of case studies and literature on the use of Blogs, there is a need for further research.

It is proposed by the authors of this chapter that the emphasis of future research should be more focused on the learner not on technologies as the learning space. In addition it is essential to consider the skills that learners will need to interact and learn in these spaces. Jenkins, Clinton, Purushotma, Robison and Weigel, (2009) suggest that this is a social participation era with far reaching changes for learning and teaching transpiring. Some specific directions highlighted by Jenkins that have potential for further research on the roles of blogs include:

- **Distributed Cognition:** the ability to interact meaningfully with tools that expand mental capacities
- **Collective Intelligence:** the ability to pool knowledge and compare notes with others toward a common goal
- **Transmedia Navigation:** the ability to follow the flow of stories and information across multiple modalities
- **Networking:** the ability to search for, synthesise, and disseminate information

- **Negotiation:** the ability to travel across diverse communities, discerning and respecting multiple perspectives, and grasping and following alternative norms.

CONCLUSION

The Monash experience is not unique within the higher education context of Australia or globally. However, it can be argued that as design specifications are developed for new physical learning and virtual spaces, definitions, frameworks and strategies for how collaboration tools such as blogs can assist students traverse from one space to another will become an increasingly important consideration.

In the Australian context, additional research is needed into the success indicators for the incorporation of collaboration tools within the learning environments of the learner along with demonstrations and case studies of successful practices in the implementation of learning environments that incorporate collaboration tools (White, 2008). In addition, further trials such as the recent tablet computer trials being developed at Monash University that seek to provide the tools and equipment to enable learners to successfully traverse the learning environment when it is appropriate for them are needed.

Blogs, when applied within the framework outlined in this chapter, will enable students to traverse the physical and the virtual, the informal and the formal spaces and activities required to become knowledge prosumers and lifelong learners. Within the blog environment the student can prepare, present and reflect on their thoughts, experiences and understanding of their learning. They can immerse themselves in and interact with the thoughts, experiences and understanding of their peers and teachers. Through practice-based blogs, they can develop a sense of community and shared understanding with their peers, members of the wider University community, and within their

profession. The blog can also serve as a means of creating and maintaining a living portfolio of their learning and work artefacts. In this way the learning space does not have to end or relocate when formal education concludes.

Blogs are one tool that may provide support for students traversing learning environments. How these tools evolve in the near future will be rapid, with increasing new and powerful iterations becoming available by some of the large internet providers such as Google and more specifically Google Wave. However against this background of rapid development and change, the considerations of support for students moving between environments will provide a stable framework on which to consider the benefits of their adoption.

REFERENCES

Alloway, N., & Dalley-Trim, L. (2009). It's all about I: Gen Ys and neoliberal discourse in new times. *Youth Studies Australia, 28*(1), 51-56. Retrieved September 28, 2009, from http://www. acys.info/ journal/ issues/ v28-n1-2009/ articles/ pp51-56

Alm, A. (2009). Blogs as protected spaces for language learners. In *Same places, different spaces. Proceedings ASCILITE Auckland 2009* (pp. 20-24). Retrieved February 23, 2010, from http:// www.ascilite.org.au/ conferences/ auckland09/ procs/ alm.pdf

Attwell, G. (2007). The personal learning environments - the future of e-learning? *eLearning Papers, 2*(1). Retrieved February22, 2010, from http:// www.elearningeuropa.info/ out/ ?doc_id=9758& rsr_id=11561

Barrett, R., Rainer, A., & Marczyk, O. (2007). Managed learning environments and an attendance crisis? *The Electronic Journal of e-Learning, 5*(1), 1–10.

Boulos, M. N. K., Maramba, I., & Wheeler, S. (2006). Wikis, blogs and podcasts: A new generation of Web-based tools for virtual collaborative clinical practice and education. *BMC Medical Education, 6*(41). Retrieved August 28, 2009, from http://www.biomedcentral.com/1472-6920/6/41

Brush, A. J. B., Bargeron, D., Grudin, J., Borning, A., & Gupta, A. (2002). Supporting interaction outside of class: Anchored discussions vs. discussion boards. In *Computer Support for Collaborative Learning: Foundations for a CSCL Community. Proceedings of CSCL 2002* (pp. 425-434). Mahway, NJ: Lawrence Erlbaum Associates.

Burbules, N. (2006). Rethinking the virtual. In Weiss, J., Nolan, J., & Hunsinger, J. (Eds.), *The international handbook of virtual learning environments* (*Vol. 1*, pp. 37–58). Dordrecht, The Netherlands: Springer. doi:10.1007/978-1-4020-3803-7_1

Chong, E. K. M. (2008). Harnessing distributed musical expertise through edublogging. *Australasian Journal of Educational Technology, 24*(2), 181–194.

Chong, E. K. M., & Soo, W. M. (2005a). *Higher-order learning in music through blogs*. Paper presented at the Redesigning Pedagogy Conference, Singapore.

Chong, E. K. M., & Soo, W. M. (2005b). *Integrative and collaborative music learning using blogs*. Paper presented at the Association for Technology in Music Instruction and College Music Society Joint-Conference, Quebec City.

Dickey, M. D. (2004). The impact of Web-logs (blogs) on student perceptions of isolation and alienation in a Web-based distance-learning environment. *Open Learning, 19*(3), 279–291. doi:10.1080/0268051042000280138

Dillenbourg, P., Schneider, D. K., & Synteta, P. (2002). Virtual learning environments. In A. Dimitracopoulou (Ed.), *Proceedings of the 3rd Hellenic Conference Information & Communication Technologies in Education* (pp. 3-18). Greece: Kastaniotis Editions.

Duffy, P., & Bruns, A. (2006). The use of blogs, wikis and RSS in education: A conversation of possibilities. In *Proceedings Online Learning and Teaching Conference 2006* (pp. 31-38). Brisbane, Australia: Queensland University of Technology.

Farmer, B., Yue, A., & Brooks, C. (2008). Using blogging for higher order learning in large cohort university teaching: A case study. *Australasian Journal of Educational Technology, 24*(2), 123–136.

Farmer, J., & Bartlett-Bragg, A. (2005). Blogs @ anywhere: High fidelity online communication. In *Proceedings of ASCILITE 2005: Balance, Fidelity, Mobility: Maintaining the momentum?* (pp. 197-203). Brisbane, Australia: Queensland University of Technology.

Ferdig, R. E., & Trammell, K. D. (2004). Content delivery in the blogosphere. *T H E Journal (Technological Horizons In Education), 12*(4), Retrieved May 10, 2010, from http://thejournal.com/articles/16626

Godwin-Jones, R. (2003). Emerging technologies blogs and wikis: Environments for on-line collaboration. *Language Learning & Technology, 7*(2), 12–16.

Green, P. (2005). Spaces of influence: A framework for analysis of an individual's contribution within communities of practice. *Higher Education Research & Development, 24*(4), 293–307. doi:10.1080/07294360500284607

Greyling, F., Kara, M., Makka, A., & van Niekerk, S. (2008). IT worked for us: Online strategies to facilitate learning in large (undergraduate) classes. *The Electronic Journal of e-Learning, 6*(3), 179–188. Retrieved September 29, 2009, from http://www.ejel.org/ Volume-6/ v6-i3/ Greyling.pdf

Guzdial, M., & Turns, J. (2000). Effective discussion through a computer-mediated anchored forum. *Journal of the Learning Sciences, 9*(4), 437–469. doi:10.1207/S15327809JLS0904_3

Hernández-Ramos, P. (2004). Web logs and online discussions as tools to promote reflective practice. *The Journal of Interactive Online Learning, 3*(1).

Hewitt, J., & Scardamalia, M. (1998). Design principles for distributed knowledge building processes. *Educational Psychology Review, 10*(1), 75–96. doi:10.1023/A:1022810231840

Jenkins, H., Clinton, K., Purushotma, R., Robison, A. J., & Weigel, M. (2009). *Confronting the challenges of participatory culture: Media education for the 21st century. An occasional paper on digital media and learning.* The John D. and Catherine T. MacArthur Foundation. Retrieved February 24, 2010, from http://digitallearning.macfound.org/ atf/ cf/ %7B7E45C7E0- A3E0-4B89- AC9C-E807E1B0AE4E%7D/ JENKINS_WHITE_PA-PER.PDF

Klamma, R., Chatti, M. A., Duval, E., Hummel, H., Hvannberg, E. H., & Kravcik, M. (2007). Social software for life-long learning. *Journal of Educational Technology & Society, 10*(3), 72–83.

Ladyshewsky, R. K., & Gardner, P. (2008). Peer assisted learning and blogging: A strategy to promote reflective practice during clinical fieldwork. *Australasian Journal of Educational Technology, 24*(3), 241–257.

Ma, A. (2009). Computer supported collaborative learning and higher order thinking skills: A case study of textile studies. *Interdisciplinary Journal of E-Learning and Learning Objects, 5*, 145-167. Retrieved September 17, 2009, from http://ijklo.org/ Volume5/ IJELLOv5p145-167 MA657.pdf

Mazzoni, E., & Gafurri, P. (2009). *Personal learning environments for overcoming knowledge boundaries between activity systems in emerging adulthood.* e-learning Papers. Retrieved February 22, 2010, from http://www.elearningeuropa.info/ out/ ?doc_id=19375& rsr_id=19744

McLoughlin, C., & Lee, M. J. W. (2007). Social software and participatory learning: Pedagogical choices with technology affordances in the Web 2.0 era. In *ICT: Providing choices for learners and learning. Proceedings ASCILITE Singapore 2007.* Retrieved September 17, 2009, from http://www.ascilite.org.au/ conferences/ singapore07/ procs/ mcloughlin.pdf

Monash University. (2009). *Flexible learning, teaching and collaboration spaces.* Retrieved July 17, 2009, from http://www.its.monash.edu.au/ staff/ projects/ collaboration-spaces/ index.html

Nicholson, S. A., & Bond, N. (2003). Collaborative reflection and professional community building: An analysis of preservice teachers' use of an electronic discussion board. *Journal of Technology and Teacher Education, 11*(2), 259–279.

Pearce, J. (2004). *An analysis of student absenteeism in first year biology students.* Institute for Science Education, University of Plymouth. Retrieved September 29, 2009, from http://www.bioscience.heacademy.ac.uk/ resources/ projects/ pearce.aspx

Piccoli, G., Ahmad, R., & Ives, B. (2001). Web-based virtual learning environments: A research framework and a preliminary assessment of effectiveness in basic IT skills training. *Management Information Systems Quarterly, 25*(4), 401–426. doi:10.2307/3250989

Richardson, W. (2009). *Blogs, wikis, podcasts, and other powerful web tools for the classroom* (2nd ed.). California: Corwin Press.

Rodgers, J. R. (2001). A panel-data study of the effect of student attendance on university performance. *Australian Journal of Education, 45*(3), 284–295.

Saulwick, I., & Muller, D. (2006). *Fearless and flexible: Views of gen Y*. Report Prepared for the Dusseldorp Skills Forum. October. Saulwick Miller Social Research.

Shoemaker, A. (2008). *If the world is our campus, where are we going?* Address given at the Australian Financial Review Higher Education Conference. Retrieved September 21, 2009, from http://www.odvce.monash.edu.au/ passport-text.html

Song, H. S. Y., & Chan, Y. M. (2008). Educational blogging: A Malaysian university students' perception and experience. In *Hello! Where are you in the landscape of educational technology? Proceedings ASCILITE Melbourne 2008*. Retrieved on February 23, 2010, from http://www.ascilite.org.au/ conferences/ melbourne07/ procs/ song.pdf

Sun, Y. C. (2009). Voice blog: An exploratory study of language learning. *Language Learning & Technology, 13*(2), 88-103. Retrieved August 28, 2009, from http://llt.msu.edu/ vol13num2/ sun.pdf

Tekinarslan, E. (2008). Blogs: A qualitative investigation into an instructor and undergraduate students' experiences. *Australasian Journal of Educational Technology, 24*(4), 402–412.

Universities Australia. (2005). *Key statistics – students*. Retrieved 29 September, 2009, from http://www.universitiesaustralia.edu.au/ documents/ publications/ stats/ Students.pdf

Webster, L., Fraser, K., & Smith, L. (2009). Research-led curriculum redesign for productive learning: A case study in the faculty of information technology. In O'Donoghue, J. (Ed.), *Technology supported environment for personalised learning: Methods and case studies*. Hershey, PA: Idea Group Inc.doi:10.4018/978-1-60566-884-0.ch013

White, G. (2008). *Digital learning: An Australian research agenda 2008*. Retrieved April 28, 2010, from Available at: http://works.bepress.com/ gerry_white/1

Wild, F., Mödritscher, F., & Sigurdarson, S. (2008). Designing for change: Mash-up personal learning environments. *eLearning Papers, 9*. Retrieved February 22, 2010, from http://www.elearningeuropa.info/ out/ ?doc_id=15055 &rsr_id=15972

Williams, J. B., & Jacobs, J. (2004). Exploring the use of blogs as learning spaces in the higher education sector. *Australasian Journal of Educational Technology, 20*(2), 232–247.

Wilson, S., Liber, O., Johnson, M., Beauvoir, P., Sharples, P., & Milligan, C. (2007). Personal learning environments: Challenging the dominant design of educational systems. *Journal of e-Learning and Knowledge Society, 3*(2), 27-38.

Wood, D., Bruner, J., & Ross, G. (1976). The role of tutoring in problem solving. *Child Psychology and Psychiatry, 17*(1), 89–100. doi:10.1111/j.1469-7610.1976.tb00381.x

Wyn, J., Cuervo, H., Smith, G., Beadle, S., & Woodman, D. (2008). *Pathways through life: Summary report on 2007 survey*. Australian Youth Research Centre, The University of Melbourne. Retrieved September 28, 2009, from http://www. edfac.unimelb.edu.au/ yrc/ life_patterns/ Path- waysSurvey2007.pdf

Young, S., & Delves, L. (2009). Expanding to fit the (blog)space: Enhancing social work education through online technologies. In *Same places, different spaces. Proceedings ASCILITE Auckland 2009*. Retrieved February 23, 2010, from http:// www.ascilite.org.au/ conferences/ auckland09/ procs/ young.pdf

ADDITIONAL READING

Rogoff, B., Matusov, E., & White, C. (1998). Models of teaching and learning: Participation in a community of learners. In Olson, D. R., & Torrance, N. (Eds.), *The Handbook of Education and Human Development* (pp. 388–414). Malden, Massachusetts: Blackwell Publishing.

Scott, L. (2009). *PLE diagram*. Retrieved September 29, 2009, from http://edtechpost.wikispaces. com/ file/ view/ swl_ple2.gif

Sher, A. (2009). Assessing the relationship of student-instructor and student-student interaction to student learning and satisfaction in web-based online learning environment. *Journal of Interactive Online Learning, 8*(2), 102–120.

Vygotsky, L. S. (1978). *Mind in society: The development of higher psychological processes*. Cambridge, MA: Harvard University Press.

Webster, L., & Mertova, P. (2007). Terms of engagement: A case study of instructional designers in a Faculty of Law. In Keppell, M. (Ed.), *Instructional design: Case studies in communities of practice* (pp. 257–274). Hershey, PA: Information Science Publishing. doi:10.4018/978-1-59904-322-7.ch013

Webster, L., & Murphy, D. (2008). Enhancing learning through technology – Challenges and responses. In Tsang, P., Kwan, R., & Fox, R. (Eds.), *Enhancing learning through technology–Research on emerging technologies and pedagogies* (pp. 1–16). Hong Kong: World Scientific Publishing. doi:10.1142/9789812799456_0001

KEY TERMS AND DEFINITIONS

Blogs (also known as a weblog): A blog is a self-published website, where content is provided by one or more authors.

Knowledge Prosumer: Individual who both consumes and creates knowledge simultaneously.

LMS (Learning Management System): A system used to organise and support online student learning and resources.

PLE (Personalised Learning Environments): Provide a more holistic learning environment which is capable of bringing together disparate sources and contexts of learning. It can assist students to take responsibility for their own learning and it may bridge the 'walled gardens' of educational institutions and the 'worlds outside'.

Virtual Environments: All tools and components that provide online access to activities, communication, resources and assessment.

Wiki: A wiki is a website that can be authored and edited by numerous people, without specific web authoring software.

Chapter 11
Ezine and iRadio as Knowledge Creation Metaphors for Scaffolding Learning in Physical and Virtual Learning Spaces

Steve Dillon
Queensland University of Technology, Australia

Deidre Seeto
University of Queensland, Australia

Anne Berry
Queensland University of Technology, Australia

ABSTRACT

eZine and iRadio represent knowledge creation metaphors for scaffolding learning in a blended learning environment. Through independent and collaborative work online participating students experience a simulated virtual publishing space in their classrooms. This chapter is presented as an auto-ethnographic account highlighting the voices of the learning designer and the teacher. Using an iterative research design, evidence is provided for three iterations of each course. A collaborative approach to the development, planning, implementation, and evaluation of two tertiary music elective courses between lecturers, tutors, learning and technological designers is narrated. The student voice is embedded in the methodology, which involved an innovative approach that blends software development and pedagogy in iterations of software and experience design. The chapter describes how the teachers and learning designers translate these data into action and design. A blended learning space was incorporated within each of these elective music courses and the movement between these learning spaces is described and problematized. The research suggests that learning design, which provides real world examples and resources integrating authentic task design, can provide meaningful and engaging experiences for students. The dialogue between learning designers and teachers and iterative review of the learning process and student outcomes has engaged students meaningfully to achieve transferable learning outcomes.

DOI: 10.4018/978-1-60960-114-0.ch011

INTRODUCTION

In this chapter, we describe the evolution of an approach to learning and teaching that focuses on developing students' understanding of their ontological relationship to discipline knowledge. The approach scaffolds student learning in physical and virtual learning spaces by engaging students in a series of assessment tasks, with supporting resources and guidance from the lecturer and tutors--the blended learning environment. Through the presentation of two long-term case study subjects, we unpack the journey of recognition of the affordances of the blended learning space, and describe the iterative design process and approach to experience design. We have chosen to incorporate an auto-ethnographic narrative to present data and the subsequent analysis. Auto-ethnography is relatively new for musicological researchers but has been adopted with considerable success amongst practice-led researchers and ethnomusicologists as it enables musicians to 'examine, understand and communicate the personal ideas behind their creative experiences' (Bartleet & Ellis, 2009). This approach echoes the focus on ontological understanding utilized in the learning and teaching discourse and amplifies the nature of the relationship between the learning designer (Deidre) and the teacher (Steve). This approach we hope will allow each of us to speak in the first person and incorporate multiple lenses on the phenomenon when we include the broad range of qualitative data we collected, synthesized and then applied to successive iterations of the learning design and blended learning practice. To aid the flow of this dialogue we will simply precede the paragraph with our names and let the dialogue between us unfold as a kind of 'choir of voices' where solo voices emerge whilst others intertwine in concert to support or contrast them in a chiasmatic dialogue.

The structure of the chapter is as follows. First, we explain what we mean by learning spaces. Second, we describe the context of the collabora-

tion. Third, we outline the research methodology. Then we elaborate on the metaphors for design and the authentic task concept design. Finally, we conclude with reflections on the iterative process and summarize the affordances and provide recommendations for learning and teaching.

Learning Spaces

Our conception of learning spaces is as follows. A learning space is a subset of a learning environment. Wilson (1995) summarizes conceptions of a learning environment as comprising learners, teachers, resources, activities, and the learning space. In the learning space, the learner acts to achieve learning goals and unintended learning outcomes by engaging in activities--independent and collaborative--using resources with guidance by teachers. The learning space can be virtual, physical or blended. The configuration of these spaces affords different opportunities for learning and teaching.

BACKGROUND: INTERROGATING THE CONTEXT

Steve: I have researched and applied transformative approaches to learning for nearly thirty years now. I began my training as an 'open space' teacher influenced by Dewey with *Art as Experience* and Experiential learning (Dewey, 1989) and Bruner's notion of Discovery learning (Bruner, 1966). Further to this I have engaged learners in conceptual and phenomenological learning through concrete experience and real world environments applying ideas explored by Gardner in the Harvard Arts Propel, Project Zero (Davidson, 1992; Gardner, 1993) which utilized domain projects in the arts and assessment using portfolios. The concept of domain projects provided an ideal setting for employing an 'intelligence fair' approach to learning and teaching. The notion of 'intelligence fair' learning refers to Gardner's theory of multiple intelligence where he suggests that some activities favour particular representations of 'intelligence' over others. It is argued that domain projects which involve large or small projects where students work collaboratively on tasks toward a 'real world' outcome offer the opportunity for students to work in different ways towards learning rather than being forced to work in more abstract ways that may not be congruent with their learning style. Arts Propel director David Perkins (1986; 1988) also extended these ideas into concepts of the 'near and far transfer' to determine the degree of generic capacity inherent in the activities. These ideas have moved into a blended learning environment with innovative projects like the Logo computers language and Lego building blocks called constructionist learning design (Papert, 1980; 1994; 1996). They extend the constructivist theories of Dewey, Piaget and Vygotsky. These kinds of theories are apparent in school curricular and in teaching practice though I have noticed that their uptake has rarely been large scale. Whilst schools present some impediments to these kinds of approaches the environment of a university presents significantly different barriers to this kind of more flexible and transformative approach to learning ranging from policy constraints through physical setting to organisational issues with timetabling and accessible technology. The setting for this project is a university in Brisbane, Australia that states its aims are 'to provide outstanding learning environments and programs that lead to excellent outcomes for graduates, enabling them to work in, and guide, a world characterized by increasing change.'

I have had some experience with creating ePortfolios for learning and assessment through an Australian Research Council Discovery (ARC) project that delivered a conceptual framework for ePortfolios in Arts learning (Dillon & Brown, 2006). At the time of conducting that research the technology was not really available to implement blended learning easily. With the more recent implementation of learning management systems in Universities and the availability of access to Web 2.0 technologies such as blogs and wikis, an opportunity was provided to apply the theoretical ideas explored with the ARC research.

Deidre: The genesis of the collaboration began in March 2006 in my role as a learning designer from a centralized learning and teaching support unit. After Steve's expression of interest was accepted by the faculty, we discussed his initial ideas about developing a blended learning environment through face-to-face presentations and virtual tutorials and discussions. This would involve transforming the original virtual learning space—created using a Learning Content Management System (LCMS) called OLT—from just resources such as readings and lecture notes to a blended collaborative learning environment integrating tasks, resources and supports to engage students.

At the time, my interest in design-based research was emerging. Recognising the gap in research and guidance available for academic staff, the project provided an opportunity to explore the development of a blended collaborative learning environment. This would involve documenting the learning design process and the outcomes of the collaboration with the aim of discovering design principles and guidelines that can be shared and used by others to improve educational practice (Seeto & Herrington, 2006). Authentic task design (Herrington, Reeves & Oliver, 2004) was an appropriate framework to guide the design of the learning environment, aligning with Steve's teaching philosophy. The learning design would engage learners in independent and collaborative tasks using tools, resources and supports provided in virtual and physical learning spaces to achieve learning objectives.

To accomplish this we needed to approach the development in phases due to time and resource constraints. Moreover, we were moving into uncharted territory, using standard tools in the LCMS innovatively. The first phase involved reviewing the assessment tasks and introducing the production of an eZine as a knowledge creation metaphor

(Paavola, Lipponen, & Hakkarainen, 2004) to engage student learning. We then created a virtual learning space that looked and functioned like an eZine providing learners with the tools to create their own articles using multimedia examples. The learning tasks were extended to include an editorial approach that involved reviewing and critiquing other students' articles.

Building on this initial work, we successfully received a small university Teaching and Learning grant in 2007 to explore these ideas with the following proposed outcomes:

- refining, implementing and evaluating a learning design centred on the production of an eZine where learners collaboratively undertake activities that integrate specific unit/discipline knowledge, skills and graduate capabilities. These activities are aligned to learning outcomes and authentic assessment tasks;
- design guidelines and resources to support implementation of the learning design into units that have similar pedagogic and educational requirements (i.e. enabling others to integrate the learning design into their units); and
- develop a design-based research framework to evaluate the blended learning environment with the objective of improving the learner experience.

Steve: Consequently we consulted with faculty colleagues with experience in radio broadcasting and creative writing who served as peer advisors and critical friends. The project involved collaboration with Deidre, a learning designer whose role was to design the virtual learning space and activities and communicate with technical developers, whilst my role was to create an approach to the learning and teaching relationship with students in both virtual space and face-to-face lecture/tutorial spaces.

Methodology

The research method adopted for this project involved a mixed method devised for simultaneous design of software and pedagogy over a series of semester length iterations. The methodology is based on what Andrew Brown calls Software Development as Research – SoDaR (Brown, 2007).

The SoDaR approach proposes three stages:

1. Identification of the learning opportunity for which software development is required and establishing an appropriate approach to take advantage of that opportunity;
2. Design and production of the software; and
3. Implementation and refinement of the software via application in an educational setting.

This methodology is a hybrid multi-method and incorporates software development cycles, extreme programming, design-based research (Van den Akker, Gravemeijer, McKenney & Nieveen, 2006), case study research, and activity theory (Nardi, 1996) as data gathering strategies. The approach has been applied successfully where both software and pedagogy are developed simultaneously through successive action cycles that are informed by user questioning, observations and quantitative data from computer records. The research took place over a three-year period with a total of six iterations across two subject units per year with a sample of 350 students per year. Both subjects are concerned with the relationship between sound and society and are examined from a musicological perspective with an emphasis upon exploring the students' personal relationship with music. This phase of the research focuses on data collected from the teaching and learning team. Data from student experiences is part of a larger scale study still underway. Data was collected in the form of interviews with learning designers, technical developers, university lecturers and tutors with data from students being drawn from artifacts of their learning posted on their personal blogs as assignments. Data was also drawn from anonymous course reviews and from a reflective editorial statement presented as part of an 'exam' in each subject. What is presented here provides a preliminary analysis and description of the interaction between teacher, learning designer and their collaboration in developing a blended learning environment that responds iteratively to learning needs of students. Whilst the student voice is significant in the research process what is presented here is the teacher and learning designer's application and synthesis of these data to learning design. An emerging model for a conceptual framework is proposed as a guide to application of these methods across disciplines. It is hoped that these tenets provide a transferable and useful framework for creative use of blended environments to engage learners.

Metaphors for the 'Real' World: Music, Identity, iRadio and eZines

Deidre: The first phase of this project focused on analysing learner characteristics, the learning space and the teaching context followed by a review of the literature and web resources to inform the design of the learning environment. The design of the assessment tasks, resources and supports drew from elements in the authentic task design framework (Herrington et al., 2004).

The initial concept proposal of an online eZine for an iRadio program sparked Steve's imagination and enthusiasm. I then created the prototype using commercial software to demonstrate how the design would support the authentic assessment tasks and would work functionally. The resulting space used existing tools in the LCMS in new ways. The affordances of the LCMS—the virtual learning space—were also considered in designing the learner experience. Standard tools in the LCMS were available to students, student created content (i.e. the team editorial and the students' individual articles) could be collocated with col-

laboration tools (i.e. the discussion forum) using a standard tool, and all artifacts could be released to the Internet easily. This enabled students to create their assessment tasks using a variety of media with authoring tools available in the LCMS, to review other students' articles and make comments in the discussion forum in one interface, and to publish the finished product to the world as an eZine. The only customisation required was the visual interface and menu structure as seen in Figure 1 to enable the students to easily navigate between volumes of the eZine. Working with a graphic designer and programmer we created the first iteration. Due to time constraints, evaluation and testing was limited to a review by two learning designers, a programmer and Steve. In hindsight, more time should have been allocated for usability testing.

Subsequent phases refined the design and also had to incorporate the migration to a new learning management system. The affordances of the new system presented challenges and constraints resulting in changes to the virtual learning space.

Steve: We began the process by using real world ideas as represented in virtual radio and magazine publishing. The affordances of these metaphors or Domain projects are that they simultaneously allow multimedia publishing in sound, visual and text forms and they also have models for editorial review and quality publication that we saw might be useful for student learning and teacher management of process and writing feedback. The outcomes from this project revealed themselves through successive iterations. In the beginning the focus on pedagogical considerations was overshadowed by impediments to uptake such as: technical problems with the Learning Management Systems, student and staff 'techno phobia' or simply bad experiences with university computing systems. The acknowledgement that the technical systems are clearly designed for security rather than ease of access was initially a major impediment for observing creative engagement with the software or the learning. The positive aspects of

Figure 1. The student workspace

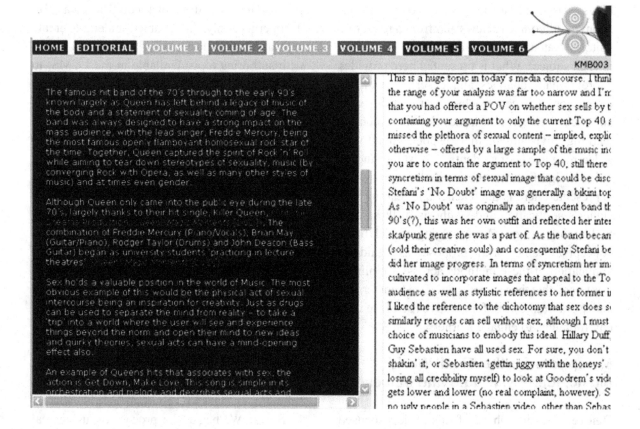

this were that an audit of what aspects worked best in virtual or physical spaces provided clear information about how each should be considered and designed. The students, learning designer and teacher's frustration of knowing the ease of access to open source free wikis and blogs such as Wikispaces.com and Ning.com created a tension with the university system for both staff and students. It also highlighted students' level of interaction with online materials with some students failing to access podcasts. One of the aspects of surveillance afforded by Learning Management Systems is their capacity to track network activity of individuals which showed students were not engaging with the wider conceptual issues required for the units online.

Phase two brought the focus to the teaching environment in tutorials and lectures. The approach revolved around three activities: first identifying the students' relationship with the phenomenon. This involved reflective questioning and small group work to determine the answer to questions such as: What music do you feel is spiritual to you? Or what music gives you flow and engages you personally? These group questions were then developed into a title for a blog article or a wiki term, an approach to researching and analysing the topic and a nominated method of presenting the work. This draft is then turned into a proposal presented on a blog or wiki. Students provide triangulated evidence comprising at least three kinds of media and text sources relevant to the phenomenon.

Over the next two sessions students in small editorial groups develop and peer edit each other's work and ideas and present the outcomes on the virtual space. These proposals are peer and teacher reviewed and marked with comment using criteria referencing that serves as an editorial or house style. Following the marking of these online, students are introduced to the key concepts of the unit, i.e. research methods – in this case we applied 'musicological element analysis' to the YouTube video clips of songs using a defined effectors and effects framework (Pratt, 1990). It is here that analytical methods are learned and applied through using students' work in class to develop the use of critical analytical tools and reporting on them. The model of effectors and effects emphasizes the embodied and ontological responses of students and then provides a clear framework for analysing what caused the effect. This aspect has been extremely successful and the quality of assignments is much higher than in prior years.

Further success was had with the idea that the work could be presented in a podcast, as a creative work: song, arrangement, visual artwork, dance or mixed media presentation. The wiki/ blog space provides a means to present artefacts of the work alongside critical analysis evidence and an exegesis describing the process and how it investigated the phenomenon. The success with this was that it became learner inclusive. We noted that for those students who had underdeveloped writing skills that their writing improved through the peer editing process. Alongside this their enthusiasm for the task showed that they increased the amount of hours spent doing the task. It was also extremely successful amongst students from non-English speaking backgrounds and enabled an understanding to be reached through symbolic forms other than language whilst also providing a forum to strengthen language development. The pride in this work was clearly demonstrated in the high quality and diversity of submissions by students. They ranged from a choreographer videotaping herself dancing the relationship between water and spirituality to a podcast interrogating the meaning of the National anthem to Indigenous and Immigrant Australians.

Whilst this engagement and quality of research and writing was encouraging and became more refined over the three iterations, the movement from the ontological to the epistemological via the key concepts for the units was not. This movement involved addressing two questions in a 'take home' progressive exam. The questions asked for a definition and evidence of each key concept from course materials, references and experiences and a reflective editorial about the changes in the way they thought about their relationship to music. This provided us with a large body of data about students' experiences with the units and what was known and valued and what aspects could be applied. For two iterations understanding of key concepts was very poor and students showed a reluctance to move beyond their own perspective and showed little understanding or ability to apply knowledge to the unit themes. Two factors influenced this. Firstly, students often did not listen to podcasts, and secondly, late in the semester attendance dropped in tutorials due to competing commitments of work and other subject assignments due. This is an indicator of a larger problem for student lives and maturity. To address these issues we have included a progressive wiki that details the students' understanding and links to key concepts. These ideas were scaffolded through classroom discussion and defined a technique for identifying and investigating all the literature and resources that refer to each key concept. Students were required then to find critical insights from this data that demonstrate they had engaged with the material each week for six weeks to scaffold their approach to learning. This utilizes the time and date stamping aspects of the LMS (Blackboard). These materials are then used by students in the take-home exam as links to evidence provided online and their engagement with it. They could then use this material to construct an essay that demonstrated their relationship to the phenomenon that showed both insight and genuine links to this evidence. Whilst results from this are in the early stages of analysis we do note that the quality of understanding presented both in class and online has been raised and even non-attending students have a strategy that moves them beyond personal opinion rants.

Whilst initially the technological affordances and constraints were foregrounded in this study, we now find that because wikis and blogs are becoming more common we can focus more clearly upon using them as a collaborative platform for publishing and sharing student work. The learning design aspects of providing an editorial space that looks and acts like an eZine and provides access to a variety of media experiences in publishing outcomes and for presenting flexibly-delivered iRadio articles as pod- or vod- casts provides a recall and flexibility not provided by live lectures and print copy essays. The idea of iRadio and eZine publishing as a real world simulation or Domain project as was used by Gardner in the Arts Propel project (Davidson, 1992) or Papert with Logo-Lego (1980) brings these notions into an environment where it is both more accessible and also accountable.

Description of the Units

Sex Drugs and Rock n Roll has been a popular elective unit at the university across disciplines for eight years now. The unit was initially a history of popular music but has been shaped by student interaction into an 'Urban' ethno-musicological subject. It simply proposes to investigate the relationships between sound and society. This has taken the form of a group presentation, an essay and an exam examining key issues. The unit was delivered as a series of lectures, performances and videos for thirteen weeks with a tutorial to discuss the emerging issues each week. When we began applying the ideas of eZine and iRadio to the unit we reduced the lecture contact time down to six live lectures, performances and videos. The lecture series was then supplemented by podcasts and vodcasts delivered online.

The unit *Music and Spirituality* continued this approach to examining the relationship between sound and society by focusing upon the connection music making has to spiritual dimensions of music. This unit also was popular and attracted a strong philosophical and theological interest from students across spiritual domains. The research approach here involves what is known as theo-ethnomusicology. The delivery of this unit also moved from thirteen lectures to podcast delivery and face-to-face tutorials.

The shift from live to online delivery lent different technological affordances to the process and required us to negotiate what was possible with a university Learning Management System whose main function was to be secure rather than flexible. This required a dynamic interaction between the learning designers and the teachers to identify what could or should be located in the virtual, what support it needed and what strategies should be developed in the present teaching environment. The affordances of hyperlinks, wikis and blogs systems allowed access to different forms of information and also different metaphors and one that emerged for us from staff professional practice was Richard Vella's A-Z of Spiritual Music which is a wiki that details the spiritual qualities of music through a definition, a podcast, an analysis and a piece of music. Initially developed as a lecture for the unit delivered live, this became an ABC website and we then adopted the model internally as a verisimilitude or real world model for learning. *Sex Drugs Rock n Roll* simply adopted a model of an eZine and iRadio station offering online publishing for a rockZine with multimedia presentations. Both provided the affordance of access, collaboration and a metaphor for dynamic development of multimedia perspectives on phenomena and multiple evidence artefacts plus a model for rigor through editing and meeting publication deadlines.

These units have become very different both in their content and the expectations placed on students. Students in these units are treated as publishing professionals and expected to use the musicological methods for analysis and the 'house style' for publishing. The key idea here is that we wanted to keep music present in the conversation about music. Many music history subjects simply write about music but we wanted to allow the sound to be present while undertaking reading and analysis. We wanted the opportunity to respond in different ways and analyse music using visual and auditory as well as practice led approaches. The online environment provides the opportunity to document and present artifacts of this kind of work that privilege the music and allow the effects and effectors of music to focus the enquiry. In teaching these units we found our teaching now became about musicological research skills using musical analysis. We developed our questioning skills to help students identify their ontological relationship to music that fed into and enhanced their personal identity. We facilitated peer editing, collaborative skills with debates about 'what music is?' and a management of philosophical, aesthetic, theoretical and theological discussions around determining the students' relationship with musical knowledge.

Authentic Task Concept Design

The learning model adopted 'authentic tasks' in the form of creating published multimedia articles online in a way that sought to integrate self, peer, group and teacher assessment processes as an ongoing element of the course. Throughout the project students worked in tutorials to edit each other's work and offer analytical and research advice. They also applied criteria-referenced assessment documents as ways of reflecting on the quality and structure of their own and peers' work in class and were required to apply them to peers' work online using the comments box. The notion of an online publishing house provides a verisimilitude and a real world model for working that has relevance to students' lives. They could examine professional eZines and iRadio sites on

the Internet and establish how they operate and determine the quality of their output.

Assessment

The design of assessment was simple:

- Project proposal – personal, social and cultural aspect of music in society, an outline of media of presentation and media examples of their musical choice;
- Project delivery using a choice of media: essay/article, creative work or podcast, documentary; and
- Reflective editorial style exam to show development of an understanding of 7 key concepts.

Criterion-referenced assessment outlines guided the peer and academic review process of each assessment item. The teaching aspect focused upon developing an ontological perspective on learning firstly in their relationship to the phenomenon followed by an exploration of the 7 key concepts so that assessment reinforces personal growth and radiates outward to conceptual understanding and application. Collaboration was developed in the assessment process through peer editorial sessions in class and online through comments.

The iterative research approach has led to several changes in assessment and emphasized the importance of ongoing assessment in maintaining/sustaining students' meaningful engagement. We found that for each step we required scaffolding through the provision of three simple steps: focusing the enquiry; researching using prescribed analytical tools; and examining and editing presentations using peer, self and teacher application of assessment criteria as a 'house style' guide.

Reflections on the Quality of Student Outcomes Based on Assessment Products and Student Feedback on the Course

Having the opportunity to reflect on experiences as part of the 'exam' for the units provided us with clear understandings of what was learnt and the quality and depth of the experiences alongside the meaning to students. The learning improved as did the quality and application of understanding when we realized that each step needed to be scaffolded by example, in live and virtual practice exercises, peer feedback and editing and clear weekly tasks with deadlines monitored by the LMS surveillance system. Whilst we initially thought this would be 'spoon feeding' or tedious because of the weekly commitment, students unanimously appreciated the clarity and consistency of a working model that it provided and the discourse about their work it provided. There was now no space for half-baked last minute submissions or an assumption that skills of critical analysis and writing/publishing had been learned elsewhere. The Meaningful Engagement Matrix (MEM) provided us with a framework and way of describing how students engaged with activity and the location of meaning for them. Whilst there is not space in this document to present this process in detail we can say

that we can determine by looking at the location of meaning: personal, social and cultural where communication is taking place and by examining the modes of engagement we can determine the nature of the activity. For example is the activity intuitive or directing? These descriptors and coding categories allow a perspective on the kind of relationship the student is experiencing and the activity they are undertaking.

Engagement and Motivation: Questions to be Asked

Ongoing issues for the units' design are: Is the unit sufficiently intrinsically motivating given the course content, design and delivery to maintain the interest and participation of the students? How can these elements be improved with each iteration of the course? What other elements may improve student participation? How can the assessment process be best designed to encourage meaningful engagement with the students to best achieve the learning outcomes?

Meaningful Engagement

Dillon and Brown have developed an approach to the evaluation of meaningful engagement (Dillon, 2003; 2004; Dillon & Brown, 2007) in real

Figure 2. The meaningful engagement matrix

	Appreciate	Select	Direct	Explore	Embody
Personal					
Social					
Cultural					

and virtual environments. It has been used in the development of generative software for children and assessment of social networks for children aged 8-14. Both Deidre and I used the Matrix to identify where the majority of activity was across the blended environments. This approach provided a means to act on the data from students and observations. We looked at how we could build motivation into the design of the experiences for students so that they received positive and encouraging feedback in personal, social and cultural interactions both in class as well as virtually. We noted that through the process of virtual representation, students were able to demonstrate understandings that may have initially been termed embodied ones because the virtual space forced them to document their processes and provide evidence of their progress. Both in class and virtually safe experiences of exploring were provided that enabled improvisation with abstract ideas and we felt that this provided multiple environments to allow tacit knowledge to move from being implicit to explicit. Personal, social and cultural feedback through self reflection, peer interaction and critique and wider peer and teacher critique provided multiple engagement opportunities and extrinsic motivations for improving quality. Furthermore it allowed us to observe different learning styles and for group interaction behaviours to emerge.

Reflections on the Iterative Research

Insight into the collaborative and iterative approach of course designers, lecturers and tutors was gained through interviews by Anne who was a non participant independent researcher and provided another lens on the phenomenon and another voice in our chorus. The aim of these interviews was to better understand how the units had evolved and the importance of the collaborative development approach. These interviews were later summarized and analyzed using the MEM as a coding mechanism that provided a way of locating and describing both the relationships and the activity.

Anne: Following an initial meeting with Steve a list of questions was devised to guide the four interviews. These questions established the roles of two learning designers, the lecturer and the tutor in relation to the two subject units, especially in regard to the development of the two units over time. Issues canvassed included both advantages and frustrations with the university's learning management system; the awareness of each of the interviewees of the personal impact on students of participation in these subjects; implications for students and administration caused by the changes in assessment practice; the impact of authentic task design (eZine and iRadio) with regard to fostering student collaboration as well as the personal growth/identity of individual students; and what are the benefits and difficulties associated with the blended learning environment – how important is the relationship aspect of face-to-face teaching?

The MEM has proved to be a useful tool for summarising the interviews which were conducted with the unit designers, tutor and lecturer. As all four of the interviewees are experienced professionals in their fields and working within their field of expertise, information summarized in the columns headed 'explore' and 'embody' proved the most interesting both in terms of comparing the interview results as well as finding critical individual experiences of engagement and motivation. The matrix allowed us to observe and document embodied/intuitive understandings so that activities could be constructed that encourage and support these formally invisible processes.

The most surprising result from the interviews and their analysis using the MEMs was the enthusiasm of all those who were interviewed when discussing their role in developing the subject units. In summarising the interviews within the construct of the MEM, I as the interviewer became the observer of the interview process. When I remembered the excitement with which Deidre described her involvement with the project, the benefits of analysis and review of the ongoing collaborative process between teachers and designers became clear. I remembered thinking that for Steve his involvement described much of his philosophy of life. For him, the element of surprise came from realising that he was actually teaching research skills and that this product of the course was really worth reporting. For Tim the web designer there was a personal challenge to do with solving technical problems in which the motivation to success had at least in part been motivated by Steve's enthusiasm for the course. It seems Tim is spurred to action by questions, that he gains a sense of personal achievement from solving these questions for others but also experiences dissatisfaction when he is aware of further issues to be solved or that the solution is not ideal. What was it for Lawrence the tutor? Lawrence enjoyed describing the way he had used musical examples to inspire the students to listen, how he had created metaphors for the students using these examples and how students had grown comfortable in discussing their process. In particular he was impressed at the value of this course in creating life-changing decisions for some students in terms of their choice of life-path. Primarily we asked participants 'what surprised you?' from data gathered in the interviews, excerpts from which follow:

Deidre's excitement revolved around three key terms: innovation, authentic task design and a collaborative approach.

Deidre: *Steve's units Music & Spirituality and Sex Drugs Rock 'n Roll were identified as priority units to be enhanced. So we met and discussed it and I said that this is a great opportunity for us to revamp it. We first started talking about pedagogy, and what he wanted to achieve and then it led to the area of authentic task design. He talked about the SoDaR model and flow theory... he had a vision about what he wanted to achieve in terms of the way the students experienced the content and experienced the unit and from that it was very much a creative process. It began with creating an authentic task for the students. From*

that emerged the design, and I said, 'why don't we base it around an eZine?' This was the unit Sex Drugs Rock 'n Roll. And we'll base it on role play...

..learning by doing, and also through reflection... 'situated learning' essentially. So we thought about the tasks, and how they would experience unit content and how they inadvertently would develop graduate capabilities...through that process how they would get in touch with themselves in terms of their connection of their own identity and the actual unit, the unit themes etc. We worked through the changes and we did some innovative things with the LMS which had never been done before. When we made the transition over to Blackboard it actually raised policy issues around technology... university for the real world, let's provide authentic learning environments for students. (I: Deidre, L, 19/08/08)

Tim's sense of achievement in dealing with the learning design issues with a creative approach is expressed in the following:

Tim: *Blackboard is a LMS and it probably really is a content management system rather than a LMS. And Steve was asking for a publication environment for students. So that was ... we bought some add-ons to Blackboard to allow students to create content. Out-of-the-box Blackboard doesn't really support that. So, we had a wiki tool which we could use across both sites. And we just had some work in trying to structure the wiki around how students could publish their journal articles, reflect on their journal articles, and then also see previous ones. Also, in OLT (previous university designed LMS) we'd been able to create a custom environment for the site with archival just built into the system and we also had a navigation system which was built into OLT which had to be recreated to Blackboard. That was actually probably the trickiest part. I designed this custom navigation system for Sex Drugs Rock 'n Roll but it went so far outside the norm of Blackboard that it had to be approved right up the university chain and it's an exception that other sites aren't allowed to do this... (I: Tim, L, 18/02/09)*

From a social/embodiment correlation using the matrix, Tim's feeling of personal connection with the importance of these units is summarized by the following:

Yeah, yeah, I did [find it interesting] and definitely the discussions I had with Steve were very rewarding, that was great. Just talking about his music software and his excitement about the design and his excitement about working with students, was really – reminds you of why we work with academics. (I: Tim, L, 18/02/09)

The benefits of a cooperative and collaborative approach between the teachers and learning designers to the units' development seem to have been mirrored in the students' achievement. Tim's comments were suggestive of an important cultural embodiment related to the significance of both the delivery and course content:

Well, I think Steve's been quite excited about the student content for both the sites and allowing the students to see each other's content has ... trying to help students with how they see each other's work because examples of what other students are doing along the way has raised the academic level and I've given these sites out as examples to other academics about how the wiki can work well. (I: Tim, L, 18/02/09)

The engagement with technological constraints of a specific LMS is not something we have time to discuss in detail here. What can be gleaned from this experience is that when the technology does not afford interaction we need to look at what can change in the teacher's behavior and approach to learning. In this case we are simply using wikis and blogs and in some cases these may be encased within an Institutional system that may make their use less user friendly. The solution is to move to the live space and interaction to implement change rather than expect the system to change or be adaptable. Technology both reveals and conceals and our job as teachers is to negotiate the ethics of these relationships and adapt ourselves to the learning approach needed.

Lawrence's summary using the MEM showed that the questions he asked himself in devising specific examples to use in tutorials were aimed at really engaging the students. Musical examples could include an unusual sound, familiar music played differently (authenticity) or including new music written during the lifetime of the students in an historic context. The careful selection of intrinsically motivating musical examples and questions to be answered seem to have been critical for engaging students and motivating them towards a deeper, more critical level of thinking as well as adding a dimension of personal development for the students.

Lawrence: *... the thing about Sex Drugs Rock 'n Roll as a Course is that it's always been about this idea of getting the students to think and apply critically like it's a critical listening, critical analysis course and a lot of students I think don't necessarily apply themselves to that necessity for thought, they kind of try and respond very quickly and they don't actually – sometimes I think it's just that they don't have the experience or interest in music deeply enough to kind of get it, but and other times...*

I'm just the tutor for the course, I'm there to facilitate people's engagement with the course and ideally open ... I've always felt strongly about opening students up to new work that they haven't come across before – new styles of music, new approaches, new sounds they haven't heard before. Often I think I've found that's been the lasting legacy of the course. I've run into people three or four later and they'll say to me, I remember when you played blah and now I'm really into that. (I: Lawrence, T, 12/02/09)

The transcript of Steve's interview as the lecturer and course coordinator reflected on many aspects of the units (I: Steve, T, 10/04/08). The MEM showed how these related and correlated to create an involved teaching approach leading to the development of generic capabilities which are often aspired to by universities including student collaboration & research skills. The four points which he emphasized in his approach were:

- critical moments and a personal history approach;
- research framework based on personal interest and studies;
- life-changing effects; and
- alternative methods of assessment to written material, i.e. podcasts & video material.

The SoDaR iterations provided the opportunity to simultaneously develop design alongside pedagogy. Each iteration revealed firstly the focus on technological impediments and how to overcome them with design, training and teaching approaches. Secondly it revealed the possibilities of an ontological approach and a multimedia presentation space to engage students in learning. Finally it revealed the difficulty of shifting from an intense self-focus to a wider appreciation of conceptual knowledge. Each negative case revealed required both a virtual and present teaching solution.

Solutions and Recommendations

The outcomes of this research have been profound for us as teachers and learning designers alike. The primary insight is that the learning and teaching can only progress in blended environments in both physical and virtual spaces, when the virtual one becomes ubiquitous and almost disappears in the process. In a 21st century student's world, the real and present is extended by the virtual and potentially relationships can be maintained beyond the classroom.

The affordances of virtual spaces we observed are that they:

- monitor time and date stamp interaction which can be more useful than thinly veiled threats to examine frequency of interaction and determine impediments to uptake and use or simply to provide scaffolded deadlines for submission;
- provide a collaborative space for development of work in clear stages which can be edited by peers and teachers;
- provide an opportunity for symbolic interaction in a variety of media forms which makes it intelligence fair;
- provide alternative repeatable spaces for non-text and text materials such as podcasts, vodcasts and websites; and
- provide a real world verisimilitude or domain project environment like a publishing house.

The affordances of physical spaces such as tutorials or lectures in a blended environment promote in the teachers focus toward an ontological and clearly structured environment that scaffolds all activity around the students' relationship to knowledge. This approach subsequently progresses to include teaching strategies that engage with conceptual knowledge. The teacher requires skills in: focusing questioning, presenting a clear understanding and examples of concepts, group management and reporting approaches, teaching of analytical processes and critical analysis, an understanding of the nature of triangulated evidence and approaches to editing and presentation skills. Further skills lie in the construction of criterion referenced assessment tools that can be used to develop, focus and improve the quality of articles.

CONCLUSION

What we have presented here is a chorus of voices about blended learning focusing on two case studies documenting three years and over a thousand students' involvement. What we believe are the transferable aspects of this process are simply that wikis and blogs provide a place where multimodal expressions can be made and the process can be documented. They provide a safe and encouraging extension of the face-to-face collaborative space. The face-to-face environment has to be managed in a way that encourages personal/ontological exploration and social collaborative activity which is extended to the cultural through editing and publication in real and virtual spaces. What was most surprising and rewarding about this experience was the quality and extended expression that being able to respond in multimedia forms afforded. The inclusion of students from non-English backgrounds was immediately apparent and those whose principle learning style was not text expression were also able to be more articulate. This also extended to the improvement in their writing because of peer review and repeated editing processes. The outcomes for students were the development of generic capabilities through learning multi-modal presentation and critical analysis and lifelong learning habits that can be carried into real-world contexts. In the 21st century we extend our relationships with others in virtual spaces mediated by technology. What this project has shown us is the importance of the physical relationship allowing students to examine their ontological relationship to knowledge, then learning skills of critical analysis to synthesize the tidal wave of knowledge available. The movement between present and virtual spaces can be almost seamless but the skills of critical and ethical engagement are necessary in both and in both we need to ask what is revealed and what is concealed and what the value of the experiences is.

ACKNOWLEDGMENT

The author of this paper acknowledge the work of Dr Christina Spurgeon and Dr Glen Thomas each of whom contributed significant consultancy information around iRadio and eZine's that shaped the design and development of this project. We also acknowledge support of the Queensland University of Technology Teaching and Learning Development Small Grants Scheme 2007 for this project. Thanks also go to Tim Plaisted (Learning Designer) and Lawrence English (Tutor) who gave their time for interviews; and Elizabeth Hall (Graphic designer) and Greg Steele (Programmer).

REFERENCES

Bartleet, B., & Ellis, C. (Eds.). (2009). *Music autoethnographies: Making autoethnography sing/making music personal*. Brisbane, Australia: Australian Academic Press.

Brown, A. (2007). Software development as music education research. *International Journal of Education & the Arts, 8*(6), 1–13.

Brown, A., & Dillon, S. (2007). Networked improvisational musical environments: Learning through online collaborative music making. In Finney, J., & Burnard, P. (Eds.), *Music education with digital technology* (pp. 96–106). London, UK: Continuum International Publishing Group.

Bruner, J. S. (1966). *Towards a theory of instruction*. Cambridge, MA: Belknap Press of Harvard University.

Davidson, L. (1992). *Arts propel: A handbook for music (with video of evaluation methods and approaches)*. Cambridge, MA: Harvard Project Zero.

Dewey, J. (1989). *Art as experience*. U.S.A.: Perigree Books.

Dillon, S. (2003). *jam2jam: Meaningful music making with computers.* Paper presented at the Artistic Practice as Research: 25th Annual Conference of the Australian Association for Research in Music Education, Brisbane, Queensland, Australia.

Dillon, S. (2004). S*ave to DISC: Documenting innovation in music learning.* Paper presented at the 26th Annual Conference of the Australian Association for Research in Music Education, Southern Cross University, Tweed Heads.

Dillon, S. (2007). *Examining meaningful engagement: Musicology and virtual music making environments.* Paper presented at the Musicological Society of Australasia.

Dillon, S., & Brown, A. (2006). The art of e-portfolios: Insights from the creative arts experience. In Jafari, A., & Kaufman, C. (Eds.), *Handbook of research on e-portfolios: Concepts, technology and case studies* (pp. 418–431). Indianapolis, IN: Idea- Group Inc.

Gardner, H. (1993). *Frames of mind: The theory of multiple intelligences.* London, UK: Fontana Press.

Herrington, J., Reeves, T. C., & Oliver, R. (2004). Designing authentic activities in Web-based courses. *Journal of Computing in Higher Education, 16*(1), 3–29. doi:10.1007/BF02960280

http://www.abc.net.au/ classic/features/ s1809663. htm

http://www.ning.com/

http://www.savetodisc.net/

http://www.wikispaces.com/

http://www.youtube.com.au/

http://www.youtube.com/ watch?v=ElBlTr74AQE

Nardi, B. (Ed.). (1996). *Context and consciousness: Activity theory and human-computer interaction.* Cambridge, MA: MIT Press.

Paavola, S., Lipponen, L., & Hakkarainen, K. (2004). Models of innovative knowledge communities and three metaphors of learning. *Review of Educational Research, 74*(4), 557–576. doi:10.3102/00346543074004557

Papert, S. (1980). *Mindstorms, children, computers and powerful ideas.* USA: Basic Books Inc.

Papert, S. (1994). *The children's machine: rethinking school in the age of the computer.* New York, NY: Harvester Wheatsheaf.

Papert, S. (1996). A word for learning. In Kafai, Y., & Resnick, M. (Eds.), *Constructionism in practice: Designing, thinking, and learning in a digital world* (p. 15). Mahwah, NJ: Lawrence Erlbaum and Associates.

Perkins, D. N. (1986). *Knowledge as design.* Hillsdale, NJ: Lawrence Earlbaum Associates.

Perkins, D. N. (1988). Teaching for transfer. *Educational Leadership, 46*(1), 22–32.

Pratt, G. (1990). *Aural awareness: Principles and practice.* United Kingdom: Open University Press.

Seeto, D., & Herrington, J. (2006). Design-based research and the learning designer. In L. Markauskaite, P. Goodyear, & P. Reimann (Eds.), *Proceedings of the 23rd Annual Conference of the Australasian Society for Computers in Learning in Tertiary Education: Who's Learning? Whose Technology?* (pp. 741-745). Sydney, Australia: Sydney University Press.

Van den Akker, J., Gravemeijer, K., McKenney, S., & Nieveen, N. (2006). *Educational design research.* London, UK: Routledge.

Wilson, B. G. (1995). Metaphors for instruction: Why we talk about learning environments. *Educational Technology, 35*(5), 25–30.

ADDITIONAL READING

Bell, J., & Opie, C. (2002). *Learning from research: Getting more from your data.* Buckingham, UK: Open University Press.

Berry, A. (1996). *Introduction to playing the cello* (video and handbook). Toowoomba: University of Southern Queensland.

Berry, A. (1997). *The development and evaluation of a multimedia approach to cello pedagogy.* Unpublished Masters Thesis, University of Southern Queensland, Toowoomba.

Berry, A. (2004, December). Teaching Australian cello music to intermediate students: An exploratory study of motivation through repertoire. In M. Chaseling (Ed.), *Australian Association for Research in Music Education: Proceedings of the XXVIth Annual Conference, 25 - 28 September 2004, Southern Cross University, Tweed Gold Coast Campus, Tweed Heads* (pp. 25-39). Melbourne: Australian Association for Research in Music Education.

Berry, A. I. (2007). *A study of motivation through repertoire in intermediate cello students.* Unpublished doctoral dissertation (PhD), University of Queensland.

Bresler, L. (1996). Basic and applied qualitative research in music education. *Research Studies in Music Education, 6,* 5–17. doi:10.1177/1321103X9600600102

Bresler, L. (2004). Knowing bodies, moving minds. In Bresler, L. (Ed.), *Landscapes the arts, aesthetics, and education.* Urbana-Champaign, Illinois, USA: Kluwer Academic Publishers.

Broughton, D., Eisner, E., & Ligtvoet, J. (1996). *Evaluating and assessing the visual arts in education.* New York: Teachers College Press.

Brown, A. (2000). *Modes of compositional engagement.* Paper read at Australasian Computer Music Conference-Interfaces, at Brisbane, Australia.

Brown, A., & Dillon, S. (2007). Networked improvisational musical environments: learning through online collaborative music making. In Finney, J., & Burnard, P. (Eds.), *Music education with digital technology* (pp. 96–106). London: Continuum International Publishing Group.

Bruner, J. S. (1973). *Beyond the information given.* New York: Norton.

Buber, M. (1969). *Between man and man* [Translation and Introduction by Ronald Gregor Smith]. London: Fontana.

Buber, M. (1975). *I and thou* [Translation and Preface by Ronald Gregor Smith]. 2nd ed.). Edinburgh: T & T Clark.

Cherry, N. (1999). *Action research: a pathway to action, knowledge and learning.* Melbourne: RMIT Publishing.

Csikszentmihalyi, M. (1994). *Flow: The psychology of happiness.* New York, USA: Random Century Group. [Original edition, 1992, Harper and Rowe]

Csikszentmihalyi, M., Rathunde, K., & Whalen, S. (1993). *Talented teenagers.* Cambridge, Great Britain: Cambridge University Press.

Davidson, L. (1992). *Arts propel: A handbook for music (with video of evaluation methods and approaches).* Cambridge, Mass: Harvard Project Zero.

Deci, E., & Ryan, R. (1992). The initiation and regulation of intrinsically motivated learning and achievement. In Boggiano, A., & Pittman, T. (Eds.), *Achievement and motivation: A social-developmental perspective* (pp. 9–36). Cambridge: Cambridge University Press.

Denzin, N. K., & Lincoln, Y. S. (2000). *Handbook of qualitative research* (2nd ed.). London: Sage Publications Inc.

DiBiase. (2002). *Using e-Portfolios at Penn State to enhance student learning.* Penn: Penn State.

Dillon, S. (2005). Meaningful engagement with music technology. In Mackinlay, E., Collins, D., & Owens, S. (Eds.), *Aesthetics and experience in music performance*. Cambridge: Cambridge Scholars Press.

Dillon, S., Adkins, B., Brown, A. R., & Hirche, K. (2008). *Communities of sound: Generative music making and virtual ensembles*. Paper read at CMA XIII: Projects, Perspectives & Conversations: Proceedings from 2008 Seminar of the Commission for Community Music Activity, Rome, Italy.

Dillon, S. C. (2009) *Examining meaningful engagement: musicology and virtual music making environments*. In: E. Mackinlay & B. Bartleet (Eds.) Islands: Proceedings of the Musicological Society of Australasia (pp. 297-310). Newcastle upon Tyne: Cambridge Scholars Publishing.

Dipert, R. R. (1993). *Artifacts art works, and agency*. Philadelphia: Temple University Press.

Ecker, D., & Baker, L. T. (1984). Multiple perception analysis: A convergence model for evaluating arts education. *Studies in Art Education, 25*(4), 245–250. doi:10.2307/1320419

Eisner, E. (Ed.). (1985). *Learning and teaching the ways of knowing. The 84th Yearbook of the National Society for the Study of Education Part II.* Chicago, USA: The University of Chicago Press.

Elliott, E., & Dweck, C. (1988). Goals: An approach to motivation and achievement. *Journal of Personality and Social Psychology, 54*(1), 5–12. doi:10.1037/0022-3514.54.1.5

Elliott, J. (1988). Educational research and outsider-insider relations. *International Journal of Qualitative Studies in Education, 1*(2), 155–165. doi:10.1080/0951839880010204

Heidegger, M. (1977). *The question concerning technology, and other essays*. New York: Garland Pub.

Jorgensen, D. L. (1989). *Participant observation: A methodology for human studies* (2nd ed.). Newbury Park, CA, USA: Sage Publications.

Lincoln, Y. S., & Guba, E. G. (1985). *Naturalistic enquiry*. Beverley Hills, CA, USA: Sage Publications Inc.

Miles, M. B., & Huberman, A. M. (1984). *Qualitative analysis: A source book of new methods*. CA, USA: Sage.

Oppenheim, A. N. (1992). *Questionnaire design, interviewing and attitude measurement* (Revised ed.). London: Continuum.

Papert, S. (1980). *Mindstorms, Children, Computers and Powerful Ideas*. USA: Basic Books Inc.

Perkins, D. N. (1994). *The intelligent eye: Learning to think by looking at art*. Santa Monica, CA: Getty Center for Education in the Arts.

Polanyi, M. (1967). *The tacit dimensions*. London: Routledge and Kegan Paul.

Reeves, T., Herrington, J., & Oliver, R. (2004). A development research agenda for online collaborative learning. *Educational Technology Research and Development, 52*(4), 53–65. doi:10.1007/BF02504718

Schon, D. (1984). *The reflective practitioner*. New York, USA: Basic Books, Harper Colophon.

Schon, D. (1987). *Educating the reflective practitioner*. San Fransisco, USA: Jossey Bass Publishers.

Schusterman, R. (1992). *Pragmatist aesthetics: Living beauty, rethinking art*. USA: Blackwell Publishers.

Scripp, L., & Gray, J. (1992). *The Arts Propel video handbook*. Cambridge, Mass: Harvard Project Zero.

Seidel, S. (2001). *The evidence project: A collaborative approach to understanding and improving teaching and learning*. Cambridge, Massachusetts: Harvard University Project Zero.

KEY TERMS AND DEFINITIONS

ABC: Australian Broadcasting Commission.

eZine: Online magazine.

iRadio: Online radio.

LMS: Learning Management System.

OLT: Online Learning and Teaching is a Learning Content Management System that was custom built by the university.

SoDaR: Software Development as Research.

DATA ORIGIN KEY

I=Interview

O=Observation

D=Document

W=Web

T=Teacher (Name)

L= learning Designer

P= Programmer

Chapter 12
Learning Spaces for the Digital Age:
Blending Space with Pedagogy

Lynne Hunt
University of Southern Queensland, Australia

Henk Huijser
University of Southern Queensland, Australia

Michael Sankey
University of Southern Queensland, Australia

ABSTRACT

This chapter shows how virtual and physical learning spaces are shaped by pedagogy. It explores the shift in pedagogy from an orientation to teaching to an emphasis on student learning. In so doing, it touches on Net Generation literature indicating that this concept has a poor fit with the diverse nature of student populations engaged in lifelong learning. The argument is that the skill set required for life-long learning is not age related. At the core of the chapter is a case study of the University of Southern Queensland (USQ) which describes a history of learning environments that have been variously shaped by pedagogy and the limits of technology. It refers to the concept of the 'edgeless university', which acknowledges that learning is no longer cloistered within campus walls, and it describes how USQ is engaging with this concept through the development of open source learning materials. An important point in the chapter is that the deliberate design of quality learning spaces requires whole-of-institution planning, including academic development for university teaching staff, themselves often ill-equipped to take advantage of the potential of new learning environments. The import of the discussion is that higher education learning spaces are shaped by deliberate design, and that student learning is optimised when that design is pedagogically informed and properly managed.

DOI: 10.4018/978-1-60960-114-0.ch012

INTRODUCTION

This chapter describes the journey from traditional learning spaces to contemporary, open learning environments, including Web 2.0 environments such as wikis, social networking spaces and virtual classrooms and worlds. The concept of 'learning space' is helpful in this respect because it provides a framework to explore emerging pedagogies and it broadens conceptualisations of learning beyond classrooms and lecture theatres. It also provides an opportunity to describe the potential of virtual learning spaces such as learning management systems and web-based learning opportunities. The term learning environment is also widely used and in this chapter the two terms are used interchangeably, as both refer to situations – physical or virtual – that are structured to assist student participation and learning. The contemporary higher education context increasingly requires flexibility of access for an increasingly diverse student cohort. Overall, therefore, this chapter argues the need for a carefully planned and appropriately managed design of learning spaces to maximise learning for all students. The key point is that pedagogy informs learning space design.

Student Characteristics and the Design of Learning Spaces

There are many factors that influence the design of contemporary learning spaces in higher education. Some of these refer to students' needs and wants, especially those of the so-called Net Generation or 'digital natives' (Prensky, 2001). That said, this chapter addresses learning spaces for diverse student populations and it draws on research that has convincingly deconstructed the discourse about the Net Generation (Kvavik, 2005; Kennedy, Judd, Churchward, Gray & Krause, 2008), arguing that it should refer to a skill set that *all* students need. Similarly, it is important to challenge the notion that lifelong learners are mature-aged students. Everyone, young or old, is a lifelong learner and

all students can be helped or hindered by learning design (Candy, Crebert & O'Leary, 1994). This reinforces the point that pedagogy is the driving force in the effective design of learning spaces.

The contemporary context of higher education has been described as 'supercomplex' (Barnett, 2000) necessitating learning environments that enable students to cope in a world that is "radically unknowable" (Barnett, 2000, p. 42). An important factor in this context is the changing political expectations of higher education, including a requirement for widened participation, which will clearly have an influence on how student learning is managed because it engages with notions of 'lifelong learning', defined as being "concerned with both flexible, convenient, relevant provision of learning opportunities and with curricula that promote lifelong learning qualities" (Walters, 2005, p. 2). In Australia, for example, the federal government has explicitly called for widening participation in higher education, firstly in terms of the numbers entering higher education, but more importantly in terms of greater participation of lower socio economic students (Heagney, 2009). Considerable incentives are planned to facilitate access to university and ambitious targets are being set. The implication is that there will be more students and greater diversity of students' learning needs that can only be accommodated through the careful design of learning spaces. To function effectively in an 'age of supercomplexity' students require multidimensional thinking and critical analysis.

We now live in a world subject to infinite interpretability. It is this world for which universities are having to prepare their students ...a situation of complexity exists where one is faced with a surfeit of data, knowledge or theoretical frames *within* one's immediate situation ... [but] professional life is increasingly becoming a matter not just of handling overwhelming data and theories *within* a given frame of reference (a situation of complexity) but also a matter of handling multiple frames of understanding, of action and of self-identity. The fundamental frameworks by which we understand the world are multiplying and are often in conflict (Barnett, 2000).

The notion of the Net Generation (Oblinger & Oblinger, 2005; Kennedy et al., 2008) seeks to capture the apparently complex and fast changing skills and knowledge sets of a new generation, rather than focusing on what this generation should be able to know and do. It ascribes specific characteristics to a generation that has grown up in a technology saturated environment. These include an ability to read visual images, visual-spatial skills, digital literacy and connectedness. Barnes, Marateo and Ferris (2007) suggest that the Net Generation is easily bored and needs active, engaged learning experiences; self-directed learning opportunities; immediacy; interactivity; experiential learning; and above all, opportunities for social interaction. If this is the case, then such characteristics have major implications for the design of learning spaces and it is not difficult to see parallels between the perceived needs of the Net Generation and the potential of a Web 2.0 learning environment. The characteristic of 'connectedness', for example, indicates a need for learning spaces that facilitate social networking opportunities. For example, traditional libraries with rules of silence and individual carrels are being replaced by 'learning commons' designed to facilitate interaction through shared desk design and break-out rooms.

Empirical research is now emerging that deconstructs generalisations about the Net Generation (Ellis & Newton, 2009; Kvavik, 2005; Lomas & Oblinger, 2006; Kennedy et al., 2008). For example, Lomas and Oblinger note that "although students have little fear of technology, they are not necessarily proficient with technology, information retrieval, or cognitive skills – what many call *information fluency*" (2006, p. 5.10). In their study of blogging for instructional purposes, Leslie and Murphy (2008) found that students did not move beyond low level information sharing, nor engaged in knowledge construction, which they

attributed to a lack of teacher presence. Further, it seems that there is considerable intra-generational variation in skill levels and in the ways in which the Net Generation uses technologies, particularly for educational purposes. For example, Kennedy et al.'s study shows that "many first year students are highly tech-savvy. However, when one moves beyond entrenched technologies and tools (e.g. computers, mobile phones, email), the patterns of access and use of a range of other technologies show considerable variation" (2008, p. 108). While they found a significant growth in students' general use of instant messaging, blogs and podcasting, they also found that the majority of students rarely or never used these technologies for study, and importantly, "the transfer from a social or entertainment technology to a learning technology is neither automatic nor guaranteed" (Kennedy et al., 2008, p. 119). The strength of Net Generation studies is that they have identified skill sets which assist in the design of learning spaces for all students. The task of university management, then, is to harness this evidence and the opportunities afforded by the internet, social networks, and collaborative online tools (Bradwell, 2009) in the design of contemporary, *pedagogically informed*, learning spaces

Pedagogy to Inform Contemporary Learning Needs

The required reorientation of thinking about pedagogies suited to contemporary learning design is paradigmatic in proportion, as Barr and Tagg (1995) recognised in their classic article, 'From teaching to learning – a new paradigm for undergraduate education'.

We are beginning to recognize that our dominant paradigm mistakes a means for an end. It takes the means or method – called "instruction" or "teaching" – and makes it the college's end or purpose. To say that the purpose of colleges is to provide instruction is like saying that General Motors' business is to operate assembly lines or that the purpose of medical care is to fill hospital beds. We now see that our mission is not instruction but rather that of producing *learning* with every student by *whatever* means work best.

Traditionally, the teacher assesses, judges and evaluates (and thus 'controls') student learning outcomes. This is understood to ensure standards, and it is a fundamental way in which individual universities build and maintain their reputations. As Geith notes, "measuring, valuing, and recognising learner performance remains an exclusive function inside formal education systems" (2008, p. 224). In contrast, pedagogies focused on student learning increase "the level of collaboration with experts and peer groups and [connects] students to an emerging global network or 'architecture of participation' that transcends the walls of the institution" (McLoughlin & Lee, 2008, p. 13). The role of teachers or instructors in this context becomes one of working "collaboratively with learners to review, edit, and apply quality assurance mechanisms to student work while also drawing on input from the wider community outside the classroom or institution" (McLoughlin & Lee, 2008, p. 14).

McLoughlin and Lee define the principles of a new approach under the heading Pedagogy 2.0: "Pedagogy 2.0 integrates Web 2.0 tools that support knowledge sharing, peer-to-peer networking, and access to a global audience with socio-constructivist learning approaches to facilitate greater learning autonomy, agency and personalisation" (2008, p. 2). They identify the main challenge as enabling "self-direction, knowledge building, and learner control by offering flexible options for students to engage in learning that is authentic and relevant to their needs and to those of the networked society *while still providing necessary structure and scaffolding*" (2008, p. 7, our emphasis). This suggests a major shift in the role of the teacher, and the level of teacher control over the learning process for which, as Mabrito and Medley note, university teachers may be poorly prepared: "while N-Gens interact with the world

through multimedia, online social networking, and routine multitasking, their professors tend to approach learning linearly, one task at a time, and as an individual activity that is centred largely around printed text" (2008, p. 4).

Much of the literature on pedagogical change is dichotomised, characterising a change from linear and didactic teaching and learning to complex and interactive approaches. The reality is that staff of all universities are variously positioned along a continuum of pedagogies and there are many instances of individual teachers taking advantage of the availability of "ubiquitous, free, and efficient online collaboration tools for teaching and learning" (Hargis & Wilcox, 2008), for example through innovative uses of blogs (Bruns & Jacobs, 2006) or by incorporating Web 2.0 environments like *Wikiversity* (Friesen & Hopkins, 2008), social networking sites (Boyd, 2008) or *Second Life* (Kelton, 2007), which provide openness and searchability, contrasting sharply with virtual learning environments that do not take advantage of network effects (Alexander, 2008). In brief, it is the *pedagogical* design of learning spaces that is important – not simply the availability of technologies. In this, the role of the teacher is paramount. However, recognising the importance of the teacher requires the development of a context in which teachers are supported in developing pedagogically informed learning spaces. The following case study shows how one university undertook a whole-of-university change process to support teachers in the redesign of learning spaces for their students. It describes how the University of Southern Queensland (USQ) managed change to enhance flexible learning spaces informed by 'Pedagogy 2.0'.

Case Study: Structural Holistic Change at USQ

The University of Southern Queensland fits the mould of an 'edgeless university' (Bradwell, 2009), which is "no longer contained within the campus, nor within the physically defined space of a particular institution ..." (Bradwell, 2009, p. 8). Some 78% of USQ's students study by distance education and about 5000 international students study USQ programs in their home countries. The University now has four decades of history in designing learning spaces for students studying off campus. The changing nature of these learning environments has been characterized in terms of five generations (Taylor, 2001):

1. First generation correspondence model;
2. Second generation multimedia model;
3. Third generation tele-learning model;
4. Fourth generation flexible learning model; and
5. Fifth generation intelligent flexible learning model.

The design of each generation of learning environments is clearly dictated by the limits of technology at the time and the pedagogies that informed the development of course materials. This case study explores the continuing interrelationship between pedagogy and the design of learning spaces by detailing the change management process and its influence on the learning design outcomes.

USQ set out to address pedagogy and learning systems. The direction of change is towards student-centred learning design and enhanced use of digital futures, including the development and use of open access learning opportunities. It is argued that both the development of new learning spaces and appropriately designed learning experiences are contingent on organisational reorientation within universities. This means that both the organisational culture and the structures that govern the institution need to change because, as Barr and Tagg (1995, p. 7) noted:

There is good reason to attend to structure. First, restructuring offers the greatest hope for increasing organizational efficiency and effectiveness. Structure is leverage. If you change the structure in which people work, you increase or decrease the leverage applied to their efforts. A change in structure can either increase productivity or change the nature of organizational outcomes. Second, structure is the concrete manifestation of the abstract principles of the organization's governing paradigm. Structures reflecting an old paradigm can frustrate the best ideas and innovations of new-paradigm thinkers.

In other words, structural changes that are aligned with a university's pedagogical direction need to be in place to effect cultural change, which in turn will affect the pedagogy underlying teaching in the university. At USQ, changes to pedagogy and learning environments required a series of adjustments. This was a challenge because, as Henshaw (2008) notes, universities are notoriously slow at adapting to major changes. Chowcat, Phillips, Popham and Jones (2008, p. 20) argue that, "the development of new pedagogies can be a substantial professional challenge: teachers must learn new skills and rethink and refashion the teacher-learner relationship". The preparation of university teachers for the paradigm shift to Pedagogy 2.0 will, therefore, require "a tremendous amount of institutional support" (Mabrito & Medley, 2008, p. 16) and a flexible 'whole-of-institution' approach (Taylor, 2001). Yet universities are traditionally monolithic systems that are "less flexible and ultimately less innovative than the granular and remixable information services now often called Web 2.0" (Unsworth, 2008, p. 229).

Part of the vision of the change management process at USQ was that cultural change will arise from structural change. Indeed, it was envisaged that changes in pedagogy might be assured, at least in terms of minimum standards, by the development of an online Course and Program Management System (CPMS). This will facilitate staff autonomy in making changes to courses and programs whilst also assuring quality and communication through built-in approval processes. This is a basic building block for improvement and it is in advance of similar products because it syndicates key information to other systems, such as e-portfolios for staff and students. This means that the CPMS will automatically deposit the outcomes of student review in staff e-portfolios, which will facilitate data collection for annual performance review and promotion. For students, the system will automatically record the graduate skills acquired in each course that they pass. This will facilitate the development of their Statement of Graduate Outcomes and hence employability. In brief, the design of the CPMS was all about getting the context right for both staff and students.

The key principle of the change management process was to avoid reliance on voluntaristic professional development and to lock in quality via the CPMS to make it difficult to avoid the essential ingredients of good learning design. Of itself, the CPMS may be seen as staff learning space. It was designed to render course design and review a business-as-usual activity. At the same time, a new, integrated system of academic professional development, including online foundation modules, was implemented to support course development. Van Note Chism (2006, p. 2.2) adopts the term 'built pedagogy', to describe how space might shape learning. However, the extent to which innovations such as the CPMS influence the adoption of new pedagogies remains to be seen. The indications are that the potential of learning spaces is contingent on the pedagogical input of university teachers. For example, Lane (2009) refers to the 'insidious pedagogy' inherent in learning management systems (LMS) because many teaching staff in universities under-utilise the potential and work at only the most basic level: "the defaults of the CMS [LMS] therefore tend to determine the way Web-novice faculty teach online, encouraging methods based on posting of material and engendering usage that focuses on administrative tasks" (Lane, 2009, p. 1). What students lacked in these contexts is what teachers traditionally offer: the design of the educational experience; the facilitation of that experience;

and subject matter expertise (Leslie & Murphy, 2008, p. 37).

The required changes in pedagogy and learning environments had implications that would affect many aspects of the University. Accordingly, in 2008, the University undertook a whole-of-university change project to enhance students' learning journeys. The approach was inevitably holistic because students want universities to deliver on a number of fronts. They want "the *combination* of consistently capable staff, with appropriate learning designs and a support system that enables them to deliver what is intended" (Scott, 2005). In their account of USQ's change management process, Hunt and Peach (2009) describe the key elements of holistic change:

There is considerable agreement about what needs to be done to lead holistic change. Burnes' (2004) model of organisational change included the need to develop: vision; participative strategies; the right culture and conditions of change; and implementation plans. ... it is holistic and recognizes the need for structural and cultural reorientation for change to be effective. The characteristics shared by these models is that they are multidimensional, systematic approaches designed to produce change-capable cultures.

The change process may be described as top-down, bottom-up and middle-out (Cummings, Phillips, Tilbrook & Lowe, 2005), the last of these being effected by the university's central Learning and Teaching Support Unit. The change management process was strategic, targeted and evidence-based. Exactly how such change might be effected is described in Hunt's (2006) community development model of change. It includes reference to key strategies including financial support, a policy framework, creating a learning mood and building capacity through inter-sectoral collaboration. At USQ, key policy changes included the introduction of a Fleximode Policy to diminish differences in the design of learning experiences between on-campus and distance education students and to guarantee to students appropriate and equal access to learning resources. Financial support was delivered through the change management project which was organised as four sub-projects: facilities; academic profile; student management; and corporate services. Worthy of note is that only one of them directly focuses on academic matters. Rather, the emphasis was on getting the context right for learning and teaching. Significant, also, is the priority given to 'facilities' to upgrade ageing infrastructure to learning spaces that enable flexible learning. For example, a key outcome of this project has been the development of plans for a new learning commons enabling access to the internet and web-based learning.

The number of degree programs and courses offered by the University was drastically reduced. This structural change was considered important in creating a learning mood because the expected outcome is that teaching staff will have more time to focus attention on improvement of the remaining courses and programs. The change process focussed on whole-of-program learning design to ensure coherence across all levels of study based on the mapping of graduate skills and assessment. The pedagogical principles of learning design are now summarised in templates and modelled in exemplars that are on the USQ Learning and Teaching website as open access learning materials. They may be used for self-help or in conjunction with the assistance of instructional designers in the development of new courses. Clarity about what is expected by way of good teaching is provided through the development of guidelines which encapsulate pedagogies suited to the development of physical and virtual flexible learning spaces. The creation of an integrated, academic professional development program that includes open access, foundation modules has improved support for staff. Further, an annual course and program management process has been developed which provides staff with one-stop-shop information about the outcomes of their courses and opportunities for reflection

by those who teach each course. This now creates a supported and reflective framework for the deliberate design and improvement of courses. In short, it is an evidence-based way of getting the context right for pedagogy to take flight.

Pedagogically Informed Learning Environments at USQ

The USQ whole-of-university change management project was designed to get the context right for learning and teaching. The aim was to achieve blended learning environments suited to the needs of a diverse and dispersed student population. The concept of blended learning environments refers to the potential links between mobile spaces, virtual spaces and physical spaces. They may also be defined as, "the combination of mobile students and mobile technologies ... [associated with] virtual spaces" (Milne, 2006, p. 11.4). They are a fluid combination of physical, online, networked and mobile spaces that are always open and subject to change. As Johnson, Levine, Smith, Smythe and Stone (2009, p. 4) note:

The learning environment is no longer limited to physical space. Today, the notion of a 'classroom' includes experiences. Experts, collaborators, peers, and resources are located all over the globe and available twenty-four hours a day. To take advantage of this trend, institutions must reflect and support the transformation of the learning environment by embracing the means that make it possible: social networking tools, semantic applications, mobile devices, virtual worlds, and other emerging technologies that facilitate collaboration, communication, and learning.

In regard to the design principles of physical learning spaces Gee's (2006) human-centered design guidelines advocate flexible and healthy environments that stimulate the senses and spaces that balance communal space and solitude. Characteristics of blended learning spaces include comfort; sensory stimulation; technology support; decenteredness (spaces that centre on learning rather than 'experts'); living-learning spaces (integrating living, leisure and learning spaces); and corridor niches which refers to ubiquitous learning not confined to the classroom (Van Note Chism, 2006, p. 2.6). These characteristics blur boundaries between learning and living spaces, and online and offline spaces. Making corridors attractive acknowledges that learning can happen anytime, anywhere, and that it is social and collaborative (Dittoe, 2006). However, "design is a process, not a product" (Oblinger, 2006, p. 1.3) and it requires vision because, as Malcolm Read observes in Bradwell's *Edgeless University*, "the aim has to be to make those running universities realise that technology isn't just something that means you build a room full of computers on your campus" (Bradwell, 2009, p. 8). Les Watson's vision for 21st century learning spaces is that they should be: inspirational, flexible, play to diversity, have a social component, create community, and have embedded technology (The Carrick Institute for Learning and Teaching in Higher Education, 2007). Learning spaces should be open-ended enough to allow for students' imagination to blossom and flexible enough for students to arrange things in their own ways and to push the boundaries of their knowledge and lifelong learning skills. This process is not always predictable, and does not necessarily align with the use of space that was envisaged. However, if there is sufficient flexibility, the learning space will enable innovation driven by imagination.

The flexibility inherent in blended learning spaces was key in USQ's change management processes because the diverse and dispersed student population must be supported at differing levels of technological sophistication and technology *per se* (*Education.au*, 2009). For example, USQ has a significant number of students in prison (around 400) who may not be permitted access to the internet, or to CD-ROM for safety reasons.

The focus is on student learning outcomes that give rise to design features including:

- a shift from instruction to active learning;
- growing emphasis on collaborative learning;
- growing commitment to project-based learning;
- emphasis on skills needed for the 21st century;
- collaborative networks that support professional learning; and
- globalisation of education through national and international networks (adapted from *Education.au*, 2009, p. 1).

USQ's vision for blended learning and more meaningful interaction between staff and students, and between students, has spawned a range of technologies and Web 2.0 approaches that are mediated by open source tools such as the Moodle learning management system and the Mahara ePortfolio software. These include:

- virtual classroom technology;
- synchronous and asynchronous voice and chat applications;
- 3D virtual worlds;
- ePortfolios and personal learning environments; and
- blog and wiki spaces, that facilitate collaboration and reflection.

The university has developed its own open source, structured content authoring system known as ICE (Integrated Content Environment) that is used for consistency in writing and developing course materials that can automatically be rendered to print, web, CD or DVD. Further, there is a separate environment for staff professional development, which is also used as a playground for trialling emerging tools. There is also an installation for engaging with the University's community and an OpenCourseWare installation, housing courses offered through the International OpenCourseWare Consortium emanating from MIT.

Bradwell notes that "social networks, Google maps, mobile internet and the immediate availability of information have found their way into the everyday lives of those on campus, but they have not yet followed students and teachers into the classroom" (2009, p. 55). Yet USQ is committed to the use of open educational resources (OER) and the further development of its own and third party open source systems. Aligned with this are the affordances offered both through cloud computing and the plethora of social networking software. This means that the learning management system, traditionally conceived of as a box-like repository of knowledge artefacts, becomes more akin to a narrow band of interaction that is used to mediate a range of activities and resources that may be syndicated into the university environment (Figure 1).

The implementation of a campus-wide approach to virtual classrooms (VCs) in 2008, using the Wimba Collaboration Suite, has allowed this technology to be embedded in the Moodle LMS, though it is hosted externally. This has facilitated the contextualized use of the VC at both a course/subject level and a university community level. The VC allows for the synchronous sharing of voice, video, presentations and application sharing, allowing these sessions to be either instructor or student led. Over the course of 2009, VCs have been used in over 110 courses/subjects in 2009 to host live interactive sessions, both in staff-to-students interactions and student-to-student interactions. Figure 2 illustrates the growth in their use from 2008 to 2009. Once a VC is established within a course anybody enrolled in that course can access this room at any time. Archives may be made of sessions to allow for recording of particular interactions for asynchronous use. This technology is intuitive enough for novices to manage, and it has allowed many students, particularly distance students, to establish new and previously unattainable networks. USQ has a high proportion of non-traditional learners, some less able to access technology enabled learning. For students unable to interact in the online sessions due to bandwidth constraints, each VC can be accessed by telephone link for the cost of a local call. Initially it was not clear how many students would require this functionality; however, within

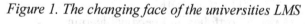
Figure 1. The changing face of the universities LMS

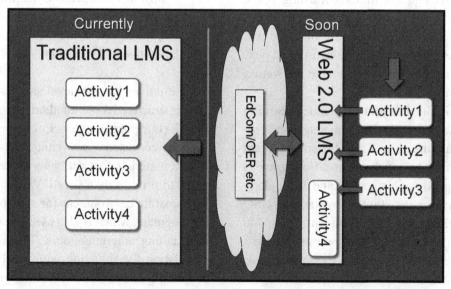

the first 10 months of use this feature was used in excess of 500 times.

The use of voice and chat applications has also been developing for many years at USQ. In previous years tools such as MSN Messenger and Skype have been used in an ad hoc way. However, the implementation of Moodle has facilitated embedding voice and text-based chat applications. Wimba voice boards allow asynchronous voice and text messaging, and the Wimba Pronto tool allows for synchronous chat with similar functionality to MSN Messenger. These two tools were not adopted until late 2008 but over 1700 sessions were recorded prior to the end of that year.

The proliferation of 3D gaming environments has opened up new possibilities for creating immersive, multi-user learning environments. This did initially present some security issues that have been largely resolved by simultaneously employing two 3D environments: Second Life (2Life) and the open source product Open Simulator (OpenSim). The latter was deployed 'within the walls' and its interoperability features take students out to 2Life as required.

For example, USQ currently has an island in the 2Life environment called Terra Incognita, hosting a range of different activities, including marketing and promotional activities for the University, a careers fair, teaching areas (Figure 3), break out rooms, a mock law court for hosting moot courts and a number of social spaces. Privacy has been a concern because anyone who can access the USQ island can drop in at any time, but OpenSim embedded in the USQ environment provides more discreet space if required.

The move towards ePortfolios for students and staff has taken an interesting turn at USQ. The Mahara software and the integration of this software with the Moodle LMS has allowed the university to provide not just a space for students to create a profile, but also an environment akin to a Personal Learning Environment (PLE). The Mahara environment allows for the creation of multiple views that students can set-up for a range of purposes (Figure 4). They can create and upload documents, house a blog, draw in content from external spaces and make a variety of these available for different people to see, and, in some cases, interact with.

Education students are using their PLEs to house records of their professional practice while also using them to complete assignments for other courses. Final year accounting students are building up their PLEs with an ePortfolio of their work-integrated learning practice. Visual Arts and multimedia students are using their PLEs as a stage from which to link to a range of other environments housing video and audio components while uploading others. These elements then all

Figure 2. The growth in the use of virtual classrooms

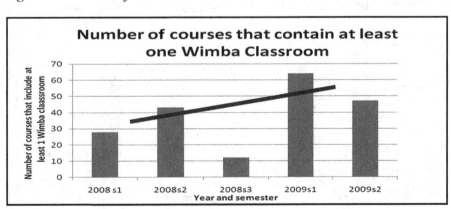

Figure 3. A USQ 2Life augmented reality room with live video conferencing (left) and a USQ Court Room (right)

appear within one or multiple views. Nursing students are encouraged in their first year of study to start creating their professional ePortfolio using the PLE environment, so that by the time they graduate they can demonstrate all the graduate skills required to enter their profession. These skills are embedded at the course level and once attained are automatically fed to their ePortfolio from the CPMS. Once there these skills can be

augmented with further examples (evidence) of how they have attained these skills. Furthermore, the maintaining of the ePortfolio is itself an important skill in a contemporary context where professional online identity development and maintenance are an increasingly important part of graduates' lives.

When a staff member undertakes a professional development (PD) activity, such as attending an

Figure 4. The Mahara software allowing for the development of personal learning environments (PLE)

assessment workshop, the official attendance and successful completion of this activity can be syndicated to their ePortfolio or PLEs from the Human Resources database. Once in this environment, this record, and any artefact that the user may want to associate with this PD event, can be managed and utilised across a range of views (see Figure 4). It may, for example, be used to support a promotion application. Evidence may be provided by linking to the university's ePrints repository that can syndicate a staff member's publication outcomes into this same environment. This is just the beginning of what is being achieved through PLEs. Notably, it saves on the double handling of data drawn from credible sources.

Finally, four work-integrated journalism professional development courses reveal what can be done to combine the potential of a range of interactive Web 2.0 environments mediated through the LMS. A program website augmented with rich media files provides baseline information pertinent to the whole program and links them to a series of wiki sites to collaborate and share good practice. This site also guides students to a series of learning environments with a range of interactive tools. These online multimodal course materials sites have been authored using USQ's Integrated Content Environment (ICE). This system has allowed the average academic staff member to author their own HTML rendered materials at their desktop, using only standard word processor. They author the base content in Word, view it in HTML and produce a print friendly PDF all in one application. The resultant multimodal courses includes multimedia enhancements and links to each course's blog, wiki, and discussion fora, all mediated through the LMS.

The use of blogging in assessment enables students to complete story writing assignments as part of their daily work at the newspaper and allows them to further engage in critical evaluation of the practices they applied in story composition. Elements such as a Newsroom Diary, a Research Record and Reflective Posts on self-selected

stories, a Court Experience Journal, and a Story Mission Statement, are built into an electronic, portfolio-based assessment model integrated into the LMS.

Each of the instances of innovative practice described in this chapter identifies the possibilities that are created by structural changes in the overall learning environment at USQ, and the importance of pedagogically informed innovation. The whole-of-institution approach supports the design of learning spaces, broadly informed by Pedagogy 2.0 principles.

CONCLUSION

The need for the transformation of learning spaces at USQ is based on a number of broad, interrelated, and mutually reinforcing trends: the changing complexity of society; changing characteristics of students (Net Generation); fast-changing information technology; and changing conceptions of learning. This chapter has argued that a whole-of-institution approach (Hunt & Peach, 2009) is required to create a context that delivers appropriate and pedagogically informed learning spaces for students. Outcomes of USQ's holistic change management project include the CPMS, the implementation of Moodle and advancement of Wimba and Camtasia, a new Course and Program Review process, templates that embed pedagogy in course and program design, assessment and graduate skills, and a new, integrated professional development program to facilitate cultural change. Without the additional funding and policy support provided by the wider change process, the outcomes would have been more limited.

The change management project concentrated on the university's top fifteen programs that serve some 80% of the university's students. This strategic approach and project methodology ensured that a holistic framework for 21st century learning spaces design is now in place. The conclusion is that appropriately designed learning spaces – 'built pedagogy' (Van Note Chism, 2006, p. 2.2) – are a necessary, but not sufficient condition for effective student learning. As Radcliffe, Wilson, Powell & Tibbetts, (2009) note, appropriately designed learning spaces will be 'positive by design', which refers to a blend of physical, online and mobile spaces characterised by openness and search-ability. The actual learning occurs when teachers begin to engage with the possibilities that are created by a consistent and pedagogically informed whole-of-university approach to the development of contemporary learning spaces.

REFERENCES

Alexander, B. (2008). Social networking in higher education . In Katz, R. N. (Ed.), *The tower and the cloud: Higher education in the age of cloud computing* (pp. 197–201). Boulder, CO: Educause.

Barnes, K., Marateo, R., & Ferris, S. (2007). Teaching and learning with the net generation. *Innovate, 3*(4). Retrieved December 4, 2008, from http://www.innovateonline.info/index.php?view=article&id=382

Barnett, R. (2000). *Realizing the university in an age of supercomplexity*. Buckingham, UK: Open University Press.

Barr, R. B., & Tag, J. (1995). From teaching to learning: A new paradigm for undergraduate education. *Change*, Nov/Dec. Retrieved October 10, 2009, from: http://ilte.ius.edu/pdf/BarrTagg.pdf

Boyd, D. (2008). Why youth (heart) social network sites: The role of networked publics in teenage social life . In Buckingham, D. (Ed.), *Youth, identity, and digital media* (pp. 119–142). Cambridge, MA: MIT Press.

Bradwell, P. (2009). *The edgeless university: Why higher education must embrace technology*. London, UK: Demos.

Bruns, A., & Jacobs, J. (Eds.). (2006). *Uses of blogs*. New York, NY: Peter Lang.

Candy, P. C., Crebert, G., & O'Leary, J. (1994). *Developing lifelong learners through undergraduate education. Commissioned Report (No. 28). National Board of Employment, Education and Training*. Canberra: AGPS.

Chowcat, I., Phillips, B., Popham, J., & Jones, I. (2008). *Harnessing technology: Preliminary identification of trends affecting the use of technology for learning*. London, UK: Becta.

Cummings, R., Phillips, R., Tilbrook, R., & Lowe, K. (2005). Middle-out approaches to reform of university teaching and learning: Champions striding between top-down and bottom-up approaches. *International Review of Research in Open and Distance Learning, 6*(1), 1–18.

Dittoe, W. (2006). Seriously cool places: The future of learning-centered built environments. In Oblinger, D. (Ed.), *Learning spaces* (pp. 3.1–3.11). Boulder, CO: Educause.

Education.au. (2009). *21st century learning spaces*. Retrieved October 10, 2009, from www.educationau.edu.au.

Ellis, A., & Newton, D. (2009). First year university students' access, usage and expectations of technology: An Australian pilot study. In [Chesapeake, VA: AACE.]. *Proceedings of World Conference on E-Learning in Corporate, Government, Healthcare, and Higher Education, 2009*, 2539–2546.

Friesen, N., & Hopkins, J. (2008). Wikiversity, or education meets the free culture movement: An ethnographic investigation. *First Monday, 13*(10). Retrieved October 16, 2008, from http://www.uic.edu/htbin/cgiwrap/bin/ojs/index.php/fm/rt/printerFriendly/2234/2031

Gee, L. (2006). Human-centered design guidelines . In Oblinger, D. (Ed.), *Learning spaces* (pp. 10.1–10.13). Boulder, CO: Educause.

Geith, C. (2008). Teaching and learning unleashed with Web 2.0 and open educational resources . In Katz, R. N. (Ed.), *The tower and the cloud: Higher education in the age of cloud computing* (pp. 219–226). Boulder, CO: Educause.

Hargis, J., & Wilcox, S. M. (2008). Ubiquitous, free, and efficient online collaboration tools for teaching and learning. *Turkish Online Journal of Distance Education, 9*(4).

Heagney, M. (2009). Australian higher education sector on the brink of a major shakeup. *Widening Participation & Lifelong Learning, 11*(1). Retrieved March 3, 2010, from http://www.staffs.ac.uk/journal/volelevenone/editorial.htm

Hunt, L. (2006). A community development model of change: The role of teaching and learning centres . In Bromage, A., Tomkinson, B., & Hunt, L. (Eds.), *The realities of change in higher education: Interventions to promote learning and teaching*. London, UK: Routledge.

Hunt, L., & Peach, N. (2009). Planning for a sustainable academic future. In *Proceedings of the iPED 4th International Conference, Researching Beyond Boundaries Academic Communities without Borders* (pp. 14-26). Coventry, UK: University TechnoCentre.

Johnson, L., Levine, A., Smith, R., Smythe, T., & Stone, S. (2009). *The Horizon Report: 2009 Australia-New Zealand edition*. Austin, TX: The New Media Consortium.

Kelton, A. J. (2007). Second Life: Reaching into the virtual world for real-world learning. *ECAR Research Bulletin*, (17).

Kennedy, G. E., Judd, T. S., Churchward, A., Gray, K., & Krause, K. (2008). First year students' experiences with technology: Are they really digital natives? *Australasian Journal of Educational Technology, 24*(1), 108–122.

Kvavik, R. B. (2005). Convenience, communications, and control: How students use technology. In D. Oblinger & J. Oblinger (Eds.), *Educating the Net generation* (pp. 7.1-7.20). Boulder, CO: Educause. Retrieved April 26, 2010 from http://net.educause.edu/ir/library/pdf/pub7101g.pdf

Lane, L. (2009). Insidious pedagogy: How course management systems impact teaching. *First Monday, 14*(10). Retrieved October 10, 2009, from http://firstmonday.org/htbin/cgiwrap/bin/ojs/index.php/fm/article/view/2530/2303

Leslie, P., & Murphy, E. (2008). Post-secondary students' purposes for blogging. *The International Review of Research in Open and Distance Learning, 9*(3). Retrieved October 24, 2008, from http://www.irrodl.org/index.php/irrodl/rt/printerFriendly/560/1099

Lomas, C., & Oblinger, D. (2006). Student practices and their impact on learning spaces . In Oblinger, D. (Ed.), *Learning spaces* (pp. 5.1–5.11). Boulder, CO: Educause.

Mabrito, M., & Medley, R. (2008). Why professor Johnny can't read: Understanding the Net generation's texts. *Innovate, 4*(6). Retrieved July 20, 2008, from http://www.innovate.info/index.php?view=article&id=510

McLoughlin, C., & Lee, M. J. W. (2008). Future learning landscapes: Transforming pedagogy through social software. *Innovate, 4*(5). Retrieved May 31, 2008, from http://www.innovate.info/index.php?view=article&id=539

Milne, A. J. (2006). Designing blended learning space to the student experience . In Oblinger, D. (Ed.), *Learning spaces* (pp. 11.1–11.15). Boulder, CO: Educause.

Oblinger, D. (2006). Space as a change agent . In Oblinger, D. (Ed.), *Learning spaces* (pp. 1.1–1.4). Boulder, CO: Educause.

Oblinger, D., & Oblinger, J. (2005). Is it age or IT: First steps toward understanding the Net generation. In D. Oblinger & J. Oblinger (Eds.), *Educating the Net generation* (pp. 2.1-2.20). Boulder, CO: Educause. Retrieved April 26, 2010, from http://net.educause.edu/ir/library/pdf/pub7101b.pdf

Prensky, M. (2001). Digital natives, digital immigrants. *On the Horizon, 9*(5). Retrieved February 14, 2007, from http://www.marcprensky.com/writing/Prensky%20-20Digital%20Natives%20Digital%20Immigrants%20-%20Part1.pdf.

Radcliffe, D., Wilson, H., Powell, D., & Tibbetts, B. (Eds.). (2009). *Learning spaces in higher education: Positive outcomes by design.* Proceedings of the Next Generation Learning Spaces 2008 Colloquium. University of Queensland, Brisbane.

Scott, G. (2005) *Accessing the student voice.* Canberra, Australia: Department of Education, Science and Training. Retrieved September 29, 2008, from http://www.dest.gov.au/sectors/higher_education/publications_resources/profiles/access_student_voice.htm

Taylor, J. (2001). *Fifth generation distance education.* Keynote address presented at the 20th ICDE World Conference, Düsseldorf, Germany.

The Carrick Institute for Learning and Teaching in Higher Education. (2007). *Places and spaces for learning seminars, September 2007. Draft report.* Sydney, Australia: Carrick Institute.

Unsworth, J. (2008). University 2.0 . In Katz, R. N. (Ed.), *The tower and the cloud: Higher education in the age of cloud computing* (pp. 227–237). Boulder, CO: Educause.

Van Note Chism, N. (2006). Challenging traditional assumptions and rethinking learning spaces . In Oblinger, D. (Ed.), *Learning spaces* (pp. 2.1–2.12). Boulder, CO: Educause.

Walters, S. (2005). Realizing a lifelong learning higher education institution . In Sutherland, P., & Crowther, J. (Eds.), *Lifelong learning: Concepts and contexts* (pp. 71–81). London, UK: Routledge.

KEY TERMS AND DEFINITIONS

Built Pedagogy: A term used by Van Note Chism (2006) to describe how space might shape learning. In other words, built pedagogy refers to the extent to which learning is influenced by the spaces or environments in which it takes place, and how this may influence learning spaces design.

Lifelong Learning: Lifelong learning is increasingly seen as a vital graduate attribute, which provides students with the disposition to keep learning, which in turn is seen as an important element of productive citizenship in the 21st century.

Net Generation: Also known as Generation Y, Millennials or Digital Natives, the Net Generation refers to a generation of students who are currently entering universities and who have grown up, immersed in an environment saturated by technology, which has arguably given them a number of distinct characteristics.

Pedagogy 2.0: "Pedagogy 2.0 integrates Web 2.0 tools that support knowledge sharing, peer-to-peer networking, and access to a global audience with socio-constructivist learning approaches to facilitate greater learning autonomy, agency and personalisation" (McLoughlin & Lee 2008, p. 2).

Personal Learning Environment (PLE): Personal learning environments are characterised by a combination of both formal and informal spaces within an environment that is managed by students themselves. PLEs, such as ePortfolios for example, allow students to develop and display digital artefacts, as well as pull in material from beyond the institution's walls.

University of Southern Queensland (USQ): One of the leading distance education providers in Australia, with more than 75% of its almost 25,000 students studying via distance or online.

Virtual and Physical Learning Spaces: In this chapter, learning spaces are broadly defined as spaces where learning takes place, which may include physical spaces, virtual spaces, and mobile spaces, or blended spaces that combine all of these to more or lesser degrees.

Whole-of-University Change: This refers to a holistic approach to learning spaces design, where the primary concern is getting the context right for learning to take place, which according to Geoff Scott (2005) involves a "combination of consistently capable staff, with appropriate learning designs and a support system that enables them to deliver what is intended".

University of Southern Queensland (USQ): One of the leading distance education providers in Australia, with more than 75% of its almost 25,000 students studying via distance or online.

Section 4
Authentic Learning Spaces

Chapter 13
Assessment in Virtual Learning Spaces

Geoffrey Crisp
University of Adelaide, Australia

ABSTRACT

This chapter examines how assessment spaces must change in response to the rapid development and uptake of new virtual learning spaces. Students are engaging in collaborative, cooperative learning activities in a spatially distributed environment, yet their assessment tasks are often delivered in traditional assessment spaces that bear little resemblance to their learning spaces. The assessment of students in virtual worlds, virtual laboratories, role-plays and serious games is examined and the case is presented for the wider use of evidence-centered assessment designs and stealth assessment techniques.

TEACHING, LEARNING, ASSESSMENT AND EDUCATIONAL PRACTICE

Introduction

Setting authentic and meaningful learning activities for students requires imagination, reflection and time; the same is true for setting meaningful assessment tasks. As teachers' epistemologies for learning and assessment are closely related, we would expect deeply held beliefs around what constitutes acceptable teaching practice to influence teachers' approaches to designing assessment tasks. It is likely that approaches to teaching that are based on the routine delivery of information will lead to the design of routine assessment tasks that reward recall; similarly, teachers who prepare imaginative learning activities for students are likely to find ways to make the related assessment tasks more imaginative.

DOI: 10.4018/978-1-60960-114-0.ch013

The spaces within which educational practices are conducted will have a significant impact on approaches to learning, teaching and assessment (Figure 1). At the centre of all educational practice is the student experience; this is influenced by the teaching, learning and assessment activities that form the educational space (Havnes, 2004). Figure 1 emphasises that educational practices, for teachers and students, develop from of a complex, synergistic relationship between the teaching, learning and assessment spaces. The student experience should be the centre of this synergistic relationship; teachers need to reflect on the impact that their teaching and assessment spaces, both physical and virtual, will have on students' approaches to learning. The alignment between assessment, learning and teaching will only occur in a space that has been appropriately designed to accentuate synergies between these three key components of the educational environment. Teachers' educational practices involve the reification of their underlying values associated with both *virtual* and *physical* teaching spaces; teachers and students require a space within which they co-construct their educational practices through meaningful interactions with each other and the concepts to be covered during a course.

This chapter will be examining assessment in *virtual learning and teaching* spaces: these spaces are realised through the use of computers and mobile digital devices. Although the examples presented throughout this chapter relate to digital environments, the principles for aligning assessment spaces with teaching and learning spaces apply equally well to physical spaces where teachers and students interact through haptic experiences. As digital resources become more sophisticated and more ubiquitous, we will see the blending of virtual and physical spaces; such spaces are already being realised through the emergence of augmented reality (Zhou, Duh & Billinghurst, 2008). This chapter will concentrate on the alignment of learning, teaching and assessment in the online spaces that are currently being used in educational institutions

Approaches to Assessment

Assessment tasks are set in order to satisfy a diverse range of needs; this means that setting meaningful assessment tasks is a complex process involving "planning, discussion, consensus building, reflection, measuring, analyzing, and improving based on the data and artefacts gathered about a learning objective" (Ramakishnan & Ramadoss,

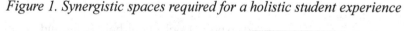

Figure 1. Synergistic spaces required for a holistic student experience

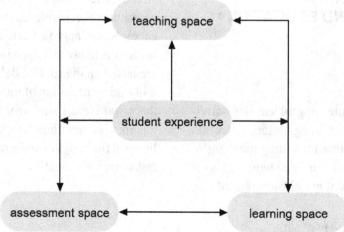

2009). Assessment tasks should provide relevant feedback on learning to both the student and the teacher; they need to document competency and skill development as well as allow students to be graded or ranked; in addition, professional organisations will use assessment results to validate certification and licence procedures and quality assurance agencies will use assessment tasks and results as benchmarks for standards (Broadfoot & Black, 2004). Teachers will need to construct a variety of assessment tasks to meet these various demands; it is unlikely that only a few, highly weighted tasks, will satisfy all of the above requirements concurrently.

The literature concerning learning and assessment has shown a gradual shift over the years from an initial emphasis on a behaviourist approach, moving towards a more constructivist view (Nichols, 1994) and recently to a discussion based on findings from neuroscience investigations (Ablin, 2008). The idea that valid and reliable inferences can be made about student learning through defining students' responses as correct or incorrect is too simple an approach to assessment design as it fails to distinguish between recall of factual (declarative) knowledge and the construction of responses based on the application of a learned strategy (http://www.gtce.org.uk/pdf/teachers/rft/neuroscience). In order to assess understanding we must be able to differentiate and reward alternative approaches to problem solving and this requires teachers to design assessment tasks that track the strategies students use to construct their responses.

Types of Assessment Tasks

Designing assessment spaces that are capable of tracking the strategies students employ to solve tasks requires that the whole student performance within the educational environment is examined. When students are required to construct responses against benchmarked standards of competency or capability, there is an increased opportunity to appropriately assess functional or procedural knowledge (how students perform or how they operate in a given context). If a student is presented with an assessment task that rewards the recall of declarative knowledge (factual information), they will frequently determine how much effort is required to temporarily store the required knowledge in order to fulfil the task and gain the reward (the marks). Current assessment spaces that use timed, paper-based examinations where students are herded into large halls and sit in rows to provide teachers with standard responses to standard questions simply encourages students to temporarily store declarative knowledge. This type of assessment space is not conducive to the assessment of functional or procedural knowledge.

Assessment should be integrated into all parts of the education process, including prior to the current learning activities, during current learning activities, and in preparation for future learning activities (Boud & Falchikov, 2006). The relationship between the different types of assessment tasks that can be set for students is summarised in Figure 2.

Before students commence a new course, teachers can require them to complete diagnostic assessments that will provide information on the current level of their declarative, procedural and functional knowledge. Both teacher and student can use this information to design strategies for interacting with the new material to be covered and the new capabilities to be developed in the course. Typical examples might include a gap analysis of specific skills or competency in solving particular problems. Students can use diagnostic tasks to determine if their prior knowledge is adequate to start the new course. During the course teachers can design formative tasks in which students are allowed to explore the development of new skills or capabilities, or test their strategies in problem solving. Both teachers and students may use the results of formative assessments to strategically map out future learning activities. If students have not engaged with and mastered specific skills or capabilities, then moving on to the next learning activity will be pointless as the students will not be able to build new approaches to learning that are underpinned by appropriate existing capabilities. Summative assessment tasks are designed to grade and judge a students' level of understanding and skill development, often for progression or certification purposes. They are most often taken at a stage when no further learning is required for the course being assessed, although summative tasks from one course can be used as the diagnostic tasks for another course.

Integrative assessment tasks are designed to influence students' approaches to future learning by providing assessment tasks that track and define strategies that students use to assess their own learning abilities and problem solving capabilities. Integrative tasks should link different content and capabilities developed throughout the entire program and can be seen as capstone experiences in some programs. Although these

culminating learning and assessment activities are often incorporated into programs, they tend be associated with final year courses; it would be more useful to incorporate these integrative assessment tasks in each course of a program so that students are able to test the development of effective strategies along their individual learning paths and not just at the exit points. The current interest in e-portfolios is facilitating the incorporation of integrative assessments throughout a program of learning. Integrative assessment tasks should incorporate elements of self- and peer-evaluation, not just on the declarative knowledge components, but more importantly on the functional and procedural knowledge components. Students need to be able to assess themselves and be able to articulate the strategies they have used to construct their responses and then assess the appropriateness of those responses.

Figure 2. Assessment types and their relationship to learning

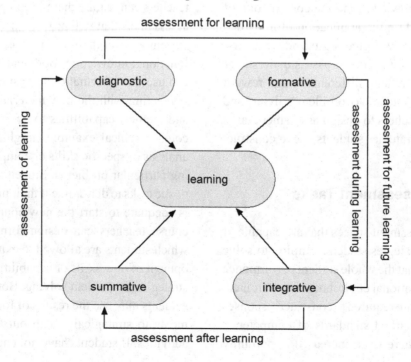

Types of Assessment Responses

All assessment responses may be divided into two types – convergent, where every student is expected to provide the same response, and divergent, where students may provide different but equally acceptable responses (Torrance & Pryor, 2001). Core knowledge (or the currently held truths for a discipline) is often assessed by convergent methodologies. Current assessment spaces for convergent responses often involve the automated marking of multiple-choice type questions using computers; it is relatively straightforward to construct an algorithm that looks for a specific piece of text or sequence of mouse clicks and assigns predetermined marks for the presence or absence of these artefacts. Standardized feedback can be readily incorporated into the design process since the feedback will be the same for all students and can be presented in a timely manner so that it has an immediate impact on the students' approach to current and (perhaps) future learning.

For divergent responses the assessor must distinguish between the range of responses and determine their relative worth; this is more difficult to do in a systematic manner with a computer. Whereas convergent assessment responses are often associated with declarative knowledge, tasks requiring divergent responses are more often associated with testing functional or procedural knowledge, including the strategies students use to construct their responses.

Online or e-assessments are often associated with the use of 'objective' questions, also known as selected response items as the student selects a response from the options offered. Typical examples would include multiple-choice, true/false, yes/no or, more recently, hotspot formats where students must recognise component parts of a digital image such as features on a geographical map or anatomical parts of a body and then use the computer mouse to click on the appropriate part. There is clearly a relationship between teachers expecting a convergent response from students and using the selected response format; this assessment space is usually chosen when teachers are testing declarative knowledge. One of the disadvantages to using online selected response formats is the restricted opportunities that students have to justify or explain their choice of responses, although this can be incorporated into e-assessments through the use of assertion-reasoning questions where both the response and the rationale for the response are offered as options.

In contrast to selected response items, constructed responses can use various combinations of text, sound or images; they can involve the manipulation or preparation of digital or physical objects, or the demonstration of a physical or virtual performance. Constructed responses normally provide more opportunities for students to justify or explain their reasoning compared to selected responses. Assessment spaces that facilitate the use of constructed responses will be the focus for many of the examples presented in this chapter. The new affordances associated with Web 2.0 have provided new opportunities for teachers to redesign their assessment tasks so that students' divergent responses can be constructed using new digital tools. This allows students to be more creative and to provide evidence of deep and holistic learning.

WHY VIRTUAL LEARNING SPACES REQUIRE NEW APPROACHES TO ASSESSMENT

We have witnessed the emergence of a wide variety of new web tools, such as those supporting global social networking and the ubiquitous availability of personal publishing using mixed media formats with minimal technical knowledge by the authors. The advent of Wikipedia has given rise to the notion that knowledge can be co-constructed and shared freely, rather than only being created by a small group of specialists and then subjected to restricted access. The new Internet has been described as Web 2.0, being characterised by participatory engagement and an underlying philosophy of collaboration, social interaction and user control. Web 2.0 examples that teachers may be familiar with include wikis, blogs, online discussions, e-portfolios, virtual worlds (such as Second Life), YouTube, Facebook, MySpace, Twitter and Flickr. Coupled with the rise in the use of mobile technology, we have also observed the ready availability of location-based communication devices (iPhone) and free services such as Google Docs and Google Maps. Traditional assessment models, based on the student as an isolated individual with limited access to resources, are not appropriate for this new environment that is collaborative, cooperative and distributed with access to almost unlimited resources.

The traditional assessment space has been described as Assessment 1.0; in this space the purpose of the assessment task is to collect evidence of student learning, often through the recall of discipline content, in a very standardized and controlled format (Elliot, 2008). The structure of an Assessment 1.0 space is designed to ensure that each student is treated in exactly the same manner, has access to the same resources, and is required to work in isolation when responding to assessment items. Traditional paper-based examinations in large halls where strict invigilation is provided would be a typical example of an Assessment 1.0 space.

Assessment 1.5 is the term proposed for much of the e-assessment activity we see today, including tasks requiring the use of e-portfolios and virtual learning environments. Although these assessment spaces offer students more flexibility in time and place, as well as item format, compared to Assessment 1.0, they still tend to replicate some of the features of Assessment 1.0 spaces, including the requirement for students to provide predominantly text-based responses, work as isolated individuals, reproduce declarative knowledge and depend predominantly on the teacher for judgements about standards and acceptability.

Many current assessment 1.0 and 1.5 tasks may be perceived by students as artificial because they are frequently designed to be delivered, collected, marked and stored in the most cost-effective manner, rather than designed around testing deep learning outcomes or contributing to future learning. Teachers will often restrict student access to online resources during a formal examination because the required response could be readily found doing a simply Google search. This restricted access to information is one of the signs that the assessment space is artificial; authentic assessment spaces allow students to access resources because the replication of the information itself is not the purpose of the task; the use of the information is what should be rewarded. Authentic assessment tasks require that the student reflects on the consequences of their response; authentic tasks will require constructed, divergent responses rather than convergent ones (Herrington & Herrington, 2006).

Many students are engaging with the Web 2.0 environment in their social lives; they have access to almost unlimited resources, including other people (Oblinger & Oblinger, 2005). One of the characteristics of today's society is that the majority of people in developed countries can, if they wish, be digitally connected to most of the rest of the world. Yet in Assessment 1.0 and 1.5 spaces, students are often isolated from this networked environment so that they can demonstrate a type of learning that is becoming less relevant to the social, cultural, economic and political context in which they live.

Web 2.0 facilitates the active participation of individuals in group activities (Franklin & van Harmelen, 2007); Wikipedia is an example of how the knowledge and understanding of a large group of individuals may be aggregated into a product. Irrespective of what one may think about the veracity of the content contained within Wikipedia pages, the format of co-constructed knowledge that is freely available to all is becoming the new information paradigm. WordPress and YouTube enable non-technical individuals to readily publish multimedia material on the Internet and blogs allow others to engage in the peer review of these products. One of the characteristics of Web 2.0 technology is that it is intuitive to use; required training is kept to a minimum and graphical user interfaces are designed to encourage immediate participation. Content can be added from a variety of sources and repurposed by the new 'author'. These new tools are specifically designed to create communities of practice, or at least communities of common interest. This type of engaging community learning space is what educational institutions should be striving to emulate, yet traditional institutions frequently fail to create these inclusive spaces because their learning and assessment spaces are not designed to encourage collaboration or ease of use. This is a new assessment space for teachers and students; it is a space that has many affordances and the potential to radically alter the assessment tasks that are set for students.

Assessment 2.0 is an emerging term used to describe tasks that are aligned with the characteristics of the Web 2.0 environment. Elliot (2008) has proposed that Assessment 2.0 has the following characteristics:

- authentic by involving real-world knowledge and skills;
- personalised by being tailored to the knowledge, skills and interests of each student;
- negotiated whereby activities and tasks are agreed between the student and the teacher;
- engaging because tasks involve the personal interests of the student;
- recognises existing skills and is willing to accredit the student's existing work;
- deep in the sense tasks assess deep knowledge and not memorisation;
- problem oriented as tasks are original and require genuine problem solving skills;

- collaboratively produced in partnership with fellow students;
- self- and peer-assessed through involving self reflection.

Assessment 2.0 spaces can facilitate opportunities for students to generate their own content through collaborative efforts; this, together with the use of self- and peer-review mechanisms, will enable students to more effectively analyse their own performances and ability levels. There are critical skills that must be developed by students in order for them to participate in future learning opportunities.

Although Web 2.0 might promise many new opportunities, without the appropriate alignment of teaching, learning and assessment into an overall integrated curriculum design, the use of Web 2.0 will add nothing to student learning or assessment quality. Students may interpret a poorly aligned assessment task as a distraction from the activities that are really being rewarded by the teacher. Similarly, students will quickly realise where their efforts should be directed if teachers require them to spend considerable time learning how to navigate within a virtual world such as Second Life, yet set traditional summative assessment tasks such as essays in a timed examination period at the end of a semester.

Much of the recent literature on e-assessment in higher education reinforces the observation that current endeavours to utilise the affordances of Web 2.0 to create new assessment spaces is still at an early stage of implementation; it is still dominated by models that attempt to replicate Assessment 1.0 and 1.5 spaces (Ripley, Harding, Redif, Ridgway & Tafler, 2009; Gilbert, Gale, Warburton & Wills, 2008). Table 1 outlines some of the formats that are offered within the Web 2.0 environment and how these may be used for Assessment 2.0 activities.

EXAMPLES OF ASSESSMENT IN VIRTUAL LEARNING AND TEACHING SPACES

Virtual or Remote Laboratories and Field Trips

Computer-based laboratory activities and field trips are associated with two distinct formats; one involves simulations that are entirely virtual and designed to provide students with a finite range of options for the manipulation of virtual data or objects; the other involves the manipulation of real objects or viewing real physical sites using the Internet for remote access. Both formats are useful as either replacements or complements to real physical activity or the physical presence of a student at a specific location. Students can be given access to remote laboratories or field sites where they can download data to their local com-

puter from a remote sensor for use in assessment tasks. This process allows students to collect and analyse authentic data which means that the assessment tasks can include requirements for students to reflect on the real life consequences of their solutions to the task (http://www.real.msu.edu). This is a particularly useful learning space for science and engineering disciplines since access to many relevant and authentic laboratory sites may be impossible because of cost or safety reasons.

There are continuing discussions on the efficacy of virtual or remote laboratory sessions compared to haptic experiences in terms of student learning outcomes (Murray, Lowe, Lindsay, Lasky & Liu, 2008). The International Journal of Online Engineering (iJOE) published an interesting series of papers on remote engineering and virtual instrumentation in a special edition of their journal in 2009 (http://www.online-journals.org/i-joe/). Virtual laboratory sessions are often

Table 1. Examples of Web 2.0 resources that could be used to assess students in the online environment

Assessment 2.0 Evidence type (Elliot, 2008)	Web 2.0 format	Current Web 2.0 example
Discovery	RSS feeds	Google Reader, Web browsers
	Social networks	Facebook, MySpace, Xing, Linkedin
	Search engines	Google, Yahoo, AltaVista
	Instant messaging	AIM, Windows Live Messenger, Yahoo! Messenger
	Content	Wikipedia, Wikiversity
Capture	Audio	Skype, Google Talk
	Bookmarking	BackFlip.com, iKeepBookmarks.com, del.icio.us
	Online polling	SnapPoll.com, Votapedia, Poll Everywhere, Zoho Polls
Creation	Wiki	Wikispaces, PBwiki
	Web data capture	Clipmarks, WetPaint,
	Virtual worlds	Second Life
	Video	BubbleShare, JumpCut, eyespot, Voicethread
	Media sharing	vimeo.com, ourmedia.org, youtube.com, video.google.com
	Podcasts	Odeo, Podomatic
Organisation	Blogs	Blogger, LiveJournal, WordPress
Storage	Email	Gmail, GoogleMail, Google Docs, Hotmail
	Audio and video presentations	YouTube, Slideshare, Flikr, Scribd
	File storage	Google Docs, Google Notebooks

used as formative activities to ensure that students are adequately prepared for engaging in a summative, hands-on laboratory session. This use of computer simulations is less controversial than the complete replacement of hands-on laboratory sessions with virtual activities, although simulations can be an appropriate replacement for experiments that pose an unacceptably high safety risk for novice students. Virtual simulations can also be used to provide students with a versatile environment in which to test hypotheses and to engage in 'what happens if I do this ...' type of activity. This experiential learning environment is aligned with a more constructivist approach to learning and teaching. The development of simulations and virtual experiments on digital representations of animals has occurred because of the heightened awareness of ethical issues associated with harming or destroying live animals (http://www.clabs.de).

An example of a simulation that allows students to experience the iterative experimental design process used by professional engineers, as well as the physical and social context found in industry, is the virtual chemical vapour deposition laboratory (Koretsky, Amatore, Barnes & Kimura, 2008). This simulation was specifically designed to replicate a reactor in a clean room environment; the Web interface integrates both formative and summative assessment tools and calculations are conducted in real time. Student feedback indicated that they felt less proficient with the learning outcome related to the virtual laboratory compared to other aspects of the course, although they perceived that the virtual activity was more effective in promoting learning compared to other hands-on laboratory activities. This uncertainty amongst students about the efficacy of learning associated with virtual activities highlights the need for an integrated approach to the design of learning and assessment spaces. Where there is a significant difference in format between the various learning or assessment environments within a course, students will be apprehensive about

the expected outcomes or level of performance. Teachers will need to reflect on this aspect of curriculum design when they are considering the introduction of tasks that rely on virtual or remote systems.

Instead of having to decide between virtual, remote or real laboratory sessions, teachers may prefer to have options available for students within an integrated approach to the practical requirements for a course. An example of such an approach is demonstrated in the Trilab project which offers students a holistic laboratory experience that incorporates activities from all three session formats; Trilab requires students to complete virtual, remote and real activities although the format could be adapted to provide options for teachers and students (Abdulwahed, Nagy & Blanchard, 2008). Similar, but not identical, learning outcomes are observed from students who have completed remote laboratory sessions compared to students who have completed hands-on sessions (Nickerson, Corter, Esche & Constantin, 2007; Corter, Nickerson, Esche, Chassapis, Im & Ma, 2007).

Although some virtual and remote laboratory experiments require students to download specialist software to their computers, many computer-based activities require only a recent version of a standard web browser using standard plugins. The JISC-funded RATATAT project (Remote Access to Academic Trials and Testing) is demonstrating how Web 2.0 technologies can assist in facilitating student use of the Internet to complete remote laboratory assessment tasks (http://ratatat. pbworks.com). The integration of virtual or remote laboratory sessions with the collaborative tools of the Web 2.0 environment would facilitate group and project work. This integration could transform the nature of laboratory sessions in higher education by facilitating student participation in larger, more complex projects that could assess many higher level capabilities.

The online 3D-compound virtual field trip system developed by Lin and Chang (2009) is an example of an integrated learning and assessment model for remote field trips. It incorporates four components, including a streaming video server, the use of instant messaging, an automatic marking and feedback system and a dedicated website for student access to the resources. Assessment tasks are linked to specific video sequences or objects in the virtual environment; selected response items will provide feedback to students. Students are able to capture still images from the video sequence and incorporate these into constructed responses. Although this type of integrated approach is still novel, it illustrates well the possibilities for new virtual and remote learning and assessment spaces that offer new experiences for students and allow teachers to assess higher level skill and capability development.

VIRTUAL WORLDS USING AVATARS, INCLUDING COLLABORATIVE 3D ENVIRONMENTS

Second Life is a well recognised example of a 3-dimensional, online virtual world that has seen a rapid uptake in many educational institutions (Linden Lab, http://lindenlab.com; http://www.secondlife.com). Second Life and Active Worlds (http://www.activeworlds.com) represent variations of multiuser online role-plays; these environments allow participants to take on a persona in the form of an avatar in order to explore or create digital objects and complete tasks as an individual or in a collaborative manner. Virtual worlds have a significant potential to facilitate authentic learning and assessment, but often require professional expertise to create the high quality digital artefacts that are seen in many of the more complex online environments. There are a number of commercial and open source software packages for constructing virtual worlds, including Second Life, Active Worlds, OpenSimulator, OLIVE, Multiverse and QWAQ. The JISC "Serious Virtual Worlds" report

contains a comprehensive list of recent virtual world platforms (de Freitas, 2008).

There is some evidence that the use of interactive digital characters can improve student motivation and retention but appropriate design principles need to be adhered to in order to obtain effective student engagement and the desired learning outcomes (Veletsianos, Miller & Doering, 2009). Designing an effective virtual world experience will require considerable time allocation from the teacher, initially for conceptually aligning the required learning outcomes with the actual activities and assessment tasks students will undertake in the virtual world, and then for the construction of the aligned environment. If teachers do not have access to professional assistance they will need to allocate enough time to develop sufficient skills to be able to construct dwellings and objects that students can use, or set learning and assessment tasks where students develop these skills and build their own virtual environments.

Users of Second Life have created their own vocabulary for their actions in order to foster a sense of community; terms such as to "rez (create) a prim (basic building block)" become a standard phrase that a "newbie" must understand in order to participate in the community of practice around creating in these virtual worlds. There is considerable hype about the potential impact that virtual worlds will have on classroom practice and some indication that the hyperbole is being questioned so that a more evidence-based interpretation will prevail of how these environments might be used to enhance learning and assessment (Fenn, Raskino & Gammage, 2009).

Virtual worlds can be designed so that participants, through their avatar, will meet and interact with other avatars as well as explore and create objects that develop particular capabilities relevant to the learning objectives for a course. Items in virtual worlds can be linked to resources on external web pages as well as external wikis, blogs or discussion boards, where students can assemble evidence of their learning (Hobbs, Brown

& Gordon, 2009). If a teacher wishes students to engage productively with a virtual world, the learning activities and associated assessment tasks must be aligned appropriately with the skills and capabilities that are being developed within the environment. This may seem to be an obvious statement, but many virtual worlds have been constructed with the view that students will spontaneously develop capabilities simply by entering or moving around inside the virtual world. Virtual worlds should be purposely built around pedagogy that clearly demonstrates the worth of undertaking the virtual activities. Virtual worlds are not required if students are expected to follow a linear sequence of prescribed tasks, there are alternative technologies that would be more appropriate and less complex, such as Flash simulations or Java applets. The teacher will need to decide which type of learning and assessment space best matches the skills and capabilities to be developed by the student and ensure that there is an obvious link between the particular space chosen and the manner in which it facilitates the development and testing of the new skills and capabilities developed (Jarmon, Traphagan, Mayrath & Trivedi, 2009).

Teachers can use the methodologies associated with experiential learning and task-based learning in order to design appropriate activities for virtual worlds; some of these methodologies can involve the use of podcasts, wikis, blogs, discussion forums, self- and peer-review and e-portfolios. Activities in virtual worlds generally emphasise performance rather than information; authentic assessment activities in these environments are therefore going to involve criteria relevant to these performances, rather than the recall or manipulation of content knowledge in isolation from context (Richardson & Molka-Danielsen, 2009; de Freitas & Neumann, 2009).

A hybrid approach to virtual worlds is the emerging technology of augmented reality; here participants are immersed in an environment containing elements from the real physical world and the digital world (Zhou, Duh & Billinghurst, 2008). Augmented Reality (AR) uses a physical device to connect the user with the virtual world, often in the form of a haptic device or heads-up or head-mounted display. This type of educational space is relatively new and found most often in disciplines such as medicine, engineering and flight or military simulations. AR has the potential to incorporate digital location data, contextual information or historical data to a real object, allowing students to interact at a much deeper level with an activity. AR has a significant potential to influence assessment spaces by providing students with a more realistic environment in which to test their capabilities and decision making. Teachers would be able to track student activity in an AR environment and obtain a detailed synopsis of key decision making points that could be used to make inferences about the strategies students used at these learning moments. The use of AR is still experimental in most educational institutions and the mainstream incorporation of AR into common teaching and assessment environments is still a number of years in the future.

Most assessment tasks are set outside of the virtual world, even when much of the student learning takes place within this environment. Even though links may be provided within the virtual world to assessment tools such as wikis, blogs, discussion forums and e-portfolios, these tools cannot provide automatic feedback to students in response to the actions of their avatar. Scripting languages within the virtual world software allows developers to create interactive activities and feedback to students, but mastering the use of the scripting language is a professional activity that takes time, frequently more time than most teachers would be able to allocate in order to construct appropriate assessment tasks and feedback for their students. What is needed by teachers, in addition to ready access to Web 2.0 tools, is a set of sophisticated quiz and survey tools within the virtual world, similar to those embedded in many learning management systems. An example of a simple version of such a tool is quizHUD (http://quizhud.avid-insight.co.uk) which has been developed for use in Second Life (Bloomfield & Livingstone, 2009). This tool integrates common selected response items from Moodle into Second Life so that an avatar can answer questions at key points within the virtual world. The question types are familiar to the student and allow the student to be tested within the virtual world, rather than outside it; the assessment tasks are seen as part of the activities within the virtual world. The advantage of quizHUD, from the teacher's perspective, is that no knowledge of scripting is required; teachers can create assessment items in a familiar format just as they would in their learning management system. Each student interacts individually with the quiz, even when multiple avatars are interacting within the virtual world.

Although quizHUD is a good example of the integration of an assessment tool within a virtual world, a more sophisticated approach would be to incorporate an evidence-centred assessment tool that allowed data to be collected about the strategies students used to move through the virtual world while engaging with a sophisticated task (Shute & Spector, 2008). This data could then be analysed by an appropriate algorithm and provide teachers with a map of the student's journey that could be translated into a mark or grade. The embedded assessment engine should be capable of providing timely feedback to students and even allow students to modify their strategies based on the feedback received. Stealth assessment has been the term introduced to describe the unobtrusive collection of data about the student and the automated scoring of this data for assessment purposes (Shute, 2009). This is particularly relevant to the virtual world space where the performance of the student is often more important than the accumulation of isolated content knowledge. The development of effective behaviours and strategies by the student need to be assessed in these virtual environments and more sophisticated assessment and feedback tools that are embedded in the software are required

so that teachers do not have to spend significant amounts of time learning to script or program assessment tasks and feedback.

The principle of using stealth assessment has developed from an analysis of participant activity in serious games (Shute, Ventura, Bauer & Zapata-Rivera, 2009). Stealth assessment relates to the systematic collection of evidence about users' actions during an online activity without interrupting the flow of that activity. Current learning and assessment spaces interrupt the flow of students' learning by separating the learning and assessment as time and location specific activities; students are given learning activities to undertake and then directed to interrupt the learning process in order to complete an assessment task, especially when the task is summative. This is the current educational model and stealth assessment would challenge this model by requiring teachers to design learning, teaching and assessment activities that were continuous and not separated by time or space; evidence of learning and capability development would be collected continuously without interrupting the flow of students' activities. The main issue would be converting this evidence into meaningful feedback, marks and grades so that appropriate weightings were applied for the summative use of the evidence.

Role-Plays and Scenario-Based Activities

Role-plays can be similar to the activities undertaken in virtual worlds, but the student normally takes on a persona as defined by the teacher and responds to a scenario as that defined persona. Although the outcomes from a role-play are not usually predetermined; the teacher would normally prescribe the characteristics of the various personas that students would take on and also the tasks to be undertaken within the exercise. Role-plays require divergent, constructed responses where students reflect on the consequences of their actions within the virtual environment. Even though an individual role-play will have the same starting point and commence with the same set of teacher-supplied documentation, the direction taken within the role-play can vary significantly as new groups of students will take the interactions and discussions in different directions. As for virtual worlds, role-plays tend to emphasise a student's performance rather than their acquisition of knowledge or factual information; they also tend to revolve around complex problems that do not have a prescribed solution. Role-plays allow students to explore the complexities of an issue and the need to consider the consequences of any solution to a problem from multiple perspectives. The assessment of scenario-based learning has much in common with that of role-plays, and should be closely aligned with rewarding the development of those skills and capabilities that are valued, not just those amenable to quantitative measurement.

Role-plays do not necessarily require specific software and all major learning management systems have discussion boards, group features and email facilities that enable online role-plays to be conducted relatively easily. Examples of role-plays performed within Moodle and Blackboard™ are available from the AUTC project site on ICT-based learning designs (http://learningdesigns.uow.edu.au) and the ALTC project EnRoLE website (http://www.uow.edu.au/cedir/enrole).

The assessment of an online role-play can be conducted using familiar Web 2.0 tools such as wikis, blogs, discussion forums and e-portfolios. Again, the assessment tasks need to reflect the capabilities that are being developed within the role-play. If the acquisition of content knowledge is the key learning objective for the activity, then a role-play is unlikely to be the appropriate space within which to develop and assess this capability. If the capabilities to be developed are around decision making, analysing the consequences of a solution from multiple social, political or cultural perspectives, negotiating outcomes with others or resolving conflicts in group situations, then a role-play is likely to be an appropriate learning and assessment space.

Whereas in a role-play the student takes on a persona and their behaviour is based on their perceptions of how that persona might act in a particular context, in scenario-based learning the student will normally behave as herself or himself, and act as they believe they should in the context presented. Scenario Based Learning Interactive (SBLi) is an example of software designed to facilitate the creation and delivery of scenarios for problem-based learning or enquiry-based learning (http://www.sblinteractive.org). An example of the use of SBLi software to construct a prescribed virtual laboratory scenario in genetics was published by Breakey, Levin, Miller and Hentges (2008); in this use of scenario-based learning the students are expected to develop capabilities in determining inheritance patterns and conducting standard screening tests. Scenario quiz questions were used as navigation tools in this particular implementation of the scenario, with students progressing through the scenario as they responded to the questions. As with role-plays, scenario-based activities do not necessarily require specific software as all of the major learning management environments have sufficient collaboration and communication tools to support group work and the documentation of reflective practice outcomes.

Serious or Educational Games

The term serious games has come into common use in higher education in order to distinguish between digital games whose primary purpose and market is leisure-based, and those that are designed for education and training (Aldrich, 2009a). Prensky (2001) was an early advocate of the use of computer games in education and training, including games to raise social awareness, to run businesses and to train military personnel. There is clearly a continuum between the types of Web 2.0 activities already discussed in this chapter, namely virtual labs, virtual worlds, role-plays and serious games. These activities do not necessarily represent discrete, quantised systems; they are all examples of highly interactive virtual environments (the HIVE model) which have the potential to facilitate authentic learning and assessment (Aldrich, 2009b). The HIVE model encourages teachers to align their learning and assessment spaces so that they match the requirements for an evidenced-centred approach to documenting the development of particular skills relevant to the learning outcomes for a course or program.

It is worth reflecting on the characteristics of well designed games; these games are characterised by an emphasis on interactivity, they contain appealing multimedia sequences and have a clearly articulated set of goals and rewards. The player develops skills as they proceed through the game, is provided with constant feedback in response to particular actions and is rewarded at regular, pre-defined milestones. Communities of practice evolve around how to master the skills and capabilities that are required to reach the new levels in the game and to attain the final goal or complete the mission. Each player will take a different path on their journey and make mistakes for which they will receive timely feedback in order to improve their performance. All of these characteristics could have been used to describe an effective learning environment in higher education.

Many of the principles proposed for good computer game designs match those for good learning designs (Pivec & Pivec, 2009). Games allow participants to enter a new world that can closely match the real world, or provide new possibilities that are not offered in the physical world. Games are particularly relevant to learning outcomes that involve the development of social and process skills, since they encourage participants to explore the options of alternative solutions and the consequences and complexities of these alternative pathways. A summary comparing the design principles for games and learning is shown in Table 2.

Assessing game-based learning will follow the same general principles outlined for virtual worlds, role-plays and scenarios. If the key learning outcomes for a course involve the development of specific skills, then drill and practice activities in a game will generally lead to improvements for

Table 2. Design principles for games compared to learning, adapted from (Pivec & Pivec, 2009; Boud & Prosser, 2002)

Game design principles	Learning design principles
Clear vision of goals or mission	Clear learning objectives
Player experience is paramount	Student-centred learning approach, active learning approach
Easily recognised structure and rules	Uses a logical sequence of learning and assessment activities that are aligned with learning outcomes
Adapts to different skill level of player	Offers open-ended tasks, acknowledges different ways of learning
Easy to learn, hard to master	Communicates high expectations, challenges students to higher level learning
Does not interrupt the flow of play	Embeds assessment tasks in learning activities
Provides frequent rewards, not penalties	Use authentic assessment activities, gives frequent and immediate feedback to students
Includes exploration and discovery	Uses active forms of learning, provides constructivist activities
New skills assist in progressing towards goal	Scaffolds student learning, assist students to become strategic learners
Intuitive interface, no need to read manual	Ready access to learning resources that can be used independently by student
Includes the ability to save progress	Use of student portfolios to demonstrate skill development

those skills (Hong, Cheng, Hwang, Lee & Chang, 2009). Examples would be upgrading a licence for machinery operators, music theory, language practice or simple math skills. Such games tend to have the assessable components embedded within the game, often using a simple form of adaptive release to guide players through the game towards the goal.

If assessment tools are external to the game (wrap around assessments), as for wikis, blogs, discussion boards and e-portfolios, the student must interrupt the flow of the game in order to complete assessable tasks. The use of stealth assessments, introduced previously for virtual worlds, would be beneficial for serious games (Shute, Ventura, Bauer & Zapata-Rivera, 2009). Embedding formative and summative assessments into serious games using an evidence-centred design approach would allow teachers to monitor a student's current level of competency. This approach could be coupled with adaptive assessment principles that could present different pathways to the student, depending on their current ability level. Well designed games encourage participants to be totally immersed in progressing through the levels so that they do not realise they are actually completing assessment tasks and receiving feedback that is influencing their strategies in terms of completing the game. This allows teachers to scaffold the development of skills aligned with the learning outcomes and the ability to offer participants increasingly complex scenarios that test their capabilities at higher levels.

Not all games require three-dimensional avatars, such as those found in virtual worlds. IMMEX (Interactive Multi-Media Exercises) could be regarded as a gaming activity that facilitates improvements in students' strategic problem-solving ability and the efficient use of resources, as it tracks the path the student takes through a problem solving activity (http://www.immex.ucla.edu). IMMEX activities model the use of authentic assessment spaces as students are provided with resources and they must decide how to use them

in the most efficient manner; there is a 'cost' to using the resources (students lose marks for using redundant or irrelevant information), just as there would be in real life. Hazmat is an example of a chemistry problem using IMMEX; student must identify an unknown compound and can request physical and chemical tests that assist them in identifying the substances (Cooper, Cox, Nammouz, Case & Stevens, 2008). Students must develop strategies for efficiently identifying unknown compounds; this skill is relevant to developing the attributes of a professional chemist who would be required to identify an unknown compound with the least number of tests.

In order to incorporate good assessment practices into serious games the following items have been proposed (Baker & Delacruz, 2008):

- An appropriate assessment architecture incorporating relevant metrics for the evaluation of participant performance based on inferences derived from expert performances.
- The use of criterion assessment where the outcomes of the game are measured against articulated levels of proficiency.
- The provision of explicit design information about the game and assessments so that appropriate evaluations can be undertaken.
- The provision of formative assessment for participants that scaffolds them more extensively in the early stages of the game and less so as their skill level rises.
- The provision of self-assessment activities that promote self-regulated learning and sustained engagement.
- The ability of the game to develop transferable skills that can be used in different contexts.

These items would allow for embedded or stealth assessment tasks to be integrated appropriately and effectively into serious games. Game design requires that both the learning and assessment activities are constructed concurrently, not sequentially; an evidence-centred approach to assessment design is required so that there is alignment between the skills being developed through the learning activities and the skills required to efficiently complete the assessment tasks.

FUTURE RESEARCH DIRECTIONS

Even as teachers come to understand the educational opportunities afforded by the Web 2.0 environment, researchers are developing the semantic web and Web 3.0 applications (Tiropanis, Davis, Millard, Weal, White & Wills, 2009). Many of these new technologies will have a profound impact on the design and delivery of training and educational programs. Semantic technologies add meaning and context to data and objects so that the relationships between items can be interpreted by a computer. This enables computers to extract meaning from an item and its context, so that a judgement can be made about your likely interest in that item. Much of the current discussion about the semantic web relates to designing standardized ontologies and the necessity for learning and assessment objects to be brought out from behind closed learning management systems and password protected databases. Although much of the detail about the semantic web are likely to appeal more to specialist rather than discipline academics, teachers will need to reconsider their teaching methods and learning and assessment spaces in the light of the affordances that will flow from ubiquitous computing and a seamless Web 3.0 semantic environment (Zhang, Cheung & Townsend, 2009). The very nature of learning and assessment will need to be redefined as students have access to sophisticated search and match tools that link data, items and context. These are new learning spaces and so require new assessment spaces to match the capabilities that students are developing and using to interact with content and context.

As teachers become more familiar with the use of evidence-centered assessment design principles we will witness a more meaningful alignment between the learning outcomes articulated for a course, the learning activities set by the teacher so that students can develop specific capabilities and the assessment tasks completed by the student to document the development of those capabilities (Shaffer, Hatfield, Svarovsky, Nash, Nulty, Bagley, Franke, Rupp & Mislevy, 2009).

CONCLUSION

Assessment spaces will change; students cannot continue to be treated as isolated individuals, cut-off from access to resources and other people during their assessment tasks. Educational institutions will need to expand their conception of assessment spaces to include virtual spaces created within the web that allow students to construct their responses with access to whatever resources are required to complete authentic tasks. Students will demand more authentic, meaningful tasks that will engage them in using the full range of capabilities they have developed during the learning process, including the knowledge, strategies, behaviours and collaborations they have developed.

If students can respond to an assessment task and receive high grades simply by using Google or Wikipedia, the problem is not with the student but with the task. We will need to stop setting assessment tasks that can be completed by copy and paste or simple recall; we will need to set tasks that require immersion, engagement and collaboration.

REFERENCES

Abdulwahed, M., Nagy, Z. K., & Blanchard, R. (2008). The TriLab, a novel view of laboratory education. In *Proceedings EE2008 Conference: Innovation, Good Practice and Research in Engineering Education* (pp.51). Loughborough, UK: Engineering Subject Centre. Retrieved April 7, 2011, from http://www.engsc.ac.uk/ downloads/ scholarart/ ee2008/p051-abdulwahed.pdf

Ablin, J. L. (2008). Learning as problem design versus problem solving: Making the connection between cognitive neuroscience research and educational practice. *Mind, Brain, and Education, 2*(2), 52–54. doi:10.1111/j.1751-228X.2008.00030.x

Aldrich, C. (2009a). *The complete guide to serious games and simulations.* Somerset, NJ: Wiley.

Aldrich, C. (2009b). Virtual worlds, simulations, and games for education: A unifying view. *Journal of Online Education, 5*(5). Retrieved April 7, 2011, from http://www.innovateonline.info /pdf/ vol5_issue5/Virtual_Worlds,_Simulations,_and_ Games_for_Education-_A_Unifying_View.pdf

Baker, E. L., & Delacruz, G. C. (2008). *What do we know about assessment in games?* Paper presented at the National Center for Research on Evaluation, Standards, and Student Testing (CRESST) American Educational Research Association AERA 2008 Annual Meeting New York, NY. Retrieved April 7, 2011, from http://www. cse.ucla.edu/ products/overheads/AERA2008 / baker_assessment.pdf

Bloomfield, P. R., & Livingstone, D. (2009). Immersive learning and assessment with quizHUD. *Computing and Information Systems Journal, 13*(1). Retrieved April 7, 2011, from http://cis. uws.ac.uk/research /journal/vol13.htm

Boud, D., & Falchikov, N. (2006). Aligning assessment with long-term learning. *Assessment & Evaluation in Higher Education, 31*(4), 399–413. doi:10.1080/02602930600679050

Boud, D., & Prosser, M. (2002). Key principles for high quality student learning in higher education: A framework for evaluation. *Educational Media International, 39*(3), 237–245. doi:10.1080/09523980210166026

Breakey, K. M., Levin, D., Miller, I., & Hentges, K. E. (2008). The use of scenario-based-learning interactive software to create custom virtual laboratory scenarios for teaching genetics. *Genetics, 179*(3), 1151–1155. doi:10.1534/genetics.108.090381

Broadfoot, P., & Black, P. (2004). Redefining assessment? The first ten years of assessment in education. *Assessment in Education, 11*(1), 7–27. doi:10.1080/0969594042000208976

Cooper, M. M., Cox, C. T. Jr, Nammouz, M., Case, E., & Stevens, R. (2008). An assessment of the effect of collaborative groups on students' problem-solving strategies and abilities. *Journal of Chemical Education, 85*(6), 886–872. doi:10.1021/ed085p866

Corter, J. E., Nickerson, J. V., Esche, S. K., Chassapis, C., Im, S., & Ma, J. (2007). Constructing reality: A study of remote, hands-on, and simulated laboratories. [TOCHI]. *ACM Transactions on Computer-Human Interaction, 14*(2), 7. doi:10.1145/1275511.1275513

de Freitas, S. (2008). *Serious virtual worlds: A scoping study.* Retrieved April 7, 2011, from http:// www.jisc.ac.uk/media/ documents/publications / seriousvirtualworldsv1.pdf

de Freitas, S., & Neumann, T. (2009). The use of exploratory learning for supporting immersive learning in virtual environments. *Computers & Education, 52*(2), 343–352. doi:10.1016/j. compedu.2008.09.010

Elliott, B. (2008). *Assessment 2.0 modernising assessment in the age of Web 2.0*. Retrieved April 7, 2011, from http://www.scribd.com/doc/ 461041/ Assessment-20

Fenn, J., Raskino, M., & Gammage, B. (2009). *Gartner's hype cycle special report for 2009*. Retrieved April 7, 2011, from http://www.gartner. com/resources /169700/169747/gartners_hype _cycle_special__169747.pdf

Franklin, T., & van Harmelen, M. (2007). *Web 2.0 for content for learning and teaching in higher education*. Retrieved April 7, 2011, from http:// www.jisc.ac.uk/media/ documents/programmes/ digitalrepositories/web2-content -learning-and-teaching.pdf

Gilbert, L., Gale, V., Warburton, B., & Wills, G. (2008). *Report on summative e-assessment quality (REAQ)*. JISC. Retrieved April 7, 2011, from http://www.jisc.ac.uk/media/ documents/projects/ reaqfinalreport.pdf

Havnes, A. (2004). Examination and learning: An activity-theoretical analysis of the relationship between assessment and educational practice. *Assessment & Evaluation in Higher Education, 29*(2), 159–176. doi:10.1080/0260293042000188456

Herrington, J., & Herrington, A. (2006). *Authentic conditions for authentic assessment: Aligning task and assessment*. In A. Bunker & I. Vardi (Eds.), *Research and development in higher education volume 29, critical visions: Thinking, learning and researching in higher education* (pp 146-151). Milperra, NSW: HERDSA.

Hobbs, M., Brown, E., & Gordon, M. (2009). Learning and assessment with virtual worlds in e-learning technologies and evidence-based assessment approaches. In C. Spratt, & P. Lajbcygier (Eds.), *AICTE book series* (pp. 55-75). Hershey, PA: Information Science Reference, IGI Global.

Hong, J.-C., Cheng, C.-L., Hwang, M.-Y., Lee, C.-K., & Chang, H.-Y. (2009). Assessing the educational values of digital games. *Journal of Computer Assisted Learning, 25*(5), 423–437. doi:10.1111/j.1365-2729.2009.00319.x

Jarmon, L., Traphagan, T., Mayrath, M., & Trivedi, A. (2009). Virtual world teaching, experiential learning, and assessment: An interdisciplinary communication course in Second Life. *Computers & Education, 53*(1), 169–182. doi:10.1016/j. compedu.2009.01.010

Koretsky, M. D., Amatore, D., Barnes, C., & Kimura, S. (2008). Enhancement of student learning in experimental design using a virtual laboratory. *IEEE Transactions on Education, 51*(1), 76–85. doi:10.1109/TE.2007.906894

Lin, M., & Chang, C. (2009). Incorporating auto-grading and feedback tools into an online 3D compound virtual field trip system. In G. Siemens & C. Fulford (Eds.), *Proceedings of World Conference on Educational Multimedia, Hypermedia and Telecommunications*, (pp. 3698-3703). Chesapeake, VA: AACE.

Murray, S. J., Lowe, D. B., Lindsay, E., Lasky, V., & Liu, D. (2008). Experiences with a hybrid architecture for remote laboratories. In D. Budny (Ed.), *FiE 2008: The 38th Annual Frontiers in Education Conference*, (pp 15-19). Piscataway, NJ: IEEE.

Nichols, P. D. (1994). A framework for developing cognitively diagnostic assessments. *Review of Educational Research, 64*(4), 575–603.

Nickerson, J. V., Corter, J. E., Esche, S. K., & Constantin, C. (2007). A model for evaluating the effectiveness of remote engineering laboratories and simulations in education. *Computers & Education, 49*(3), 708–725. doi:10.1016/j. compedu.2005.11.019

Oblinger, D. G., & Oblinger, J. L. (Eds.). (2005). *Educating the Net generation*. Retrieved April 7, 201a, from http://www.educause.edu/ educatingthenetgen

Pivec, M., & Pivec, P. (2009) IMAGINE report on Game-Based Learning projects within the European community and good practice case studies spread across all levels of education. Retrieved April 7, 2011, http://www.imaginegames.eu/ eng/ Reports

Prensky, M. (2001). *Digital games-based learning*. New York, NY & London, UK: McGraw Hill.

Ramakishnan, S., & Ramadoss, B. (2009). Assessment using multi-criteria decision approach for "higher order skills" learning domains. *International Journal on E-Learning*, 8(2), 241–262.

Richardson, D., & Molka-Danielsen, J. (2009). Assessing student performance. In Molka-Danielsen, J., & Deutschmann, M. (Eds.), *Learning and teaching in the virtual world of Second Life* (pp. 52–60). Trondheim, Norway: Tapir Academic Press.

Ripley, M., Harding, R., Redif, H., Ridgway, J., & Tafler, J. (2009). *Review of advanced e-assessment techniques (RAeAT) final report*. Retrieved April 7, 2011, from http://www.jisc.ac.uk/media /documents/projects/ raeat_finalreport.pdf

Shaffer, D. W., Hatfield, D., Svarovsky, G. N., Nash, P., Nulty, A., & Bagley, E. (2009). Epistemic network analysis: A prototype for 21st century assessment of learning. *International Journal of Learning and Media*, 1(2), 33–53. doi:10.1162/ ijlm.2009.0013

Shute, V. J. (2009). Simply assessment. *International Journal of Learning and Media*, 1(2), 1–11. doi:10.1162/ijlm.2009.0014

Shute, V. J., & Spector, J. M. (2008). *SCORM 2.0 white paper: Stealth assessment in virtual world*. Retrieved April 7, 2011, from http://www.adlnet.gov/ Technologies/Evaluation/Library /Additional%20Resources/ LETSI%20White%20Papers/ Shute%20-%20Stealth%20Assessment%20 in%20 Virtual%20Worlds.pdf

Shute, V. J., Ventura, M., Bauer, M., & Zapata-Rivera, D. (2009). Melding the power of serious games and embedded assessment to monitor and foster learning: Flow and grow. In U. Ritterfeld, M. Cody & P. Vorderer (Eds.), *Serious games: Mechanisms and effects* (pp. 293-319). New York, NY: Taylor & Francis Group. Retrieved April 7, 2011, from http://21st-century-assessment. wikispaces. com/file/ view/GAMES_Shute _FINAL.pdf

Tiropanis, T., Davis, H., Millard, D., Weal, M., White, S., & Wills, G. (2009). *JISC SemTech project report*. Retrieved April 7, 2011, from http://www.jisc.ac.uk/media/ documents/projects/ semtech-report.pdf

Torrance, H., & Pryor, J. (2001). Developing formative assessment in the classroom: Using action research to explore and modify theory. *British Educational Research Journal*, 27(5), 615–631. doi:10.1080/01411920120095780

Veletsianos, G., Miller, C., & Doering, A. (2009). EnALI: A research and design framework for virtual characters and pedagogical agents. *Journal of Educational Computing Research*, 41(2), 171–194. doi:10.2190/EC.41.2.c

Zhang, Z., Cheung, K.-H., & Townsend, J. P. (2009). Bringing Web 2.0 to bioinformatics. *Briefings in Bioinformatics*, 10(1), 1–10. doi:10.1093/ bib/bbn041

Zhou, F., Duh, H. B.-L., & Billinghurst, M. (2008). Trends in augmented reality tracking, interaction and display: A review of ten years of ISMAR. In *Proceedings of the 7th IEEE/ACM International Symposium on Mixed and Augmented Reality* (pp. 193-202). Washington, DC: IEEE Computer Society.

ADDITIONAL READING

Lin, X., Chen, H., Mather, R., & Fletcher, H. (2009). Adaptive assessment – A practice of classification on small-size training sets. In I. Gibson, R. Weber, K. McFerrin, R. Carlsen & D. A. Willis, (Eds.), *Proceedings of Society for Information Technology and Teacher Education International Conference 2009* (pp 3168-3181). Retrieved April 7, 2011, from http://www.editlib.org /p/31131.

KEY TERMS AND DEFINITIONS

Assessment 2.0: An emerging term used to describe tasks that are aligned with the characteristics of the Web 2.0 environment.

Augmented Reality: Blending of virtual and physical spaces.

Convergent Response: Where every student is expected to provide the same response to an assessment task.

Divergent Response: Where students may provide different but equally acceptable responses to an assessment task.

Integrative Assessment: Tasks designed to influence students' approaches to future learning by tracking the strategies students use to assess their own learning abilities and problem solving capabilities.

Serious Games: Digital games whose primary purpose and market is education and training.

Stealth Assessment: Describes the unobtrusive collection of data about a student's performance and capabilities without interrupting the flow between learning and assessment activities.

Web 2.0: An Internet experience based on participatory engagement and an underlying philosophy of collaboration, social interaction and user control.

Chapter 14

The Charles Darwin University vHospital®:
Creating an Authentic Virtual Learning Environment for Undergraduate Nursing Students

Gylo (Julie) Hercelinskyj
Charles Darwin University, Australia

Beryl McEwan
Charles Darwin University, Australia

ABSTRACT

This chapter presents an overview of an innovative teaching approach in an undergraduate nursing degree at Charles Darwin University (CDU). The authors describe the development and initial integration into the first year clinical nursing subject of a virtual learning space using a case-based approach to address some of the issues associated with an externalised Bachelor of Nursing program. In addition, the use of the CDU vHospital® in supporting early role socialisation into nursing and professional identity of first year nursing students will be explored. The findings and outcomes of formal and informal evaluations of the resource are also presented. Lastly, the authors identify recommendations for future development and areas for potential future research.

INTRODUCTION

In an externalized nursing program, it is a challenge to facilitate an awareness of, and engagement with, the complexity and reality of tertiary education and nursing practice. This chapter describes an innovative teaching approach in an undergraduate nursing degree in Australia designed to enhance the learning opportunities and early professional engagement for students enrolled in a program by distance learning. Through the presentation of an exemplar case, the development process and initial integration of the Charles Darwin University Virtual Hospital® (CDU vHospital®) into

DOI: 10.4018/978-1-60960-114-0.ch014

the Bachelor of Nursing program as a web-based learning platform is described and the benefits and relevance for students and the program are discussed.

Background

Australia's Northern Territory (NT) is located primarily above the Tropic of Capricorn and has both desert and dry tropic environments. There are five major population centres in the NT. Darwin, the capital city, is located on the northern coast and is geographically closer to Indonesia than to other Australian capital cities. Alice Springs is located in the geographical centre of Australia and is the next largest city in the NT. In between are the smaller centres of Katherine and Tennant Creek and, on the eastern side of the north coast is Nhulunbuy, a site of significant bauxite mining operations (Tourism NT, 2005-2009).

The NT has a small, culturally diverse and geographically spread population, with around 30% of the population being Indigenous Australians (Australian Bureau of Statistics, 2008). Approximately 50% of the NT population lives in the Darwin area, with the remaining 50% spread across the four regional cities or towns and in many small and remote indigenous communities (Tourism NT, 2005-2009).

The health profile of the NT population differs somewhat from the rest of Australia. There are higher rates of chronic diseases and indigenous clients are more likely to present with multiple morbidities. Specifically, health concerns of the NT population include self-harm and suicide, diabetes, renal and cardiovascular disease (Australian Institute of Health and Welfare, 2006a, 2006b).

Charles Darwin University (CDU) is located in the NT and is the Territory's major tertiary institution with approximately 19,000 students enrolled. CDU is a dual-sector education provider that offers pathways for students from secondary school-based vocational training to advanced research degrees. The student cohort is diverse,

with students coming from local, national and international backgrounds (Charles Darwin University, 2009). Challenges for the University are to meet the needs of the diverse and geographically spread population of the NT and, for health related programs in particular, to ensure that graduates are adequately prepared to meet the needs of the NT as well as the broader Australian health sector.

The nursing program at CDU commenced in 1991 after the transfer of the local hospital-based nurse training to the University sector and, in consultation with industry and the profession, the program is continuously being revised to meet the changing needs of the community and the health care sector (Charles Darwin University, 2007). The program prepares students for practice as registered nurses in Australia and, because of the availability of an external study mode, attracts students from all Australian States and Territories. It is also a regulatory requirement that graduates, at the end of their program, meet the required professional competencies and standards of practice in Australia (Nursing and Midwifery Board of the Northern Territory, 2008).

The program is available full or part time and is normally completed in three (3) years full time. Clinical skills teaching blocks (CTBs) and clinical placements occur in all three years of the program. Students enrolled in the CDU Bachelor of Nursing are primarily of mature age and many are practicing as licensed second level nurses (referred to in Australia as Enrolled or Division 2 Nurses) or as unlicensed health care workers (in Australia referred to as assistants in nursing or personal care assistants) in a diverse range of health care settings and geographical locations across Australia. In 2009, the student cohort is predominantly mixed mode, (approximately 90%) with only around 10% of students enrolled internally. Four percent (4%) are international students, mainly from the South East Asian region.

There are two-entry points into the Bachelor of Nursing program. Students can enter at the first year level, either directly from school or as non-school leavers (this includes mature age students). Alternatively, students can enter with advanced standing in the initial nursing subjects because of previous lower level nursing qualifications (for example, enrolled or Division 2 nurse) or completion of equivalent subjects elsewhere. In 1997 the CDU Bachelor of Nursing program was externalized. External study mode enables students to complete theoretical components of the program off campus and the flexibility to determine their study timetable in consideration of their specific life/work/study commitments (Hewitt-Taylor, 2003; Jacobsen, 2006).

Initially students enrolled externally in the CDU Bachelor of Nursing were supported by print based learning resources and communicated with the University lecturers by telephone or email. These approaches were in line with the traditional distance learning resources described by Zawacki-Richter, Brown and Delport (2009). When the University moved to a web-based learning platform around 2005, external students were supported by learning materials and resources using electronic formats. Today, external students are supported by a range of electronic resources such as direct links to appropriate material, live classrooms and online discussion boards or chat rooms. Most print based material is now presented directly online or as downloadable documents accessed via the web-based learning platform.

Regardless of study mode or entry level, students find university studies challenging (Andrew, McGuiness, Reid, & Corcoran, 2009). In particular, first year students may struggle with the transition from school-based learning to the university setting and have issues adjusting to the expectations of the university, the self-directed nature of learning and the personal responsibilities required to be successful independent learners (Andrew et al., 2009). In addition, nursing is a practice based discipline and a "supportive learning environment has been identified as pivotal for the transfer of learning into a clinical context" (Henderson, Twentyman, Heel & Lloyd, 2006, p.

564). Therefore, as well as adjusting to new ways of learning and university life in general, there is an educational imperative for nursing students to develop their understanding of the requirements and knowledge essential for professional nursing practice early in their studies and to understand the context in which it applies.

One of the issues with external study that nursing academics at CDU have identified is that many students do not physically engage with the University unless they are required to attend on campus for some reason. The external nature of the Bachelor of Nursing means that many students do not engage with the clinical aspects of the program until they attend required CTBs on campus. This has implications for their role socialisation, development of a professional nursing identity and their understanding and appreciation of the role and scope of nursing practice, particularly for students not exposed to clinical settings until required to do so as part of their studies.

Whilst nursing practice involves many psychomotor tasks, the processes which underpin nursing interventions are "problem solving, decision making and clinical judgements" (Reilly & Oermann 1992, cited in Morales-Mann & Kaitell, 2001, p. 14). This requirement is also explicitly stated in the professional nursing standards in Australia (Australian Nursing & Midwifery Council 2006). In order to develop the requisite problem solving skills to meet the increasing demands and complexity of contemporary health care (Tiwari, Lai, So, & Yuen, 2006), students need opportunities to engage in problem solving activities that promote sound decision making and to expand their scope of practice throughout the duration of their studies. Whilst graduate nurse programs, offered by health care facilities, provide support and orientation during the initial transition period, on completion of their preparatory programs graduates are expected to carry a full patient load and to "hit the floor running" (Kilstoff & Rochester, 2004, p. 13).

During an internal revision of the Bachelor of Nursing (BN) curriculum at CDU in 2006, it was recognized that some of these issues identified above were evident in CDU nursing students, particularly those enrolled externally. The review identified that students needed increased opportunities to integrate a range of knowledge, attitudes and skills to critique and analyse practice problems in order to foster the development of their professional identity and facilitate role transition (Andrew et al., 2009; Elliot, Efron, Wright, & Martinelli, 2003; Morales-Mann & Kaitell, 2001). It was also acknowledged that external students needed support and feedback to be able to effectively engage with these aspects of the learning process.

Given the large numbers of externally based students enrolled in the Bachelor of Nursing program, it was also evident there was a high priority to provide a more flexible, easily accessible and potentially portable learning resource and, as a result, the CDU vHospital® project commenced in 2006. The aims of the CDU vHospital® were to develop a content rich learning space that would:

- present patient journeys in an interactive environment
- provide experiential learning opportunities for students,
- promote early development of professional identity,
- as part of early role socialisation, expose students to clinical nursing practice in preparation for required clinical placement, and
- provide opportunities for formative assessment either as part of subject requirements or as individual self-assessment by students.

This chapter is an overview of the CDU vHospital® as a learning space; a description of the case development process; and reports on the initial integration into the CDU Bachelor of Nursing program. The evaluation findings from the first students to use the resource and suggestions for the future directions of the CDU vHospital® are also reported.

CHARLES DARWIN UNIVERSITY VHOSPITAL®

The CDU vHospital® is an English language learning space developed for undergraduate nursing students that uses clinical cases to present nursing concepts and knowledge to address some of the issues identified during a review of the program. The work by Lave and Wenger (1991) and Wenger (1998) provides a context to understand the way in which the CDU vHospital® was conceptualised and designed to be an authentic learning space to prepare students for clinical nursing practice.

The CDU vHospital® as a Learning Space

To foster the acquisition of the necessary knowledge, behaviours and attitudes by CDU nursing students studying externally across Australia, CDU has a responsibility to ensure all students are able to access the necessary learning resources in a way that is flexible, responsive and contemporary and encourages students to engage with the profession early in their program.

Traditionally, learning spaces have been defined as concrete places that students attend to gain the knowledge and skills necessary for the successful completion of the program. However, in the contemporary world, learning spaces are becoming increasingly less concrete and more intangible with access no longer restricted to those able to attend campus or other venues for learning. Further, students expect to have greater flexibility in the way and when they access learning materials and communicate with the University (Weir, 2008). More flexible learning spaces and accessibility to learning resources enables students to structure their study commitments to meet their specific personal, social and work requirements and further promotes self-directed and independent learning.

Some of the challenges in this environment for any discipline at CDU is to create learning spaces that foster professional engagement and that situates students in a context for learning discipline specific knowledge and inter-professional collaborative practice (Stone, 2010) in a student cohort that is primarily off campus. The limited contact with peers and discipline specific academics impedes student introduction to the community of practice and the development of a professional identity (Lave & Wenger, 1991). It also restricts the opportunities to engage in critical thinking and problem solving related to the specific area of professional practice.

In nursing, this has implications for the ability of nursing students to gain entry into the community of nursing practice and to participate in legitimate peripheral learning that fosters role socialisation and development of their professional nursing identity (Lave & Wenger, 1991; Wenger, 1998). It also reduces their ability to develop the critical thinking, problem-solving and collaborative behaviours required for the delivery of contemporary health care in Australia (Morales-Mann & Kaitell, 2001; Tiwari, Lai, So & Yen, 2006).

For the large external cohort enrolled in the CDU Bachelor of Nursing individual student learning spaces are largely constituted outside of the traditional confines of the University. During the CDU vHospital® development phase, the academic development team conceptualised learning spaces as any environment in which a student could access and interact with learning resources required for their studies and that foster early engagement with professional nursing practice.

The CDU vHospital® immerses students in the health experience of individual patients and the social and professional context of health care provision in Australia. It provides an environment through which students can engage with clinicians, patients and their families in a range of health settings, including community and hospital based care settings and prepare them for further experiential learning actual clinical settings during clinical placements. The literature has consistently demonstrated that the clinical nursing practice environment is a major learning context for nursing students (Smedley & Morey, 2009; Henderson et al., 2006). Prior to entering real clinical practice settings as a learning environment, students must be supported by theoretical content that presents an authentic picture of the complexity and reality of clinical nursing practice.

Embedded activities within each case promote active learning and facilitate nursing knowledge acquisition and foster student exploration of professional nursing issues. The CDU vHospital® enables students to practice activities such as completing documentation, drug calculations and patient assessment under the guidance or moderation of the lecturer. It also provides an introduction into the teamwork and communication between nurses and patients, nurses and other health professionals and between nurses in different practice settings as part of patient care. In traditional learning spaces these activities would be undertaken in tutorial sessions or integrated into weekly clinical laboratory sessions prior to the student attending clinical practice in a health care setting.

The CDU vHospital® therefore provides a safe, authentic learning space for beginning students where they can explore the range of professional interactions and decisions related to clinical care, and reflect on the outcomes of the choices they make for each patient. This situated learning (Lave & Wenger, 1991) "acts as a bridge between" (p. 35) the cognitive and experiential learning that is essential for students to develop the requisite knowledge and skills for professional nursing practice and to gain entry to the community of nursing practice (Wenger, 1998).

Case-Based Learning

There are two different approaches to using cases in teaching and learning: case-based or problem-based learning (Stjernquist & Crang-Svalenius, 2007). Case-based learning uses cases, whether real or fictional, to tell a patient story and to present information as an example of specific circumstances or clinical presentations that may be seen in a health setting (Brauer et al., 2009; Marriner Tomey, 2003). Problem based learning is an alternative to case-based learning that has been popular nationally and internationally in health programs since the 1960's but differs from case-based learning slightly in its approach, degree of student activity and the resources required to successfully use it (Stjernquist & Crang-Svalenius, 2007). While Stjernquist and Crang-Svalenius (2007) suggest that cases should be based on real life scenarios, Brauer et al. (2009) urges caution when developing cases using this method as there is the potential for personal or experiential biases or limitations during case development.

Regardless of whether case or problem-based learning is used, there is evidence from the literature that using cases prompts problem solving and knowledge seeking behaviour by students (Stjernquist & Crang-Svalenius, 2007) and results in better outcomes for students, particularly in clinical settings (Spencer, 2003). Therefore, use of case scenarios in nursing studies is useful in assisting students to view the patient in a holistic way and to see that how the patient responds in any situation is related to their current health problems. It also enables students to understand how the social determinants of health, such as socio-economic status, can impact on an individual's current well being.

Case-based learning is less resource intensive than problem-based learning, is better suited to larger student numbers and has different requirement for student activity and for the role of the teacher (Brauer et al., 2009). Because of the large external cohort of nursing students at CDU, often completing their studies at a distance from the University, the constraints on staff availability and limited infrastructure at CDU, case-based learning was seen as the preferred approach in the CDU vHospital®. The CDU vHospital® development team believed that the content and context richness of case-based learning would stimulate students to focus on the holistic care of patients rather than specific problem resolution that is implicit in problem based learning.

Contextualizing student learning in real case experiences facilitates the development of the professional knowledge, skills and behaviours expected of a registered nurse, and assists students to develop their professional identity, fosters their role socialisation (Andrew et al., 2009) and builds their skills to effectively contribute as a member of a multi-disciplinary team in the clinical setting. The use of cases allowed the development team to present detailed clinical stories that guided students through the patient journey in a way that assists students to develop their understanding of how to care for a patient as opposed to the problem-based method that provides triggers to stimulate student thinking about situations that require explanation (Stjernquist & Crang-Svalenius, 2007).

In addition, students, particularly early on in their studies, tend to focus on the procedural tasks rather than the holistic nursing care requirements of the patient which can result in a fragmented and incomplete picture of nursing care and the requirements of professional nursing practice (Andrew et al., 2009). The use of an interactive case-based learning environment presents content in a way that reinforces the fundamental concept that the patient is the central focus in nursing (Meleis, 2005) and that nursing care is concerned with the psychosocial as well as physical health of the patient.

Overview of the CDU vHospital®

There are currently six patients admitted to the CDU vHospital®.

- *Peter Abbot* is the member for Larapinta who finds that he is unable to pass urine.
- *Judy Thompson* an Australian aid worker who has recently developed flu like symptoms after returning from working as a nurse near the Thai/Lao border.
- *Robert Bogan* is a tough, tattooed bike enthusiast who develops a painful case of ulcerative colitis and subsequently requires a colostomy. His care incorporates surgical nursing and mental health nursing care. This case is a precursor to the case of Bikey Bob (see below).
- *Beth Sheba* is in a rush to get to work but has a horrific car crash, crushing her right arm and leg and causing her a head injury. Beth's care incorporates emergency nursing (including triage and trauma) post-operative care and orthopaedic nursing care.
- *John Wayne* is an Aboriginal man living in a remote Northern Territory community. John is diagnosed with diabetes and a secondary ulcer on his foot by the community physician. John's hospital nursing care is to help him with his diabetes self-management and to assess and treat his neuropathic foot ulcer.
- *Bikey Bob* is a continuation of Robert Bogan, the tough tattooed bike enthusiast who required a colostomy to manage his ulcerative colitis. Here students return to Bob who is presenting with mental health issues associated with managing and accepting his colostomy.

Student Access

Students access the site via the online learning materials for the relevant subject. Using a secure login, students are able to access the available cases and can navigate through cases as directed or as they wish. They are also able to access information and resources for additional learning.

Online Presentation

The initial logon page (see Figure 1) provides a video introduction to the vHospital and information about how to navigate the cases and the resources available on the site. When the plan in the top right hand corner is highlighted, there is a brief description of the clinical setting (ward), the patients that are likely to be admitted to the ward and the types of clinical procedures they may experience.

Each patient journey is presented like a book, with specific times or places presented as a *Chapter*. All cases begin with a *Patient Story* outlining the patient history, why they have been admitted to hospital and their experiences in the emergency department. Students then follow the patient through the *Chapters* representing their subsequent admission to hospital.

As they move through the cases, students are asked to complete nursing documentation or other activities, to make clinical decisions and are able to see the consequences of their decisions. Cases also include video, voice or sound recordings of procedures, clinical assessment findings and nursing communication with the patient, other nurses and other health professionals as well as interactive or animated student learning tasks.

CDU vHospital® Development Team

The project team established to develop and implement the first stage of the CDU vHospital® included a range of CDU staff including a web-based learning consultant, technical staff with relevant software and database management expertise and expert nurse academics from the CDU School of Health Sciences.

Figure 1. CDU vHospital® logon page (Source: CDU vHospital®)

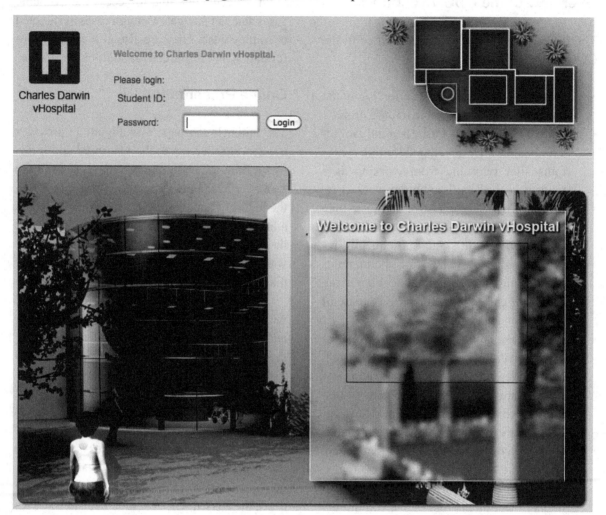

The Web and Multimedia Group (WAMM) in the Teaching Learning Quality Group (TLQG) at Charles Darwin University are the development team behind the CDU vHospital®. Working in conjunction with the Project Manager, WAMM produces the patient cases and advises the Project Team on the design and development of the CDU vHospital®.

The initial stages of the project involved identifying the key stages and where specific aspects should occur, for example, case development, online prototype production and field testing. The main stages of the project were concept development, prototype production, content development, production and upload to the web-based learning platform and field testing. Concept development identified the audience, purpose of the case and details of the learning approaches. Prototype production created the first version of the product to enable an interface for initial peer testing and to test proposed site navigation. After initial development, the first case became the template for the other cases to be developed in the first stage of the project.

A major stage is development of content where all the resources for each case are compiled and sequenced. The production phase develops the software resource and allows significant internal testing to be undertaken. Once these phases have been completed, the case is loaded onto the web-based learning platform so that testing of the links between the CDU vHospital® and the learning platform to assessment tasks or resources can occur. Field testing is a major feature in the development stage and once all other phases are completed there is extensive field testing of each case with end users and clinical and teaching experts to ensure accuracy and currency of content and to test usability and navigation.

CASE DEVELOPMENT AND PRODUCTION

The development of each case is a multi-stage process that draws on a broad range of expertise to bring the patient journey to life. The case of CDU vHospital® patient *John Wayne* will be presented here to demonstrate the practical implementation of the case development process.

The first step is to identify a 'typical' case for development.

Background to John Wayne*: Diabetes is a serious problem in the NT. It is a chronic disease 'causing substantial morbidity, premature death, disability, reduced quality of life and financial cost' (Australian Institute of Health and Welfare, 2009). Aboriginal and Torres Strait Islander people experience a higher burden of disease than the rest of the Australian population with the rate for diabetes in Indigenous communities being three times higher than non indigenous communities (Australian Institute of Health and Welfare, 2008). Given this background it was decided that a case presenting this chronic illness in the context of the NT was an appropriate choice for the CDU vHospital®. As a result, John Wayne was born.*

Each case is developed by a lead author and is a cumulative story based on real cases they have encountered in their clinical experience (Brauer et al., 2009; Stjernquist & Crang-Svalenius, 2007). To minimise the potential for bias or limitation (Brauer et. al., 2009), the case was also reviewed by several other nurse academics and clinical nurse specialists which further strengthened the authenticity of the story. Initially, a story is built that includes a 250-word background, 50 words on the patient's condition and a map of the patient journey identifying the pathway from admission to discharge (see Figure 2). A list of the health professionals patients will see, procedures they will undergo and the hospital forms, medications and any other relevant information is also developed at this stage. This information does not appear in the final online page but is essential to ensure continuity of story development.

John Wayne' story: *John is an Aboriginal man living in a remote Northern Territory community who is diagnosed with diabetes and a secondary ulcer on his foot by the community physician. John's hospital nursing care is to help him with his diabetes self-management and to assess and treat his neuropathic foot ulcer.*

Once the initial story and the content and context of the story have been established, the case *Chapters* can be developed. The first *Chapter,* the *Patient Story,* tells the reader about the unique life story of the patient and describes events that led to their admission. Subsequent *Chapters* follow the patient journey through the remainder of their admission. Breaking the cases into *Chapters* helps the student to focus their learning on a specific aspect of the case within the whole patient story.

*The story for **John Wayne** sets the scene. Students are introduced to **John Wayne**, the person, before they met **John Wayne** the patient. This is essential to reinforce to students that patients must be viewed in a broader framework than merely an illness or medical diagnosis. It also promotes an awareness of the cultural sensitivities that need to be considered.*

Figure 2. Example of flowchart used to develop John Wayne's case

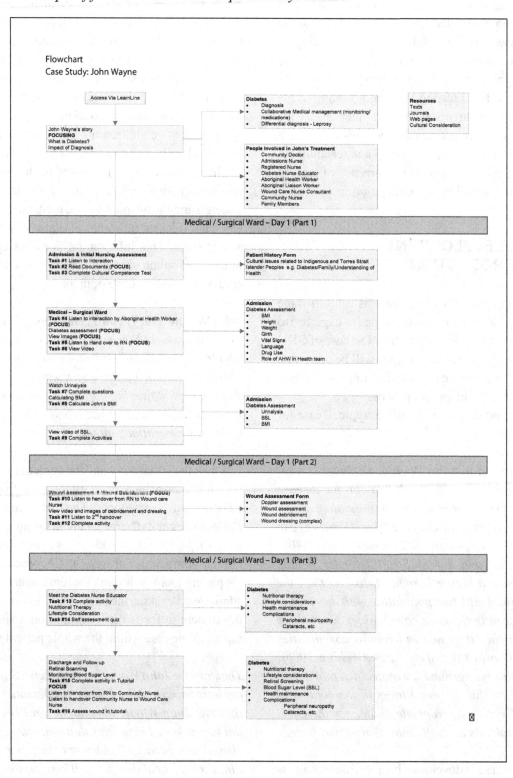

John's Patient Story: *John is 55 years old and leads a relatively sedentary lifestyle. He works as the Environmental Program Supervisor which is an office based job. During the weekends he likes to go hunting with his grandchildren, but nowadays he mostly drives the "troupie" [a four wheel drive vehicle] to the waterhole and gets the fire ready while the young ones go out hunting. In the past few months, he has been experiencing unusual thirst, dizziness, occasional blurred vision, and an awkward feeling of numbness in his right foot....*

In the development phase the text and media plans for voice and video recordings are also developed to provide the 'script' or scenarios in preparation for recording and/or photography or filming. Included in these resources are the scripts for nursing Handovers. Handover is an important communication tool in nursing that is used to communicate information about the patient from one nurse to another in a variety of circumstances. Clinical handover is a complex skill and one which is traditionally learnt through repeated exposure and role modelling in the clinical setting (Meißner et al., 2007; Kerr, 2002).

When undertaking clinical experience as part of their program, students often find it difficult to understand the information that is being given at handover and, when required to give a handover, struggle with what information to include or exclude, particularly in the early stages of their clinical experience. Given the high turnover of patients through many health settings it is essential that students begin to develop their skills in giving a concise and accurate patient handover early in their clinical experience (Kerr, 2002; O'Connell & Penney, 2001).

Figure 3. John Wayne (Source: CDU vHospital®)

In the CDU vHospital®, Handovers are short scripts of about 100-150 words scripted by the case creator that describe the patient condition at a given moment of their journey. The Handovers link one Chapter or event to the next and provide students with information regarding the current health status and care of the patient.

Figure 4 is an example of a handover related to John Wayne. It illustrates to students a number of key concepts as well as the type of information required in relation to a health handover. In addition, it highlights the multi-disciplinary nature of health care and how cultural sensitivities can be addressed. There are important cues related to John's personal situations, and past health history. The AHW worker also provides information about John's current health status and she also indicates who else will be contacted about John. Relevant terminology is introduced and students are guided to explore what this language means in the total context of patient management in the learning materials.

All *Chapters* and *Handovers* are reviewed by internal and external processes before production commences. Internally, they are proof read and edited by academic and teaching support staff to ensure they meet the objectives of the units where they are to be used as well as teaching and learning standards. To ensure clinical currency and accuracy (Brauer et.al., 2009), they are proof read and edited by specialist nurses with expertise in the relevant area of nursing practice and/or clinical setting.

*In **John Wayne**, the case author had extensive experience as a remote area nurse and in wound management. To ensure clinical currency a Wound Nurse Consultant and Diabetes Nurse from the local health service were invited to peer review the nursing care for the case.*

The Media Plan details the various media elements that need to be created for the web version of the patient case and includes things such as video clips, still images and interactive activities. The plan also identifies the setting and resources that will be required during the filming or photography session. In some cases, it requires negotiation with local health facilities and relevant clinical staff in the facilities to film or photograph in a specific clinical area or to arrange for staff to be available to play a role in the material being filmed or photographed. In others, the voluntary support of local academic and other university

Figure 4. Example of handover from the John Wayne case. This handover is being given by the Aboriginal Health Worker (AHW) to the Registered Nurse (RN). (Source: CDU vHospital®)

Trudy: *Hi Robert, this is John Wayne. He's a 53 and lives in a community near Katherine. He turned up to the local clinic with a foot wound where he was diagnosed with diabetes. The ulcer on his left foot is infected and needs cleaning and dressing. The ulcer on his heel was caused by him a stepping on a stone. He doesn't know when he did it as he didn't feel it due to his diabetic neuropathy. I checked his foot pulses they are present but weak and are the same on both sides. John's blood pressure is 140/90, pulse 106, respirations 20, temperature 37.5 and his oxygen saturation is 99% on room air. He doesn't have any pain. John smokes about 25 cigarettes a day and drinks a few beers once a week. He doesn't have any other medical or surgical problems and doesn't have a family history of diabetes. John has two relatives living near here. I will contact Sharon the hospital's Aboriginal Liaison Officer to find out where John's relatives are. If you have any questions call me on my pager.*

staff is sought for people to portray the patient, any relatives or friends and the range of health professionals included in the case. Before any filming or photography, all potential participants were briefed on what was required of them and the story background and asked to give consent for their participation and use of any material containing their images.

*The media plan for **John Wayne** included a visit to a small regional centre about 3 hours from Darwin to get still photos for the Patient Journey chapter and photos in the local health service facility for use throughout the case story. Appropriate charts and diagrams were also sourced for inclusion or as a template for the development of interactive charts (see Figure 5) for students to complete online.*

In addition, a *script* is produced by the multimedia personnel and the case author to provide a plan for the specific recording session. This is essential as it requires combined expertise to ensure that what is required can be produced in a realistic yet feasible way. The multi-media personnel were invaluable in advising the most appropriate filming and photography techniques while the case author or clinical nursing expert ensured that the setting and events reflect current and appropriate nursing practice.

A production leader is critical to ensure that the people, scripts or plans, and physical resources are available on the day when filming or photography is planned. They are essential to oversee the production elements to ensure the *Media Plan* is followed and, in conjunction with the case author, arrange the staff to be involved, the required resources and locations to be available and, on the day of filming, to direct actors and to shoot still photographs or video clips.

Following filming, the media personnel edit the still photographs and video clips in preparation for insertion into the relevant *Chapter.* Any required voice recordings are done concurrently with image editing or at the time of filming. Further quality checking and proofing is undertaken during the production phases of each case to ensure currency and accuracy of information and that the *Patient Story* remains contextually realistic.

Each case must be authorized by the commissioning author and/or the clinical expert before it can be made available to students. In addition, the commissioning author and WAMM undertake further revision and editing to ensure errors and omissions are identified and corrected. Final authorization of each case is a three stage process. WAMM, the commissioning author and appropriate Faculty staff must all give approval for the case to be made available before it is made live to staff or students for active use.

INTEGRATION INTO THE BACHELOR OF NURSING PROGRAM

The CDU vHospital® was integrated into the Bachelor of Nursing program in August 2008 in the first year clinical nursing subject. The theory component of the subject was available online through the web-based platform used by the University (Blackboard) and students were able to access the CDU vHospital® through a link in their online learning resources.

At this time, two completed cases were available for students to access and explore. Students were provided with instructions that requested that they 'visit' the CDU vHospital® hospital setting to gain an understanding of the clinical environment of a hospital, how nurses practice, and how patient care is managed and delivered. For some students, this was their first 'experience' of a clinical setting of any description. It also provided further opportunity for live testing in a controlled environment of the resource and the web-based platform through which it is delivered.

In 2009, the CDU vHospital® was used again in the same first year nursing subject and introduced into the mental health nursing subject. Follow-

Figure 5. This is a concept map of the aspects to address in a wound assessment (see Figure 5a). The camera is used here to indicate there are photos for students to view (Source: CDU vHospital®). Students are directed to click on any area around the camera which then takes them to a picture of John's wound. Students are instructed to view John's wound then to use an interactive pen tool to draw a circle around the wound (see Figure 5b). (Source: CDU vHospital®) Students are then directed to click the link to compare their assessment against that performed by the Wound Nurse (see Figure 5c). Source: (CDU vHospital®).

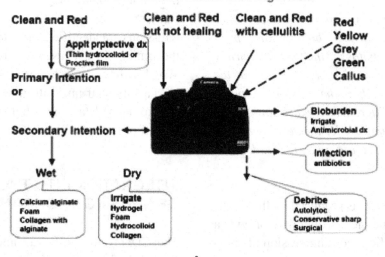

a

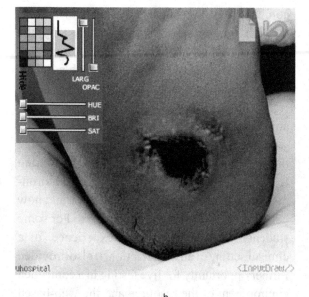

b

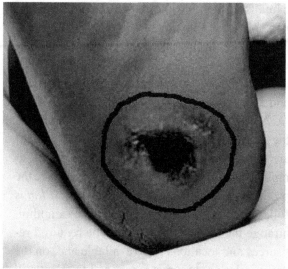

c

ing feedback from students and the authors' own informal review after the initial integration, the directions and instructions on how to access and use the CDU vHospital® were revised with more explicit information being provided to guide students. The CDU vHospital® will be introduced into the second year nursing theory subject in the near future and there are plans to broaden access to the resource across the entire nursing program.

EVALUATION

There have been several evaluations conducted throughout the development and initial integration of the CDU vHospital® into the Bachelor of Nursing program. In November 2007, initial user pilot testing was conducted to test the navigation of the resource and identify any areas of concern. This was followed by an evaluation by independent educational designers in April 2008.

In addition, and as part of the ongoing development process, clinical experts were asked to review the cases to ensure clinical currency and content before cases went live to students. It was felt there was no need to formally evaluate this aspect as there was close collaboration between clinicians and nurse academics during the case development process. However, it did identify some minor amendments and has reinforced the need to plan regular review of cases to maintain clinical accuracy and currency (Brauer et. al., 2009).

Key stakeholders (for example, academic staff, clinicians and students) were invited to view and test the CDU vHospital® in its first developmental stage to provide feedback on usability and navigation and to ensure clinical currency and accuracy of the content in June 2008. The final user testing commenced in August 2008 following integration into the first year nursing subject. Students enrolled in the subject were invited to complete an evaluation and to provide informal feedback over the course of the semester. Here we report on

the initial user and integration evaluation results as they represent key points in the development of the CDU vHospital®.

Initial User Pilot Testing

The initial pilot testing of the CDU vHospital® project took place in 2007. A purposive sample of seven students from undergraduate and postgraduate nursing programs at CDU was invited to come and use the vHospital under observation of the development team. The aim was to observe a range of users as they navigated one case and for participants to record their responses to the case. Participants were asked to identify any areas for improvement in relation to the introduction, usability and content relevance and to record their level of interest in the case.

The majority of participants found the introduction to the CDU vHospital® clear in terms of the aim of the vHospital as a teaching and learning resource. However, they felt more information about how to navigate around the hospital would have been helpful in some places. Six of the seven participants found the interface appealing. There were a number of comments regarding the size of the pop-up windows, with a number of participants trying several times to unsuccessfully maximise the windows. Many participants did not find the site easy to navigate, however the hospital layout map at the top of the screen was effective.

All participants found the content engaging and easy to follow but had a varied response to completing the assessment tasks. The quizzes were considered self explanatory but the instructions for completing documentation activities were not clear. The interactive features of the CDU vHospital® were viewed positively by participants, particularly the ability to replay videos. Participants described their experience of using the CDU vHospital® as positive and identified the concept as a good educational medium.

Following this evaluation, there was a revision of the instructions for completing activities and minor editing was undertaken to correct identified errors. This feedback also informed the ongoing development of the other five cases.

Following Integration into a Nursing Subject

As part of the initial live access to the CDU vHospital® by students, formal and informal evaluations and feedback were sought from students enrolled in the subject. Over the course of the semester students were also encouraged to provide anecdotal feedback during telephone or face to face conversations or when emailing the subject coordinator and, at the end of the semester, a formal survey using an online tool was made available. The subject coordinator was also asked to reflect on her thoughts and comment on the resource as a learning tool in the subject.

Only 10% of students responded to the formal survey but around 25% posted comments on an online discussion board that was part of the learning resources for the subject. There were also numerous informal comments made during communication related to the subject throughout the semester. The team was disappointed with the response to the formal evaluation, but acknowledged that the timing of the survey at the end of semester may have contributed to the low response rate. In spite of this issue, the results of the formal survey reflected the anecdotal and informal feedback received during the course of the semester. Here we report on the combined results of the formal and informal evaluation by students using the CDU vHospital® for the first time.

Overall, students enjoyed the CDU vHospital® and have found it engaging and interactive. It helped them to place learning in a context that assisted them to understand the nursing role and responsibilities as well as how nurses work with others in providing patient care (Andrew et al., 2009; Stjernquist & Crang-Svalenius, 2007).

Placing Learning in Context

For students with no or limited experience in a clinical setting the CDU vHospital® was useful in putting the subject content into a context that assisted their learning and understanding. It also highlighted the complexity and reality of nursing practice in a hospital setting. They were excited at being able to 'visit' a hospital setting and to see what was involved in nursing and the teamwork and communication between nurses and the broader multi-disciplinary team.

I just wanted to say that this experience using the computer to view the hospital was great, a look at actual processes in the hospital, it's helped you understand what is involved in nursing, the team work and communication between staff members is so important

I am quite impressed with the vhospital concept. I found I a great learning tool especially for those of us who are more audial [sic], practical based learners. Listening to the nurses and patients and seeing the interventions were for me far more useful that reading pages and pages of text books

Because the two cases did not overtly demonstrate first year clinical nursing activities such as providing personal hygiene, some students struggled with understanding how the cases related to the subject content. For example, one student asked *"Why was all that other 'stuff' included if it is not part of my current practice?"* Using cases that demonstrate the potential range of patients and health related problems students will encounter when undertaking clinical placements enables discussion related to their current scope of nursing practice. It also assists students to identify the specific nursing activities they are able to provide at different points in their studies.

The CDU vHospital® is, therefore, providing a safe environment for them to explore what their role and scope would be in preparation for clinical placement (Andrew et al., 2009; Elliot et al., 2003; Morales-Mann & Kaitell, 2001). It situates learning in a legitimate nursing environment, allows their supervised and controlled participation in patient care and provides an initial introduction to the nursing practice community (Wenger, 1998).

Access, Usability and Navigation

Most students found the site accessible and, once familiar with it, easy to navigate. There were some initial problems until they had worked out how to move between pages. Students also disliked not being able to maximise the pages, having to move backwards and forwards between pages when completing embedded activities and the lack of sound on some videos. Some also found using the CDU vHospital® time consuming and one student was not overly impressed with accessing what they viewed as just another resource on the internet.

...although for most people it is convenient, I think that too many things are reliant on the internet, and it just adds more too [sic] the stack.

Some students were unable to access some or all of the CDU vHospital®, for example, the embedded videos. Most of the problems were related to their web browser, system components and their download capacity. One student was not able to access the CDU vHospital®, at all because of intermittent satellite internet access and download capacity. Whilst the University stipulates the recommended minimum system requirements, the necessary infrastructure to support this is not always available due to the geographical location or isolation of some students participating in the program.

Only have dial up connection, connection so slow everything took hours to download or to go to

...quite a few things either don't load or take a long time to load (possibly due to my internet connection)...

There were a number of students who did not access the CDU vHospital® at all. The reasons for this are not known as they had not responded to the formal survey or provided informal feedback to the subject coordinator. Reasons for not accessing the CDU vHospital® has been identified as an area of future research.

Personal Reflections of Subject Coordinator

Overall the subject coordinator found CDU vHospital® of benefit to students and could see further potential through better integration into the subject and improved direction to students. To some extent, there is also a sense that, it helped them to prepare for their first clinical placement which has also been identified by the authors as an area that requires future research.

The CDU vHospital® enhanced student understanding of nursing work and the nursing role and helped students gain a more graphic picture of how nurses managed or coordinated the care of patients. It was particularly beneficial in demonstrating the team work and communication which are essential to patient care. Using the same cases when students attended the clinical intensive (CTB) was particularly valuable and enhanced the ability of staff and students to relate concepts to particular patients or situations. In addition, some students were delighted to meet staff who had portrayed characters on the CDU vHospital®. It is felt that the CDU vHospital®, as well as the required visit to campus for CTB, increases student connection to the University and academic staff, especially for those who are enrolled as external students.

For ease of navigation and because of how the CDU vHospital® was used in the subject, instructions to students were to enter anything in the activities to enable them to move easily through the cases. However, this proved problematic as some students demonstrated a tentativeness to experiment in the safe, virtual environment and became quite concerned about not being able to complete activities 'correctly'. On the other hand, other students became quite absorbed in the cases and spent a lot of time finding out the information required to complete the activities, sometimes at the expense of the intended subject content.

It was difficult to use the CDU vHospital® in lectures or tutorials because of the size of the page and the inability to maximise the windows. Initially it took a significant amount of additional time to become familiar with the cases and to support students to access, navigate the site and to complete interactive activities. It was also clearly evident that there was a need for better instructions and directions on how to use the resource, particularly in relation to subject content as many students had difficulty in understanding what was required of them or what information was required for some activities.

Outcomes from Evaluation

The development team were pleased with student evaluations and, although they highlighted a number of issues, feel that the CDU vHospital® is a valuable learning resource for nursing students.

Following the completion of the subject in which the CDU vHospital® was initially integrated and a review of the students evaluations, the initial logon and instructions for navigating the site have been reviewed and now contain more specific information about how to use and move through the cases. There is also more explanation of the cases and how they link to subject content. The technical and presentation issues have been identified for review in Stage 2 of the project due to commence in 2010.

FUTURE DIRECTIONS

In a health sector where the health needs of the Australian population and the requirements for professional nursing practice in Australia are not static, the challenge with a resource like the CDU vHospital® is to ensure that it continues to maintain its relevance and appropriateness as a teaching and learning resource. To achieve this, the CDU vHospital® has to continue to present cases which reflect contemporary health and nursing practice issues in Australia, and in particular, the Northern Territory. It is also essential that students are able to actively engage in learning both individually and as part of a collaborative effort and that the learning reflects contemporary health care delivery models and best practice standards for professional nursing in Australia.

Maintaining a quality, engaging, interactive and current resource presents a number of challenges, including the ongoing technical development of the resource, ensuring the clinical accuracy of the current cases and the need to develop further cases to increase the integration of the vHospital in all subjects in the CDU Bachelor of Nursing program.

The evaluations identified a number of recurring issues related to access to, and usability of, the CDU vHospital®. Feedback related to clarity of instructions was addressed by the academic developers and implemented in 2009. There has since been little indication of problems related to access, and navigation of, the site. Instructions for academic staff using the CDU vHospital® were also developed which has helped them become familiar with the site more quickly.

Maintaining the Quality of the CDU vHospital®

Evaluations have highlighted that the ongoing development of the CDU vHospital® requires a rigorous process to be in place for maintaining clinical accuracy and story quality as well as ensuring that the CDU vHospital® is supported by current technological advances in infrastructure and web-based learning delivery. In view of this, the authors have proposed that as part of its ongoing development, the quality processes must include a review of all current cases and consideration of and, where possible, improvement of the ongoing technical issues such as those related to the online presentation (e.g., the pop-up windows) which has continued to be problematic. These will be addressed in Stage 2 of the project due to commence in 2010 and will be embedded as an integral part of the ongoing development of the CDU vHospital® beyond completion of Stage 2.

It must be noted that the technical issues related to internet access and download capacity are sometimes beyond the scope of the University to address. The authors have been exploring how they may be able to link in with digital initiatives that offer opportunities to connect to national networks in the broader educational and health sectors as well as other online resources such as 'Second Life' (see http://secondlife.com/?v=1.1.)

Expanding the CDU vHospital®

As with any innovation there is a need to continue developing what the resource is able to offer. Health care does not take place only within the acute hospital setting. Activities around health promotion, health education, and health care take place in a range of community and clinical settings. Professional nurses need to be prepared to work in a variety of contexts and as active contributors to health care policy development, implementation and evaluation (ANMC, 2006).

The CDU Bachelor of Nursing Program is currently undergoing a major revision and, as a result of a needs analysis and stakeholder feedback, the new curriculum will be underpinned by a primary health care framework. The decision to take this approach reflects the Australian Government policy direction to move toward a health care system that focuses on disease prevention and maintenance of health not just the treatment of disease (Primary Health Care Reform in Australia, 2009). The new curriculum also supports the recent view that education of health professionals such as nurses, should be dynamic, broadly based, delivered in a flexible manner, and contain a focus on chronic illness, communication and quality of life (Bryce, 2009).

It is intended that the CDU vHospital® will play an integral part in the new curriculum with cases being designed and embedded within specific subjects. This will give the development team the ability to produce cases that illustrate a range of health issues with increasing levels of complexity and that demonstrate patient care in variety of clinical settings. Future plans include the development of new cases set in the hospital setting that students can continue to follow after discharge home or to other care settings such as aged or community care. The broader focus will also offer students a resource that will help to prepare them for professional nursing practice in a diverse range of practice contexts and for a population with diverse health care needs.

Future Research

As Andrew et al. (2009) point out, beginning students in nursing must navigate through a number of challenges in their transition to tertiary study and clinical practice. The CDU vHospital® has been developed with the intent to facilitate student understanding of nursing practice and the development of critical thinking and problem solving skills required for practice (Morales-Mann & Kaitell, 2001). The authors are interested in exploring how the CDU vHospital® assists first year students with role socialisation, professional engagement, the development of professional identity and how it supports their transition to their first clinical placement and, on completion of their program, to professional nursing practice. In addition, given the evidence that not all students are accessing the CDU vHospital®, the authors are also keen to explore what factors facilitate and hinder students' use of online learning technologies such as the CDU vHospital®. Other potential research areas include how the CDU vHospital® can be utilised in clinically based graduate nurse programs and as a professional development tool for registered nurses, either as part of a post graduate nursing qualification or as an informal learning resource.

CONCLUSION

The purpose of this book is to consider how higher education institutions and administrators need to reconceptualise, re-design and re-think the way learning resources are provided for students entering university in the 21st Century.

This chapter has presented an overview of the authors' involvement in the development, implementation and evaluation of an online learning resource designed to facilitate the learning opportunities of students studying a Bachelor of Nursing program in the Northern Territory of Australia.

The majority of students studying at CDU complete their studies predominantly as external students and this limits the degree of direct contact they have with the University, academic staff and their student colleagues.

The CDU vHospital® is a content and context rich learning environment which presents realistic stories of people experiencing health issues that facilitates situated learning (Lave & Wenger, 1991) and an entry point into the community of nursing practice (Wenger, 1998). The exemplar case of John Wayne illustrates the process of case development and presents a unique picture of an important chronic health issue in the Northern Territory. The complexity and richness of nursing work is demonstrated through the sequencing of John's story and also demonstrates the way in which professional nurses work collaboratively with patients, families and health care colleagues.

It also enhances students' sense of connection to the University.

Evaluation results indicated that the CDU VHospital® has been well received by students in terms of content, learning strategies and as an introduction to the role and scope of professional nursing practice. A number of issues related to technical aspects of the CDU vHospital® remain and there continues to be a need to explore more reliable means of access and delivery of materials.

Finally, as with any project the CDU vHospital® is a work in progress. The authors have presented a number of recommendations for the future development of this teaching and learning resource that centre around addressing the identified technical issues, maintaining the quality of the project, expanding the vHospital into stage 2 and future research directions.

ACKNOWLEDGMENT

The CDU vHospital® would not be possible if it were not for the time and input from many other people at CDU and local health services. We acknowledge these people and their important roles in developing and implementing this innovative learning resource. In particular, we acknowledge the support of the administration and clinical staff from the NT Department of Health and Families for the allowing the Development Team access to their facilities and to the clinical nurses from local health services who acted as clinical referees. We also acknowledge the people who voluntarily gave their time to play the characters in each of the patient stories.

We also thank the staff from the CDU Teaching and Learning Quality Group (TLQG) who prepared the images for use in this chapter.

REFERENCES

Andrew, N., McGuiness, C., Reid, G., & Corcoran, T. (2009). Greater than the sum of its parts: Transition into the first year of undergraduate nursing. *Nurse Education in Practice*, *9*(1), 13–21. doi:10.1016/j.nepr.2008.03.009

Australian Bureau of Statistics. (2008). *Experimental estimates of Aboriginal and Torres Strait Islander Australians, June 2006* (No. 3238.0.55.001). Canberra, Australian Capital Territory: ABS, Canberra. Retrieved October 28, 2009, from http://www.abs.gov.au/ausstats/abs@. nsf/Latestproducts /3238.0.55.001Main%20 Features 1Jun%202006?opendocument &tabname=Summary&prodn o=3238.0.55.001& issue=Jun %202006&num=&view=

Australian Institute of Health and Welfare. (2006a). *Ill-health conditions: Overview*. Canberra. Retrieved October 28, 2009, from http:// www.aihw.gov.au/ indigenous/health/ health_conditions.cfm

Australian Institute of Health and Welfare. (2006b). *Mental health: Overview*. Canberra. Retrieved October 28, 2009, from http://www. aihw.gov.au/ indigenous/health/mental.cfm

Australian Institute of Health and Welfare. (2008). *Diabetes: Australian facts 2008*. Canberra. Retrieved October 28, 2009, from http://www.aihw. gov.au/ publications/cvd/daf08/daf08.pdf

Australian Institute of Health and Welfare. (2009). *Diabetes prevalence in Australia: An assessment of national data sources*. Canberra. Retrieved October 28, 2009, from http://www.aihw.gov.au/ publications/cvd /cvd-46-10639/ cvd-46-10639. pdf

Australian Nursing and Midwifery Council (ANMC). (2006). *National competency standards for the registered nurse and the enrolled nurse*. Dickson, ACT. Retrieved November 3, 2009, from http://www.anmc.org.au /userfiles/file/competency_standards/Competency_ standards_RN.pdf

Brauer, P., Hanning, R. M., Arocha, J. F., Royall, D., Goy, R., & Grant, A. (2009). Creating case scenarios or vignettes using factorial design methods. *Journal of Advanced Nursing*, *65*(9), 1937–1945. doi:10.1111/j.1365-2648.2009.05055.x

Bryce, J. (2009). A consensus view in primary health care. *Australian Nursing Journal*, *16*(7), 21.

Charles Darwin University. (2007). *Bachelor of Nursing curriculum document*. Charles Darwin University.

Charles Darwin University. (2009). *Territory 2030: Charles Darwin University response June 2009*. Darwin, Australia: Charles Darwin University.

Elliot, K., Efron, D., Wright, M., & Martinelli, A. (2003). Educational technologies that integrate problem based learning principles: Do these resources enhance student learning? In G. Crisp, D Thiele, I. Scholten, S. Barker & J. Baron (Eds), *20th Annual Conference of the Australian Society for Computers in Learning in Tertiary Education*. Adelaide, South Australia.

Henderson, A., Twentyman, M., Heel, A., & Lloyd, B. (2006). Students' perception of the psychosocial clinical learning environment: An evaluation of placement models. *Nurse Education Today*, *26*(7), 564–571. doi:10.1016/j.nedt.2006.01.012

Hewitt-Taylor, J. (2003). Facilitating distance learning in nurse education. *Nurse Education in Practice*, *3*(1), 23–29. doi:10.1016/S1471-5953(02)00052-5

Jacobsen, H. E. (2006). A comparison of on-campus first year undergraduate nursing students' experiences with face-to-face and on-line discussions. *Nurse Education Today*, *26*(6), 494–500. doi:10.1016/j.nedt.2006.01.005

Kerr, M. P. (2002). A qualitative study of shift handover practice and function from a socio-technical perspective. *Journal of Advanced Nursing*, *37*(2), 125–134. doi:10.1046/j.1365-2648.2002.02066.x

Kilstoff, K. K., & Rochester, S. (2004). Hitting the floor running: Transitional experiences of graduates previously trained as enrolled nurses. *The Australian Journal of Advanced Nursing*, *22*(1), 13–17.

Lave, J., & Wenger, E. (1991). *Situated learning: Legitimate peripheral participation*. Cambridge, UK: Cambridge University Press.

Marriner Tomey, A. (2003). Learning with cases. *Journal of Continuing Education in Nursing*, *34*(1), 34–38.

Meißner, A., Hasselhorn, H. M., Estryn-Behar, M., Nezet, O., Pokorski, J., & Gould, D. (2007). Nurses' perceptions of shift handovers in Europe-results from the European nurses' early exit study. *Journal of Advanced Nursing*, *57*(5), 535–542. doi:10.1111/j.1365-2648.2006.04144.x

Meleis, A. F. (2005). *Theoretical nursing: Development and progress* (3rd ed.). Philadelphia, PA: Lippincott, Williams & Wilkins.

Morales-Mann, E. T., & Kaitell, C. A. (2001). Problem-based learning in a new Canadian curriculum. *Journal of Advanced Nursing*, *33*(1), 13–19. doi:10.1046/j.1365-2648.2001.01633.x

Nursing and Midwifery Board of the Northern Territory. (2008). *Standards for the accreditation of education providers delivering nursing and midwifery courses*. Health Professionals Licensing Authority, NT Dept of Health and Families.

O'Connell, B., & Penney, W. (2001). Challenging the handover ritual: Recommendations for research and practice. *Collegian (Royal College of Nursing, Australia)*, *8*(3), 14–18. doi:10.1016/S1322-7696(08)60017-7

Primary Health Care Reform in Australia. (2009). *Report to support Australia's first national primary healthcare strategy*. Canberra, Australia: Commonwealth of Australia.

Smedley, A., & Morey, P. (2009). Improving learning in the clinical nursing environment: Perceptions of senior Australian bachelor of nursing students. *Journal of Research in Nursing*, *15*(1), 75–88. doi:10.1177/1744987108101756

Spencer, J. (2003). ABC of learning and teaching in medicine: Learning and teaching in the clinical environment. *BMJ (Clinical Research Ed.)*, *326*(7389), 591–594. doi:10.1136/bmj.326.7389.591

Stjernquist, M., & Crang-Svalenius, E. (2007). Problem based learning and the case method-medical students change preferences during clerkship. *Medical Teacher*, *29*(8), 814–820. doi:10.1080/01421590701601592

Stone, J. (2010). Attempting to speak the same language: Interprofessional collaborative practice (ICP) - definitions and terminology. *Nursing Review, February*, 10-11.

Tiwari, A., Lai, P., So, M., & Yuen, K. (2006). A comparison of the effects of problem-based learning and lecturing on the development of students' critical thinking. *Medical Education*, *40*(6), 547–554. doi:10.1111/j.1365-2929.2006.02481.x

Tourism, N. T. (2005-2009). *About NT. Key facts: The people*. Retrieved October 28, 2009, from http://en.travelnt.com/about-nt /key-facts/people.aspx

Weir, S. (2008). Teachers advocating m-learning. *The International Journal of Technology, Knowledge and Society, 4*(5), 9–16.

Wenger, E. (1998). *Communties of practice: Learning, meaning and identity*. Cambridge, UK: Cambridge University Press.

Zawacki-Richter, O., Brown, T., & Delport, R. (2009). Mobile learning: From single project status into the mainstream? *European Journal of Open, Distance and E-Learning*. Retrieved May 27, 2010, from http://www.eurodl.org/materials/contrib/2009/Richter_Brown _Delport.htm

KEY TERMS AND DEFINITIONS

Australia: Commonwealth of Australia.

Case-Based Learning: The use of cases, whether real or fictional, to tell a patient story and to present information as an example of specific circumstances or clinical presentations that may be seen in a health setting.

CDU vHospital®: Online teaching resource, offering case-based learning scenarios. Developed by and registered to Charles Darwin University.

Evaluation: The process used to gather feedback from student users and key stakeholders regarding the usability and effectiveness of the CDU vHospital® as a teaching/learning resource.

Nursing Education: Undergraduate degrees designed to prepare graduates for registration as Registered Nurses in Australia.

Nursing Practice: The provision of nursing care which demonstrate the appropriate application of knowledge, skills, attitudes and behaviours as identified in professional nursing standards in Australia.

Online Learning: The delivery of educational materials via a web-based platform and incorporating text, visual and audio teaching strategies.

Undergraduate Nursing Students: Students enrolled in a Bachelor of Nursing program at a University.

Chapter 15
Re-Imagining Teaching for Technology-Enriched Learning Spaces:
An Academic Development Model

Caroline Steel
University of Queensland, Australia

Trish Andrews
University of Queensland, Australia

ABSTRACT

New technology-enriched learning spaces are a focus of institutional investment to address the identified shortcomings of traditional teaching and learning environments. Academic development, an area that has received little attention in this context, can be designed to provide strong opportunities for university teachers to re-imagine their teaching for these new spaces while also building their leadership capacity. This chapter discusses challenges that teachers face in transforming their teaching practices and proposes a model for academic development to support this. Two case studies demonstrate the flexibility and efficacy of the model and provide pointers for further adoption in the higher education context.

INTRODUCTION

This chapter highlights the need for a stronger focus on academic development to enable teachers to re-imagine their teaching for technology-enriched learning spaces. In order to assist academics to adapt to new teaching and learning environments a translation process is required. This process should include identifying the opportunities offered by technology-enriched formal learning spaces for teachers' own contexts and re-designing student learning with peer support and review. Specifically, the model outlined here seeks to improve support for academic teachers in the design of pedagogical activities for technology-enriched learning spaces while simultaneously building leadership capacity to sustain change at local disciplinary levels.

DOI: 10.4018/978-1-60960-114-0.ch015

BACKGROUND

In recent years the higher education sector has recognised that the spaces within which university teaching takes place can have a major impact on student learning.

The spaces in which we work, live and learn can have profound effects on how we feel, how we behave, how we perform ... spaces can also limit the possibilities of our activity, restricting us to old modes of working and thinking (Watson, 2007, p.260).

Consequently, many universities have realised that in order to promote more active, student-centred teaching and learning activities, different physical and virtual spaces are required to those traditionally available in most higher education institutions. Accordingly, sizeable investment is being made in designing and creating technology-enriched formal spaces across higher education institutions (Oblinger, 2005; Watson, 2007). These spaces are innovative physical learning environments equipped with a wide-range of technology tools and are designed to support new ways of teaching and learning. While there are significant differences in the types and purposes of the spaces being provided, common characteristics that define these innovative formal spaces are:

- the use of technology to support learning and teaching activities and
- the requirement for flexibility; and increasingly adaptability.

These new technology-enriched learning spaces are designed and built to support active, social, collaborative and independent learning. Consequently, these spaces, which offer a rapidly expanding range of technologies and configurations, confront traditional assumptions about teaching and learning. In turn, this creates challenges for teachers working in these new spaces to re-imagine their teaching, learning designs and practices and actively promote more student engagement in the learning process.

Physically, these new learning spaces are usually visually attractive, designed for a range of educational purposes and equipped with state-of-the-art technologies. However, there is reportedly some tension between the desire to justify the expenditure on these new spaces in terms of enriched student learning, and the support of innovative teaching and learning practices (Pearshouse, et al., 2009). While the spaces have been designed with a view to transforming student learning and knowledge creation (Punie, 2007), little attention has been given to helping mainstream university teachers to transform or re-imagine their teaching practices in ways that these spaces and technologies can afford. When confronted with these new technology-enriched spaces, many university teachers feel ill-equipped to re-imagine their teaching practices so have reservations in relation to the commitment required to capitalise on the affordances enabled by these spaces. Furthermore, a focus on research in the promotion processes of many higher education institutions leaves little time to develop new pedagogical understandings and skills to effectively utilise technology-enriched learning spaces. University teachers require opportunities and time to reconcile their pedagogical beliefs, beliefs about technologies and the pedagogical affordances inherent in these spaces with their pedagogical contexts (Steel, 2009a). A crucial part of this re-imagining process is to create opportunities for teachers to rethink their learning designs so that they can effectively harness the potential teaching and learning opportunities offered by these spaces.

THE COMPLEXITIES OF RE-IMAGINING TEACHING

A significant problem for higher education institutions is that the complexities involved in changing educational practices for these new technology-enriched spaces are often overlooked in terms of both leadership and academic development. Such a change requires an equivalent shift in teacher and student roles and relationships and is not necessarily comfortable or economic for many university teachers. As with any change to daily practices, people need to be convinced of why change should take place (Vrakking, 1995) and inspired and supported to make that change. Providing opportunities for 'supported mutual introspection' (Carew, Lefoe, Bell, & Amour, 2008) through peer review processes is one approach to motivating academics to undertake changes to their teaching practices. Building leadership capacity throughout this process addresses the continuing need for academic leadership development in higher education, particularly in relation to teaching and learning practices. Academic development programs need to explicitly promote the development of leadership skills necessary to undertake the 'radical change to the status quo' required to effect new teaching and learning practices (Lefoe, 2010).

Leadership as a Critical Component

Leadership is crucial to ensuring that university learning and teaching change initiatives have the best possible chance of success. However leadership capacity development is an area of higher education that has been ad hoc, particularly beyond the realms of management and administration (Lefoe, 2010). Changes in teacher practices require different levels of distributive leadership that can empower, enable and support teachers while appreciating and engaging with their cultural codes and assumptions. Leadership is needed at various levels to enable university teachers to be part of the vision for change and to help teachers address the challenges that they face personally, as teachers, and as part of a cultural organisation.

Universities are places of great teacher diversity (Steel & Levy, 2009) as well as homes to many disciplinary and faculty based cultures. Teachers hold different beliefs about their disciplinary knowledge, how it is taught, how students should learn and the role and value of technology. Their beliefs and teaching practices are also influenced by institutional and local teaching cultures. These cultures represent differing and sometimes conflicting interests, disciplines, beliefs and values. From a cultural perspective, these are "the informal codes and shared assumptions of the individuals who participate in an organisation" (Tierney, 1996, p. 372). They can also be expressed in relation to educational practices such as those that might take place in new learning spaces. Trowler and Cooper (2002) suggest that these cultures can be understood within the notion of teaching and learning regimes (TLR). TLRs comprise an interrelated collection of local "rules, assumptions, practices and relationships related to teaching and learning issues in higher education" (Trowler & Cooper, 2002, p. 221). For example, negativity around changes to practices can be derived from the local rules around what comprises appropriate teaching practices (Sahin & Thompson, 2006). Expectations around transforming teaching practices can be at odds with local TLRs. Thus, there is a need to build capacity for educational leadership at local levels and with teachers who are privy to those codes and also open to moving beyond them. Some have suggested that distributive leadership, as a mechanism for the sharing of knowledge, practice and reflection on practice, can be an effective collegial tool for moving teaching and learning innovations forward (e.g. Knight & Trowler, 2001; Lefoe, 2010). Distributive leadership offers distributive power sharing in order to transform TLRs and help colleagues re-interpret teaching practices meaningfully in connection with cultural rules and assumptions for new technology-enriched learning spaces. This kind of distributive leadership can be further strengthened by the involvement of academic developers as both colleagues and partners in initiating and supporting change and learning. The benefits of these kinds of collegial-partner leadership roles lies in the ability to meaningfully interpret local TLRs through localised leadership in partnership with higher education researchers and specialists (academic developers).

Staff development is a critical part of any change process. Changes in learning and teaching methods can require significant changes in both academic and support staff roles. In order to enable staff to get the most out of their new roles there need to be development opportunities made available (JISC, 2009).

The field of academic development has recently been described as 'elastic practice' (Carew, et al., 2008) because academic developers are able to draw on a 'toolkit' of theories, strategies, techniques, ideas, values and experiences in order to respond to the varying contexts they work within. Across the discipline of Higher Education they are leaders, educational researchers, practitioners, scholars and change agents whose role, in part, is to stimulate the kinds of academic conversations and reflective practices that underpin pedagogical growth and transformation. Academic development is a more valued and valuable experience when integrated into a distributive leadership environment that forms constructive partnerships with faculty-based leaders, senior management and leaders in related areas (such as IT and support). As Kotter (1996, p. 6) suggests, without "a sufficiently powerful guiding coalition" change initiatives experience "countervailing forces" such as tradition, self-interest and passive resistance.

The Need for Academic Development for 21st Century Learning

With the current demands placed upon university teachers for technology-enriched 21st Century learning and purpose-built 21st Century learning spaces, the need for academic development strategies to enable academic teachers to move forward,

are critical (Hughes, 2009). As Diaz et al. (2009), point out, while academic development needs are not new, new areas of need are emerging:

21st-century faculty ... will need support in new areas as well: keeping up with an increasingly technological workplace, developing ways to further integrate technology into the instructional experience (p. 48).

Hooker, (2008), suggests that while technologies provide many opportunities for teachers they also create many challenges. Not only do teachers need to be able to develop the technical skills to use the new technologies effectively, they also have a need to consider the pedagogical aspects of using these tools. Academics can be sceptical of the stated learning benefits of using technologies in teaching and learning largely due to the overwhelming emphasis on the technology in contrast to any overarching pedagogical framework (Waldron, Dawson, & Burnett, 2005, p. 4). As part of the process of developing skills and identifying affordances in relation to the use of ICTS, Hooker, (2008) quoting Papert (1990), emphasises the importance of providing "opportunities for teachers to reflect on their practice as they make use of the technologies so that they can become *active generators* rather than *passive consumers* of knowledge" (p. 2). However, to become active generators, strategies need to be formulated that enable academics to overcome critical issues in relation to their ability to rapidly and effectively adopt pedagogically appropriate technologies for a range of teaching and learning contexts in higher education. Indeed, the identified need for improved ICT skills amongst academic teachers is critical in overcoming the 'digital divide' in the provision of higher education in a 'web 2.0 world' (Hughes, 2009). However, further to this, Young (2008) highlights the importance of not losing sight of the 'endgame' and cautions that the key focus of academic professional development needs to be the enhancement of student learning. With that in mind we need to consider how we can assist teachers to "develop increasingly sophisticated and complex conceptions of teaching so that they might more readily think about teaching in new ways" (Young, 2008, p. 42).

As new learning and teaching spaces are usually designed with pedagogical transformation in mind, context-specific academic development needs to be integral to the development and implementation of new technology-enriched learning and teaching spaces. Academic development strategies need to address local TLRs, personal belief systems and help teachers renegotiate their pedagogical vision and student-teacher roles and relationships. Teachers need convincing of how these spaces can be used with different technologies to positively influence student learning. Furthermore, academic development opportunities need to be targeted at better equipping teachers to identify the affordances and constraints of these spaces and technologies in relation to their belief systems and the pedagogical and cultural contexts they operate within.

Persistent Issues Around Technology Adoption and Integration

While not focused on learning spaces in particular, technology adoption and integration into university teaching and learning practices continues as a persistent issue. Although various technologies have been widely available for some time and promoted for their ability to transform learning, this promise has not yet been realised (Hedberg, 2006). There are a number of recursive and interactive factors that influence teachers' decision-making around technology use. These include teachers' own pedagogical beliefs and beliefs about the value and application of technologies as well as their own cultural and pedagogical contexts. Successful academic development for effective technology integration into teaching and learning needs to be cognizant of the multiple aspects of the teaching

and learning environment and provide a number of strategies and approaches.

Diaz et al., (2009), in a recent study into the professional development needs for 21st century teachers, found that successful models for 21st century academic development require flexibility and multiple approaches that should:

include mentoring, delivery in a variety of on-campus and off-campus formats (face-to-face, blended, online, self-initiated/self-paced), and anyplace/anytime programming to accommodate just-in-time needs. Faculty members are learners with needs and constraints similar to those of students. Support programs must be valuable, relevant, current, and engaging. They should also demonstrate best practices in providing a participatory, facilitated learning environment (p.5).

Jonas-Dwyer and Pospisil (2004) also suggest adopting a holistic approach to academic development for preparing academics for teaching the rapidly growing numbers of millennial students now attending university. They highlight the importance of developing more student-centred approaches and aligning such approaches both with the needs of the teachers and the needs of the institution. In addressing the complexity of teacher needs, Jonas-Dwyer and Pospisil (2004) propose that an appropriate model should assist academics to "develop a greater awareness of student needs and learning styles, teaching styles, educational design, and to increase their technology skills" (p.202) and that the model should include the following seven factors:

1. Consideration of the university's strategic direction
2. Awareness of the current and evolving academic/university culture within the university
3. Knowledge of the students' characteristics

4. Encourage teachers to be aware of their own preferred teaching style and philosophy and to experiment with other approaches
5. Encourage teachers to become conversant in applying educational design principles, or engage expert educational designers to assist
6. Consider technological innovations
7. Investigate the university's infrastructure to establish feasibility (p. 204).

This model recognises the complexity of the context within which academic development occurs and the need to respond to a broad range of issues. The model also suggests the importance of teachers recognising their approach to teaching and learning and consequently considering new ways of teaching with technologies.

The recognition of the importance of teacher beliefs as part of professional development program is essential (Steel, 2009a; 2009b). In particular, a professional development model for teaching with technology should acknowledge that teachers' prior experiences with technology along with their beliefs in relation to technology in teaching and learning are of critical importance and can have a significant impact on the ways in which teachers use technologies in their classrooms. Steel (2009a), discussing the complexities of technology adoption, proposes that "even if teachers are confident and proficient in their use of technologies, this does not mean that they believe they are valuable tools when used for educational purposes" (p. 399). Further, a significant predictor of teachers' technology uptake and use is the beliefs that teachers hold about their application in their educational contexts (Mahdizadeh, Biemans, & Mulder, 2008; Miller, et al., 2003). Therefore teachers require opportunities to surface and resolve tensions across their own belief systems and practices in relation to their own pedagogical context, their belief systems and the technologies on offer (Steel, 2009a). These are essential elements in any academic development approach designed to sustain transformative practices in technology-enriched learning and teaching spaces.

Pedder and colleagues (Pedder, Storey, & Opfer, 2008) in their study that explored different stakeholders view of what constitutes successful professional development for teaching and learning with technology in schools found that both teachers and leaders found similar approaches of value. School leaders felt that professional development activities that enabled learning through experimentation and practice in the classroom, reflection, student and peer feedback and participation in teacher networks promoted successful outcomes. Teachers valued opportunities for classroom experimentation and practice and being able to make changes based on student or peer feedback. Significantly both groups identified the importance of peer feedback and opportunities for practice.

Many professional development approaches, strategies and programmes advocate the value of peer learning. As Eisen (2001), points out:

Peer learning is a model well suited to the development of professionals, who are no longer novices, because it promotes sharing of partners' experiences through action and reflection (p.31).

Peer learning is defined as "voluntary reciprocal relationships between individuals of comparable status, who share a common or closely related learning/development objective" (Eisen, 2001, p. 32). Boud (2001), also considers reciprocity in his definition of peer learning. He takes the view that "peer learning needs to involve reciprocal interaction between participants. Peer learning should be mutually beneficial and involve the sharing of knowledge ideas and experience between the participants" (p. 3). While reciprocity is common across definitions of peer learning, Topping (2007) introduces the notion of active helping. "Peer learning can be defined as the acquisition of knowledge and skill through active helping and supporting among status equals or matched companions" (Topping, 2007, p. 631). Approaches to peer learning that provide constructive feedback and suggestions could be considered as 'active helping'. The P2P project (2006) which explored peer learning across schools in several European countries found that professional development that involved peer learning had a positive impact on student learning. This reflects Young's (2008) injuncture, that academic development activities need to keep a focus on student learning. This focus on student learning needs to be at the forefront of any potential solutions or recommendations to dealing with the complexities inherent in the development and implementation of new learning spaces.

Academic Development for Learning Spaces

Currently there is very little literature relating to what constitutes effective academic development activities to support teacher practices in new learning spaces. While universities are enthusiastic about building new student-centred and technology-enriched learning spaces, there is less emphasis on how teachers are helped to re-conceptualise their learning designs for these spaces. The juncture between learning spaces, learning design and teacher beliefs is an under-theorised area that is pivotal to future space developments and successful student outcomes in these spaces. However in spite of this limitation, work in relation to supporting the adoption and integration of technology into higher education and schools provides useful models and insights that can be considered in relation to developing professional development approaches for new learning spaces.

The limited work that is available in relation to academic development for learning spaces highlights the complexity of the issue. In a recent (extended) blog comment, Long (2009) refers to the issue of timing as a key aspect of successful academic development for learning spaces.

Long makes the important point that academic development activities for learning spaces need to be implemented at an early stage in the space development process.

What absolutely CANNOT happen regarding professional development for these spaces is to wait until they are built (blog comment, Long, 2009).

However, in the majority of cases, preparing teachers to engage with new spaces is seldom considered prior to the completion of the space. Further, Long suggests that one-off professional development activities delivered by an expert, while they have their uses, falls well short of meeting the complexity and diversity of teachers needs in relation to learning spaces. Consequently, he suggests a multi-faceted model that allows for:

real time modelling of good (and new) practice, team teaching, real time support, group work, mixed groupings, lead lessons, small group work with the whole team working, learning and gaining confidence together. This is not a one hour session – this takes some days to really embed in, along with return visits (blog comment, Long, 2009).

The Challenges of Teaching in New Learning Spaces

Taking into consideration the multiple complexities and challenges associated with teachers translating their practices for technology-enriched learning spaces it is surprising that so little attention has been focused on academic development to assist teachers to transform their practices for these spaces. Approaches are needed that assist teachers to recognise both the pedagogical and other affordances and constraints of the technologies and spaces relevant for their own teaching context. Figure 1 summarises teacher challenges that need to be addressed through academic development strategies. In addressing these challenges, it is possible to harness the benefits of distributive

Figure 1. Challenges of teaching in new learning spaces

leadership in partnership with academic development while being respectful of local cultural perspectives (such as TLRs).

This diagram highlights recurring challenges that teachers face when confronted with new technologies and learning spaces. It also emphasises the heightened significance of teachers as designers of student learning in these innovative technology-enriched learning spaces. These elements are further explored below.

Pedagogical Beliefs and Beliefs About Technologies and Spaces

Teachers' pedagogical beliefs about teaching, learning and the use of technologies are highly influential technology practices (Bates & Poole, 2003; Park & Ertmer, 2007; Steel, 2009a). Consequently, academic development programs that encourage re-imagining teaching practices for new teaching and learning environments need to start making teachers' beliefs systems explicit. Teachers' pedagogical beliefs and their beliefs about the value, use and role of technologies and new learning spaces are highly influential on the way teachers conceptualise their teaching practices for these new spaces. Furthermore, using these spaces often involves a shift away from teachers' usual educational practices and teacher beliefs can act as a filter to change (Yerrick, Parke, & Nugent, 1997). Therefore opportunities to discuss and explore these beliefs should be considered critical to translating practices for new spaces.

Contemporary design of physical learning spaces is often underpinned by the assumption that they will be used in ways that are student-centred rather than teacher centred. Some teachers hold pedagogical beliefs that are more aligned with teacher-centred practices while others may not have experienced using the spaces and/or technologies to express their pedagogical beliefs. How a teacher conceptualises these roles internally has implications for their educational practices, use of technologies and for student learning. Even when a more student-centred learning design is developed, teacher-centred approaches may prevail.

Indeed some teachers may not see a role, or any value, in using the spaces or the technologies in their teaching. While this may well be justifiable, models for academic development need to provide opportunities for teachers to make their beliefs explicit in order to properly explore the affordances and constraints of the spaces and to reconcile their beliefs with the possibilities that may be identified as part of the academic development process.

Pedagogical Vision for Use of Technology-Enriched Spaces

Given that most teachers are unfamiliar with the ways that new technology-enriched spaces can be used for teaching and learning, teachers need time and scaffolding to develop a pedagogical vision. Developing a clear pedagogical vision enables teachers to convey the relevance of their use of spaces and technologies, and consequent pedagogical changes, to students. Learners need to understand how their learning is meant to occur through their use of these technology-enriched spaces. As with any learning design, students are likely to engage if they are clear about how learning tasks are linked to their academic success.

In an examination of educationally sophisticated technology-using university teachers, Steel (2009b) found that the interrelationship between a number of factors contributed to a strong pedagogical vision for technology use. These factors were derived from the fact that these teachers held coherent pedagogical beliefs and were well equipped to draw on their beliefs about technologies, the characteristics of their pedagogical contexts and their experiences with technologies to help them identify the affordances and constraints of technologies that they needed to resolve in practice. For mainstream teachers, there is benefit in guiding them to consider these kinds of linkages and experiences. A good way to start conceptualising a pedagogical vision is for teachers to explore examples of how other academics are using technology-enriched spaces, to have exposure to pedagogical models that convey possibilities and to test and modify ideas in a safe peer-supported environment.

Discipline, Curriculum and Assessment Agendas

Translating curriculum and assessment to blended and online models is inherently problematic. Academics are prone to transporting their existing practices to new environments (Kirkup & Kirkwood, 2005) and need encouragement and support to change their curriculum and assessment practices. Academic development programs need to assist teachers in identifying uses of spaces and technologies that solve teaching and learning problems inherent to their particular disciplines. Examples of well structured technology-enriched learning designs from a variety of disciplines can provide teachers with models to assist them to change their curriculum approaches to take advantage of the affordances offered by these environments. Opportunities to test these models in their own contexts and to receive constructive feedback from peers can strengthen teacher's confidence to change their curriculum practices.

Student Profiles, Needs and Challenges

Modern teaching and learning environments are characterised by student diversity. Curriculum design that addresses the diversity of student needs and characteristics, can promote student engagement and retention. However adequately preparing students for these new learning environments is a critical part of the challenge (Kennedy, et al., 2009). In preparing teachers to use these new learning environments consideration needs to be given to the digital literacy of students, the wide variation they present in this regard and ways in which this might effectively be addressed. Furthermore, teachers need to develop skills in assisting students to understand what learning means in a 'web 2.0 world' (Fitzgerald et al., 2009; Hughes, 2009). Students' ability to learn with technologies is a key aspect of these environments. Overlooking this can result in poor student learning outcomes in these new spaces (Kennedy, et al., 2009). Additionally, these new learning environments can mean changes in the ways in which students participate in learning activities creating feelings of isolation, alienation and anxiety. Academic development programs need to provide opportunities to explore these issues and find strategies to address them.

Pedagogical Effectiveness vs. Real Constraints of Pedagogical Context

While some learning designs are highly effective they may not be very efficient or vice-versa (Hornby, 2003). Moreover some learning designs may be suitable for one teacher's pedagogical context but not for another. The pedagogical context includes variables such as teacher and student characteristics and preferences, the pedagogical approach employed by specific disciplines, the organisation of the learning environment as well as disciplinary and institutional culture and norms. It encompasses the variables 'woven together in the act of learning, rather than around it, as conveyed by the word 'environment'' (de Figueiredo & Afonso, 2006) and can be understood as 'the relationship between a setting and how participants interpret that setting, including the meaning of practices' (Moschkovich & Brenner, 2000).

When re-imagining teaching for technology-enriched learning spaces teachers can benefit from testing the pedagogical effectiveness of a learning design in a peer-supported environment that is conducive to safe constructive feedback and reflection. For example, an excellent learning design may be conceptualised that is actually an add-on to the curriculum rather than integral to it. Or due to students being located in different international time zones some features of the design may not be feasible. Workload is of course a crucial issue. Many teachers have implemented highly effective teaching and learning strategies only to find that their own workload has been highly exacerbated. There is high value in trying to troubleshoot these kinds of issues ahead of time as teachers quickly loose enthusiasm for innovation when troublesome issues arise.

Affordances and Constraints of Technologies and Space

If teachers have not used or experienced available technologies and spaces, it is very difficult to be able to identify the affordances and constraints of the technologies and spaces. The terms 'affordances' and 'constraints' suffer a lack of clarity in contemporary literature particularly as applied to the use of technologies in teaching and learning (Conole & Dyke, 2004; McGrenere & Ho, 2000).

Figure 2. A model of academic development for technology-enriched learning spaces

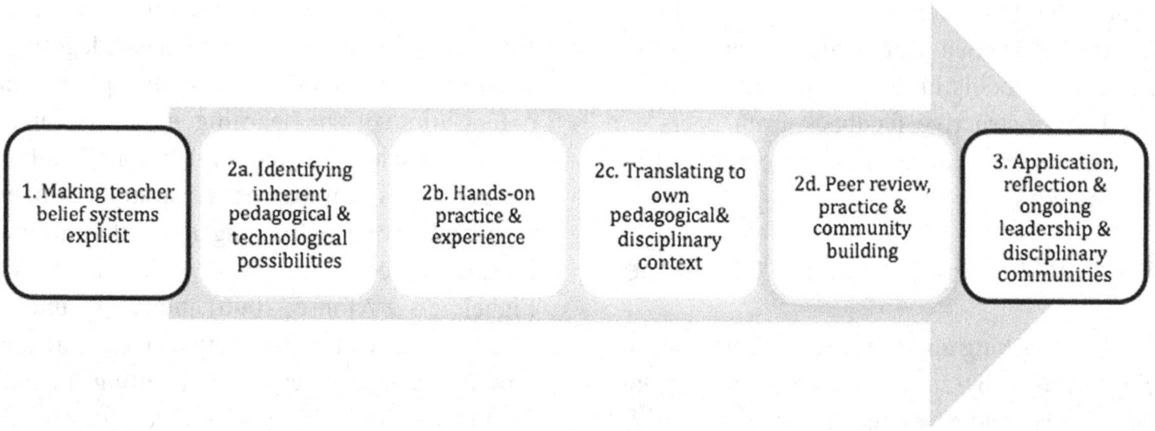

A more interrelational view of the concept was offered by Kennewell (2001). He pursued the idea of exploring affordances and constraints not only in relation to the inherent properties of the object and the perceptions of the actor, but also in relation to the whole pedagogical context. Kennewell (2001) defines affordances as "the attributes of the setting which provide potential for action" and constraints as "the conditions and relationships amongst attributes which provide structure and guidance for the course of actions" (p. 106). As with pedagogical effectiveness, teachers need opportunities to consider the affordances and constraints of technology-enriched spaces in relation to their pedagogical context and educational aims.

Considering the issues and challenges for teachers who are confronted with the need to re-imagine their teaching for technology-enriched environments, it is surprising that so little attention has been given to supporting teachers to enact quality teaching practices in these environments. The next section offers a model of academic development for technology-enriched learning spaces that draws on and builds capacity toward distributive leadership while being inclusive of different disciplinary perspectives and TLRs.

DEVELOPING A MODEL OF ACADEMIC DEVELOPMENT FOR TECHNOLOGY-ENRICHED LEARNING SPACES

With a clear knowledge of the considerable challenges that teachers are confronted with when trying to re-imagine their teaching for innovative technology-enriched learning spaces, a model for academic development was developed to help individuals and disciplinary communities move forward (Figure 2). The model itself is also aimed at developing capacity for leadership and building communities so that progress and growth are championed, sustained and encompassing. As noted by Lefoe (2010), there is an urgent need in Australian universities to build leadership capacity that will enable distributive leadership in all aspects of teaching and learning. She also quotes Fullan, Hill and Crévola (2006) as proposing that "capacity building involves the use of strategies that increase the collective effectiveness of all levels of the system in developing and mobilizing knowledge, resources and motivation, all of which are needed to raise the bar and close the gap of student learning across the system" (p.88). It is with these aims in mind that the model was created. As a model of academic development for technology-enriched learning spaces it aims to:

- facilitate a process whereby academics can translate their practices in ways that harness the potential of these spaces and technologies for their own pedagogical context
- build leadership capacity that can influence
- build collegial peer-based disciplinary communities

Further, congruent with the notion of academic development as 'elastic practice' (Carew, et al., 2008), the model is designed to be applicable in different modes, disciplinary contexts and with different teacher cohorts (higher education and K12). It is also flexible in terms of the kinds of activities that can achieve the different components of the model. This kind of inherent flexibility is meant to accommodate different academic developers'/ facilitators' styles and preferences. Two applications of the model are detailed later in this section.

The model, as visually displayed in Figure 2, depicts a staged process that addresses the challenges previously outlined in Figure 1 with a particular focus on teachers' learning designs for use in technology-enriched spaces.

Stage 1: Teachers' Pedagogical Beliefs and Beliefs About Technologies and Spaces

The initial stage of the model begins with the provision of opportunities for teachers to make their pedagogical beliefs and beliefs about technologies and spaces explicit. Many academics have not necessarily had the opportunity to articulate these beliefs and as such this can be a reflective and revealing process. This step is also an opportunity for some teachers to start to conceptualise their pedagogical vision for the use of the space and the technologies on offer.

Stages 2a-2d: Orienting to the Possibilities and Re-Imagining Practice in a Peer-Supported Environment

These next four components of the model are integrated rather than a linear staged process. They may occur together at different times and serve to further surface teachers' belief systems and assist in conceptualising their pedagogical vision for the use of the technology-enriched spaces. These four elements are designed to help teachers envisage learning designs that are appropriate to the spaces and to their own pedagogical and disciplinary context. In 2a, teachers engage with discipline relevant models that exemplify some of the pedagogical and technological affordances of the spaces. During their engagement they are encouraged to identify and discuss both affordances and constraints for their own pedagogical context, discipline, curriculum and assessment agendas. Teachers are also encouraged to consider their student profiles, needs and challenges. In 2b, opportunities are made available for hands-on training and practice in the spaces using various technologies. Teachers also experience a student perspective of the use of the spaces and technologies during their participation in exemplar teaching models. Most academics have not learnt with technologies or in technology-enriched spaces, so providing them with opportunities to participate as both student and teacher are important. As teachers have competing priorities for their time, it is also essential to ensure that there is time (preferably both during and outside of academic development) to translate a part of their curriculum into learning designs that harness the potential they have identified for the space. Therefore 2c is integral to enabling teachers to re-imagine their teaching practices for technology-enriched learning spaces. As learning designs emerge and mature, peer review and sharing can be used to catalyse disciplinary communities (2d). Such peer-supported communities can be encouraged

Table 1. Teacher challenges mapped to model

Teacher challenges (Figure 1)	Mapped to Model (Figure 2)
a. Pedagogical beliefs and beliefs about technologies	1, 2c, 2d
b. Pedagogical vision for use of space	1, 2a, 2b, 2c, 2d
c. Discipline, curriculum and assessment agendas	2a, 2c, 2d
d. Student profiles, needs and challenges	2c, 2d
e. Pedagogical effectiveness vs. real constraints of pedagogical context	2a, 2b, 2c, 2d, 3
f. Affordances and constraints of technologies and space	2a, 2b, 2c, 2d

to provide a safe, non-competitive space for discussing possibilities, pedagogical effectiveness, affordances and constraints.

Stage 3: Consolidating Designs, Enacting Leadership and Sustaining Community Learning

Finally in stage 3, teachers apply their designs to their own pedagogical context, supported by their disciplinary communities and leadership both within that community and institutionally. Reflection has been interwoven throughout the model, however teachers are strongly encouraged to reflect on the application of their designs and evaluate their pedagogical effectiveness. Having completed the academic development model that underpins the process with a network of peers, teachers are being positioned to lead further iterations of the model either in partnership with academic developers or with community members in their cohort. The model itself is made explicit, resources are made available and the expectation of leadership has been interlaced throughout the academic development process. Further to this, teachers have experienced the potential of socially-mediated community-based learning and are provided with a range of strategies to continue this practice both with established community members and with other teachers in their local cultural communities.

The teacher challenges outlined in Figure 1 are mapped to the model in Table 1.

APPLYING THE MODEL TO TWO CASE STUDIES

The following two teacher development programs were designed to help teachers address barriers to technology innovation while enabling them to identify and realise the affordances and constraints of new learning environments enriched with technologies. Each culminated in a portfolio of learning designs that were appropriate to their own pedagogical contexts.

Masters of Educational Studies Course

The development of a postgraduate course in a Masters of Educational Studies program provided an opportunity to test the model of academic development for technology-enriched spaces over two iterations. The course is aimed at helping teachers to integrate technologies into their teaching and become future leaders in their home school environment. As this was a predominantly online course, both virtual and physical learning spaces were explored. Enrolled teachers engaged in the course through a Learning Management System (LMS) and used a range of other technologies throughout the course. They attended campus-based workshops three times over the semester.

The course objectives were as follows:

1. Review and reflect on the common enablers and barriers to technology integration and the

use of different learning spaces in relation to your educational context

2. Express and evaluate your beliefs about technology, teaching and learning and their influence on your own use of technologies and different learning spaces

3. Compare and evaluate various pedagogical and learning theories in relation to the use of educational technologies and consequential pedagogical affordances and constraints for current and emerging technologies

4. Critically analyse and debate contested issues associated with existing and emergent technologies with reference to scholarly research and theories

5. Design and justify a range of your own learning designs for new technology-enriched spaces with reference to your beliefs, learning theories and pedagogies, attributes of effective technology practices and potential barriers to implementation.

The assessment items for the course were:

1. Concept map and reflective essay on teachers' beliefs about teaching and learning and technology use

2. An online discussion on a contested issue and submission of debate synthesis

3. Project: Portfolio of learning designs that included

   ◦ A presentation of a design with peer review

   ◦ A portfolio of learning designs for technology-enriched learning spaces

Teachers were initially required to introduce themselves online and complete an online icebreaker. The icebreaker was designed to 'hook' teachers in, place them in the course context and promote strong interaction in order to stimulate an initial sense of community. A short, provocative YouTube video was used and stimulus questions provided in a dedicated discussion forum in the

LMS. Teachers were exposed to various models of technology and space use during the course, and the course itself was designed to model possibilities inherent in the technologies and spaces explored.

Their first assessment sought to help teachers make their beliefs explicit in order to challenge their ideas of what is possible in their own teaching context as well as expose them to the beliefs and practices of their fellow teachers. Throughout the course they were exposed to various technologies either through their own exploration or as part of the course (e.g. a virtual field trip into the virtual world of Second Life™). The course challenged teachers to think through the enablers and barriers of both technologies and different spaces from their own pedagogical context and belief systems and also in terms of their own hands-on experiences.

An online discussion, again on a provocative and contemporary issue, gave teachers the opportunities to expose and question some of their beliefs about the value and risks of using technologies in their teaching practices. Finally, each teacher created a portfolio of learning designs for technology-enriched learning spaces for their own teaching context. This was accompanied by a rationale for each activity that articulated their underlying beliefs and thinking for their designs. A template was provided for this activity to encourage them to relate their designs to their pedagogical context and affordances and constraints they identified. Peer review of designs promoted cross-fertilisation of ideas and access to other teachers' examples of practice. As a cohesive online community developed participants gave constructive feedback and supported each other.

Although class sizes were relatively small (5-12 teachers), participants were able to work on their own disciplinary areas, create peer networks and engage in authentic activities that were aimed at helping them re-imagine their teaching. Teachers responded well to both iterations of the course (offered so far) as indicated in email correspondence:

Iteration 1 (we had one extra assessment item which was a blog for reflections on course readings):

I have enjoyed the subject immensely and see immediate applications in my teaching and planning for next year.

I thought the course overall was excellent and I learned a lot of practical ways to implement new knowledge in my teaching. Also, the mode of the course was great with so much online and the assessment really worked to reinforce what we were learning. The only negative I would say is that it was quite time consuming, in that there seemed to be more assessment for this course than for other Masters courses I've done.

Iteration 2

I have found this course so interesting – its about what is happening now. There is so much talk about connecting study to the real world but very little of it actually happens. Most of the assignments I do are so dull and boring – it is worse than watching paint dry. I find this course not only challenging and exciting but providing me with new strategies, new challenges in teaching and learning strategies – for classrooms and in my own life.

Thank you so much for this course. I have learnt so much and it has made me think more about technology in the classroom.

Teacher Continuing Professional Development Program

In 2010 an urban private school was planning to open its new teaching and learning complex. The building consists of collaborative teaching and learning spaces (CTLCs) and advanced concept teaching spaces similar to those at The University of Queensland (UQ) (http://www. uq.edu.au/~webaf/index.html). These advanced, technology-enriched teaching and learning spaces are intended to support more collaborative, interactive and engaged approaches to teaching and learning at the school and will have a major impact on teaching and learning at the school. It is envisaged that the use of these spaces will improve students learning experiences and help support students' transition to university learning. This would occur through the familiarisation with technology-enriched learning spaces and approaches that are evolving at the university through the use of such spaces.

Recognising the need to prepare teachers to work in these new spaces and build their capacity for leadership within their disciplinary areas, senior levels of leadership within the school were proactive in addressing teacher development ahead of the completion of their new centre. This is consistent with Long's view (2009) that teacher development for new technology-enriched spaces should occur prior to the building completion. An initial group of eighteen teachers were selected to participate in a continuing professional development program to provide distributive leadership in the use and applications of these spaces across the rest of the school community.

The continuing professional development program was offered through a combination of whole day face-to-face workshops supported by online modules over a period of four months (see Table 2). It was aimed at helping teachers address the challenges outlined in Figure 1. Tasks and discussion were designed to help teachers reconcile their own pedagogical beliefs, and beliefs about technologies and spaces, with their own learning experiences in different physical spaces and online using a variety of pedagogical models. In this way teachers were encouraged to develop their own pedagogical vision for use of the space that was meaningful for their own discipline, curriculum and assessment agenda as well as mindful of their own student profiles, needs and challenges. The workshops in

Table 2. Summary of continuing professional development program for technology-enriched spaces

Modules and workshops	Activities
Online module 1: Pre-workshop online activities:	Participants were required to read some introductory material and complete the following tasks: • Post a personal bio photo, experience with technologies, teaching profile/experience, discipline, aspirations for this CPD) to the LMS – maximum 250 words • Create and submit a concept map on their pedagogical beliefs and a short reflect piece on how these beliefs might be expressed in a technology-enriched learning space – the challenges, enablers and barriers.
Face-to-face workshop 1	• Overview of two different learning spaces • Discussion and evaluation of teaching and learning models derived from innovative teacher practices in different discipline contexts and spaces (virtual and physical) • Discussion of teacher beliefs, enablers and barriers
Online module 2	• Identification and rationale for unit of work to be translated into a learning design for technology-enriched spaces • Reflection on anticipated changes to teacher and student roles
Face-to face workshop 2	• Hands on training and practice in UQ learning spaces • Activity stations set up with explicit pedagogical approaches that used the spaces and a variety of technologies in different ways • Time allocated to work on learning designs (template provided for optional use)
Online module 3	• Preparation for developing learning designs for peer review and for peer review process
Face-to-face workshop 3	• Further hands on training and practice in UQ learning spaces • Presentation of learning design concept for peer feedback and discussion • Time allocated for further developing learning designs incorporating feedback
Face-to-face workshop 4	• Participants conducted mini-teaching sessions for selected spaces • Time was allocated for peer questioning/comments and all teachers received written peer feedback • Discussion around leadership and strategies for sustaining peer knowledge sharing via disciplinary and cross disciplinary communities • Wrap up and presentation of certificates

particular, provided an array of opportunities to compare the pedagogical effectiveness of various pedagogical models with the affordances and constraints of the spaces, technologies and their own pedagogical context.

The workshop facilitators utilised both the technological and spatial features of the learning spaces, so that teachers could explore different theoretical approaches to teaching and learning such as inquiry learning, independent learning and discovery-based learning. They were provided with many reflective opportunities to examine their own belief systems and how they might be translated into learning designs for technology-enriched learning environments, including the challenges and enablers. The teachers all participated in hands-on training in both physical spaces and a familiarization with the classroom management software that will be used in their own spaces, LMS technologies, virtual

worlds, mobile technologies and Web 2.0 technologies. This enabled teachers to develop an understanding of the affordances and constraints of the space and the technologies and develop a coherent vision for how they might utilise the space for their own teaching and learning activities.

The final workshops enabled teachers to test their learning designs in their selected space with feedback from peers. The peer reviews were conducted with an emphasis on providing with a safe and respectful space to practice the implementation of their designs with constructive and supportive peer feedback (Eisen, 2001; Pedder, et al., 2008). This concluding component was also designed to enable teachers to re-visit their beliefs and to promote leadership, strong communities of practice and mentoring strategies. The mini-teaching sessions were highly successful with teachers demonstrating a wide variety of approaches to utilising the spaces. There was a strong emphasis on active and collaborative learning in the presentations, signalling a shift for many in their teaching and learning approaches. Many teachers were also keen to explore opportunities for team teaching offered by the new centre.

The combination of online modules and face-to-face workshops were derived from the model of academic development for technology-enriched learning spaces (Figure 2). Throughout the program teachers became increasingly supportive of one another and prepared to share their ideas, knowledge and expertise. The course was fully evaluated throughout and that data is currently being analysed. Additionally, a follow-up evaluation will take place in mid 2010 once teachers have experienced teaching in their own spaces. Each workshop was rated individually and qualitative data was gathered to monitor learning and identify learning gaps. Facilitators were then able to respond to evaluations at subsequent workshops. Feedback from teachers generally indicated that participants were happy with the quality and content of the workshops. In particular, they indicated that the opportunities the program provided for practice and peer-learning were highly valued. The online modules, though integrated with the workshops, were not received as well. Teachers found that allocating time outside of the face-to-face sessions was difficult.

Leadership was also a critical factor. Initially a distributive leadership model was established between the academic developers and the school with a strong sense of partnership and commitment on both sides. With changes in leadership in the school, this partnership was not sustained at the same level and this had a notable impact on the teachers' behaviours. Although the program was successful, the academic developers all believed that the outcomes would have been even more powerful if the distributive leadership approach had continued with equal commitment and momentum.

FUTURE RESEARCH DIRECTIONS AND RECOMMENDATIONS

Evaluation of the impact of academic development on teacher practices and student learning in technology-enriched learning spaces, and development and testing of models of academic development that support teachers to re-imagine their teaching for these spaces, are key areas for further research. The positive outcomes experienced by teachers who participated in the programs outlined here suggests that opportunities for practice in the new spaces accompanied by peer feedback, in particular 'active helping' (Topping, 2007), should be considered as critical elements. Programs designed to support teachers to develop the skills to successfully capitalise on the affordances of technology-enriched learning spaces are crucial to the success of these initiatives. Institutions need to consider how such programs can be integrated into their overall academic development programs in a timely manner (Long, 2009). Incorporation of models such as the one offered here should also be offered through formal post-graduate higher education programs to encourage teacher participation and address the challenges outlined in this chapter.

In conjunction with dedicated time for appropriate academic development and distributive leadership, reward structures, vision, and social-cultural factors are influential to the use of technology-enriched learning spaces. Enabling teachers to participate in change means using motivational strategies and addressing perceived barriers. For example, reward incentives can be as powerful an influence as lack of time for some faculty members (Newton, 2003; Zhou & Xu, 2007). With competing priorities it is important that both leaders and faculty are allocated sufficient time and recognised and valued for their efforts to transform their teaching (Pajo & Wallace, 2001). Some university teachers have felt that there is a 'lack of respect', institutionally, for the development of teaching materials because it is not a research-related activity (Newton, 2003). These kinds of perceptions need to be constantly and specifically addressed through all levels of leadership in order for teaching cultures to buy into change. Implementing change strategies that are culturally aligned with institutional, disciplinary and pedagogical beliefs and priorities are more likely to be successful (Kezar & Eckel, 2002).

CONCLUSION

In order to see a strong cost-benefit return for the significant financial and capital investment these spaces command, a substantial investment in the academic development needs of university teachers needs to be made. Teachers require time and experience using technologies to translate their pedagogical beliefs and beliefs about technologies and re-imagine their teaching in these spaces (Hai, 2008). This chapter offers a model for academic development for technology-enriched spaces that has been well received in the contexts it has been applied thus far. As outlined here such academic development programs need to draw on the benefits of academic developers' 'elastic practice' (Carew, et al., 2008), in conjunction with a focus on distributive leadership. Such approaches have been seen to go some way towards addressing the range of challenges faced by teachers and disciplinary cultures in adapting to technology-enriched learning environments. Additionally, these approaches can be powerful in encouraging teachers to develop a strong pedagogical vision for their use of these technology-enriched spaces.

REFERENCES

P2P. (2006). *Policy peer review ICT in schools: Methodology*. Retrieved April 27, 2010, from http://insight.eun.org/ shared/data/insight/ documents/ P2PMethodology.pdf

Bates, A. W., & Poole, G. (2003). *Effective teaching with technology in higher education: Foundations for success*. San Francisco, CA: Jossey-Bass.

Boud, D. (2001). *Peer learning in higher education: Learning from and with each other*. London, UK: Kogan Page.

Carew, A. L., Lefoe, G., Bell, M., & Amour, L. (2008). Elastic practice in academic developers. *The International Journal for Academic Development*, *13*(1), 51–66. doi:10.1080/13601440701860250

Conole, G., & Dyke, M. (2004). What are the affordances of information and communication technologies? *ALT-J*, *12*(2), 113–124. doi:10.1080/0968776042000216183

de Figueiredo, A. D., & Afonso, A. P. (2006). Context and learning: A philosophical framework. In de Figueiredo, A. D., & Afonso, A. P. (Eds.), *Managing learning in virtual settings: The role of context* (pp. 1–22). London, UK: Information Science Publishing. doi:10.4018/9781591404880. ch001

Diaz, V., Garret, P., Kinley, E., Moore, J., Schwartz, C., & Kohrman, P. (2009). Faculty development for the 21st century. *EDUCAUSE Review*, *44*(3), 46–55.

Eisen, M.-J. (2001). Peer-based professional develoment viewed through the lens of transformation. *Holistic Nursing Practice*, *16*(1), 30–42.

Fitzgerald, R., Barrass, S., Campbell, J., Hinton, S., Ryan, Y., Whitelaw, M., et al. (2009). *Digital learning communities: Investigating the application of social software to support networked learning*. Australian Learning and Teaching Council. Retrieved from http://eprints.qut.edu. au /18476/1/c18476.pdf

Fullan, M., Hill, P., & Crévola, C. (2006). *Breakthrough*. Toronto, Canada: Corwin Press.

Hai, B. (2008). Facilitating development of student teachers positive beliefs about educational technologies through electronic modelling, reflection and technology experience. *International Journal of Instructional Technology and Distance Learning, 5*(1). Retrieved May 27, 2010, from http://www.itdl.org/Journal/ Jan_08/article04.htm

Hedberg, J. G. (2006). E-learning futures? Speculations for a time yet to come. *Studies in Continuing Education, 28*(2), 171–183. doi:10.1080/01580370600751187

Hooker, M. (2008). *Models and best practice in teacher professional development*. Retrieved April 27, 2010, from http://www.gesci.org/old/ files/ docman/Teacher_Professional_ Development_Models.pdf

Hornby, W. (2003). *Case studies in streamlining assessment*. Aberdeen, UK: Centre for the Enhancement of Learning and Teaching, The Robert Gordon University.

Hughes, A. (2009). *Higher education in the Web 2.0 world*. Retrieved April 27, 2010, from http://www.jisc.ac.uk/ publications/documents / heweb2.aspx.

JISC. (2009). *Effective practice in a digital age: A guide to technology-enhanced learning and teaching*. Retrieved April 27, 2010 from http://www.jisc.ac.uk/media/ documents/publications/effectivepracticedigitalage.pdf

Jonas-Dwyer, D., & Pospisil, R. (2004). The millennial effect: Implications for academic development. In *Transforming Knowledge into Wisdom: Holistic Approaches to Teaching and Learning, Proceedings of the 27th Annual HERDSA Conference* (pp. 194-206). Miri, Sarawak.

Kennedy, G., Dalgarno, B., Bennet, S., Gray, C., Judd, T., Waycott, J., et al. (2009). *Education and the net generation: Implications for learning and teaching in Australian universities*. Australian Learning and Teaching Council. Retrieved May 27, 2010, from http://www.altc.edu.au/system / files/resources/CG6-25_Melbourne _Kennedy_ Final%20Report _July09_v2.pdf

Kennewell, S. (2001). Using affordances and constraints to evaluate the use of information and communications technology in teaching and learning. *Journal of Information Technology for Teacher Education, 10*(1&2), 101–116.

Kezar, A., & Eckel, P. D. (2002). The effect of institutional culture on change strategies in higher education. *The Journal of Higher Education, 73*(4), 435–460. doi:10.1353/jhe.2002.0038

Kirkup, G., & Kirkwood, A. (2005). Information and communications technologies (ICT) in higher education teaching: A tale of gradualism rather than revolution. *Learning, Media and Technology, 30*(2), 185–199. doi:10.1080/17439880500093810

Knight, P., & Trowler, P. (2001). *Department leadership in higher education*. Buckingham, UK: SRHE and Open University.

Kotter, J. P. (1996). *Leading change*. Boston, MA: Harvard Business School Press.

Lefoe, G. (2010). Creating the future: Changing culture through leadership capacity development. In U. D. Ehlers & D. Schneckenberg (Eds.), *Changing cultures in higher education. A handbook for strategic change* (189-204). Heidelberg, Germany: Springer Verlag.

Long, G. (2009). *Professional development for 21st century learning and teaching*. Retrieved from http://blog.garethl.com/2009/ 04/proessional-development-for-21st.html

Mahdizadeh, H., Biemans, H., & Mulder, M. (2008). Determining factors of the use of e-learning environments by university teachers. *Computers & Education*, *51*(1), 142–154. doi:10.1016/j.compedu.2007.04.004

McGrenere, J., & Ho, W. (2000). Affordances: Clarifying and evolving a concept. In *Proceedings of the Graphics Interface Conference* (pp. 179-186). Montreal, Canada.

Miller, S., Meier, E., Payne-Bourcy, L., Shablak, S., Newmann, D. L., Wan, T. Y., et al. (2003). Technology use as a catalyst for change: A leadership framework for transforming urban teacher preparation. *International Electronic Journal for Leadership in Learning, 7*(12). Retrieved May 27, 2010, from http://iejll.synergiesprairies.ca/ iejll/ index.php/iejll/ article/viewFile/427/89

Moschkovich, J. N., & Brenner, M. E. (2000). Integrating a naturalistic paradigm into research on mathematics and science cognition and learning. In Kelly, A. E., & Lesh, R. A. (Eds.), *Handbook of research design in mathematics and science education* (pp. 457–486). Mahwah, NJ: Lawrence Erlbaum Associates.

Newton, R. (2003). Staff attitudes to the development and delivery of e-learning. *New Library World, 104*(1193), 412–425. doi:10.1108/03074800310504357

Oblinger, D. (2005). Leading the transition from classrooms to learning spaces. *EDUCAUSE Quarterly*, *28*(1), 14–18.

Pajo, K., & Wallace, C. (2001). Barriers to the uptake of Web-based technology by university teachers. *Journal of Distance Education, 16*(1), 70–84.

Park, S. H., & Ertmer, P. A. (2007). Impact of problem-based learning (PBL) on teachers' beliefs regarding technology use. *Journal of Research on Technology in Education, 40*(2), 247–267.

Pearshouse, I., Bligh, B., Brown, E., Lewthwaite, S., Graber, R., & Hartnell-Young, E. (2009). *A study of effective evaluation models and practices for technology supported physical learning spaces (JELS)*. Nottingham, UK: Learning Sciences Research Institute, University of Nottingham.

Pedder, D., Storey, A., & Opfer, V. D. (2008). *Schools and continuing professional development (CPD) in England - State of the nation research project: A report commissioned by the Training and Development Agency for Schools*. Cambridge University and the Open University.

Punie, Y. (2007). Learning spaces: An ICT-enabled model of future learning in the knowledge-based society. *European Journal of Education, 42*(2), 185–199. doi:10.1111/j.1465-3435.2007.00302.x

Sahin, I., & Thompson, A. (2006). Using Rogers' theory to interpret instructional computer use by COE faculty. *Journal of Research on Technology in Education, 39*(1), 81–104.

Steel, C. H. (2009a). Reconciling university teacher beliefs to create learning designs for LMS environments. *Australasian Journal of Educational Technology, 25*(3), 399–420.

Steel, C. H. (2009b). *The interrelationship between university teachers' pedagogical beliefs, beliefs about Web technologies and Web practices*. Brisbane: Unpublished PhD, Griffith University.

Steel, C. H., & Levy, M. (2009). Creativity and constraint: Understanding teacher beliefs and the use of LMS technologies. In R. Atkinson & C. McBeath (Eds.), *Same places, different spaces. Proceedings of ASCILITE Conference Auckland 2009* (pp. 1013-1022). Auckland, New Zealand: Auckland University.

Tierney, W. G. (1996). Leadership and postmodernism: On voice and the qualitative method. *The Leadership Quarterly, 7*(3), 371–383. doi:10.1016/S1048-9843(96)90026-0

Topping, K. (2007). Trends in peer learning. *Educational Psychology*, *25*(6), 631–645. doi:10.1080/01443410500345172

Trowler, P., & Cooper, A. (2002). Teaching and learning regimes: Implicit theories and recurrent practices in the enhancement of teaching and learning through educational development programmes. *Higher Education Research & Development*, *21*(3), 221–240. doi:10.1080/0729436022000020742

Vrakking, W. J. (1995). The implementation game. *Journal of Organisational Change*, *8*(3), 31–46. doi:10.1108/09534819510090141

Waldron, N., Dawson, S., & Burnett, B. (2005). Academic staff development in online learning and teaching: Developing online pedagogies. In *Proceedings of AUSweb 2005*. Gold Coast. Retrieved May 27, 2010, from http://ausweb.scu.edu.au/aw05 /papers/refereed/waldron /index.html

Watson, L. (2007). Building the future of learning. *European Journal of Education*, *42*(2), 255–263. doi:10.1111/j.1465-3435.2007.00299.x

Yerrick, R., Parke, H., & Nugent, J. (1997). Struggling to promote deeply rooted change: The filtering effect of teachers' beliefs on understanding transformational views of teaching science. *Science Education*, *81*(2), 137–159. doi:10.1002/(SICI)1098-237X(199704)81:2<137::AID-SCE2>3.0.CO;2-G

Young, S. F. (2008). Theoretical frameworks and models of learning: Tools for developing conceptions of teaching and learning. *The International Journal for Academic Development*, *13*(1), 41–49. doi:10.1080/13601440701860243

Zhou, G., & Xu, J. (2007). Adoption of educational technology ten years after setting strategic goals: A Canadian university case study. *Australasian Journal of Educational Technology*, *23*(4), 508–528.

ADDITIONAL READING

Andrews, T., & Powell, D. (2009) Collaborative Teaching and Learning Centres at the University of Queensland. In D., Radcliffe, H., Wilson, D. Powell, & B. Tibbetts, (Eds.), *Learning spaces in higher education: Positive outcomes by design: Proceedings of the Next Generation Learning Spaces 2008 Colloquium* (pp 41-48) Brisbane: University of Queensland.

Brinkerhoff, J. (2006). Effects of long-duration professional development academy on technology skills, computer efficacy and technology integration beliefs and practices. *Journal of Research on Technology in Education*, *39*(1), 22–43.

Chen, C. H. (2007). Cultural diversity in instructional design for technology-based education. *British Journal of Educational Technology*, *38*(6), 1113–1116. doi:10.1111/j.1467-8535.2007.00738.x

Chen, Y. L. (2008). Modelling the determinants of technology use. *Computers & Education*, *51*(2), 545–558. doi:10.1016/j.compedu.2007.06.007

Conole, G., & Fill, K. (2005). A learning design toolkit to create pedagogically effective learning activities. *Journal of Interactive Media in Education*. Retrieved May 27, 2010, from http://jime.open.ac.uk/2005/08/

Cox, M., & Marshall, G. (2007). Effects of ICT: Do we know what we should know? *Education and Information Technologies*, *12*(2), 59–70. doi:10.1007/s10639-007-9032-x

Cranton, P. (1996). *Professional development as transformative learning: New perspectives for teachers of adults*. San Francisco, CA: Jossey-Bass.

Cranton, P., & Carusetta, E. (2002). Reflecting on teaching: The influence of context. *The International Journal for Academic Development*, *7*(2), 167–176. doi:10.1080/1360144032000071288

Dearn, J., Fraser, K., & Ryan, Y. (2002). *Investigation into the provision of professional development for university teaching in Australia: A discussion paper*. Canberra: Department of Education, Science and Training.

Downes, S. (2005) *E-learning 2.0*, National Research Council of Canada. Retrieved May 27, 2010, from http://elearnmag.org/ subpage. cfm?section= articles&article=29-1.

Entwistle, N., Skinner, D., Entwistle, D., & Orr, S. (2000). Conceptions and beliefs about 'good teaching': An integration of contrasting research. *Higher Education Research & Development*, *19*(1), 5–26. doi:10.1080/07294360050020444

Ertmer, P. (2005). Teacher pedagogical beliefs: The final frontier in our quest for technology integration? *Educational Technology Research and Development*, *53*(4), 25–39. doi:10.1007/BF02504683

Ertmer, P., Ross, E. M., & Gopalakrishnan, S. (2000). Technology-using teachers: How powerful visions and student-centered beliefs fuel exemplary practice. In C. Crawford, D. A. Willis, R. Carlsen, I. Gibson, K. McFerrin, J. Price & R. Weber (Eds.), *Proceedings of Society for Information Technology and Teacher Education International Conference 2000* (pp. 1519-1524). Chesapeake, VA: AACE.

Ertmer, P. A., Ottenbreit-Leftwich, A., & York, C. S. (2006-2007). Exemplary technology-using teachers: Perceptions of factors influencing success. *Journal of Computing in Teacher Education*, *23*(2), 55–61.

Ferman, T. (2002). Academic professional development practice: What lecturers find valuable. *The International Journal for Academic Development*, *7*(2), 146–158. doi:10.1080/1360144032000071305

Gaible, E., & Burns, M. (2005). Using Technology to Train Teachers (Online). Retrieved April 27, 2010, from http://www.infodev.org/en /Publication.13.html.

Hatch, T., Bass, R., Iiyoshi, T., & Mace, D. P. (2004). Building knowledge for teaching and learning. *Change*, September/October, *36*(5): 62-66.

Ho, A., Watkins, D., & Kelly, M. (2001). The conceptual change approach to improving teaching and learning: An evaluation of a Hong Kong staff development programme. *Higher Education*, *42*(2), 143–169. doi:10.1023/A:1017546216800

Jimoyiannis, A., & Komis, V. (2007). Examining teachers' beliefs about ICT in education: Implications of a teacher preparation programme. *Teacher Development*, *11*(2), 149–173. doi:10.1080/13664530701414779

JISC. (2006). Designing spaces for effective learning: A guide to 21st Century learning space design. Retrieved May 27, 2010, from http://www. jisc.ac.uk/ publications/programmerelated/2006/pub_spaces.aspx.

Laurillard, D. (2002). Rethinking teaching for the knowledge society. *Educause, January/February*, 16-25.

Lim, C. P., & Chai, S. C. (2007). Teachers' pedagogical beliefs and their planning and conduct of computer-mediated classroom lessons. *British Journal of Educational Technology*, *38*(2), 272–286.

Matzen, N. J., & Edmunds, J. A. (2007). Technology as a catalyst for change: The role of professional development. *Journal of Research on Technology in Education*, *39*(4), 417–430.

Miller, S., Meier, E., Payne-Bourcy, L., Shablak, S., Newmann, D. L., Wan, T. Y., et al. (2003). Technology use as a catalyst for change: A leadership framework for transforming urban teacher preparation. *International Electronic Journal for Leadership in Learning, 7*(12). Retrieved May 27, 2010, from http://www.ucalgary.ca /iejll/miller_et_al.

Mumtaz, S. (2000). Factors affecting teachers' use of information and communications technology: A review of the literature. *Journal of Information Technology for Teacher Education, 9*(3), 319–341.

Oblinger, D. (2005). Leading the transition from classrooms to learning spaces. *EDUCAUSE Quarterly, 28*(1), 14–18.

Pelgrum, W. J., & Law, N. (2003). *ICT in education around the world: Trends, problems and prospects*. Paris: UNESCO.

Prensky, M. (2007). How to teach with technology: Keeping both teachers and students comfortable in an era of exponential change. *Emerging Technologies for Learning, BECTA., 2*(9), 40–46.

Roche, V. (2001). Professional development models and transformative change: A case study of indicators of effective practice in higher education. *The International Journal for Academic Development, 6*(2), 120–129. doi:10.1080/13601440110090767

Samuelowicz, K., & Bain, J. D. (2001). Revisiting academics' beliefs about teaching and learning. *Higher Education, 41*(3), 299–325. doi:10.1023/A:1004130031247

Smarkola, C. (2007). Technology acceptance predictors among student teachers and experienced classroom teachers. *Journal of Educational Computing Research, 37*(1), 65–82. doi:10.2190/J3GM-3RK1-2907-7U03

Sugar, W., Crawley, F., & Fine, B. (2004). Examining teachers' decisions to adopt technology. *Journal of Educational Technology & Society, 7*(4), 201–213.

Webb, M., & Cox, M. (2004). A review of pedagogy related to information and communication technology. *Technology, Pedagogy and Education, 13*(3), 235–286. doi:10.1080/14759390400200183

Windschitl, M., & Sahl, K. (2002). Tracing teacher's use of technology in a laptop computer school: The interplay of teacher beliefs, social dynamics and institutional culture. *American Educational Research Journal, 39*(1), 165–205. doi:10.3102/00028312039001165

Wozney, L., Venkatesh, V., & Abrami, P. C. (2006). Implementing computer technologies: Teachers' perceptions and practices. *Journal of Technology and Teacher Education, 14*(1), 173–207.

KEY TERMS AND DEFINITIONS

Academic Developers: Scholarly professionals with expertise in the discipline of Higher Education who focus on providing a link between pedagogical practice, research and theory.

Academic Development: Opportunities to develop the link between pedagogical practice, research and theory.

Affordances: The action possibilities inherent in technologies and spaces that can be realised by a teacher in relation to their own pedagogical context.

Distributive Leadership: Leadership that is enacted through power sharing of knowledge and ideas by collegial groups.

Learning Designs: Curriculum-based framework that includes tasks and interactions that are designed to promote student learning.

Pedagogical Context: The variable that are interwoven into the act of learning and teachings such as teacher and student characteristics and preferences, the pedagogical approach employed by specific disciplines, the organisation of the learning environment as well as disciplinary and institutional culture and norms.

Teacher Beliefs: A complex and inter-related system of personal and professional beliefs that are often held implicitly and serve as cognitive maps that underlie teachers' practices.

Technology-Enriched Spaces: Innovative physical learning environments that are equipped with a range of technology tools and designed to support new ways of learning and teaching.

Chapter 16
Experiential Space

Chris Cheers
Holmesglen Institute, Australia

Chen Swee Eng
Holmesglen Institute, Australia

Glen Postle
University of Southern Queensland, Toowoomba, Australia

ABSTRACT

The description of learning environments as physical or virtual spaces focuses on the tools and infrastructure that support learning as opposed to the learning interactions. The authors of this chapter advocate the view that to maximise the potential of any learning environment, educators need to understand how students learn in the first instance and then design the learning environment based on these insights. Throughout this chapter, formal learning is conceived as an individualised experience within an organised learning community, and as such, it is suggested that this learning environment is described as an experiential space. Within this chapter, an approach to designing an experiential space that uses problem based learning to engage students and facilitate their active construction of knowledge is described. The Holmesglen built environment degree program is used as a case study to illustrate a particular solution to designing an experiential learning space.

INTRODUCTION

We live in a world that has been described as a 'digital ecosystem' where the physical and the virtual are fully intertwined and functioning through well-designed, well-integrated social and technical architecture working together in a wireless mesh that is persistent, pervasive, and mobile. This digital ecosystem can, and has, enhanced our abilities to connect with other people, share ideas, work collaboratively and form communities (Suter et al., 2005). There is growing evidence to suggest that educational approaches that leverage on the strengths of this digital ecosystem can provide alternative educational experiences that challenge the legitimacy of location-based models as the best way to deliver quality education (JISC Web 2.0 Report, 2009). Quality learning can be undertaken independent of time and distance, no longer constrained by administrative requirements

DOI: 10.4018/978-1-60960-114-0.ch016

Table 1. (Adapted from Kimball, 2002)

From	To
Face-to-face learning and teaching is the ideal environment for learning and other modes represent a compromise.	Diverse learning environments utilised in a pedagogically appropriate way can support high quality learning.
Learning only occurs when teachers interact with students at a fixed time and space.	Learning is ongoing and boundary-less and is most successful when learners take ownership of their own learning.
Managing online learning is about learning how to use the latest technology.	Managing online learning requires greater understanding about the learning process.

surrounding the use of lecture/tutorial structures and their associated timetables. Interactive elements of learning can be recorded and archived and thus allow the student to utilise a diverse range of resources that can be revisited, reflected upon, modified, and challenged. This promotes a view of learning that is non-linear and fluid and more in tune what is known about learning.

These digital technologies provide us with increased opportunities to promote exemplary learning and teaching strategies. Ideas such as personalised (individualised) learning, situated (authentic) learning and problem-based learning have been educational ideals for many years due to the fact that these approaches engage the student in deep, authentic and contextualised learning. Unfortunately, the dominance of the transmission model (reinforced by widespread use of instructivist teaching approaches and top-down management structures) has prevailed (Laurillard, 2006). Instructivism has inappropriately installed location-based education as the traditional mode of learning and teaching, which is a premise that needs to be challenged. Although, the digital age has provided technologies with the potential to challenge this notion, there is still a need to ensure that instructivism in digital environments is not being perpetuated.

If used appropriately, these technologies have the potential to radically improve the way students engage with knowledge and negotiate ideas. However, this potential will only be realised if educators begin with an understanding of how students learn, and design the use of learning

technologies and learning environments from this standpoint (Laurillard, 2002). Virtual learning environments and social networking solutions have the capacity to cater for a diverse range of learner initiatives and learner interactions. The learner is provided with opportunities to interact with the tutor, other learners, course content (readings and other resources), and external experts. Learners therefore, have access to a rich socio-cultural context. Unfortunately, the adoption of these technologies seems to have been more about the preservation of the status quo than any paradigm shift. Kimball (2002) argues that it is now not a question of how we can engage learners via learning technologies but rather a question of how we can engage learners in more meaningful learning activities. To make the most of the opportunities provided by our world's digital ecosystem we need to support new learning dynamics in an integrated manner across physical and virtual spaces. We need to shift our thinking as educators ...

Today's learners increasingly have access to, and use a broad range of social networking tools and technologies that provide a constantly evolving multiplicity of interactive resources for information and communication. As such learners will expect to see this diversity reflected in their educational experiences. They will increasingly have little patience with learning and teaching approaches which are modelled only on location-based approaches and without the blending of digital technologies. There is a need to conceive of learning as an experience, and therefore rather than defining the learning space in terms of a location with physical or virtual dimensions we need to start with the experience and support this experience with a range of appropriate tools which may include physical and/or virtual environments.

EXPERIENTIAL SPACE

Learning environments are multi-dimensional and complex, and students are individually unique in their perception and engagement with the learning experience. Although the actions and experiences of individual students are somewhat unpredictable, by applying concepts from Complexity Science, it is possible to generalise patterns in this complex environment and identify principles that can be used to design learning environments that 'encourage' certain dynamics. When designing for educational experiences there is a need to "Shift thinking away from single events or processes towards thinking in terms of patterns, interrelated processes, and relationships" (Stroebel et al., 2005). A complexity paradigm views the world as complex and unpredictable, where relationships are non-linear and dynamic. It is made up of complex adaptive systems where intelligent agents anticipate the behaviour of others and the external environment and modify their behaviour accordingly. The engagement of the learner in a learning experience or journey, interacting with other learners and tutors, assisted by learning resources and tools makes for a contextually situated definition of an experiential space. An experiential space can be seen as an activity system (Engestrom, 1987), which is a complex adaptive system, and learners are self organising intelligent agents within that system.

Defining an Experiential Space

An architect might talk about space as something we experience in relation to how we traverse the space and negotiate the different aspects of the space. Physical space could be defined by contain-ment (walls, ceiling, floor) and the (experiential) quality of that space which is influenced by textures, colours, shapes and volumes. What a person feels about the space is dependent on his or her own perceptions, values and attitudes.

Designing for the educational experience can enable learners to use technologies to support their learning in ways that best suit their individual needs, in comfortable spaces of their choice and with a range of tools to support their activities. These spaces and tools can be virtual, physical or blended. Any planned learning space needs to accommodate individual journeys (experiences), within design parameters which support pre-defined curriculum outcomes. Designing for educational experience is designing for engagement and interaction in a community of learning (Barab & Duffy, 2000; Wenger, 1999), where the interactions are based on trust, openness and dialogue between learners & learners, learners & tutors and interaction with the environment, which may include cognitive tools that students implicitly or explicitly use (Jonassen & Reeves, 1996). In effect a community of learning within an experiential space, is the result of the collective behaviour of a group with shared objectives. In formal educational settings, this involves sharing common processes, values, experiences and intellectual exchange. Communities are living entities. They need the flow of energy and activities to keep them healthy. They consist of individuals who have made a choice to participate in the collective activities of the community.

An experiential space may be defined by containment in four dimensions, three dimensions would be the tutor and students (interactive), the learning resources (directive) and the tools (facilitative). These are the elements that are manipulated when designing an experiential space. The experiential space is then the experiential activity (or learning journey) that the student(s) occupy, interacting with other fellow learners and tutors and moving along the 4th dimension of time. Whether the activity takes place in a physical or

Table 2. Characteristics of authentic activity (Reeves et al, 2002)

No.	Characteristic of authentic activity	Supporting authors, researchers and theorists
1.	Have real-world relevance	(Lebow & Wager, 1994) (Cronin, 1993) (Oliver & Omari, 1999) (Brown et al., 1989) (Cognition and Technology Group at Vanderbilt, 1990a) (Jonassen, 1991) (Resnick, 1987) (Winn, 1993) (Young, 1993)
2.	Are ill-defined, requiring students to define the tasks and sub-tasks needed to complete the activity	(Sternberg, Wagner, & Okagaki, 1993) (Lebow & Wager, 1994) (Bransford, Vye, Kinzer, & Risko, 1990) (Young, 1993) (Brown et al., 1989) (Cognition and Technology Group at Vanderbilt, 1990a) (Winn, 1993)
3.	Comprise complex tasks to be investigated by students over a sustained period of time	(Lebow & Wager, 1994) (Bransford, Vye et al., 1990) (Cognition and Technology Group at Vanderbilt, 1990b) (Jonassen, 1991)
4.	Provide the opportunity for students to examine the task from different perspectives, using a variety of resources	(Sternberg et al., 1993) (Bransford, Vye et al., 1990) (Young, 1993) (Cognition and Technology Group at Vanderbilt, 1990b)
5.	Provide the opportunity to collaborate	(Lebow & Wager, 1994) (Young, 1993) (Gordon, 1998)
6.	Provide the opportunity to reflect and involve students' beliefs and values	(Young, 1993) (Myers, 1993) (Gordon, 1998)
7.	Can be integrated and applied across different subject areas and lead beyond domain-specific outcomes	(Bransford, Sherwood et al., 1990 (Bransford, Vye et al., 1990) (Jonassen, 1991)
8.	Are seamlessly integrated with assessment	(Reeves & Okey, 1996) (Young, 1995) (Herrington & Herrington, 1998)
9.	Create polished products valuable in their own right rather than as preparation for something else	(Barab, Squire, & Dueber, 2000) (Gordon, 1998)
10.	Allow competing solutions and diversity of outcome	(Duchastel, 1997) (Bottge & Hasselbring, 1993) (Young & McNeese, 1993) (Bransford, Sherwood et al.,1990) (Bransford, Vye et al., 1990)

virtual space should not be a driving factor in the learning design, each space with its particular affordances is but another tool supporting each learner's journey. Each space should meet three criteria: comfort (usability), utility and user well-being. In other words learning is more productive when the student is comfortable, utilises tools that suit their individual learning style and is facilitated in a way that values the student's unique approach to the learning task.

Experiential Space as a Problem Space

The experiential space of the Holmesglen Built Environment Degree Programs is designed to provide students with the opportunity to experience and explore what it is to be a professional in the building and construction industry. Students engage in authentic learning activities that have real-world relevance as outlined in Table 2. The learning activities are designed to engage the

participants, empower them to contribute and feel that they have something to contribute, and connect the individual and collective experiences.

The Problem Based Learning (PBL) approach used in the Holmesglen Built Environment Degree Program engages students through the use of stimulating and challenging Learning Triggers. Learning triggers are realistic, ill-structured problems which act as a catalyst for investigation and learning. Empowerment is inherent in the learner-centred philosophy and processes of the degree program where 'instructors' are facilitators, mentors, coaches, co-learners and peers rather than authority figures; and active learning generates meaningful experiences individually and collectively (Savin-Baden, 2003). PBL requires active learning, where the learner plays an authentic role in carrying out complex tasks. In PBL the focus is on the learning process not on the course content. In addition, the information and communication technologies used throughout the degree program are chosen to complement educational

Figure 1. PBL activity system (adapted from Engestrom, 1987)

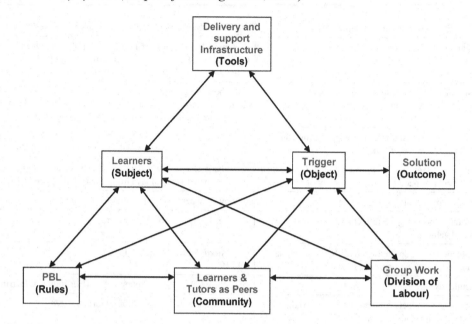

approaches that emphasise problem solving, inquiry and critical thinking rather than simple acquisition of factual knowledge, and when the learner is an active constructor of knowledge (Jonassen, 1999; Garrison & Anderson, 2003).

Experiential Space as an Activity System

In Activity Theory human activity is seen as an Activity System as outlined in Figure 1.

The Subject refers to the individual or group of learners engaged in the problem-based learning activities whereas the Object refers to the Learning Trigger for the activities. The learners are assisted in this process with physical and symbolic, external and internal mediating instruments or Tools. The Community comprises multiple individuals and/or groups who share the same Object. The Division of Labor refers to both the horizontal division of tasks between the members of the community and to the vertical division of power and status. The Rules refer to the explicit and implicit regulations, norms and conventions that constrain actions and interactions within the activity system, which in this case are those of Problem Based Learning (PBL). The learning that takes place is personal and unique to each learner within the activity system. The learning process is the journey (in time) through the experiential space with each learner taking a different route through the space. The learning experience is the stimulation, change, and meaning experienced by the learner in interacting and journeying through the experiential space. In this way the activity system maps the major aspects of the experiential space as the learner undertakes this complex journey.

HOLMESGLEN BUILT ENVIRONMENT DEGREE PRORAM

The Holmesglen Program, with its requirement for integration of problem-based learning, on-line and off-line interaction and learning materials as a seamless connection of physical and virtual, has provided an excellent opportunity to explore how educational experiences can be designed to leverage on the strengths of our world's digital ecosystem. The program has been designed to prepare students for professional roles in the building and construction industry using authentic interactions that are relevant in this professional role. The ability to work effectively with stakeholders at a distance, internationally, and in some cases in virtual teams, has become a core skill for such professional roles.

The learning design developed for the Holmesglen Built Environment Degree Program is underpinned by a number of elements:

1. *Students are Empowered:* Learners are placed in the role of professionals solving challenging, real world, problems. Their learning is their responsibility and tutors are seen as peers and a resource. Activity is triggered by an authentic industry problem (Learning Trigger) and driven by Milestones and Deliverables

2. *Learning Journey:* Each Subject's activities are seen as a Learning Journey.

3. *Learning Triggers:* At the core of a Problem Based Learning approach is the Learning Trigger, which can be described as an issue, disorientating dilemma, or problem. Such a trigger must be engaging, encompass all intended learning outcomes, and act as a catalyst for student inquiry. The Learning Trigger is used to:
    ◦ start the learning process
    ◦ stimulate student engagement
    ◦ set boundaries and direction for the learning

To provide stimulating relevant triggers current authentic construction and building industry projects are used.

An example of such a trigger is the Darling Harbour Barangaroo Project (http://www.barangaroo.com/) used in the 3rd year subject LSD363 – Large Scale Mixed-Use Sustainable Development. In this subject

Figure 2. Learning journey

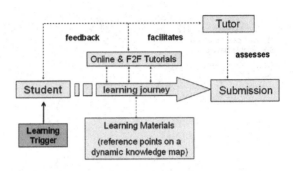

a range of complex and interrelated issues are examined including macroeconomics, environmental economics and large-scale economic investment, social and cultural diversity issues, cost benefit analysis and large-scale economic investments, sustainability, risk analysis and project management all as they relate to a large-scale mixed-use sustainable development. Learners are placed in the role of a Consultant who has been tasked to conduct a Feasibility Study of the Barangaroo Darling Harbour redevelopment in Sydney NSW. They are required to produce a comprehensive report which is to be presented to the CEO of their company.

4. *Student Learning Process Maps:* A Student Learning Process Map (SLPM) provides learners with an overview of the subject, guides them through their learning journey, and supports and guides effective time management over the Trimester (Figure 3).

The SLPMs vary in structure from levels 1 - 3 across the degree program. More structure and guidance is provided to 1st year students to support them as they acclimatise themselves to the PBL process. Less scaffolding is provided to third year students who are expected to be ready to enter the workplace as professionals.

5. *Communication Tools:* These tools can include discussion forums and messaging through Moodle and Basecamp, mobile

Figure 3. LSD363 SLPM

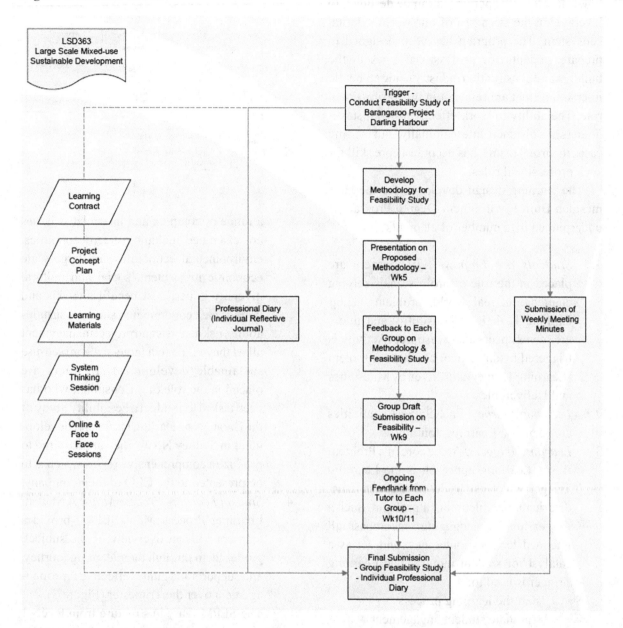

phone text and voice, instant messaging and email. Use of discussion forums is strongly encouraged with discussion threads created to reflect each aspect of the subject. They can range from mini case studies to highlight an important concept, to project management processes, to simple Q&A areas. Discussions also take place in face-to-face sessions however the interaction between learners and learners, and tutors and learners, is not dependent on place. These communications are part of the energy flow and connections that evolve across the learning community.

6. *Project Management Tools:* Basecamp is a commercially developed web-based project management solution that provides students

Figure 4. Built environment degree subject performance chart 2009

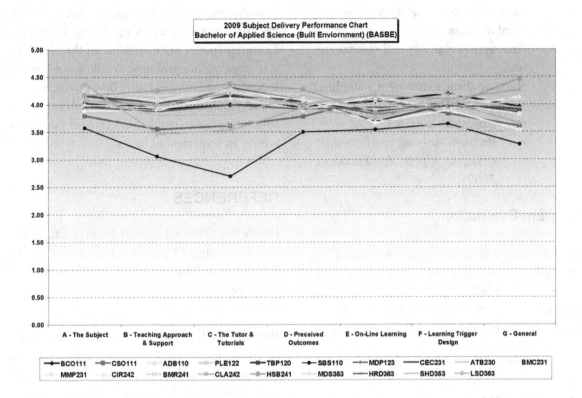

with tools to effectively and transparently manage their work. They can create To-Do lists, allocate Tasks, set Milestones, share Files and communicate with their group members to keep work on track.

7. *Learning Materials:* The curriculum is more than the content. Learning materials are 'Markers' on a dynamic and incomplete knowledge map. Students navigate their own unique learning journeys with reference to these markers, and through research find and explore additional materials. These are all used to support the development of a solution to the problem scenario/learning trigger.

8. *Additional Scaffolding for Interaction:* A range of other strategies have also been implemented to scaffold student interaction. These include:
   - Learning Contracts,
   - Weekly Meeting Minutes,
   - Reflective Journals, and
   - Peer Assessment.

9. *Assessment:* Assessment is recognised as a major driver of student behaviour and is integrated into the design of the experiential space. It is focused on improvement and is developmental as opposed to being summative. The social context, through problem-based learning, promotes developmental assessment. Students are provided with opportunities to actively explore and learn from mistakes through draft submissions and feedback in the course of discussions. Formative assessment is used to guide learners throughout their learning journey. These assessment practices:
   - Align with curriculum objectives;
   - Are based on real world contexts;
   - Encourage learners to reflect and learn continually;

- ○ Provide learners with the opportunity to demonstrate what they know and what they can do;
- ○ Encourage creativity and risk taking; and
- ○ Pursue holistic assessment, including:
  - ▪ Teamwork,
  - ▪ Research skills, and
  - ▪ Problem solving performance. (Cheers, Chen & Zarakhsh, 2009)

Program Evaluation

Subject evaluation surveys, using a 5 point Likert Scale, are conducted on completion of each Trimester. As seen in Figure 4, which illustrates student evaluations for a full cycle of subjects, student response to the Degree Program has been overwhelming positive.

CONCLUSION

In a Higher Education context, learning is an individual experience within a learning community that traverses physical and virtual learning space. Such a community no longer needs to be bound by temporal or spatial limitations as the concept of experiential space explained throughout this chapter has suggested. In addition the concept of a digital ecosystem suggests a promising direction for higher education. Experiential space focuses on utilising the best space available to achieve learning outcomes and allows learners to connect with other people, share ideas and work collaboratively anywhere and at anytime.

The challenge in relation to experiential space is to design educational experiences that leverage on the strengths of this digital ecosystem. These learning experiences need to be designed for engagement and interaction in a community of learning, and support learning dynamics in an integrated manner across physical and virtual spaces. Education practices must evolve if we are to make the most of the opportunities provided by this constantly evolving digital ecosystem. Learning spaces are central to all this, however it is more meaningful now to talk about learning spaces as experiential rather than physical or virtual. As such, educational design needs to focus on supporting the dynamics and flow of interaction within an Experiential Space.

REFERENCES

Barab, S., & Duffy, T. (2000). From practice fields to communities of practice. In Jonassen, D. D., & Land, S. M. (Eds.), *Theoretical foundations of learning environments*. Mahwah, NJ: Lawrence Erlbaum Associates.

Barab, S. A., Squire, K. D., & Dueber, W. (2000). A co-evolutionary model for supporting the emergence of authenticity. *Educational Technology Research and Development*, *48*(2), 37–62. doi:10.1007/BF02313400

Bottge, B. A., & Hasselbring, T. S. (1993). Taking word problems off the page. *Educational Leadership*, *50*(7), 36–38.

Bransford, J. D., Sherwood, R. D., Hasselbring, T. S., Kinzer, C. K., & Williams, S. M. (1990). Anchored instruction: Why we need it and how technology can help. In Nix, D., & Spiro, R. (Eds.), *Cognition, education and multimedia: Exploring ideas in high technology* (pp. 115–141). Hillsdale, NJ: Lawrence Erlbaum.

Bransford, J. D., Vye, N., Kinzer, C., & Risko, V. (1990). Teaching thinking and content knowledge: Toward an integrated approach. In Jones, B. F., & Idol, L. (Eds.), *Dimensions of thinking and cognitive instruction* (pp. 381–413). Hillsdale, NJ: Lawrence Erlbaum Associates.

Brown, J. S., Collins, A., & Duguid, P. (1989). Situated cognition and the culture of learning. *Educational Researcher, 18*(1), 32–42.

Cheers, C., Chen, S. E., & Zarakhsh, K. (2009). *Bringing e-learning to life - student engagement and empowerment.* Paper presented at HERDSA Conference, Darwin, Australia.

Cognition and Technology Group at Vanderbilt. (1990a). Anchored instruction and its relationship to situated cognition. *Educational Researcher, 19*(6), 2–10.

Cognition and Technology Group at Vanderbilt. (1990b). Technology and the design of generative learning environments. *Educational Technology, 31*(5), 34–40.

Cronin, J. C. (1993). Four misconceptions about authentic learning. *Educational Leadership, 50*(7), 78–80.

Duchastel, P. C. (1997). A Web-based model for university instruction. *Journal of Educational Technology Systems, 25*(3), 221–228. doi:10.2190/UFF9-KB1X-NGG4-UHKL

Engeström, Y. (1987). *Learning by expanding: An activity-theoretical approach to developmental research.* Helsinki, Finland: Orienta-Konsultit.

Garrison, D. R., & Anderson, T. (2003). *E-learning in the 21st century: A framework for research and practice.* London, UK: Routledge Falmer. doi:10.4324/9780203166093

Gordon, R. (1998). Balancing real-world problems with real-world results. *Phi Delta Kappan, 79*, 390–393.

Herrington, J., & Herrington, A. (1998). Authentic assessment and multimedia: How university students respond to a model of authentic assessment. *Higher Education Research & Development, 17*(3), 305–322. doi:10.1080/0729436980170304

JISC. (2009). *Higher Education in a Web 2.0 world.* JISC Report. Retrieved March 1, 2010, from http://www.jisc.ac.uk/ publications/documents /heweb2.aspx

Jonassen, D. (1991). Evaluating constructivistic learning. *Educational Technology, 31*(9), 28–33.

Jonassen, D. H. (1999). Designing constructivist learning environments. In Reigeluth, C. M. (Ed.), *Instructional design theories and models: Their current state of the art* (2nd ed.). Mahwah, NJ: Lawrence Erlbaum Associates.

Jonassen, D. H. (1999). Designing constructivist learning environments. In Reigeluth, C. M. (Ed.), *Instructional design theories and models: A new paradigm of instructional technology* (*Vol. 2*, pp. 215–240). Mahwah, NJ: Lawrence Erlbaum Associate.

Jonassen, D. H., & Reeves, T. C. (1996). Learning with technology: Using computers as cognitive tools. In Jonassen, D. H. (Ed.), *Handbook of research for educational communications and technology* (1st ed., pp. 693–719). New York, NY: Macmillan.

Kimball, L. (2002). Managing distance learning: New challenges for faculty. In Hazemi, R., & Hailes, S. (Eds.), *The digital university: Building a learning community.* London, UK: Springer. doi:10.1007/978-1-4471-0167-3_3

Laurillard, D. (2002). *Rethinking university teaching: A conversational framework for the effective use of learning technologies* (2nd ed.). London, UK: Routledge Falmer. doi:10.4324/9780203304846

Laurillard, D. (2006). E-learning in higher education. In Ashwin, P. (Ed.), *Changing higher education: The development of learning and teaching* (pp. 1–12). London, UK: Routledge.

Lebow, D., & Wager, W. W. (1994). Authentic activity as a model for appropriate learning activity: Implications for emerging instructional technologies. *Canadian Journal of Educational Communication*, 23(3), 231–244.

Myers, S. (1993). A trial for Dmitri Karamazov. *Educational Leadership*, 50(7), 71–72.

Oliver, R., & Omari, A. (1999). Using online technologies to support problem based learning: Learners responses and perceptions. *Australian Journal of Educational Technology*, 15, 158–179.

Reeves, T. C., Herrington, J., & Oliver, R. (2002). Authentic activities and online learning. *Annual Conference Proceedings of Higher Education Research and Development Society of Australasia*. Perth, Australia.

Reeves, T. C., & Okey, J. R. (1996). Alternative assessment for constructivist learning environments. In Wilson, B. G. (Ed.), *Constructivist learning environments: Case studies in instructional design* (pp. 191–202). Englewood Cliffs, NJ: Educational Technology Publications.

Resnick, L. (1987). Learning in school and out. *Educational Researcher*, 16(9), 13–20.

Savin-Baden, M. (2003). *Facilitating problem-based learning*. Maidenhead, UK: Open University Press.

Sternberg, R. J., Wagner, R. K., & Okagaki, L. (1993). Practical intelligence: The nature and role of tacit knowledge in work and at school. In Puckett, J. M., & Reese, H. W. (Eds.), *Mechanisms of everyday cognition* (pp. 205–227). Hillsdale, NJ: Lawrence Erlbaum Associates.

Stroebel, C. K., McDaniel, R. R., Crabtree, B. F., Miller, W. L., Nutting, P. A., & Stange, K. C. (2005). How complexity science can inform a reflective process for improvement in primary care practices. *Joint Commission Journal on Quality and Patient Safety*, 31(8), 438–446.

Suter, V., Alexander, B., & Kaplan, P. (2005). The future of F2F. *Educause Review*, 40(1). Retrieved March 1, 2010, from http://www. educause.edu/ EDUCAUSE+Review/ EDU-CAUSEReviewMagazineVolume40/TheFuture-ofF2F/157954

Wenger, E. (1999). *Communities of practice: Learning, meaning, and identity*. Cambridge, UK: Cambridge University Press.

Winn, W. (1993). Instructional design and situated learning: Paradox or partnership. *Educational Technology*, 33(3), 16–21.

Young, M. F. (1993). Instructional design for situated learning. *Educational Technology Research and Development*, 41(1), 43–58. doi:10.1007/BF02297091

Young, M. F. (1995). Assessment of situated learning using computer environments. *Journal of Science Education and Technology*, 4(1), 89–96. doi:10.1007/BF02211586

Young, M. F., & McNeese, M. (1993). A situated cognition approach to problem solving with implications for computer-based learning and assessment. In Salvendy, G., & Smith, M. J. (Eds.), *Human-computer interaction: Software and hardware interfaces*. New York, NY: Elsevier Science Publishers.

ADDITIONAL READING

Gagne, R. M., Briggs, L. J., & Wager, W. W. (1992). *Principles of instructional design* (4th ed.). Orland, FL: Harcourt, Brace, Jovanovich.

Lave, J., & Wenger, E. (1991). *Situated learning: Legitimate peripheral participation*. Cambridge: Cambridge University Press.

Mayes, J. T., & de Freitas, S. (2004). *Review of e-Learning theories, frameworks and models: JISC e-Learning models desk study stage 2* Retrieved March 1, 2010 from http://www.jisc.ac.uk/uploaded_documents/Stage%202%20Learning%20Models%20(Version%201).pdf

Reeves, T. C., & Laffey, J. M. (1999). Design, assessment, and evaluation of a problem-based learning environment in undergraduate engineering. *Higher Education Research and Development Journal, 18*(2), 219–232. doi:10.1080/0729436990180205

Chapter 17
Student Mentors in Physical and Virtual Learning Spaces

Keith Kirkwood
Victoria University, Australia

Gill Best
Victoria University, Australia

Robin McCormack
Victoria University, Australia

Dan Tout
Victoria University, Australia

ABSTRACT

This chapter explores the human element in the learning space through the notion that once a learning space is inhabited, it becomes a learning place of agency, purpose and community involving both staff and students. The School of Languages and Learning at Victoria University in Melbourne has initiated a multifaceted peer learning support strategy, 'Students Supporting Student Learning' (SSSL), involving the deployment of student peer mentors into various physical and virtual learning spaces. The chapter discusses the dynamics of peer learning across these learning space settings and the challenges involved in instituting the shift from teacher- to learning-centred pedagogies within such spaces. Both physical and virtual dimensions are considered, with the SNAPVU Platform introduced as a strategy for facilitating virtual learning communities of practice in which staff, mentors, and students will be able to engage in mutual learning support. The chapter concludes with calls for the explicit inclusion of peer learning in the operational design of learning spaces.

INTRODUCTION

The purpose of this chapter is to initiate a discussion around a critical parameter in the design and implementation of learning spaces: the learners who inhabit these spaces. Too much attention has been focussed on the architectural design and the technological infrastructure as opposed to the learners who inhabit these spaces. We suggest a reframing of discussions concerning the design

DOI: 10.4018/978-1-60960-114-0.ch017

and development of learning spaces toward one concerned with the development of learning *places*; peopled, positioned and purposeful. Harrison and Dourish (1996, p. 69) posit a distinction between notions of space and place, in that "we are located in 'space', but we act in 'place'"; so, "a space is always what it is, but a place is how it's used". Learning spaces can be understood to possess particular affordances that "encourage or constrain behaviour" (Hunley & Schaller, 2006, p. 32), while the agents interacting with and within such a space possess particular capabilities for action or interaction themselves (Ingold, 1992, p. 46). Consequently, what Hunley and Schaller (2009, p. 34) identify as the "reciprocal interaction between a learning space and its users" may be understood as an ongoing negotiation and interaction between the affordances of a space and the capabilities of its users engaged in the participatory processes of transforming *space* into *place*. As Harrison and Dourish (1996, p. 70) conclude: a "sense of place must be forged by the users [and] cannot be inherent in the system itself", it can however be "designed *for*"; in other words, "a space can only be made a place by its occupants ... [t]he best that the designers can do is to put the tools into their hands" (p. 74).

This chapter explores the human element in the learning space and focuses on learners and on peer-to-peer pedagogies within a variety of learning spaces. At Victoria University (VU) in Melbourne, the School of Language and Learning employs a range of strategies to enable students to support other students in their learning, including peer mentors in traditional classrooms and student rovers in the Learning Commons. We are also in the process of developing a virtual peer-learning platform, SNAPVU, based on a synthesis of Web 2.0 technologies. Together, these strategies form a new learning support initiative, 'Students Supporting Student Learning' (SSSL). Through an exploration of these peer learning support strategies and the spaces within which they operate, we suggest that a peer-learning approach may unlock

the potential affordances of physical and virtual learning spaces as environments facilitative of student learning and engagement. This approach provides a visible and practical link between learners and teachers by providing voice and agency to: student mentors, peers or near-peers who can mediate the joint processes of community building and knowledge making.

Peer Learning Pedagogy

Peer learning is defined as "students learning from and with each other in both formal and informal ways" (Boud, Cohen & Sampson, 2001, p. 4). It is influenced by constructivism, specifically, in Vygotsky's (1978) key concept of the "zone of proximal development"; that is, "the distance between the actual development as determined by individual problem solving and the level of potential development as determined through problem solving under adult guidance or in collaboration with more capable peers" (p. 86). Peer learning has at its heart the principle that students can effectively assist other students with their learning. Van der Meer and Scott (2008) argue that peer-assisted learning approaches are particularly important for first-year tertiary education and call for "shifting the balance from an instruction focus of learning support staff to facilitating or supporting peer learning" (p. 73). However, as Boud, et al. (2001, p. 3) point out, "[p]eer learning is not a single, undifferentiated educational strategy. It encompasses a broad sweep of activities." Such is the case at Victoria University, where a variety of peer learning and peer mentoring strategies have been combined within the overarching strategy of Students Supporting Student Learning (SSSL).

STUDENTS SUPPORTING STUDENT LEARNING (SSSL) AT VU

This chapter explores the dimensions of peer learning at Victoria University's School of Language and Learning in the context of various university learning spaces: a faculty-wide Peer Mentoring program, a Student Rover program in the multi-campus Learning Commons, and the virtual learning support platform SNAPVU. Each of these programs operates within different physical or virtual learning spaces, and each presents its own challenges and opportunities with respect to the affordances of peer learning in these spaces or places.

Learning Support Strategies

Victoria University is a dual sector university which has a mission to provide education to the western region of Melbourne, a region of below-average household incomes, high unemployment and a large migrant and refugee population (Sheehan & Wiseman, 2004). VU's student population reflects this region's social and economic diversity with many of the students from migrant and refugee backgrounds and/or the first in their families to attend university. In addition a majority of both domestic and international students attending the university have a language background other than English (Keating, Kent, & McLennan, 2008, pp. 299-300).

The student peer learning/mentoring strategies described in this chapter, and their relation to learning spaces, form part of the SSSL peer learning support strategy deployed by VU's School of Language and Learning in response to these challenges. The authors regard student peer learning as a key to unlocking and developing VU's culturally and linguistically diverse student population. A discussion of learning support strategies for students from diverse and disadvantaged backgrounds and how they relate to learning spaces is timely given the publication of the Bradley report in late 2008, which recommended that:

By 2020, 20 per cent of undergraduate enrolments in [Australian] higher education should be stu-

dents from low socio-economic backgrounds. All institutions in receipt of Commonwealth funds for teaching will be expected to establish initiatives to increase both the enrolment of, and success of, students from disadvantaged backgrounds (Bradley, Noonan, Nugent, & Scales, 2008, n.p.).

This shift to student retention and success has major implications for all teaching staff of universities including learning support staff.

Moving Towards Peer Learning

Contemporary universities support their students' academic and emotional development through dedicated academic support units and counselling centres. This support is complex and it is difficult to determine the most effective strategies to meet the various needs of diverse cohorts. Student cohorts may include 'first-generation', 'LOTE (language other than English)' and 'low socio-economic', etc. The challenge from a learning support perspective is that the labelling of students identifies them within a 'deficit framework', which focuses attention on their weaknesses in terms of academic writing skills or cultural capital as opposed to the potential and existing knowledge and skills they bring to the institution. Underlying this model is a "fix it" model of learning support (Huijser, Kimmins, & Galligan, 2008, p. A24).

This view of learning support is perpetuated by the dynamics of the dominant form of learning space utilised within learning support centres: the individual staff office. Students traditionally seek extra academic support in one-to-one individual consultations with learning support experts. However in this context both the learning space and the learning support knowledge are owned by the staff member working with the individual student. Despite this dynamic, which we question, such assistance can impact significantly on English language and other skills (Chanock, 2007). Consequently, individual consultations remain an essential element in the range of learn-

Figure 1. Timeline of VU learning support strategies

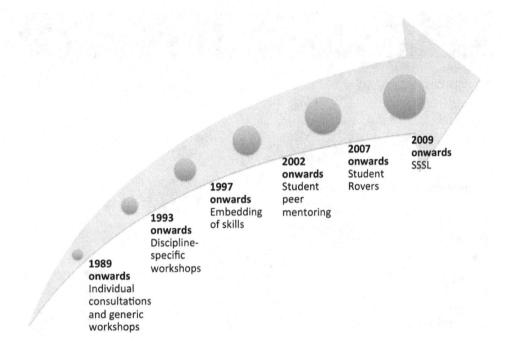

2009 onwards SSSL

2007 onwards Student Rovers

2002 onwards Student peer mentoring

1997 onwards Embedding of skills

1993 onwards Discipline-specific workshops

1989 onwards Individual consultations and generic workshops

ing support required in universities, particularly for culturally and linguistically diverse students. In addition finite resources mean that this form of academic assistance is unable to be provided to every student which lead us to investigate how learning support can be implemented with large numbers of students. Over a twenty-year period, VU's learning support staff have attempted to develop strategies designed to work synergistically with its student body to address more appropriate models of learning support. Figure 1 represents these changes in learning support provision at VU.

The emergence of student peer learning, outlined in Figure 1, reflects an increasing awareness and acceptance of Astin's (1975) work that places primary importance on involving students in the life of the university, as well as the more recent realisation that students' part-time work and other off-campus demands result in a limited on-campus presence for many students (Krause, Hartley, James, & McInnis, 2005). The increasing deployment of student peer learning is also a deliberate strategy to honour, celebrate and utilise

VU's student diversity and knowledge (McCormack, Best, & Kirkwood, 2009) by acknowledging students' existing knowledge and their ability to share this knowledge with others.

In response to these changes and challenges, VU's learning support staff in collaboration with their colleagues in the faculties and library, have set up a variety of student peer learning programs both inside and outside the classroom and within physical and virtual spaces. Staff expertise is utilised to devise student peer learning programs particularly in the areas of program design, development and evaluation as well as in supporting the students themselves in their role as peer mentors or student rovers. Staff become facilitators, while the student peer mentors control both the learning space and the learning content. In our conceptualisation of learning spaces, students are at the centre of the university community as active, authentic sources of knowledge alongside staff, reflecting Bickford and Wright's (2006, pp. 4.2-4.3) vision of a community:

281

Figure 2. VU learning support spaces

Type of Learning Support	Individual staff offices	Classrooms	Learning Commons	Subject staff offices	Mentor Space	Virtual space
Individual consultations	■					
Generic workshops		■				
Discipline-specific workshops		■				
Embedding of skills		■		■		
Student peer mentoring		■				
Rovers			■			
Students Support Students Learning (S³L)			■		■	■

A real community…exists only when its members interact in a meaningful way that deepens their understanding of each other and leads to learning. Many equate learning with the acquisition of facts and skills by students; in a community, the learners—including faculty—are enriched by collective meaning-making, mentorship, encouragement, and an understanding of the perspectives and unique qualities of an increasingly diverse membership.

Mentors in the MentorSpace

Along with this shift to student peer learning support there has been a corresponding shift in the types of learning spaces used for the provision of learning support. Figure 2 reveals the types of learning spaces occupied by each kind of learning support strategy discussed above. With the move towards peer learning support, we perceive an increasing potential for occupying a diverse range of learning spaces.

By acknowledging the power of peer learning and the construction of student peer mentoring programs we have enhanced learning by encouraging students to support students in their learning. We have also observed VU students inhabiting new and different learning spaces. Increasingly, learning spaces are being created for and by students. At the beginning of 2009, within VU's School of Language and Learning, an office previously occupied by staff was given to student mentors. Students currently use the space, referred to as the *MentorSpace*, to conduct student peer mentor preparation sessions and events as well as to house peer mentor resources. Following the news that the space was to be enlarged, staff actively requested design input from the student mentors who requested an open space unhindered by posts, poles and computers. These suggestions and alterations echo Anders, Calder, Elder and Logan's (2007, p. 43) findings regarding the impact of colour, artwork, furniture and open spaces on student learning spaces.

Entering Other Learning Spaces

As demonstrated by our experience with the *MentorSpace* outlined above, it seems that once access is either gained or granted, it is likely that students can, and will, enter into an increasing number of institutional spaces, a key one being the space of decision-making processes. Cook-Sather (2002) argues cogently for the inclusion of students in decision-making:

Because of who they are, what they know, and how they are positioned, students must be recognized as having knowledge essential to the development of sound educational policies and practices. Because of who we are, what we know, and how we are positioned, we need to authorize students' perspectives by changing the participant structures as well as the participants in policymaking and practice-shaping conversations about education (p. 12).

In a recent student peer mentoring development at VU, it was recommended that Senior Mentors be granted membership of the newly created Student Peer Mentoring Governance Committee. The ease with which this proposal was accepted may arguably signal an important shift towards growing acceptance of student involvement in policy-making decisions, and opens up another space for students to enter and actively participate within. This may prove to provide another learning space that offers legitimacy to student voices and experiences and, in this case, might allow staff and students the opportunity of convening in the same space for the same purpose: to improve student learning. Allowing students to negotiate and find voice within the policy-making space of the university may form an important sphere of student-centred engagement and one that can potentially influence, as Bruffee (1993, p. 96) maintains, "university governance, from department curriculum to long-range institutional planning." In the next section, issues surrounding students supporting student learning in the Learning Commons, VU's student rovers, will be explored.

Placing Student Rovers in the Learning Commons

Corresponding to the "move in higher education away from a teaching culture and toward a culture of learning" (Bennett, 2005, p. 10), there has been a progressive shift in emphasis from traditional teaching spaces toward learning spaces, as well as a reframing of academic libraries initially as "information commons" and later as "learning commons". Despite the complexities involved in measuring the impact of learning spaces on learning outcomes (Hunley & Schaller, 2006, p. 13-15), research has found that learning is strongly supported by student engagement in an academic community (Bennett, 2005; Bensimon, 2007; Hunley & Schaller, 2006, 2009). It follows that the focus of learning space design and development should be the fostering of engagement and the nurturing of communities of learning. This is an implication of the term learning *commons*.

A commons, as defined by Benkler (2003, p. 6), constitutes "a particular type of institutional arrangement for governing the use and disposition of resources [within which] no single person has exclusive control over the use and disposition of any particular resource". In the context of the learning space, this implies that the resources and affordances are made equally available for use by all members of the learning community. In addition, the extent to which a learning commons can be said to exist is determined by the communities of learners sharing those resources and affordances. Learning commons, then, refers to a shared *place* - the commons - made available for shared *practices* oriented towards the shared *purpose* of learning. Pang (2009, p. 91) also sees an active and recursive relationship between the concept of the commons and the activities it facilitates, similar to the reciprocal relation between space and place described above. In this sense the concept of a learning commons anticipates the shared agency, participation and purpose of those who inhabit it.

In this context, the transformation of VU's Information Commons into Learning Commons may be conceptualised as constituting a new kind of learning space; a space that does not simply provide technologies, information, services and resources for student learning, but more importantly provides a shared and participatory learning *place* where student learning and engagement is actively supported and enhanced. There were two primary elements to this more intervention-ist approach: firstly, architectural features were redesigned to be more attractive and cater more holistically to a wider range of student activities, including silent study, noisy collaborative teams, relaxed coffee drinking, solitary reading and web surfing; and secondly, learning support services were introduced into the Learning Commons space. These learning support services in turn consisted of two components: traditional learn-ing support services provided by staff, as well as a new student rover program in which students supported the learning of other students as part of VU's SSSL strategy as outlined above. The role of the student rovers was specified as:

- Assisting with basic student queries related to using and locating core facilities, infor-mation resources, software and hardware;
- Helping students to clarify and articulate basic issues related to their learning strate-gies, and
- Directing and referring students to fur-ther information or assistance, includ-ing IT, Library or Learning Support staff within the Learning Commons, as well as other services beyond the confines of the Learning Commons such as Faculty Advisors or Student Counsellors.

The Rovers' Role

Rovers have characteristics of both staff and stu-dents and are located ambiguously between the roles of staff and student. Rovers are liminal and do not fit seamlessly into existing institutional identities and roles within the learning commons. This indeterminacy allows others to project their own competing assumptions and understandings onto the rovers, assumptions that are perhaps re-vealed most dramatically around the issue of the spatial placement of rovers. Designing spaces and assigning places within spaces is not neutral, and decisions around space and place form the terrain on which complex issues of institutional status, relationships, power and authority are negotiated. Four scenarios might be posited for framing the socio-institutional identity and status of rovers. Each scenario suggests a different spatial place-ment of rovers within the Learning Commons:

1. 'Students-as-staff' rovers adds a new tier within the existing service model;
2. Student mentor rovers focus on assisting other students with generic academic skills;
3. Another newly emergent role focuses on rovers who support the learning of other students, and
4. Another hybrid role for rovers involves moving back and forth between the lived world of students and the abstract realities of the academic institution.

These different perspectives intersect with the concrete physical spatiality of the three Learning Commons at Victoria University. After three years of operation and trialling a range of placements, what has become clear is that there is no gener-ally shared consensus on how to physically *place* rovers in the learning space across the three com-mons. The spatial particularities of each Learning Commons as an architectural space impacts on both the range of possible placements for rovers and on the socio-institutional meanings assigned to the rovers through these placements. There is continuing debate about whether rovers should have a fixed place within the space or whether they should be mobile moving throughout the space to interact with students. The fact that this issue of a settled, visible place versus nomadic roving has arisen repeatedly at all three Learning Commons suggests that the nature of space is an influencing factor.

Different Places for Different Spaces

The following discussion explores these issues in terms of the specificities of VU's three current Learning Commons, together with some representative tensions and anecdotes. *Learning Commons A* accommodates around 160 students and no identifiable place was architecturally designated or marked for rovers in this space. Rovers were welcomed as adding a dimension that alleviated pressure off library service staff coping with enquiries from students. Rovers eventually determined that they would like to establish their own 'place', a 'rover station'. Rovers in this team insisted that an identifiable place gave them a higher profile and established their identity within the learning space, arguing that students would now know where to go for assistance. Currently rovers within this Learning Commons are operating across an eclectic range of placement styles including the designated rover station, while others move around the space and others are invited to work at the library service desk.

In clear contrast *Learning Commons B* is a large open space that has been redesigned to provide more computer seats, tables for collaborative work, and lounge areas for student socialising. The library service desk was made less intrusive and a rover station was established closer to the student computer seating area. However as with all furniture in learning spaces it is important to carefully consider its purpose and flexibility in relation to the proposed function. In this case the dimensions of the rover station created an intimi-

dating boundary between rovers and students. This has made it harder for rovers to develop friendly relations with both staff and students but on the other hand it established a strongly defined place and identity for rovers, distinct from the service desk

Learning Commons C is located on a small campus and consists of a small redesigned space catering for around 40 students. It comprises three consulting rooms for IT, learning and career support services, plus a room of computer desks for students to access language and learning support staff. Rovers were given no designated place or station, nor were they invited to be part of the existing service delivery team, as occurred in *Learning Commons A*. Due to the size of the space it was difficult to determine whether the rover should move around the space or remain seated at the rover station. Perhaps an enlargement of space and increased student numbers will enable the rovers to move around the space, whilst also allowing for the establishment of a designated rover station separate from the library service desk. One rover describes her experience within the learning commons in acting as a 'broker'.

It isn't really a table for science students, but I am a very pro-active student which means that I get to know a lot of students. I guess because I talk to anyone, they bring their friends over and from there, the circle widens. I place a great emphasis in my role as a rover on getting to know other students and trying to help them feel welcome. It is funny how my science table can quickly turn into a business or TAFE table depending on the movement of people in and out of lectures. Usually if I head into the library directly after lab/lecture, there are many science students who 'tag' along and so a table is formed. It is usually a bunch of students who are planning on working, and so I find that if I am also rostered on, I will leave my stuff at that table and just keep 'roving' around. Many other students from other courses that I know will also come and join us on the table.

Figure 3. The Evolution of Virtual Learning Spaces

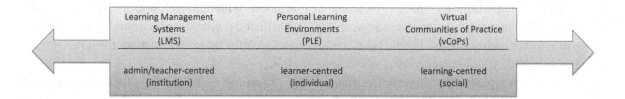

SNAPVU: VU Virtual Learning Community

We have explored the role of peer mentors and rovers at VU in physical learning spaces and the Learning Commons, and discussed some of the challenges arising through the negotiation of space within the institutional setting. The concept of communities of practice developed by Etienne Wenger (Wenger, 1998b) suggests that members of a community of practice are involved in negotiating meaning through the *reification* of knowledge—the production of "abstractions, tools, symbols, stories, terms, and concepts" related to the practice (p. 59) and, *participation* in defining, shaping, and organising the community itself. A community is bound together by three dimensions: joint enterprise, mutual engagement, and shared repertoire (p. 73).

The Evolution of Virtual Learning Spaces

Online learning environments have evolved from Learning Management Systems (LMS) such as Blackboard, Sakai and Moodle, through Personal Learning Environments (PLE), Networks (PLN) or Ecosystems (PLE) (Bogdanov, Salzmann, Helou, & Gillet, 2008; Chatti, Jarke, & Frosch-Wilke, 2007) and finally to the virtual Community of Practice (vCoP). This evolution of online learning platforms seems to reveal a shift from teacher- to

learner- and finally to learning-centred pedagogy, as represented in Figure 3.

The third kind of e-learning platform, the vCoP, represents a shift from a learner to a learning focus, centrally situating the social or cooperative nature of learning and necessitating a pedagogical shift of focus and intent. As Stefanou and Salisbury-Glennon (2002, p. 78) maintain: "Unlike a more traditional approach to instruction, learning communities foster the social construction of knowledge, cooperative learning, active learning, an emphasis on integration and synthesis of diverse student perspectives, as well as student-student, student-staff, and staff-staff collaboration." The vCoP aims to facilitate these elements in both its design and implementation; its purpose is to make visible the knowledge-making activities of the community, to collect and organise the tacit knowledge of its members, and to encourage their ongoing participation. In our conceptualisation, virtual learning spaces constitute community places where both teachers and learners can be involved in a shared practice; it provides a platform for the development of virtual learning communities of practice.

Enabling Virtual Learning Communities of Practice

The social and community-building affordances of Web 2.0 technologies, or *social software*, are well documented and appreciated (Akoumianakis, 2009; Chatti, et al., 2007). Since their develop-

Table 1. Social software tools for a virtual learning CoP

Tool	Knowledge-building features	Community-building features
Discussion forums	Informal sharing (Kreijns, Kirschner, & Jochems, 2003); negotiation; Q&A; peer production	Direct contact with other users; participation is visible
Blogs	Instructors and mentors share expertise and model knowledge making process; reflective practice (Ladyshewsky & Gardner, 2008)	Students can witness and learn from the participation of instructors and near-peers (Ackerman, Pipek, & Wulf, 2003)
Wikis	Collaborative resource creation	Students participate in collaborative exchange and learn the benefits of social capital, trust (Augar, Raitman, Lanham, & Zhou, 2006)
Podcasts and vodcasts	Peer-production of resource development; development of media literacies (Huijser, 2006; Lee, McLoughlin, & Chan, 2008)	Adds affective elements of aural and visual immediacy and personalising
Social bookmarking	Sharing of discovered web or research-based resources (Carbonaro, 2006)	Cooperative sharing of intellectual capital for the public good (van den Hooff, Elving, Meeuwsen, & Dumoulin, 2003)
Social networking profiles (including thumbnail avatars)	Enables students to find others with similar tasks, research interests; enables 1:1 communication across network	Makes visible the active users of the community and their activity/contributions
Tagging: controlled vocabularies and folksonomies	Collective and personal management of information and resources	Negotiation and articulation of subject headings and lists of community resources (Limpens, Gandon, & Buffa, 2008; Lux & Dosinger, 2007)
RSS feeds and application widgets	Allows the student to pull together useful resources from across the platform	User agency in manipulating and sharing elements of the vCoP (Wilson, Sharples, & Griffiths, 2008)
Commentary (on blogposts, forum posts, vodcasts, other resources)	Students can contribute to and improve a resource by adding personal amendments and observations	The hub of communicative exchange: develops community cohesion, vitality and personality
Rating, polling, recommendations, feedback systems	Community mediation of quality assurance and appropriateness of resources	Allows for visibility of group consensus and empowerment

ment, the face of the Web has been altered significantly, with users allowed the opportunity to contribute to content creation, community building and networking. Web 2.0 tools and functionalities appear to have developed out of a desire to make the Web more communal and participatory and more socially meaningful. The application of these affordances to virtual learning spaces fosters what Pang (2009) calls "participatory design". This move toward participatory design of virtual learning spaces may represent a move to challenge LMS and transmission models of teaching.

However, as Wesch (2009, n.p.) observes, "the current information revolution", aided by Web 2.0 services, "is a social revolution, not a technological one, and its most revolutionary aspect may be the ways in which it empowers us to rethink education and the teacher-student relationship in an almost limitless variety of ways". In developing virtual learning communities of practice the instructor takes on new and fluid roles, as "knowledge broker, knowledge co-creator, mentor, coordinator and facilitator of the learning experience" (Chatti, et al., 2007, p. 412). Virtual learning spaces then become places for knowledge construction and management and social software tools should enable the management of social knowledge making that forms the basis of virtual learning communities of practice. Table 1 identifies some of these tools and summarises their knowledge- and community-building features as we perceive them:

The interactions within these spaces may be informal and may focus on process-oriented learning, consisting of the learning of meta-skills we perceive as essential in the development of a learner: the ability to negotiate meaning, to critically assess resources for personal and overall value, to develop a meaningful taxonomic structure, to participate in the development of a collective practice, to work cooperatively and develop personal and social confidence and competence. These are potentially transformative skills, and emphasise graduate attributes that students may need in their professional lives.

The SNAPVU Platform @ VU and the Role of Peer Production

The School of Language and Learning has developed a virtual learning platform for students at Victoria University based on some of the principles described above. This platform is called SNAPVU, or *Social Networking for Academic Purposes at VU* (http://snap.vu.edu.au). SNAPVU uses a wide array of the social software listed above to encourage the development of virtual learning communities of practice with a particular focus on learning support (Kirkwood, 2009). The platform has been built with the open source content management system (CMS) Drupal, because of Drupal's flexibility and extensibility. SNAPVU is intended to be a departure from traditional learning support websites in that it infuses principles of peer learning, like the VU Peer Mentoring and Student Rover programs. The approach seeks to employ both the explicit and tacit knowledge of VU's student population to reveal current practice through a system of student forums, commentary, ratings, polling, and other feedback mechanisms. The core static resources on the site are created by the professional university community, while most of the resources are dynamic content generated by the students themselves.

Within this space, staff act as knowledge managers and modellers, and participants of knowledge making. As Wenger (1998a, n.p.) maintains, "knowledge managers must go beyond creating informational repositories that take knowledge to be a 'thing,' toward supporting the whole social and technical ecology in which knowledge is retained and created". Staff are also involved in forum contributions, developing a group blog and a social bookmarking resource, to share informal ideas and point to resource-rich material on the Web. The social presence of 'experts' is an acknowledged asset in building a CoP, and students have been found to appreciate the timely contributions of teaching staff (Palloff & Pratt, 2007).

The near-peers of peer mentors and student rovers play a critical role in the SNAPVU social learning environment. Like staff, they act as content contributors and administrators of the platform, developing group blogs, adding to the social bookmarks, and creating resources in the form of short vodcasts. In the last few years, free simple-to-use video screen-capture services have appeared on the Web as well as ubiquitous video capture in mobile phones and digital cameras, making the creation of short learning support videos a viable medium of knowledge sharing. With free, sharable Web-based hosting on services such as YouTube and iTunes U, the storage and dissemination of this resource has become intuitive. Teams of mentors/rovers have worked to develop hundreds of these vodcasts, which are now hosted on SNAPVU as shareable, rateable, and comment-able resources.

As part of VU's SSSL strategy outlined at the beginning of this chapter, the student mentors and rovers play an active and central role in the forming and facilitation of the SNAPVU virtual learning community, and in generating and encouraging the participation of their peers. Kaulback and Bergtholdt (2008, p. 29) describe this type of role as community stewardship: "The goal of stewardship of a vCoP is to engage members and to create and hold a space where they can interact, learn, and create the next iteration of their practice ... The stewards do the work of analysing, facilitating, coordinating, and developing an inventory while enabling the birthing of knowledge."

Unlike an online teaching subject, the intention of the SNAPVU social learning environment is to create a virtual learning community of practice. It is a place where students can go for academic and social engagement that is removed from the institutional pressures of official tasks, timelines and assessment regimes. It is envisaged as a dedicated virtual learning commons/community, in which the learning is more informal than formal, more about process than product, and more about learning meta-skills than memorizing content. SNAPVU has been designed and developed as a virtual learning place. In such a platform,

[t]he focus shifts from organizing content or subject matter, to designing opportunities for varying levels of participation in practice. Questions for educational designers shift from "what knowledge, skills, or attitudes do learners need to acquire?" and "how should this content be organized to facilitate acquisition?" to "what are the attributes of particular practice communities?" and "how can I create spaces for learners to engage in practices, to create identities, develop relationships, and make new meanings in the context of these practice communities?" (Hayes, 2009, n.p.)

This pedagogical shift posits students as at the wheel and hub of the learning process, and at the centre of virtual learning spaces. At the heart of this 'electronic pedagogy' (Palloff & Pratt, 2007), both students and teachers may be required to renegotiate their roles and participate as equal members of the academic commons. These potential forms of participatory learning and community building may prove to be transformational. Motschnig-Pitrik (2008, p. 4) describes what she calls "significant learning communities" as those that develop around human resource and knowledge development, and are a self-organised, interdependent "way of becoming" leading to a "way of becoming knowledgeable".

Solutions and Recommendations

It has been our suggestion that the successful design, development and use of learning spaces may necessitate a significant shift in emphasis toward consideration of not only physical and technological aspects, but also the social and community affordances offered by these spaces, whether physical or virtual. With this in mind, we have suggested the placement of peer mentors and student rovers within learning spaces—as well as the additional reconceptualisation of learning spaces as learning places—as a possible strategy for instituting this reemphasis. The shift we are proposing arises within a pedagogical perspective that places (and keeps) learners at the centre, as agents of learning rather than recipients of teaching. From this perspective, the design of the learning environment and experience can and should accommodate the social dimensions of learning. The role of peer mentoring and peer learning in the learning space and commons has been proposed as a means of operationalising the social aspects of learning within such spaces.

Mentors provide a bridge between novice and expert knowledge, and facilitate knowledge-making and management within learning communities. We have explored the community of practice model as a potential way of thinking about the relationships and involvements between learners; in particular, as giving us a model for the facilitative role of learning support staff, the participatory role of students, and the mediatory role of student mentors. In learning communities, mentors provide a focus and impetus for student engagement through their own active participation and the informal sharing and modeling of reflective learning practice, thereby transforming these learning spaces into inhabited learning places.

FUTURE RESEARCH DIRECTIONS

We have suggested that careful consideration is warranted with respect to existing social and institutional structures and relationships when peer mentors are introduced into physical and virtual learning spaces. Placing learning at the centre of these spaces means that learners will need support and accommodation from the institution to be(come) effective agents of learning. This may also mean allowing them to be agents of self-directed action and change, and may include the recognition and validation of new, as yet undefined, learning practices initiated by the mentors and students themselves.

Our experience at Victoria University with peer mentor and student rover programs suggests a need to further explore these dynamics of 'placing' peer learning into learning spaces. Different physical placements suggest subtle shifts of knowledge authority and power brokerage that may help or hinder learning. As learning institutions experiment with enabling student-centred spaces, it will be important to monitor and assess these shifts and address counterproductive influences as they are discovered. It may also be worth considering the impact and compatibility of institutional hierarchies and information silos upon learning spaces, and how universities might be redesigned to better align with the fundamental objective of developing and facilitating learning communities.

Virtual learning communities of practice, as holistic social learning environments, are still in their formative stages. While over the last number of years a great deal has been learned about the affective requirements of online learning communities (Palloff & Pratt, 2007), there is still much to discover about the knowledge-making affordances of social software and Web 2.0 technologies. It will be of interest, particularly with regard to student motivation and participation, to further research the community-building potential of mentors and peer learning in the online environment.

CONCLUSION

This chapter has constituted a preliminary discussion of the possible impacts of placing peer-learning programs within a variety of learning spaces, both physical and virtual. In particular, it has considered the potential of peer learning for enabling these learning spaces to become learning places; peopled, positioned and purposeful. Our experience at Victoria University with peer mentor and student rover programs has suggested that more attention needs to be directed to the dynamics of 'placing' peer mentors into learning spaces. Subtle differences in physical or abstract placement can project subtle differences of perception. As learning institutions implement the challenging shift from teacher- to learning-centred pedagogies, it will be important to attend closely to these differences and their effects.

REFERENCES

Ackerman, M., Pipek, V., & Wulf, V. (Eds.). (2003). *Sharing expertise: Beyond knowledge management*. Cambridge, UK: The MIT Press.

Akoumlanakls, D. (Ed.). (2009). *Virtual community practices and social interactive media: Technology lifecycle and workflow analysis*. Hershey, PA: Information Science Reference. doi:10.4018/978-1-60566-340-1

Anders, D., Calder, A., Elder, K., & Logan, A. (2007, July). *Investigating the dynamics of an integrated learning space at James Cook University*. Paper presented at the Next Generation Learning Spaces Colloquium, University of Queensland, QLD.

Astin, A. W. (1975). *Preventing students from dropping out*. San Francisco, CA: Jossey-Bass.

Augar, N., Raitman, R., Lanham, E., & Zhou, W. (2006). Building virtual learning communities. In Ma, Z. (Ed.), *Web-based intelligent e-learning systems: Technologies and applications* (pp. 72–100). Hershey, PA: Information Science Publishing.

Benkler, Y. (2003). The political economy of commons. *UPGRADE: European Journal for the Informatics Professional, 4*(3), 6-9. Retrieved June 22, 2010, from http://www.upgrade-cepis. org/index.html

Bennett, S. (2005). Righting the balance. In *Library as place: Rethinking roles, rethinking space* (pp. 10–24). Washington, DC: Council on Library and Information Resources.

Bensimon, E. M. (2007). The underestimated significance of practitioner knowledge in the scholarship on student success. *Review of Higher Education, 30*(4), 441–469.

Bickford, D. J., & Wright, D. J. (2006). Community: The hidden context for learning. In Oblinger, D. G. (Ed.), *Learning spaces* (pp. 4.1–4.22). EDUCAUSE.

Bogdanov, E., Salzmann, C., Helou, S. E., & Gillet, D. (2008). *Social software modeling and mashup based on actors, activities and assets.* Paper presented at the First International Workshop on Mashup Personal Learning Environments (MUPPLE08), Maastricht, The Netherlands.

Boud, D. J., Cohen, R., & Sampson, J. (2001). *Peer learning in higher education: Learning from & with each other.* London, UK: Kogan Page.

Bradley, D., Noonan, P., Nugent, H., & Scales, B. (2008). *Review of Australian higher education - final report.* Australian Government, Department of Education, Employment and Workplace Relations. Retrieved February 11, 2009, from http://www.deewr.gov.au/ HigherEducation/Review/Pages/default.aspx

Bruffee, K. A. (1993). *Collaborative learning: Higher education, interdependence, and the authority of knowledge.* Baltimore, MD: The John Hopkins University Press.

Carbonaro, A. (2006). Defining personalized learning views of relevant learning objects in a collaborative bookmark management system. In Ma, Z. (Ed.), *Web-based intelligent e-learning systems: Technologies and applications* (pp. 139–155). Hershey, PA: Information Science Publishing.

Chanock, K. (2007). Valuing individual consultations as input into other modes of teaching. *Journal of Academic Language & Learning, 1*(1), A1-A9. Retrieved June 22, 2010, from http://journal.aall. org.au/ index.php/jall/issue/view/2

Chatti, M. A., Jarke, M., & Frosch-Wilke, D. (2007). The future of e-learning: A shift to knowledge networking and social software. *International Journal of Knowledge and Learning, 3*(4-5), 404–420. doi:10.1504/IJKL.2007.016702

Cook-Sather, A. (2002). Authorizing students' perspectives: Toward trust, dialogue, and change in education. *Educational Researcher, 31*(4), 3–14. doi:10.3102/0013189X031004003

Harrison, S., & Dourish, P. (1996, February). *Re-place-ing space: The roles of place and space in collaborative systems.* Paper presented at the ACM Conference on Computer Supported Cooperative Work (CSCW), Boston, MA.

Hayes, E. (2009). *Becoming a (virtual) skateboarder: Communities of practice and the design of e-learning.* Retrieved September 9, 2009, from http://www.academiccolab.org/ resources/ documents/Becoming %20a%20_Virtual_%20 Skateboarder.pdf

Huijser, H. (2006). Refocusing multiliteracies for the net generation. *International Journal of Pedagogies and Learning, 2*(1), 22–34.

Huijser, H., Kimmins, L., & Galligan, L. (2008). Evaluating individual teaching on the road to embedding academic skills. *Journal of Academic Language & Learning, 2*(1), A23-A38. Retrieved June 22, 2010, from http://journal.aall.org.au/index.php/jall/issue/view/5

Hunley, S., & Schaller, M. (2006). Assessing learning spaces. In Oblinger, D. G. (Ed.), *Learning spaces* (pp. 13.1–13.11). EDUCAUSE.

Hunley, S., & Schaller, M. (2009). Assessment: The key to creating spaces that promote learning. *EDUCAUSE Review, 44*(2), 26-35. Retrieved June 22, 2010, from http://www.educause.edu/ EDUCAUSE+Review/ EDUCAUSEReviewMagazine Volume44/AssessmentTheKeyto CreatingSpac/163797

Ingold, T. (1992). Culture and the perception of the environment. In Croll, E., & Parkin, D. (Eds.), *Bush base: Forest farm - culture, environment and development* (pp. 39–56). London, UK & New York, NY: Routledge.

Kaulback, B., & Bergtholdt, D. (2008). Holding the virtual space: The roles and responsibilities of community stewardship. In Kimble, C., Hildreth, P., & Bourdon, I. (Eds.), *Communities of practice: Creating learning environments for educators* (pp. 25–43). Charlotte, NC: Information Age Publishing, Inc.

Keating, S., Kent, P. G., & McLennan, B. (2008). Putting learners at the centre: The learning commons journey at Victoria University. In Schader, B. (Ed.), *Learning commons: Evolution and collaborative essentials* (pp. 297–323). Oxford, UK: Chandos Publishing.

Kirkwood, K. (2009). *The SNAP! platform: Social networking for academic purposes, peer learning, and communities of practice*. Paper presented at the ICICTE Conference 2009, Corfu, Greece.

Krause, K., Hartley, R., James, R., & McInnis, C. (2005). *The first year experience in Australian universities: Findings from a decade of national studies*. Retrieved 2009, from http://www.dest.gov.au/sectors/ higher_education/policy_issues_reviews/key_issues/assuring_quality_in_higher_education/ first_year_experience_aust_uni.htm

Kreijns, K., Kirschner, P. A., & Jochems, W. (2003). Identifying the pitfalls for social interaction in computer-supported collaborative learning environments: A review of the research. *Computers in Human Behavior, 19*(3), 335–353. doi:10.1016/S0747-5632(02)00057-2

Ladyshewsky, R. K., & Gardner, P. (2008). Peer assisted learning and blogging: A strategy to promote reflective practice during clinical fieldwork. *Australasian Journal of Educational Technology, 24*(3), 241–257.

Lee, M. J. W., McLoughlin, C., & Chan, A. (2008). Talk the talk: Learner-generated podcasts as catalysts for knowledge creation. *British Journal of Educational Technology, 39*(3), 501–521. doi:10.1111/j.1467-8535.2007.00746.x

Limpens, F., Gandon, F., & Buffa, M. (2008, September). *Bridging ontologies and folksonomies to leverage knowledge sharing on the social Web: A brief survey*. Paper presented at the First International Workshop on Social Software Engineering and Applications, L'Aquila, Italy.

Lux, M., & Dosinger, G. (2007). From folksonomies to ontologies: Employing wisdom of the crowds to serve learning purposes. *International Journal of Knowledge and Learning, 3*(4-5), 515–528. doi:10.1504/IJKL.2007.016709

McCormack, R., Best, G., & Kirkwood, K. (2009). *Students supporting student learning*. Melbourne, VIC: Victoria University.

Motschnig-Pitrik, R. (2008). Significant learning communities - a humanistic approach to knowledge and human resource development in the age of the Internet. In Lytras, M. D., Carroll, J. M., Damiani, E., Tennyson, R. D., Avison, D., Vossen, G., & Ordonez de Pablos, P. (Eds.), *The open knowledge society: A computer science and information systems manifesto* (pp. 1–10). Berlin, Germany: Springer-Verlag. doi:10.1007/978-3-540-87783-7_1

Palloff, R., & Pratt, K. (2007). *Building online learning communities: Effective strategies for the virtual classroom* (2nd ed.). San Francisco, CA: Jossy-Bass.

Pang, N. (2009). The role of participatory design in constructing the virtual knowledge commons. In Akoumianakis, D. (Ed.), *Virtual community practices and social interactive media: Technology lifecycle and workflow analysis* (pp. 86–100). Hershey, PA: IGI Global. doi:10.4018/978-1-60566-340-1.ch005

Sheehan, P., & Wiseman, J. (2004). *Investing in Melbourne's West: A region in transition*. Retrieved June 22, 2010, from http://www.cfses.com/documents/Investing_in_Melbournes_West.pdf

Stefanou, C., & Salisbury-Glennon, J. (2002). Developing motivation and cognitive learning strategies through an undergraduate learning community. *Learning Environments Research, 5*(1), 77–97. doi:10.1023/A:1015610606945

van den Hooff, B., Elving, W., Meeuwsen, J. M., & Dumoulin, C. (2003). Knowledge sharing in knowledge communities. In M. Huysman, E. Wenger & V. Wulf (Eds.), *Community and Technologies: Proceedings of the First International Conference on Communities and Technologies; C&T 2003* (pp. 119-141). Dordrecht, The Netherlands: Kluwer Academic Publishers.

van der Meer, J., & Scott, C. (2008). Shifting the balance in first-year learning support: From staff instruction to peer-learning primacy. *Australasian Journal of Peer Learning, 1*(1). Retrieved June 22, 2010 from http://ro.uow.edu.au/ ajpl/vol1/iss1/9

Vygotsky, L. S. (1978). *Mind in society: The development of higher psychological processes*. Cambridge, MA: Harvard University Press.

Wenger, E. (1998a). Communities of practice: Learning as a social system. *Systems Thinker, 9*(5). Retrieved June 22, 2010, from http://www.co-i-l.com/coil/ knowledge-garden/cop/lss.shtml

Wenger, E. (1998b). *Communities of practice: Learning, meaning, and identity*. Cambridge, UK: Cambridge University Press.

Wesch, M. (2009, January 7). From knowledgable to knowledge-able: Learning in new media environments. Retrieved from http://www.academic-commons.org/ commons/essay/ knowledgable-knowledge-able

Wilson, S., Sharples, P., & Griffiths, D. (2008, September). *Distributing education services to personal and institutional systems using widgets*. Paper presented at the First International Workshop on Mashup Personal Learning Environments (MUPPLE08), Maastricht, The Netherlands.

ADDITIONAL READING

Allen, C. (2004, October 13). Tracing the evolution of social software [Web log post]. Archived at http://www.lifewithalacrity.com/ 2004/10/ tracing_the_evo.html

Darling, L. W. (1986). The mentoring mosaic: A new theory of mentoring. In Gray, W. A., & Gray, M. M. (Eds.), *Mentoring: Aid to excellence in career development, business, and the professions* (*Vol. 2*, pp. 1–7). Vancouver, BC: International Association for Mentoring.

Foreman, J. (2004). Game-based learning: How to delight and instruct in the 21st Century. *EDUCAUSE Review, 39*(5), 50–66. Retrieved from http://www.educause.edu/EDUCAUSE+Review/EDUCAUSEReviewMagazine Volume39/Game-BasedLearning HowtoDelighta/157927.

Jamieson, P., Taylor, P. G., Fisher, K., Trevitt, T., & Gilding, T. (2000). Place and space in the design of new learning environments. *Higher Education Research & Development, 19*(2), 221–237. doi:10.1080/072943600445664

Tuomi-Grohn, T., Engestrom, Y., & Young, M. (2003). From transfer to boundary-crossing between school and work as a tool for developing vocational education: An introduction. In Tuomi-Grohn, T., & Engestrom, Y. (Eds.), *Between school and work: new perspectives on transfer and boundary-crossing* (pp. 1–15). Amsterdam, The Netherlands: Pergamon.

Weinberger, D. (2007). *Everything is miscellaneous: The power of the new digital disorder.* New York, NY: Henry Holt and Company.

Wenger, E., McDermott, R., & Snyder, W. M. (2002). *Cultivating communities of practice.* Boston, MA: Harvard Business School Press.

Wenger, E., White, N., & Smith, J. D. (2009). *Digital habitats: Stewarding technology for communities.* Portland, OR: CPSquare.

KEY TERMS AND DEFINITIONS

Community of Practice: A community of practice (CoP) is an informal, fluid community of people engaged in a common practice. A CoP is not an institutionally-dictated entity nor a group working towards a single goal (like a team); rather, membership is voluntary and self-selecting. The community gathers around the development of a repertoire of knowledge, mutual enterprise and participation.

Peer Mentor: A peer student engaged in helping other students learn in both formal and informal ways. At Victoria University, peer mentors are engaged in subject-based programs administered jointly by faculties and the School of Language and Learning, in which they facilitate study and review sessions for self-selecting students.

Social Software: Software and online tools that support social interaction and the development of an online community (Allen, 2004). Web 2.0, or the 'read/write web', carries this connotation as well, though the term *social software* may be considered the broader term.

Student Rover: At Victoria University, student rovers are peer-learning students who operate as learning support agents in the Learning Commons.

Compilation of References

Abdulwahed, M., Nagy, Z. K., & Blanchard, R. (2008). The TriLab, a novel view of laboratory education. In *Proceedings EE2008 Conference: Innovation, Good Practice and Research in Engineering Education* (pp.51). Loughborough, UK: Engineering Subject Centre. Retrieved April 7, 2011, from http://www.engsc.ac.uk/downloads/scholarart/ ee2008/p051-abdulwahed.pdf

Ablin, J. L. (2008). Learning as problem design versus problem solving: Making the connection between cognitive neuroscience research and educational practice. *Mind, Brain, and Education, 2*(2), 52–54. doi:10.1111/j.1751-228X.2008.00030.x

Aldrich, C. (2009a). *The complete guide to serious games and simulations.* Somerset, NJ: Wiley.

Aldrich, C. (2009b). Virtual worlds, simulations, and games for education: A unifying view. *Journal of Online Education, 5*(5). Retrieved April 7, 2011, from http://www.innovateonline.info /pdf/vol5_issue5/Virtual_Worlds ,_Simulations,_and_Games_for_Education-__A_Unifying_View.pdf

Alexander, S. (1999). An evaluation of innovative projects involving communication and information technology in higher education. *Higher Education Research & Development, 18*(2), 173. doi:10.1080/0729436990180202

Alexander, B. (2008). Social networking in higher education. In Katz, R. N. (Ed.), *The tower and the cloud: Higher education in the age of cloud computing* (pp. 197–201). Boulder, CO: Educause.

Allan, C., Kent, K., & Klomp, N. (2004). Walking the talk in environmental management. In *University Regional and Rural Engagement. Conference Proceedings 2004.* Sydney, Australia: Australian Universities Community Engagement Alliance.

Allen, R., Bowen, J. T., Clabough, S., DeWitt, B., Francis, J., Kerstetter, J., & Rieck, D. (1996). *Classroom design manual* (3rd ed.). College Park, MD: Academic Information Technology Services, The University of Maryland.

Allen, M. (1998). Has the discourse of teaching/learning killed the radical and the spontaneous in university education? In B. Black, & N. Stanley, (Eds.), *Teaching and learning in changing times. Proceedings of the 7th Annual Teaching Learning Forum* (pp. 12-16). Perth, Australia: The University of Western Australia.

Aller, B. M., Kline, A. A., Tsang, E., Aravamuthan, R., Rasmusson, A. C., & Phillips, C. (2005). WeBAL: A Web-based assessment library to enhance teaching and learning in engineering. *IEEE Transactions on Education, 48*(4), 764–771. doi:10.1109/TE.2005.858390

Alloway, N., & Dalley-Trim, L. (2009). It's all about I: Gen Ys and neoliberal discourse in new times. *Youth Studies Australia, 28*(1), 51-56. Retrieved September 28, 2009, from http://www.acys.info/journal/ issues/ v28-n1-2009/ articles/ pp51-56

Alm, A. (2009). Blogs as protected spaces for language learners. In *Same places, different spaces. Proceedings ASCILITE Auckland 2009* (pp. 20-24). Retrieved February 23, 2010, from http://www.ascilite.org.au/ conferences/ auckland09/ procs/ alm.pdf

AMA (Alexi Marmot Associates). (2006). *Spaces for learning. A review of learning spaces in further and higher education.* Edinburgh, UK: Scottish Funding Council.

AMI. (Academic Management Information Section, Office of Registry Services). (2008). *A projection of the number of classrooms required for the 334 curriculum.* Hong Kong: The Chinese University of Hong Kong.

Anderson, T. (2005). Design-based research and its application to a call center innovation in distance education. *Canadian Journal of Learning and Technology, 31*(2). Retrieved March 6, 2010, from http://www.cjlt.ca/index.php/cjlt/article/view/143/136

Andrew, N., McGuiness, C., Reid, G., & Corcoran, T. (2009). Greater than the sum of its parts: Transition into the first year of undergraduate nursing. *Nurse Education in Practice, 9*(1), 13–21. doi:10.1016/j.nepr.2008.03.009

Ashling, J. (2007). Transforming research communication. *Information Today, 24*(5), 29–30.

Association of Language Testers in Europe. (2005). *EAQUALS-ALTE Portfolio Project*. Retrieved Novemver 13, 2009, from http://www.eelp.org/eportfolio/index.html

Attwell, G. (2007). The personal learning environment: The future of elearning? *Elearning papers, 2*(1), 1-7.

Attwell, G. (2007). The personal learning environments - the future of e-learning? *eLearning Papers, 2*(1). Retrieved February 22, 2010, from http://www.elearningeuropa.info/out/ ?doc_id=9758& rsr_id=11561

Australian Bureau of Statistics. (2008). *Experimental estimates of Aboriginal and Torres Strait Islander Australians, June 2006* (No. 3238.0.55.001). Canberra, Australian Capital Territory: ABS, Canberra. Retrieved October 28, 2009, from http://www.abs.gov.au/ausstats/abs@.nsf/Latestproducts /3238 0 55.001Main%20Features 1Jun%20 2006?opendocument &tabname=Summary&prodn o=3238.0.55.001&issue=Jun %202006&num=&view=

Australian Institute of Health and Welfare. (2006a). *Ill-health conditions: Overview*. Canberra. Retrieved October 28, 2009, from http://www.aihw.gov.au/ indigenous/ health/ health_conditions.cfm

Australian Institute of Health and Welfare. (2006b). *Mental health: Overview*. Canberra. Retrieved October 28, 2009, from http://www.aihw.gov.au/ indigenous/ health/mental.cfm

Australian Institute of Health and Welfare. (2008). *Diabetes: Australian facts 2008*. Canberra. Retrieved October 28, 2009, from http://www.aihw.gov.au/ publications/ cvd/daf08/daf08.pdf

Australian Institute of Health and Welfare. (2009). *Diabetes prevalence in Australia: An assessment of national data sources*. Canberra. Retrieved October 28, 2009, from http://www.aihw.gov.au/ publications/cvd/cvd-46-10639/ cvd-46-10639.pdf

Australian Nursing and Midwifery Council (ANMC). (2006). *National competency standards for the registered nurse and the enrolled nurse*. Dickson, ACT. Retrieved November 3, 2009, from http://www.anmc.org. au /userfiles/file/competency _standards/Competency_ standards_RN.pdf

Baker, E. L., & Delacruz, G. C. (2008). *What do we know about assessment in games?* Paper presented at the National Center for Research on Evaluation, Standards, and Student Testing (CRESST) American Educational Research Association AERA 2008 Annual Meeting New York, NY. Retrieved April 7, 2011, from http://www.cse. ucla.edu/ products/overheads/AERA2008 /baker_assessment.pdf

Ball, S. J. (1994). *Education reform: A critical and post-structural approach*. Buckingham, UK: Open University Press.

Ball, S. J. (1995). Intellectuals or technicians? The urgent role of theory in education studies. *British Journal of Education, 43*(3), 255–271.

Bannan-Ritland, D. (2003). The role of design in research: The integrative learning design framework. *Educational Researcher, 32*(1), 21–24. doi:10.3102/0013189X032001021

Barab, S. A., Squire, K. D., & Dueber, W. (2000). A co-evolutionary model for supporting the emergence of authenticity. *Educational Technology Research and Development, 48*(2), 37–62. doi:10.1007/BF02313400

Barab, S., & Duffy, T. (2000). From practice fields to communities of practice. In Jonassen, D. D., & Land, S. M. (Eds.), *Theoretical foundations of learning environments*. Mahwah, NJ: Lawrence Erlbaum Associates.

Barnes, K., Marateo, R., & Ferris, S. (2007). Teaching and learning with the net generation. *Innovate, 3*(4). Retrieved December 4, 2008, from http://www.innovateonline.info/ index.php?view=article&id=382

Barnett, R. (2011). *Being a university*. New York, NY: Routledge.

Barnett, R. (2000). *Realizing the university in an age of supercomplexity*. Buckingham, UK & Philadelphia, PA: Society for Research into Higher Education & Open University Press.

Barnett, R. (2005). *Reshaping the university: New relationships between research, scholarship and teaching*. Maidenhead, UK & New York, NY: Society for Research into Higher Education & Open University Press.

Barnett, R. (2000). *Realizing the university in an age of supercomplexity*. Buckingham, UK: Open University Press.

Barr, R. B., & Tag, J. (1995). From teaching to learning: A new paradigm for undergraduate education. *Change*, Nov/Dec. Retrieved October 10, 2009, from: http://ilte.ius.edu/pdf/BarrTagg.pdf

Barret, H. (2008). *Categories of ePortfolio tools*. Retrieved November 13, 2009, from http://electronicportfolios.com/categories.html

Barrett, H. (2009). *Researching lifelong ePortfolios and Web 2.0*. Retrieved April 26, 2010 from http://electronicportfolios.org.

Barrett, R., Rainer, A., & Marczyk, O. (2007). Managed learning environments and an attendance crisis? *The Electronic Journal of e-Learning, 5*(1), 1–10.

Bartleet, B., & Ellis, C. (Eds.). (2009). *Music autoethnographies: Making autoethnography sing/ making music personal*. Brisbane, Australia: Australian Academic Press.

Bates, A. W., & Poole, G. (2003). *Effective teaching with technology in higher education: Foundations for success*. San Francisco, CA: Jossey-Bass.

Bauman, Z. (2000). *Liquid modernity*. Cambridge, UK: Polity Press.

Beetham, H., & Sharpe, R. (Eds.). (2007). *Rethinking pedagogy for a digital age: Designing and delivering e-learning*. London, UK: Routledge Falmer.

Bennett, S., Maton, K., & Kervin, L. (2008). The 'digital natives' debate: A critical review of the evidence. *British Journal of Educational Technology, 39*(5), 775–786. doi:10.1111/j.1467-8535.2007.00793.x

Bernath, U., Szücs, A., Tait, A., & Vidal, M. (2009). *Distance and e-learning in transition*. London, UK: ISTE.

Bickford, D. J., & Wright, D. J. (2006). Community: The hidden context for learning. In D. G. Oblinger (Ed.), *Learning spaces*, (pp. 4.1 – 4.22). Retrieved September 9, 2009, from http://www.educause.edu/learningspaces

Biggs, J. B., & Tang, C. (2007). *Teaching for quality learning at University* (3rd ed.). Maidenhead, UK: Open University Press/McGraw Hill.

Biggs, J. (2003). *Teaching for quality learning at university* (2nd ed.). Buckingham, UK: SRHE and Open University Press.

Bion, W. R. (1984). *Elements of psycho-analysis*. London, UK: Karnac.

Blackboard Inc. (2009). *Blackboard release 9*. Retrieved September 6, 2009, from http://www.blackboard.com/Release9/Release-9/What-is-New-in-9/Facebook.aspx

Bloomfield, P. R., & Livingstone, D. (2009). Immersive learning and assessment with quizHUD. *Computing and Information Systems Journal, 13*(1). Retrieved April 7, 2011, from http://cis.uws.ac.uk/research /journal/vol13.htm

Bottge, B. A., & Hasselbring, T. S. (1993). Taking word problems off the page. *Educational Leadership, 50*(7), 36–38.

Boud, D., & Falchikov, N. (2006). Aligning assessment with long-term learning. *Assessment & Evaluation in Higher Education, 31*(4), 399–413. doi:10.1080/02602930600679050

Boud, D., & Prosser, M. (2002). Key principles for high quality student learning in higher education: A framework for evaluation. *Educational Media International, 39*(3), 237–245. doi:10.1080/09523980210166026

Boud, D. (2001). *Peer learning in higher education: Learning from and with each other*. London, UK: Kogan Page.

Boulos, M. N. K., & Wheeler, S. (2007). The emerging Web 2.0 social software: An enabling suite of sociable technologies in health and health care education. *Health Information and Libraries Journal, 24*(1), 2–23. doi:10.1111/j.1471-1842.2007.00701.x

Boulos, M. N, K., Maramba, I., & Wheeler, S. (2006). Wikis, blogs and podcasts: A new generation of Web-based tools for virtual collaborative clinical practice and education. *BMC Medical Education, 6*(41). Retrieved August 28, 2009, from http://www.biomedcentral.com/1472-6920/ 6/ 41

Bouslama, F., Lansari, A., Al-Rawi, A., & Abonamah, A. A. (2003). A novel outcome-based educational model and its effect on student learning, curriculum development, and assessment. *Journal of Information Technology Education, 2*, 203–214.

Boyd, D. (2008). Why youth (heart) social network sites: The role of networked publics in teenage social life. In Buckingham, D. (Ed.), *Youth, identity, and digital media* (pp. 119–142). Cambridge, MA: MIT Press.

Boyd, D. M., & Ellison, N. B. (2007). Social network sites: Definition, history, and scholarship. *Journal of Computer-Mediated Communication, 13*(1). Retrieved April 28, 2010, from http://jcmc.indiana.edu/vol13/issue1/boyd.ellison.html

Boyle, T., & Cook, J. (2004). Understanding and using technological affordances: A commentary on Conole and Dyke. *ALT-J, 12*(3), 295–299. doi:10.1080/0968776042000259591

Bradwell, P. (2009). *The edgeless university: Why higher education must embrace technology.* Retrieved March 6, 2010, from http://www.demos.co.uk/publications/the-edgeless-university

Brakke, D. F., & Brown, D. T. (2002). Assessment to improve student learning. In Narum, J. L., & Conover, K. (Eds.), *Building robust learning environments in undergraduate science, technology, engineering, and mathematics: New directions for higher education* (pp. 119–122). San Francisco, CA: Jossey-Bass.

Bransford, J., Brown, A., & Cocking, R. (Eds.). (2000). *How people learn: Brain, mind, experience and school.* Washington, DC: National Academy Press.

Bransford, J. D., Vye, N., Kinzer, C., & Risko, V. (1990). Teaching thinking and content knowledge: Toward an integrated approach. In Jones, B. F., & Idol, L. (Eds.), *Dimensions of thinking and cognitive instruction* (pp. 381–413). Hillsdale, NJ: Lawrence Erlbaum Associates.

Bransford, J. D., Sherwood, R. D., Hasselbring, T. S., Kinzer, C. K., & Williams, S. M. (1990). Anchored instruction: Why we need it and how technology can help. In Nix, D., & Spiro, R. (Eds.), *Cognition, education and multimedia: Exploring ideas in high technology* (pp. 115–141). Hillsdale, NJ: Lawrence Erlbaum.

Brauer, P., Hanning, R. M., Arocha, J. F., Royall, D., Goy, R., & Grant, A. (2009). Creating case scenarios or vignettes using factorial design methods. *Journal of Advanced Nursing, 65*(9), 1937–1945. doi:10.1111/j.1365-2648.2009.05055.x

Brawn, R. (2006). From teaching spaces to learning spaces. [University of Bristol Learning Technology Support Service]. *Interact, 32*, 3–4.

Breakey, K. M., Levin, D., Miller, I., & Hentges, K. E. (2008). The use of scenario-based-learning interactive software to create custom virtual laboratory scenarios for teaching genetics. *Genetics, 179*(3), 1151–1155. doi:10.1534/genetics.108.090381

Britain, S., & Liber, O. (1999). *A framework for pedagogical evaluation of virtual learning environments.* Retrieved March 30, 2010, from http://www.jisc.ac.uk/publications/reports/1999/pedagogicalvlefinal.aspx

Broadfoot, P., & Black, P. (2004). Redefining assessment? The first ten years of assessment in education. *Assessment in Education, 11*(1), 7–27. doi:10.1080/0969594042000208976

Brockbank, A., & McGill, I. (2007). *Facilitating reflective learning in higher education.* Maidenhead, UK: Open University Press.

Brooks, R., & Everett, G. (2008). The impact of higher education on lifelong learning. *International Journal of Lifelong Education, 27*(3), 239–254. doi:10.1080/02601370802047759

Brown, J. S., Collins, A., & Duguid, P. (1989). Situated cognition and the culture of learning. *Educational Researcher, 18*(1), 32–42.

Brown, M., & Lippincott, J. (2003). Learning spaces: More than meets the eye. *EDUCAUSE Quarterly, 26*(1), 14–16.

Brown, J. S., & Duguid, P. (2000). *The social life of information.* Boston, MA: Harvard Business School.

Brown, A. (2007). Software development as music education research. *International Journal of Education & the Arts*, *8*(6), 1–13.

Brown, J. S., Collins, A., & Duguid, P. (1989). Situated cognition and the culture of learning. *Educational Researcher*, *18*(1), 32–42.

Brown, A., & Dillon, S. (2007). Networked improvisational musical environments: Learning through online collaborative music making. In Finney, J., & Burnard, P. (Eds.), *Music education with digital technology* (pp. 96–106). London, UK: Continuum International Publishing Group.

Brown, M. (2005). Learning spaces. In D. G. Oblinger & J. L. Oblinger (Eds.). *Educating the Net generation*. Boulder, CO: EDUCAUSE. Retrieved April 25, 2010, from http://www.educause.edu/LearningSpaces/6072

Browne, T., Jenkins, M., & Walker, R. (2006). A longitudinal perspective regarding the use of VLEs by higher education institutions in the United Kingdom. *Interactive Learning Environments*, *14*(2), 177–192. doi:10.1080/10494820600852795

Brownlee, J., & Berthelsen, D. (2008). Developing relational epistemology through relational pedagogy: New ways of thinking about personal epistemology in teacher education. In Khine, M. S. (Ed.), *Knowing, knowledge and beliefs: Epistemological studies across diverse cultures* (pp. 404–421). Perth, Western Australia: Springer Science and Business Media.

Bruner, J. S. (1966). *Towards a theory of instruction*. Cambridge, MA: Belknap Press of Harvard University.

Bruns, A., & Jacobs, J. (Eds.). (2006). *Uses of blogs*. New York, NY: Peter Lang.

Brush, A. J. B., Bargeron, D., Grudin, J., Borning, A., & Gupta, A. (2002). Supporting interaction outside of class: Anchored discussions vs. discussion boards. In *Computer Support for Collaborative Learning: Foundations for a CSCL Community. Proceedings of CSCL 2002* (pp. 425-434). Mahway, NJ: Lawrence Erlbaum Associates.

Bryce, J. (2009). A consensus view in primary health care. *Australian Nursing Journal*, *16*(7), 21.

Burbules, N. (2006). Rethinking the virtual. In Weiss, J., Nolan, J., & Hunsinger, J. (Eds.), *The international handbook of virtual learning environments* (*Vol. 1*, pp. 37–58). Dordrecht, The Netherlands: Springer. doi:10.1007/978-1-4020-3803-7_1

Callahan, J. (2004). *Effects of different seating arrangements in higher education computer lab classrooms on student learning, teaching style, and classroom appraisal*. Unpublished Master's thesis, University of Florida, Gainesville, FL.

Campbell, M. (2008). Teaching, communities of practice and the police. In Barrow, M., & Sutherland, K. (Eds.), *HERDSA 2008: Engaging Communities* (pp. 106–116). Milperra, NSW: HERDSA.

Candy, P. C., Crebert, G., & O'Leary, J. (1994). *Developing lifelong learners through undergraduate education. Commissioned Report (No. 28). National Board of Employment, Education and Training*. Canberra: AGPS.

Capell, K. (2006). Europe's politicians embrace Web 2.0. *BusinessWeek Online*. Retrieved 24 October, 2006, from http://www.businessweek.com/bwdaily/dnflash/content/oct2006/db20061024_653130.htm

Careers Wales Association. (2006). *E-progress file project*. Retrieved November 13, 2009, from http://www2.careerswales.com/progressfile/

Carew, A. L., Lefoe, G., Bell, M., & Amour, L. (2008). Elastic practice in academic developers. *The International Journal for Academic Development*, *13*(1), 51–66. doi:10.1080/13601440701860250

Castells, M. (1996). *The rise of the network society* (*Vol. 1*). Oxford, UK: Blackwell.

Castells, M. (1997). *The power of identity* (*Vol. 2*). Oxford, UK: Blackwell.

Castells, M. (1998). *End of millennium* (*Vol. 3*). Oxford, UK: Blackwell.

Castells, M., Flecha, R., Freire, P., Giroux, H. A., Macedo, D., & Willis, P. (1999). *Critical education in the new information age*. Lanham, MD: Rowan & Littlefield.

Castells, M. (2000). *The rise of the network society* (2nd ed.). Oxford, UK: Blackwell.

Castells, M., Fernández-Ardèvol, M., Qiu, J. L., & Sey, A. (2007). *Mobile communication and society: A global perspective*. Cambridge, MA: MIT Press.

Centre for International ePortfolio Development. (2006). *Joining up organisations supporting engineering pathways into higher education*. Retrieved November 13, 2009, from http://www.nottingham.ac.uk/eportfolio/JOSEPH/

Centre for International ePortfolio Development. (2007). *DELIA*. Retrieved November 13, 2009, from http://www.nottingham.ac.uk/eportfolio/delia/

Charles Darwin University. (2007). *Bachelor of Nursing curriculum document*. Charles Darwin University.

Charles Darwin University. (2009). *Territory 2030: Charles Darwin University response June 2009*. Darwin, Australia: Charles Darwin University.

Cheers, C., Chen, S. E., & Zarakhsh, K. (2009). *Bringing e-learning to life - student engagement and empowerment*. Paper presented at HERDSA Conference, Darwin, Australia.

Chickering, A. W. (2008). Strengthening democracy and personal development through community engagement. *New Directions for Adult and Continuing Education, 118*, 87–95. doi:10.1002/ace.298

Chong, E. K. M. (2008). Harnessing distributed musical expertise through edublogging. *Australasian Journal of Educational Technology, 24*(2), 181–194.

Chong, E. K. M., & Soo, W. M. (2005a). *Higher-order learning in music through blogs*. Paper presented at the Redesigning Pedagogy Conference, Singapore.

Chong, E. K. M., & Soo, W. M. (2005b). *Integrative and collaborative music learning using blogs*. Paper presented at the Association for Technology in Music Instruction and College Music Society Joint-Conference, Quebec City.

Chowcat, I., Phillips, B., Popham, J., & Jones, I. (2008). *Harnessing technology: Preliminary identification of trends affecting the use of technology for learning*. London, UK: Becta.

Churchill, D. (2009). Educational applications of Web 2.0: Using blogs to support teaching and learning. *British Journal of Educational Technology, 40*(1), 179–183. doi:10.1111/j.1467-8535.2008.00865.x

Clark, B. R. (2004). Delineating the character of the entrepreneurial university. *Higher Education Policy, 17*(4), 355–370. doi:10.1057/palgrave.hep.8300062

Clarke, M. (2003). *The reflective journal: Implications for professional learning*. Paper presented at the NZARE/AARE Conference, Auckland, New Zealand.

Clegg, S., Hudson, A., & Steel, J. (2003). The emperor's new clothes: Globalisation and e-learning in higher education. *British Journal of Sociology of Education, 24*(1), 39–53. doi:10.1080/01425690301914

Coates, H., James, R., & Baldwin, G. (2005). A critical examination of the effects of Learning Management Systems on university teaching and learning. *Tertiary Education and Management, 11*, 19–36. doi:10.1080/13583883.2005.9967137

Cognition and Technology Group at Vanderbilt. (1990a). Anchored instruction and its relationship to situated cognition. *Educational Researcher, 19*(6), 2–10.

Cognition and Technology Group at Vanderbilt. (1990b). Technology and the design of generative learning environments. *Educational Technology, 31*(5), 34–40.

Collins, A., Brown, J. S., & Newman, S. E. (1989). Cognitive apprenticeship: Teaching the crafts of reading, writing and mathematics. In Resnick, L. B, (Ed.), *Knowing, learning and instruction: Essays in honor of Robert Glaser* (pp. 453–494). Hillsdale, NJ: Lawrence Erlbaum Associates.

Collis, B., & De Boer, W. (2004). E-learning by design. *Teachers as learners: Embedded tools for implementing a CMS, 48*(6), 7-12.

Collom, G., Dallas, A., Jong, R., & Obexer, R. (2002, December). *Six months in a leaky boat: Framing the knowledge and skills needed to teach well online*. Paper presented at the ASCILITE 2002 - Winds of Change in the Sea of Learning: Charting the Course of Digital Education, Auckland, NZ. Retrieved March 3, 2010, from http://www.ascilite.org.au/conferences/auckland02/proceedings/papers/181.pdf

Colman, F. (2005). Affect. In Parr, A. (Ed.), *The Deleuze dictionary* (pp. 11–13). Edinburgh, UK: Edinburgh University Press.

Conole, G., & Dyke, M. (2004). Understanding and using technological affordances: A response to Boyle and Cook. *ALT-J, 12*(3), 301–308. doi:10.1080/0968776042000259609

Conole, G., & Dyke, M. (2004). What are the affordances of information and communication technologies? *ALT-J, 12*(2), 113–124. doi:10.1080/0968776042000216183

Cooper, M. M., Cox, C. T. Jr, Nammouz, M., Case, E., & Stevens, R. (2008). An assessment of the effect of collaborative groups on students' problem-solving strategies and abilities. *Journal of Chemical Education, 85*(6), 886–872. doi:10.1021/ed085p866

Corcoran, E. (1993). Why kids love computer nets. *Fortune.* Retrieved March 18, 2010, from http://money.cnn.com/magazines/fortune/fortune_archive/1993/09/20/78335/index.htm

Corter, J. E., Nickerson, J. V., Esche, S. K., Chassapis, C., Im, S., & Ma, J. (2007). Constructing reality: A study of remote, hands-on, and simulated laboratories. [TOCHI]. *ACM Transactions on Computer-Human Interaction, 14*(2), 7. doi:10.1145/1275511.1275513

Cronin, J. C. (1993). Four misconceptions about authentic learning. *Educational Leadership, 50*(7), 78–80.

Crook, C. (2002). The campus experience of networked learning. In Steeples, C., & Jones, C. (Eds.), *Networked learning: Perspectives and issues* (pp. 293–308). London, UK: Springer.

CSU. (2003). *Charles Sturt University annual report. For the public good.* Retrieved April 8, 2010, from http://www.csu.edu.au/ division/ marketing/ annualreports/ ar03/ index.html

Cummings, R., Phillips, R., Tilbrook, R., & Lowe, K. (2005). Middle-out approaches to reform of university teaching and learning: Champions striding between top-down and bottom-up approaches. *International Review of Research in Open and Distance Learning, 6*(1), 1–18.

Curtin University. (2006). *Graduate attributes policy* Retrieved September 7, 2009, from http://policies.curtin.edu.au/policies/teachingandlearning.cfm

Czerniewicz, L., Williams, K., & Brown, C. (2009). Students make a plan: Understanding student agency in constraining conditions. *ALT-J, 17*(2), 75–88. doi:10.1080/09687760903033058

Daniel, J. S. (1996). *Mega-universities and knowledge media: Technology strategies for higher education.* London, UK: Kogan Page.

Davidson, L. (1992). *Arts propel: A handbook for music (with video of evaluation methods and approaches).* Cambridge, MA: Harvard Project Zero.

Davies, A., & LeMahieu, P. (2003). Reconsidering portfolios and research evidence. In Segers, M., Dochy, F., & Cascallar, E. (Eds.), *Optimising new modes of assessment: In search of qualities and standards* (pp. 141–170). Dordrecht, The Netherlands/ Boston, MA/ London, UK: Kluwer Academic Publishers. doi:10.1007/0-306-48125-1_7

de Figueiredo, A. D., & Afonso, A. P. (2006). Context and learning: A philosophical framework. In de Figueiredo, A. D., & Afonso, A. P. (Eds.), *Managing learning in virtual settings: The role of context* (pp. 1–22). London, UK: Information Science Publishing. doi:10.4018/9781591404880.ch001

de Freitas, S., & Neumann, T. (2009). The use of exploratory learning for supporting immersive learning in virtual environments. *Computers & Education, 52*(2), 343–352. doi:10.1016/j.compedu.2008.09.010

de Freitas, S. (2008). *Serious virtual worlds: A scoping study.* Retrieved April 7, 2011, from http://www.jisc.ac.uk/media/ documents/publications /seriousvirtual-worldsv1.pdf

De Landa, M. (2002). *Intensive science and virtual philosophy.* New York, NY: Continuum International Publishing Group.

Deleuze, G. (1993). *The fold: Leibniz and the baroque.* Minneapolis, MN: University of Minnesota Press.

Deleuze, G., & Guattari, F. (1983). *Anti-Oedipus: Capitalism and schizophrenia* (Hurley, R., Seem, M., & Lane, H. R., Trans.). Minneapolis, MN: University of Minnesota Press.

Deleuze, G., & Guattari, F. (1987). *A thousand plateaus: Capitalism and schizophrenia* (Massumi, B., Trans.). Minneapolis, MN: University of Minnesota Press.

Department of Education. Employment and Workplace Relations (DEEWR). (2009). *Experience the digital education revolution*. Retrieved March 6, 2010, from http://www.digitaleducationrevolution.gov.au

Department of Education. Employment and Workplace Relations (DEEWR). (2009a). *Building the education revolution*. Retrieved March 6, 2010, from http://www.deewr.gov.au/Schooling/BuildingTheEducationRevolution

Design-Based Research Collective. (2003). Design-based research: An emerging paradigm for educational inquiry. *Educational Researcher, 32*(1), 5–8. doi:10.3102/0013189X032001005

Dewey, J. (1989). *Art as experience*. U.S.A.: Perigree Books.

Diaz, V., Garret, P., Kinley, E., Moore, J., Schwartz, C., & Kohrman, P. (2009). Faculty development for the 21st century. *EDUCAUSE Review, 44*(3), 46–55.

Dickey, M. D. (2004). The impact of Web-logs (blogs) on student perceptions of isolation and alienation in a Web-based distance-learning environment. *Open Learning, 19*(3), 279–291. doi:10.1080/0268051042000280138

Dillenbourg, P. (1999). What do you mean by collaborative learning? In Dillenbourg, P. (Ed.), *Collaborative-learning: Cognitive and computational approaches* (pp 1–19). Oxford, UK: Elsevier.

Dillenbourg, P., Schneider, D., & Synteta, P. (2002). Virtual learning environments. In A. Dimitracopoulou (Ed.). *Proceedings of the 3rd Hellenic Conference: Information & Communication Technologies in Education* (pp. 3–18). Greece: Kastaniotis Editions.

Dillenbourg, P., Schneider, D. K., & Synteta, P. (2002). Virtual learning environments. In A. Dimitracopoulou (Ed.), *Proceedings of the 3rd Hellenic Conference Information & Communication Technologies in Education* (pp. 3-18). Greece: Kastaniotis Editions.

Dillon, S., & Brown, A. (2006). The art of e-portfolios: Insights from the creative arts experience. In Jafari, A., & Kaufman, C. (Eds.), *Handbook of research on e-portfolios: Concepts, technology and case studies* (pp. 418–431). Indianapolis, IN: Idea- Group Inc.

Dillon, S. (2003). *jam2jam: Meaningful music making with computers*. Paper presented at the Artistic Practice as Research: 25th Annual Conference of the Australian Association for Research in Music Education, Brisbane, Queensland, Australia.

Dillon, S. (2004). S*ave to DISC: Documenting innovation in music learning*. Paper presented at the 26th Annual Conference of the Australian Association for Research in Music Education, Southern Cross University, Tweed Heads.

Dillon, S. (2007). *Examining meaningful engagement: Musicology and virtual music making environments*. Paper presented at the Musicological Society of Australasia.

Dirckinck-Holmfeld, L., Jones, C., & Lindström, B. (2009). *Analysing networked learning practices in higher education and continuing professional development*. Rotterdam, The Netherlands: Sense Publishers B.V.

Dittoe, W. (2006). Seriously cool places: The future of learning-centered built environments. In Oblinger, D. (Ed.), *Learning spaces* (pp. 3.1–3.11). Boulder, CO: Educause.

Dowling, D. (2006). Designing a competency based program to facilitate the progression of experienced engineering technologists to professional engineer status. *European Journal of Engineering Education, 31*(1), 95–107. doi:10.1080/03043790500429542

Duchastel, P. C. (1997). A Web-based model for university instruction. *Journal of Educational Technology Systems, 25*(3), 221–228. doi:10.2190/UFF9-KB1X-NGG4-UHKL

Duffy, P., & Bruns, A. (2006). The use of blogs, wikis and RSS in education: A conversation of possibilities. In *Proceedings Online Learning and Teaching Conference 2006* (pp. 31-38). Brisbane, Australia: Queensland University of Technology.

Eberhard, J. P., & Patoine, B. (2004). Architecture with the brain in mind. *Cerebrum, 6*(Spring), 71–84.

Education.au. (2009). *21st century learning spaces*. Retrieved October 10, 2009, from www.educationau.edu.au

Edwards, B. (2000). *University architecture*. London, UK: Spon Press.

Edwards, P. N. (2003). Infrastructure and modernity: Force, time, and social organization in the history of sociotechnical systems. In Misa, T. J., Brey, P., & Feenberg, A. (Eds.), *Modernity and technology* (pp. 185–225). Cambridge, MA: MIT Press.

Eisen, M.-J. (2001). Peer-based professional develoment viewed through the lens of transformation. *Holistic Nursing Practice, 16*(1), 30–42.

Elliot, K., Efron, D., Wright, M., & Martinelli, A. (2003). Educational technologies that integrate problem based learning principles: Do these resources enhance student learning? In G. Crisp, D Thiele, I. Scholten, S. Barker & J. Baron (Eds), *20th Annual Conference of the Australian Society for Computers in Learning in Tertiary Education.* Adelaide, South Australia.

Elliott, B. (2008). *Assessment 2.0 modernising assessment in the age of Web 2.0.* Retrieved April 7, 2011, from http://www.scribd.com/doc/ 461041/Assessment-20

Ellis, A., & Newton, D. (2009). First year university students' access, usage and expectations of technology: An Australian pilot study. In [Chesapeake, VA: AACE.]. *Proceedings of World Conference on E-Learning in Corporate, Government, Healthcare, and Higher Education, 2009,* 2539–2546.

Engeström, Y. (1987). *Learning by expanding: An activity-theoretical approach to developmental research.* Helsinki, Finland: Orienta-Konsultit.

Etzkowitz, H. (2004). The evolution of the entrepreneurial university. *International Journal of Technology and Globalisation, 1*(1), 64–77.

European Commission. (2000). *A memorandum on lifelong learning.* Retrieved April 20, 2009, from http://www.bologna-berlin2003.de/pdf/MemorandumEng.pdf

Fallows, S. (2003). Teaching and learning for student skill development. In H. Fry, S. Ketteridge, & S. Marshall (Eds.). *A handbook for teaching and learning in higher education: Enhancing academic practice* (2nd ed.) (pp. 121-133). London, UK & Sterling, VA: Kogan Page.

Farinon, A. M. (2005). *Endoscopic surgery of the potential anatomical spaces.* Dordrecht, The Netherlands & London, UK: Springer. doi:10.1007/1-4020-2846-6

Farmer, B., Yue, A., & Brooks, C. (2008). Using blogging for higher order learning in large cohort university teaching: A case study. *Australasian Journal of Educational Technology, 24*(2), 123–136.

Farmer, J., & Bartlett-Bragg, A. (2005). Blogs @ anywhere: High fidelity online communication. In *Proceedings of ASCILITE 2005: Balance, Fidelity, Mobility: Maintaining the momentum?* (pp. 197-203). Brisbane, Australia: Queensland University of Technology.

Fenn, J., Raskino, M., & Gammage, B. (2009). *Gartner's hype cycle special report for 2009.* Retrieved April 7, 2011, from http://www.gartner.com/resources/169700/169747/gartners_hype _cycle_special__169747.pdf

Ferdig, R. E., & Trammell, K. D. (2004). Content delivery in the blogosphere. *T H E Journal (Technological Horizons In Education), 12*(4), Retrieved May 10, 2010, from http://thejournal.com/ articles/ 16626

Field, J., & Leicester, M. (2003). *Lifelong learning: Education across the lifespan.* London: UK RoutledgeFalmer.

Fitzgerald, R., Barrass, S., Campbell, J., Hinton, S., Ryan, Y., Whitelaw, M., et al. (2009). *Digital learning communities: Investigating the application of social software to support networked learning.* Australian Learning and Teaching Council. Retrieved from http://eprints.qut.edu.au /18476/1/c18476.pdf

Flutter, J. (2006). This place could help you learn: Student participation in creating better school environments. *Educational Review, 58*(1), 183–193. doi:10.1080/00131910600584116

Fox, R. (2007). Teaching through technology: Changing practices in two universities. *International Journal on E-Learning, 6*(2), 187–203.

Fox, R. (2009). *CUHK future classrooms.* Shatin, Hong Kong: The Chinese University of Hong Kong, Centre for Learning Enhancement And Research.

Fox, R. (2005, June). *Universities in knowledge-based economies: The challenge for change.* Invited keynote speech at the International Conference on Capacity Building for Information Technology Integration in Teaching and Learning, Hong Kong Baptist University, Hong Kong.

Fox, R., & Stuart, C. (2009). Creating learning spaces through collaboration: How one library refined its approach. *Educause Quarterly, 32*(1). Retrieved April 27, 2010, from http://www.educause.edu/EDUCAUSE+Quarterly/EDUCAUSEQuarterlyMagazineVolum/CreatingLearningSpacesThroughC/163850

Franklin, T., & van Harmelen, M. (2007). *Web 2.0 for content for learning and teaching in higher education.* Retrieved April 7, 2011, from http://www.jisc.ac.uk/media/documents/programmes/digitalrepositories/web2-content -learning-and-teaching.pdf

Friesen, N., & Hopkins, J. (2008). Wikiversity, or education meets the free culture movement: An ethnographic investigation. *First Monday, 13*(10). Retrieved October 16, 2008, from http://www.uic.edu/htbin/cgiwrap/bin/ojs/index.php/fm/rt/printerFriendly/2234/2031

Fullan, M., Hill, P., & Crévola, C. (2006). *Breakthrough.* Toronto, Canada: Corwin Press.

Gale, H. (2006). Flexible learning needs flexible spaces. [University of Bristol Learning Technology Support Service]. *Interact, 32*, 14–15.

Gardner, H. (1993). *Frames of mind: The theory of multiple intelligences.* London, UK: Fontana Press.

Garrison, R., & Vaughan, H. (2008). *Blended learning in higher education: Framework, principles and guidelines.* San Francisco, CA: Jossey-Bass.

Garrison, D. R., & Anderson, T. (2003). *E-learning in the 21st century: A framework for research and practice.* London, UK: Routledge Falmer. doi:10.4324/9780203166093

Gaver, W., Dunne, T., & Pacenti, E. (1999). Design: Cultural probes. *Interaction, 6*(1), 21–29. doi:10.1145/291224.291235

Gay, P., Salaman, G., & Rees, B. (1996). The conduct of management and the management of conduct: Contemporary managerial discourse and the constitution of the competent manager. *Journal of Management Studies, 33*(3), 263–282. doi:10.1111/j.1467-6486.1996.tb00802.x

Gee, L. (2006). Human-centered design guidelines. In Oblinger, D. (Ed.), *Learning spaces* (pp. 10.1–10.13). Boulder, CO: Educause.

Geith, C. (2008). Teaching and learning unleashed with Web 2.0 and open educational resources. In Katz, R. N. (Ed.), *The tower and the cloud: Higher education in the age of cloud computing* (pp. 219–226). Boulder, CO: Educause.

Gerbic, P., & Stacey, E. (2009). Conclusion. In Stacey, E., & Gerbic, P. (Eds.), *Effective blended learning practices: Evidence-based perspectives in ICT-facilitated education* (pp. 298–311). Hershey, PA/New York, NY: Information Science Reference. doi:10.4018/978-1-60566-296-1.ch016

Geser, G., Hornung-Prähauser, V., & Schaffert, S. (2007). Observing open e-learning content: A roadmap for educational policy and institutions and hands-on tips for practitioners. In *Proceedings of the Interactive Computer Aided Learning Conference (ICL).* Villach, Austria.

Gilbert, L., Gale, V., Warburton, B., & Wills, G. (2008). *Report on summative e-assessment quality (REAQ).* JISC. Retrieved April 7, 2011, from http://www.jisc.ac.uk/media/documents/projects/reaqfinalreport.pdf

Godwin-Jones, R. (2003). Emerging technologies blogs and wikis: Environments for on-line collaboration. *Language Learning & Technology, 7*(2), 12–16.

Goldschmid, B., & Goldschmid, M. L. (1976). Peer teaching in higher education: A review. *Higher Education, 5*(1), 9–33.

Goodyear, P., Banks, S., Hodgson, V., & McConnell, D. (2004). *Advances in research on networked learning.* Dordrecht, The Netherlands: Kluwer.

Goodyear, P., Jones, C., Asensio, M., Hodgson, V., & Steeples, C. (2001). *Effective networked learning in higher education: Notes and guidelines.* Lancaster, UK: CSALT, Lancaster University. Retrieved April 10, 2011, from http://csalt.lancs.ac.uk/jisc/

Gordon, R. (1998). Balancing real-world problems with real-world results. *Phi Delta Kappan, 79*, 390–393.

Grabowski, U. (2004). Erfolgsfaktor persönlichkeit: Anforderungen an eine ganzheitliche ingenieurausbildung. *Global Journal of Engineering Education, 8*(3), 269–274.

Graham, C. (2006). Blended learning systems. Definitions, current trends and future directions. In Bonk, C., & Graham, C. (Eds.), *The handbook of blended learning: Global perspectives, local designs.* San Francisco, CA: John Wiley and Sons.

Green, P. (2005). Spaces of influence: A framework for analysis of an individual's contribution within communities of practice. *Higher Education Research & Development, 24*(4), 293–307. doi:10.1080/07294360500284607

Greyling, F., Kara, M., Makka, A., & van Niekerk, S. (2008). IT worked for us: Online strategies to facilitate learning in large (undergraduate) classes. *The Electronic Journal of e-Learning, 6*(3), 179–188. Retrieved September 29, 2009, from http://www.ejel.org/ Volume-6/ v6-i3/ Greyling.pdf

Guest, G. (2006). Lifelong learning for engineers: A global perspective. *European Journal of Engineering Education, 31*(3), 273–281. doi:10.1080/03043790600644396

Guribye, F., & Lindström, B. (2009). Infrastructures for learning and networked tools - The introduction of a new tool in an inter-organisational network. In Dirckinck-Holmfeld, L., Jones, C., & Lindström, B. (Eds.), *Analysing networked learning practices in higher education and continuing professional development* (pp. 103–116). Rotterdam, The Netherlands: Sense Publishers.

Guribye, F. (2005). *Infrastructures for learning - ethnographic inquiries into the social and technical conditions of education and training.* Doctoral Thesis, University of Bergen, Norway. Retrieved April 10, 2011, from http://hdl.handle.net/1956/859

Guzdial, M., & Turns, J. (2000). Effective discussion through a computer-mediated anchored forum. *Journal of the Learning Sciences, 9*(4), 437–469. doi:10.1207/S15327809JLS0904_3

Hai, B. (2008). Facilitating development of student teachers positive beliefs about educational technologies through electronic modelling, reflection and technology experience. *International Journal of Instructional Technology and Distance Learning, 5*(1). Retrieved May 27, 2010, from http://www.itdl.org/Journal/ Jan_08/article04.htm

Hanna, D. E. (2008). Organizational change in higher distance education. In M. G. Moore (Ed.), *Handbook of distance education* (pp. 501-514). Mahway, NJ & London, UK: Lawrence Erlbaum Associates.

Hargis, J., & Wilcox, S. M. (2008). Ubiquitous, free, and efficient online collaboration tools for teaching and learning. *Turkish Online Journal of Distance Education, 9*(4).

Havenstein, H. (2007). Customers courted with Web 2.0. *Computerworld, 41*(8), 1–36.

Havnes, A. (2004). Examination and learning: An activity-theoretical analysis of the relationship between assessment and educational practice. *Assessment & Evaluation in Higher Education, 29*(2), 159–176. doi:10.1080/0260293042000188456

Hawthorne, J. (2002). What about the tables and chairs? [Oxford Brookes University]. *Teaching Forum, 50*, 46–47.

Heagney, M. (2009). Australian higher education sector on the brink of a major shakeup. *Widening Participation & Lifelong Learning, 11*(1). Retrieved March 3, 2010, from http://www.staffs.ac.uk/journal/volelevenone/editorial.htm

Hedberg, J. G. (2006). E-learning futures? Speculations for a time yet to come. *Studies in Continuing Education, 28*(2), 171–183. doi:10.1080/01580370600751187

Heinrich, E., Bhattacharya, M., & Rayudu, R. (2007). Preparation for lifelong learning using ePortfolios. *European Journal of Engineering Education, 32*(6), 653–663. doi:10.1080/03043790701520602

Heinrich, E. (2008, July 1-4). *Supporting continuous improvement in teaching development through electronic teaching portfolios.* Paper presented at the 31st HERDSA Annual Conference, Rotorua, New Zealand.

Hektner, J. M., Schmidt, J. A., & Csikszentmihalyi, M. (2006). *Experience sampling method: Measuring the quality of everyday life.* London, UK: Sage.

Henderson, A., Twentyman, M., Heel, A., & Lloyd, B. (2006). Students' perception of the psycho-social clinical learning environment: An evaluation of placement models. *Nurse Education Today, 26*(7), 564–571. doi:10.1016/j.nedt.2006.01.012

Hernández-Ramos, P. (2004). Web logs and online discussions as tools to promote reflective practice. *The Journal of Interactive Online Learning, 3*(1).

Hernon, P. (2006). Methods of data collection. In Hernon, P., Dugan, R. E., & Schwartz, C. (Eds.), *Revisiting outcomes assessment in higher education* (pp. 135–150). Westport, CT & London, UK: Libraries Unlimited.

Herrington, J., Reeves, T. C., & Oliver, R. (2004). Designing authentic activities in Web-based courses. *Journal of Computing in Higher Education, 16*(1), 3–29. doi:10.1007/BF02960280

Herrington, J., & Herrington, A. (1998). Authentic assessment and multimedia: How university students respond to a model of authentic assessment. *Higher Education Research & Development, 17*(3), 305–322. doi:10.1080/0729436980170304

Herrington, J., & Herrington, A. (2006). *Authentic conditions for authentic assessment: Aligning task and assessment.* In A. Bunker & I. Vardi (Eds.), *Research and development in higher education volume 29, critical visions: Thinking, learning and researching in higher education* (pp 146-151). Milperra, NSW: HERDSA.

Hewitt, J., & Scardamalia, M. (1998). Design principles for distributed knowledge building processes. *Educational Psychology Review, 10*(1), 75–96. doi:10.1023/A:1022810231840

Hewitt-Taylor, J. (2003). Facilitating distance learning in nurse education. *Nurse Education in Practice, 3*(1), 23–29. doi:10.1016/S1471-5953(02)00052-5

Higher Education Funding Council for England. (2009). *Lifelong learning networks.* Retrieved November 13, 2009, from http://www.hefce.ac.uk/widen/lln/

Hill, J. (2006). Flexible learning environments: Leveraging the affordances of flexible delivery and flexible learning. *Innovative Higher Education, 31*, 187–197. doi:10.1007/s10755-006-9016-6

Hine, C. (2000). *Virtual ethnography.* London, UK: SAGE Publications Ltd.

Hobbs, M., Brown, E., & Gordon, M. (2009). Learning and assessment with virtual worlds in e-learning technologies and evidence-based assessment approaches. In C. Spratt, & P. Lajbcygier (Eds.), *AICTE book series* (pp. 55-75). Hershey, PA: Information Science Reference, IGI Global.

Holahan, C. (2006). Fantasy football 2.0. *BusinessWeek Online,* p. 6. Retrieved November 11, 2009, from http://www.businessweek.com/technology/content/sep2006/tc20060901_880554.htm

Holahan, C. (2007). Close harmony: Bands and Web 2.0. *BusinessWeek Online,* p. 10 Retrieved November 11, 2009, from http://www.businessweek.com/technology/content/mar2007/tc20070326_958216.htm

Hong, J.-C., Cheng, C.-L., Hwang, M.-Y., Lee, C.-K., & Chang, H.-Y. (2009). Assessing the educational values of digital games. *Journal of Computer Assisted Learning, 25*(5), 423–437. doi:10.1111/j.1365-2729.2009.00319.x

Hooker, M. (2008). *Models and best practice in teacher professional development.* Retrieved April 27, 2010, from http://www.gesci.org/old/files/docman/Teacher_Professional_Development_Models.pdf

Hornby, W. (2003). *Case studies in streamlining assessment.* Aberdeen, UK: Centre for the Enhancement of Learning and Teaching, The Robert Gordon University.

Howell, C. (2008). *Space.* Project Report. Learning Landscape Project, University of Cambridge. Retrieved March 15, 2011, from http://www.caret.cam.ac.uk/blogs/llp/wp-content/uploads/llp_public_t1report_l3_space_final_v06.pdf

http://www.abc.net.au/classic/features/s1809663.htm

http://www.ning.com/

http://www.savetodisc.net/

http://www.wikispaces.com/

http://www.youtube.com.au/

http://www.youtube.com/watch?v=ElBlTr74AQE

Hub, D. E. (2010). *About.* Retrieved February 17, 2010, from http://dehub.edu.au

Hughes, A. (2009). *Higher education in the Web 2.0 world*. Retrieved April 27, 2010, from http://www.jisc.ac.uk/ publications/documents /heweb2.aspx.

Hunt, L. (2006). A community development model of change: The role of teaching and learning centres. In Bromage, A., Tomkinson, B., & Hunt, L. (Eds.), *The realities of change in higher education: Interventions to promote learning and teaching*. London, UK: Routledge.

Hunt, L., & Peach, N. (2009). Planning for a sustainable academic future. In *Proceedings of the iPED 4th International Conference, Researching Beyond Boundaries Academic Communities without Borders* (pp. 14-26). Coventry, UK: University TechnoCentre.

ISLE. (2005). *Individualised support for learning through e-Portfolios*. Retrieved November 13, 2009, from http://isle.paisley.ac.uk/default.aspx

Jackson, N. J. (2010). From a curriculum that integrates work to a curriculum that integrates life: Changing a university's conceptions of curriculum. *Higher Education Research & Development, 29*(5), 491–505. doi:10.1080/07294360.2010.502218

Jacobsen, H. E. (2006). A comparison of on-campus first year undergraduate nursing students' experiences with face-to-face and on-line discussions. *Nurse Education Today, 26*(6), 494–500. doi:10.1016/j.nedt.2006.01.005

James, R. (2008). The theories of teaching and learning underpinning space and design decisions. In Huijser, H., Elson-Green, J., Reid, I., Walta, C., Challis, D., & Harris, K.-L. (Eds.), *Places and spaces for learning seminars (draft report)*. Sydney, Australia: Carrick Institute for Learning and Teaching in Higher Education.

Jamieson, P., Fisher, K., Gilding, T., Taylor, P. G., & Trevitt, A. C. F. (2000). Place and space in the design of new learning environments. *Higher Education Research & Development, 19*(2), 221–237. doi:10.1080/072943600445664

Jamieson, P. (2005). *Understanding a happy accident: Learning to build new learning environments. Report of ECE Research Project on Learning Communities*. Brisbane, Australia: TEDI, The University of Queensland.

Jamieson, P., Taylor, P., Fisher, K., Trevitt, A. C. F., & Gilding, T. (2000). Place and space in the design of new learning environments. *Higher Education Research & Development, 19*(2), 221–236. doi:10.1080/072943600445664

Jarmon, L., Traphagan, T., Mayrath, M., & Trivedi, A. (2009). Virtual world teaching, experiential learning, and assessment: An interdisciplinary communication course in Second Life. *Computers & Education, 53*(1), 169–182. doi:10.1016/j.compedu.2009.01.010

Jarvis, P. (2004). From adult education to lifelong learning: A conceptual framework. In Jarvis, P. (Ed.), *Adult education and lifelong learning: Theory and practice* (pp. 39–65). London, UK & New York, NY: Routledge Falmer.

Jenkins, H., Clinton, K., Purushotma, R., Robison, A. J., & Weigel, M. (2009). *Confronting the challenges of participatory culture: Media education for the 21st century. An occasional paper on digital media and learning*. The John D. and Catherine T. MacArthur Foundation. Retrieved February 24, 2010, from http://digitallearning.macfound.org/ atf/ cf/ %7B7E45C7E0- A3E0-4B89- AC9C-E807E1B0AE4E%7D/ JENKINS_WHITE_PAPER.PDF

JISC. (2006). *Designing spaces for effective learning: A guide to 21st century learning space design*. Retrieved April 8, 2010, from http://www.jisc.ac.uk/ media/ documents/ publications/ learningspaces.pdf

JISC. (2006). *Designing spaces for effective learning: A guide to 21st century learning space design*. Bristol, UK: JISC Development Group. Retrieved February 27, 2010, from http://www.jisc.ac.uk/eli_learningspaces.html

JISC. (2006). *Regional interoperability project on progression for lifelong learning*. Retrieved November 13, 2009, from http://www.nottingham.ac.uk/rippll/

JISC. (2007). *Student expectations study: Key findings from online research*. Discussion evenings held in June 2007 for the Joint Information Systems Committee. London, UK: JISC. Retrieved April 10, 2011, from http://www.jisc.ac.uk/publications/publications/studentexpectations

JISC. (2009). *Effective practice in a digital age: A guide to technology-enhanced learning and teaching*. Retrieved April 27, 2010 from http://www.jisc.ac.uk/media/ documents/publications/ effectivepracticedigitalage.pdf

JISC. (2009). *E-return*. Retrieved November 13, 2009, from http://www.jisc.ac.uk/whatwedo/programmes/elearningcapital/xinstit2/ereturn

JISC. (2009). *Higher Education in a Web 2.0 world.* JISC Report. Retrieved March 1, 2010, from http://www.jisc.ac.uk/ publications/documents /heweb2.aspx

John, P., & Sutherland, R. (2005). Affordance, opportunity and the pedagogical implications of ICT. *Educational Review, 57*(4), 405–413. doi:10.1080/00131910500278256

Johnson, L., Smith, R., Levine, A., & Haywood, K. (2010). *The 2010 horizon report: Australia–New Zealand edition.* Austin, TX: The New Media Consortium.

Johnson, L., Smith, R., Willis, H., Levine, A., & Haywood, K. (2011). *The 2011 horizon report.* Austin, TX: The New Media Consortium.

Johnson, C., & Lomas, C. (2005). Design of the learning space: Learning and design principles. *EDUCAUSE Review, 40*(4), 16–28.

Johnson, L., Levine, A., Smith, R., Smythe, T., & Stone, S. (2009). *The Horizon Report: 2009 Australia-New Zealand edition.* Austin, TX: The New Media Consortium.

Joint Information Systems Committee (JISC). (2006). *Designing spaces for effective learning: A guide to 21st century learning space design.* Retrieved March 6, 2010, from http://www.jisc.ac.uk/media/documents/publications/learningspaces.pdf

Jonas-Dwyer, D., & Pospisil, R. (2004). The millennial effect: Implications for academic development. In *Transforming Knowledge into Wisdom: Holistic Approaches to Teaching and Learning, Proceedings of the 27th Annual HERDSA Conference* (pp. 194-206). Miri, Sarawak.

Jonassen, D. (1991). Evaluating constructivistic learning. *Educational Technology, 31*(9), 28–33.

Jonassen, D. H., & Reeves, T. C. (1996). Learning with technology: Using computers as cognitive tools. In Jonassen, D. H. (Ed.), *Handbook of research for educational communications and technology* (1st ed., pp. 693–719). New York, NY: Macmillan.

Jonassen, D. H. (1999). Designing constructivist learning environments. In Reigeluth, C. M. (Ed.), *Instructional design theories and models: Their current state of the art* (2nd ed.). Mahwah, NJ: Lawrence Erlbaum Associates.

Jones, C., & Asensio, M. (2001). Experiences of assessment: using phenomenography for evaluation. *Journal of Computer Assisted Learning, 17*(3), 314–321. doi:10.1046/j.0266-4909.2001.00186.x

Jones, C., Dirckinck-Holmfeld, L., & Lindström, B. (2006). A relational, indirect, meso-level approach to cscl design in the next decade. *International Journal of Computer-Supported Collaborative Learning, 1*(1), 35–56. doi:10.1007/s11412-006-6841-7

Jones, C., Ramanau, R., Cross, S. J., & Healing, G. (2010). Net generation or digital natives: Is there a distinct new generation entering university? *Computers & Education, 54*(3), 722–732. doi:10.1016/j.compedu.2009.09.022

Jones, C., & Dirckinck-Holmfeld, L. (2009). Analysing networked learning practices: An introduction. In Dirckinck-Holmfeld, L., Jones, C., & Lindström, B. (Eds.), *Analysing networked learning practices in higher education and continuing professional development* (pp. 1–28). Rotterdam, The Netherlands: Sense Publishers B.V.

Jones, C. (2008). Infrastructures, institutions and networked learning. In V. Hodgson, C. Jones, T. Kargidis, D. McConnell, S. Retalis, D. Stamatis, & M. Zenios (Eds.), *Proceedings of the Sixth International Conference on Networked Learning 2008*. Lancaster, UK: Lancaster University.

Jones, C. (2009). A context for collaboration: The institutional selection of an infrastructure for learning. In C. O'Malley, D. Suthers, P. Reimann, & A. Dimitracopoulou (Eds.), *Proceedings of the 8th International Conference on Computer Supported Collaborative Learning Practices (CSCL2009)*. Rhodes, Greece: Lulu.com.

Jørgensen, M., & Phillips, L. (2002). *Discourse analysis as theory and method*. London, UK: Sage.

Kahneman, D., Krueger, A. B., Schkade, D. A., Schwarz, N., & Stone, A. A. (2004). A survey method for characterizing daily life experience: The day reconstruction method. *Science, 306*(5702), 1776–1780. doi:10.1126/science.1103572

Katz, R. (2005). Foreword: Growing up digital. In J. B. Caruso & R. Kvavik (Eds.), *ECAR study of students and information technology, 2005: Convenience, connection, control, and learning* (pp 5-8). EDUCAusE. Retrieved November 11, 2009, from http://net.educause.edu/ir/library/pdf/ers0506/rs/ERS0506w.pdf

Kelton, A. J. (2007). Second Life: Reaching into the virtual world for real-world learning. *ECAR Research Bulletin*, (17).

Kennedy, G. E., Judd, T. S., Churchward, A., Gray, K., & Krause, K. (2008). First year students' experiences with technology: Are they really digital natives? *Australasian Journal of Educational Technology, 24*(1), 108–122.

Kennedy, G., Dalgarno, B., Bennet, S., Gray, C., Judd, T., Waycott, J., et al. (2009). *Education and the net generation: Implications for learning and teaching in Australian universities.* Australian Learning and Teaching Council. Retrieved May 27, 2010, from http://www.altc.edu.au/system /files/resources/CG6-25_Melbourne _Kennedy_Final%20Report _July09_v2.pdf

Kennedy, G., Judd, T. S., Churchward, A., Gray, K., & Krause, K. (2008). First year students' experiences with technology: Are they really digital natives? Questioning the net generation: A collaborative project in Australian higher education. *Australasian Journal of Educational Technology, 24*(1), 108-122. Retrieved April 20, 2009, from http://www.ascilite.org.au/ajet/ajet24/kennedy.html

Kennewell, S. (2001). Using affordances and constraints to evaluate the use of information and communications technology in teaching and learning. *Journal of Information Technology for Teacher Education, 10*(1&2), 101–116.

Kenny, J. (2002). Managing innovation in educational institutions. *Australian Journal of Educational Technology, 18*(3), 359–376.

Keppell, M. J. (2010). *Blended and flexible learning standards.* Charles Sturt University.

Kerr, M. P. (2002). A qualitative study of shift handover practice and function from a socio-technical perspective. *Journal of Advanced Nursing, 37*(2), 125–134. doi:10.1046/j.1365-2648.2002.02066.x

Kezar, A., & Eckel, P. D. (2002). The effect of institutional culture on change strategies in higher education. *The Journal of Higher Education, 73*(4), 435–460. doi:10.1353/jhe.2002.0038

Kilstoff, K. K., & Rochester, S. (2004). Hitting the floor running: Transitional experiences of graduates previously trained as enrolled nurses. *The Australian Journal of Advanced Nursing, 22*(1), 13–17.

Kimball, L. (2002). Managing distance learning: New challenges for faculty. In Hazemi, R., & Hailes, S. (Eds.), *The digital university: Building a learning community.* London, UK: Springer. doi:10.1007/978-1-4471-0167-3_3

Kirkup, G., & Kirkwood, A. (2005). Information and communications technologies (ICT) in higher education teaching: A tale of gradualism rather than revolution. *Learning, Media and Technology, 30*(2), 185–199. doi:10.1080/17439880500093810

Klamma, R., Chatti, M. A., Duval, E., Hummel, H., Hvannberg, E. H., & Kravcik, M. (2007). Social software for life-long learning. *Journal of Educational Technology & Society, 10*(3), 72–83.

Klomp, N. (2008). Learning places and head spaces – are we leading by example? In Huijser, H., Elson-Green, J., Reid, I., Walta, C., Challis, D., & Harris, K.-L. (Eds.), *Places and spaces for learning seminars (draft report).* Sydney, Australia: Carrick Institute for Learning and Teaching in Higher Education.

Knapper, C. K., & Cropley, A. J. (2000). *Lifelong learning in higher education* (3rd ed.). London, UK: Kogan Page.

Knight, P., & Trowler, P. (2001). *Department leadership in higher education.* Buckingham, UK: SRHE and Open University.

Koper, R., & Tattersall, C. (Eds.). (2005). *Learning design: A handbook on modeling and delivering networked education and training.* Berlin, Germany: Springer.

Koretsky, M. D., Amatore, D., Barnes, C., & Kimura, S. (2008). Enhancement of student learning in experimental design using a virtual laboratory. *IEEE Transactions on Education, 51*(1), 76–85. doi:10.1109/TE.2007.906894

Kotter, J. P. (1996). *Leading change.* Boston, MA: Harvard Business School Press.

Kuhn, T. S. (1957). *The Copernican revolution: Planetary astronomy in the development of Western thought.* Cambridge, MA: Harvard University Press.

Kuhn, T. S. (1962). *The structure of scientific revolutions* (1st ed.). Chicago, IL: University of Chicago Press.

Kukulska-Hulme, A. (2010). Mobile learning as a catalyst for change. *Open Learning: The Journal of Open and Distance Learning, 25*(3), 181–185. doi:10.1080/0268 0513.2010.511945

Kvavik, R. B. (2005). Convenience, communications, and control: How students use technology. In D. Oblinger & J. Oblinger (Eds.), *Educating the Net generation* (pp. 7.1-7.20). Boulder, CO: Educause. Retrieved April 26, 2010 from http://net.educause.edu/ir/library/pdf/pub7101g.pdf

Ladyshewsky, R. K., & Gardner, P. (2008). Peer assisted learning and blogging: A strategy to promote reflective practice during clinical fieldwork. *Australasian Journal of Educational Technology, 24*(3), 241–257.

Land, R., Meyer, J., & Smith, J. (2008). *Threshold concepts within the disciplines.* Rotterdam, The Netherlands: Sense Publishers.

Lane, L. (2009). Insidious pedagogy: How course management systems impact teaching. *First Monday, 14*(10). Retrieved October 10, 2009, from http://firstmonday.org/htbin/cgiwrap/bin/ojs/index.php/fm/article/view/2530/2303

Larsen, M. (2010). Troubling the discourse of teacher centrality: A comparative perspective. *Journal of Education Policy, 25*(2), 207–231. doi:10.1080/02680930903428622

Laurillard, D. (2002). *Rethinking university teaching: A conversational framework for the effective use of learning technologies* (2nd ed.). London, UK & New York, NY: Routledge Falmer. doi:10.4324/9780203304846

Laurillard, D. (2006). E-learning in higher education. In Ashwin, P. (Ed.), *Changing higher education: The development of learning and teaching* (pp. 1–12). London, UK: Routledge.

Lave, J., & Wenger, E. (1991). *Situated learning: Legitimate peripheral participation.* Cambridge, UK: Cambridge University Press.

Lawson, B. (2001). *The language of space.* Oxford, UK: Architectural Press.

Le Grew, D. (2008). The place of learning. In Huijser, H., Elson-Green, J., Reid, I., Walta, C., Challis, D., & Harris, K.-L. (Eds.), *Places and spaces for learning seminars (draft report).* Sydney, Australia: Carrick Institute for Learning and Teaching in Higher Education.

Lea, M. R., & Nicoll, K. (2002). *Distributed learning: Social and cultural approaches to practice.* New York, NY: RoutledgeFalmer.

Learning Landscape Project Team. (2008). *The Cambridge pathfinder journey: The experience of the learning landscape project.* Retrieved March 15, 2011, from http://www.caret.cam.ac.uk/blogs/llp/wp-content/uploads/llp_pathfinder_journey_v03.pdf

Lebow, D., & Wager, W. W. (1994). Authentic activity as a model for appropriate learning activity: Implications for emerging instructional technologies. *Canadian Journal of Educational Communication, 23*(3), 231–244.

Lee, C. H., Lam, P., Lee, W. K., Ho, A., & Fox, R. M. (2009). Role of computers in student learning. In W. Kwan, R. Fox, A. Chan, et al. (Eds.). *ICT2009,* (p. 12). Hong Kong, Hong Kong SAR: Open University of Hong Kong.

Lee, N., Dixon, J., & Andrews, T. (2008). *A comprehensive learning space evaluation model: ALTC project proposal.* Retrieved March 6, 2010, from http://www.altc.edu.au/project-comprehensive-learning-space-swinburne-2008

Lefebvre, H. (1991). *The production of space.* Oxford, UK: Blackwell.

Lefebvre, H., & Goonewardena, K. (2008). *Space, difference, everyday life: Reading Henri Lefebvre.* New York, NY: Routledge.

Lefoe, G. (2010). Creating the future: Changing culture through leadership capacity development. In U. D. Ehlers & D. Schneckenberg (Eds.), *Changing cultures in higher education. A handbook for strategic change* (189-204). Heidelberg, Germany: Springer Verlag.

Leitch, S. (2006). *Leitch review of skills: Prosperity for all in the global economy - world class skills.* London, UK: HM Treasury. Retrieved August 25, 2009, from http://www.hm-treasur,/.gov.uk/media/6/4/leitch final-report051206.pdf

Leslie, P., & Murphy, E. (2008). Post-secondary students' purposes for blogging. *The International Review of Research in Open and Distance Learning, 9*(3). Retrieved October 24, 2008, from http://www.irrodl.org/index.php/irrodl/rt/printerFriendly/560/1099

Levin, C. (2008). *Leading by example: From sustainable campuses to a sustainable world.* Climate Lecture Series, University of Copenhagen. Retrieved April 8, 2010, from http://opa.yale.edu/ president/ message.aspx? id=1

Lin, M., & Chang, C. (2009). Incorporating auto-grading and feedback tools into an online 3D compound virtual field trip system. In G. Siemens & C. Fulford (Eds.), *Proceedings of World Conference on Educational Multimedia, Hypermedia and Telecommunications,* (pp. 3698-3703). Chesapeake, VA: AACE.

Littlejohn, A., & Pegler, C. (2007). *Preparing for blended e-learning.* London, UK: Routledge.

Lomas, C., & Oblinger, D. (2006). Student practices and their impact on learning spaces. In Oblinger, D. (Ed.), *Learning spaces* (pp. 5.1–5.11). Boulder, CO: Educause.

Lombardi, M. M. (2008). *Making the grade: The role of assessment in authentic learning.* Retrieved April 26, 2010, from http://net.educause.edu/ir/library/pdf/ELI3019.pdf

Lombardo, T. (2007), *Understanding and teaching future consciousness.* Retrieved August 25, 2009, from http://oth-newlearning.wikispaces.com/Understanding+and+Teaching+Future+Consciousness

Long, G. (2009). *Professional development for 21st century learning and teaching.* Retrieved from http://blog.garethl.com/2009/ 04/proessional-development-for-21st.html

Longworth, N. (2003). *Lifelong learning in action: Transforming education in the 21st century. London, UK & Sterling.* VA: Kogan Page.

Ma, A. (2009). Computer supported collaborative learning and higher order thinking skills: A case study of textile studies. *Interdisciplinary Journal of E-Learning and Learning Objects, 5,* 145-167. Retrieved September 17, 2009, from http://ijklo.org/ Volume5/ IJELLOv5p145-167MA657.pdf

Mabrito, M., & Medley, R. (2008). Why professor Johnny can't read: Understanding the Net generation's texts. *Innovate, 4*(6). Retrieved July 20, 2008, from http://www.innovate.info/index.php?view=article&id=510

MacMillan, D. (2007). Family trees 2.0. *BusinessWeek Online,* p. 23 Retrieved November 11, 2009, from http://www.businessweek.com/technology/content/jun2007/tc20070617_133514.htm

MacPhee, L. (2009). Learning spaces: A tutorial. *Educause Quarterly, 32*(1). Retrieved February 2, 2010, from http://www.educause.edu/EDUCAUSE+Quarterly/EDUCAUSEQuarterlyMagazineVolum/LearningSpacesATutorial/163854

Madge, C., Meek, J., Wellens, J., & Hooley, T. (2009). Facebook, social integration and informal learning at university: It is more for socialising and talking to friends about work than for actually doing work. *Learning, Media and Technology, 34*(2), 141–155. doi:10.1080/17439880902923606

Mahdizadeh, H., Biemans, H., & Mulder, M. (2008). Determining factors of the use of e-learning environments by university teachers. *Computers & Education, 51*(1), 142–154. doi:10.1016/j.compedu.2007.04.004

Marginson, S. (1997). *Markets in education.* Melbourne, Australia: Allen & Unwin.

Marriner Tomey, A. (2003). Learning with cases. *Journal of Continuing Education in Nursing, 34*(1), 34–38.

Massey University. (2008). *Lifelong learning policy.* Retrieved November 13, 2009, from http://science.massey.ac.nz/eportfolios/lllPolicy.asp

Mazzoni, E., & Gafurri, P. (2009). *Personal learning environments for overcoming knowledge boundaries between activity systems in emerging adulthood.* e-learning Papers. Retrieved February 22, 2010, from http://www.elearningeuropa.info/ out/ ?doc_id=19375& rsr_id=19744

McAlister, G., & Alexander, S. (2003). Key aspects of teaching and learning in information and computer sciences. In H. Fry, S. Ketteridge, & S. Marshall (Eds.), *A handbook for teaching and learning in higher education: Enhancing academic practice* (2nd ed.) (pp. 278-300). London, UK & Sterling, VA: Kogan Page.

McAndrew, P., Goodyear, P., & Dalziel, J. (2006). Patterns, designs and activities: Unifying descriptions of learning structures. *International Journal of Learning Technology, 2*(2–3), 216–242. doi:10.1504/IJLT.2006.010632

McCann, D., Christmass, J., Nicholson, P., & Stuparich, J. (1998). *Educational technology in higher education.* Canberra, Australia: Department of Employment, Education, Training and Youth Affairs.

McCroskey, J. C., & McVetta, R. W. (1978, April 25–29). *Classroom seating arrangements: Instructional communication theory versus student preferences.* Paper presented at the annual meeting of the International Communication Association, Chicago, IL.

MCEETYA. (2008). *Learning in an online world: Learning spaces framework.* Retrieved March 2, 2010, from http://www.mceecdya.edu.au/verve/_resources/ICT_LearningOnlineWorld-LearningSpacesFWork.pdf

McGrenere, J., & Ho, W. (2000). Affordances: Clarifying and evolving a concept. In *Proceedings of the Graphics Interface Conference* (pp. 179-186). Montreal, Canada.

McLoughlin, C., & Lee, M. J. W. (2009). Personalised learning spaces and self-regulated learning: Global examples of effective pedagogy. In R. Atkinson & C. McBeath, *Same places, different space. Proceedings ascilite Auckland 2009* (pp. 639-645). Retrieved March 29, 2011, from http://www.ascilite.org.au/conferences/auckland09/procs/mcloughlin.pdf

McLoughlin, C., & Lee, M. J. W. (2007). Social software and participatory learning: Pedagogical choices with technology affordances in the Web 2.0 era. In *ICT: Providing choices for learners and learning. Proceedings ASCILITE Singapore 2007.* Retrieved September 17, 2009, from http://www.ascilite.org.au/ conferences/ singapore07/ procs/ mcloughlin.pdf

McLoughlin, C., & Lee, M. J. W. (2008). Future learning landscapes: Transforming pedagogy through social software. *Innovate, 4*(5). Retrieved May 31, 2008, from http://www.innovate.info/index.php?view=article&id=539

McNaught, C. (2005). *Criteria for the design of a classroom for active and interactive teaching and learning.* Unpublished paper, CLEAR, The Chinese University of Hong Kong.

McNaught, C., & Lam, P. (2009). Institutional strategies for embedding blended learning in a research-intensive university. *Proceedings of the elearn2009 Conference, Bridging the development gap through innovative eLearning environments.* St Augustine, Trinidad and Tobago: The University of the West Indies. Retrieved April 27, 2010, from http://elearn2009.com/public/downloads/papers/MCNAUGHT_Carmel.pdf

McWilliam, E. L. (1998). Teacher IM/material: Challenging the new pedagogies of instructional design. *Educational Researcher, 27*(8), 29–35.

McWilliam, E. L. (2005). Unlearning pedagogy. *Journal of Learning Design, 1*(1), 1–11.

Meißner, A., Hasselhorn, H. M., Estryn-Behar, M., Nezet, O., Pokorski, J., & Gould, D. (2007). Nurses' perceptions of shift handovers in Europe- results from the European nurses' early exit study. *Journal of Advanced Nursing, 57*(5), 535–542. doi:10.1111/j.1365-2648.2006.04144.x

Meleis, A. F. (2005). *Theoretical nursing: Development and progress* (3rd ed.). Philadelphia, PA: Lippincott, Williams & Wilkins.

Meyer, J., & Land, R. (2006). *Overcoming barriers to student understanding: Threshold concepts and troublesome knowledge.* London, UK & New York, NY: Routledge.

Meyer, J., & Land, R. (2003). Threshold concepts and troublesome knowledge: Linkages to ways of thinking and practicing within the disciplines. In C. Rust (Ed.), *Improving student learning theory and practice - 10 years on* (pp. 412-424). Oxford, UK: Oxford centre for Staff & Learning Development Oxford Brookes University.

Miller, S., Meier, E., Payne-Bourcy, L., Shablak, S., Newmann, D. L., Wan, T. Y., et al. (2003). Technology use as a catalyst for change: A leadership framework for transforming urban teacher preparation. *International Electronic Journal for Leadership in Learning, 7*(12). Retrieved May 27, 2010, from http://iejll.synergiesprairies.ca/ iejll/index.php/iejll/ article/viewFile/427/89

Milne, A. J. (2006). Designing blended learning space to the student experience. In Oblinger, D. (Ed.), *Learning spaces* (pp. 11.1–11.15). Boulder, CO: Educause.

Mitchell, D. S., Croft, I., Harrison, T., & Webster-Mannison, M. (2001). *Water management on the Thurgoona campus of Charles Sturt University*. Paper presented at the Advancing On-site Wastewater Systems, University of New England, Armidale.

Mitchell, G., Winslett, G., & Howell, G. (2009). Lab 2.0. In D. Radcliffe, H. Wilson, D. Powell, & B. Tibbetts (Eds.), *Learning spaces in higher education – positive outcomes by design. Proceedings of the Next Generation Learning Spaces 2008 Colloquium* (Ch. 5.9). Brisbane, Australia: University of Queensland.

Monash University. (2009). *Flexible learning, teaching and collaboration spaces.* Retrieved July 17, 2009, from http://www.its.monash.edu.au/ staff/ projects/ collaboration-spaces/ index.html

Morales-Mann, E. T., & Kaitell, C. A. (2001). Problem-based learning in a new Canadian curriculum. *Journal of Advanced Nursing, 33*(1), 13–19. doi:10.1046/j.1365-2648.2001.01633.x

Morgan-Klein, B., & Osborne, M. (2007). *The concepts and practices of lifelong learning*. London, UK & New York, NY: Routledge.

Moschkovich, J. N., & Brenner, M. E. (2000). Integrating a naturalistic paradigm into research on mathematics and science cognition and learning. In Kelly, A. E., & Lesh, R. A. (Eds.), *Handbook of research design in mathematics and science education* (pp. 457–486). Mahwah, NJ: Lawrence Erlbaum Associates.

MOSEP. (2006). *More self esteem with my e-Portfolio*. Retrieved November 13, 2009, from http://www.mosep.org

Mouzelis, N. (1995). *Sociological theory: What went wrong?* New York, NY: Routledge.

Muffo, J. A. (2001). Assessing student competence in engineering. In Palomba, C. A., & Banta, T. W. (Eds.), *Assessing student competence in accredited disciplines* (pp. 159–175). Sterling, VA: Stylus.

Murray, S. J., Lowe, D. B., Lindsay, E., Lasky, V., & Liu, D. (2008). Experiences with a hybrid architecture for remote laboratories. In D. Budny (Ed.), *FiE 2008: The 38th Annual Frontiers in Education Conference*, (pp 15-19). Piscataway, NJ: IEEE.

Myers, S. (1993). A trial for Dmitri Karamazov. *Educational Leadership, 50*(7), 71–72.

Nardi, B., & O'Day, V. (1999). *Information ecologies: Using technology with heart*. Cambridge, MA: MIT Press.

Nardi, B. (Ed.). (1996). *Context and consciousness: Activity theory and human-computer interaction*. Cambridge, MA: MIT Press.

Newcastle University. (2007). *The first EPICS project*. Retrieved November 13, 2009, from http://www.eportfolios.ac.uk/EPICS/?pid=173

Newcastle University. (2009). *EPICS-2: North East regional collaboration for personalised, work-based, and life-long learning*. Retrieved November 13, 2009, from http://www.eportfolios.ac.uk/EPICS

Newton, R. (2003). Staff attitudes to the development and delivery of e-learning. *New Library World, 104*(1193), 412–425. doi:10.1108/03074800310504357

Nichols, P. D. (1994). A framework for developing cognitively diagnostic assessments. *Review of Educational Research, 64*(4), 575–603.

Nicholson, S. A., & Bond, N. (2003). Collaborative reflection and professional community building: An analysis of preservice teachers' use of an electronic discussion board. *Journal of Technology and Teacher Education, 11*(2), 259–279.

Nickerson, J. V., Corter, J. E., Esche, S. K., & Constantin, C. (2007). A model for evaluating the effectiveness of remote engineering laboratories and simulations in education. *Computers & Education, 49*(3), 708–725. doi:10.1016/j.compedu.2005.11.019

Norman, D. (1988). *The psychology of everyday things*. New York, NY: Basic Books.

Nursing and Midwifery Board of the Northern Territory. (2008). *Standards for the accreditation of education providers delivering nursing and midwifery courses*. Health Professionals Licensing Authority, NT Dept of Health and Families.

Oblinger, D. G. (2005). Leading the transition from classrooms to learning spaces. *EDUCAUSE Quarterly, 28*(1), 14–18.

Oblinger, D. (2005). Leading transition from classrooms to learning spaces. *Educause 28*(1). Retrieved April 8, 2010, from http://www.educause.edu/EDUCAUSE+Quarterly/ EDUCAUSE QuarterlyMagazineVolum/ LeadingtheTransitionfromClassr/ 157328

Oblinger, D. (Ed.). (2006). *Learning spaces*. EDUCAUSE. Retrieved March 6, 2010, from www.educause.edu/ learningspaces

Oblinger, D. G. (2006). Space as a change agent. In D. G. Oblinger (Ed.), *Learning spaces*, (pp. 1.1–1.4). Educause. Retrieved September 9, 2009 from http://www.educause. edu/learningspaces

Oblinger, D. G., & Oblinger, J. L. (Eds.). (2005). *Educating the Net generation*. Retrieved April 7, 201a, from http:// www.educause.edu/ educatingthenetgen

Oblinger, D., & Oblinger, J. (2005). Is it age or IT: First steps toward understanding the Net generation. In D. Oblinger & J. Oblinger (Eds.), *Educating the Net generation* (pp.2.1-2.20). Boulder, CO: Educause. Retrieved April 26, 2010, from http://net.educause.edu/ir/library/ pdf/pub7101b.pdf

O'Connell, B., & Penney, W. (2001). Challenging the handover ritual: Recommendations for research and practice. *Collegian (Royal College of Nursing, Australia)*, *8*(3), 14–18. doi:10.1016/S1322-7696(08)60017-7

OECD. (2005). E-learning in tertiary education: Where do we stand? In OECD (Ed.), *IT infrastructure: Use of learing management system (LMS) and other applications* (pp. 138-178). Paris, France: OECD Publishing.

Ofcom. (2008). *Social networking: A quantitative and qualitative research report into attitudes, behaviours and use*. Retrieved September 29, 2009, from http:// www.ofcom.org.uk/advice/media_literacy/medlitpub/ medlitpubrss/socialnetworking/report.pdf

Oliver, M. (2005). The problem with affordance. *E-learning*, *2*(4), 402–413. doi:10.2304/elea.2005.2.4.402

Oliver, R., & Omari, A. (1999). Using online technologies to support problem based learning: Learners responses and perceptions. *Australian Journal of Educational Technology*, *15*, 158–179.

Osguthorpe, R. T., & Graham, C. R. (2003). Blended learning environments definitions and directions. *The Quarterly Review of Distance Education*, *4*(3), 227–233.

Otala, L. (1997). Implementing lifelong learning in partnership with the educational sector and the work place. *The International Information & Library Review*, *29*(3-4), 455–460. doi:10.1006/iilr.1997.0063

Overton, T. (2003). Key aspects of teaching and learning in experimental sciences and engineering. In H. Fry, S. Ketteridge, & S. Marshall (Eds.), *A handbook for teaching and learning in higher education: Enhancing academic practice* (2nd ed.) (pp. 255-277). London, UK & Sterling, VA: Kogan Page.

P2P. (2006). *Policy peer review ICT in schools: Methodology*. Retrieved April 27, 2010, from http://insight.eun. org/ shared/data/insight/ documents/ P2PMethodology.pdf

Paavola, S., Lipponen, L., & Hakkarainen, K. (2004). Models of innovative knowledge communities and three metaphors of learning. *Review of Educational Research*, *74*(4), 557–576. doi:10.3102/00346543074004557

Pajo, K., & Wallace, C. (2001). Barriers to the uptake of Web-based technology by university teachers. *Journal of Distance Education*, *16*(1), 70–84.

Palfrey, J., & Gasser, U. (2008). *Born digital: Understanding the first generation of digital natives*. New York, NY: Basic Books.

Papert, S. (1980). *Mindstorms, children, computers and powerful ideas*. USA: Basic Books Inc.

Papert, S. (1994). *The children's machine: rethinking school in the age of the computer*. New York, NY: Harvester Wheatsheaf.

Papert, S. (1996). A word for learning. In Kafai, Y., & Resnick, M. (Eds.), *Constructionism in practice: Designing, thinking, and learning in a digital world* (p. 15). Mahwah, NJ: Lawrence Erlbaum and Associates.

Park, S. H., & Ertmer, P. A. (2007). Impact of problem-based learning (PBL) on teachers' beliefs regarding technology use. *Journal of Research on Technology in Education*, *40*(2), 247–267.

Passportfolio. (2008). *Passportfolio project*. Retrieved November 13, 2009, from https://www.passportfolio.com

Pearce, J. (2004). *An analysis of student absenteeism in first year biology students*. Institute for Science Education, University of Plymouth. Retrieved September 29, 2009, from http://www.bioscience.heacademy.ac.uk/ resources/ projects/ pearce.aspx

Pearshouse, I., Bligh, B., Brown, E., Lewthwaite, S., Graber, R., & Hartnell-Young, E. (2009). *A study of effective evaluation models and practices for technology supported physical learning spaces (JELS)*. Nottingham, UK: Learning Sciences Research Institute, University of Nottingham.

Pedder, D., Storey, A., & Opfer, V. D. (2008). *Schools and continuing professional development (CPD) in England - State of the nation research project: A report commissioned by the Training and Development Agency for Schools*. Cambridge University and the Open University.

Perkins, D. (1999). The many faces of constructivism. *Educational Leadership, 57*(3), 6–11.

Perkins, D. N. (1986). *Knowledge as design*. Hillsdale, NJ: Lawrence Earlbaum Associates.

Perkins, D. N. (1988). Teaching for transfer. *Educational Leadership, 46*(1), 22–32.

Perkins, D. (2008). Beyond understanding. In Land, R., Meyer, J., & Smith, J. (Eds.), *Threshold concepts within the disciplines* (pp. 3–19). Rotterdam, The Netherlands: Sense Publishers.

Perraton, H., & Moses, K. (2004). Technology. In Perraton, H. D., & Lentell, H. (Eds.), *Policy for open and distance learning* (pp. 141–157). London, UK: RoutledgeFarmer. doi:10.4324/9780203464403_chapter_8

Phillips, R. (1998). What research says about learning on the Internet. In McBeath, C., & Atkinson, R. (Eds.), *Planning for Progress, Partnership and Profit. Australian Society for Educational Technology. EduTech 98* (pp. 203–207). Perth, Australia: Australian Society for Educational Technology.

Piccoli, G., Ahmad, R., & Ives, B. (2001). Web-based virtual learning environments: A research framework and a preliminary assessment of effectiveness in basic IT skills training. *Management Information Systems Quarterly, 25*(4), 401–426. doi:10.2307/3250989

Pitman, T., & Broomhall, S. (2009). Australian universities, generic skills and lifelong learning. *International Journal of Lifelong Education, 28*(4), 439–458. doi:10.1080/02601370903031280

Pivec, M., & Pivec, P. (2009) IMAGINE report on Game-Based Learning projects within the European community and good practice case studies spread across all levels of education. Retrieved April 7, 2011, http://www.imaginegames.eu/ eng/Reports

Poole, G. (2008). *A place to call a learning home*. Key address at ASCILITE 2008, Hello! Where are you in the landscape of educational technology, Melbourne, Australia. Retrieved February 27, 2010, from http://www.ascilite.org.au/conferences/melbourne08/keynotegary.htm

Pratt, G. (1990). *Aural awareness: Principles and practice*. United Kingdom: Open University Press.

Pratt, J. G. (2003). Decision making, rationality, and the adoption of online learning technologies in Australian higher education. In *Conference Proceedings - Surfing the Waves: Management Challenges, Management Solutions, 17th Annual Conference of the Australian and New Zealand Academy of Management (ANZAM)* (pp. 1-11). Fremantle, Australia: ANZAM.

Prensky, M. (2001). Digital natives, digital immigrants. *Horizon, 9*(5), 1–6. doi:10.1108/10748120110424816

Prensky, M. (2001). *Digital games-based learning*. New York, NY & London, UK: McGraw Hill.

Prensky, M. (2001). Digital natives, digital immigrants. *On the Horizon, 9*(5). Retrieved February 14, 2007, from http://www.marcprensky.com/writing/Prensky%20 -20Digital%20Natives%20Digital%20Immigrants%20 -%20Part1.pdf.

Primary Health Care Reform in Australia. (2009). *Report to support Australia's first national primary healthcare strategy*. Canberra, Australia: Commonwealth of Australia.

Prosser, M., & Trigwell, K. (1999). *Understanding learning and teaching: The experience in higher education*. Buckingham, UK & Philadelphia, PA: Society for Research into Higher Education & Open University Press.

Prosser, M., & Jamieson, P. (2008). *Spatial-pedagogy matrix for different types of classroom settings*. Unpublished manuscript, The University of Hong Kong.

Punie, Y. (2007). Learning spaces: An ICT-enabled model of future learning in the knowledge-based society. *European Journal of Education, 42*(2), 185–199. doi:10.1111/j.1465-3435.2007.00302.x

Radcliffe, D. (2009). A pedagogy-space-technology (PST) framework for designing and evaluating learning spaces. In D. Radcliffe, H. Wilson, D. Powell, & B. Tibbetts (Eds.), *Learning spaces in higher education – positive outcomes by design. Proceedings of the Next Generation Learning Spaces 2008 Colloquium* (Chapter 1.0). Brisbane, Australia: University of Queensland.

Radcliffe, D., Wilson, H., Powell, D., & Tibbetts, B. (2008). *Designing next generation places of learning: Collaboration at the pedagogy-space-technology nexus*. ALTC Priority Project #627. The University of Queensland. Retrieved March 6, 2010, from http://www.uq.edu.au/nextgenerationlearningspace/

Radcliffe, D., Wilson, H., Powell, D., & Tibbetts, B. (Eds.). (2009). *Learning spaces in higher education: Positive outcomes by design*. Proceedings of the Next Generation Learning Spaces 2008 Colloquium. University of Queensland, Brisbane.

Radloff, P. (1998). Proceedings of the 7th Annual Teaching Learning Forum. In B. Black & N. Stanley (Eds.), *Teaching and learning in changing times*. Perth, Australia: The University of Western Australia. Retrieved April 30, 2010, from http://lsn.curtin.edu.au/ tlf/ tlf1998/ radloff-p.html

Rafferty, J. (2011). Design of outdoor and environmentally integrated learning spaces. In Keppell, M. J., Riddle, M., & Souter, K. (Eds.), *Physical and virtual learning spaces in higher education: Concepts for the modern learning environment*. Hershey, PA: IGI Global.

Rafferty, J. M. (2007). *The continuing myth of school reform*. Paper presented at the Australian Association for Research in Education International Education Research Conference, Fremantle, Western Australia.

Ramakishnan, S., & Ramadoss, B. (2009). Assessment using multi-criteria decision approach for "higher order skills" learning domains. *International Journal on E-Learning, 8*(2), 241–262.

Reeves, T. C., & Okey, J. R. (1996). Alternative assessment for constructivist learning environments. In Wilson, B. G. (Ed.), *Constructivist learning environments: Case studies in instructional design* (pp. 191–202). Englewood Cliffs, NJ: Educational Technology Publications.

Reeves, T. C., Herrington, J., & Oliver, R. (2002). Authentic activities and online learning. *Annual Conference Proceedings of Higher Education Research and Development Society of Australasia*. Perth, Australia.

Resnick, L. (1987). Learning in school and out. *Educational Researcher, 16*(9), 13–20.

Reushle, S. (2009). *PaSsPorT for designing learning spaces*. Unpublished USQ discussion paper.

Reushle, S. (2009a). *eValuation model using design-based research*. Unpublished USQ discussion paper, University of Southern Queensland, Queensland

Richardson, W. (2009). *Blogs, wikis, podcasts, and other powerful web tools for the classroom* (2nd ed.). California: Corwin Press.

Richardson, D., & Molka-Danielsen, J. (2009). Assessing student performance. In Molka-Danielsen, J., & Deutschmann, M. (Eds.), *Learning and teaching in the virtual world of Second Life* (pp. 52–60). Trondheim, Norway: Tapir Academic Press.

Riddle, M., & Arnold, M. (2007). *The day experience method: A resource kit*. Retrieved April 10, 2011, from http://www.matthewriddle.com/papers/Day_Experience_Resource_Kit.pdf

Riddle, M., & Howell, C. (2008). You are here: Students map their own ICT landscapes. In R. Atkinson & C. Mc-Beath (Eds.), *Hello! Where are you in the landscape of educational technology? Proceedings ascilite Melbourne 2008* (pp. 802-808). Retrieved March 29, 2011, from http://www.ascilite.org.au/conferences/melbourne08/procs/riddle.pdf.

Ripley, M., Harding, R., Redif, H., Ridgway, J., & Tafler, J. (2009). *Review of advanced e-assessment techniques (RAeAT) final report*. Retrieved April 7, 2011, from http://www.jisc.ac.uk/media /documents/projects/ raeat_final-report.pdf

Rodgers, J. R. (2001). A panel-data study of the effect of student attendance on university performance. *Australian Journal of Education, 45*(3), 284–295.

Rosenzweig, R. M. (2001). *The political university: Policy, politics, and presidential leadership in the American research university*. Baltimore, MD: Johns Hopkins University Press.

Russell, C., & Hodson, D. (2002). Whalewatching as critical science education? *Canadian Journal of Science. Mathematics and Technology Education, 2*(4), 485–504. doi:10.1080/14926150209556537

Sachs, J. (2001). Teacher professional identity: Competing discourses, competing outcomes. *Journal of Education Policy, 16*(2), 149–161. doi:10.1080/02680930116819

Sahin, I., & Thompson, A. (2006). Using Rogers' theory to interpret instructional computer use by COE faculty. *Journal of Research on Technology in Education, 39*(1), 81–104.

Salaway, G., Caruso, J. B., & Nelson, M. R. (2008). *The ECAR study of undergraduate students and Information Technology, 2008. Research study* (vol. 8). Boulder, CO: EDUCAUSE. Retrieved April 10, 2011, from http://www.educause.edu/ecar

Saulwick, I., & Muller, D. (2006). *Fearless and flexible: Views of gen Y*. Report Prepared for the Dusseldorp Skills Forum. October. Saulwick Miller Social Research.

Savin-Baden, M. (2008). *Learning spaces: Creating opportunities for knowledge creation in academic life*. Maidenhead, UK: Open University Press.

Savin-Baden, M. (2003). *Facilitating problem-based learning*. Maidenhead, UK: Open University Press.

Scanlon, L. (2006). Graduate attributes and the transition to higher education. In Hager, P. J., & Holland, S. (Eds.), *Graduate attributes, learning and employability* (Vol. 6, pp. 125–148). Netherlands: Springer. doi:10.1007/1-4020-5342-8_7

Schuetze, H. G., & Casey, C. (2006). Models and meanings of lifelong learning: Progress and barriers on the road to a learning society. *Compare: A Journal of Comparative and International Education, 36*(3), 279-287.

Schwartz, C. (2006). Managing electronic portfolios. In Hernon, P., Dugan, R. E., & Schwartz, C. (Eds.), *Revisiting outcomes assessment in higher education* (pp. 151–164). Westport, CT & London, UK: Libraries Unlimited.

Schwarz, C. V., Meyer, J., & Sharma, A. (2007). Technology, pedagogy, and epistemology: Opportunities and challenges of using computer modeling and simulation tools in elementary science methods. *Journal of Science Teacher Education, 18*(2), 243–269. doi:10.1007/s10972-007-9039-6

Sclater, N., & Weller, M. (2009). *Podcast for H800 Technology-enhanced learning: Practices and debates*. Retrieved April 11, 2011 from http://nogoodreason.typepad.co.uk/no_good_reason/2009/04/vle-vs-ple-fight-club.html

Scott, G. (2005) *Accessing the student voice*. Canberra, Australia: Department of Education, Science and Training. Retrieved September 29, 2008, from http://www.dest.gov.au/sectors/higher_education/publications_resources/profiles/access_student_voice.htm

Seeto, D., & Herrington, J. (2006). Design-based research and the learning designer. In L. Markauskaite, P. Goodyear, & P. Reimann (Eds.), *Proceedings of the 23rd Annual Conference of the Australasian Society for Computers in Learning in Tertiary Education: Who's Learning? Whose Technology?* (pp. 741-745). Sydney, Australia: Sydney University Press.

Sfard, A. (1998). On two metaphors for learning and the dangers of choosing just one. *Educational Researcher, 27*(2), 4–13.

Shaffer, D. W., Hatfield, D., Svarovsky, G. N., Nash, P., Nulty, A., & Bagley, E. (2009). Epistemic network analysis: A prototype for 21st century assessment of learning. *International Journal of Learning and Media*, *1*(2), 33–53. doi:10.1162/ijlm.2009.0013

Shoemaker, A. (2008). *If the world is our campus, where are we going?* Address given at the Australian Financial Review Higher Education Conference. Retrieved September 21, 2009, from http://www.odvce.monash.edu.au/ passport-text.html

Shulman, L. S. (2005). Signature pedagogies in the professions. *Daedalus*, (June): 52–59. doi:10.1162/0011526054622015

Shute, V. J. (2009). Simply assessment. *International Journal of Learning and Media*, *1*(2), 1–11. doi:10.1162/ijlm.2009.0014

Shute, V. J., & Spector, J. M. (2008). *SCORM 2.0 white paper: Stealth assessment in virtual world.* Retrieved April 7, 2011, from http://www.adlnet.gov/ Technologies/Evaluation/Library /Additional%20Resources/ LETSI%20White%20Papers/ Shute%20-%20Stealth%20 Assessment%20in%20 Virtual%20Worlds.pdf

Shute, V. J., Ventura, M., Bauer, M., & Zapata-Rivera, D. (2009). Melding the power of serious games and embedded assessment to monitor and foster learning: Flow and grow. In U. Ritterfeld, M. Cody & P. Vorderer (Eds.), *Serious games: Mechanisms and effects* (pp. 293-319). New York, NY: Taylor & Francis Group. Retrieved April 7, 2011, from http://21st-century-assessment. wikispaces.com/file/ view/GAMES_Shute _FINAL.pdf

Sibeon, R. (2004). *Rethinking social theory.* London, UK: Sage publications.

Siemens, G. (2006). *Knowing knowledge.* Lulu.com.

Simsek, A., & Hooper, S. (1992). The effects of cooperative versus individual videodisc learning on student performance and attitudes. *International Journal of Instructional Media*, *19*(3), 209–218.

Skamp, K. (2008). *Teaching primary science constructively* (3rd ed.). South Melbourne, Victoria, Australia: Cengage Learning.

Smedley, A., & Morey, P. (2009). Improving learning in the clinical nursing environment: Perceptions of senior Australian bachelor of nursing students. *Journal of Research in Nursing*, *15*(1), 75–88. doi:10.1177/1744987108101756

Soley, L. (1995). *Leasing the ivory tower: The corporate takeover of academia.* Boston, MA: South End Press.

Song, H. S. Y., & Chan, Y. M. (2008). Educational blogging: A Malaysian university students' perception and experience. In *Hello! Where are you in the landscape of educational technology? Proceedings ASCILITE Melbourne 2008.* Retrieved on February 23, 2010, from http://www.ascilite.org.au/ conferences/ melbourne07/ procs/ song.pdf

Souter, K. Riddle, M., Keppell, M. J., & Sellers, W. (2010). *Spaces for knowledge generation.* Retrieved March 29, 2011, from http://www.skgproject.com/

Spencer, J. (2003). ABC of learning and teaching in medicine: Learning and teaching in the clinical environment. *BMJ (Clinical Research Ed.)*, *326*(7389), 591–594. doi:10.1136/bmj.326.7389.591

Steck, H. (2003). Corporatization of the university: Seeking conceptual clarity. *The Annals of the American Academy of Political and Social Science*, *585*(1), 66–83. doi:10.1177/0002716202238567

Steel, C. H. (2009a). Reconciling university teacher beliefs to create learning designs for LMS environments. *Australasian Journal of Educational Technology*, *25*(3), 399–420.

Steel, C. H. (2009b). *The interrelationship between university teachers' pedagogical beliefs, beliefs about Web technologies and Web practices.* Brisbane: Unpublished PhD, Griffith University.

Steel, C. H., & Levy, M. (2009). Creativity and constraint: Understanding teacher beliefs and the use of LMS technologies. In R. Atkinson & C. McBeath (Eds.), *Same places, different spaces. Proceedings of ASCILITE Conference Auckland 2009* (pp. 1013-1022). Auckland, New Zealand: Auckland University.

Sternberg, R. J., Wagner, R. K., & Okagaki, L. (1993). Practical intelligence: The nature and role of tacit knowledge in work and at school. In Puckett, J. M., & Reese, H. W. (Eds.), *Mechanisms of everyday cognition* (pp. 205–227). Hillsdale, NJ: Lawrence Erlbaum Associates.

Stevens, M. (2007). Social video: Videoblogging & YouTube. *Library Technology Reports*, *43*(5), 52–57.

Stjernquist, M., & Crang-Svalenius, E. (2007). Problem based learning and the case method-medical students change preferences during clerkship. *Medical Teacher*, *29*(8), 814–820. doi:10.1080/01421590701601592

Stone, J. (2010). Attempting to speak the same language: Interprofessional collaborative practice (ICP) - definitions and terminology. *Nursing Review, February*, 10-11.

Stroebel, C. K., McDaniel, R. R., Crabtree, B. F., Miller, W. L., Nutting, P. A., & Stange, K. C. (2005). How complexity science can inform a reflective process for improvement in primary care practices. *Joint Commission Journal on Quality and Patient Safety*, *31*(8), 438–446.

Sun, Y. C. (2009). Voice blog: An exploratory study of language learning. *Language Learning & Technology, 13*(2), 88-103. Retrieved August 28, 2009, from http://llt.msu.edu/ vol13num2/ sun.pdf

Suter, V., Alexander, B., & Kaplan, P. (2005). The future of F2F. *Educause Review*, *40*(1). Retrieved March 1, 2010, from http://www.educause.edu/ EDUCAUSE+Review/ EDUCAUSEReviewMagazineVolume40 /TheFuture-ofF2F/157954

Sutherland, P., & Crowther, J. (2006). *Lifelong learning: Concepts and contexts*. London, UK & New York, NY: Routledge.

Tapscott, D. (1998). *Growing up digital: The rise of the Net generation*. New York, NY: McGraw-Hill.

Tapscott, D. (2009). *Grown up digital: How the Net generation is changing your world*. New York, NY: McGraw-Hill.

Taylor, J. (2001). *Fifth generation distance education*. Keynote address presented at the 20th ICDE World Conference, Düsseldorf, Germany.

Tchounikine, P. (2008). Operationalising macro-scripts in CSCL technological settings. *International Journal of Computer-Supported Collaborative Learning, 3*(2), 193–233. doi:10.1007/s11412-008-9039-3

Teghe, D., & Knight, B. A. (2004). Neo-liberal higher education policy and its effects on the development of online courses. *Campus-Wide Information Systems, 21*(4), 151–156. doi:10.1108/10650740410555025

Tekinarslan, E. (2008). Blogs: A qualitative investigation into an instructor and undergraduate students' experiences. *Australasian Journal of Educational Technology, 24*(4), 402–412.

Temple, P. (2008). Learning spaces in higher education: An under-researched topic. *London Review of Education, 6*(3), 229–241. doi:10.1080/14748460802489363

Temple, P., & Barnett, R. (2007). Higher education space: Future directions. *Planning for Higher Education, 36*(1), 5–15.

The Carrick Institute for Learning and Teaching in Higher Education. (2007). *Places and spaces for learning seminars, September 2007. Draft report*. Sydney, Australia: Carrick Institute.

The Chinese University of Hong Kong. (2009). *Campus master plan*. Retrieved March 10, 2010 from http://www.cuhk.edu.hk/cmp/en/

Tierney, W. G. (1996). Leadership and postmodernism: On voice and the qualitative method. *The Leadership Quarterly, 7*(3), 371–383. doi:10.1016/S1048-9843(96)90026-0

Tiropanis, T., Davis, H., Millard, D., Weal, M., White, S., & Wills, G. (2009). *JISC SemTech project report*. Retrieved April 7, 2011, from http://www.jisc.ac.uk/media/ documents/projects/ semtech-report.pdf

Tiwari, A., Lai, P., So, M., & Yuen, K. (2006). A comparison of the effects of problem-based learning and lecturing on the development of students' critical thinking. *Medical Education, 40*(6), 547–554. doi:10.1111/j.1365-2929.2006.02481.x

Topping, K. (2007). Trends in peer learning. *Educational Psychology, 25*(6), 631–645. doi:10.1080/01443410500345172

Torrance, H., & Pryor, J. (2001). Developing formative assessment in the classroom: Using action research to explore and modify theory. *British Educational Research Journal, 27*(5), 615–631. doi:10.1080/01411920120095780

Tourism, N. T. (2005-2009). *About NT. Key facts: The people.* Retrieved October 28, 2009, from http://en.travelnt.com/about-nt /key-facts/people.aspx

Trowler, P., & Cooper, A. (2002). Teaching and learning regimes: Implicit theories and recurrent practices in the enhancement of teaching and learning through educational development programmes. *Higher Education Research & Development, 21*(3), 221–240. doi:10.1080/0729436022000020742

Tynan, B., & Lee, M. J. W. (2009). Tales of adventure and change: Academic staff members' future visions of higher education and their professional development needs. *Horizon, 17*(2), 98–108. doi:10.1108/10748120910965485

Tynan, B., Lee, M. J. W., & Barnes, C. (2008). Polar bears, black gold and light bulbs: Creating stable futures for tertiary education through instructor training and support in the use of ICTs. In *Proceedings of World Conference on Educational Multimedia, Hypermedia and Telecommunications,* (pp. 3557-64). Chesapeake, VA: AACE.

UNESCO. (2001). *Report on the UNESCO Programme — LEARNTEC 2001.* Retrieved August 23, 2009, from http://webworld.unesco.org/c_learning/new/report.shtml

Universities Australia. (2005). *Key statistics – students.* Retrieved 29 September, 2009, from http://www.universitiesaustralia.edu.au/ documents/ publications/ stats/ Students.pdf

University of Leeds. (2008a). *The enhancing learner progression project.* Retrieved November 13, 2009, from http://www.leeds.ac.uk/medicine/meu/elp/index.html

University of Leeds. (2008b). *Leeds practice.* Retrieved November 13, 2009, from http://www.leeds.ac.uk/PDP/leedspractice.htm

University of Leicester. (2007). *Skills for sustainable communities lifelong learning network.* Retrieved November 13, 2009, from http://www.le.ac.uk/ssclln/

University of Nottingham. (2005). *PADSHE project.* Retrieved November 13, 2009, from http://www.nottingham.ac.uk/padshe/

Unsworth, J. (2008). University 2.0. In Katz, R. N. (Ed.), *The tower and the cloud: Higher education in the age of cloud computing* (pp. 227–237). Boulder, CO: Educause.

Van den Akker, J., Gravemeijer, K., McKenney, S., & Nieveen, N. (2006). *Educational design research.* London, UK: Routledge.

Van Note Chism, N. (2006). Challenging traditional assumptions and rethinking learning spaces. In Oblinger, D. (Ed.), *Learning spaces* (pp. 2.1–2.12). Boulder, CO: Educause.

Van Note Chism, N. (2006). Challenging traditional assumptions and rethinking learning spaces. In D. G. Oblinger (Ed.), *Learning spaces,* (pp. 2.1 – 2.12). Educause. Retrieved February 27, 2010, from http://www.educause.edu/learningspaces

Veletsianos, G., Miller, C., & Doering, A. (2009). EnALI: A research and design framework for virtual characters and pedagogical agents. *Journal of Educational Computing Research, 41*(2), 171–194. doi:10.2190/EC.41.2.c

Velocity Magazine. (2008). *Hot desking.* Retrieved March 6, 2010, from http://vlmmagazine.com/2008/11/01/hot-desking/

Vrakking, W. J. (1995). The implementation game. *Journal of Organisational Change, 8*(3), 31–46. doi:10.1108/09534819510090141

Vygotsky, L. S., & Cole, M. (1978). *Mind in society: The development of higher psychological processes.* Cambridge, UK: Harvard University Press.

Waldron, N., Dawson, S., & Burnett, B. (2005). Academic staff development in online learning and teaching: Developing online pedagogies. In *Proceedings of AUSweb 2005.* Gold Coast. Retrieved May 27, 2010, from http://ausweb.scu.edu.au/aw05 /papers/refereed/waldron /index.html

Walters, S. (2005). Realizing a lifelong learning higher education institution. In Sutherland, P., & Crowther, J. (Eds.), *Lifelong learning: Concepts and contexts* (pp. 71–81). London, UK: Routledge.

Watson, L. (2003). *Lifelong learning in Australia (3/13)*. Canberra, Australia: Commonwealth of Australia.

Watson, L. (2007). Building the future of learning. *European Journal of Education*, *42*(2), 255–263. doi:10.1111/j.1465-3435.2007.00299.x

Weaver, B. (2009). Collaboration with users to design learning spaces: Playing nicely in the sandbox. *Educause Quarterly*, *32*(1). Retrieved February 2, 2010, from http://www.educause.edu/EDUCAUSE+Quarterly/EDUCAUSEQuarterlyMagazineVolum/Collaboratingwith UserstoDesign/163855

Webster, L., Fraser, K., & Smith, L. (2009). Research-led curriculum redesign for productive learning: A case study in the faculty of information technology. In O'Donoghue, J. (Ed.), *Technology supported environment for personalised learning: Methods and case studies*. Hershey, PA: Idea Group Inc.doi:10.4018/978-1-60566-884-0.ch013

Weir, S. (2008). Teachers advocating m-learning. *The International Journal of Technology. Knowledge and Society*, *4*(5), 9–16.

Weller, M. (2007). *Virtual learning environments: Using, choosing and developing your VLE*. London, UK: Routledge.

Wenger, E., McDermott, R. A., & Snyder, W. (2002). *Cultivating communities of practice: A guide to managing knowledge*. Boston, MA: Harvard Business School Press.

Wenger, E. (1998). *Communties of practice: Learning, meaning and identity*. Cambridge, UK: Cambridge University Press.

Wenger, E. (1999). *Communities of practice: Learning, meaning, and identity*. Cambridge, UK: Cambridge University Press.

Wenger, E. (2003). Communities of practice and social learning systems. In D. Nicolini, S.Gherardi, & D. Yanow (Eds.), *Knowing in organizations: A practice-based approach* (pp. 76-99). New York, NY: Armonk.

Wheeler, S., Yeomans, P., & Wheeler, D. (2008). The good, the bad and the wiki: Evaluating student-generated content for collaborative learning. *British Journal of Educational Technology*, *39*(6), 987–995. doi:10.1111/j.1467-8535.2007.00799.x

White, G. (2008). *Digital learning: An Australian research agenda 2008*. Retrieved April 28, 2010, from Available at: http://works.bepress.com/ gerry_white/1

WikiEducator. (2009). *About*. Retrieved February 17, 2010, from http://wikieducator.org/WikiEducator:About

Wild, F., Mödritscher, F., & Sigurdarson, S. (2008). Designing for change: Mash-up personal learning environments. *eLearning Papers*, *9*. Retrieved February 22, 2010, from http://www.elearningeuropa.info/ out/?doc_id=15055 &rsr_id=15972

Williams, J. B., & Jacobs, J. (2004). Exploring the use of blogs as learning spaces in the higher education sector. *Australasian Journal of Educational Technology*, *20*(2), 232–247.

Wilson, B. G. (1995). Metaphors for instruction: Why we talk about learning environments. *Educational Technology*, *35*(5), 25–30.

Wilson, S., Liber, O., Johnson, M., Beauvoir, P., Sharples, P., & Milligan, C. (2007). Personal learning environments: Challenging the dominant design of educational systems. *Journal of e-Learning and Knowledge Society*, *3*(2), 27-38.

Winn, W. (1993). Instructional design and situated learning: Paradox or partnership. *Educational Technology*, *33*(3), 16–21.

Winnicott, D. W. (1953). Transitional objects and transitional phenomena. *The International Journal of Psycho-Analysis*, *34*, 89–97.

Winnicott, D. W. (1971). *Playing and reality*. London, UK: Tavistock.

Wittel, A. (2001). Towards a network sociality. *Theory, Culture & Society*, *18*(6), 51–76.

Wood, D., Bruner, J., & Ross, G. (1976). The role of tutoring in problem solving. *Child Psychology and Psychiatry*, *17*(1), 89–100. doi:10.1111/j.1469-7610.1976.tb00381.x

Woudstra, A., & Adria, M. (2008). Network and virtual forms of distance education. In M. G. Moore (Ed.), *Handbook of distance education* (pp. 501-514). Mahway, NJ & London, UK: Lawrence Erlbaum Associates.

Wyn, J., Cuervo, H., Smith, G., Beadle, S., & Woodman, D. (2008). *Pathways through life: Summary report on 2007 survey*. Australian Youth Research Centre, The University of Melbourne. Retrieved September 28, 2009, from http://www.edfac.unimelb.edu.au/yrc/life_patterns/PathwaysSurvey2007.pdf

Yerrick, R., Parke, H., & Nugent, J. (1997). Struggling to promote deeply rooted change: The filtering effect of teachers' beliefs on understanding transformational views of teaching science. *Science Education, 81*(2), 137–159. doi:10.1002/(SICI)1098-237X(199704)81:2<137::AID-SCE2>3.0.CO;2-G

Young, S. F. (2008). Theoretical frameworks and models of learning: Tools for developing conceptions of teaching and learning. *The International Journal for Academic Development, 13*(1), 41–49. doi:10.1080/13601440701860243

Young, M. F. (1993). Instructional design for situated learning. *Educational Technology Research and Development, 41*(1), 43–58. doi:10.1007/BF02297091

Young, M. F. (1995). Assessment of situated learning using computer environments. *Journal of Science Education and Technology, 4*(1), 89–96. doi:10.1007/BF02211586

Young, M. F., & McNeese, M. (1993). A situated cognition approach to problem solving with implications for computer-based learning and assessment. In Salvendy, G., & Smith, M. J. (Eds.), *Human-computer interaction: Software and hardware interfaces*. New York, NY: Elsevier Science Publishers.

Young, S., & Delves, L. (2009). Expanding to fit the (blog)space: Enhancing social work education through online technologies. In *Same places, different spaces. Proceedings ASCILITE Auckland 2009*. Retrieved February 23, 2010, from http://www.ascilite.org.au/conferences/auckland09/procs/young.pdf

Zawacki-Richter, O., Brown, T., & Delport, R. (2009). Mobile learning: From single project status into the mainstream? *European Journal of Open, Distance and E-Learning*. Retrieved May 27, 2010, from http://www.eurodl.org/materials/contrib/2009/Richter_Brown_Delport.htm

Zhang, Z., Cheung, K.-H., & Townsend, J. P. (2009). Bringing Web 2.0 to bioinformatics. *Briefings in Bioinformatics, 10*(1), 1–10. doi:10.1093/bib/bbn041

Zhou, G., & Xu, J. (2007). Adoption of educational technology ten years after setting strategic goals: A Canadian university case study. *Australasian Journal of Educational Technology, 23*(4), 508–528.

Zhou, F., Duh, H. B.-L., & Billinghurst, M. (2008). Trends in augmented reality tracking, interaction and display: A review of ten years of ISMAR. In *Proceedings of the 7th IEEE/ACM International Symposium on Mixed and Augmented Reality* (pp. 193-202). Washington, DC: IEEE Computer Society.

About the Contributors

Mike Keppell is currently Director, The Flexible Learning Institute and Professor of Higher Education at Charles Sturt University, Australia. Prior to this, he worked from 2003 – 2007 at the Hong Kong Institute of Education as Associate Professor and Head of the Centre for Learning, Teaching and Technology (LTTC). Before this, he was Head of the Biomedical Multimedia Unit, Faculty of Medicine, Dentistry and Health Science, The University of Melbourne, Australia from 1998-2002 and Head of the Interactive Multimedia Unit, Division of Distance and Continuing Education, Central Queensland University, Australia from 1994-1998. He has a background in learning and teaching, curriculum, evaluation, and more specifically, instructional design. His research focuses on blended learning, learning-oriented assessment, authentic learning, learning spaces and transformative learning using design-based research. He is currently President of *ascilite*. In 2007 he edited a book through IGI Global titled *Instructional Design: Case Studies in Communities of Practice* with authors from eight different countries.

Kay Souter is Associate Dean (Academic) at La Trobe University, in Melbourne Australia. She is the leader of the 'Spaces for Knowledge Generation project' (www.skgproject.com), and has been associated with several other major pedagogical research projects. She teaches and researches mostly in the areas of psychoanalytic literary theory and the representations of the female body, and has published widely in these areas. She is currently working on collaborative research projects with colleagues in Melbourne and Delhi, including an anthology of mother-daughter relationships in Indian literature, *An Endless Winter's Night anthology of Mother-Daughter relationships in Indian Literature,* with Ira Raja (New Delhi, Women Unlimited Press, 2010).

Matthew Riddle is a Senior Lecturer in Academic Development in the Faculty of Law and Management at La Trobe University, Australia. He has been working in the field of tertiary education since 1993. He has worked as an educational researcher at the University of Cambridge and educational designer at the University of Melbourne, Australia. He is interested in a broad range of higher education issues, particularly in virtual and physical learning spaces, curriculum design and e-learning, and has designed innovative online role-plays. His research uses a combination of quantitative and qualitative methods in order to build a rich evidence base about student perspectives on daily technology use in the context of their broader learning experience. This research is attempting to change the way we think about learning spaces by examining what students do with their time, where they go, and how they feel about learning spaces.

* * *

Trish Andrews has worked in the field of higher education for over fifteen years and has considerable experience in the areas of open, distance, flexible, and blended learning. She has extensive experience in supporting innovative curriculum development with a particular focus on integrating technologies into higher education programs. Trish has had several educational development and research grants including current ALTC grants in the area of rich media and learning spaces and has published widely in the area of educational innovation. Trish's current research interests include learning spaces, mobile learning and distance learning.

Anne Berry is a cellist, AMEB cello examiner, and freelance researcher currently based in Newcastle, Australia. In addition to instrumental pedagogy, Anne's research interests include Australian cello music, Australian indigenous culture and communities, community participation in music making, learning and academically gifted children, neuro-plasticity, performance confidence, and motivation. Anne was awarded her PhD (Music Education & Pedagogy) from The University of Queensland, Australia in 2007. She studied the influence of repertoire choice on intrinsic motivation in intermediate cello students. Other research projects have included the production of a video teaching package for beginning cellists with non-cellist teachers.

Gill Best is a Lecturer in the School of Learning Support Services and the Coordinator, Students Supporting Student Learning (S3L) at Victoria University. Gill has spent many years utilising traditional forms of learning support methodologies with students from diverse family and academic backgrounds. Since the late 1990's Gill has led the development of S3L as an additional and central student learning support strategy for Victoria University students.

Yuliya Bozhko is currently a PhD student at the School of Engineering and Advanced Technology, Massey University, New Zealand. Her research interests include lifelong learning in higher education, personal learning environments, and e-portfolio processes. In 2008, Yuliya completed her Master of Science Degree with Honours in Information Control Systems and Technologies at National University "Kyiv-Mohyla Academy," Ukraine. While completing her Master's Degree, she was involved in the TEMPUS Joint European Projects and in eFolio development for student learning portals. She has previously been working in the software development industry and in higher education.

Chris Cheers has a broad international background in education having taught, coordinated, and developed courses in university, polytechnic, TAFE, and industry settings. His work has focused on the design, development, and implementation of e-learning and student-centred approaches such as problem, case, and project based learning. After working in Singapore for 10 years in educational design and development and faculty development at Ngee Ann Polytechnic and Nanyang Technological University, he currently holds the position of Academic Development Manager for the Built Environment Degree Program at Holmesglen Institute, Melbourne, Australia, and is a PhD candidate at the University of Southern Queensland, Faculty of Education, Australia. His research interests focus on the design of learning triggers and the scaffolding of critical reflection in digital ecosystems for higher education.

Merilyn Childs is Deputy Director of the Flexible Learning Institute at Charles Sturt University, Australia. She has long been an advocate for the recognition of prior learning (also known as APEL) in higher education as a way of legitimizing learning gained in learning spaces outside the academy. She is a career adult educator, and sees education as a practice of freedom and active citizenship. In her current role, she provides mentoring and advocacy for learning and teaching approaches that foster blended learning and create spaces for innovative practices such as student-designed materials.

Geoffrey Crisp is the Director of the Centre for Learning and Professional Development and Director of Online Education at the University of Adelaide, Australia. He completed a PhD in chemistry, undertook postdoctoral research in Germany and the USA, and commenced his academic career as a lecturer in chemistry at the University of Melbourne, Australia before moving to the University of Adelaide where he continued as a discipline academic in chemistry until 2000. Geoff was an Associate Dean for Learning and Teaching for the Faculty of Science when he became actively involved in online learning and e-assessment. He was appointed the Director of the Online Learning and Teaching Unit in 2001 and made the permanent move to educational development and online learning in 2002. Geoff has received the University of Adelaide's Excellence in Teaching Award, the Royal Australian Chemical Institute Stranks Medal for Chemical Education, an Australian Learning and Teaching Council Associate Fellowship in 2006, and National Teaching Fellowship in 2009. Geoff is currently President of HERDSA.

Steve Dillon is founding director of the save to DISC (Documenting Innovation in Sound Communities) Research Network which examines and documents the qualities and relationships between music, meaning, cognitive and social benefit, health, and well being. Steve is a Senior Lecturer of Music and Sound and music education in the Faculty of Creative Industry, Queensland University of Technology, Australia. His research focuses upon meaningful engagement with music making in schools and communities. Steve is Project Leader for the Australasian Cooperative Research Centre for Interaction Design (ACID). He is focussed on network jamming research creating generative media performance systems and ways of learning. He has published widely in music education and community music with a strong emphasis upon the role of technology in 21st century learning and social contexts. He is active as a professional singer and songwriter and a review panellist and series editor for international arts, technology, musicological and music education journals and book series.

Chen Swee Eng is the Academic Director, Higher Education and Chair Professor of Building and Property at Holmesglen Institute in Melbourne, Australia. Prior to joining Holmesglen, he was Professor for Building in the Faculty of Engineering and Built Environment at the University of Newcastle, Australia. He has more than 20 years of research and experience with innovative approaches to education including student-centred learning, problem and project based learning (PBL), and e-learning. He has developed and taught problem-based learning courses in architecture, construction management, and property. He has consulted internationally and across a number of different disciplines in the development of PBL courses. Professor Chen was an invited keynote speaker at the 4th Asia Pacific Conference on Problem-Based Learning in Hat Yai in 2002, and also at the International Conference on PBL in Lahti, Finland, in 2005. His research interests in education include student perceptions of their learning environment, student-centred learning environments and assessment practices.

Robert Fox has over 30 years experience in teaching and research in South East Asia, Australia, and Great Britain. His research interests focus on teacher professional development; innovative use of information and communication technology (ICT); technological practice and change in higher education; blended learning; change and leadership in technology supported educational innovation; and the impact of technology in new teaching and learning places and environments. He is an Associate Professor, Division of Information and Technology Studies in the Faculty of Education and a Deputy Director of the Centre for Information Technology in Education (CITE), The University of Hong Kong (HKU). He has taught on undergraduate and post-graduate programs and supervised Master's and doctoral students. In 2006, he was awarded the HKU University Teaching Fellowship (UTF) for excellence in teaching. The UTF is awarded on average to four academic staff per year.

Eva Heinrich teaches computer science and Information Technology at Massey University, New Zealand. Eva's research interests include higher education and e-learning, and more specifically in e-portfolio supported lifelong learning and assessment. Initially, Eva focussed on the technology side of e-learning, and then moved toward pedagogy issues related to e-learning and the scholarship of teaching and learning in higher education. Eva was awarded a Darrylin O'Dea Award in the field of e-learning by Massey University in 2010. Eva has conducted research projects and published widely.

Gylo (Julie) Hercelinskyj is a Registered Nurse and a Senior Lecturer in the School of Health at Charles Darwin University, Australia. Her clinical speciality is in mental health nursing, and she teaches across all mental health nursing units in the Bachelor of Nursing Program. Gylo's teaching and learning activities and interests include curriculum development, m-learning, and simulation as a teaching and learning approach. She has worked in collaboration with clinical and academic nurse colleagues on the development of the mental health curriculum for the Bachelor of Nursing program and the CDU vHospital. Gylo's research interests include the use of m-learning with externally based students, workforce issues in mental health nursing and the oral history of mental health nursing. Gylo has also recently completed her doctoral thesis.

Henk Huijser is a Lecturer of Learning Enhancement (Communication) in the Learning and Teaching Support Unit, and a researcher in the Public Memory Research Centre at the University of Southern Queensland, Australia. His research interests and publications include technology enhanced learning and teaching, cross-cultural communication and cultural studies. His current interests include mobile learning and social networking technology, and their potential applications in higher education. Henk has published and presented widely: http://www.usq.edu.au/users/huijser/Research.htm.

Lynne Hunt is Pro Vice-Chancellor (Learning and Teaching) at the University of Southern Queensland, Australia. She won the 2002 Prime Minister's Award for Australian University Teacher of the Year. Subsequently, she received an Australian Executive Endeavour Award to explore quality assurance in university learning and teaching in Malaysia. She publishes in the field of sustainable planning to promote university teaching. Her co-edited book *The realities of change in higher education: Interventions to promote learning and teaching* was published in 2006. She is currently a member of the International Advisory Board of the Malaysian Journal of Teaching and Learning in Higher Education (JTLHE). Professor Hunt was a member of the Board of the Australian Learning and Teaching Council and two of its sub-committees from its inception until March 2008. She has also served internationally in external review roles for the University of Pretoria and the University of Botswana.

Christopher R. Jones is a Reader in the Institute of Educational Technology at the Open University, UK. He writes course materials for the Masters programme and coordinates the Online and Distance Education strand of the Doctorate in Education. His research focuses on the utilization of the metaphor of networks to the understanding of learning in tertiary education. Chris is the principal investigator for a UK Funding Council project *The Net generation encountering e-learning at university*. He was co-leader of the European Union funded Kaleidoscope Research Team *Conditions for productive networked learning environments,* and Chris has been a co-director of a number of research and evaluation projects. Chris has published over 50 refereed journal articles, book chapters, and conference papers. He is the joint editor of *Networked Learning: Perspectives and Issues*, Springer (2002) and *Analysing Networked Learning Practices in Higher Education and Continuing Professional Development,* Sense Publishers, BV (2009).

Keith Kirkwood is a Lecturer in the School of Learning Support at Victoria University. His academic and professional backgrounds also include e-learning design and information management. He has been involved in writing about and developing participatory learning platforms since 2001. Keith pioneered the development of the SNAP-VU virtual learning platform at Victoria University.

Paul Lam is an Assistant Professor at the Centre for Learning Enhancement And Research (CLEAR) at The Chinese University of Hong Kong. He is involved in many teaching and learning (T&L) research studies and services such as promotion of outcomes-based approaches to T&L, the enhancement of T&L spaces, and the use of technology for T&L. Paul's additional research interests include case-based T&L, learners' characteristics, self and peer assessment, and English language teaching (ELT).

Robin McCormack spent many years working to formulate a coherent theory and practice for Adult Basic Education as a rounded education for 'second chance adults'. From the mid-90s he worked at Batchelor Institute of Indigenous Tertiary Education, Northern Territory, focusing on the development of academic and civic literacy for indigenous adults. Now at Victoria University, Melbourne, he manages teams of student rovers employed as peer mentors to assist other students in the Learning Commons.

Beryl McEwan is a Registered Nurse and Midwife who has been involved in nursing in the Northern Territory for over 30 years. Her clinical speciality is neonatal intensive and special care and she has experience as a clinical nurse educator in that setting. Beryl teaches in the general nursing units and clinical intensives in the Bachelor of Nursing program at Charles Darwin University (CDU), Australia. Her academic, teaching and research interests include the CDU vHospital®, e-learning and external students, role transition in nursing, and the development of professional identity in nursing students and new graduate nurses. Beryl is currently a PhD candidate exploring the role transition of new graduate nurses who were previously enrolled nurses.

Kerryn Newbegin has been working in the online learning field for over ten years, with a number of publications in the field. She has formerly worked for the Department of Marketing and the Faculty of Law, and is currently with the Centre for the Advancement of Learning and Teaching at Monash University, Australia. Kerryn was a co-recipient of the Vice Chancellor's Award for Excellence for her work in implementing the university's content management system, and is co-designer of the InterLearn, LEX and InterLex personal learning environments.

Glen Postle During his 30 years at the University of Southern Queensland (USQ), Australia, Professor Glen Postle has assumed roles and responsibilities in mathematics education, curriculum theory, research and evaluation, and open and distance learning. Over this time he has held a range of positions, including: Foundation Director of the Toowoomba Education Centre; Head, Centre for Research and Development in Curriculum; Head, Department of Higher Education Studies; Foundation Co-ordinator, Open Access Support Centre, Department of Education; Director, Office of Preparatory and Continuing Studies; and Associate Director (Academic), Distance Education Centre. His research interests and publications are in the areas of educational design for open and distance learning, teaching and learning online, access and equity, and technology enhanced learning. He has also been involved in funded consultancies in the Solomon Islands (World Bank), Pakistan (Asian Development Bank and Commonwealth of Learning), and Malawi (Malawi Ministry of Education).

John Rafferty is a Lecturer in Science Education at Charles Sturt University (CSU), Australia. John is actively involved in a number of diverse projects designed to maximize staff, student, and community engagement with CSU's environmentally sensitive Thurgoona campus. His teaching and research interests focus on science and environmental education. Through his research and management of CSU environmental education outreach initiatives, John is linked with a network of community based environmental action groups. John works with pre-service teachers, schools, and community groups developing educational responses to issues concerning education for sustainability. John is also a Research Fellow with CSU's Research Institute for Professional Practice, Learning and Education (RIPPLE).

Shirley Reushle is the Manager of Technology-Enhanced Learning in the University of Southern Queensland's (USQ) Australian Digital Futures Institute, a cross-institutional multidisciplinary institute with two work-streams - one pertaining to e-learning and the other to e-research. Shirley is also a Senior Lecturer in Online Pedagogies and teaches Master's and Doctoral students for the Faculty of Education. Shirley has worked in the Australian school and higher education sectors for all of her professional career, and for the last fifteen years, has taught online at USQ. Her research is in professional development for online educators, facilitating transformative flexible learning experiences, pedagogical applications of new and emerging technologies and learning space design.

Michael Sankey is currently the Director of the Learning and Teaching Support Unit at the University Southern Queensland in Australia. He specialises in the areas of e-learning pedagogies, multimodal and Web design, visual and multiliteracies. His recent research has focused on the multiple representations of concepts when utilising multimedia and Web 2.0 technologies, and how the use of hybridized electronic environments can enhance learning opportunities for students, particularly for those studying at a distance. With a background in art and design, he is passionate about the ways in which aesthetically enhanced learning environments can better transmit concepts to students of all backgrounds. Michael is an active member of the Australasian Society for Computers in Learning in Tertiary Education (*ascilite*), and is a life member of the International Visual Literacy Association (IVLA).

Deidre Seeto is Coordinator of Educational Technologies with the Teaching and Educational Development Institute (TEDI), University of Queensland, Australia. She has an active interest in learning design, educational technology, and its practical implementation in the higher education sector. Deidre's research and development interests include authentic task design, sustainable approaches to educational innovation, communities of practice and Web 2.0, design-based research, work-integrated learning, and interactive multimedia. She is a reviewer for national and international journals in educational technology and publishes in this area.

Warren Sellers devoted the late 20th Century to what is now called the creative industries sector, as a designer, director, and producer. At the most recent *Fin de siècle,* a long-standing critical interest in education returned him to scholarly inquiries that earned a Master's degree and a Doctorate of Philosophy in Education. His distinctive publications, interweaving text and imagery, work to unpack densities in complexities. He has filled several educational research roles involving e-learning and the scholarship of teaching and learning in Aotearoa, New Zealand. Warren now works at La Trobe University, Victoria, Australia as the Project Manager for the *Spaces for Knowledge Generation* project, and for the whole of institution curriculum project *Design for Learning.*

Caroline Steel is a Lecturer in Higher Education (eLearning) in the Teaching and Educational Development Institute (TEDI) at the University of Queensland, Australia. Her research into current and emerging technologies is focused on teacher beliefs, learning spaces, mobile technologies, 3D immersive environments, and identifying the pedagogical affordances of technologies that have the potential to enhance the quality of university learning and teaching. She completed her PhD on the interrelationship between university teacher's pedagogical beliefs, beliefs about Web technologies and their Web practices in 2009. In recent years, Caroline has facilitated workshops in Hong Kong, Singapore, Sweden, and Australia that have assisted teachers to re-imagine their teaching practices for technology-enriched learning spaces. Caroline is Vice President of the Australasian Society for Computers in Tertiary Education (ascilite) – see www.ascilite.org.

Dan Tout has worked at Language Australia and Centre for Adult Education (CAE) in Melbourne, and is currently employed as a research assistant in the School of Learning Support Services at Victoria University, Melbourne. Dan is currently involved in a number of research projects with a particular focus on the interplay between learning spaces and learning space users. Current projects include the ALTC funded project entitled 'A Comprehensive Learning Space Design Evaluation Model' (http://www.altc. edu.au/project-comprehensive-learning-space-swinburne-2008). This project has the aim of developing an evaluation framework for institutional learning spaces. He is also undertaking an evaluation focussed on 'Student Rovers in the Learning Commons' at Victoria University.

Belinda Tynan is Academic Director, Faculty of the Professions, University of New England, Australia. Professor Tynan has held numerous academic positions in the UK, Australia, and Japan. She leads numerous grants and is Director for the DEHub: Innovation in distance education, which is a commonwealth funded research project. Her research and publications cover areas such as distance education, academic staff development, new technologies, and regional issues. She is also the Treasurer for the Open and Distance Learning Association Australia (ODLAA).

Regine Wagner is currently Director of Higher Education Programs in the School of Education at RMIT University, Australia. Regine sees herself as an organisational development agent. Her work predominantly relates to the 'unfreezing' of structures and practices that no longer serve the best interest of the institution, its members and clients. Regine is an Adult Educator, and her teaching philosophy is grounded in critical social pedagogy, the application of an interdisciplinary action focus with the aim to balance power inequities, and economic, social, and political disadvantage. Regine is a 'pedagogy activist' with a strong commitment to improving access and outcomes for non-traditional students. She holds a PhD from the University of Technology, Berlin.

Leonard Webster is the Educational Adviser for Teaching in the Centre for the Advancement of Learning and Teaching (CALT), Monash University, Australia. His experience includes research in teaching and learning in higher education with special interests in educational development research and learning environments supported through technology. He has a particular interest is in the application of narrative inquiry research methods, having recently published a book on the use of narrative inquiry for complex and human-centred activities. As an educational theorist, Leonard has sought to link educational theory with learning and research models to provide educationally sound learning environments. This work has been recognized in an award made to Leonard by the Australian Society for Computers in Teaching and Learning (1999) for his co-creation of the online interactive environment 'InterLearn' and an Innovations Patent (2005).

Nathan Wise has a BA Hons from the University of Wollongong, Australia and a PhD in history from the University of New South Wales, Australia. Nathan was formerly employed as an Associate Lecturer at the University of New South Wales and as a Research Officer with the Refugee Review Tribunal. He is currently an Adjunct Lecturer in the School of Humanities at UNE and the Manager and Adjunct Lecturer within the DEHub: Innovation in distance education project.

Index